DATABASE PROCESSING

EDITION

DATABASE PROCESSING
Fundamentals, Design, and Implementation
• • • • • • • • • • • • • • • •

David M. Kroenke

 Prentice Hall, Upper Saddle River, N.J. 07458

Library of Congress Cataloging-in-Publication Data
Kroenke, David M.
　　Database processing : fundamentals, design, and implementation /
　David M. Kroenke. — 6th ed.
　　　p.　　cm.
　　Includes bibliographical references and index.
　　ISBN 0-13-737842-4
　　1. Database management.　I. Title.
　QA76.9.D3K737　1997
　005.74—dc21　　　　　　　　　　　　　　　　　97-62
　　　　　　　　　　　　　　　　　　　　　　　　　　CIP

Acquisitions Editor: Jo-Ann DeLuca
Editorial Assistant: Marc Oliver
Executive Marketing Manager: Nancy Evans
Editor-in-Chief: PJ Boardman
Director of Production and Manufacturing: Joanne Jay
Managing Editor: Katherine Evancie
Production Editor: Susan Rifkin
Production Coordinator: Cindy Spreder
Manufacturing Manager: Vincent Scelta
Senior Manufacturing Supervisor: Paul Smolenski
Manufacturing Buyer: Alana Zdinak
Electronic Art Supervisor: Warren Fischbach
Artist: Annie Bartell
Senior Designer: Suzanne Behnke
Interior Design: Rosemarie Votta
Cover Design: Paul Gourham
Composition: Carlisle Communications, Ltd.
Cover Art/Photo: Delaunay, Robert. Simultaneous Contrasts: Sun and Moon. (Dated on painting 1912.) Oil on canvas, 53" in diameter. The Museum of Modern Art, New York. Purchase.

Copyright © 1998, 1995, 1992, 1988, and 1983 by Prentice Hall, Inc.
A Simon & Schuster Company
Upper Saddle River, New Jersey 07458

Microsoft and Windows are registered trademarks of the Microsoft Corporation in the U.S.A. and other countries. Screen shots and icons reprinted with permission from Microsoft Corporation. This book is not sponsored or endorsed by or affiliated with the Microsoft Corporation.

Printed in the United States of America
10 9 8 7 6 5 4 3 2

ISBN 0-13-737842-4

Prentice-Hall International (UK) Limited, London
Prentice-Hall of Australia Pty. Limited, Sydney
Prentice-Hall Canada, Inc., Toronto
Prentice-Hall Hispanoamericana, S.A., Mexico
Prentice-Hall of India Private Limited, New Delhi
Prentice-Hall of Japan, Inc., Tokyo
Simon & Schuster Asia Pte. Ltd., Singapore
Editora Prentice-Hall do Brasil, Ltda., Rio de Janeiro

BRIEF CONTENTS

CONTENTS

CHAPTER ◆18◆ **The Hierarchical and**
                Network Data Models   449

APPENDIX   **Data Structures for**
            Database Processing   479

This text is intended for use in a one-term course on database processing. The purpose of this text is, first and foremost, to teach the fundamental skills students need to be successful developing personal databases on their own and working as members of a team when building workgroup and enterprise databases. Given this foundation, the second purpose is to discuss and illustrate emerging technology and applications.

■ COURSE FOUNDATIONS

Data Modeling
Relational Database Design
Knowledge of SQL
Application Design Fundamentals
Practice with Different Examples
Multi-User Processing

For a database to be effective, its structure must logically reflect the users' view of their world. Such consistency does not arise automatically. No wizard will provide it. Instead, it must be developed through the hard work of understanding the users' model of their world. This means that any person or team who hopes to build effective databases and database applications must be able to create data models of the users' needs. Hence, I believe learning solid modeling skills is critically important in this course—in fact, the single most important skill to be learned.

Of course, once the users' requirements have been modeled, they must be translated into a database design that accurately represents this model. Therefore, the second foundation skill of this course is database design. Today, the graduates of this course will encounter relational databases almost exclusively; hence, this text presents the skills necessary to transform data models into relational database designs.

In fact, with the exceptions of Chapter 17, which presents object-oriented database processing, and Chapter 18, which surveys the DL/I and the CODASYL DBTG models, all of this text assumes the use of relational database technology. This leads to the third foundational skill: knowledge of SQL.

SQL is the lingua franca of database processing. While one could argue that SQL has failed as an end-user query tool, supplanted today by Query by Example and Query by Form, there is no question that SQL is the standard means by which application programs access and update relational databases. SQL statements are important for creating views for forms and reports as well.

No organization wants a database for the sheer joy of having a database. People want to keep track of things and they want to pose queries and generate reports to gain information about those things. Database applications are the means by which this is done, and therefore, a knowledge of the relationship of application design to database design and the users' data model is another foundation skill. This topic overlaps with the systems development course. To avoid conflict and repetition with that course, this text focuses on application design considerations that pertain directly to databases and data models. See, for example, Chapter 8 and the ODBC section in Chapter 14. Hence, whether or not the student has already taken the systems class, the material presented here should be understandable and useful.

Finally, there is no substitute for experience. To ensure that every student can have hands-on experience with a software product for creating data models and database designs, this text is accompanied by the commercial version of SALSA for the Desktop. Of course, if your university has licenses for other products such as Microsoft Access, you will also want to use those products. The goal in providing

SALSA is to ensure that students have at least one commercial product at their disposal. More information on the use of Access and SALSA is presented later in the Preface.

Years ago, database products were so difficult to use that the students had time to develop, at best, a single database. Often even that was too much work. Today, however, with the productivity inherent in modern products, students should be able to develop several data models, if not complete databases. If the projects are suitably chosen, the students will learn firsthand how different data models impact the design and characteristics of the databases and related applications.

Finally, many databases are used by more than one person at a time. This means students need to learn the special requirements, techniques, and technologies of multi-user processing including concurrency control, reliability, security, and database administration.

■ IMPORTANT NEW TOPICS IN THIS EDITION

ODBC

Data Warehousing

Intranet and Internet Databases

Multimedia DBs

Object Databases

SQL3 and ODMB

Databases are everywhere. Whereas at one time databases were the sole province of the MIS department that applied the technology only to enterprise databases on mainframes behind locked doors, today we find databases on personal computers, in client-server workgroup settings, and as the backbone of data warehouses, multimedia applications, and network databases on corporate intranets and the Internet.

This text discusses a number of new technologies that support these applications. The Open Database Connectivity standard has become important in client-server applications and will increasingly be important for network applications as well. Many organizations are currently attempting to increase their return on their data resource by developing data warehouses. Both intranets and the Internet have become new delivery mechanisms for database applications. Such networks are likely to dramatically increase the need for skilled database designers. In addition, databases are being used to support multimedia applications. In the future, it is likely that most database applications will include at least some multimedia elements.

Object-oriented databases are also becoming important, although, at present, they are far less common than relational databases. As object-oriented programming continues to increase in popularity, the demand for such databases will grow. It is difficult to assess whether such databases will result as an outgrowth of relational databases (along the lines of the SQL3 standard), or whether organizations will find a way to migrate to DBMS with completely new architectures (along the lines of the ODMG standard). Today, I believe the wise course of action is to follow both, while focusing the bulk of this course on the current form of the relational model.

■ ORGANIZATION OF THIS BOOK

This text is organized into six parts. Part I provides an introduction. A number of different types of databases and applications are presented in Chapter 1, along with a brief history of database processing. Chapter 2 illustrates the components of a DBMS and provides an overview of the process of building a database and its applications.

The focus of Part II is on data modeling. Chapter 3 explains the concepts and constructs of the entity-relationship model and illustrates its use. Chapter 4 presents the semantic object in a similar way. Either of these models can be used to express the users' data requirements.

Part III discusses the transformation of data models into relational database designs. Chapter 5 sets the stage by discussing the relational model and normalization. Normalization techniques are then used in Chapter 6 to explain the transformation of entity-relationship data models into relational designs and in Chapter 7 to explain the transformation of semantic object data models into relational designs. Chapter 8 concludes Part III by discussing database application design. The presentation in this chapter is limited to those aspects of application design that pertain directly to database structures.

The implementation of relational databases is presented next in Part IV. Chapter 9 discusses the foundations of relational implementation and briefly surveys relational algebra. Chapter 10 is devoted to a thorough discussion of SQL and Chapter 11 illustrates the implementation of a personal database using the features and functions of Microsoft Access.

Part V discusses concepts, techniques, technology, and products that are important for multi-user databases. Chapter 12 introduces multi-user processing alternatives and describes reliability, security, and database administration. It contains a brief survey of distributed database alternatives, as well. Chapter 13 illustrates the implementation of multi-user data using DB2. This chapter is important not only because it describes a mainframe DBMS, but also because it illustrates the means by which SQL can be embedded in application programs. Client-server database processing and ODBC are the subjects of Chapter 14, and the sharing of enterprise data and data warehousing are discussed in Chapter 15. Part V concludes with Chapter 16 and its discussion of the use of database technology on intranets and the Internet. This chapter also discusses the design of two different multimedia databases.

Nonrelational database processing is addressed in Part VI. Chapter 17 discusses object-oriented databases and standards. It includes a brief summary of object-oriented programming, along with a description of the need for object persistence and a discussion of persistence via traditional file structures, relational databases, and ODBMS. Both the SQL3 and ODMG standards are summarized. Finally, Chapter 18 discusses the major elements of DL/I and the CODASYL DBTG models. Little new development is done with the models, but students may encounter them when working on maintenance or database conversion projects.

I have endeavored to limit the discussions in Chapters 14 through 18 so that all of this material could be presented in one course. The needs of employers vary from one locality to another, and it may be that some of this material is unimportant to your students. If so, Chapters 14 through 18 can be read in any order and any of the chapters can be omitted without loss of continuity.

■ USE OF MICROSOFT ACCESS AND SALSA FOR THE DESKTOP

I have used Microsoft Access to illustrate discussion points throughout this text. I understand that many institutions do not have a license for students to use this product, and further, not every professor would choose this product for illustration. Using Access is an attempt to balance, on the one hand, the need for the student to see how abstract concepts apply to a real DBMS, and, on the other, the desire not to indicate that Access is the only choice. In fact, Access is an excellent personal DBMS product, and it also happens to be, by a wide margin, the world's most popular DBMS product. Hence, students are most likely to encounter it. IBM (Lotus's) Approach and Borland's Paradox for Windows are two other excellent products.

This text includes a copy of SALSA for the Desktop. Except for a section in Chapter 17, I have not illustrated the use of this product in this text. I have, however, presented the semantic object model, as a model, using product-independent illustrations. I have done this because I believe that students will find the semantic object model easy to use and powerful. Dan Rogers, writing in the *VB Tech Journal,* said, "The arrangement (of semantic objects) feels quite natural and it leads me to believe that (semantic object modeling) is a break-through modeling technique that can bridge the gap between the business and technical worlds."[1]

Using SALSA is entirely optional; no section in the text depends on it. As stated earlier, however, I believe that the students' experiences in data modeling will be significantly enhanced if they do perform exercises and accomplish some of the end-of-chapter projects. Be aware that SALSA, however, is designed to hide the technology that this course teaches. Thus, after building a semantic object model, the user clicks a button and all of the relations, foreign keys, intersection tables, SQL, and so forth are generated behind the scenes. Thus, while SALSA can be used to create models and to observe the impact of changes in those models on forms and reports, the students will need to cause SALSA to print supplementary reports to determine the relational structure that is generated from their models. Or, if you have Microsoft Access, the students can have SALSA generate an Access database and then examine that database in Access. These issues are discussed in the SALSA projects at the end of Chapters 4 and 7.

My hope is that using SALSA can raise the level of discourse in this class. Instead of spending many hours discussing the placement of foreign keys, we can spend some time on foreign keys, but invest the bulk of the time discussing how well a particular data model represents the needs of the business that it is intended to support. I believe that this hope is consistent with the general trend in technology. Over time, all DBMS vendors will find ways to hide more and more of the underlying data structures, and data modeling will become the primary focus of the database development process.

■ ACKNOWLEDGMENTS

I would like to thank the following reviewers of this book who provided many helpful and insightful comments:

Linda Behrens, *University of Central Oklahoma*

Donna Davis, *University of Southern Mississippi*

Gordon Everest, *University of Minnesota*

William R. Friend, *Edmonds Community College*

Richard D. Heath, *St. Cloud State University*

Andrew Kreutzer, *Richard Stockton College*

Julian M. Scher, *New Jersey Institute of Technology*

Also, at Prentice Hall, I would like to thank my editor, Jo-Ann DeLuca; her assistant, Marc Oliver; and Susan Rifkin, who managed the production of this book.

Thanks also to Jim Simpson, John Wall, Kevin Vitale, and John Nicol of Wall Data, who have supported the development of SALSA and who generously agreed to include SALSA for the Desktop in this text. I am indebted to all of the SALSA developers—thanks especially to Chris Olds and Kawai Kenji with whom I have had many enjoyable conversations. Finally, a special thanks to Marvin Mall without whom SALSA might not ever have been finished.

David Kroenke
Seattle, Washington

---

[1]Roger, Dan "Manage Data with Modeling Tools" *VB Tech Journal,* December 1996, p. 30.

DATABASE
PROCESSING

Part I introduces the topic of database processing. Chapter 1 surveys the topic and describes four applications that typify the wide range of databases in use today, as well as the benefits and evolution of database technology. Chapter 2 introduces the development of databases and database applications and describes the elements of a database and the functions of a DBMS as well.

The goal of this part is to set the stage for the discussion of data modeling that begins in Chapter 3.

INTRODUCTION

INTRODUCTION TO DATABASE PROCESSING

This book presents the fundamental skills you will need to be able to design and develop a database and its related applications. Many students find this subject enjoyable and interesting, even though it can be challenging. Learning this material will certainly be worth the effort you put forth as these skills are in great demand, and many fulfilling and well-paying database development positions are available. The reason for this demand is that almost every business person needs the benefits of database technology, but very few know how to use that technology and few want to learn. Hence, there is a great need for people who can serve as liaisons between business users and database technology. The goal of this book is to help you learn the knowledge and skills you will need to provide that service.

FOUR DATABASE EXAMPLES

The purpose of a database is to help people keep track of things. The classical database applications concern the tracking of items like orders, customers, jobs, employees, phone calls, or other items of interest to a business person. Recently, as databases have become more readily available, database technology has been applied to new areas such as databases for the Internet or for organizational intranets. Also, databases are increasingly used to create and maintain multimedia applications. Consider several typical examples.

■ MARY RICHARDS HOUSEPAINTING

Mary Richards is a professional housepainter who owns and operates a small company consisting of herself, another professional painter, and, when needed, part-time painters. Mary has been in business for ten years and has earned a reputation as a high-quality painter who works for a reasonable rate. Mary gets most of her work through repeat business from customers who hire her to paint their houses and also from their word-of-mouth referrals. In addition, Mary gets some work from building contractors and professional interior designers.

Customers remember Mary far better than she remembers them. Indeed, sometimes she is embarrassed when a customer calls and says something like, "Hi Mary, this is John Maples. You painted my house three years ago." Mary knows she

FIGURE 1-1   *Tables of Data for Mary Richards Housepainting*

is supposed to remember the caller and the work she did for him, but since she paints more than fifty houses a year, it usually is difficult for her to do so. This situation becomes worse when the customer says something like, "My neighbor liked the job you did on our house and would like something similar done to her house."

In order to help her memory and to keep better track of her business records, Mary had a consultant develop a database and database application that she uses on her personal computer. The database stores records regarding customers, jobs, and sources in the form of tables, as shown in the example in Figure 1-1.

It is the job of a program called a database management system (DBMS) to store and retrieve the data in these tables. Unfortunately, when such data are in the form of tables, they are not very useful to Mary. Rather, she would like to know how customers and jobs and referrals relate to one another, for example, what jobs she has done for a particular customer or what customers have been referred by a particular person.

To provide this capability, Mary's consultant created a database application that processes data entry forms and produces reports. Consider the example form in Figure 1-2. Here, Mary keys in data about customers such as name, phone, and address. She also links the customer to a particular referral source and keys in data about jobs performed for the customer. This data can then be displayed in reports like the one shown in Figure 1-3.

It is the function of the database application and the DBMS to process the form and store the data that are entered into tables like those in Figure 1-1. Similarly, the application and DBMS extract data from tables like those in Figure 1-1 to create a report like the one in Figure 1-3.

Consider again the data in Figure 1-1, and notice that the rows in the tables cross-reference and are linked to one another. Each JOB contains the Customer_ID of the CUSTOMER who purchased that JOB, and each CUSTOMER contains the Source_ID of the person who referred that customer. These references are used to

FIGURE 1-2   *Example Data Entry Form for Mary Richards Housepainting*

FIGURE 1-3   *Example Report for Mary Richards Housepainting*

produce forms and reports like those shown in Figures 1-2 and 1-3. Other uses of the database include recording bid estimates, tracking referral sources, and producing mailing labels for the direct sales literature that Mary sends out from time to time.

As you can imagine, Mary is unlikely to know how to design the tables in Figure 1-1, how to use a DBMS to create those tables, and how to develop the application to create the forms and reports. But by the time you have finished this course, you should know how to use database technology to create this database and its application. You should also know how to design and manipulate tables to create forms and reports of far greater complexity.

FIGURE   1-4   *Local Area Network with Database Server Used by Treble Clef Music*

■ TREBLE CLEF MUSIC

Mary Richards's database is called a *single-user* database because only one user accesses the database at a given time. In some cases, this limitation is too restrictive; multiple people need to access the database simultaneously from multiple computers. Such *multi-user* databases are more complicated because the DBMS and the application must keep one user's work from interfering with another's.

Treble Clef Music uses a database application to keep track of musical instruments that it rents. It needs a multi-user database application because, during busy periods, several salespeople may rent musical instruments at the same time. Also, the store manager needs to access the rental database to determine when to order more instruments of a given type. She does not want to interrupt the rental process when she does this.

The Treble Clef store has a local area network that connects several microcomputers to a server computer that holds the rental database as shown in Figure 1-4. Each clerk has access to a database application that has the three forms illustrated in Figure 1-5. The Customer form is used to maintain Customer data, the Rental Agreement form is used to track the instruments that have been rented and whether or not they have been returned, and the Instrument form is used to record the purchase of instruments and keep track of their condition.

To understand the problems that must be overcome in a multi-user database, consider what happens when two customers attempt to rent the same B-flat clarinet at the same time. The DBMS and the application programs must somehow detect that this situation is occurring and inform one of the clerks that he or she must choose a different instrument.

■ STATE LICENSING AND VEHICLE REGISTRATION BUREAU

Now consider an even larger application of database technology. This example is of a state licensing and auto registration bureau. It has fifty-two centers that conduct drivers' tests and issue and renew drivers' licenses and also thirty-seven offices that sell vehicle registrations.

The personnel in these offices access a database to perform their jobs. Before a person can be issued or can renew a driver's license, his or her records in the database are checked for traffic violations, accidents, or arrests. This data are used to determine whether the license can be renewed and, if so, whether it should carry

FIGURE 1-5

Three Forms Used by Treble Clef Music: (a) Customer Form, (b) Rental Agreement Forms, and (c) Instrument Form

(a)

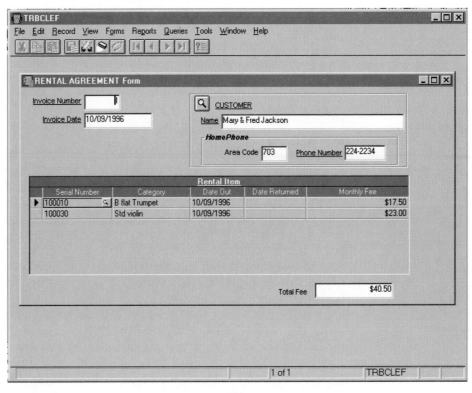

(b)

(c)

any limitations. Similarly, personnel in the auto registration department access the database to determine whether an auto has been registered before and, if so, to whom, and whether there are any outstanding matters that should prohibit the registration.

This database has hundreds of users, including not only the license and registration personnel but also the people in the state department of revenue and in law enforcement. Not surprisingly, the database is large and complex, with more than forty different tables of data, several of which contain hundreds of thousands of rows of data.

■ ROSE HARBOR YACHT SALES

The databases used by Mary Richards, Treble Clef, and the state licensing bureau involve the storage of business records consisting of character data like names, addresses, prices, and dates. Databases, however, can be used to store other types of data such as pictures, sounds, or animations, as well. Consider, for example, the case of Rose Harbor Yacht Sales. Rose Harbor sells and leases medium-to-large sailboats. It has two full-time partners, four salespeople, and an office administrator. Rose Harbor maintains its own marina, where it keeps most of the boats that it has for sale. Its salespeople also cooperate with personnel from other brokerages to sell boats that are not part of its own inventory.

Rose Harbor Yachts has found the Internet to be an effective sales and marketing technique. Consequently, the partners hired a consultant to develop a multimedia database application that displays pictures and data. Their application displays pictures of boat types as well as of specific boat listings. Additionally, their application displays pictures of each of the Rose Harbor sales associates as well as a recording of the salesperson describing his or her own boating experience and interests. Figure 1-6 shows one of the forms that is displayed over the Internet.

FIGURE 1-6   *Sample Multimedia Database Application Form Used by Rose Harbor Yachts*

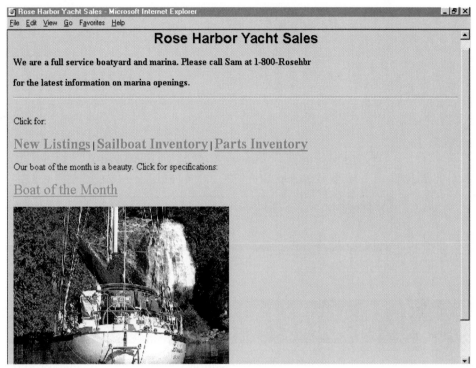

The storage and processing of multimedia data is one of the newest and most interesting types of database application. There will be many opportunities in the future for people who have the knowledge and skills to build such applications.

■ COMPARISON OF DATABASE APPLICATIONS

These examples represent a sampling of the uses of database technology. Hundreds of thousands of databases are like the one used by Mary Richards House Painting, single-user databases with a relatively small amount of data—say, less than ten megabytes. The forms and reports for these are generally simple and straightforward.

Other databases are like the one used by Treble Clef Music; they have more than one user but usually fewer than twenty or thirty users all together. They contain a moderate amount of data, say, fifty or a hundred megabytes. The forms and reports need to be complex enough to support several different business functions.

The largest databases are like those in the auto registration case, which have hundreds of users and trillions of bytes of data. Many different applications are in use, each application having its own forms and reports. Finally, some databases involve the storage and processing of not just character data but of multimedia data such as pictures, sounds, animations, movies, and the like. Often, these applications are made available over the Internet or an intranet. The characteristics of these types of databases are summarized in Figure 1-7.

When you finish this book, you should be able to design and create a database and database application like those used by Mary Richards and Treble Clef. You will probably not be able to create one as large and complicated as the vehicle registration database, but you will be able to serve as an effective member of a team that does design and create such a database. You should also be able to create a database containing multimedia data like the one used by Rose Harbor Yacht Sales.

FIGURE 1-7 *Characteristics of Different Types of Databases*

Type	Example	Typical Number of Concurrent Users	Typical Size of Database
Personal	Mary Richards House Painting	1	<10 Megabytes
Workgroup	Treble Clef Music	<25	<100 Megabytes
Organizational	Licensing and Registration	Hundreds	>1 Trillion Bytes
Multimedia	Rose Harbor Yacht Sales	Possibly Hundreds	<Several Hundred Megabytes

THE RELATIONSHIP OF APPLICATION PROGRAMS AND THE DBMS

All of the preceding examples and, indeed, all database applications have the general structure shown in Figure 1-8: The user interacts with a database application, which in turn interfaces with the DBMS, which accesses the database data.

At one time, the boundary between the application program and the DBMS was clearly defined. Applications were written in third-generation languages like COBOL, and those applications called on the DBMS for data management services. In fact, this still is done, most frequently on large mainframe databases.

Today, however, the features and functions of many DBMS products have grown to the point that the DBMS itself can process sizable portions of the application. For example, most DBMS products contain report writers and form generators that can be integrated into an application. (SALSA for the Desktop, the product included in the back of this text, will, in fact, generate a complete application.) This fact is important to us for two reasons. First, although the bulk of this text considers the design and development of databases, we will often refer to the design and development of database applications. After all, no user wants just a database. Instead, users want forms, reports, and queries that are based on their data.

Second, from time to time you will note an overlap between the material discussed in this class and that discussed in your systems development class, because developing effective database applications requires many of the skills that you have learned or will learn in your systems development class. Likewise, most systems development classes today also include the design of databases. The difference between the two courses is one of emphasis. Here, our emphasis is on the design and construction of the database. In a systems class, the emphasis is on the development of information systems—most of which use database technology.

FILE-PROCESSING SYSTEMS

The best way to understand the general nature and characteristics of databases today is to look at the characteristics of systems that predated the use of database technology. These systems reveal the problems that database technology has solved.

Relationships of User, Database Application, DBMS, and Database

Two File-Processing Systems

The first business information systems stored groups of records in separate files and were called **file-processing systems.** Figure 1-9, for example, depicts two file-processing systems that Treble Clef could use. One system processes CUSTOMER data, and the other one processes RENTAL data.

Although file-processing systems are a great improvement over manual record-keeping systems, they have important limitations:

- Data are separated and isolated.
- Data are often duplicated.
- Application programs are dependent on file formats.
- Files are often incompatible with one another.
- It is difficult to represent data in the users' perspectives.

■ SEPARATED AND ISOLATED DATA

The salespeople at Treble Clef need to relate their customers to the instruments that they rent. For the system in Figure 1-9, the data need to be extracted somehow from CUSTOMER and RENTAL files and combined into a single file. With file-processing, this is difficult. First, systems analysts and computer programmers must determine which parts of each of the files are needed; then they must decide how the files are related to one another; last, they must coordinate the processing of the files so that the correct data are extracted. Coordinating two files is difficult enough, but imagine the task of coordinating ten or more of them!

■ DATA DUPLICATION

In the Treble Clef example, a customer's name, address, and other data may be stored many times. That is, the data are stored once for CUSTOMER and again for each RENTAL agreement the customer has. Although these duplicate data waste file space, that is not the most serious problem; rather, the most serious problem with duplicated data concerns **data integrity.**

A collection of data has integrity if the data are logically consistent. Poor data integrity can often be seen in file-processing systems. For example, if a customer changes his or her name or address, then all those files containing that data must be updated, but the danger is that all of the files might *not* be updated, causing discrepancies among them. In the Treble Clef example, the customer might have one address for one RENTAL record and a different address for a second RENTAL record.

Data integrity problems are serious. If data items differ, they will produce inconsistent results. For example, if a report from one application disagrees with a report from another application, who will be able to tell which one is correct? When results are inconsistent, the credibility of the stored data, and even the MIS function itself, comes into question.

■ APPLICATION PROGRAM DEPENDENCY

With file processing, application programs depend on the file formats. Usually in file-processing systems the physical formats of files and records are part of the application code. In COBOL, for example, file formats are written in the DATA DIVISION. The problem with this arrangement is that when changes are made in the file formats, the application programs also must be changed.

For example, if the customer record is modified to expand the zip-code field from five to nine digits, all programs using that customer record must be modified, even if they do not use the zip-code field. Because there might be twenty programs that process the customer file, such a change means that a programmer has to identify all the affected programs, modify them, and then retest them—all time-consuming and error-prone tasks. Also, requiring programmers to modify programs that do not use the field whose format has changed is a waste of money.

■ INCOMPATIBLE FILES

One of the consequences of program data dependency is that file formats depend on the language or product used to generate them. Thus, the format of a file processed by a COBOL program is different from the format of a file processed by a BASIC program, which is different still from the format of a file processed by a C program.

As a result, files cannot be readily combined or compared. Suppose, for example, FILE-A contains CUSTOMER data that includes CustomerNumber, and FILE-B contains RENTAL data that also includes CustomerNumber. Suppose an application requires that we combine records that have matching CustomerNumbers. If FILE-A were processed by a COBOL program and FILE-B were processed by a C program, we would need to convert both files to a common structure before we could combine the records. This would be time-consuming and, sometimes, difficult. Such problems grow worse as the number of files to be combined increases.

■ THE DIFFICULTY OF REPRESENTING DATA IN THE USERS' PERSPECTIVES

It is difficult to represent file-processing data in a form that seems natural to users. Users want to see RENTAL data in a format like that in Figure 1-5(b). But in order to show the data in this way, several different files need to be extracted, combined, and presented together. This difficulty arises because with file processing, relationships among records are not readily represented or processed. Since a file-processing system cannot quickly determine which CUSTOMERs have rented which instruments, producing a form showing CUSTOMER preferences is quite difficult.

DATABASE PROCESSING SYSTEMS

Database technology was developed largely to overcome the limitations of file-processing systems. To understand how, compare the file-processing system in Figure 1-9 with the database system in Figure 1-8. File-processing programs directly access files of stored data. In contrast, database-processing programs call the DBMS to access the stored data. This difference is significant because it makes the application-programming job easier; that is, application programmers do not have to be concerned with the ways in which data are physically stored. Rather, they are free to concentrate on matters important to the user instead of matters important to the computer system.

■ INTEGRATED DATA

In a database system, all the application data is stored in a single facility called the **database.** An application program can ask the DBMS to access customer data or sales data or both. If both are needed, the application programmer specifies only how the data are to be combined, and the DBMS performs the necessary operations to do it. Thus, the programmer is not responsible for writing programs to consolidate the files, as must be done for the system in Figure 1-9.

■ REDUCED DATA DUPLICATION

With database processing, the duplication of data is minimal. For example, in Treble Clef's database, the customer's number, name, and address are stored only once. Whenever these data are needed, the DBMS can retrieve them, and when they are modified, only one update is necessary. Because data are stored in only one place, data integrity problems are less common—there is less opportunity for discrepancies among multiple copies of the same data item.

■ PROGRAM/DATA INDEPENDENCE

Database processing reduces the dependency of programs on file formats. All record formats are stored in the database itself (along with the data), and they are accessed by the DBMS, not by application programs. Unlike file-processing programs, database application programs need not include the format of all the files and records they process. Instead, application programs must contain only a definition (the length and data type) of each of the data items they need from the database. The DBMS maps the data items into records and handles other similar transformations.

Program/data independence minimizes the impact of data format changes on application programs. Format changes are input to the DBMS, which in turn updates the data it maintains concerning the structure of the database. For the most part, application programs are unaware that the format has changed. This also means that whenever data items are added, changed, or deleted from the database, only those programs that use these particular data items have to be modified. For applications consisting of dozens of programs, this can be a considerable savings of time.

■ EASIER REPRESENTATION OF THE USERS' PERSPECTIVES

As you will discover throughout this text, database technology makes it possible to represent, in a straightforward fashion, the objects found in the user's world. The forms in Figure 1-5 can readily be produced from a database because the relationships among the records of data are stored as part of the database.

DEFINITION OF A DATABASE

The term *database* suffers from many different interpretations. It has been used to refer to everything from a collection of index cards to the volumes and volumes of data that a government collects about its citizens. In this text, we use this term with a specific meaning: *A database is a self-describing collection of integrated records.* It is important to understand each part of this definition.

■ A DATABASE IS SELF-DESCRIBING

A database is self-describing: It contains, in addition to the user's source data, a description of its own structure. This description is called a **data dictionary** (or **data directory,** or **metadata**).

In this sense, a database is similar to a library, which can be thought of as a self-describing collection of books. In addition to the books, the library contains a card catalog describing them. In the same way, the data dictionary (which is part of the database, just as the card catalog is part of the library) describes the data contained in the database.

Why is this self-describing characteristic of a database so important? First, it promotes program/data independence. That is, it makes it possible to determine the structure and content of the database by examining the database itself. We do not need to guess what the database contains, nor do we need to maintain external documentation of the file and record formats (as is done in file-processing systems).

Second, if we change the structure of the data in the database (such as adding new data items to an existing record), we enter only that change in the data dictionary. Few, if any, programs will need to be changed. In most cases, only those programs that process the altered data items must be changed.

If you are familiar with COBOL, you know that the structure of the data for file-processing programs is described in the DATA DIVISION. Compared with database processing, this practice is inefficient. It is like putting a copy of your library's card catalog in the home or office of every library user. Then when the library buys a new book, the card catalog has to be changed in dozens or hundreds of places!

You may have learned in your COBOL or other programming courses that it is good practice to store the files' structure in a copy library and extract this structure from the library when the files are compiled. A similar strategy is used with databases. The structure of the database is extracted from the database and loaded into the program before the program is compiled.

■ A DATABASE IS A COLLECTION OF INTEGRATED RECORDS

The standard hierarchy of data is as follows: Bits are aggregated into bytes or characters; characters are aggregated into fields; fields are aggregated into records; and records are aggregated into files (see Figure 1-10[a]). It is tempting to follow the pattern of that statement and say that files are aggregated into databases. Although this statement is true, it does not go far enough.

A database does include files of user data, but it also contains more. As we mentioned earlier, a database contains a description of itself in **metadata.** In addition, a database includes **indexes** that are used to represent relationships among the data and also to improve the performance of database applications. Finally, the database often contains data about the applications that use the database. The structure of a data entry form, or a report, is sometimes part of the database. This last category of data we call **application metadata.** Thus a database contains

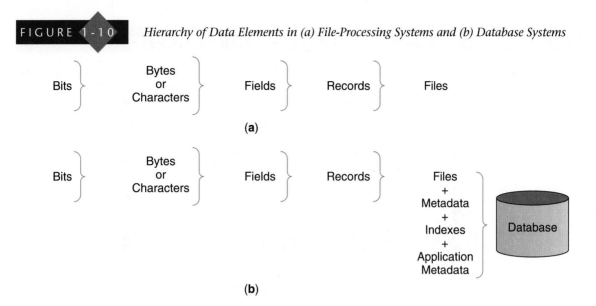

FIGURE 1-10   *Hierarchy of Data Elements in (a) File-Processing Systems and (b) Database Systems*

the four types of data shown in Figure 1-10(b): files of user data, metadata, indexes, and application metadata.

■ A DATABASE IS A MODEL OF A MODEL

A database is a model. It is tempting to say that a database is a model of reality or of some portion of reality as it relates to a business. This, however, is not true. A database does not model reality or some portion thereof. Instead, a database is a model of the *users' model*. For example, Mary Richards's database is a model of the way in which Mary Richards views her business. As she sees it, her business has customers, jobs, and referrals. Her database, therefore, contains representations of facts concerning those entities. The names and addresses of customers, the dates and descriptions of her jobs, and the names of her referral sources all are measurements that are important to her view of her business.

Databases vary in their level of detail. Some are simple and crude. A list of customers and the amounts they owe is an approximate representation of Mary's mental model. A more detailed representation includes jobs, referrals, and the trips made for each job. And a very detailed representation contains the amount and type of paint used on each job, the number of paintbrushes required, and the hours of labor on specific job tasks such as taping, painting woodwork, painting walls, cleanup, and the like.

The degree of detail that should be incorporated into a database depends on the information desired. Clearly, the more information that is wanted, the more detail the database must have. Deciding on the appropriate amount of detail is an important part of the job of designing a database. As you will discover, the principal criterion is the level of detail that exists in the minds of the users.

The database model must be dynamic because businesses change. People come and go. Products are introduced and phased out. Money is earned and spent. As these changes occur, the data that represents the business also must be altered. If not, the data will become outdated and inaccurately represent the business.

Transactions are representations of events. When events take place, the transactions for the events must be processed against the database. To do this, someone (a data entry clerk, a salesperson, or a teller, for example) activates a transaction-processing program and enters the transaction data. The program then calls on the DBMS to alter the database. Transaction-processing programs usually produce displays or print responses such as order confirmations or receipts.

THE HISTORY OF DATABASE PROCESSING

Database processing was originally used in major corporations and large organizations as the basis of large transaction-processing systems. An example is the licensing and vehicle registration example considered earlier. Later, as microcomputers gained popularity, database technology migrated to micros and was used for single-user, personal database applications like that described for Mary Richards. Next, as micros were connected together in work groups, database technology moved to the workgroup setting such as in the Treble Clef example. Finally, databases are being used today for multimedia applications, some of which are shared on public and private networks.

■ THE ORGANIZATIONAL CONTEXT

The initial application of database technology was to resolve problems with the file-processing systems discussed earlier in this chapter. In the mid-1960s, large corporations were producing data at phenomenal rates in file-processing systems, but the data were becoming difficult to manage, and new systems were becoming increasingly difficult to develop. Furthermore, management wanted to be able to relate the data in one file system to those in another.

The limitations of file processing prevented the easy integration of data. Database technology, however, held out the promise of a solution to these problems, and so large companies began to develop organizational databases. Companies centralized their operational data, such as orders, inventory, and accounting data, in these databases. The applications were primarily organization-wide, transaction-processing systems.

At first, when the technology was new, database applications were difficult to develop, and there were many failures. Even those applications that were successful were slow and unreliable: The computer hardware could not handle the volume of transactions quickly; the developers had not yet discovered more efficient ways to store and retrieve data; and the programmers were still new at accessing databases, and sometimes their programs did not work correctly.

Companies found another disadvantage of database processing: vulnerability. If a file-processing system fails, only that particular application will be out of commission. But if the database fails, all of its dependent applications will be out of commission.

Gradually, the situation improved. Hardware and software engineers learned how to build systems powerful enough to support many concurrent users and fast enough to keep up with the daily workload of transactions. New ways of controlling, protecting, and backing up the database were devised. Standard procedures for database processing evolved, and programmers learned how to write more efficient and more maintainable code. By the mid-1970s, databases could efficiently and reliably process organizational applications. With many of the early problems resolved, management turned its attention to finding new uses for this new huge pool of organizational data.

Managers knew that somehow all of those data could provide information for both tactical (short-term) and strategic (long-term) decision making. To do this, however, the users had to access the data themselves, as they could not be expected to wait weeks or months for programmers to "get the information out of the computer."

Unfortunately, most of the applications had to be developed in procedural languages such as COBOL and PL/I, but the users did not have the time or resources to become professional programmers. Besides, they were interested only in getting the answers to their questions, not in learning COBOL or navigating through a database to extract just the right bytes of data. It seemed that users and computers were existing in two different worlds. And yet all those data were there waiting to be put to even more good uses, a situation that set the stage for the next major development in database processing: the relational model.

■ THE RELATIONAL MODEL

In 1970, E. F. Codd published a landmark paper[1] in which he applied concepts from a branch of mathematics called relational algebra to the problem of storing large amounts of data. Codd's paper started a movement in the database community that in a few years led to the definition of the **relational database model.** This model is a particular way of structuring and processing a database, and we discuss it at length in Chapters 5 and 9 through 13.

BENEFITS OF THE RELATIONAL MODEL   The advantage of the relational model is that data are stored in a way that minimizes duplicated data and eliminates certain types of processing errors that can occur when data are stored in other ways. Data are stored as tables, with rows and columns, like the data in Figure 1-1.

According to the relational model, not all tables are equally desirable. Using a process called *normalization,* a table that is not desirable can be changed into two or more that are. You will learn about the normalization process in detail in Chapter 5.

Another key idea of the relational model is that columns can be used to contain data that relate one row to another. For example, in Figure 1-1, CUSTOMER_ID in the JOB table relates to CUSTOMER_ID in the CUSTOMER table. This makes the relationships among rows visible to the user.

At first, it was thought that the relational model would enable users to obtain information from databases without the assistance of MIS professionals. Part of the rationale of this idea was that tables are simple constructs that are intuitively understandable. Additionally, since the relationships are stored in the data, the users would be able to combine rows when necessary. For example, to access a RENTAL record, a user at Treble Clef would be able to combine a row of the CUSTOMER table with rows of a RENTAL table.

It turned out that this process was too difficult for most users. Hence, the promise of the relational model as a means for nonspecialists to access a database was never realized. In retrospect, the key benefit of the relational model has turned out to be that it provides an effective way for specialists (like you!) to structure and process a database.

RESISTANCE TO THE RELATIONAL MODEL   Initially the relational model encountered a good deal of resistance. Relational database systems require more computer resources, and so at first they were much slower than the systems based on earlier database models. Although they were easier to use, the slow response time was often unacceptable. To some extent, relational DBMS products were impractical until the 1980s when faster computer hardware was developed and the price–performance ratio of computers fell dramatically.

The relational model also seemed foreign to many programmers, who were accustomed to writing programs in which they processed data one record at a time. But relational DBMS products process data most naturally an entire table at a time. Accordingly, programmers had to learn a new way to think about data processing.

Because of these problems, even though the relational model had many advantages, it did not gain true popularity until computers became more powerful. In particular, as microcomputers entered the scene, more and more CPU cycles could be devoted to a single user. Such power was a boon to relational DBMS products and set the stage for the next major database development.

---

[1]E. F. Codd, "A Relational Model of Data for Large Shared Databanks," *Communications of the ACM,* June 1970, pp. 377–387.

■ MICROCOMPUTER DBMS PRODUCTS

In 1979, a small company called Ashton-Tate introduced a microcomputer product, dBase II (pronounced "d base two"), and called it a relational DBMS. In an exceedingly successful promotional tactic, Ashton-Tate distributed—nearly free of charge—more than 100,000 copies of its product to purchasers of the then-new Osborne microcomputers. Many of the people who bought these computers were pioneers in the microcomputer industry. They began to invent microcomputer applications using dBase, and the number of dBase applications grew quickly. As a result, Ashton-Tate became one of the first major corporations in the microcomputer industry. Later, Ashton-Tate was purchased by Borland, which now sells the dBase line of products.

The success of this product, however, confused and confounded the subject of database processing. The problem was this: According to the definition prevalent in the late 1970s, dBase II was neither a DBMS nor relational. In fact, it was a programming language with generalized file-processing (not database-processing) capabilities. The systems that were developed with dBase II appeared much more like those in Figure 1-9 than the ones in Figure 1-8. The million or so users of dBase II thought they were using a relational DBMS when, in fact, they were not.

Thus, the terms *database management system* and *relational database* were used loosely at the start of the microcomputer boom. Most of the people who were processing a microcomputer database were really managing files, and so they were not receiving the benefits of database processing, although they did not realize it. Today, the situation has changed as the microcomputer marketplace has become more mature and sophisticated. dBase IV and the dBase products that followed it are truly *relational* DBMS products.

Although dBase did pioneer the application of database technology on microcomputers, at the same time, other vendors began to move their products from the mainframe to the microcomputer. Oracle, Focus, and Ingress are three examples of DBMS products that were ported down to microcomputers. They are truly DBMS programs, and most would agree that they are truly relational as well. In addition, other vendors developed new relational DBMS products especially for micros. Paradox, Revelation, MDBS, Helix, and a number of other products fall into this category.

One impact of the move of database technology to the micro was the dramatic improvement in DBMS user interfaces. Users of microcomputer systems are generally not MIS professionals, and they will not put up with the clumsy and awkward user interfaces common on mainframe DBMS products. Thus, as DBMS products were devised for micros, user interfaces had to be simplified and made easier to use. This was possible because micro DBMS products operate on dedicated computers and because more computer power was available to process the user interface. Today, DBMS products provide rich and robust user interfaces using graphical user interfaces such as Microsoft Windows. Two such products are Microsoft's Access and Wall Data's SALSA for the Desktop.

The combination of microcomputers, the relational model, and vastly improved user interfaces enabled database technology to move from an organizational context to a personal-computing context. When this occurred, the number of sites that used database technology exploded. In 1980 there were about ten thousand sites using DBMS products in the United States; today there are well over ten million such sites!

■ CLIENT-SERVER DATABASE APPLICATIONS

In the middle to late 1980s, end users began to connect their separated microcomputers using local area networks (LANs). These networks enabled computers to send data to one another at previously unimaginable rates. The first applications of this technology shared peripherals, such as large-capacity fast disks, expensive printers and plotters, and facilitated intercomputer communication via electronic mail. In time, however, end users wanted to share their databases as well, which led to the development of multi-user database applications on local area networks.

The LAN-based multi-user architecture is considerably different from the multi-user architecture used on mainframe databases. With a mainframe, only one CPU is involved in database application processing, but with LAN systems, many CPUs can be simultaneously involved. Because this situation was both advantageous (greater performance) and more problematic (coordinating the actions of independent CPUs), it led to a new style of multi-user database processing called the **client–server database architecture.**

Not all database processing on a local area network is client–server processing. A simple, but less robust, mode of processing is called **file-sharing architecture.** A company like Treble Clef could most likely use either type since it is a relatively small organization with modest processing requirements. Larger workgroups, however, would require client–server processing. We will describe these approaches and discuss them in detail in Chapter 14.

■ MULTIMEDIA AND NETWORK DATABASES

As shown in the example of Rose Harbor Yacht Sales, database technology is being used today to store and process multimedia data such as pictures, sounds, movies, and animations. While at first this may seem surprising, it makes sense because a large portion of multimedia applications processing concerns keeping track of disparate files and relating them to each other. In a traditional database application, a SALES ORDER relates a CUSTOMER to a SALESPERSON to a set of ITEMS on the order. In the same way, a PAGE of a multimedia presentation relates an IMAGE to a background SOUND to a set of PICTURES to be shown sequentially as a slide show. Since database technology can support the first application, it can also support the second.

At present, the principle way of delivering multimedia applications (other than computer games) is via the Internet or organizational intranets. Since this is the case, multimedia database applications are often coupled with large public or private networks.

In fact, as far as database processing is concerned, such networks are simply a means of delivering an application to its users. The application need not be a multimedia application; any database application can be delivered across a network. For example, the human resources department of a corporation could create a traditional database application for in-house training sessions and deliver that application over the corporate intranet. Employees would access the application and use it to sign up for training sessions.

Thus, the availability of the Internet and other intranets simply increases the need for database applications—whether they are multimedia applications or not. Hence, the incredible popularity of network processing will serve to increase the demand for database technology. We will discuss such applications in greater detail in Chapter 16.

■ DISTRIBUTED DATABASE PROCESSING

Before concluding this survey of the history of database processing, we need to discuss two aspects of database technology that are important in theory but have not been, at least so far, widely adopted. The first is distributed database processing, and the second is object-oriented databases. We discuss these topics in more detail in Chapters 13 and 17, respectively.

Organizational database applications solve the problems of file processing and allow more integrated processing of organizational data. Personal and workgroup database systems bring database technology even closer to the user by allowing him or her access to locally managed databases. **Distributed databases** combine these types of database processing by allowing personal, workgroup, and organizational databases to be combined into integrated but distributed systems. As such, in theory, they offer even more flexible data access and processing, but they also unfortunately pose many unsolved problems.

The essence of distributed databases is that all of the organization's data are spread over many computers—micros, LAN servers, and mainframes—that communicate with one another as they process the database. The goals of distributed database systems are to make it appear to each user that he or she is the only user of the organization's data and to provide the same consistency, accuracy, and timeliness that he or she would have if no one else were using the distributed database.

Among the more pressing problems with distributed databases are those of security and control. Enabling so many users to access the database (there can be hundreds of concurrent users) and controlling what they do to that distributed database are complicated tasks.

Coordinating and synchronizing the data can be difficult. If one user group downloads and updates part of the database and then transmits the changed data back to the mainframe, how does the system prevent, in the meantime, another user from attempting to use the version of the data it finds on the mainframe? Imagine this problem involving dozens of files and hundreds of users using scores of pieces of computer equipment.

In fact, the concept of a distributed database actually blurs the definition of a database. Supposedly a database is a centralized, controlled collection of data and relationships. But if we fragment it and copy it onto many different computers, we have altered the original database concept.

Whereas the transitions from organizational to personal to workgroup database processing were relatively easy, the difficulties facing the database designers and engineers of the distributed DBMS are monumental. In truth, even though work on distributed database systems has been underway for more than twenty-five years, significant problems remain. Effective distributed database processing is still the child of the laboratory.

■ OBJECT-ORIENTED DBMS (ODBMS)

In the late 1980s a new style of programming called *object-oriented programming* (OOP) began to be used, which has a substantially different orientation from that of traditional programming, as is explained in Chapter 17. In brief, the data structures processed with OOP are considerably more complex than those processed with traditional languages. These data structures also are difficult to store in existing relational DBMS products. As a consequence, a new category of DBMS products called *object-oriented database systems* is evolving to store and process OOP data structures.

For a variety of reasons, OOP has not yet been widely used for business information systems. First, it is difficult to use, and it is very expensive to develop OOP applications. Second, most organizations have millions or billions of bytes of data already organized in relational databases, and they are unwilling to bear the cost and risk required to convert those databases to an ODBMS format. Finally, most ODBMS have been developed to support engineering applications, and they do not have features and functions that are appropriate or readily adaptable to business information applications.

Consequently, for the foreseeable future, ODBMS are likely to occupy a niche in commercial information systems applications. We will discuss OOP and object-oriented databases in Chapter 17, but the bulk of the discussion in this text will concern the relational model, since it concerns technologies that you are likely to use in the first five years of your career.

SUMMARY

Database processing is one of the most important courses in the information systems curriculum. Almost all business people need the benefits of database technology, but few know how to use it themselves. Thus, there is a great demand for people who can serve as a liaison between the technology and the business users.

Database technology is used in a variety of applications. Some serve only a single user on a single computer; others are used by work groups of twenty or thirty people on a local area network; still others are used by hundreds of users and involve trillions of bytes of data. Recently, database technology has been used to support multimedia applications and public and private networks.

The components of a database application are the database, the database management systems (DBMS), and application programs. Sometimes the application programs are entirely separate from the DBMS; other times substantial portions of the application are provided by features and functions of the DBMS.

File-processing systems store data in separate files, each of which contains a different type of data. File-processing systems have several limitations. With separated files, it is difficult to combine data stored in separate files, as the data are often duplicated among files, leading to data integrity problems. Application programs are dependent on file formats, causing maintenance problems when the formats change and the files become incompatible, requiring file conversions. And it is difficult to represent data from the users' perspectives.

Database-processing systems were developed to overcome these limitations. In the database environment, the database management system is the interface between application programs and the database. The data are integrated, and their duplication is reduced. Only the DBMS is affected by changes in the physical formats of stored data. And if data items are changed, added, or deleted, few application programs will require maintenance. With database technology, it is easier to represent objects in the users' environments.

A database is a self-describing collection of integrated records. It is self-describing because it contains a description of itself in a data dictionary. A data dictionary is also known as a data directory or metadata. A database is a collection of integrated records because the relationships among the records are stored in the database. This arrangement enables the DBMS to construct even complicated objects by combining data on the basis of the stored relationships. Relationships are often stored in overhead data. Thus, the three parts of a database are the application data, the data dictionary, and the overhead data.

Database technology developed in several stages. Early databases focused on the transaction processing of organizational data. Then, the relational model, together with the microcomputer, led to the use of personal database applications. With the advent of local area networks, departments began to implement workgroup client–server databases. Today, multimedia applications are being developed, and they, along with traditional database applications, are being delivered over the Internet and private networks. Distributed processing and object-oriented databases are important topics in database processing. To date, however, neither has been commercially successful or seen widespread use in business applications.

GROUP I QUESTIONS

1.1   Why is database processing an important subject?

1.2   Describe the nature and characteristics of a single-user database application used by an individual like Mary Richards.

1.3   Describe the nature and characteristics of a database application used by a workgroup like Treble Clef Music.

1.4   Describe the nature and characteristics of a database application used by a state's licensing and vehicle registration bureau.

1.5   Describe the nature and characteristics of a database application used by Rose Harbor Yacht Sales.

1.6   Explain the nature and function of each of the components of Figure 1-8.

1.7   How is the relationship between application programs and the DBMS changing over time?

1.8   List the limitations of file-processing systems as described in this chapter.

1.9   Explain how database technology overcomes the limitations you listed in your answer to Question 1.8.

1.10 Define the term *database*.

1.11 What are metadata? What are indexes? What are application metadata?

1.12 Explain why a database is a model. Describe the difference between a model of reality and a model of a user's model of reality. Why is this difference important?

1.13 Give an example, other than one in this chapter, of a personal database application.

1.14 Give an example, other than one in this chapter, of a workgroup database application.

1.15 Give an example, other than one in this chapter, of a large-enterprise database application.

1.16 What were some of the weaknesses of early organizational database applications?

1.17 What are the two primary advantages of the relational model?

1.18 Why was the relational model initially resisted?

1.19 Summarize the events in the development of microcomputer DBMS products.

1.20 What was the major factor that gave rise to workgroup database applications?

1.21 How does the client–server architecture differ from mainframe multi-user architectures?

1.22 Explain the general nature of distributed processing. What are some of the difficult problems to be faced?

1.23 Describe the purpose of an object–oriented database. Why have such databases not been more accepted for information systems applications?

◆ GROUP II QUESTIONS

1.24 Should a database course be required for an information systems major? Give reasons to support your answer. (It might be interesting to save your reasons and review them at the end of the course.)

1.25 Interview a salesperson at a local computer store. Ask for information on microcomputer database management systems. Does the store distinguish between file management systems and database management systems? If so, what are the differences? Does the store distinguish between relational and nonrelational DBMS products? If so, what are the differences?

1.26 Interview people who use a database application. What business functions are served? What information is produced? What objects are involved? Is this application a personal, workgroup, or organizational application?

INTRODUCTION TO DATABASE DEVELOPMENT

• • • • • • • • • • • • • • • • •

This chapter presents a broad overview of the development of a database and a database application. We begin with a description of the elements of a database and a discussion of the features and functions of a DBMS. Next we illustrate the creation of a database and a database application. Finally, we discuss common strategies of database development. The goal of this chapter is to create a perspective for the detailed descriptions of the technology in following chapters.

THE DATABASE

Figure 2-1 shows the main components of a database system. The **database** is processed by the **DBMS,** which is used by both developers and users, who can use the DBMS either directly or indirectly via **application programs.** We discuss the database in this section and the DBMS and applications in subsequent sections.

As described in Chapter 1, a database contains four main elements: user data, metadata, indexes, and application metadata.

■ USER DATA

Today, most databases represent user data as relations. We formally define the term relation in Chapter 5. For now, consider a relation to be a table of data. The columns of the table contain fields or attributes, and the rows of the table contain records for particular entities in the business environment.

Not all relations are equally desirable; some relations are better structured than others. Chapter 5 describes a process called normalization that is used to create well-structured relations. To get an idea of the difference between poorly structured and well-structured relations, consider the relation R1 (StudentName, StudentPhone, AdviserName, AdviserPhone) with the following data:

StudentName	StudentPhone	AdviserName	AdviserPhone
Baker, Rex	232-8897	Parks	236-0098
Charles, Mary	232-0099	Parks	236-0098
Johnson, Beth	232-4487	Jones	236-0110
Scott, Glenn	232-4444	Parks	236-0098
Zylog, Frita	232-5588	Jones	236-0110

The problem with this relation is that it has data concerning two different topics, students and advisers. A relation structured in this way presents a number of problems when it is updated. For example, if adviser Parks changes his or her telephone number, three rows of data must be changed. For this reason, the data would be better represented by the two relations R2(StudentName, StudentPhone, AdviserName) with data

StudentName	StudentPhone	AdviserName
Baker, Rex	232-8897	Parks
Charles, Mary	232-0099	Parks
Johnson, Beth	232-4487	Jones
Scott, Glenn	232-4444	Parks
Zylog, Frita	232-5588	Jones

and R3(AdviserName, AdviserPhone) with data

AdviserName	AdviserPhone
Parks	236-0098
Jones	236-0110

FIGURE 2-1   *Components of Database Systems*

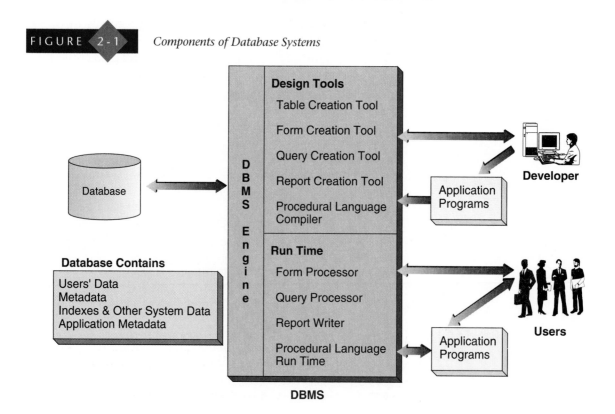

Now if an adviser changes his or her phone, only one row of R3 has to be changed. Of course, to produce a report that shows the names of students along with their advisers' phone numbers, the rows of these two tables will need to be combined. It turns out, however, that it is far better to store the relations separately and combine them when producing a report than to store them as one combined table.

■ METADATA

As defined in Chapter 1, a database is self-describing, which means that it contains a description of its structure as part of itself. This description of the structure is called **metadata.** Since DBMS products are designed to store and manipulate tables, most products store the metadata in the form of tables, sometimes called **system tables.**

Figure 2-2 shows an example of metadata stored in two system tables. The first stores a list of tables that are in the database, indicating how many columns are in each table and what column(s) is the primary key. This key is the unique identifier of a row. The second table stores a list of columns in each table and the data type and length of each column. These two tables are typical of system tables; other such tables store lists of indexes, keys, rules, and other portions of the database structure.

Storing metadata in tables is not only efficient for the DBMS; it is also convenient for users because they can use the same query tools for metadata as they do for user data. Thus, once a user learns how to use the DBMS's query facility to query a user table, he or she can use that same facility to query system tables. Later in this book we discuss a language called SQL that is used to query and update tables for both metadata and user data.

FIGURE 2-2   *Examples of Metadata*

SysTables Table

Table Name	Number of Columns	Primary Key
Student	4	Student Number
Adviser	3	AdviserName
Course	3	ReferenceNumber
Enrollment	3	{StudentNumber, ReferenceNumber}

SysColumns Table

Column Name	Table Name	Data Type	Length*
StudentNumber	Student	Integer	4
FirstName	Student	Text	20
LastName	Student	Text	30
Major	Student	Text	10
AdviserName	Adviser	Text	25
Phone	Adviser	Text	12
Department	Adviser	Text	15
ReferenceNumber	Course	Integer	4
Title	Course	Text	10
NumberHours	Course	Decimal	4
StudentNumber	Enrollment	Integer	4
ReferenceNumber	Enrollment	Integer	4
Grade	Enrollment	Text	2

* Lengths are stated in bytes, which are the same as characters of text data.

As an example of how you might use SQL for this purpose, suppose that you have developed a database with fifteen tables and two hundred columns. You remember that several of the columns have the data type *currency,* but you cannot remember which ones. By using SQL, you can access the SysColumns Table to find out which columns have that data type.

■ INDEXES

A third type of database data improves the performance and accessibility of the database. These data, which are sometimes called **overhead data,** consist principally of indexes, although other types of data structures, such as linked lists, are sometimes used (see the appendix for a discussion of indexes and linked lists).

Figure 2-3 shows a table of student data and two indexes. To demonstrate the necessity of having these indexes, suppose that the data are stored on disk in ascending order of StudentNumber and that the user wants to print a report of student data sorted by LastName. To do this, all of the data could be extracted from the source table and sorted, but unless the table is small, this is a time-consuming process.

Alternatively, an index like the LastName index in Figure 2-3 could be created. The entries in this index are sorted by value of LastName, so the entries of the index can be read and used to access the student data in sorted order. Suppose further that student data must also be printed in order of student major. Again, the

FIGURE 2-3 *Examples of Database Indexes*

Example STUDENT Table

Student Number	FirstName	LastName	Major
100	James	Baker	Accounting
200	Mary	Abernathy	Info Systems
300	Beth	Jackson	Accounting
400	Eldridge	Johnson	Marketing
500	Chris	Tufte	Accounting
600	John	Smathers	Info Systems
700	Michael	Johnson	Accounting

LastName Index

LastName	StudentNumber
Abernathy	200
Baker	100
Jackson	300
Johnson	400, 700
Smathers	600
Tufte	500

Major Index

Major	StudentNumber
Accounting	100, 300, 500, 700
Info Systems	200, 600
Marketing	400

data could be extracted from the source table and sorted, or an index like the Major index could be constructed and used as just described.

Indexes are used not only for sorting but also for quick access to data. For example, a user wants to access only those students who have the value "Info Systems" for Major. Without an index, the entire source table must be searched. But with the index, the index entry can be found and used to find all of the qualifying rows. Although indexes are not needed for a table with as few rows as the STUDENT table in Figure 2-3, consider a table that has ten thousand or twenty thousand rows of data. In that case, sorting or searching the entire table would be very slow.

Indexes are indeed helpful for sorting and searching operations, but at a cost. Every time a row in the STUDENT table is updated, the indexes must also be updated. This is not necessarily bad; it just means that indexes are not free and so should be reserved for cases in which they are truly needed.

■ APPLICATION METADATA

The fourth and final type of data that is stored in the database is **application metadata,** which is used to store the structure and format of user forms, reports, queries, and other application components. Not all DBMS products support application components and, of those products that do, not all store the structure of those components as application metadata in the database. However, most of the modern DBMS products do store such data as part of the database. In general, neither the database developers nor the users access the application metadata directly. Instead, they use tools in the DBMS to process it.

THE DBMS

DBMS products vary considerably in the features and functions that they provide. The first such products were developed for use on mainframes in the late 1960s, and they had very primitive features. Since then, DBMS products have been continually enhanced and improved not only to process database data better but also to incorporate features that facilitate the creation of database applications.

In this chapter we use Microsoft Access to illustrate the capabilities of DBMS products, because it provides features and functions that typify the characteristics of a modern DBMS. Microsoft Access is not, however, the only such DBMS, and our selecting it is not meant to be an endorsement of it over other, similar products, such as Lotus Approach, Borland's Paradox for Windows, or Wall Data's SALSA for the Desktop.

As shown in Figure 2-1, the features and functions of a DBMS can be divided into three subsystems: the design tools subsystem, the run-time subsystem, and the DBMS engine.

■ THE DESIGN TOOLS SUBSYSTEM

The design tools subsystem has a set of tools to facilitate the design and creation of the database and its applications. It typically includes tools for creating tables, forms, queries, and reports. DBMS products also provide programming languages and interfaces to programming languages. For example, Access has two languages, a macro language that does not require in-depth programming knowledge and a version of BASIC called Visual Basic. When using the form, query, and report design tools, these languages can be used to develop application features and functions that extend beyond those currently available.

■ RUN-TIME SUBSYSTEM

The run-time subsystem[1] processes the application components that are developed using the design tools. For example, Access has a run-time facility that materializes forms and connects form elements with table data. For example, a form has been defined that includes a text box to display the value of StudentNumber of the STUDENT table. During execution, when the form is opened, the form run-time processor extracts the value of StudentNumber from the current STUDENT row and displays it in the form. All of this is automatic; neither the user nor the developer need do anything once the form is created. Other run-time processors answer queries and print reports. In addition, there is a run-time component that processes application program requests for reading and writing database data.

Although not shown in Figure 2-1, DBMS products must also provide an application program interface for standard languages such as COBOL, C++, and ANSI BASIC. Some type of subprogram call library or a similar facility enables programs written in standard languages to read table data, to add and update data, and even to define new tables and queries.

■ THE DBMS ENGINE

The third component of the DBMS is the DBMS engine, which is the intermediary between the design tools and run-time subsystems and the data. The DBMS engine receives requests from the other two components—stated in terms of tables, rows, and columns—and translates those requests into commands to the operating system to read and write data on physical media.

The DBMS engine is also involved with transaction management, locking, and backup and recovery. As we show in Chapter 13, actions against the database often must be made as a complete unit. When processing an order, for example, changes in the CUSTOMER, ORDER, and INVENTORY tables should be made as a group: Either all of them should be made, or none of them should be made. The DBMS engine helps coordinate the activities to ensure that either all of the group or none of the group is applied.

◆ CREATING THE DATABASE

A *database schema* defines a database's structure, its tables, relationships, domains, and business rules. A database schema is a design, the foundation on which the database and the applications are built.

■ AN EXAMPLE OF A SCHEMA

To illustrate a schema and why it is important, consider an example. Highline College is a small liberal arts college in the Midwest. Its student activities department sponsors intramural athletic leagues, but it has a problem keeping track of the athletic equipment that has been checked out to various team captains.

---

[1]Do not confuse the term *run-time subsystem* with the term *run-time product*. Some vendors use the term *run-time product* to refer to a product that includes the run-time and DBMS engine components but not the design tools subsystem. Such a product can be used to process an application that has already been developed. The purpose of run-time products is to reduce the cost of the application to the end user. Normally, the run-time product is much less expensive (sometimes even free) than the full DBMS product. Hence, only the developer buys the full product that includes the design tools subsystem; the end users buy only the run-time product.

TABLES   To address this problem, the department created a database consisting of the following two tables:[2]

CAPTAIN (CaptainName, Phone, Street, City, State, Zip)

and

ITEM (Quantity, Description, DateOut, DateIn)

where the table names are shown outside the parentheses and the column names are shown inside the parentheses.

Neither CaptainName nor Description is necessarily a unique name, as two captains could just as easily be named 'Mary Smith' and there certainly are many items called 'Soccer Balls'. In order to make sure that each row can be identified (the importance of this will be made clearer in later chapters), we add two columns of unique numbers to these tables, as follows:

CAPTAIN (CAPTAIN_ID, CaptainName, Phone, Street, City, State, Zip)

ITEM (ITEM_ID, Quantity, Description, DateOut, DateIn)

RELATIONSHIPS   The relationship between these two tables is as follows: One row of CAPTAIN relates to many rows of ITEM, but a row of ITEM relates to one, and only one, row of CAPTAIN. The general notation for a relationship like this is **1:N** and is pronounced "one to N" or "one to many." The term 1:N means that one row of the first table is related to many rows of the second.

For the tables shown here, there is no way to tell which row of CAPTAIN relates to which rows of ITEM. Therefore, to show that relationship, we add CAPTAIN_ID to ITEM. The complete structure of the two tables is as follows:

CAPTAIN (CAPTAIN_ID, CaptainName, Phone, Street, City, State, Zip)

ITEM (ITEM_ID, Quantity, Description, DateOut, DateIn, CAPTAIN_ID)

With this structure, it is easy to determine which captain has checked out a given ITEM. For example, to find out who has checked out item 1234, we examine the row for item 1234 and find the value of CAPTAIN_ID stored in that row. We can then use that value to determine the name and phone number of that captain.

DOMAINS   A domain[3] is a set of values that a column may have. Consider the domains for the columns of ITEM. Suppose that both ITEM_ID and Quantity have the domain of integer numbers, that Description is text of length 25, that both DateOut and DateIn have the domain of date, and that CAPTAIN_ID also has the domain of integer numbers. In addition to the physical format, we also need to decide whether any of the domains are to be unique to the table. For our example, we want ITEM_ID to be unique and so must specify its domain in that way. Since a captain may have more than one ITEM checked out, CAPTAIN_ID is not unique to the ITEM table.

The domains of the columns of CAPTAIN also must be specified. CAPTAIN_ID is integer, and all the rest of the columns are text of different lengths. CAPTAIN_ID must be unique to the CAPTAIN table.

BUSINESS RULES   The last element of a database schema is business rules, which are restrictions on the business's activities that need to be reflected in the database and database applications. The following are examples of business rules for Highline College:

---

[2]As we show in Chapters 3 through 6, the most important and difficult task in database development is designing the table structure. By starting this example with the tables already defined, we have skipped a major portion of the project.

[3]This discussion is simplified considerably so as to focus on the components of a database system. A more complete discussion of domains appears in Chapter 4.

1. In order to check out any equipment, a captain must have a local phone number.
2. No captain may have more than seven soccer balls checked out at any one time.
3. Captains must return all equipment within five days after the end of each semester.
4. No captain may check out more equipment if he or she has any overdue.

Business rules are an important part of the schema because they specify the constraints on allowed data values that must be enforced no matter how the data changes reach the DBMS engine. Regardless of whether the request for a data change comes from the user of a form, a query/update request, or from an application program, the DBMS should ensure that the change violates no rules.

Unfortunately, DBMS products today offer only limited enforcement of business rules, and many such rules must be enforced by the application programs and procedures carried out by the user. This situation is changing, however, and DBMS products are being developed to enforce more and more types of business rules.

■ CREATING TABLES

Once the schema has been designed, the next step is creating the database tables using the DBMS's table creation tools. Figure 2-4 shows the form used with Microsoft Access to create the ITEM table. Each table column name is typed in the Field Name form column, and the data type of the column is specified in the Data Type column. Additional data about the column—such as text length, field format, caption, and other data—are specified in the entry fields in the lower left-hand column of the form.

In Figure 2-4, the focus is on the ITEM_ID column. Observe that the indexed property at the bottom of the form has been set to Yes (No Duplicates), which

FIGURE 2-4   *Creating a Table with Microsoft Access*

Field Name	Data Type	Description
ITEM_ID	Number	
Quantity	Number	
Description	Memo	
DateOut	Date/Time	
DateIn	Date/Time	
CAPTAIN_ID	Number	

Field Properties

General | Lookup

Field Size	Long Integer
Format	
Decimal Places	Auto
Input Mask	
Caption	
Default Value	
Validation Rule	
Validation Text	
Required	No
Indexed	Yes (No Duplicates)

A field name can be up to 64 characters long, including spaces. Press F1 for help on field names.

Design view. F6 = Switch panes. F1 = Help.   CAPS

FIGURE 2-5 *Declaring a Relationship with Microsoft Access*

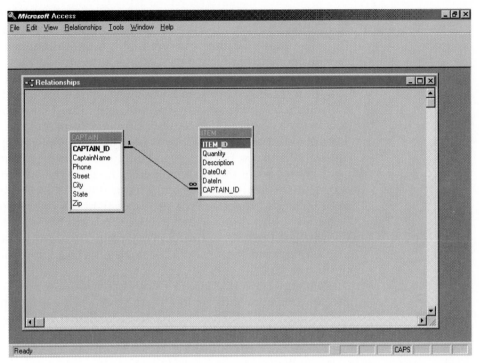

means that an index of unique values is to be created for the ITEM_ID column. To complete the database definition, the CAPTAIN table is created in a similar way.

■ DEFINING RELATIONSHIPS

The relationship between CAPTAIN and ITEM is 1:N, which we represent in the schema by placing the key of CAPTAIN in ITEM. In Figure 2-4, we place CAPTAIN_ID in the ITEM table. A column like CAPTAIN_ID in the ITEM table is sometimes called a **foreign key** because it is the key of a table that is foreign to the table in which it resides. When creating forms, queries, and reports, the DBMS can provide more services and help to the developer if it knows that CAPTAIN_ID in ITEM is a foreign key of CAPTAIN.

DBMS products vary in the way that they declare this status. With Microsoft Access, the declaration is made by drawing the relationship between the key and the foreign key, as shown in Figure 2-5. CAPTAIN_ID of the primary table (CAPTAIN) is set equal to CAPTAIN_ID of the related table (ITEM). The 1 and infinity sign indicate a 1-to-many relationship.

One of the advantages of declaring a relationship to the DBMS is that whenever columns from the two tables are placed in a form, query, or report, the DBMS will know how to relate the rows of the tables. Although this can be declared each time for each form, query, or report, declaring it once saves time and reduces the chance of errors. Once the tables, columns, and relationships have been defined, the next step is to build the application components.

COMPONENTS OF APPLICATIONS

A database application consists of forms, queries, reports, menus, and application programs. As shown in Figure 2-1, the forms, queries, and reports can be defined using tools supplied with the DBMS. Application programs must be written in either a language that is part of the DBMS or a standardized language and connected to the database through the DBMS.

■ FORMS

Figure 2-6 shows a data entry form that is used at Highline College to enter both captain and item checkout data. The user enters the captain data at the top of the form and the item checkout data in a grid below the captain data.

The form shown in Figure 2-6 was developed using the Access form generation tool. Figure 2-7 shows how this tool was used to locate text boxes, like the one that contains the CaptainName column. Using the form tool, a text box was drawn on a blank form. The left-hand box is the box label, which is set to 'CaptainName'. The right-hand text box is used to hold values of the CaptainName column.

Once the box is drawn, its properties are set in the property sheet (the window shown on the right-hand side of the figure titled 'Label: CaptainName Label'). The Control Source property of the text box will be set to CaptainName. This informs Access that the values entered into this text box should be stored in the CaptainName column of the CAPTAIN table. Then, when the form is used to display existing data, the value of CaptainName is taken from the table and displayed in this text box.

You may be wondering how Access knows to use the CAPTAIN table. Before the situation shown in Figure 2-7, the user set the source property of the form equal to CAPTAIN, thereby telling Access to base the form on the columns of the CAPTAIN table.

In this application, neither CAPTAIN_ID nor ITEM_ID is visible in the form in Figure 2-6. Such IDs are hidden from the user. Whenever the user creates a new CAPTAIN by opening a blank form, an application program in the background assigns a value for CAPTAIN_ID. Similarly, whenever the user clicks on the ITEM grid to create a new row in the grid, the background application creates

FIGURE 2-6   *Example Highline College Data Entry Form*

FIGURE 2-7   *Creating a Form with Microsoft Access*

a new value of ITEM_ID, and it also assigns the current value of CAPTAIN_ID to the new ITEM row.

Why are these IDs hidden? The reason is that they have no meaning to the users. Highline does not assign IDs to captains or to particular items that are checked out. If they did, then these IDs would be used and would be made visible. Instead, these IDs have been created only so that each row of each table will be uniquely identifiable to Access. Since these IDs have no meaning to the user, they are hidden.

■ QUERIES

From time to time, users want to query the data to answer questions or to identify problems or particular situations. For example, suppose that at the start of the fall semester, 1996, one of the users wants to know whether any equipment that was checked out before September 1, 1996, has not yet been checked back in. If it has not, the user wants to know the name of the captain, his or her phone number, and the quantity and description of the items checked out.

There are a number of ways that such a query can be expressed. One is to use the data access language SQL, which is explained in Chapter 8. Another way is to use **query by example (QBE).** Figure 2-8 shows the creation of this query using QBE in Microsoft Access. To create a query, the user places into the query window the names of the tables that are to be queried. This has already been done in the upper section of the form shown in Figure 2-8. Since the relationship between CAPTAIN and ITEM has already been defined for Access (in Figure 2-5), Access knows that the two tables are linked by CAPTAIN_ID, as shown by the line drawn between CAPTAIN_ID in the two table boxes in Figure 2-8.

Next the query creator indicates which columns of data are to be returned by the query. With Access, this is done by dragging and dropping the names of the columns from the table boxes into the grid in the bottom half of the form. In Figure 2-8, the columns CaptainName, Phone, Quantity, Description, DateOut, and

FIGURE 2-8   *Creating a Query with Microsoft Access*

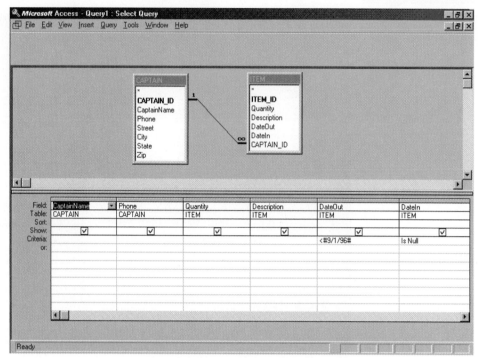

DateIn have been placed into the query. Then the query criteria are specified in the row labeled Criteria. These criteria are that data must be before (<) 9/1/96. (In Access, dates are surrounded by pound signs [#].) Also, the value of DateIn is to be equal to Null, which means that no value for DateIn has been specified. The result of this query for sample data is shown in Figure 2-9. Note that all of the equipment shown was checked out before 9/1/96, as was required in the query definition.

With Access and most other DBMS products, queries can be saved as part of the application so that they can be rerun as necessary. In addition, queries can be parameterized, meaning that they can be constructed so as to accept criteria values at the time they are run. For example, the query in Figure 2-8 can be parameterized so that the user enters the value of DateOut when the query is run. Any items that were checked out before that date but that have not yet been checked back in will be shown.

A third type of query, one that is easier for users, is called **query by form.** With it, the user types query constraints on a data entry form and presses the search button. The DBMS finds all instances that meet the given constraints. For the example query, for the form in Figure 2-6, the user would enter <#9/1/1996# in the DateOut field and Is Null in the DateIn field and press the QueryByForm button. The DBMS would find the records for all captains who meet the query constraints. Query by form is a newer and more modern way to query data than query by example, and is likely to replace query by example in many applications.

■ REPORTS

A report is a formatted display of database data, an example of which is shown in Figure 2-10. This report, which is shown as it would be displayed on a computer screen, contains a section for each team captain and a list of the items checked out by that captain in the section. For example, the items checked out by captain 'Miyamoto Mary' are shown in the first section of the report.

FIGURE 2-9   *Result of Example Query in Figure 2-8*

FIGURE 2-10   *Example Report for Highline College*

FIGURE 2-11   *Developing a Report with Microsoft Access*

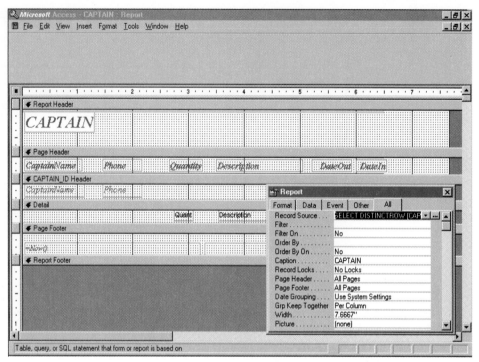

Developing a report is similar to developing a data entry form, although in some ways it is easier because a report is used only for displaying data. In other ways, constructing a report is more difficult because reports often have a more complicated structure than forms do.

Figure 2-11 shows the display of the Access report definition tool that was used to create the report in Figure 2-10. The text 'CaptainName Phone Quantity . . . ' has been typed in the section labeled Page Header, an action that causes Access to print these labels at the top of each page of the report. Next a section has been defined by creating the CAPTAIN_ID Header. Two fields have been entered in this header, one for CaptainName and another for Phone. Defining such a section causes Access to create the captain groups shown in Figure 2-10. Finally, the columns that are to be shown in each captain section are placed in the Detail section. In Figure 2-11, the Description, Quantity, DateOut, and DateIn columns are to be displayed.

In general, reports can have many sections. In a more complex example, say course/student enrollment, a report could be grouped by COLLEGE, by DEPART-MENT, by COURSE, and by STUDENT. In this case the report would have three Header sections and a detail line.

■ MENUS

Menus are used to organize the application components so as to make them more accessible to the end user and to provide control over the user's activities. Figure 2-12 shows an example menu for the Highline application. The line across the top of the form presents the highest-level options: File, Forms, Queries, Reports, and Help. The underlined letters represent keyboard shortcut keys. If the user types <Alt> plus the underlined letter, the submenu choices will be displayed.

In Figure 2-12, the user has keyed <Alt> plus the letter S. The submenu choices are Select All Records, Select by Name, and Select by Phone. Again, keyboard shortcut keys can be used to select one of these items by typing <Alt> and

FIGURE 2-12   *Example Menu*

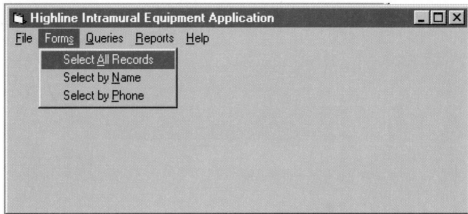

the underlined letter of the choice. Menus make the application more accessible to the user by showing what options are available and helping the users select those actions they want performed. Menus can also be used to control user access to forms, reports, and programs. Some applications take advantage of this by dynamically changing menu items after the user signs on.

■ APPLICATION PROGRAMS

The final component of a database application is application programs. As we mentioned earlier, such programs can be written in a language that is specific to the DBMS or in a standard language that interfaces with the DBMS through a predefined program interface. Here we use the version of BASIC included with Microsoft Access.

Consider the problem of assigning IDs to new rows of data. Whenever the user creates a new record via a form, Access generates an Insert event. The application programmer can trap or intercept the processing of this event by naming a function to be called when a row is inserted. Figure 2-13 illustrates how this is done for the CAPTAIN form. The properties of the form are in the window labeled 'Form'. The property named Before Insert is used to declare the name of the routine that is to be called when a new row is to be inserted through the form. Here this property is set to call the function GetNextID. It passes the name of the current form and a number that the application uses to identify the CAPTAIN table.

Figure 2-14 shows two Visual Basic functions. It is not necessary to understand the details of them; indeed, there is more in them than we can or need to discuss at this point. Instead, look at the two functions to get a general idea of how an application program references a database.

The Highline application contains a table called WTableList that keeps data about all of the tables in the database. This table is metadata created by the application. One of the columns in this table is named MaxID. When a table is opened, the value of this column is read from the database and entered into an array named *ObjectID*. The position of the tables in this array depends on their table number. CAPTAIN has been allocated table 1 and so occupies the first position in the array.

When GetNextID is called, the first line of code checks to see whether ObjectID (TableNum) equals zero. If so, the table is not yet open, and so the function OpenDBTable is called to open it. If ObjectID(TableNum) is not zero, then one is added to the value in this array, and the new value is placed in the form. The third statement is peculiar to Access Basic and simply is used to set the value of the text box named Text1 to the value of ObjectID(TableNum). Since Text1 has been

FIGURE 2-13

Trapping an Event on the Captain Form

FIGURE 2-14

Access BASIC Example

```
Function GetNextID (FormName As String, TableNum As Long)
'ObjectID is an array common to all run time routines
'it is filled when the table is first opened

Dim T as Variant

        If ObjectID(TableNum) = 0 Then T = OpenDBTable(TableNum)
        ObjectID(TableNum) = ObjectID(TableNum) + 1
        Forms(FormName).Text1 = ObjectID(TableNum)

End Function

Function OpenDBTable (TableNum As Long)
'ObjectID is an array common to all run time routines
'DB is type Database and is common
'TableTable is type Table and is common

   If ObjectID(TableNum) <> 0 Then Exit Function

   Set DB = CurrentDB()                      'establish DB variable
   Set TableTable = DB.OpenTable("WTableList") 'open table of tables
   TableTable.Index = "PrimaryKey"           'set up seek

   TableTable.Seek "=", TableNum             'find row for this table
   If TableTable.NoMatch = -1 Then
           Call ProcessError(TNumProblem)    'process error
           Exit Function
   End If

   ObjectID(TableNum) = TableTable!MaxID     'fill entry in ObjectID
   TableTable.Close

End Function
```

bound to the column named CAPTAIN_ID, this statement causes the new ID to be entered into that column.

If OpenDBTable is called, then the table named WTableList is opened, and the row for table TableNum is found with the statement

TableTable.Seek "=", TableNum

Then ObjectID(TableNum) is set to the value of the column MaxID, by means of the statement

ObjectID(TableNum) = TableTable!MaxID.

Not shown in Figure 2-14 is a third function that is called when the form is closed. At that time, the current value of the array ObjectID is written out to the column MaxID in the WTableList table.

Again, do not be alarmed if you do not understand the syntax of these statements. They are peculiar to Microsoft Access and not important to us at this point. Your objective here should be to get a general idea of how the forms, tables, and application programs interact to create the application.

DATABASE DEVELOPMENT PROCESSES

Volumes and volumes have been written on the development of information systems in general and on the development of database applications in particular. Therefore, we do not need to discuss here systems development processes in any depth, but we will conclude this chapter with an overview of the processes used to develop databases and database applications.

■ GENERAL STRATEGIES

A database is a model of the users' model of their business activities. Therefore, in order to build an effective database and related applications, the development team must become thoroughly familiar with the users' model. To do this, they build a data model that identifies the things to be stored in the database and defines their structure and the relationships among them. This familiarity must be obtained early in the development process, by interviewing the users and building a statement of requirements. Most such statements include the use of **prototypes,** which are sample databases and applications that represent various aspects of the system to be created.

There are two general strategies for developing a database: top-down and bottom-up. **Top-down development** proceeds from the general to the specific. It begins with a study of the strategic goals of the organization, the means by which those goals can be accomplished, the information requirements that must be satisfied to reach those goals, and the systems necessary to provide that information. From such a study, an abstract data model is constructed.

Using this high-level model, the development team progressively works downward toward more and more detailed descriptions and models. Intermediate-level models also are expanded with more detail until the particular databases and related applications can be identified. One or more of these applications is then selected for development. Over time, the entire high-level data model is transformed into lower-level models, and all of the indicated systems, databases, and applications are created.

Bottom-up development operates in the reverse order of abstraction, by beginning with the need to develop a specific system. The means of selecting the first system vary from organization to organization. In some organizations, a steering committee chooses the application; in others, the users may choose it themselves; in still others, the loudest voice in the executive office wins out.

By whatever means, a particular system is selected for development. The development team then obtains statements of requirements by considering the outputs and inputs of any existing computer-based systems, by analyzing the forms and reports for existing manual systems, and by interviewing the users to find out their need for new reports, forms, queries, and other requirements. From all of this, the team develops the information system. If the system involves a database, the team uses the requirement specifications to build a data model, and from the model, it designs and implements the database. When this system is finished, other projects are started in order to build additional information systems.

Proponents of the top-down approach claim that it is superior to the bottom-up approach because the data models (and subsequent systems) are constructed with a global perspective. They believe that such systems have better interfaces to one another, are more consistent, and require far less rework and modification.

Proponents of the bottom-up approach claim that it is superior to top-down because it is faster and less risky. They assert that top-down modeling results in many studies that are difficult to complete and that the planning process often ends in analysis paralysis. Although bottom-up modeling does not necessarily produce the best set of systems, it does produce useful systems quickly. The benefits of these systems begin accruing much faster than with top-down modeling, and they can more than compensate for any rework or modification that will need to be done to adjust the system to a global perspective.

This text explains the tools and techniques that can be used with either style of systems development. For example, although both entity-relationship modeling (Chapter 3) and semantic object modeling (Chapter 4) work with either top-down or bottom-up development, the entity-relationship approach is particularly effective with top-down development, and the semantic object approach is particularly effective with bottom-up development.

■ DATA MODELING

As we stated, the most important goal of the requirements phase is creating a model of the users' data. Whether this is done in top-down or bottom-up fashion, it involves interviewing users, documenting requirements, and, from those requirements, building the data model and prototypes. Such a model identifies what is to be stored in the database and defines their structure and the relationships among them.

For example, consider Figure 2-15(a), a list of orders made by a salesperson during a specific period of time. For this report to be produced by a database application, the database must contain the data shown, so the database developers need to examine the report and work backward to the data that must be stored in the database. In this case, there must be data concerning salespeople (name and region) and data concerning orders (company, order date, and amount).

Database development is complicated by the fact that there is not just one requirement but many and that the requirements usually overlap. The report in Figure 2-15(b) is also about salespeople, but, instead of orders, it lists commission checks. From this report, we can surmise that there are different types of orders and that each type has a different commission rate.

The orders implied by the report in Figure 2-15(b) somehow relate to the orders listed in Figure 2-15(a), but how they do so is not entirely clear. The development team must determine this relationship by inference from reports and forms, from interviews with users, from the team's knowledge of the subject matter, and from other sources.

DATA MODELING AS INFERENCING   When the users say they need forms and reports with specific data and structures, their statement implies a model that the users have of the things in their world. The users may not, however, be able to de-

FIGURE 2-15   *Examples of Two Related Reports: (a) Sample SALES Report and (b) Sample COMMISSION Report*

Salesperson Order List
14-Jun-96

Name	Region	CompanyName	OrderDate	Amount
Kevin Dougherty	Western			
		Cabo Controls	9/12/96	$2,349.88
				$2,349.88
Mary B. Wu	Western			
		Ajax Electric	9/17/96	$23,445.00
		American Maxell	9/24/96	$17,339.44
				$40,784.44
			Grand Total:	$43,134.32

(a)

Salesperson Commission Check Report
14-Jun-96

Name	LocalNumber	CheckDate	CType	CAmount
Kevin Dougherty	232-9988			
		9/30/96	XZ	$487.38
				$487.38
Mary B. Wu	232-9987			
		9/30/96	C	$237.44
		9/30/96	A	$1,785.39
				$2,022.83
			Grand Total:	$2,510.21

(b)

scribe exactly what that model is. If a developer were to ask the typical user, "What is the structure of the data model in your brain regarding salespeople?" the user would, at best, look quizzical, because most users do not think in that way.

Instead, the developers must infer, from the users' statements about forms and reports, the structure and relationships of the things to be stored in the database. The developers then record these inferences in a data model that is transformed into a database design, and that design is implemented using a DBMS. Applications that produce the reports and forms for the users are then constructed.

Building a data model is thus a process of inference. Reports and forms are like shadows projected on a wall. The users can describe the shadows, but they cannot describe the shapes that give rise to the shadows. Therefore the developers must infer, work backward, and reverse-engineer the structures and relationships of those shapes from the shadows.

This inferencing process is, unfortunately, more art than science. It is possible to learn the tools and techniques for data modeling; in fact, such tools and techniques are the subject of the next two chapters, but using those tools and techniques is an art that requires experience guided by intuition.

The quality of the model is important. If the documented data model accurately reflects the data model in the users' minds, there is an excellent chance that the resulting reports will be close to the users' needs. But if the documented data model inaccurately reflects this data model, it is unlikely that the report to be produced will be close to what the users really want.

MODELING IN MULTIUSER SYSTEMS   The data modeling process becomes even more complicated for multiuser workgroup and organizational databases, because many users may envision many different data models. Occasionally these data models are inconsistent, although sometimes the inconsistencies can be resolved. For example, the users may be employing the same term for different things or different terms for the same things.

Sometimes, however, the differences cannot be reconciled. In such cases, the database developer must document the differences and help the users resolve them, and this usually means that some people have to change the way they view their world.

An even greater challenge is presented by large systems in which no single user has a model of the complete structure. Each user understands some of the workgroup's or organization's data model, but no single user understands all of it. In such cases, the database becomes the logical union of the pieces of the workgroup's or organization's model, and the developers must document that logical union in the data model. And this can be quite difficult.

CONFUSION ABOUT THE TERM *MODEL*   The next two chapters present two alternative tools for building data models: the entity-relationship model and the semantic object model. Both models are structures for describing and documenting users' data requirements. To avoid confusion, note the different uses of the term *model*. The development team analyzes the requirements and builds a *users' data model* or a *requirements data model*. This model is a representation of the structure and relationships of what needs to be in the database to support the users' requirements. To create the users' data model, the development team uses tools called entity-relationship and the semantic object data models, which consist of language and diagramming standards for representing the users' data model. Their role in database development is similar to that of flowcharting and pseudocode in programming.

SUMMARY

The components of a database system are the database, the DBMS, and application programs, which are used by both developers and users. A database contains data, metadata, indexes, and application metadata. Most databases today represent data as relations or tables, although not all relations are equally desirable. Undesirable relations can be improved through a process called normalization. Metadata is often stored in special tables called system tables.

A DBMS's features and functions can be grouped into three subsystems. The design tools subsystem defines the database and the structure of applications or application components. The functions of the run-time subsystem are to materialize the forms, reports, and queries by reading or writing database data. The DBMS engine is the intermediary between the other two subsystems and the operating system. It receives requests stated in terms of tables and rows and columns and translates those requests into read and write requests.

A schema is a description of the structure of a database and includes descriptions of tables, relationships, domains, and business rules. The rows of one table can be related to the rows of other tables. This chapter illustrated a 1:N relationship between table rows; there are other relationship types as well, as we will discuss in the next chapter.

A domain is a set of values that a column may have. We must specify a domain for each column of each table.

Finally, business rules are restrictions on the business's activities that must be reflected in the database and database applications.

The facilities of the DBMS are used to create table structures, to define relationships, and to create forms, reports, queries, and menus. DBMS products also include facilities for interacting with application programs written in either DBMS-specific languages or standard languages like COBOL.

Since a database is a model of the users' model of the business, database development begins by learning and recording this model. Sometimes it is expressed in prototypes of the application or application components to be constructed.

The two general styles of development are top-down development, which proceeds from the general to the specific, and bottom-up development, which proceeds from the specific to the general. With top-down, applications are developed with a global perspective; with bottom-up, applications are developed more quickly. Sometimes a combination of the two approaches is used.

Data models are constructed by a process that involves inferencing from users' statements. Forms, reports, and queries are gathered, and the developers work backward to infer the structures that the users envision. This is necessary because most users cannot describe their data models directly. Data modeling can be especially difficult and challenging in multi-user applications, in which the users' views may contradict one another's and no single user can visualize the entire view of the business activity.

The term *data model* is used in two ways, to refer to a model of the users' view of their data and to refer to the tools used to define the users' view of their data.

GROUP I QUESTIONS

2.1   Name the major components of a database system, and briefly explain the function of each.

2.2   Give an example, other than the one in this chapter, of a relation that is likely to have problems when it is updated. Use relation R1 as an example.

2.3   Transpose the relation in your answer to Question 2.2 into two or more relations that do not have update problems. Use relations R2 and R3 as examples.

2.4   Explain the roles of metadata and system tables.

2.5   What is the function of indexes? When are they desirable, and what is their cost?

2.6   What is the function of application metadata? How does it differ from metadata?

2.7   Explain the features and functions of the design tools subsystem of a DBMS.

2.8   Describe the features and functions of a DBMS's run-time subsystem.

2.9   Explain the features and functions of the DBMS engine.

2.10 What is a database schema? List its components.

2.11 How are relationships represented in a relational database design? Give an example of two tables with a 1:N relationship, and explain how the relationship is expressed in the data.

2.12 What is a domain, and why is it important?

2.13 What are business rules? Give an example of possible business rules for the relations in your answer to Question 2.11.

2.14 What is a foreign key? Which column(s) in your answer to Question 2.11 is a foreign key?

2.15 Explain the purpose of forms, reports, queries, and menus.

2.16 Explain the difference between query by example and query by form.

2.17 What is the first important task in developing a database and related applications?

2.18 What is the role of a prototype?

2.19 Describe top-down development. What are its advantages and disadvantages?

2.20 Describe bottom-up development. What are its advantages and disadvantages?

2.21 Explain the two different meanings of the term *data model.*

GROUP II QUESTIONS

2.22 Implement a database with the relations CAPTAIN and ITEM in any DBMS to which you can gain access. Use one of the DBMS products facilities to enter data into each of these relations. Create and process a query to use the DBMS's facility to process a query that identifies those items checked out before September 1, 1996, that have not yet been checked back in. Print the name of the captain, his or her phone number, and the quantity and description of any such items.

2.23 Interview a professional database application developer, and find out the process that this person uses to develop databases. Is this top-down development, bottom-up development, or some other strategy? How does this developer build data models and with what tools? What are the biggest problems usually encountered in developing a database?

2.24 Consider the statement "A database is a model of the users' model of reality." How does it differ from "A database is a model of reality"? Suppose two developers disagree about a data model, and one of them asserts, "My model is a better representation of reality." What does this person really mean? What differences are likely to result when a developer believes the first statement more than the second statement?

DATA MODELING

Data modeling is the process of creating a representation of the users' view of the data. It is the most important task in the development of effective database applications. If the data model incorrectly represents the users' view of the data, the users will find the applications difficult to use, incomplete, and very frustrating. Data modeling is the basis for all subsequent work in the development of databases and their applications.

Part II describes two different data modeling tools: Chapter 3 considers the entity-relationship model, which was introduced in 1976 and has a considerable following among CASE vendors and others, and Chapter 4 describes the semantic-object model, which was introduced in 1988. As the newer model, it has a smaller following, but some consider it to be richer and easier to use than the E-R model. It is the basis of SALSA for the DESKTOP™, the applications generation tool included with this textbook.

These two models provide a language for expressing the users' data model, or the structure of data and data relationships in the users' work environment. Data modeling is used to express a logical data design just as pseudocode, or flowcharting, is used to express a logical program design.

THE ENTITY– RELATIONSHIP MODEL

This chapter describes and illustrates the use of the **entity-relationship model (E-R model)** which was introduced by Peter Chen in 1976.[1] In this paper, Chen set out the foundation of the model, which has since been extended and modified by Chen and many others.[2] In addition, the E-R model has been made part of a number of CASE tools, which also have modified it. Today, there is no single, generally accepted standard E-R model but, instead, a set of common constructs from which most of the E-R variants are derived. This chapter describes these common constructs and shows how they are used. Be aware, however, that during your career you may encounter variants of the approach presented here.[3] In addition, the symbols used to express the E-R model differ considerably. Those used here are typical and popular, but they are by no means the only symbols that you will encounter.

ELEMENTS OF THE ENTITY–RELATIONSHIP MODEL

Key elements of the E-R model are entities, attributes, identifiers, and relationships. Consider each of these in turn.

ENTITIES

An **entity** is something that can be identified in the users' work environment, something that the users want to track. Example entities are EMPLOYEE Mary Doe, CUSTOMER 12345, SALES-ORDER 1000, SALESPERSON John Smith, and PRODUCT A4200. Entities of a given type are grouped into **entity classes.** Thus, the EMPLOYEE entity class is the collection of all EMPLOYEE entities. In this text, entity classes are printed in capital letters.

It is important to understand the differences between an entity class and an entity instance. An entity class is a collection of entities and is described by the

---

[1]P. P. Chen, "The Entity-Relationship Model—Towards a Unified View of Data," *ACM Transactions on Database Systems,* January 1976, pp. 9–36.
[2]T. J. Teorey, D. Yang, and J. P. Fry, "A Logical Design Methodology for Relational Databases Using the Extended Entity-Relationship Model," *ACM Computing Surveys,* June 1986, pp. 197–222.
[3]Thomas A. Bruce, *Designing Quality Databases with IDEF1X Information Models* (New York: Dorset House Publishing, 1992).

FIGURE 3-1   *CUSTOMER: An Example of an Entity*

CUSTOMER
entity contains:
    CustNumber
    CustName
    Address
    City
    State
    Zip
    ContactName
    PhoneNumber

Two instances of CUSTOMER:

12345	67890
Ajax Manufacturing	Jefferson Dance Club
123 Elm St	345-10th Avenue
Memphis	Boston
TN	MA
32455	01234
P. Schwartz	Frita Bellingsley
223-5567	210-8896

structure or format of each of the entities in that class. An instance of an entity class is the representation of a particular entity, such as CUSTOMER 12345; it is described by the values of attributes of the entity. There are usually many instances of an entity in an entity class. For example, within the class CUSTOMER, there are many instances—one for each customer represented in the database. See Figure 3-1.

■ ATTRIBUTES

Entities have **attributes** or, as they are sometimes called, **properties** that describe the entity's characteristics. Examples of attributes are EmployeeName, DateOfHire, and JobSkillCode. In this text, attributes are printed in both uppercase and lowercase letters. The E-R model assumes that all instances of a given entity class have the same attributes.

As defined in the original E-R model, attributes can be single or multiple valued, or they can be composite. For example, in CUSTOMER, the composite attribute Address can be defined as the group {Street, City, State, Zip}. Most implementations of the E-R model, however, do not allow multivalued or composite attributes.

■ IDENTIFIERS

Entity instances have **identifiers,** which are attributes that name, or identify, entity instances. For example, EMPLOYEE instances could be identified by SocialSecurityNumber, EmployeeNumber, or EmployeeName. EMPLOYEE instances are not likely to be identified by attributes like Salary or DateOfHire because normally these attributes are not used in a naming role. Similarly, CUSTOMERs could be identified by CustomerNumber or CustomerName, and SALES-ORDERs could be identified by OrderNumber.

The identifier of an entity instance consists of one or more of the entity's attributes. An identifier may be either **unique** or **nonunique.** If it is unique, its value will identify one, and only one, entity instance. If it is nonunique, the value will identify a set of instances. EmployeeNumber is most likely a unique identifier, while EmployeeName is most likely a nonunique identifier (there may be many John Smiths, for example).

Identifiers that consist of two or more attributes are called **composite identifiers.** Examples are {AreaCode, LocalNumber}, {ProjectName, TaskName}, and {FirstName, LastName, PhoneExtension}.

■ RELATIONSHIPS

Entities can be associated with one another in **relationships.** The E-R model contains both relationship classes and relationship instances. Relationship classes are associations among entity classes, and relationship instances are associations among entity instances. Relationships can have attributes.

As defined in the original E-R model, a relationship can include many entities; the number of entities in a relationship is the **degree** of the relationship. In Figure 3-2(a), the SP-ORDER relationship is of degree 2 because each instance of the relationship involves two entity instances: a SALESPERSON entity instance and an ORDER entity instance.[4] In Figure 3-2(b), the PARENT relationship is of degree 3, since each instance involves three entities: MOTHER, FATHER, and CHILD. Relationships of degree 2 are very common and are often referred to by the term **binary relationships.**

THREE TYPES OF BINARY RELATIONSHIPS   Figure 3-3 shows the three types of binary relationships. In a 1:1 (read "one-to-one") relationship, a single-entity instance of one type is related to a single-entity instance of another type. In Figure 3-3(a), the AUTO-ASSIGNMENT relationship associates a single EMPLOYEE with a single AUTO. According to this diagram, no employee has more than one automobile assigned, and no automobile is assigned to more than one employee.

Figure 3-3(b) shows the second type of relationship, 1:N (read "one to N" or "one to many"). In this relationship, called a DORM-OCCUPANT relationship, a single instance of DORMITORY relates to many instances of STUDENT. According to this sketch, a dormitory has many students, but a student has only one dormitory.

The positions of the 1 and the N are significant. The 1 is close to the line connecting DORMITORY, which means that the 1 refers to the DORMITORY side of the relationship, and the N is close to the line connecting STUDENT, which means that the N refers to the STUDENT side of the relationship. If the 1 and the N were reversed and the relationship were written N:1, a DORMITORY would have one STUDENT, and a STUDENT would have many DORMITORIES. This is not, of course, the case.

Figure 3-3(c) shows the third type of binary relationship, N:M (read "N to M" or "many to many"). This relationship is named STUDENT-CLUB, and it relates instances of STUDENT to instances of CLUB. A student can join more than one club, and a club can have many students as members.

FIGURE 3-2   *Relationships of Different Degrees: (a) Example Relationship of Degree 2 and (b) Example Relationship of Degree 3*

(a)   (b)

---

[4]For brevity, we sometimes drop the word *instance* when the context makes it clear that an instance rather than an entity class is involved.

FIGURE 3-3 *Three Types of Binary Relationships: (a) 1:1 Binary Relationship, (b) 1:N Binary Relationship, (c) N:M Binary Relationship, and (d) Relationship Representation with Crow's Feet*

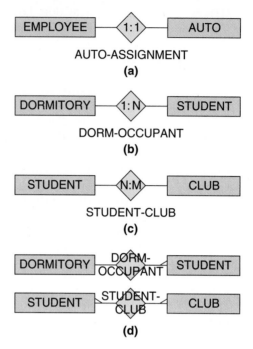

The numbers inside the relationship diamond show the maximum number of entities that can occur on one side of the relationship. Such constraints are called the relationship's **maximum cardinality.** The relationship in Figure 3-3(b), for example, is said to have a maximum cardinality of 1:N. But the cardinalities are not restricted to the values shown here. It is possible, for example, for the maximum cardinality to be other than 1 and N. The relationship between BASKETBALL-TEAM and PLAYER, for example, could be 1:5, indicating that a basketball team has at most five players.

Relationships of the types shown in Figure 3-3 are sometimes called **HAS-A relationships.** This term is used because an entity *has a* relationship with another entity. For example, an EMPLOYEE has an AUTO; a STUDENT has a DORMITORY; and a CLUB has STUDENTs.

ENTITY–RELATIONSHIP DIAGRAMS   The sketches in Figure 3-3 are called **entity-relationship** or **E-R diagrams.** Such diagrams are standardized, but only loosely. According to this standard, entity classes are shown by rectangles, relationships are shown by diamonds, and the maximum cardinality of the relationship is shown inside the diamond.[5] The name of the entity is shown inside the rectangle, and the name of the relationship is shown near the diamond.

Although in some E-R diagrams the name of the relationship is shown inside the diamond, this can make the diagram look awkward, since the diamonds may have to be large and out of scale in order to include the relationship name. To avoid this, relationship names are sometimes written over the diamond. When the

---

[5]The graphical symbols that originated with the model (which are the symbols described here) are not the best ones for displaying a model in a GUI system such as the Macintosh or Microsoft Windows. In fact, the E-R model was developed long before any GUI system was popular. Consequently, as vendors developed GUI CASE tools, they chose to invent new symbols for presenting their designs. The result is that an E-R CASE tool may use symbols different from these. This kind of problem is common in the information systems industry: Standards must be extended as technology evolves.

Relationship with Minimum Cardinality Shown

DORM-OCCUPANT

Recursive Relationship

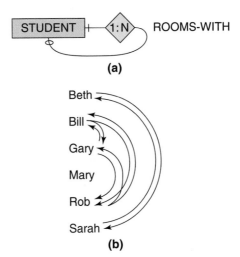

name is placed inside or on top of the diamond, the relationship cardinality is shown by placing crow's feet on the lines connecting to the entity(ies) on the many side of the relationship. Figure 3-3(d) shows the DORM-OCCUPANT and STUDENT-CLUB relationships with such crow's feet.

As we stated, the maximum cardinality indicates the maximum number of entities that can be involved in a relationship. The diagrams do not indicate the minimum. For example, Figure 3-3(b) shows that a student is related, at maximum, to one dormitory, but it does not show whether a student *must be* related to a dormitory instance.

A number of different ways are used to show **minimum cardinality.** One way, illustrated in Figure 3-4, is to place a hash mark across the relationship line to indicate that an entity must exist in the relationship and to place an oval across the relationship line to indicate that there may or may not be an entity in the relationship. Accordingly, Figure 3-4 shows that a DORMITORY must have a relationship with at least one STUDENT but that a STUDENT is not required to have a relationship with a DORMITORY. The complete relationship restrictions are that a DORMITORY has a minimum cardinality of one and a maximum cardinality of many STUDENT entities. A STUDENT has a minimum cardinality of zero and a maximum cardinality of one DORMITORY entity.

A relationship may exist among entities of the same class. For example, the relationship ROOMS-WITH could be defined on the entity STUDENT. Figure 3-5(a) shows such a relationship, and Figure 3-5(b) shows instances of entities that conform to this relationship. Relationships among entities of a single class are sometimes called **recursive relationships.**

SHOWING ATTRIBUTES IN ENTITY–RELATIONSHIP DIAGRAMS   In some versions of E-R diagrams, the attributes are shown in ellipses and are connected to the entity or relationship to which they belong. Figure 3-6(a) shows the DORMITORY and STUDENT entities and the DORM-OCCUPANT relationship with the attributes.

FIGURE 3-6

Showing Properties in Entity-Relationship Diagrams: (a) Entity-Relationship Diagram with Properties Shown and (b) Entity-Relationship Diagram with Properties Listed Separately

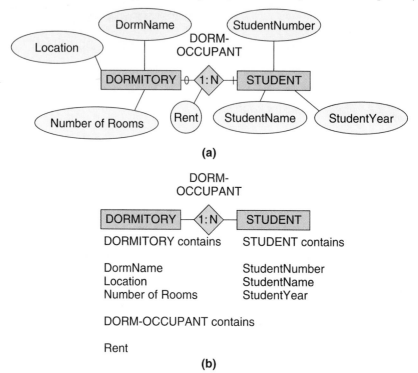

As shown, DORMITORY has DormName, Location, and NumberOfRooms attributes, and STUDENT has Student, StudentName, and StudentYear attributes. The relationship DORM-OCCUPANT has the attribute Rent, which shows the amount of rent paid by a particular student in a particular dorm.

If an entity has many attributes, listing them in this way on the E-R diagram may make the diagram cluttered and difficult to interpret. In these cases, entity attributes are listed separately, as shown in Figure 3-6(b). Many CASE tools show such attributes in pop-up windows.

■ WEAK ENTITIES

The entity-relationship model defines a special type of entity called a **weak entity.** Such entities are those that cannot exist in the database unless another type of entity also exists in the database. An entity that is not weak is called a **strong entity.**

To understand weak entities, consider a human resource database with EMPLOYEE and DEPENDENT entity classes. Suppose the business has a rule that an EMPLOYEE instance *can exist* without having a relationship to any DEPENDENT entity, but a DEPENDENT entity *cannot exist* without having a relationship to a particular EMPLOYEE entity. In such a case, DEPENDENT is a weak entity. This means that DEPENDENT data can be stored in the database only if the DEPENDENT has a relationship with an EMPLOYEE entity.

As shown in Figure 3-7(a), weak entities are signified by rounding the corners of the entity rectangle. In addition, the relationship on which the entity depends for its existence is shown in a diamond with rounded corners. Alternatively, in some E-R diagrams (not shown here), weak entities are depicted by using a double line for the boundary of the weak entity rectangle and double diamonds for the relationship on which the entity depends.

Weak Entities: (a) Example of a Weak Entity and (b) ID-Dependent Entity

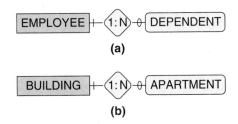

The E-R model includes a special type of weak entity called an **ID-dependent entity.** Such an entity is one in which the identifier of one entity includes the identifier of another entity. Consider the entities BUILDING and APARTMENT. Suppose the identifier of BUILDING is BuildingName, and the identifier of APARTMENT is the composite identifier {BuildingName, ApartmentNumber}. Since the identifier of APARTMENT contains the identifier of BUILDING (BuildingName), then APARTMENT is ID-dependent on BUILDING. Contrast Figure 3-7(b) with Figure 3-7(a). Another way to think of this is that, both logically and physically, an APARTMENT cannot exist unless a BUILDING exists.

ID-dependent entities are common. Another example is the entity VERSION in the relationship between PRODUCT and VERSION, where PRODUCT is a software product and VERSION is a release of that software product. The identifier of PRODUCT is ProductName, and the identifier of VERSION is {ProductName, ReleaseNumber}. A third example is EDITION in the relationship between TEXTBOOK and EDITION. The identifier of TEXTBOOK is Title, and the identifier of EDITION is {Title, EditionNumber}.

Unfortunately, there is an ambiguity hidden in the definition of weak entity, and this ambiguity is interpreted differently by different database designers (as well as different textbook authors). The ambiguity is this: In a strict sense, if a weak entity is defined as any entity whose presence in the database depends on another entity, then any entity that participates in a relationship having a minimum cardinality of 1 to a second entity is a weak entity. Thus, in an academic database, if a STUDENT must have an ADVISOR, then STUDENT is a weak entity, because a STUDENT entity cannot be stored without an ADVISOR. This interpretation, however, seems too broad to some people. A STUDENT is not physically dependent on an ADVISOR (unlike APARTMENTs and BUILDINGs), and a STUDENT is not logically dependent on an ADVISOR (in spite of how it might appear to either the student or the advisor!); therefore, a STUDENT should be considered a strong entity.

To avoid such situations, some people interpret the definition of weak entity more narrowly. To be a weak entity, an entity must logically depend on another entity. According to this definition, both DEPENDENT and APARTMENT would be considered weak entities, but STUDENT would not. A DEPENDENT cannot be a dependent unless it has someone to depend on, and an APARTMENT cannot exist without a BUILDING to reside in. A STUDENT, however, can logically exist without an ADVISOR, even if a business rule requires it.

To illustrate this interpretation, consider several examples. Suppose a data model includes the relationship between an ORDER and a SALESPERSON. While we might say that an ORDER must have a SALESPERSON, it does not necessarily require one for its existence (the ORDER could be a cash sale in which the salesperson is not recorded). Hence, the minimum cardinality of 1 arises from a business rule, not from logical necessity. Thus, ORDER requires a SALESPERSON but is not existence-dependent on it, and ORDER would be considered a strong entity.

Now, however, consider the relationship of PATIENT and PRESCRIPTION. Here, a PRESCRIPTION cannot logically exist without a PATIENT. Hence, not only is the minimum cardinality 1, but also, the PRESCRIPTION is existence dependent on PATIENT. PRESCRIPTION is thus a weak entity. Finally, consider ASSIGNMENT, where the key of ASSIGNMENT contains the key of PROJECT. Here, not only does ASSIGNMENT have a minimum cardinality of 1, and not only is ASSIGNMENT existence-dependent on PROJECT, but it is also ID-dependent on PROJECT, since its key includes the key of another entity. Thus, ASSIGNMENT is a weak entity.

In this text we will assume the less inclusive definition of weak entity. To be weak, an entity must logically depend on another entity. This means that some (but not all) objects that have a minimum cardinality of 1 in relationship with another entity are weak, and it means that all ID-dependent entities are weak. Also, every weak entity has a minimum cardinality of 1 on the entity on which it depends, but every entity that has a minimum cardinality of 1 need not necessarily be weak.[6]

■ SUBTYPE ENTITIES

Some entities contain optional sets of attributes, or subtypes.[7] Consider, for example, CLIENT, with attributes ClientNumber, ClientName, and AmountDue. Suppose that a CLIENT can be an individual, a partnership, or a corporation and that additional data are to be stored depending on the type. Assume that these additional data are as follows:

INDIVIDUAL-CLIENT:
Address, SocialSecurityNumber
PARTNERSHIP-CLIENT:
ManagingPartnerName, Address, TaxIdentificationNumber
CORPORATE-CLIENT:
ContactPerson, Phone, TaxIdentificationNumber

One possibility is to allocate all of these attributes to the entity CLIENT, as shown in Figure 3-8(a). In this case, some of the attributes are not applicable. ManagingPartnerName has no meaning for an individual or corporate client, and so it cannot have a value.

A closer-fitting model would instead define three subtype entities, as shown in Figure 3-8(b). Here the INDIVIDUAL-CLIENT, PARTNERSHIP-CLIENT, and CORPORATE-CLIENT entities are shown as **subtypes** of CLIENT. CLIENT, in turn, is a **supertype** of the INDIVIDUAL-CLIENT, PARTNERSHIP-CLIENT, and CORPORATE-CLIENT entities.

The ∈ next to the relationship lines indicates that INDIVIDUAL-CLIENT, PARTNERSHIP-CLIENT, and CORPORATE-CLIENT are subtypes of CLIENT. Each subtype entity must belong to the supertype CLIENT. The curved line with a 1 next to it indicates that a CLIENT entity must belong to one, and only one, subtype. It means that the subtypes are exclusive and that one of them is required.

Subtypes are not always mutually exclusive, however, nor are they always required. Figure 3-8(c) shows the CLIENT-USING subtypes within CLIENT. The *m* indicates that CLIENT may belong to from zero to many CLIENT-USING subtypes.

Structures of subtypes and supertypes are sometimes called **generalization hierarchies** because CLIENT is a generalization of the three subtypes. Sometimes, too, this relationship type is called an **IS-A relationship,** since, in Figure 3-8(b), INDIVIDUAL-CLIENT *is a* CLIENT, just as PARTNERSHIP-CLIENT and CORPORATE-CLIENT also are CLIENTs.

---

[6]This discussion omits the cases in which the minimum cardinality is greater than 1. The logic is similar, but the entity depends on a set of entities.
[7]Subtypes were added to the E-R model after the publication of Chen's initial paper, and they are part of what is called the *extended E-R model.*

FIGURE 3-8 *Subtype Entities: (a) CLIENT Without Subtype Entities, (b) CLIENT with Subtype Entities, and (c) Nonexclusive Subtypes with Optional Supertype*

CLIENT Contains

ClientNumber
ClientName
AmountDue
Address
SocialSecurityNumber
ManagingPartnerName
TaxIdentificationNumber
ContactPerson
Phone

(a)

CLIENT Contains	INDIVIDUAL-CLIENT Contains
ClientNumber ClientName AmountDue	Address SocialSecurityNumber
PARTNERSHIP-CLIENT Contains	CORPORATE-CLIENT Contains
ManagingPartnerName Address TaxIdentificationNumber	ContactPerson Phone TaxIdentificationNumber

(b)

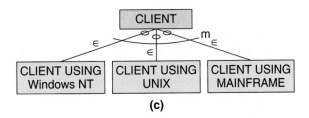

(c)

A way to verify that the term *IS-A* is appropriate is to consider the identifier of all four of these entities. They all have the same identifier, ClientNumber, and so they all have the same name and hence refer to the same entity. Contrast this situation with the HAS-A relationships shown in Figure 3-3.

Generalization hierarchies have a special characteristic called **inheritance,** which means that the entities in subtypes inherit attributes of the supertype entity class. PARTNERSHIP-CLIENT, for example, inherits ClientName and AmountDue from CLIENT.

Figure 3-9 is an example E-R diagram that contains all of the elements of the E-R model that we have been discussing. It shows the entities and relationships for an engineering consulting company that analyzes the construction and condition of houses and other buildings and facilities.

There is an entity class for the company's employees. Because some EMPLOYEEs are ENGINEERs, there is a subtype relationship between EMPLOYEE and ENGINEER. Every ENGINEER must be an EMPLOYEE; ENGINEER has a 1:1

FIGURE 3-9 *Example Entity-Relationship Diagram*

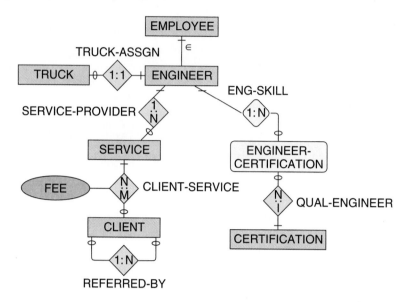

relationship to TRUCK; and each TRUCK must be assigned to an ENGINEER, but not all ENGINEERs have a TRUCK.

ENGINEERs provide SERVICEs to CLIENTs. An ENGINEER can provide from zero to many services, but a given SERVICE must be provided by an ENGINEER and can be provided by only that ENGINEER. CLIENTs have many SERVICEs, and a SERVICE can be requested by many CLIENTs. A CLIENT must have purchased at least one SERVICE, but SERVICE need not have any CLIENTs. The CLIENT-SERVICE relationship has an attribute Fee, which shows the amount that a particular CLIENT paid for a particular SERVICE. (Other attributes of entities and relationships are not shown in this diagram.)

Sometimes CLIENTs refer one another, which is indicated by the recursive relationship REFERRED-BY. A given CLIENT can refer one or more other CLIENTs. A CLIENT may or may not have been referred by another CLIENT, and a CLIENT may be referred by only one CLIENT.

The ENGINEER-CERTIFICATION entity shows that a given engineer has completed the education and testing required to earn a particular certificate. An ENGINEER may have earned CERTIFICATIONS. ENGINEER-CERTIFICATION's existence is dependent on ENGINEER through the relationship ENG-SKILL. CERTIFICATION is the entity that describes a particular certification.

■ DOCUMENTATION OF BUSINESS RULES

Chapter 2 defined a database schema as consisting of tables, relationships, domains, and business rules. We can obtain or infer the first three of these from an E-R model, but we cannot obtain business rules from the model. Thus, these rules are sometimes added to the E-R model during the data modeling stage.

The E-R model is developed from an analysis of requirements obtained from users. During this analysis, business rules often are brought up, and, indeed, systems analysts should make it a point to ask about them.

Consider the entities TRUCK and ENGINEER in Figure 3-9. Does the business have rules concerning who is assigned a TRUCK? If there are not enough TRUCKs for one to be assigned to every ENGINEER, what rules determine who gets a TRUCK? It might be that the database application is to assign trucks on the basis of which ENGINEER has the most number of SERVICEs scheduled during some period of time, the most number of SERVICEs out of the office, or some other rule.

Another example concerns the allocation of ENGINEERs to SERVICEs. There probably are rules concerning the type of ENGINEERING-CERTIFICATION that an ENGINEER must have in order to be assigned to particular types of SERVICE. To inspect an apartment building, for example, the ENGINEER may need to be licensed as a professional ENGINEER. Even if there is no law that dictates this rule, it may be the policy of the company to enforce it.

Business rules may or may not be enforced by the DBMS or by the application program. Sometimes business rules are written in manual procedures that the users of the database application are to follow. At this point, the way in which the rules are to be enforced is not important. What is important is to document these rules so that they become part of the system's requirements.

■ THE ENTITY–RELATIONSHIP MODEL AND CASE TOOLS

Developing a data model using the entity-relationship model has become easier in recent years, because the tools for building E-R diagrams are included in many popular CASE products. Products such as IEW, IEF, DEFT, ER-WIN, and Visio have drawing and diagramming facilities to create E-R diagrams. Such products also integrate entities with the database relations that represent them, which can facilitate the administration, management, and maintenance of the database.

We do not assume the use of a CASE tool for the discussions in this text. But if your university has such a tool, by all means use it to create E-R diagrams for exercises you are assigned. The E-R diagrams created using these tools are generally more visually pleasing, and they are far easier to change and adapt.

◆ EXAMPLES

The best way to gain proficiency with any modeling tool is to study examples and to use the tool to make your own models. The remainder of this chapter presents two case applications to help you with the first task. After working through these examples, you should then work the example problems at the end of the chapter.

■ EXAMPLE 1: THE JEFFERSON DANCE CLUB

The Jefferson Dance Club teaches social dancing and offers both private and group lessons. Jefferson charges $45 per hour per student (or couple) for a private lesson and $6 per hour per student for a group lesson. Private lessons are offered throughout the day, from noon until 10 P.M., six days a week. Group lessons are offered in the evenings.

Jefferson employs two types of instructor: full-time salaried instructors and part-time teachers. The full-time instructors are paid a fixed amount per week, and the part-time instructors are paid either a set amount for an evening or a set amount for teaching a particular class.

In addition to the lessons, Jefferson sponsors two weekly social dances featuring recorded music. The admission charge is $5 per person. The Friday night dance is the more popular and averages around eighty people; the Sunday night dance attracts about thirty attendees. The purpose of the dances is to give the students a place in which to practice their skills. No food or drinks are served.

Jefferson would like to develop an information system to keep track of students and the classes they have taken. Jefferson's managers would also like to know how many and which types of lessons each teacher has taught and to be able to compute the average cost per lesson for each of their instructors.

■ ENTITIES

The best way to begin an entity-relationship model is to determine potential entities. Entities are usually represented by nouns (places, persons, concepts, events, equipment, and so on) in documents or interviews. A search of the previous example for important nouns that relate to the information system reveals the following list:

- Private lesson
- Group lesson
- Teacher
- Full-time teacher
- Part-time teacher
- Dance
- Customer

Clearly, the nouns *private lesson* and *group lesson* have something in common, as do the nouns *teacher, full-time teacher,* and *part-time teacher.* One solution is to define an entity LESSON, with subtypes PRIVATE-LESSON and GROUP-LESSON, and another entity TEACHER, with subtypes FULL-TIME-TEACHER and PART-TIME-TEACHER. Additional entities are DANCE and CUSTOMER.

As stated in Chapter 2, data modeling is as much art as it is science. The solution just described is one of several feasible solutions. A second solution is to eliminate LESSON and TEACHER from the list in the preceding paragraph and to eliminate all subtypes. A third solution is to eliminate LESSON (since lesson was never mentioned by itself as a noun) but to keep TEACHER and its subtypes. Here we choose the third case because it seems to be the best fit for the information we have. Thus, the list of entities is PRIVATE-LESSON, GROUP-LESSON, TEACHER, FULL-TIME-TEACHER, PART-TIME-TEACHER, DANCE, and CUSTOMER.

Choosing among these alternatives requires analyzing the requirements and considering the design implications of each of them. Sometimes it helps to consider the attributes of the entities. If, for example, the entity LESSON has no attributes other than its identifier, then it is not necessary.

■ RELATIONSHIPS

To begin, TEACHER has two subtype entities, FULL-TIME-TEACHER and PART-TIME-TEACHER. A given teacher must be one or the other, so the subtypes are mutually exclusive.

Consider next the relationships between TEACHER and PRIVATE-LESSON and GROUP-LESSON. A TEACHER can teach many PRIVATE-LESSONs, and normally a PRIVATE-LESSON is taught by a single TEACHER. However, further discussion with Jefferson's management reveals that for advanced dancers, especially those preparing for competitions, sometimes two teachers are involved in a private lesson. Therefore the relationship between TEACHER and PRIVATE-LESSON must be many to many. Assume, however, that only one teacher is involved in a group lesson. The relationships just described are shown in Figure 3-10.

CUSTOMERs can take either PRIVATE-LESSONs or GROUP-LESSONs. Sometimes a lesson is taken by a single individual and sometimes by a couple. There are two ways in which this situation can be modeled. An entity COUPLE can be defined as having a one-to-two relationship with CUSTOMER, or either CUSTOMER or COUPLE can have a relationship with PRIVATE-LESSON. We assume that couples do not take group lessons or that if they do, it is not important to store that fact in the database. This alternative is shown in Figure 3-11(a).

PRIVATE-LESSON's existence is dependent on CUSTOMER or COUPLE. That is, a lesson cannot exist unless it is given to either a CUSTOMER or a COUPLE. The 1

FIGURE 3-10

Initial E-R Diagram for the Jefferson Dance Club

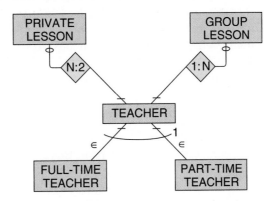

FIGURE 3-11

Alternatives for Representing CUSTOMER: (a) E-R Diagram Showing COUPLE Entity and (b) E-R Diagram Without Couples

(a)

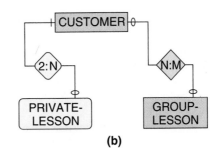

(b)

next to the horizontal line underneath CUSTOMER and COUPLE indicates that PRIVATE-LESSON must have at least one CUSTOMER or one COUPLE, which makes sense, since PRIVATE-LESSON is dependent on them.

Another alternative is not to represent couples but, instead, to model the relationship between CUSTOMER and PRIVATE-LESSON as many to many. More precisely, this relationship is one or two to many and is shown in Figure 3-11(b). Although the model is not as detailed as that in Figure 3-11(a), it may very well suffice for Jefferson's purposes.

The last relationship possibility is that between DANCE and other entities. Both customers and teachers attend dances, and the developers must decide whether it is important to store these relationships. Does Jefferson really need to know which customers attended which dances? Do Jefferson's managers really want to record attendance in a computer-based information system as customers enter the door? Do the customers want that fact recorded? Most likely, this is not a relationship that need or should be stored in the database.

The situation between DANCE and TEACHER is different. Jefferson likes some of its teachers to be present at each dance. In order to be fair about this requirement, Jefferson's management has drawn up a schedule for the teachers' attendance at dances. Developing and recording this schedule requires that the database contain the DANCE-TEACHER relationship, which is many to many.

■ FINAL E–R DIAGRAM FOR THE JEFFERSON DANCE CLUB

Figure 3-12 shows an E-R diagram for the model described in this section. We have not named the relationships in this diagram. Although doing so would make the diagrams more true to form, for our data, naming relationships would add little.

PRIVATE-LESSON's existence is dependent on CUSTOMER, but GROUP-LESSON's is not, because group lessons are scheduled long before any customer signs up, and they will be held even if no customers show up. This situation is not true, however, for private lessons, as they are scheduled only at the customer's request. Also notice that this model does not represent couples.

Once a model such as this is developed, its accuracy and completeness in regard to the requirements should be verified. Usually this is done with the users.

■ EVALUATING THE E–R DATA MODEL

It is easier and cheaper to correct errors early in the database development process rather than later. For example, changing the maximum cardinality of a relationship from 1:N to N:M in the data modeling stage is simply a matter of recording the change in the E-R diagram. But once the database has been designed and loaded with data and application programs written to process the database, making such a change requires considerable rework, possibly even weeks of labor. It is important, therefore, to evaluate the data model before designing it.

One evaluation technique is to consider the E-R data model in the context of possible queries that might be posed to a database with the structure implied by the model. For example, look at the diagram in Figure 3-12. What questions could be answered from a database that was implemented according to this design?

The Final E-R Diagram for Jefferson Dance Club

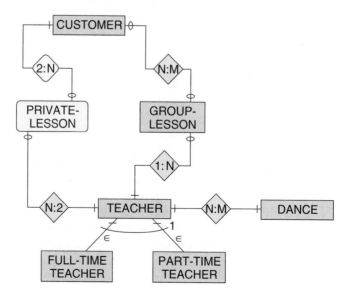

- Who has taught which private lessons?
- Which customers have taken a private lesson from Jack?
- Who are the full-time teachers?
- Which teachers are scheduled to attend the dance on Friday?

When evaluating an E-R data model, you can construct such questions and show them to the users, who can then be asked to draw up their own list of questions. Their questions can then be posed against the design in order to check its appropriateness. For example, suppose that the users asked which customers attended last week's Friday night dance. The designers of the data model in Figure 3-12 would conclude that their design was not correct, because it is not possible to answer this question using their E-R model. If it must be answered, a relationship between CUSTOMER and DANCE must be constructed.

Clearly, such an informal and loosely structured process cannot be used to *prove* that a design is correct. It is, however, a pragmatic technique that can be used to verify the potential correctness of a design. And it is far better than no evaluation at all!

■ EXAMPLE 2: SAN JUAN SAILBOAT CHARTERS

San Juan Sailboat Charters is an agent that leases sailboats to customers for a fee. San Juan does not own any sailboats but instead leases them on behalf of boat owners who wish to earn income when they are not using their boats. San Juan charges a fee for its service. San Juan specializes in boats that can be used for multi-day or weekly charters—the smallest sailboat in their inventory is twenty-eight feet and the largest is fifty-one feet.

Each sailboat is fully equipped at the time it is leased. Most of the equipment is provided by the owners, but some is added by San Juan. The owner-provided equipment includes what is fixed on the boat, such as radios, compasses, depth indicators and other instrumentation, stoves, and refrigerators. Other owner-provided equipment is not installed as part of the boat. Such equipment includes sails, lines, anchors, dinghies, life preservers, and, in the cabin, dishes, silverware, cooking utensils, bedding, and the like. San Juan provides consumable equipment, which could also be considered supplies, such as charts, navigation books, tide and current tables, soap, dish towels, toilet paper, and similar items.

An important part of San Juan's responsibilities is keeping track of the equipment on the boat. Much of it is expensive, and some of it, particularly what is not attached to the boat, can easily be lost or stolen. Customers are responsible for all equipment during the period of their charter.

San Juan likes to keep accurate records of its customers and the charters, not only for marketing but also for recording the trips that customers have taken. Some itineraries and weather conditions are more dangerous than others, and so San Juan likes to know which customers have what experience.

Most of San Juan's business is bare-boat chartering, which means that no skipper or other crew is provided. In some cases, however, customers request the services of a skipper or other crew member, and so San Juan hires such personnel on a part-time basis.

Sailboats often need maintenance. San Juan is required by its contracts with the boat owners to keep accurate records of all maintenance activities and costs, including normal activities, such as cleaning or engine-oil changes, and unscheduled repairs. In some cases, repairs are necessary during a charter. A boat engine, for example, might fail while the boat is far away from San Juan's facility. In this case, the customers radio the San Juan dispatcher, who determines the best facility to make the repair and sends the facility's personnel to the disabled boat. To make these decisions, the dispatchers need information about repair facilities as well as past histories of repair quality and costs.

Before you continue reading, try to produce an entity-relationship diagram on your own. Examine the preceding statements and look for nouns that seem important to the design. Then check the possible relationships among the entities. Finally, list the likely attributes for each entity or relationship.

■ ENTITIES

The data model required for San Juan Charters is more complicated than that for the Jefferson Dance Club. Potential entities are shown in Figure 3-13(a).

Consider first the equipment-related entities. There are a number of different kinds of equipment, and this fact suggests the possibility of modeling subtypes. However, why does San Juan care about equipment? It does not really want to know the characteristics of each item—the chain length on each anchor, for example. Instead, its goal is to keep track of the items and their type so that it can determine if any has been lost or damaged. This can be done without keeping detailed records of the particular subtypes of equipment. Thus, for this design, we place all types of equipment into the entity EQUIPMENT.

Ownership of equipment is established by defining a relationship between EQUIPMENT and OWNER. If San Juan Charters is allowed to be an instance of OWNER, all of the equipment that it owns can be carried by this relationship. Similarly, from the case description, there is no reason to define the equipment that is attached to the boat differently from that not attached. An accurate list can be produced without this division. Figure 3-13(b) shows the final list of entities.

FIGURE 3-13   *Entities for San Juan Charters*

```
LEASE
BOAT
CUSTOMER
OWNER
EQUIPMENT
OWNER-PROVIDED-EQUIPMENT
FIXED OWNER-EQUIPMENT
REMOVABLE OWNER-EQUIPMENT
SAN-JUAN-PROVIDED-EQUIPMENT
ITINERARY/WEATHER
CHARTER
PART-TIME-CREW
SCHEDULED-MAINTENANCE
UNSCHEDULED-MAINTENANCE
REPAIRS
REPAIR-FACILITY

(a) Possible entities for San Juan Charters

LEASE or CHARTER(synonyms)
BOAT
CUSTOMER
OWNER
EQUIPMENT
ITINERARY/WEATHER
PART-TIME-CREW
SCHEDULED-MAINTENANCE
REPAIR or UNSCHEDULED-MAINTENANCE(synonyms)
REPAIR-FACILITY

(b) Entities selected for the E-R design
```

FIGURE 3-14   *E-R Diagram for San Juan Charters*

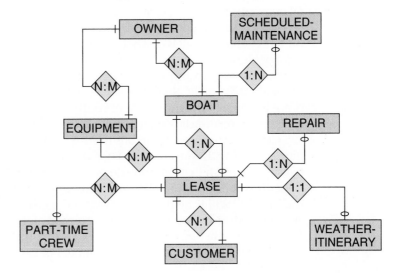

Note that LEASE and CHARTER are synonyms; they refer to the same transaction. We show both names here so that they can be related to the case description.

It is possible that SCHEDULED-MAINTENANCE should be combined with UN-SCHEDULED-MAINTENANCE. One way to decide is to examine the attributes of each of these entities. If they are the same, the two entity classes should be merged into one. Also observe that REPAIR and UNSCHEDULED-MAINTENANCE are defined as synonyms.

■ RELATIONSHIPS

Figure 3-14 is an entity-relationship diagram for San Juan Charters. For the most part, the relationships in this diagram are straightforward, but the relationship between EQUIPMENT and LEASE is arguable. One might say that EQUIPMENT should be related to BOAT and not to LEASE or that some EQUIPMENT should be related to BOAT (the equipment that stays with the boat) and the other equipment should be related to LEASE. These changes would be feasible alternatives to the design shown in Figure 3-14.

Notice, too, that SCHEDULED-MAINTENANCE is related to BOAT but that RE-PAIR (UNSCHEDULED-MAINTENANCE) is related to LEASE. This implies that no repair action is required when the boat is not being leased. Perhaps this is unrealistic.

Finally, LEASE and ITINERARY-WEATHER have a 1:1 relationship, and they also have the same identifying attributes. Therefore, it would be possible, and might even be preferable, to combine them into one entity class.

◆ DATABASES AS MODELS OF MODELS

As you can see, there are many different ways of modeling a business situation, and the variety becomes even greater as the application grows more complex. Often, dozens of models are feasible, and it can be difficult to choose among them.

Sometimes when evaluating alternatives, project team members discuss and argue about which data model best represents the real world. These discussions are misguided. Databases do not model the real world, although it is a common misconception that they do. Rather, databases are models of the users' models of the world (or, more to the point, of their business world). The question to ask when evaluating alternative data models is not "Does this design accurately represent the real world?" but, rather, "Does this design accurately represent the users' model of his or her environment?" The goal is to develop a design that fits the users' mental conception.

In fact, Immanuel Kant and other philosophers argued that it is impossible for humans to build models of what actually exists, claiming that the essence of things is forever unknowable by humans.[8] Extending this line of argument to computer systems, Winograd and Flores stated that in societies, humans construct systems of tokens that enable them to operate successfully in the world. A series of tokens is not a model of the infinitude of reality but, rather, only a social system that enables users to coordinate their activities successfully, and nothing more can be said.[9]

Computer systems therefore need to model and represent their users' communications with one another. They do not model anything other than that system of tokens and communications. So learn to ask these questions of yourself: "Does this model accurately reflect the users' perceptions and mental models of their world? Will it help the users respond consistently and successfully with one another and with their clients?" It is pointless for one analyst to claim that his or her model is a better representation of reality. Instead, the point is to develop a model that well represents the user's model of his or her business environment.

SUMMARY

The entity-relationship model was developed by Peter Chen. With this model, entities—which are identifiable things of importance to the users—are defined. All of the entities of a given type form an entity class. A particular entity is called an instance. Entities have attributes that describe their characteristics, and one or more attributes identify an entity.

Relationships are associations among entities. The E-R model explicitly defines relationships; each relationship has a name; and there are relationship classes as well as relationship instances. Relationships may have attributes.

The degree of the relationship is the number of entities participating in the relationship. Most relationships are binary. The three types of binary relationships are 1:1, 1:N, and N:M.

In entity-relationship diagrams, the entities are shown in rectangles, and the relationships are shown in diamonds. The maximum cardinality of the relationship is shown inside the diamond. The minimum cardinality is indicated by a hash mark or an oval. Relationships that connect entity instances of the same class are recursive. Attributes can be shown in an E-R diagram in ellipses or in a separate table.

A weak entity is one whose existence depends on another entity; an entity that is not weak is called a strong entity. Weak entities are shown in rectangles with rounded corners, and the relationship on which the entity depends is indicated by a diamond with rounded corners. In this text, we further define a weak entity to be an entity that logically depends on another entity. An entity can have a minimum cardinality of 1 in a relationship with another entity and not necessarily be a weak entity.

Some entities have subtypes that define subsets of similar entities. Subtypes inherit attributes from their parent, the supertype. HAS-A relationships connect en-

---

[8]"We cannot, indeed, beyond all possible experience, form a definitive concept of what things in themselves may be. Yet we are not at liberty to abstain entirely from inquiring into them; for experience never satisfies reason fully, but, in answering questions, refers us further and further back and leaves us dissatisfied with regard to the complete solution." Immanuel Kant, *Prolegomena to Any Future Metaphysics* (Indianapolis: Bobbs-Merrill, 1950), p. 100.
[9]Terry Winograd and F. Flores, *Understanding Computers and Cognition* (Reading, MA: Addison-Wesley, 1986).

tities of different types, and the identifiers of the entities are different. IS-A relationships are subtypes, and the identifiers of the entities are the same.

Once a data model is developed, the designers should consider business rules that may restrict processing against entities. Each entity in the model should be evaluated in light of possible data additions, changes, and deletions. Deletions, in particular, often are the source of important processing restrictions. When business rules are discovered, they should be documented in the data model.

The E-R model is an important part of many CASE products. These products provide tools for constructing and storing E-R diagrams. Some CASE tools integrate the E-R constructs with data constructs in the CASE repository.

Once they are completed, E-R models should be evaluated. One technique is to list queries that could be answered using the data model. This list is then shown to the users, who are asked to think of additional questions. The design is then evaluated against these questions to ensure that the model can answer them.

Databases do not model the real world but instead model the users' model of their business world. The appropriate criterion for judging a data model is whether the model fits the users' model. Arguing about which model best fits the real world is pointless.

GROUP I QUESTIONS

3.1 Define *entity* and give an example.

3.2 Explain the difference between an entity class and an entity instance.

3.3 Define *attribute* and give examples for the entity you described in Question 1.

3.4 Explain what a composite attribute is and give an example.

3.5 Which attribute defined in your answer to Question 3.3 identifies the entity?

3.6 Define *relationship* and give an example.

3.7 Explain the difference between a relationship class and a relationship instance.

3.8 Define *degree of relationship*. Give an example, other than the one in this text, of a relationship greater than degree 2.

3.9 List and give an example of the three types of binary relationships. Draw an E-R diagram for each.

3.10 Define the terms *maximum cardinality* and *minimum cardinality*.

3.11 Name and sketch the symbols used in entity-relationship diagrams for (a) entity, (b) relationship, (c) weak entity and its relationship, (d) recursive relationship, and (e) subtype entity.

3.12 Give an example E-R diagram for the entities DEPARTMENT and EMPLOYEE, which have a 1:N relationship. Assume that a DEPARTMENT does not need to have any EMPLOYEE but that every EMPLOYEE does have a DEPARTMENT.

3.13 Give an example of a recursive relationship and show it in an E-R diagram.

3.14 Show example attributes for DEPARTMENT and EMPLOYEE (from Question 3.12). Describe the two ways that attributes can appear on or with E-R diagrams.

3.15 Define the term *weak entity* and give an example other than the one in this text.

3.16 Explain the ambiguity in the definition of the term *weak entity*. Explain how this text interprets this term. Give examples, other than those in this text, of each type of weak entity.

3.17 Define the term *ID-dependent entity* and give an example other than one in this text.

3.18 Describe subtype entities and give an example other than those in this text.

3.19 Explain the term *inheritance* and show how it applies to your answer to Question 3.18.

3.20 Explain the difference between a HAS-A relationship and an IS-A relationship, and give an example of each.

3.21 How are business rules treated in an E-R model?

3.22 Describe why it is important to evaluate a data model once it has been created. Summarize one technique for evaluating a data model, and explain how that technique could be used to evaluate the data model in Figure 3.14.

GROUP II QUESTIONS

3.23 Change the E-R diagram in Figure 3-12 to include an entity LESSON. Let PRIVATE-LESSON and GROUP-LESSON be subtypes of LESSON. Modify the relationships as necessary.

3.24 Change the E-R diagram in Figure 3-12 to exclude TEACHER. Modify the relationships as necessary.

3.25 Which of the models in Figure 3-12 and in your answers to Questions 3.23 and 3.24 do you prefer? Explain the reason for your preference.

3.26 Change the E-R diagram in Figure 3-14 to include subtypes of equipment. Assume that the equipment owned by San Juan Charters pertains to LEASE and that other equipment pertains to BOAT. Model the differences between the BOAT-related equipment that is fixed on the boats and the BOAT-related equipment that is not fixed. What benefits does the added complexity of this model bring?

PROJECT

Develop an E-R diagram for a database to support the tracking needs of the following organization: The Metropolitan Housing Agency (MHA) is a nonprofit organization that advocates the development and improvement of low-income housing. The MHA operates in a metropolitan area of approximately 2.2 million people in a midwestern city.

The MHA maintains data about the location, availability, and condition of low-income housing in eleven different census tracts in the metropolitan area. Within the boundaries of these tracts are approximately 250 different buildings that provide low-income housing. On average, each building contains twenty-five apartments or other units.

The MHA keeps data about each census tract, including geographic boundaries, median income of the population, elected officials, principal businesses, principal investors involved in attributes in that tract, and other demographic and economic data. It also maintains a limited amount of data about crime. For each building, the MHA stores the name, address, size, owner(s)'s name and address, mortgagor(s)'s name and address, renovations and repairs, and availability of facilities for handicapped people. In addition, the MHA keeps a list of each of the units within each building, including the type of unit, size, number of bedrooms, number of baths, kitchen and dining facilities, location in the building, and any special remarks. The MHA would like to maintain data regarding the average occupancy rates for each unit, but, to date, it has been unable to collect or store such data. The MHA does, however, keep data about whether a given unit is occupied.

The MHA serves as an information clearinghouse and offers three basic services. First, it works with politicians, lobbyists, and advocacy groups to support legislation that encourages the development of low-income housing through tax incentives, developmental zoning preferences, and other legislative inducements. To accomplish this, the MHA provides information about low-income housing to state, county, and city governments. Second, through speeches, seminars, displays at conventions, and other public relations activities, the MHA officials strive to raise the community's consciousness about the need for low-income housing. Finally, the MHA provides information about the availability of low-income housing to other agencies that work with the low-income and homeless populations.

THE SEMANTIC OBJECT MODEL

• • • • • • • • • • • • • • •

This chapter discusses the semantic object model, which, like the E-R model discussed in Chapter 3, is used to build data models to understand and document the users' requirements. As shown in Figure 4-1, the development team interviews users; analyzes the users' reports, forms, and queries; and from these constructs a model of the users' data. This data model is later transformed into a database design.

The particular form of the data model depends on the constructs used to build it. If an E-R model is used, the model will have entities, relationships, and the like. If a semantic model is used, the model will have semantic objects and related constructs, which are discussed in this chapter.

The E-R model and the semantic object model are like lenses through which the database developers look when studying and documenting the users' data. Both lenses work, and they both ultimately result in a database design. They use different lenses to form that design, however, and because the lenses create different images, the designs they produce may not be exactly the same. When developing a database, you must decide which approach to use, just as a photographer needs to decide which lens to use. Each approach has strengths and weaknesses, which we discuss at the end of this chapter.

The semantic object model was first presented in the third edition of this text, in 1988. It is based on concepts that were developed and published by Codd and by Hammer and McLeod.[1] The semantic object model is a data model. It is different from **object-oriented database processing** which we will discuss in Chapter 17. There you will learn how the purposes, features, and constructs of semantic object modeling differ from object-oriented database processing.

SEMANTIC OBJECTS

The purpose of a database application is to provide forms, reports, and queries so that the users can record data and obtain the information they need about entities or objects important to their work. The main goals of the early stages of database

[1] E. F. Codd, "Extending the Relational Model to Capture More Meaning," *ACM Transactions on Database Systems,* December 1976, pp. 397–424; and Michael Hammer and Dennis McLeod, "Database Description with SDM: A Semantic Database Model," *ACM Transactions on Database Systems*, September 1981, pp. 351–386.

FIGURE 4-1 *Using Different Data Models for Database Designs*

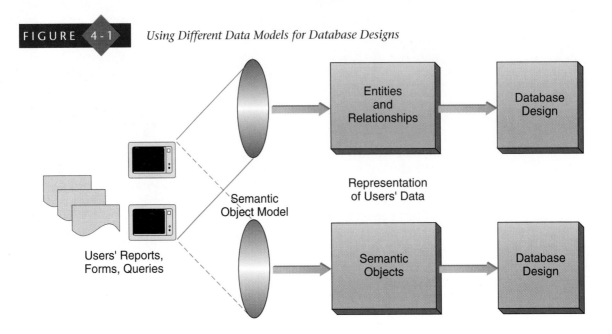

development are to build a data model that documents the things to be represented in the database, to determine the characteristics of those things that need to be stored, and to establish the relationships among them.

In Chapter 3, we referred to these things as entities. In this chapter, we refer to them as semantic objects, or sometimes as just objects. The word *semantic* means meaning, and a semantic object is one that models, in part, the meaning of the users' data. Semantic objects model the users' perceptions more closely than does the E-R model. We use the adjective *semantic* with the word *object* to distinguish the objects discussed in this chapter from the objects defined in object-oriented programming (OOP) languages.

■ DEFINING SEMANTIC OBJECTS

Entities and objects are similar in some ways, and they are different in other ways. We begin with the similarities. A semantic object is a representation of some identifiable thing in the users' work environment. More formally, a semantic object is a *named collection of attributes that sufficiently describes a distinct identity.*

Like entities, semantic objects are grouped into classes. An object class has a *name* that distinguishes it from other classes and that corresponds to the names of the things it represents. Thus, a database that supports users who work with student records has an object class called STUDENT. Note that object class names, like entity class names, are spelled with capital letters. A particular semantic object is an instance of the class. Thus, 'William Jones' is an instance of the STUDENT class, and 'Accounting' is an instance of the DEPARTMENT class.

Like entities, an object has a *collection of attributes*. Each attribute represents a characteristic of the identity being represented. For instance, the STUDENT object could have attributes like Name, HomeAddress, CampusAddress, DateOfBirth, DateOfGraduation, and Major. This collection of attributes also is a *sufficient description*, which means that the attributes represent all of the characteristics that the users need in order to do their work. As we stated at the end of Chapter 3, things in the world have an infinite set of characteristics; we cannot represent all of them. Instead, we represent those necessary for the users to satisfy their information needs so that they can successfully perform their jobs. Sufficient description also means that the objects are complete in themselves. All of the data required about a CUSTOMER, for example, is located in the CUSTOMER object, so we need not look anywhere else to find data about CUSTOMERs.

Objects represent *distinct identities*; that is, they are something that users recognize as independent and separate and that users want to track and report. These identities are the nouns about which the information is to be produced. To understand better the term *distinct identity*, recall that there is a difference between objects and object instances. CUSTOMER is the name of an object, and 'CUSTOMER 12345' is the name of an instance of an object. When we say that an object represents a distinct identity, we mean that users consider each *instance* of an object to be unique and identifiable in its own right.

Finally, note that the identities that the objects represent may or may not have a physical existence. For example, EMPLOYEEs physically exist, but ORDERs do not. Orders are, themselves, models of a contractual agreement to provide certain goods or services under certain terms and conditions. They are not physical things but, rather, representations of agreements. Thus, something need not be physical in order to be considered an object; it need only be identifiable in its own right in the minds of the users.

■ ATTRIBUTES

Semantic objects have attributes that define their characteristics. There are three types of attributes. **Simple attributes** have a single value. Examples are DateOfHire, InvoiceNumber, and SalesTotal. **Group attributes** are composites of other attributes. One example is Address, which contains the attributes {Street, City, State, Zip}; another example is FullName, which contains the attributes {FirstName, MiddleInitial, LastName}. **Semantic object attributes** are attributes that establish a relationship between one semantic object and another.

To understand these statements better, look at Figure 4-2(a), which is an example of a **semantic object diagram**, or **object diagram.** Such diagrams are used by development teams to summarize the structures of objects and to present them visually. Objects are shown in portrait-oriented rectangles, in which the name of the object appears at the top. Attributes are written in order after the object name.

The DEPARTMENT object contains an example of each of the three types of attributes: DepartmentName, PhoneNumber, and FaxPhoneNumber all are simple attributes, each of which represents a single data element. CampusAddress is a group attribute containing the simple attributes Building and OfficeNumber. Finally,

 FIGURE 4-2   *DEPARTMENT Object Diagram: (a) DEPARTMENT Object and (b) DEPARTMENT Object with Cardinalities*

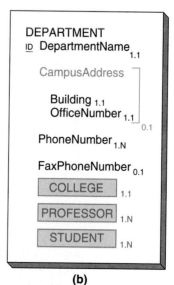

(a)   (b)

COLLEGE, PROFESSOR, and STUDENT each are semantic object attributes, which means that those objects are connected to and logically contained in DEPARTMENT.

The object attributes, or **object links** as they are sometimes called, mean that when a user thinks about a DEPARTMENT, he or she thinks not only about DepartmentName, Address, Phone, and FaxPhone but also about the COLLEGE, PROFESSORs, and STUDENTs who are related to that department. Since COLLEGE, PROFESSOR, and STUDENT also are objects, the complete data model contains object diagrams for them, too. The COLLEGE object contains attributes of the college; the PROFESSOR object contains attributes of the faculty; and the STUDENT object contains attributes of the students.

ATTRIBUTE CARDINALITY Each attribute in a semantic object has both a minimum cardinality and a maximum cardinality. The minimum cardinality indicates the number of instances of the attribute that must exist in order for the object to be valid. Usually this number is either 0 or 1. If it is 0, the attribute is not required to have a value. If it is 1, the attribute must have a value. Although it is unusual, the minimum cardinality can sometimes be larger than 1. For example, the attribute PLAYER in an object called BASKETBALL-TEAM might have a minimum cardinality of 5, since this is the smallest number of players required to make up a basketball team.

The maximum cardinality indicates the maximum number of instances of the attribute that the object may have. It is usually either 1 or N. If it is 1, the attribute can have no more than one instance; if it is N, the attribute can have many values, and the absolute number is not specified. Sometimes the maximum cardinality is a specific number such as 5, meaning the object can contain no more than exactly five instances of the attribute. For example, the attribute PLAYER in BASKETBALL-TEAM might have a maximum cardinality of 15, which would indicate that no more than fifteen players could be assigned to a team's roster.

Cardinalities are shown as subscripts of attributes in the format **n.m,** where n is the minimum cardinality and m is the maximum. In Figure 4-2(b), the minimum cardinality of DepartmentName is 1 and the maximum is also 1, which means that exactly one value of DepartmentName is required. The cardinality of PhoneNumber is 1.N, meaning that a DEPARTMENT is required to have at least one PhoneNumber but may have many. The cardinality of 0.1 in FaxPhoneNumber means that a DEPARTMENT may have either zero or one FaxPhoneNumber.

The cardinalities of groups and the attributes in groups can be subtle. Consider the attribute CampusAddress. Its cardinalities are 0.1, meaning a DEPARTMENT may have zero or one address (indicating the users' model is such that a DEPARTMENT's address does not have to be specified). Now examine the attributes in CampusAddress. Both Building and OfficeNumber have the cardinalities 1.1. You might be wondering how a group can be optional if the attributes in that group are required. The answer is that the cardinalities operate only between the attribute and the container of that attribute. The minimum cardinality of CampusAddress indicates that there need not be a value for address *in DEPARTMENT*. But the minimum cardinalities of OfficeNumber and Building indicate that both OfficeNumber and Building must exist *in CampusAddress*. Thus a CampusAddress group need not appear, but if one does, it must have a value for both OfficeNumber and Building.

Showing all of the cardinalities of an object sometimes clutters the diagram. In the diagrams in this text, we assume that all simple attributes have the cardinality 0.1. As long as this is true, we do not show the cardinality of simple attributes. We always show the cardinalities of group and semantic object attributes.

OBJECT INSTANCES The object diagrams for DEPARTMENT shown in Figure 4-2 are a format, or general structure, that can be used for any department. An instance of the DEPARTMENT object is shown in Figure 4-3, with each attribute's value for a particular department. The DepartmentName is Information Systems, and it is located in Room 213 of the Social Science Building. Observe that there are three values for PhoneNumber—the Information Systems Department has three phone

FIGURE 4-3   *An Instance of the DEPARTMENT Object in Figure 4-2*

lines in its office. Other departments may have fewer or more, but every department has at least one.

Furthermore, there is one instance of COLLEGE, the College of Business, and there are multiple values for the PROFESSOR and STUDENT object attributes. Each of these object attributes is a complete object; each has all the attributes defined for an object of that type. To keep this diagram simple, only the identifying names are shown for each of the instances of object attribute.

An object diagram is a picture of the user's perception of an object in the work environment. Thus, in the user's mind, the DEPARTMENT object includes all of this data. A DEPARTMENT logically contains data about the COLLEGE in which it resides, as well as the PROFESSORs and STUDENTs who are related to that department.

PAIRED ATTRIBUTES   The semantic object model has no one-way object relationships. If an object contains another object, the second object will contain the first. For example, if DEPARTMENT contains the object attribute COLLEGE, then COLLEGE will contain the matching object attribute DEPARTMENT. These object attributes are called **paired attributes,** since they always occur as a pair.

Why must object attributes be paired? The answer lies in the way in which human beings think about relationships. If Object A has a relationship with Object B, then Object B will have a relationship with Object A. At the least, B is related to A in the relationship of "things that are related to B." If this argument seems obscure, try to envision a one-way relationship between two objects. It cannot be done.

■ OBJECT IDENTIFIERS

An **object identifier** is one or more object attributes that the users employ to identify object instances. Such identifiers are potential names for a semantic object. In CUSTOMER, for example, possible identifiers are CustomerID and CustomerName. Each of these are attributes that users consider to be valid names of CUSTOMER instances. Compare these identifiers with attributes like DateOfFirstOrder, StockPrice, and NumberOfEmployees. Such attributes are not identifiers because the users do not think of them as names of CUSTOMER instances.

A **group identifier** is an identifier that has more than one attribute. Examples are {FirstName, LastName}, {FirstName, PhoneNumber} and {State, License Number}.

Object identifiers may or may not be unique, depending on how the users view their data. For example, InvoiceNumber is a unique identifier for ORDER, but StudentName is not a unique identifier for STUDENT. There may, for example, be two students named 'Mary Smith.' If so, the users will employ StudentName to identify a group of one or more students and then, if necessary, use values of other attributes to identify a particular member of that set.

In semantic object diagrams, object identifiers are denoted by the letters *ID* in front of the attribute. If the identifier is unique, these letters will be underlined. In Figure 4-2(b), for example, the attribute DepartmentName is a unique identifier of DEPARTMENT.

Normally, if an attribute is to be used as an identifier, its value is required. Also, generally there is no more than one value of an identifier attribute for a given object. In most cases, therefore, the cardinality of an ID attribute is 1.1, and so we use this value as a default.

There are (relatively few) cases, however, in which the cardinality of an identifier is other than 1.1. Consider, for example, the attribute Alias in the semantic object PERSON. A person need not have an alias, or he or she may have several aliases. Hence, the cardinality of Alias would be 0.N.

■ ATTRIBUTE DOMAINS

The **domain** of an attribute is a description of an attribute's possible values. The characteristics of a domain depend on the type of the attribute. The domain of a simple attribute consists of both a physical and a semantic description. The physical description indicates the type of data (for example, numeric versus string), the length of the data, and other restrictions or constraints (such as the first character must be alphabetic, or the value must not exceed 9999.99). The semantic description indicates the function or purpose of the attribute—it distinguishes this attribute from other attributes that might have the same physical description.

For example, the domain of DepartmentName could be defined as "the set of strings of up to seven characters that represent names of departments at Highline University." The phrase *strings of up to seven characteristics* is the physical description of the domain, and the phrase *that represent names of departments at Highline University* is the semantic description. The semantic description differentiates strings of seven characters that represent names of departments from similar strings that represent, say, names of courses or buildings or some other attribute.

In some cases, the physical description of a simple attribute domain is an **enumerated list,** the set of an attribute's specific values. The domain of the attribute PartColor, for example, might be the enumerated list {'Blue', 'Yellow', 'Red'}.

The domain of a group attribute also has a physical and a semantic description. The physical description is a list of all of the attributes in the group and the order of those attributes. The semantic description is the function or purpose of the group. Thus the physical domain description of CampusAddress (in Figure 4-2) is the list OfficeNumber, Building; the semantic description is *the location of an office at Highline University.*

The domain of an object attribute is the set of object instances of that type. In Figure 4-2, for example, the domain of the PROFESSOR object attribute is the set of all PROFESSOR object instances in the database. The domain of the COLLEGE object is the set of all COLLEGEs in the database. In a sense, the domain of an object attribute is a dynamically enumerated list; the list contains all of the object instances of a particular type.

■ SEMANTIC OBJECT VIEWS

Users access the values of object attributes through database applications that provide data entry forms, reports, and queries. In most cases, such forms, reports, and

FIGURE 4-4   *StudentListing and Staff Views of the DEPARTMENT Semantic Object*

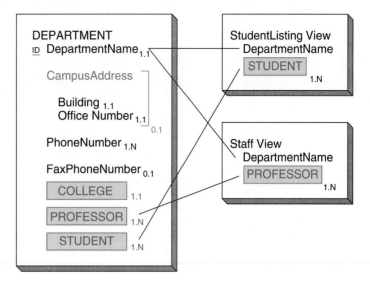

queries do not require access to all of an object's attributes. For example, Figure 4-4 shows two application views of DEPARTMENT. Some attributes of DEPARTMENT (its DepartmentName, for example) are visible in both application views. Other attributes are visible in only one. For example, STUDENT is seen only in the Student-Listing View, but PROFESSOR is visible in only the Staff View.

The portion of an object that is visible to a particular application is called the **semantic object view** or simply the **view.** A view consists of the name of the object plus a list of all of the attributes visible from that view.

Views are used in two ways. When you are developing a database, you can use them to develop the data model. Look at Figure 4-1 again. As shown, when developing the data model, the database and application developers work backward. That is, they begin with the forms, reports, and queries that the users say they need and then work backward to the database design. To do this, the team selects a required form, report, or query and determines the view that must exist in order for the form, report, or query to be created. Then the team selects the next form, report, or query and does the same. These two views are then integrated. This process is repeated until the structure of the entire database has been created.

The second way in which views are used occurs after the database structure has been created. At this point, views are constructed to support new forms, reports, and queries based on the existing database structure. Examples of this second use are shown in Part IV when we discuss database implementation.

CREATING DATA MODELS WITH SEMANTIC OBJECTS

This section illustrates a process for developing semantic objects in which the developers examine the application interface—forms, reports, and queries—and work backward (or reverse-engineer) to derive the object structure. For example, to model the structure of a DEPARTMENT object, we first gather all of the reports, forms, and queries based on DEPARTMENT. From them, we define a DEPARTMENT object that enables those reports, forms, and queries to be constructed.

For a totally new application, however, there will be no computer-based reports, forms, or queries to examine. In this case, the developers begin by determining what objects the users need to track. Then through interviews with the users, the team finds out what object attributes are important. From this, proto-types of forms and reports can be constructed that are then used to refine the data model.

AN EXAMPLE: THE HIGHLINE UNIVERSITY ADMINISTRATION DATABASE

Suppose that the administration at Highline University wants to keep track of department, faculty, and student major data. Suppose further that the application needs to produce four reports (Figures 4-5, 4-7, 4-9, and 4-11). Our goal is to examine these reports and, using reverse engineering, determine the objects and attributes that must be stored in the database.

THE COLLEGE OBJECT   The example report in Figure 4-5, is about a college—specifically, the College of Business. This example is only one instance of the report; Highline University has similar reports about other colleges, such as the College of Arts and Sciences and the College of Social Sciences. When creating a data model, it is important to gather enough examples to form a representative sample of all of the college reports. Here we assume that the report in Figure 4-5 is representative.

In examining the report, we find data specific to the college—such as the name, dean, telephone number, and campus address—and also facts about each of the departments within the college. This *suggests* that the database might contain COLLEGE and DEPARTMENT objects, with a relationship between the two.

These preliminary findings are documented in the object diagrams in Figure 4-6. Notice that we have omitted cardinalities from the simple attributes. The ID attributes have a cardinality of 1.1; otherwise, all the simple attributes have a cardinality of 0.1.

The cardinality of DEPARTMENT within COLLEGE is 1.N, indicating that a COLLEGE must have at least one DEPARTMENT and that it may have many. This minimum cardinality cannot be deduced from the report in Figure 4-5; rather, it was obtained by asking the users whether or not a college could exist with no departments. Their answer was no.

Also note that the structure of DEPARTMENT is inferred from the data shown in Figure 4-5. Since object attributes are always paired, COLLEGE is shown in DEPARTMENT, even though, strictly speaking, this fact cannot be determined from Figure 4-5. As with the DEPARTMENT attribute in COLLEGE, the users were asked

FIGURE 4-5   *Example COLLEGE Report*

College of Business Mary B. Jefferson, Dean			
Phone: 232-1187		Campus Address: Business Building, Room 100	
Department	Chairperson	Phone	Total Majors
Accounting	Jackson, Seymour P.	232-1841	318
Finance	HeuTeng, Susan	232-1414	211
Info Systems	Brammer, Nathaniel D.	236-0011	247
Management	Tuttle, Christine A.	236-9988	184
Production	Barnes, Jack T.	236-1184	212

FIGURE 4-6   *First Version of COLLEGE and DEPARTMENT Objects*

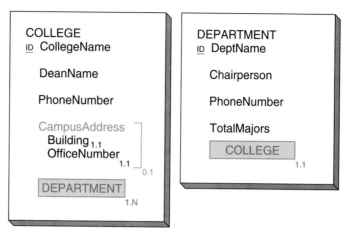

to determine the cardinalities of the COLLEGE attribute. They are 1.1, meaning that a DEPARTMENT must be related to one, and only one, COLLEGE.

As an aside, we have interpreted the report in Figure 4-5 to mean that the groups of repeating data refer to DEPARTMENT as an independent object. In fact, such repeating groups are often a signal that the repeating group is data concerning another object. *This is not always the case, however.* The repeating group can also be a group attribute that happens to have several values.

You may be wondering how to tell the difference between repeating-object data and repeating-group data. There is no hard and fast rule, because the answer depends on the ways that the users view their world. Consequently, the best approach is to consult the users about the semantics of the data. Ask whether these repeating-group data are only a part of the college or whether they refer to something else that stands on its own. If the former, they constitute a group attribute; if the latter, a semantic object. Also, look for other reports (or forms or queries). Do the users have one for departments? If so, then the assumption that DEPARTMENT is a semantic object would be confirmed. In fact, the personnel at Highline use two reports regarding Departments. This fact further substantiates the notion that a DEPARTMENT object must be defined.

Also, groups of attributes that represent an independent object generally have obvious identifying attribute(s). Automobiles have a VinNumber or LicenseNumber; Products have a ProductNumber or SKU. Orders have an OrderNumber. However, the group of attributes {DateOfMeasure, TirePressure}

FIGURE 4-7   *Example DEPARTMENT Report*

Information Systems Department
College of Business

Chairperson: Brammer, Nathaniel D
Phone: 236-0011
Campus Address: Social Science Building, Room 213

Professor	Office	Phone
Jones, Paul D.	Social Science, 219	232-7713
Parks, Mary B	Social Science, 308	232-5791
Wu, Elizabeth	Social Science, 207	232-9112

FIGURE 4-8   *Adjusted DEPARTMENT and New PROFESSOR Objects*

does not have an obvious identifier. When you ask a user about that group's identifier, he or she will say something like "Tire pressure of what?" It will be tire pressure of a car or a truck or a trailer or some vehicle. Hence, such a group would be a group attribute within another object—the object that is the answer to the "of what" question.

THE DEPARTMENT OBJECT   The department report shown in Figure 4-7 contains departmental data, along with a list of the professors who are assigned to those departments. Note that this report contains data concerning the department's campus address. Since these data do not appear in the object in Figure 4-6, we need to add them to the DEPARTMENT object, as has been done in Figure 4-8. This adjustment is typical of the data modeling process. That is, the semantic objects are continually adjusted as new reports, forms, and queries are identified and analyzed.

THE PROFESSOR OBJECT   The report in Figure 4-7 not only indicates that a DEPARTMENT object needs to be modeled but also, it suggests that another object may be needed to represent professor data. Accordingly, a PROFESSOR object was added to the model, as shown in Figure 4-8. The ID of PROFESSOR, which is Professor Name, is not unique; this is denoted by not underlining the ID in Figure 4-8.

According to the object diagrams in Figure 4-8, a DEPARTMENT must have at least one PROFESSOR and may have several, but a PROFESSOR must have one, and only one, DEPARTMENT. Thus, according to this model, joint appointments are prohibited. This restriction is part of the business rules and data semantics that must be obtained from interviews with the users.

FIGURE 4-9   *Second Example DEPARTMENT Report*

Student Major List Information Systems Department		
Chairperson: Brammer, Nathaniel D Phone: 236-0011		
Major's Name	Student Number	Phone
Jackson, Robin R.	12345	237-8713
Lincoln, Fred J.	48127	237-8713
Madison, Janice A.	37512	237-8713

FIGURE 4-10   *Adjusted DEPARTMENT and New STUDENT Objects*

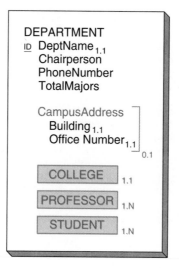

Figure 4-9 shows a second report about a department. This one concerns a department and the students who major in that area. Having two reports about an object is typical; they are simply documenting different views of the same thing. Moreover, the existence of this second report strengthens the notion that department is an object in the minds of the users.

THE STUDENT OBJECT   The report in Figure 4-9 gives data about students who major in a department's area, implying that students are also an object. Therefore the DEPARTMENT object must contain a STUDENT object as well as a PROFESSOR object, as in Figure 4-10.

The student object in Figure 4-10 contains the attributes StudentName, StudentNumber, and PhoneNumber, the attributes listed on the report in Figure 4-9. Note that both StudentName and StudentNumber are identifiers. StudentNames are not unique, but StudentNumbers are.

Figure 4-11 is an example of another report about a student—the acceptance letter that Highline sends to its incoming students. Even though this is a letter, it is also a report; the letter was probably produced using mail merge with a word-processing program.

Those data items in the letter that should be stored in the database are shown in boldface type. In addition to data regarding the student, the letter also contains data regarding the student's major DEPARTMENT and the student's adviser. Since an adviser is a PROFESSOR, this letter substantiates the need for a separate PROFESSOR object. Object diagrams from the revised PROFESSOR and STUDENT objects are shown in Figure 4-12. According to the STUDENT object, both DEPARTMENT and PROFESSOR are single valued (they have a maximum cardinality of 1). Hence, a student at this university has, at most, one major department and one adviser and is required to have both.

The STUDENT object in Figure 4-12 corresponds to the data shown in the letter in Figure 4-11. It may turn out, however, that the student actually has more than one major, in which case both PROFESSOR and STUDENT would be multivalued. This fact cannot be determined from this single form letter, so additional letters and interviews are needed to find out whether multiple majors are permitted. Here we assume that only one major is allowed.

The format of the student's name is given first in the format *first name last name* at the top of the letter and then in the format *last name* in the salutation. If presenting names in this format is a requirement, then the single attribute

FIGURE 4-11   *Acceptance Letter*

Mr. Fred Parks
123 Elm Street
Los Angeles, CA 98002

Dear **Mr. Parks**:

You have been admitted as a major in the **Accounting** Department at Highline University, starting in the **Fall Semester**, **1993**. The office of the Accounting Department is located in the **Business** Building, Room **210**.

Your adviser is professor **Elizabeth Johnson**, whose telephone number is **232-8740** and whose office is located in the **Business** building, Room **227**. Please schedule an appointment with your adviser as soon as you arrive on campus.

Congratulations and welcome to Highline University!

Sincerely,

Jan P. Smathers
President

JPS/rkp

StudentName (in Figure 4-10) will not suffice, and instead the group FirstName, LastName must be defined. This has been done in Figure 4-12. Note also that the adviser's name is in the format *first name, last name*, which means that the name of PROFESSOR should be changed as well.

In addition, this letter indicates that names in addresses and salutations must be preceded by the title *Mr.* or *Ms.* If this is to be done, an additional attribute must be placed in STUDENT. One alternative is to record the gender of the student and to select the title based on this attribute. Another alternative is to store the title it-

FIGURE 4-12   *Adjusted PROFESSOR and STUDENT Objects*

self. The advantage of this second alternative is that titles other than *Mr.* and *Ms.* can be stored. An example is the title *Dr.*

As currently documented, the model does not require a title other than Mr. or Ms. It seems plausible, however, that additional titles might be needed; hence, the second alternative seems more robust, and therefore the attribute Title has been added to STUDENT in Figure 4-12.

Again, these changes illustrate the iterative nature of data modeling. Design decisions often need to be rethought and revised again and again. Such iteration does not mean that the design process is faulty; in fact, it is typical and expected.

■ SPECIFYING OBJECTS

Figure 4-13 shows the completed object diagrams for the Highline University database. A few changes have been made: Both DeanName and Chairperson have been modeled in the format {FirstName, LastName} so that all names are in a similar format. And to improve the precision of the model, the PROFESSOR attribute in

FIGURE 4-13   *A Complete Set of Semantic Object Diagrams*

FIGURE 4-14

Object Specifications for the Highline University Database: (a) Semantic Object Specifications and (b) Domain Specifications

Object Name	Property Name	Min Card	Max Card	ID Status	Domain Name
COLLEGE	CollegeName	1	1	<u>ID</u>	CollegeName
	DeanName	1	1		PersonName
	FirstName	0	1		FirstName
	LastName	1	1		LastName
	PhoneNumber	0	1		Phone
	CampusAddress	0	1		CampusAddress
	Building	1	1		Building
	OfficeNumber	1	1		OfficeNumber
	DEPARTMENT	1	N		DEPARTMENT
DEPARTMENT	DeptName	1	1	<u>ID</u>	DeptName
	Chairperson	1	1		PersonName
	FirstName	0	1		FirstName
	LastName	1	1		LastName
	PhoneNumber	0	1		Phone
	TotalMajors	0	1		MajorCount
	CampusAddress	0	1		CampusAddress
	Building	1	1		Building
	OfficeNumber	1	1		OfficeNumber
	COLLEGE	1	1		COLLEGE
	PROFESSOR	1	N		PROFESSOR
	STUDENT	1	N		STUDENT
PROFESSOR	ProfessorName	1	1	ID	PersonName
	FirstName	0	1		FirstName
	LastName	1	1		LastName
	CampusAddress	0	1		CampusAddress
	Building	1	1		Building
	OfficeNumber	1	1		OfficeNumber
	PhoneNumber	0	1		Phone
	DEPARTMENT	1	1		DEPARTMENT
	ADVISER	1	N		STUDENT
STUDENT	StudentName	1	1	ID	PersonName
	FirstName	0	1		FirstName
	LastName	1	1		LastName
	StudentNumber	1	1	<u>ID</u>	StudentNumber
	PhoneNumber	0	1		Phone
	HomeAddress	1	1		Address
	Title	0	1		Title
	EnrollmentDate	0	1		QuarterDate
	DEPARTMENT	1	1		DEPARTMENT
	ADVISER	1	1		PROFESSOR

(a)

STUDENT has been renamed Adviser. The PROFESSOR instance that is connected to a STUDENT instance through this attribute is not just any of the STUDENT's professors; it is the particular PROFESSOR who serves as that STUDENT's adviser, and the term *Adviser* is more precise than the term *PROFESSOR*.

The domain of this attribute is unchanged. The domain of Adviser is PROFESSOR, just as the domain of the attribute PROFESSOR was PROFESSOR. This attribute still points to or connects to instances of the PROFESSOR semantic object. The name change is only that: an improvement in specifying the role that the PROFESSOR domain plays in the STUDENT semantic objects. A similar change was made in PROFESSOR. The STUDENT attribute was renamed ADVISEE, but this attribute is still connected to objects from the STUDENT domain.

Figure 4-14 presents a tabular specification of the data model. The semantic objects and attributes are defined in the semantic object specification, and the

FIGURE 4-14 (Continued)

Domain Name	Type[a]	Semantic Description	Physical Description
Address	G	A U.S. address	Street City State Zip
Building	S	A name of a building on campus	Text 20
CampusAddress	G	An address on campus	Building OfficeNumber
City	S	A city name	Text 25
COLLEGE	SO	One of Highline's ten colleges	See semantic object specification table
CollegeName	S	The official name of a college at Highline	Text 25
DEPARTMENT	SO	An academic department on campus	See semantic object specification table
DeptName	S	The official name of an academic department	Text 25
FirstName	S	The first-name portion of PersonName	Text 20
LastName	S	The last-name portion of PersonName	Text 30
MajorCount	F	Count of the students assigned to a given department	Integer; values {0 to 999}; format 999.
OfficeNumber	S	The number of an office on campus	Text 4
PersonName	G	First and last names of an administrator, professor, or student	FirstName LastName
Phone	S	Phone number within local area code	Text 4
PROFESSOR	SO	The name of a full-time member of Highline's faculty	See semantic object specification table
QuarterDate	S	An academic quarter and year	Text 3; values {q99, where q = one of {'F', 'W', 'S', 'M'} and 99 is decimal number from 00 to 99.}
State	S	A two-digit state abbreviation	Text 2
Street	S	A street address	Text 30
STUDENT	SO	A person who has been admitted for study at Highline	See semantic object specification table
StudentNumber	S	The ID assigned to a student admitted to Highline	Integer; values {10000 to 99999}; format 99999
Title	S	The title of individuals to be used in addresses	Text 3; values {Mr., Ms.}
Zip	S	A nine-digit zip code	Text 10; format 99999-9999

[a]F = formula
G = Group
S = Simple
SO = semantic object

(b)

domains are defined in the domain specification. The first table is an alternative presentation of the information in the semantic object diagrams, and its interpretation is straightforward.

The second table, the domain table, supplies information about domains that is not available from the semantic object diagrams. As we stated earlier, a domain has both a semantic and a physical description. The semantic description of each domain is shown in the Description column, and the physical description is shown in the Specification column. The Description column is self-explanatory.

The specification for domains includes a physical description and, in some cases, a set of values and a format. StudentNumber, for example, is specified as integer with values between 10000 and 99999 and with a format of five decimal digits. (In this table, a 9 in a format specification means a decimal digit.) Other domains are documented in a similar way. Title is an example of an enumerated domain whose values for Title are Mr., Ms.. The physical description of a group domain consists of a list of the domains included in the group. The physical description of a semantic object domain is just a reference to the semantic object description.

The TotalMajors domain is an example of a fourth type of domain, the **formula domain.** Formulas represent attributes computed from other values. The MajorCount domain is the count of the STUDENT objects that are connected to a given DEPARTMENT object. We shall not try to document the means by which this computation is to be carried out in the domain definition. At this point, all that is important is documenting the need for and the specification of the formula.

TYPES OF OBJECTS

This section describes and illustrates seven types of objects. For each type, we examine a report or form and show how to model that report or form with an object. Later, in Chapter 7, we transform each of these types of objects into database designs.

Three new terms are used in this section. A **single-valued attribute** is an attribute whose maximum cardinality is 1. A **multivalued attribute** is one whose maximum cardinality is greater than 1. And a **nonobject attribute** is a simple or a group attribute.

■ SIMPLE OBJECTS

A **simple object** is a semantic object that contains only single-valued, nonobject attributes. An example is shown in Figure 4-15. Part (a) of this figure shows two instances of a report called an *Equipment Tag*. Such tags are applied to items of office equipment in order to help keep track of inventory. These tags can be considered a report.

Figure 4-15(b) shows a simple object, EQUIPMENT, that models Equipment Tag. The attributes of the object include the items shown on the tag: EquipmentNumber, Description, AcquisitionDate, and PurchaseCost. Note that none of these attributes is multivalued, and none is an object attribute. Hence, EQUIPMENT is a simple object.

■ COMPOSITE OBJECTS

A **composite object** is a semantic object that contains one or more multivalued, nonobject attributes. The Hotel Bill shown in Figure 4-16(a) gives rise to the need for a composite object. The bill includes data that concerns the bill as a whole: InvoiceNumber, ArrivalDate, CustomerName, and TotalDue. It also contains a

FIGURE 4-15   *Example of a Simple Object: (a) Reports Based on a Simple Object and (b) EQUIPMENT Simple Object*

EQUIPMENT TAG:
   EquipmentNumber: 100   Description: Desk
   AcquisitionDate: 2/27/96   PurchaseCost: $350.00

EQUIPMENT TAG:
   EquipmentNumber: 200   Description: Lamp
   AcquisitionDate: 3/1/96   PurchaseCost: $39.95

(a)

EQUIPMENT
ID EquipmentNumber
    Description
    AcquisitionDate
    PurchaseCost

(b)

FIGURE 4-16   *Example of a Composite Object: (a) Report Based on a Composite Object and (b) HOTEL-BILL Composite Object*

GRANDVIEW HOTEL
Sea Bluffs, California

Invoice Number: 1234   Arrival Date: 10/12/96
Customer Name: Mary Jones

10/12/96	Room	$ 99.00
10/12/96	Food	$ 37.55
10/12/96	Phone	$ 2.50
10/12/96	Tax	$ 15.00
10/13/96	Room	$ 99.00
10/13/96	Food	$ 47.90
10/13/96	Tax	$ 15.00
	Total Due	$ 315.95

(a)

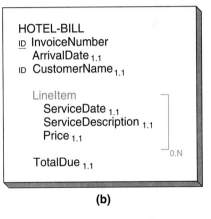

HOTEL-BILL
ID InvoiceNumber
   ArrivalDate $_{1.1}$
ID CustomerName $_{1.1}$

   LineItem
      ServiceDate $_{1.1}$
      ServiceDescription $_{1.1}$
      Price $_{1.1}$
                 0.N
   TotalDue $_{1.1}$

(b)

group of attributes that is repeated for services provided to the guest. Each group includes ServiceDate, ServiceDescription, and Price.

Figure 4-16(b) shows an object diagram for the HOTEL-BILL object. The attribute LineItem is a group attribute having a maximum cardinality of N, which means that the group ServiceDate, ServiceDescription, Price can occur many times in an instance of the HOTEL-BILL semantic object.

LineItem is not modeled as an independent semantic object; instead, it is considered to be an attribute within a HOTEL-BILL. This design is appropriate because the hotel does not view one line of a guest's charges as a separate thing, so line items on the guest's bill do not have identifiers of their own. No employee attempts to enter a LineItem except in the context of a bill. The employee enters the data for bill number 1234 and then, in the context of that bill, enters the charges. Or the employee retrieves an existing bill and enters additional charges in the context of that bill.

FIGURE 4-17   *A Composite Object with Two Groups: (a) HOTEL-BILL with Multivalued Customer Names and (b) HOTEL-BILL with Two Multivalued Groups*

GRANDVIEW HOTEL
Sea Bluffs, California

Invoice Number: 1234   Arrival Date: 10/12/96
Customer Name: Mary Jones
                        Fred Jones
                        Sally Jones

10/12/96	Room	$ 99.00
10/12/96	Food	$ 37.55
10/12/96	Phone	$ 2.50
10/12/96	Tax	$ 15.00
10/13/96	Room	$ 99.00
10/13/96	Food	$ 47.90
10/13/96	Tax	$ 15.00
	Total Due	$ 315.95

(a)

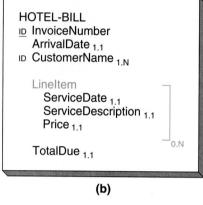

(b)

The minimum cardinality of LineItem is 0, which means that a HOTEL-BILL object can exist without any LineItem data. This allows a bill to be started when the customer checks in and before there are any charges. If the minimum cardinality were 1, then no HOTEL-BILL could be started until there was at least one charge. This design decision must be made in light of the business rules. It may be that the hotel's policy is not to start the bill until there has been a charge. If so, then the minimum cardinality of LineItem should be 1.

A composite object can have more than one multivalued attribute. Figure 4-17(a) shows a hotel bill that has a multivalued attribute for CustomerName, as well as a multivalued group for service charges. Each of these groups is independent of the other. The second instance of CustomerName, for example, is not logically associated with the second LineItem.

Figure 4-17(b) is an object diagram for the hotel bill in Figure 4-17(a). CustomerName is shown as a multivalued attribute. It is not included in the bracket of service charges because the repetitions of CustomerName have nothing to do with the repetitions of services. The two are independent, as we just noted.

Both simple and group attributes can be multivalued. In Figure 4-17(a), for example, CustomerName is a multivalued, simple attribute. By itself, it is sufficient for the object to be considered a composite object.

Multivalued attributes can also be nested within one another. For example, suppose it is important to keep track of individual expenses within a LineItem. In the form in Figure 4-18(a), the charges are subdivided. Food, for example, is broken down by meal. An object diagram for such nested attributes is presented in Figure 4-18(b) and shows that any service charge can have subitems.

To repeat, a composite object is an object that contains one or more multivalued simple or group attributes. It has no object attributes.

■ COMPOUND OBJECTS

A **compound object** contains at least one object attribute. Figure 4-19(a) shows two different data entry forms. One form, used by the company's motor pool, is used to keep track of the vehicles. The second form is used to maintain data about

FIGURE 4-18

A Composite Object with Nested Groups: (a) HOTEL-BILL with Service Subdescriptions and (b) HOTEL-BILL with Nested Multivalued Groups

GRANDVIEW HOTEL
Sea Bluffs, California

Invoice Number: 1234   Arrival Date: 10/12/96
Customer Name: Mary Jones

10/12/96	Room		$ 99.00
10/12/96	Food		
	Breakfast	$ 15.25	
	Dinner	$ 22.30	
			$ 37.55
10/12/96	Phone		$ 2.50
10/12/96	Tax		$ 15.00
10/13/96	Room		$ 99.00
10/13/96	Food		
	Breakfast	$ 15.25	
	Snack	$ 5.50	
	Dinner	$ 27.15	
			$ 47.90
10/13/96	Tax		$ 15.00
	Total Due		$ 315.95

(a)

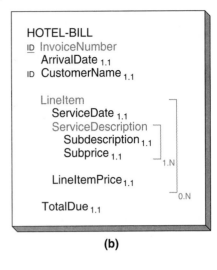

(b)

FIGURE 4-19

Compound Objects with 1:1 Paired Properties: (a) Example Vehicle and Employee Data Entry Forms and (b) EMPLOYEE and VEHICLE Compound Objects

VEHICLE DATA			
License number	Serial number		
Make	Type	Year	Color
Employee assignment			

EMPLOYEE WORK DATA			
Employee name		Employee ID	
Mailing address		Division	Phone
Pay code	Skill code	Hire date	Auto assigned

(a)

(b)

the employees. According to these forms, a vehicle is assigned to at most one employee, and an employee has at most one auto assigned.

We cannot tell from these forms whether an auto must be assigned to an employee or whether every employee must have an auto. To obtain that information, we would have to ask the users in the motor pool or human resources departments. Assume that we find out that an EMPLOYEE need not have a VEHICLE but that a VEHICLE must be assigned to an employee.

Figure 4-19(b) shows object diagrams for EMPLOYEE and VEHICLE. An EMPLOYEE contains VEHICLE as one of its attributes, and VEHICLE, in turn, contains EMPLOYEE as one of its attributes. Since both EMPLOYEE and VEHICLE contain object attributes, they both are compound objects. Furthermore, since neither attribute is multivalued, the relationship from EMPLOYEE to VEHICLE is one to one, or 1:1.

In Figure 4-19(a), the Employee and Vehicle forms contain each other. That is, Vehicle Data has a field Employee assignment, and Employee Work Data has a field Auto assigned. But this is not always the case; sometimes the relationship can appear in only one direction. Consider the report and form in Figure 4-20(a), which concern two objects: DORMITORY and STUDENT. From the Dormitory Occupancy Report, we can see that users think of a dorm as having attributes regarding the dorm (Name, ResidentAssistant, Phone) and also attributes regarding the students (StudentName, StudentNumber, Class) who live in the dorm.

On the other hand, the Student Data Form shows only student data; it does not include any dormitory data. (The local address might contain a dorm address, but this, if true, is apparently not important enough to document on the form. In a database development project, this possibility should be checked out with the users in an interview. Here we will assume that the Student Data Form does not include dormitory data.)

As we stated earlier, object attributes always occur in pairs. Even if the forms, reports, and queries indicate that only one side of the relationship can be seen, both sides of the relationship always exist. By analogy, a bridge that connects two islands touches both islands and can be used in both directions, even if the bridge is, by custom or law, a one-way bridge.

When no form or report can be found to document one side of a relationship, the development team must ask the users about the cardinality of that relationship. In this case, the team would need to find out how many DORMITORYs a STUDENT could have and whether a STUDENT must be related to a DORMITORY. Here let us suppose the answers to these questions are that a STUDENT is related to just one DORMITORY and may be related to no DORMITORY. Thus in Figure 4-20(b), DORMITORY contains multiple values of STUDENT, and STUDENT contains one value of DORMITORY, so the relationship from DORMITORY to STUDENT is one to many, or 1:N.

A third illustration of compound objects appears in Figure 4-21(a). From these two forms, we can deduce that one book can be written by many authors (from the Book Stock Data form) and that one author can write many books (from the Books in Stock, by Author form). Thus in Figure 4.21(b), the BOOK object contains many values of AUTHOR, and AUTHOR contains many values of BOOK. Hence the relationship from BOOK to AUTHOR is many to many, or N:M. Furthermore, a BOOK must have an AUTHOR, and an AUTHOR (to be an author) must have written at least one BOOK. Therefore, both of these objects have a minimum cardinality of one.

Figure 4-22 summarizes the four types of compound objects. In general, OBJECT-1 can contain a maximum of one or many OBJECT-2s. Similarly, OBJECT-2 can contain one or many OBJECT-1s. We use this table when we discuss database design in Chapter 7.

FIGURE 4-20 *Compound Objects with 1:N Paired Properties: (a) Example Dormitory Report and Student Data Form and (b) DORMITORY and STUDENT Compound Objects*

DORMITORY OCCUPANCY REPORT		
Dormitory	Resident Assistant	Phone
Ingersoll	Sarah and Allen French	3-5567
Student name	Student Number	Class
Adams, Elizabeth	710	SO
Baker, Rex	104	FR
Baker, Brydie	744	JN
Charles, Stewart	319	SO
Scott, Sally	447	SO
Taylor, Lynne	810	FR

STUDENT DATA FORM

Student Name	Student Number
Major	Adviser
Class	High School

Prior College

Local Address
Phone

Permanent Address
Phone

(a)

DORMITORY
ID DormName
ID ResidentAssistant
   Phone

> STUDENT   1.N

STUDENT
ID StudentName
ID StudentNumber
   Major
   Adviser
   Class
   HighSchool
   Prior College
   LocalAddress
   LocalPhone
   PermanentAddress
   PermanentPhone

> DORMITORY   0.1

(b)

FIGURE 4-21

Compound Objects with N:M Paired Properties: (a) Bookstore Data Entry Forms and (b) BOOK and AUTHOR Objects

(a)

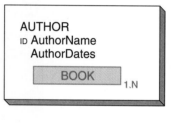

(b)

FIGURE 4-22

Four Types of Compound Objects

		Object1 Can Contain	
Object2		One	Many
Can	One	1:1	1:N
Contain	Many	M:1	M:N

■ HYBRID OBJECTS

As the term implies, **hybrid objects** are combinations of objects of two types. In particular, a hybrid object is a semantic object with at least one multivalued group attribute that includes a semantic object attribute.

Figure 4-23(a) is a second version of the report about dormitory occupancy shown in Figure 4-20(a). The difference is that the third column of the student data contains Rent instead of Class. This is an important difference because rent is not an attribute of STUDENT but pertains to the combination of STUDENT and DORMITORY and is an attribute of DORMITORY.

Figure 4-23(b) is an object diagram that models this form. DORMITORY contains a multivalued group with both the object attribute STUDENT and the nonobject attribute Rent. This means that Rent is paired with STUDENT in the context of DORMITORY.

Now examine the alternative DORMITORY object in Figure 4-23(c). This is an *incorrect* model of the report in Figure 4-23(a), as it shows that Rent and STUDENT

FIGURE 4-23   *DORMITORY Hybrid Object: (a) Dormitory Report with Rent Property, (b) Correct DORMITORY and STUDENT Objects, and (c) Incorrect DORMITORY and STUDENT Objects*

DORMITORY OCCUPANCY REPORT

Dormitory	Resident Assistant	Phone
Ingersoll	Sarah and Allen French	3-5567

Student name	Student Number	Rent
Adams, Elizabeth	710	$175.00
Baker, Rex	104	$225.00
Baker, Brydie	744	$175.00
Charles, Stewart	319	$135.00
Scott, Sally	447	$225.00
Taylor, Lynne	810	$175.00

(a)

DORMITORY
ID DormName
ResidentAssistant
Phone
StudentRent
STUDENT $_{1.1}$
Rent $_{0.1}$ $_{1.N}$

STUDENT
ID StudentName
ID StudentNumber $_{1.1}$
DORMITORY $_{0.1}$

(b)

DORMITORY
ID DormName
ResidentAssistant
Phone
STUDENT $_{1.N}$
Rent $_{0.N}$

STUDENT
ID StudentName
ID StudentNumber
DORMITORY $_{0.1}$

(c)

are independently multivalued, which is incorrect because Rent and STUDENT are multivalued as a pair.

Figure 4-24(a) shows a form based on another hybrid object. This Sales Order form contains data about an order (SalesOrderNumber, Date, Subtotal, Tax, and Total), data about a CUSTOMER and a SALESPERSON, and a multivalued group that itself contains data about items on the order. Furthermore, ITEM data (item number, description, and unit price) appear within the multivalued group.

Figure 4-24(b) shows the SALES-ORDER semantic object. It contains the nonobject attributes SalesOrderNumber, Date, Subtotal, Tax, and Total. It also contains the CUSTOMER and SALESPERSON object attributes and a multivalued group that represents each line item on the sales order. The group contains nonobject attributes Quantity and ExtendedPrice and the object attribute ITEM.

The object diagrams in Figure 4-24(b) are ambiguous in one aspect that may or may not be important, depending on the application. According to the ITEM

FIGURE 4-24   *Hybrid SALES-ORDER and Related Objects: (a) Sales Order Form and (b) Objects to Model Sales Order Form*

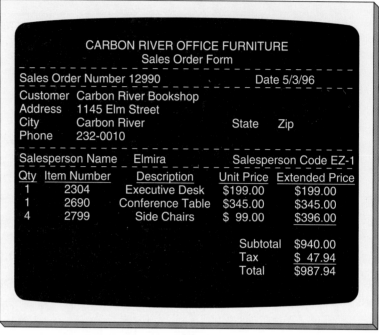

CARBON RIVER OFFICE FURNITURE
Sales Order Form

Sales Order Number 12990   Date 5/3/96

Customer   Carbon River Bookshop
Address   1145 Elm Street
City   Carbon River   State   Zip
Phone   232-0010

Salesperson Name   Elmira   Salesperson Code EZ-1

Qty	Item Number	Description	Unit Price	Extended Price
1	2304	Executive Desk	$199.00	$199.00
1	2690	Conference Table	$345.00	$345.00
4	2799	Side Chairs	$ 99.00	$396.00

Subtotal $940.00
Tax $ 47.94
Total $987.94

(a)

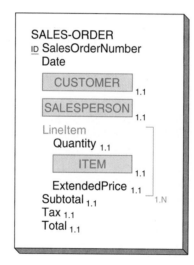

SALES-ORDER
ID SalesOrderNumber
  Date
  CUSTOMER 1.1
  SALESPERSON 1.1
  LineItem
    Quantity 1.1
    ITEM 1.1
    ExtendedPrice 1.1
  Subtotal 1.1   1.N
  Tax 1.1
  Total 1.1

ITEM
ID ItemNumber
  ItemDescription
  UnitPrice 1.1
  SALES-ORDER 0.N

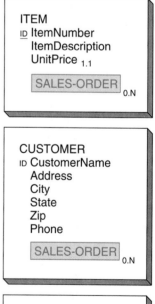

CUSTOMER
ID CustomerName
  Address
  City
  State
  Zip
  Phone
  SALES-ORDER 0.N

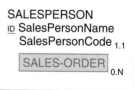

SALESPERSON
ID SalesPersonName
  SalesPersonCode 1.1
  SALES-ORDER 0.N

(b)

object diagram, an ITEM can be connected to more than one SALES-ORDER. But since the multivalued group LineItem is encapsulated (hidden within) SALES-ORDER, it is not clear from this diagram whether an ITEM can occur *once or many times* on the same SALES-ORDER.

In general, there are four interpretations of maximum cardinality for the paired attributes in the SALES-ORDER hybrid object:

1. An ITEM can appear on only one SALES-ORDER and in only one of the LineItems within that SALES-ORDER.

2. An ITEM can appear on only one SALES-ORDER but in many different LineItems within that SALES-ORDER.

3. An ITEM can appear on many different SALES-ORDERs but in only one LineItem within each of those SALES-ORDERs.

4. An ITEM can appear on many different SALES-ORDERs and in many different LineItems within those SALES-ORDERs.

When it is important to distinguish among these cases, the following notation should be used: If either Case 1 or 2 is in force, the maximum cardinality of the hybrid object attribute should be set to 1. Thus, for this example, the maximum cardinality of SALES-ORDER in ITEM is set to 1. If an ITEM is to appear in only one LineItem of the SALES-ORDER (Case 1), it should be marked as having a unique ID in that group. Otherwise (Case 2), it need not be marked. These two cases are shown in Figure 4-25 (a) and (b).

If either Case 3 or 4 is in force, the maximum cardinality of the hybrid object attribute is set to N. Thus, for this example, the maximum cardinality of SALES-ORDER in ITEM is set to N. Furthermore, if an ITEM is to appear in only one LineItem of a SALES-ORDER (Case 3), it should be marked as having a unique ID in that group. Otherwise (Case 4), it need not be marked. These two cases are shown in Figure 4-25(c) and (d).

■ Association Objects

An **association object** is an object that relates two (or more) objects and stores data that are peculiar to that relationship. Figure 4-26(a) on page 97 shows a report and two data entry screens that give rise to the need for an association object. The report contains data about an airline flight and data about the particular airplane and pilot assigned to that flight. The two data entry forms contain data about a pilot and an airplane.

In Figure 4-26(b), the object FLIGHT is an association object that associates the two objects AIRPLANE and PILOT and stores data about their association. FLIGHT contains one each of AIRPLANE and PILOT, but both AIRPLANE and PILOT contain multiple values of FLIGHT. This particular pattern of associating two (or more) objects with data about the association occurs frequently, especially in applications that involve the assignment of two or more things. Other examples are a JOB that assigns an ARCHITECT to a CLIENT, a TASK that assigns an EMPLOYEE to a PROJECT, and a PURCHASE-ORDER that assigns a VENDOR to a SERVICE.

For the example in Figure 4-26, the association object FLIGHT has an identifier of its own, the group {FlightNumber, Date}. Often association objects do not have identifiers of their own, in which case the identifier is the combination of the identifiers of the objects that are associated.

To understand this better, consider Figure 4-27(a) on page 98, which shows a report about the assignment of architects to projects. Although the assignment has no obvious identifier, in fact the identifier is the combination {ProjectName, Name}. These attributes, however, belong to PROJECT and ARCHITECT and not to ASSIGNMENT. The identifier of ASSIGNMENT is thus the combination of those identifiers of the things that are assigned.

FIGURE 4-25

Examples of the Four Cases of Maximum Cardinality in a Hybrid Object: (a) ITEM in One LineItem of One ORDER, (b) ITEM in (Possibly) Many LineItems of One ORDER, (c) ITEM in One LineItem of (Possibly) Many ORDERs, and (d) ITEM in (Possibly) Many LineItems of (Possibly) Many ORDERs

(a)

(b)

(c)

(d)

FIGURE 4-26

Examples of an Association Object: (a) Example Flight Report and Forms and (b) FLIGHT, PILOT, AIRPLANE Objects

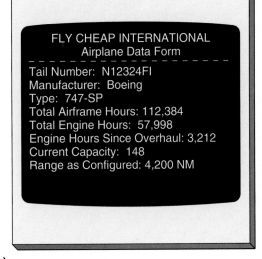

(a)

FLIGHT
ID FlightID
    FlightNumber
    Date
  OriginatingCity
  Destination
  FuelOnTakeOff
  WeightOnTakeOff

   AIRPLANE   1.1
   PILOT   1.1

AIRPLANE
ID TailNumber
  Manufacturer
  Type
  TotalAirframeHours
  TotalEngineHours
  EngHoursPastOH
  CurrentCapacity
  RangeAsConfig

   FLIGHT   0.N

PILOT
ID FCI-ID
ID Name
ID SocialSecurityNumber
  Street
  City
  State
  Zip
  Phone
  EmergPhone
  DateOfLastCheckOut
  Hours
  DateOfLastPhysical

   FLIGHT   0.N

(b)

FIGURE 4-27   *ASSIGNMENT Association Object: (a) Example Assignment Report and (b) ASSIGNMENT Object with Semantic Object ID*

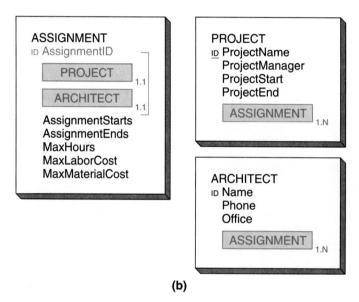

Figure 4-27(b) shows the object diagrams for this situation. Both PROJECT and ARCHITECT are object attributes of ASSIGNMENT, and the group {PROJECT, ARCHITECT} is the identifier of ASSIGNMENT. This means that the combination of an instance of PROJECT and an instance of ARCHITECT identifies a particular ASSIGNMENT.

Note that the AssignmentID identifier in Figure 4-27(b) is not unique, thereby indicating that an architect may be assigned to a project more than once. If this is not the case, the identifier should be declared to be unique. Also, if an employee may be assigned to a project more than once and if for some reason it is important to have a unique identifier for an ASSIGNMENT, the attribute Date or some other time-indicating attribute (Week, Quarter, and so forth) should be added to the group.

■ PARENT/SUBTYPE OBJECTS

To understand parent and subtype objects, consider the object EMPLOYEE in Figure 4-28(a). Some of the attributes in EMPLOYEE pertain to all employees, and others pertain only to employees who are managers. The object in Figure 4-28(a)

FIGURE 4-28   *Need for MANAGER Subtype: (a) EMPLOYEE Without Subtype and (b) EMPLOYEE with MANAGER Subtype*

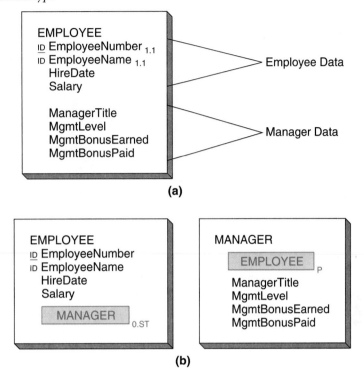

is not very precise because the manager-oriented attributes are not suitable for nonmanager employees.

A better model is shown in Figure 4-28(b), in which the EMPLOYEE object contains a subtype object, MANAGER. All of the manager-oriented attributes have been moved to the MANAGER object. Employees who are not managers have one EMPLOYEE object instance and no MANAGER object instances. Employees who are managers have both an EMPLOYEE instance and a MANAGER instance. In this example, the EMPLOYEE object is called a *parent object* or *supertype object*, and the MANAGER object is called a *subtype object*.

The first attribute of a subtype is the parent attribute and is denoted by the subscript P. Parent attributes are always required. The identifiers of the subtype are the same as the identifiers of the parent. In Figure 4-28, EmployeeNumber and EmployeeName are identifiers of both EMPLOYEE and MANAGER.

Subtype attributes are shown with the subscript 0.ST or 1.ST. The first digit (0 or 1) is the minimum cardinality of the subtype. If 0, the subtype is optional, and if 1, the subtype is required. (A required subtype does not make sense for this example but will for the more complicated examples to follow.) The *ST* indicates that the attribute is a subtype, or IS-A attribute.

Parent/subtype objects have an important characteristic called inheritance. A subtype acquires, or *inherits*, all of the attributes of its parent, and therefore a MANAGER inherits all of the attributes of an EMPLOYEE. In addition, the parent acquires all of the attributes of its subtypes, and an EMPLOYEE who is a MANAGER acquires all of the attributes of MANAGER.

A semantic object may contain more than one subtype attribute. Figure 4-29 shows a second EMPLOYEE object that has two subtype attributes, MANAGER and PROGRAMMER. Since all of these attributes are optional, an EMPLOYEE can have neither, one, or both of these subtypes. This means that some employees are neither managers nor programmers, some are managers but not programmers, some are programmers but not managers, and some are both programmers and managers.

FIGURE 4-29   *EMPLOYEE with Two Subtype Properties*

Sometimes subtypes exclude one another. That is, a VEHICLE can be an AUTO or a TRUCK, but not both. A CLIENT can be an INDIVIDUAL, a PARTNERSHIP, or a CORPORATION, but only one of these three types. When subtypes exclude one another, they are placed into a subtype group, and the group is assigned a subscript of the format *X.Y.Z.* X is the minimum cardinality and is 0 or 1, depending on whether or not the subtype group is required. Y and Z are counts of the number of

FIGURE 4-30   *Exclusive (a) and Nested (b) Subtypes*

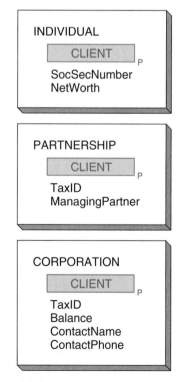

(a)

```
┌─────────────────────────────┐      ┌─────────────────────────────┐
│ CORPORATION                 │      │ TAXABLE CORP                │
│   ┌───────────────┐         │      │   ┌───────────────┐         │
│   │   CLIENT      │ P       │      │   │  CORPORATION  │ P       │
│   └───────────────┘         │      │   └───────────────┘         │
│   TaxID                     │      │   TaxRate                   │
│   Balance                   │      └─────────────────────────────┘
│   ContactName               │
│   ContactPhone              │      ┌─────────────────────────────┐
│   ┌───────────────┐         │      │ NONTAXABLE CORP             │
│   │ TAXABLE CORP  │ 0.ST    │      │   ┌───────────────┐         │
│   └───────────────┘    ┐    │      │   │  CORPORATION  │ P       │
│   ┌───────────────┐    │1.1.1│     │   └───────────────┘         │
│   │NONTAXABLE CORP│ 0.ST│   │      │   ExemptionID               │
│   └───────────────┘    ┘    │      │   ┌───────────────┐         │
└─────────────────────────────┘      │   │  GOV-AGENCY   │ 0.ST    │
                                      │   └───────────────┘    ┐    │
                                      │   ┌───────────────┐    │1.1.1│
                                      │   │    SCHOOL     │ 0.ST│   │
                                      │   └───────────────┘    ┘    │
                                      └─────────────────────────────┘

┌─────────────────────────────┐      ┌─────────────────────────────┐
│ GOV-AGENCY                  │      │ SCHOOL                      │
│   ┌───────────────┐         │      │   ┌───────────────┐         │
│   │NONTAXABLE CORP│ P       │      │   │NONTAXABLE CORP│ P       │
│   └───────────────┘         │      │   └───────────────┘         │
│   FederalIDNumber           │      │   SchoolDistrictName        │
└─────────────────────────────┘      └─────────────────────────────┘
```

(b)

attributes in the group that are allowed to have a value. Y is the minimum number required, and Z is the maximum number allowed.

Figure 4-30(a) shows three types of CLIENT as a subtype group. The subscript of the group, 0.1.1, means that the subtype is not required, but if it exists, a minimum of one and a maximum of one (or exactly one) of the subtypes in the group must exist. Note that each of the subtypes has the subscript 0.ST, meaning that they all are optional, as they must be. If they all were required, the maximum count would have to be three, not one. This notation is robust enough to allow for situations in which three out of five or seven out of ten of a list of subtypes must be required.

Even more complex restrictions can be modeled when subtypes are nested. The subtype group in Figure 4-30(b) models a situation in which the subtype CORPORATION must be either a TAXABLE-CORP or a NONTAXABLE-CORP. If it is a NONTAXABLE-CORP, it must be either GOV-AGENCY or a SCHOOL. Only a few nonobject attributes are shown in this example. In reality, if such a complex structure were required, there would likely be more attributes.

■ ARCHETYPE/VERSION OBJECTS

The final type of object is the **archetype/version object**. An archetype object is a semantic object that produces other semantic objects that represent versions, releases, or editions of the archetype. For example, in Figure 4-31, the archetype object TEXTBOOK produces the version objects EDITIONs. According to this model, the attributes Title, Author, and Publisher belong to the object TEXTBOOK, and the attributes EditionNumber, PublicationDate, and NumberOfPages belong to the EDITION of the TEXTBOOK.

The ID group in EDITION has two portions, TEXTBOOK and EditionNumber; this is the typical pattern for an ID of a version object. One part of the ID contains the archetype object, and the second part is a simple attribute that identifies the

FIGURE 4-31   *Example of an Archetype/Version Object*

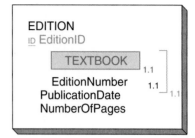

FIGURE 4-32   *Another Example of an Archetype/Version Object*

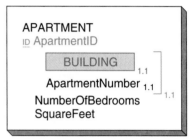

version within the archetype. Figure 4-32 shows another instance of archetype/version objects.

COMPARING THE SEMANTIC OBJECT AND THE E-R MODEL

The E-R model and the semantic object model have both similarities and differences. They are similar in that they both are tools for understanding and documenting the structure of the users' data. They both strive to model the structure of the things in the users' world and the relationships among them.

The principal difference between the two models is one of orientation. The E-R model sees the concept of *entity* as basic. Entities and their relationships are considered the atoms, if you will, of a data model. These atoms can be combined to form what the E-R model calls *user views,* which are combinations of entities whose structure is similar to that of semantic objects.

The semantic object model takes the concept of *semantic object* as basic. The set of semantic objects in a data model is a map of the essential structure of the things that the user considers important. These objects are the atoms of the users' world and are the smallest distinguishable units that the users want to process. They may be decomposed into smaller parts inside the DBMS (or application), but those smaller parts are of no interest or utility to the users.

According to the semantic object perspective, entities, as defined in the E-R model, do not exist. They are only pieces or chunks of the real entities. The only entities that have meaning to users are, in fact, semantic objects. Another way to state this is to say that semantic objects are *semantically self-contained* or *semantically complete.* Consider an example. Figure 4-33 shows four semantic objects, SALES-ORDER, CUSTOMER, SALESPERSON, and ITEM. When a user says, "Show me sales order number 2000," he or she means show SALES-ORDER as modeled in

FIGURE 4-33   *SALES-ORDER and Related Semantic Objects*

Figure 4-33. That includes, among other attributes, CUSTOMER data. Because CUSTOMER is part of SALES-ORDER, the SALES-ORDER object includes CUSTOMER.

Figure 4-34 is an E-R model of this same data and contains the SALES-ORDER, CUSTOMER, SALESPERSON, LINE-ITEM, and INVENTORY entities. The SALES-ORDER entity includes the attributes OrderNumber, Date, Subtotal, Tax, and Total. Now if a user were to say, "Show me sales order number 2000" and be given only the attributes Date, Subtotal, Tax, and Total, he or she would be disappointed. Most likely the user's response would be, "Where's the rest of the data?" That is,

FIGURE 4-34   *Entity-Relationship Model of SALES-ORDER and CUSTOMER*

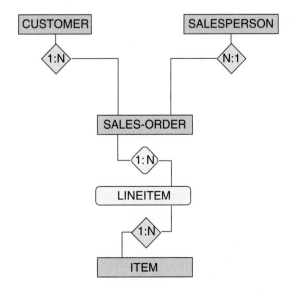

the entity SALES-ORDER does not represent the user's meaning of the distinct identity SALES-ORDER. The entity is only a part of SALES-ORDER.

At the same time, when a user (perhaps even the same user) says, "Show me customer 12345," he or she means show all of the data modeled for CUSTOMER in Figure 4-33, including CustomerName, all of the attributes of the group Address, and all of the SALES-ORDERs for that CUSTOMER. The entity CUSTOMER in Figure 4-34 has only the attributes CustomerName, Street, City, State, Zip. If the user were to say, "Show me customer ABC" and be given only this data, he or she again would be disappointed: "No, that's only part of what I want."

According to the semantic object view, E-R entities are unnecessary. Semantic objects can be readily transformed into database designs without ever considering E-R model entities. They are halfway houses, so to speak, constructed in the process of moving away from the paradigm of the computer file to the paradigm of the user.

Another difference is that the semantic objects contain more metadata than do the entities. In Figure 4-33, the semantic object model records the fact that CustomerNumber is a unique identifier in the users' minds. It may or may not be used as an identifier for the underlying table, but that fact is not important to the data model. In addition, CustomerName is a nonunique identifier to the users. Furthermore, the semantic objects represent the fact that there is a semantic group of attributes called *Address*. This group contains other attributes that form the address. The fact that this group exists will become important when forms and reports are designed. Finally, the semantic objects indicate that an ITEM may relate to more than one SALES-ORDER but that it can relate to only one LineItem within that SALES-ORDER. This fact cannot be shown on the entity-relationship diagram.

In the final analysis, decide which of Figures 4-33 and 4-34 gives you a better idea of what the database should contain. Many people find that the boundaries drawn around the semantic objects and the brackets around the group attributes help them get a better idea of the overall picture of the data model.

SUMMARY

Both the E-R and the semantic object models are used to interpret requirements and to build models of the users' data. These models are like lenses through which developers look when studying and documenting the users' data. Both ultimately lead to a database design.

A semantic object is a named collection of attributes that sufficiently describes a distinct identity. Semantic objects are grouped into classes, and both classes and instances of semantic objects have names. For example, the name of a class is EMPLOYEE, and the name of an instance is EMPLOYEE 2000.

Attributes represent characteristics of the identities being represented. The set of attributes is sufficient in that it represents all of the characteristics that the users need to do their work. Objects represent distinct identities, instances that the users view as independent and separate. The distinct identities represented may or may not be physical; indeed, they may themselves be representative, such as a contract.

Object attributes can be simple data items, groups, or other semantic objects. Object diagrams summarize the structure of objects. Object names are spelled in capital letters at the top of the diagram. Nonobject attributes are written with initial capitals, and attribute groups are indicated by brackets.

All attributes have a minimum cardinality that indicates how many instances of the attribute must exist in order for the object to be valid. They also have a maximum cardinality that indicates the maximum number of instances of the attribute allowed. Cardinality is written in the format m.n, where m is the minimum cardinality and n is the maximum. To reduce the clutter in an object diagram, if the cardinality of a simple value attribute is 0.1, it is not shown. But cardinality is always shown for group and object attributes.

Object attributes are always paired. If one object has a relationship with a second, the second must have a relationship with the first. Object identifiers are attributes that serve, in the users' minds, to identify objects. Identifiers can be unique or not unique. Any type of attribute can be an identifier. Identifiers are shown with the letters ID in front of the attribute. If the attribute is unique, then the letters ID are underlined. The cardinalities of an identifier are normally 1.1.

The domain of an attribute is the set of all possible values that the attribute can have. Domains have both a physical and a semantic definition. There are three types of domains: simple, group, and semantic object.

Applications process objects through users' views. A view of an object consists of the name of the object and all of the attributes visible from that view. View and object definition is often an iterative process.

The process of developing a set of object diagrams is iterative. Reports or forms are examined; an initial set of objects is documented; and the new reports and forms are then checked to reveal new objects and changes in existing objects. This process continues until all the forms and reports have been examined.

There are seven types of objects. Simple objects have no multivalued attributes and no object attributes. Composite objects have multivalued attributes but no object attributes. Compound objects have object attributes, and hybrid objects combine composite and compound objects. Association objects relate two or more other objects. Subtype objects are used to represent the specializations of objects. Finally, archetype/version objects are used to model objects that contain base data along with multiple variations, or versions.

The E-R model considers entities as basic, whereas the semantic object model considers semantic objects as basic. The semantic object model also contains more information about the meaning of the data than does the entity relationship model.

GROUP I QUESTIONS

4.1 Explain why the E-R model and the semantic object model are like lenses.

4.2 Define *semantic object*.

4.3 Explain the difference between an object class name and an object instance name. Give an example of each.

4.4 What is required for a set of attributes to be a sufficient description?

4.5 Explain the words *distinct identity* as they pertain to the definition of a semantic object.

4.6 Explain why a line item of an order is not a semantic object.

4.7 List the three types of attributes.

4.8 Give an example of each of the following:

   a. a simple, single-valued attribute

   b. a group, single-valued attribute

   c. a simple, multivalued attribute

   d. a group, multivalued attribute

   e. a simple object attribute

   f. a multivalued object attribute

4.9 What is minimum cardinality? How is it used? Which types of attributes have minimum cardinality?

4.10 What is maximum cardinality? How is it used? Which types of attributes have maximum cardinality?

4.11 What are paired attributes? Why are they needed?

4.12 What is an object identifier? Give an example of a simple attribute object identifier and an example of a group attribute object identifier.

4.13 Define *attribute domain*. What are the types of attribute domain? Why is a semantic description necessary?

4.14 What is a semantic object view? Give an example of an object and two views other than those in this text.

4.15 Give an example of a simple object other than the one discussed in this chapter.

4.16 Give three examples of composite objects other than those in this chapter. One of your examples should have just one composite group; one should have two independent composite groups; and the third should have nested composite groups.

4.17 Give an example of four sets of compound objects other than those in this chapter. One set should have a 1:1 relationship; one set should have a 1:N relationship; one set should have an M:1 relationship; and one set should have an M:N relationship.

4.18 Give an example of a hybrid object other than the one in this chapter.

4.19 Give an example of one association and two compound objects other than those in this chapter.

4.20 Give an example of a supertype object with three subtype objects other than those in this chapter.

4.21 Give an example of archetype/version objects other than those in this chapter.

4.22 Explain the similarities between the E-R model and the semantic object model.

4.23 Explain the major differences between the E-R model and the semantic object model.

4.24 Explain the reasoning that entities, as defined in the E-R model, do not truly exist.

4.25 Show how both the E-R model and the semantic object model would represent the data underlying the SALES ORDER form in Figure 4-24(a), and explain the main differences.

GROUP II QUESTIONS

4.26 Collect as many forms or reports as you can about your relationship with your college or university. Examples are acceptance letters, class schedules, transcripts, bills, class-change forms, and grades. Using the E-R model, create a data model of the entities that underlie your relationship with your school.

4.27 To answer Question 4.26, use the semantic-object model instead.

4.28 Compare your answers to Questions 4.26 and 4.27. How are they similar? How are they different? Are the differences important? Do you think one model is uniformly superior to the other? Justify your answers.

PROJECTS USING SALSA FOR THE DESKTOP

The end-sheets of this textbook enclose a CD-ROM that contains SALSA for the Desktop™. The following projects require you to use this product. To complete these projects you should install SALSA on a 486 or higher IBM-compatible computer with at least 12 megabytes of RAM and 35 megabytes of available disk storage. The license on this disk allows you to use SALSA for the Desktop for educational purposes only. If you wish to use it for commercial purposes, you should contact the vendor at the telephone number on the disk.

The following projects will be much easier to accomplish if you take the time to work through the Tour Bus (on the Learning Studio help map). You might want to use the other Learning Studio components as well.

The notation used in SALSA for the Desktop varies somewhat from the notation used in this text. Specifically, group attributes and identifying status are shown differently. SALSA for the Desktop uses an animated tab symbol to expand and contract groups. Attributes that are identifiers are indicated by asterisks: one asterisk denotes a nonunique identifier; two asterisks denote a unique identifier.

This version of SALSA for the Desktop will generate a database in either of two formats. It will either produce a database in its own, internal, relational engine, or it will generate one using the Microsoft Access 2.0 or higher engine. If you have a version of Microsoft Access loaded on your computer, you can cause SALSA to generate Access format databases by selecting that option from the Options/Database menu item.

■ PROJECT 1

Use SALSA to create the model in Figure 4-13. Do this in a number of stages.

a. First create the COLLEGE and DEPARTMENT objects in Figure 4-6. You can drag and drop templates from SALSA's catalog. (SALSA uses the term *template* for what this text calls a *domain*.) Your job will be easier if you create a template for the CampusAddress group. Once you have created the model in Figure 4-13, use SALSA to generate the application. Key in the example data from Figure 4-5 as well as your own example data.

b. Create the objects in Figure 4-8. You will need to create a new object PROFESSOR and the DEPARTMENT to include it. Generate the application, and add the data in Figure 4-7 as well as your own sample data.

c. Add STUDENT object shown in Figure 4-10, and modify DEPARTMENT to include it. Generate the application, and add sample data from Figure 4-9 as well as your own sample data.

d. Adjust the PROFESSOR and STUDENT objects as shown in Figure 4-12. Create a new group template for PersonName, and use it to create ProfessorName and StudentName attributes. Add sample data that would be necessary to generate the letter in Figure 4-11. Add your own sample data.

e. Use SALSA to print the COLLEGE, DEPARTMENT, PROFESSOR, and STUDENT reports. Explain how the structure of these reports reflects the structure of the semantic objects.

■ PROJECT 2

Use SALSA to create objects of the following types. Pick any subjects for your objects, but choose ones that are realistic examples for each type. Use subjects that are different from those in this text.

a. Simple object

b. Composite object with one repeating group

c. Composite object with two repeating groups, not nested within each other

d. Composite object with two repeating groups, one nested inside the other

e. Compound object with a 1:1 relationship

f. Compound object with a 1:N relationship

g. Compound object with an N:M relationship

h. Hybrid object

i. Association object

j. Archetype/version objects

k. SALSA does not support parent/subtype objects. Simulate a parent/subtype object with compound objects having a 1:1 relationship. Comment on the effectiveness of this simulation.

l. Generate an application having these objects. Explain how the structure of the forms that are generated reflects the structure of the underlying objects.

The chapters in Part III discuss the design of databases and database applications. Chapter 5 presents the relational model and normalization. The relational model is important because it is the standard in which most database designs are expressed; it is also the foundation of most of today's DBMS products. Normalization is important because it is a technique for checking the quality of a relational design. Given the groundwork in Chapter 5, we then consider, in Chapter 6, the process of transforming entity-relationship data models into DBMS-independent, relational designs. Next, Chapter 7 describes the process for transforming semantic object data models into such designs. Finally, in Chapter 8, we address application design and examine the relationship between database structure and application structure and processing.

DATABASE AND DATABASE APPLICATION DESIGN

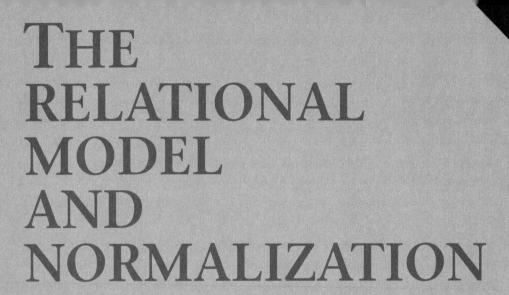

THE RELATIONAL MODEL AND NORMALIZATION

The relational model is important for two reasons. First, since the constructs of the relational model are broad and general, it can be used to express DBMS-independent database designs. Second, the relational model is the basis for an important category of DBMS products. Understanding the concepts of this model will help you implement databases using one of these products.

This chapter presents the basics of the relational model and explains the fundamental concepts of *normalization*. We begin with the fact that not all relations are equal, that some are better than others. Normalization is a process for converting a relation that has certain problems to two or more relations that do not have these problems. Even more important, normalization can be used as a guideline for checking the desirability and correctness of relations. Much theoretical work has been done on the question of what a well-structured relation is. This work is termed *normalization* because one of the pioneers in database technology, E. F. Codd, defined various normal forms of relations. In this chapter we survey normalization, including the results of theorems that are useful and significant to database practitioners. The proofs of these theorems and a formal, more rigorous treatment of this subject can be found in the work of Date and of Ullman.[1]

THE RELATIONAL MODEL

A **relation** is a two-dimensional table. Each row in the table holds data that pertain to some thing or a portion of some thing. Each column of the table contains data regarding an attribute. Sometimes rows are called **tuples** (rhymes with "couples"), and columns are called **attributes.**

The terms *relation*, *tuple*, and *attribute* arose from relational mathematics, which is the theoretical source of this model. MIS professionals find more comfortable the analogous terms *file*, *record*, and *field*, and most users find the terms *table*, *row*, and *column* most sensible. Figure 5-1 summarizes this terminology.

[1]C. J. Date, *An Introduction to Database Systems* (Reading, MA: Addison-Wesley, 1992); and J. D. Ullman, *Principles of Database Systems* (New York: Computer Science Press, 1982).

FIGURE 5-1 *Relational Terminology*

Relational Model	Programmer	User
Relation	File	Table
Tuple (Row)	Record	Row
Attribute	Field	Column

FIGURE 5-2 *EMPLOYEE Relation*

	Attribute1 Name	Attribute2 Age	Attribute3 Sex	Attribute4 EmployeeNumber
Tuple 1	Anderson	21	F	010110
Tuple 2	Decker	22	M	010100
.	Glover	22	M	101000
.	Jackson	21	F	201100
.	Moore	19	M	111100
.	Nakata	20	F	111101
Tuple 7	Smith	19	M	111111

For a table to be a relation, it must meet certain restrictions.[2] First, the cells of the table must be single valued; neither repeating groups nor arrays are allowed as values.[3] All of the entries in any column (attribute) must be of the same kind. For example, if one column contains employee numbers, it must have employee numbers for every row of the table. Each column has a unique name, and the order of the columns in the table is insignificant. Finally, no two rows (tuples) in a table may be identical, and the order of the rows is insignificant.

Figure 5-2 is a sample table. Notice that it has seven rows (tuples) made up of four columns (attributes). If we were to rearrange the order of the columns (say, by placing EmployeeNumber at the far left) or to reorder the rows (perhaps in ascending sequence on Age), we would have an equivalent table.

Figure 5-2 shows one occurrence, or instance, of a table. The generalized format, EMPLOYEE (Name, Age, Sex, EmployeeNumber), is called the relation structure, and it is what most people mean when they use the term *relation*.

To understand the relational model and normalization, we need to define two important terms, *functional dependency* and *key*.

■ FUNCTIONAL DEPENDENCIES

A **functional dependency** is a relationship between or among attributes. Suppose that if we are given the value of one attribute, we can obtain (or look up) the value of another attribute. For example, if we know the value of CustomerAccountNumber, we can find the value of CustomerBalance. If this is true, we can say that CustomerBalance is *functionally dependent* on CustomerAccountNumber.

In more general terms, attribute Y is functionally dependent on attribute X if the value of X determines the value of Y. Stated differently, if we know the value of X, we can obtain the value of Y.

[2]E. F. Codd, "A Relational Model of Data for Large Shared Databanks," *Communications of the ACM,* June 1970, pp. 377–387.
[3]This does not mean that the values must be a fixed length. A variable-length memo field, for example, is a perfectly legitimate value. Only *one* such value is allowed, however.

Equations represent functional dependencies. For example, if we know the price of an item and the quantity of items purchased, we can calculate the total price of those items, as follows:

TotalPrice = ItemPrice × Quantity

In this case, we would say that TotalPrice is functionally dependent on ItemPrice and Quantity.

The functional dependencies between attributes in a relation usually do not involve equations. For example, suppose that students have a unique identification number, SID, and that every student has one, and only one, major. Given the value of an SID, we can find out that student's major, so Major is functionally dependent on SID. Or consider microcomputers in a computer lab. Each has one, and only one, size of main memory, so MemorySize is functionally dependent on ComputerSerialNumber.

Unlike an equation, such functional dependencies cannot be solved using arithmetic; instead, they are listed in the database. In fact, one can argue that the storage and retrieval of functional dependencies is the only reason for having a database.

Functional dependencies are written using the following notation:

SID → Major

ComputerSerialNumber → MemorySize

The first expression is read as "SID functionally determines Major," "SID determines Major," or "Major is dependent on SID." The attributes on the left side of the arrow are called **determinants.**

As stated, if SID determines Major, a particular value of SID will be paired with only *one* value of Major. Conversely, however, a value of Major may be paired with *one or more* different values of SID. Suppose the student whose SID is 123 majors in accounting. Whenever SID and Major are found together in a relation, the SID value of 123 will always be paired with the Major value of Accounting. The opposite is not true, however, as the Major Accounting may be paired with many values of SID (many students may major in accounting). Consequently, we can say that the relationship of SID with Major is many to one (N:1). In general, we can say that if A determines B, the relationship of the values of A to B is N:1.

Functional dependencies can involve groups of attributes. Consider the relation GRADES (SID, ClassName, Grade). The combination of a SID and a ClassName determines a grade, a functional dependency that is written

(SID, ClassName) → Grade

Note that both SID and ClassName are needed to determine a Grade. We cannot subdivide the functional dependency because neither SID nor ClassName determines Grade by itself.

Notice the difference in the following two patterns: If X → (Y, Z), then X → Y and X → Z. For example, if SID → (StudentName, Major), then SID → StudentName and SID → Major. But if (X, Y) → Z, then in general, it is not true that X → Y or Y → Z. Hence, if (SID, ClassName) → Grade, then neither SID nor ClassName by itself determines Grade.

■ KEYS

A **key** is a group of one or more attributes that uniquely identifies a row. Consider the relation ACTIVITY in Figure 5-3, whose attributes are SID, Activity, and Fee. The meaning of a row is that a student engages in the named activity for the specified fee. Assume that a student is allowed to participate in only one activity at a time. In this case, a value of SID determines a unique row, and so it is a key.

FIGURE 5-3   *ACTIVITY Relation*

ACTIVITY (SID, Activity, Fee)
Key: SID
Sample Data

SID	Activity	Fee
100	Skiing	200
150	Swimming	50
175	Squash	50
200	Swimming	50

FIGURE 5-4   *Relation with a Two-Attribute Key*

SID	Activity	Fee
100	Skiing	200
100	Golf	65
150	Swimming	50
175	Squash	50
175	Swimming	50
200	Swimming	50
200	Golf	65

Keys can also be composed of a group of attributes taken together. For example, if students were allowed to enroll in many activities at the same time, it would be possible for one value of SID to appear in two or more rows of the table, so SID could not uniquely identify the row. Some combination of attributes, perhaps (SID, Activity), would be required.

As an aside, there is a subtle but important point in the preceding paragraph. Whether or not attributes are keys and whether or not they are functional dependencies are determined not by an abstract set of rules but, rather, by the users' semantics—by the users' mental models and by the business rules of the organization developing the database. In this example, whether SID is the key or whether (SID, Activity) is the key or whether some other combination is the key is determined entirely by the underlying semantics of the people in the organization using the database. We must ask the users to resolve these questions. As we continue, keep in mind that all the assumptions we make about functional dependencies, keys, and the like are determined by the users' mental models.

After interviewing the users, suppose we discover that students are, in fact, allowed to participate in several activities at one time. This situation is represented by the relation ACTIVITIES, shown in Figure 5-4. As we stated, SID is *not* a key of this relation. Student 100, for example, has enrolled in both skiing and golf, and the SID value of 100 occurs in two different rows. In fact, for this relation, no single attribute is a key, so the key must be a combination of two or more attributes.

Consider the combinations of two attributes from this table. There are three possibilities: (SID, Activity), (SID, Fee), and (Activity, Fee). Is any one of these combinations a key? To be a key, it must uniquely identify a row. Again, to decide questions like this, we must ask the users. We cannot simply depend on sample data like those in Figure 5-4 or rely on our own assumptions to make the decision.

After talking with the users, suppose we find out that several activities can charge the same fee. Since this is the case, the combination (SID, Fee) cannot determine a unique row. Student 100, for example, could engage in two different activities, both of which cost $200. This would mean that the combination (100, $200) occurs twice in the table, so this combination cannot be a key.

Can the combination (Activity, Fee) be a key? Does the combination (Skiing, $200) determine a unique row? No, it does not, because many students can participate in skiing. What about (SID, Activity)? Given what we know from the users, can a combination of values for SID and Activity determine a unique row? Yes, it can, so long as we are not required to keep records of the different occasions on which a student enrolled in a given activity. In other words, is this table to be used to record only a student's current activities, or is it supposed to keep records of past activities as well?

Again, we must consult the users to answer this question. Suppose we learn that only records of current activities are to be kept. Then the combination (SID, Activity) can determine a unique row, and consequently, (SID, Activity) is the key for this relation. If the users specified that records of current and past activities were to be kept, the relation in Figure 5-3 would have duplicate rows. Since this is prohibited by the definition of relation, we would need to add other attributes such as Date.

This brings up an important point. Every relation has at least one key. This must be true because no relation can have duplicate rows and hence, at the extreme, the key consists of all of the attributes of the relation.

▨ FUNCTIONAL DEPENDENCIES, KEYS, AND UNIQUENESS

Many students confuse the concepts of functional dependencies, keys, and uniqueness. To avoid that confusion, consider the following: A determinant of a functional dependency may or may not be unique to a relation. If we know that A determines B and that A and B are in the same relation, we still do not know whether A is unique in that relation. We only know that A determines B.

For example, in the ACTIVITIES relation, Activity functionally determines Fee, and yet there can be many instances of a particular Activity in the relation. The functional dependency states only that wherever Activity occurs with Fee, it always occurs with the same value of Fee. That is, skiing always costs $200, regardless of how many times the value skiing occurs in the table.

Unlike determinants, keys are always unique. A key functionally determines the entire row. If the value of the key were duplicated, the entire tuple would be duplicated. But this is not allowed because, by definition, rows in a relation must be unique. Thus, when we say that an attribute (or combination) is a key, we know that it will be unique. If (SID, Activity) is a key, then, for example, the combination (100, skiing) will occur only once in a relation.

To test your understanding of these concepts, try to explain why, in the ACTIVITY relation in Figure 5-3, SID is both a determinant and a key but Activity is a determinant and not a key. (Keep in mind that the relation in Figure 5-3 reflects the school's policy that a student may participate in, at most, one activity at a time.)

◆ NORMALIZATION

Unfortunately, not all relations are equally desirable. A table that meets the minimum definition of a relation may not have an effective or appropriate structure. For some relations, changing the data can have undesirable consequences, called **modification anomalies.** Anomalies can be eliminated by redefining the relation into two or more relations. In most circumstances, the redefined, or **normalized,** relations are preferred.

■ MODIFICATION ANOMALIES

Again consider Activity in Figure 5-3. If we delete the tuple for Student 100, we will lose not only the fact that Student 100 is a skier but also the fact that skiing costs $200. This is called a **deletion anomaly;** that is, by deleting the facts about one entity (that Student 100 is a skier), we inadvertently delete facts about another entity (that skiing costs $200). With one deletion, we lose facts about two entities.

The same relation can be used to illustrate an **insertion anomaly.** Suppose we want to store the fact that scuba diving costs $175, but we cannot enter this data into the ACTIVITY relation until a student takes up scuba diving. This restriction seems silly. Why should we have to wait until someone takes the activity before we can record its price? This restriction is called an insertion anomaly. We cannot insert a fact about one entity until we have an additional fact about another entity.

The relation in Figure 5-3 can be used for some applications, but it obviously has problems. We can eliminate both the deletion and the insertion anomalies by dividing the ACTIVITY relation into two relations, each one dealing with a different theme. For example, we can put the SID and Activity attributes into one relation (we will call the new relation STU-ACT for student activity), and we can put the Activity and Fee attributes into a relation called ACT-COST (for activity cost). Figure 5-5 shows the same sample data stored in these two new relations.

Now if we delete Student 100 from STU-ACT, we do not lose the fact that skiing costs $200. Furthermore, we can add scuba diving and its fee to the ACT-COST relation even before anyone enrolls. Thus, the deletion and the insertion anomalies have been eliminated.

Separating one relation into two relations has a disadvantage, however. Suppose a student tries to sign up for a nonexistent activity. For instance, Student 250 wants to enroll in racquetball. We can insert this new tuple in STU-ACT (the row would contain 250, RACQUETBALL), but should we? Should a student be allowed to enroll in an activity that is not in the relation ACT-COST? Put another way, should the database applications somehow prevent student rows from being added if the value of the ACTIVITY is not in the ACT-COST table? The answer to this question lies with the users' requirements. If the action should be prohibited, this constraint must be documented as part of the schema design. Later, in implementation, the constraint will be defined to the DBMS if the product in use provides such constraint checking. If not, the constraint must be enforced by application programs.

Suppose the user specifies that activities can exist before any student enrolls in them but that no student may enroll in an activity that does not have a fee assigned to it (that is, no activities that are not in the ACT-COST table). We can document this constraint in any of several ways in the database design: Activity in STU-ACT is a subset of Activity in ACT-COST, or STU-ACT [Activity] is a subset of ACT-COST [Activity], or STU-ACT [Activity]⊆ACT-COST [Activity].

According to this notation, the brackets [ ] denote a column of data that is extracted from a relation. These expressions simply mean that the values in the

FIGURE 5-5   *The Division of ACTIVITY into Two Relations*

STU-ACT (SID, Activity)
Key: SID

ACT-COST (Activity, Fee)
Key: Activity

SID	Activity
100	Skiing
150	Swimming
175	Squash
200	Swimming

Activity	Fee
Skiing	200
Swimming	50
Squash	50

Activity attribute of STU-ACT must exist in the Activity attribute of ACT-COST. It also means that before we allow an Activity to be entered into STU-ACT, we must check to make sure that it is already present in ACT-COST. Constraints like this are called **referential integrity constraints.**

■ ESSENCE OF NORMALIZATION

The anomalies in the ACTIVITY relation in Figure 5-3 can be stated in the following intuitive way: Problems occur because ACTIVITY contains facts about two different themes:

- the students who participate in each activity
- how much each activity costs

When we add a new row, we must add data about two themes at once, and when we delete a row, we are forced to delete data about two themes at once.

Remember your eighth-grade English teacher? He or she claimed that a paragraph should have a single theme. If a paragraph had more than one theme, you were taught to break up the paragraph into two or more paragraphs so that each paragraph would have only one theme. Similar statements apply to relations. Every normalized relation has a single theme. Any relation having two or more themes should be broken up into two or more relations, each of which has a single theme. This process is the essence of normalization. When we find a relation with modification anomalies, we eliminate them by splitting the relation into two or more separate ones, each containing a single theme.

Every time we break up a relation, however, we may create a referential integrity constraint. Hence, it is good practice to check for such constraints every time you break a relation into two or more.

In the remainder of this chapter, you will learn a number of rules about normalization. All of these rules are special cases of the process just described.

■ CLASSES OF RELATIONS

Relations can be classified by the types of modification anomalies to which they are vulnerable. In the 1970s, relational theorists chipped away at these types. Someone would find an anomaly, classify it, and think of a way to prevent it. Each time this happened, the criteria for designing relations improved. These classes of relations and the techniques for preventing anomalies are called **normal forms.** Depending on its structure, a relation may be in first normal form, second normal form, or some other normal form.

In the work that followed his landmark 1970 paper, E. F. Codd and others defined first, second, and third normal forms (1NF, 2NF, 3NF). Later, Boyce–Codd normal form (BCNF) was specified, and then fourth and fifth normal forms were defined. As shown in Figure 5-6, these normal forms are nested. That is, a relation

FIGURE 5-6   *Relationship of Normal Forms*

First Normal Form (1NF)
Second Normal Form (2NF)
Third Normal Form (3NF)
Boyce–Codd Normal Form (BCNF)
Fourth Normal Form (4NF)
Fifth Normal Form (5NF)

* Domain/Key Normal Form (DK/NF)

in second normal form is also in first normal form, and a relation in 5NF (fifth normal form) is also in 4NF, BCNF, 3NF, 2NF, and 1NF.

These normal forms were helpful, but they had a serious limitation. No theory guaranteed that any of them would eliminate all anomalies; each form could eliminate just certain ones. This changed, however, in 1981 when R. Fagin defined a new normal form called **domain/key normal form (DK/NF).** In an important paper, Fagin showed that a relation in domain/key normal form is free of all modification anomalies, regardless of their type.[4] He also showed that any relation that is free of modification anomalies must be in domain/key normal form.

Until DK/NF was defined, it was necessary for relational database theorists to continue looking for more and more anomalies and more and more normal forms. Fagin's proof, however, simplified the situation. If we can put a relation in DK/NF, then we can be sure that it will have no anomalies. The trick is knowing how to put relations in DK/NF.

FIRST THROUGH FIFTH NORMAL FORMS

Any table of data that meets the definition of a relation is said to be in **first normal form.** Remember that for a table to be a relation, the following must hold: The cells of the table must be single valued, and neither repeating groups nor arrays are allowed as values. All entries in any column (attribute) must be of the same kind. Each column must have a unique name, but the order of the columns in the table is insignificant. Finally, no two rows in a table may be identical, and the order of the rows is insignificant.

The relation in Figure 5-3 is in first normal form. As we have seen, however, relations in first normal form may have modification anomalies. To eliminate those anomalies, we split the relation into two or more relations. When we do this, the new relations are in some other normal form—just which one depends on the anomalies we have eliminated, as well as the ones to which the new relations are vulnerable.

■ SECOND NORMAL FORM

To understand second normal form, consider the ACTIVITIES relation in Figure 5-4. This relation has modification anomalies similar to the ones we examined earlier. If we delete the tuple for Student 175, we will lose the fact that squash costs $50. Also, we cannot enter an activity until a student signs up for it. Thus, the relation suffers from both deletion and insertion anomalies.

The problem with this relation is that it has a dependency involving only part of the key. The key is the combination (SID, Activity), but the relation contains a dependency, Activity -> Fee. The determinant of this dependency (Activity) is only part of the key (SID, Activity). In this case, we say that Fee is *partially dependent* on the key of the table. There would be no modification anomalies if Fee were dependent on all of the key. To eliminate the anomalies, we must separate the relation into two relations.

This example leads to the definition of second normal form: *A relation is in second normal form if all its nonkey attributes are dependent on all of the key.* According to this definition, if a relation has a single attribute as its key, then it is automatically in second normal form. Since the key is only one attribute, by default, every nonkey attribute is dependent on *all* of the key; there can be no partial dependencies. Thus, second normal is of concern only in relations that have composite keys.

---

[4]R. Fagin, "A Normal Form for Relational Databases That Is Based on Domains and Keys," *ACM Transactions on Database Systems,* September 1981, pp. 387–415.

FIGURE 5-7   *Elimination of Transitive Dependency: (a) Relation with Transitive Dependency and (b) Relations Eliminating the Transitive Dependency*

HOUSING (SID, Building, Fee)
Key: SID
Functional
dependencies: Building → Fee
                    SID → Building → Fee

SID	Building	Fee
100	Randolph	1200
150	Ingersoll	1100
200	Randolph	1200
250	Pitkin	1100
300	Randolph	1200

(a)

STU-HOUSING (SID, Building)
Key: SID

SID	Building
100	Randolph
150	Ingersoll
200	Randolph
250	Pitkin
300	Randolph

BLDG-FEE (Building, Fee)
Key: Building

Building	Fee
Randolph	1200
Ingersoll	1100
Pitkin	1100

(b)

ACTIVITIES can be decomposed to form two relations in second normal form. The relations are the same as those in Figure 5-5, namely, STU-ACT and ACT-COST. We know the new relations are in second normal form because they both have single-attribute keys.

■ THIRD NORMAL FORM

Relations in second normal form can also have anomalies. Consider the HOUSING relation in Figure 5-7(a). The key is SID, and the functional dependencies are SID → Building and Building → Fee. These dependencies arise because each student lives in only one building and each building charges only one fee. Everyone living in Randolph Hall, for example, pays $1,200 per quarter.

Since SID determines Building and Building determines Fee, then, indirectly SID → Fee. An arrangement of functional dependencies like this is called a **transitive dependency,** since SID determines Fee through the attribute Building.

The key of HOUSING is SID, which is a single attribute, and hence the relation is in second normal form (both Building and Fee are determined by SID). Despite this, however, HOUSING has anomalies because of the transitive dependency.

What happens if we delete the second tuple shown in Figure 5-7(a)? We lose not only the fact that Student 150 lives in Ingersoll Hall but also the fact that it costs $1100 to live there. This is a deletion anomaly. And how can we record the fact that the Fee for Carrigg Hall is $1500? We cannot until a student decides to move in. This is an insertion anomaly.

To eliminate the anomalies from a relation in second normal form, the transitive dependency must be removed, which leads to a definition of third normal form: *A relation is in third normal form if it is in second normal form and has no transitive dependencies.*

The HOUSING relation can be divided into two relations in third normal form. This has been done for the relations STU-HOUSING (SID, Building) and BLDG-FEE (Building, Fee) in Figure 5-7(b).

The ACTIVITY relation in Figure 5-3 also has a transitive dependency. In ACTIVITY, SID determines Activity and Activity determines Fee. Therefore, ACTIVITY is not in third normal form. Decomposing ACTIVITY into the relations STU-ACT (SID, Activity) and ACT-COST (Activity, Fee) eliminates the anomalies.

■ BOYCE–CODD NORMAL FORM

Unfortunately, even relations in third normal form can have anomalies. Consider the ADVISER relation in Figure 5-8(a). Suppose the requirements underlying this relation are that a student (SID) can have one or more majors (Major), a major can have several faculty members (Fname) as advisers, and a faculty member (Fname) advises in only one major area.

Since students can have several majors, SID does not determine Major. Moreover, since students can have several advisers, SID also does not determine Fname. Thus, SID, by itself, cannot be a key.

The combination (SID, Major) determines Fname, and the combination (SID, Fname) determines Major. Hence, either of the combinations can be a key. Two or more attributes or attribute collections that can be a key are called **candidate keys.** Whichever of the candidates is selected to be *the* key is called the **primary key.**

FIGURE 5-8   *Boyce–Codd Normal Form: (a) Relation in Third Normal Form but Not in Boyce–Codd Normal Form and (b) Relations in Boyce–Codd Normal Form*

ADVISER (SID, Major, Fname)

Key (primary): (SID, Major)
Key (candidate): (SID, Fname)

Functional
dependencies: Fname→Major

SID	Major	Fname
100	Math	Cauchy
150	Psychology	Jung
200	Math	Riemann
250	Math	Cauchy
300	Psychology	Perls
300	Math	Riemann

(a)

STU-ADV (SID, Fname)
Key: SID, Fname

SID	Fname
100	Cauchy
150	Jung
200	Riemann
250	Cauchy
300	Perls
300	Riemann

ADV-SUBJ (Fname, Subject)
Key: Fname

Fname	Subject
Cauchy	Math
Jung	Psychology
Riemann	Math
Perls	Psychology

(b)

In addition to the candidate keys, there is another functional dependency to consider: Fname determines Major (any faculty member advises in only one major. Therefore, given the Fname, we can determine the Major). Thus, Fname is a determinant.

By definition, ADVISER is in first normal form. It is also in second normal form, since any nonkey attributes are dependent on the entire key (no matter which candidate key we select). And it also is in third normal form because it has no transitive dependencies. Despite all this, however, it has modification anomalies.

Suppose Student 300 drops out of school. If we delete Student 300's tuple, we will lose the fact that Perls advises in psychology. This is a deletion anomaly. Similarly, how can we store the fact that Keynes advises in economics? We cannot until a student majors in economics. This is an insertion anomaly.

Situations like this lead to the definition of Boyce–Codd normal form (BCNF): *A relation is in BCNF if every determinant is a candidate key.* ADVISER is not in BCNF, since it has a determinant, Fname, that is not a candidate key.

As with the other examples, ADVISER can be decomposed into two relations having no anomalies. For example, the relations STU-ADV (SID, Fname) and ADV-SUBJ (Fname, Subject) have no anomalies.

Relations in BCNF have no anomalies in regard to functional dependencies, and this seemed to put the issue of modification anomalies to rest. It was soon discovered, however, that anomalies can arise from situations other than functional dependencies.

◼ FOURTH NORMAL FORM

Consider the STUDENT relation in Figure 5-9, showing the relationship among students, majors, and activities. Suppose that students can enroll in several different majors and participate in several different activities. Since this is so, the only key is the combination of attributes (SID, Major, Activity). Student 100 majors in music and accounting, and she also participates in swimming and tennis. Student 150 majors only in math and participates in jogging.

What is the relationship between SID and Major? It is not a functional dependency because students can have several majors. A single value of SID can have many values of Major. Also, a single value of SID can have many values of Activity.

This attribute dependency is called a **multivalued dependency.** Multivalued dependencies lead to modification anomalies. To begin, note the data redundancy in Figure 5-9. Student 100 has four records, each of which shows one of her majors paired with one of her activities. If the data were stored with fewer rows—say there were only two tuples, one for music and swimming and one for accounting

FIGURE 5-9   *Relation with Multivalued Dependencies*

STUDENT (SID, Major, Activity)
Key: (SID, Major, Activity)

Multivalued
dependencies: SID →→ Major
                 SID →→ Activity

SID	Major	Activity
100	Music	Swimming
100	Accounting	Swimming
100	Music	Tennis
100	Accounting	Tennis
150	Math	Jogging

FIGURE 5-10   *STUDENT Relations with Insertion Anomalies: (a) Insertion of a Single Tuple and (b) Insertion of Two Tuples*

STUDENT (SID, Major, Activity)
Key: (SID, Major, Activity)

SID	Major	Activity
100	Music	Skiing
100	Music	Swimming
100	Accounting	Swimming
100	Music	Tennis
100	Accounting	Tennis
150	Math	Jogging

(a)

SID	Major	Activity
100	Music	Skiing
100	Accounting	Skiing
100	Music	Swimming
100	Accounting	Swimming
100	Music	Tennis
100	Accounting	Tennis
150	Math	Jogging

(b)

and tennis—the implications would be misleading. It would *appear* that Student 100 swam only when she was a music major and played tennis only when she was an accounting major. But this interpretation is not logical. Her majors and her activities are completely independent of each other. So to prevent such a misleading conclusion, we store all the combinations of majors and activities.

Suppose that because Student 100 decides to sign up for skiing, we add the tuple [100, MUSIC, SKIING], as in Figure 5-10(a). The relation at this point implies that Student 100 skis as a music major but not as an accounting major. In order to keep the data consistent, we must add one row for each of her majors paired with skiing. Thus, we must also add the row [100, ACCOUNTING, SKIING], as in Figure 5-10(b). This is an update anomaly—too much updating needs to be done to make a simple change in the data.

In general, a multivalued dependency exists when a relation has at least three attributes, two of them are multivalued, and their values depend on only the third attribute. In other words, in a relation R (A, B, C), a multivalued dependency exists if A determines multiple values of B, A determines multiple values of C, and B and C are independent of each other. As we saw in the previous example, SID determines multiple values of Major and SID determines multiple values of Activity, but Major and Activity are independent of each other.

Refer again to Figure 5-9. Notice how multivalued dependencies are written: SID $\rightarrow\rightarrow$ Major, and SID $\rightarrow\rightarrow$ Activity. This is read "SID multidetermines Major, and SID multidetermines Activity." This relation is in BCNF (2NF because it is all key; 3NF because it has no transitive dependencies; and BCNF because it has no non-key determinants). However, as we have seen, it has anomalies: If a student adds a major, we must enter a tuple for the new major, paired with each of the student's activities. The same holds true if a student enrolls in a new activity. If a student drops a major, we must delete each of his records containing that major. If he participates in four activities, there will be four tuples containing the major he has dropped, and each of them must be deleted.

FIGURE 5-11   *Elimination of Multivalued Dependency*

STU-MAJOR (SID, Major)
Key: (SID, Major)

SID	Major
100	Music
100	Accounting
150	Math

STU-ACT (SID, Activity)
Key: (SID, Activity)

SID	Activity
100	Skiing
100	Swimming
100	Tennis
150	Jogging

To eliminate these anomalies, we must eliminate the multivalued dependency. We do this by creating two relations, each one storing data for only one of the multivalued attributes. The resulting relations do not have anomalies. They are STU-MAJOR (SID, Major) and STU-ACT (SID, Activity), as seen in Figure 5-11.

From these observations, we define fourth normal form in the following way: *A relation is in fourth normal form if it is in BCNF and has no multivalued dependencies.* After we have discussed domain/key normal form later in this chapter, we will return to describe multivalued dependencies in another, more intuitive way.

■ FIFTH NORMAL FORM

Fifth normal form concerns dependencies that are rather obscure. It has to do with relations that can be divided into subrelations, as we have been doing, but then cannot be reconstructed. The condition under which this situation arises has no clear, intuitive meaning. We do not know what the consequences of such dependencies are or even if they have any practical consequences. For more information about fifth normal form, refer to the work by Date that was cited earlier in this chapter.

◆ DOMAIN/KEY NORMAL FORM

Each of the normal forms we have discussed was identified by researchers who found anomalies with some relations that were in a lower normal form: Noticing modification anomalies with relations in second normal form led to the definition of third normal form, etc. Although each normal form solved some of the problems that had been identified with the previous one, no one could know what problems had not yet been identified. With each step, progress was made toward a well-structured database design, but no one could guarantee that no more anomalies would be found. In this section we study a normal form that guarantees that there will be no anomalies of any type. When we put relations into that form, we know that even the obscure anomalies associated with fifth normal form cannot occur.

In 1981, R. Fagin published an important paper in which he defined domain/key normal form (DK/NF).[5] He showed that a relation in domain/key normal form has no modification anomalies and, furthermore, that a relation having no modification anomalies must be in domain/key normal form. This finding establishes a bound on the definition of normal forms, and so no higher normal form is needed, at least in order to eliminate modification anomalies.

Equally important, DK/NF involves only the concepts of key and domain, concepts that are fundamental and close to the heart of database practitioners. They are readily supported by DBMS products (or could be, at least). In a sense, Fagin's

[5]*Ibid.*

work formalized and justified what many practitioners believed intuitively but were unable to express formally.

◼ DEFINITION

In concept, DK/NF is quite simple: A relation is in DK/NF if every constraint on the relation is a logical consequence of the definition of keys and domains. Consider the important terms in this definition: constraint, key, and domain.

Constraint in this definition is intended to be very broad. Fagin defines a constraint as any rule governing static values of attributes that is precise enough that we can ascertain whether or not it is true. Edit rules, intrarelation and interrelation constraints, functional dependencies, and multivalued dependencies are examples of such constraints. Fagin expressly excludes constraints pertaining to changes in data values, or time-dependent constraints. For example, the rule "Salesperson salary in the current period can never be less than salary in the prior period" is excluded from Fagin's definition of constraint. Except for time-dependent constraints, Fagin's definition is both broad and inclusive.

A **key** is a unique identifier of a tuple, as we have already defined. The third significant term in the definition of DK/NF is **domain.** In Chapter 4, we stated that a domain is a description of an attribute's allowed values. It has two parts: a physical description and a semantic, or logical, description. The physical description is the set of values the attribute can have, and the logical description is the meaning of the attribute. Fagin's proof refers to both parts.

Informally, a relation is in domain/key normal form if enforcing key and domain restrictions causes all of the constraints to be met. Moreover, since relations in domain/key normal form cannot have modification anomalies, the DBMS can prohibit them by enforcing key and domain restrictions.

Unfortunately, there is no known algorithm for converting a relation to DK/NF, nor is it even known which relations can be converted to DK/NF. Finding, or designing, DK/NF relations is more of an art than a science.

In spite of this, in the practical world of database design, DK/NF is an exceedingly useful design objective. If we can define relations in a way that constraints on them are logical consequences of domains and keys, then there will be no modification anomalies. For many designs, this objective can be accomplished. When it cannot, the constraints must be built into the logic of application programs that process the database. We will see more of this later in this chapter and in Chapter 8.

The following three examples illustrate DK/NF.

◼ EXAMPLE 1 OF DOMAIN/KEY NORMAL FORM

Consider the STUDENT relation in Figure 5-12, which contains attributes SID, GradeLevel, Building, and Fee. Building is the building in which the student lives, and Fee is the amount the student pays to live in that building.

FIGURE 5-12   *Example 1 of DK/NF*

STUDENT (SID, GradeLevel, Building, Fee)

Key: SID

Constraints: Building → Fee
              SID must not begin with digit 1

SID functionally determines the other three attributes, so SID is a key. Assume we also know, from the requirements definition, that Building → Fee and that SIDs must not begin with 1. If we can express these constraints as logical consequences of domain and key definitions, we can be certain, according to Fagin's theorem, that there will be no modification anomalies. For this example, it will be easy.

To enforce the constraint that student numbers not begin with 1, we simply define the domain for student numbers to incorporate this constraint (Figure 5-13). Enforcing the domain restriction guarantees that this constraint will be met.

Next we need to make the functional dependency Building → Fee a logical consequence of keys. If Building were a key attribute, Building → Fee would be a logical consequence of a key. Therefore, the question becomes how to make Building a key. It cannot be a key in STUDENT because more than one student lives in the same building, but it can be a key of its own relation. Thus, we define the relation BLDG-FEE with Building and Fee as its attributes. Building is the key of this relation. Having defined this new relation, we can remove Fee from STUDENT. The final domain and relation definitions for this example appear in Figure 5-13.

This is the same result we obtained when converting a relation from 2NF to 3NF to remove transitive dependencies. In this case, however, the process was simpler and the result more robust. It was simpler because we did not need to know that we were eliminating a transitive dependency. We simply needed to find creative ways to make all the constraints logical consequences of domain and key definitions. The result was more robust because when converting the relation to 3NF, we knew only that it had fewer anomalies than when it was in 2NF. By converting the relation to DK/NF, we know that the relations have no modification anomalies whatsoever.

■ EXAMPLE 2 OF DOMAIN/KEY NORMAL FORM

The next example involves the relation described in Figure 5-14 and is more complicated than the previous one. The PROFESSOR relation contains data about professors, the classes they teach, and the students they advise. FID (for Faculty ID) and Fname uniquely identify a professor. SID uniquely identifies a student, but Sname does not necessarily identify a SID. Professors can teach several classes and advise several students, but a student is advised by only one professor. FIDs start with a 1, but SIDs must not start with a 1.

FIGURE 5-13   *Domain/Key Definition of Example 1*

Domain Definitions

SID	in	CDDD, where C is decimal digit not = 1; D = decimal digit
GradeLevel	in	{'FR', 'SO', 'JR', 'SN', 'GR'}
Building	in	CHAR(4)
Fee	in	DEC(4)

Relation and Key Definitions

STUDENT (SID, GradeLevel, Building)
Key: SID

BLDG-FEE
(Building, Fee)
Key: Building

Example 2 of DK/NF

```
PROFESSOR (FID, Fname, Class, SID, Sname)
Key: (FID, Class, SID)
Constraints:       FID →► Fname
                   Fname →► FID
                   FID →► →► Class | SID
                   Fname →► →► Class | SID
                   SID →► FID
                   SID →► Fname
                   SID →► Sname
                   FID must start with 1; SID must not start with 1
```

These statements can be expressed more precisely by the functional and multivalued dependencies shown in Figure 5-14. FID and Fname functionally determine each other (in essence, they are equivalent). FID and Fname multidetermine Class and SID. SID functionally determines FID and Fname. SID determines Sname.

In more complex examples such as this one, it is helpful to consider DK/NF from a more intuitive light. Remember that the essence of normalization is that every relation should have a single theme. Considered from this perspective, there are three themes in PROFESSOR. One is the correspondence between FIDs and Fnames. Another concerns the classes that a professor teaches, and the third concerns the identification number, name, and adviser of a given student.

Figure 5-15 shows three relations that reflect these themes. The FACULTY relation represents the equivalence of FID and Fname. FID is the key and Fname is an alternative key, which means that both attributes are unique to the relation. Because both are keys, the functional dependencies FID → Fname and Fname → FID are logical consequences of keys.

The PREPARATION relation contains the correspondence of faculty and classes; it shows the classes that a professor is prepared to teach. The key is the combination (Fname, Class). Both attributes are required in the key because a professor may teach several classes. Finally, STUDENT represents the student and adviser names for a particular SID. Observe that each of these relations has a single

FIGURE 5-15   Domain/Key Definition of Example 2

```
Domain Definitions

    FID        in    CDDD, C = 1; D = decimal digit
    Fname      in    CHAR(30)
    Class      in    CHAR(10)
    SID        in    CDDD, C is decimal digit, not = 1;
                     D = decimal digit
    Sname      in    CHAR(30)

Relation and Key Definitions

    FACULTY (FID, Fname)
    Key (primary):    FID
    Key (candidate):  Fname

    PREPARATION (Fname, Class)
    Key: Fname, Class

    STUDENT (SID Sname, Fname)
    Key: SID
```

theme. These relations express all of the constraints of Figure 5-14 as a logical consequence of domains and key definitions. These relations are, therefore, in DK/NF.

Note that separating the PREPARATION theme from the STUDENT theme has eliminated the multivalued dependencies. When we examined fourth normal form, we found that in order to eliminate multivalued dependencies, we had to separate the multivalued attributes into different relations. Our approach here is to break a relation with several themes into several relations, each with one theme. In doing that, we eliminated a multivalued dependency. In fact, we arrived at the same solution using both approaches.

■ EXAMPLE 3 OF DOMAIN/KEY NORMAL FORM

The next example concerns a situation that was not addressed by any of the other normal forms but that occurs frequently in practice. This relation has a constraint among data values within a tuple that is neither a functional dependency nor a multivalued dependency.

Consider the constraints in the relation STU-ADVISER in Figure 5-16. This relation contains information about a student and his or her adviser. SID determines Sname, FID, Fname, and GradFacultyStatus and is therefore the key. FID and Fname identify a unique faculty member and are equivalent to each other, as in Example 2. Both FID and Fname determine GradFacultyStatus. Finally, the new type of constraint is that only members of the graduate faculty are allowed to advise graduate students.

The domain restrictions are that SID must not begin with a 1, SID must begin with a 9 for graduate students, FID must begin with a 1, and GradFacultyStatus is 0 for undergraduate faculty and 1 for graduate faculty. With these domain definitions, the constraint that graduate students must be advised by graduate faculty can be expressed as a constraint on row values. Specifically, if the SID starts with 9, the value of GradFacultyStatus must be 1.

To put this relation in DK/NF, we proceed as in Example 2. What are the basic themes of this relation? There is one regarding faculty personnel that relates FID, Fname, and GradFacultyStatus. Since FID and Fname determine GradFacultyStatus, either of these attributes can be the key, and this relation is in DK/NF (see Figure 5-17).

Now consider the data regarding students and advisers. Although it may first appear that there is only one theme, that of advising, the constraint that only graduate faculty can advise graduate students implies otherwise. Actually, there are two themes: graduate advising and undergraduate advising. Thus, Figure 5-17 contains a G-ADV relation for graduate students and a UG-ADV relation for undergraduates.

FIGURE 5-16   *Example 3 of DK/NF*

STU-ADVISER (SID, Sname, FID, Fname, GradFacultyStatus)

Key: SID

Constraints:
FID → Fname
Fname → FID
FID and Fname → GradFacultyStatus
Only graduate faculty can advise graduate students
FID begins with 1
SID must not begin with 1
SID of graduate student begins with 9
GradFacultyStatus = { 0 for undergraduate faculty
{ 1 for graduate faculty

FIGURE 5-17   *Domain/Key Definition of Example 3*

<u>Domain Definitions</u>

FID	in	CDDD, where C = 1; D = decimal digit
Fname	in	CHAR (30)
Grad-faculty-status	in	[0, 1]
GSID	in	CDDD, where C = 9; D = decimal digit; graduate student
UGSID	in	CDDD, WHERE C ≠ 1 and C ≠ 9; D = decimal digit; undergraduate student
Sname	in	CHAR (30)

<u>Additional Domain Definitions</u>

Gfname	in	{Fname of FACULTY, where GradFacultyStatus = 1}

<u>Relations and Key Definitions</u>

FACULTY (FID, Fname, GradFacultyStatus)
Key: FID or Fname

G-ADV (GSID, Sname, Gfname)
Key: GSID

UG-ADV (UGSID, Sname, Fname)
Key: UGSID

FIGURE 5-18   *Summary of Normal Forms*

Form	Defining Characteristic
1NF	Any relation
2NF	All nonkey attributes are dependent on all of the keys.
3NF	There are no transitive dependencies.
BCNF	Every determinant is a candidate key.
4NF	There are no multivalued dependencies.
5NF	Not described in this discussion.
DK/NF	All constraints on relations are logical consequences of domains and keys.

Look at the domain definitions: GSID starts with a 9; Gfname is the Fname of a FACULTY tuple with GradFacultyStatus equal to 1; and UGSID must not begin with 1 or 9. All the constraints described in Figure 5-16 are implied by the key and domain definitions in Figure 5-17. These relations are therefore in DK/NF and have no modification anomalies.

To summarize, Figure 5-18 lists the normal forms and presents the defining characteristic of each.

THE SYNTHESIS OF RELATIONS

In the previous section, we approached relational design from an analytical perspective. The question we asked was, Given a relation, is it in good form? Does it have modification anomalies? In this section, we look at relational design from a different perspective—a synthetic one. From this perspective, we ask, Given a set of attributes with certain functional dependencies, what relations should we form?

First, observe that two attributes, say A and B, can be related in three ways:

1. They determine each other:

$A \rightarrow B$ and $B \rightarrow A$

Hence A and B have a one-to-one attribute relationship.

2. One determines the other.

$A \rightarrow B$, but B not $\rightarrow A$

Hence A and B have a many-to-one relationship.

3. They are functionally unrelated.

A not $\rightarrow$ B and B not $\rightarrow$ A

Hence, A and B have a many-to-many attribute relationship.

■ ONE-TO-ONE ATTRIBUTE RELATIONSHIPS

If A determines B and B determines A, the values of the attributes have a one-to-one relationship. This must be because if A determines B, the relationship between A and B is many to one. It is also true, however, that if B determines A, the relationship between B and A must be many to one. For both statements to be true at the same time, the relationship between A and B must actually be one to one (which is a special case of many to one), and the relationship between B and A is also actually one to one. Therefore, the relationship is one to one.

This case is illustrated by FID and Fname in Examples 2 and 3 in the previous section on domain/key normal form. Each of these attributes uniquely identifies a faculty person. Consequently, one value of FID corresponds to exactly one value of Fname, and vice versa.

Three equivalent statements can be drawn from the example of FID and Fname:

- If two attributes functionally determine each other, the relationship of their data values is one to one.

- If two attributes uniquely identify the same thing (entity or object), the relationship of their data values is one to one.

- If two attributes have a one-to-one relationship, they functionally determine each other.

When creating a database with attributes that have a one-to-one relationship, the two attributes must occur together in at least one relation. Other attributes that are functionally determined by these (an attribute that is functionally determined by one of them is functionally determined by the other as well) may also reside in this same relation.

Consider FACULTY (FID, Fname, GradFacultyStatus) in Example 3 in the previous section. FID and Fname determine each other. GradFacultyStatus can also occur in this relation because it is determined by FID and Fname. Attributes that are not functionally determined by these attributes may not occur in a relation with them. Consider the relations FACULTY and PREPARATION in Example 2, in which both FID and Fname occur in FACULTY, but Class (from PREPARATION) may not. Class can have multiple values for a faculty member, so Class is not dependent on FID or Fname. If we added Class to the FACULTY relation, the key of FACULTY would need to be either (FID, Class) or (Fname, Class). In this case, however, FACULTY would not be in DK/NF because the dependencies between FID and Fname would not be logically implied by either of the possible keys.

These statements are summarized in the first column of Figure 5-19, and the record definition rules are listed in Figure 5-20. If A and B have a 1:1 relationship, they can reside in the same relation, say R. A determines B, and B determines A.

FIGURE 5-19   *Summary of Three Types of Attribute Relationships*

	Type of Attribute Relationship		
	One-to-One	Many-to-One	Many-to-Many
Relation Definition*	R(A,B)	S(C,D)	T(E,F)
Dependencies	A → B B → A	C → D D ↛ C	E ↠ F F ↠ E
Key	Either A or B	C	(E,F)
Rule for Adding Another Attribute	Either A or B → C	C → E	(E,F) → G

* The letters used in these relation definitions match those used in Figure 5-20

FIGURE 5-20   *Summary of Rules for Constructing Relations*

Concerning One-to-One Relationships

- Attributes that have a one-to-one relationship must occur together in at least one relation. Call the relation *R* and the attributes *A* and *B*.
- Either *A* or *B* must be the key of *R*.
- An attribute can be added to *R* if it is functionally determined by *A* or *B*.
- An attribute that is not functionally determined by *A* or *B* cannot be added to *R*.
- *A* and *B* must occur together in *R*, but should not occur togehter in other relations.
- Either *A* or *B* should be consistently used to represent the pair in relations other than *R*.

Concerning Many-to-One Relationships

- Attributes that have a many-to-one relationship can exist in a relation together. Assume *C* determines *D* in relation *S*.
- *C* must be the key of *S*.
- An attribute can be added to *S* if it is determined by *C*.
- An attribute that is not determined by *C* cannot be added to *S*.

Concerning Many-to-Many Relationships

- Attributes that have a many-to-many relationship can exist in a relation together. Assume two such attributes, *E* and *F*, reside together in relation *T*.
- The key of *T* must be (*E*,*F*).
- An attribute can be added to *T* if it is determined by the combination (*E*,*F*).
- An attribute may not be added to *T* if it is not determined by the combination (*E*,*F*).
- If adding a new attribute, *G*, expands the key to (*E*,*F*,*G*), then the theme of the relation has been changed. Either *G* does not belong in *T* or the name of *T* must be changed to reflect the new theme.

The key of the relation can be either A or B. A new attribute, C, can be added to R if either A or B functionally determines C.

Attributes having a one-to-one relationship must exist together in at least one relation in order to establish their equivalence (FID of 198, for example, refers to Professor Heart). It is generally undesirable to have them occur together in more than one relation, however, because this causes needless data duplication. Often, one or both of the two attributes occur in other relations. In Example 2, Fname occurs in both PREPARATION and STUDENT. Although it would be possible to place Fname in PREPARATION and FID in STUDENT, this generally is bad practice, because when attributes are paired in this way, one of them should be selected to represent the pair in all other relations. Fname was selected in Example 2.

■ MANY-TO-ONE ATTRIBUTE RELATIONSHIPS

If attribute A determines B but B does not determine A, the relationship among their data values is many to one. In the adviser relationship in Example 2, SID determines FID. Many students (SID) are advised by a faculty member (FID), but each student is advised by only one faculty member. This, then, is a many-to-one relationship.

For a relation to be in DK/NF, all constraints must be implied by keys, and thus every determinant must be a key. If A, B, and C are in the same relation and if A determines B, then A must be the key (meaning it also determines C). If, instead, (A, B) determines C, then (A, B) must be the key. In this latter case, no other functional dependency, such as A determines B, is allowed.

You can apply these statements to database design in the following way: When constructing a relation, if A determines B, the only other attributes you can add to the relation must also be determined by A. For example, suppose you have put SID and Building together in a relation called STUDENT. You may add any other attribute determined by SID, such as Sname, to this relation. But if the attribute Fee is determined by Building, you may not add it to this relation. Fee can be added only if SID -> Fee.

These statements are summarized in the center column of Figure 5-19. If C and D have an N:1 relationship, they may reside together in a relation, say S. C will determine D, but D will not determine C. The key of S will be C. Another attribute, E, can be added to S only if C determines E.

■ MANY-TO-MANY ATTRIBUTE RELATIONSHIPS

If A does not determine B and B does not determine A, the relationship among their data values is many to many. In Example 2, Fname and Class have a many-to-many relationship. A professor teaches many classes, and a class is taught by many professors. In a many-to-many relationship, both attributes must be a key of the relation. For instance, the key of PREPARATION in Example 2 is the combination (Fname, Class).

When constructing relations that have multiple attributes as keys, you can add new attributes that are functionally dependent on all of the key. NumberOf TimesTaught is functionally dependent on both (Fname, Class) and can be added to the relation. FacultyOffice, however, cannot be added because it would be dependent only on Fname, not on Class. If FacultyOffice needs to be stored in the database, it must be added to the relation regarding faculty, not to the relation regarding preparations.

These statements are summarized in the right column of Figure 5-19. If E and F have an M:N relationship, E does not determine F, and F does not determine E. Both E and F can be put into a relation T, and if this is done, the key of T will be the composite (E,F). A new attribute, G, can be added to T if it is determined by all of (E,F). It cannot be added to T if it is determined by only one of E or F.

Consider a similar, but different, example. Suppose we add ClassroomNumber to PREPARATION. Is ClassroomNumber functionally determined by the key of PREPARATION, (Fname, Class)? Most likely it is not, because a professor could teach a particular class in many different rooms.

The composite (Fname,Class) and ClassroomNumber have an M:N relationship. Since this is so, the rules in Figure 5-19 can be applied, but with E representing (Fname, Class) and F representing ClassroomNumber. Now we can compose a new relation, T, with attributes Fname, Class, and ClassroomNumber. The key becomes (Fname, Class, ClassroomNumber). In this situation, we have created a new relation with a new theme. Consider relation T, which contains faculty names, classes, and classroom numbers. The theme of this relation is therefore no longer PREPARATION but, rather, WHO-WHAT-WHERE-TAUGHT.

Changing the theme may or may not be appropriate. If ClassroomNumber is important, the theme does need to be changed. In that case, PREPARATION is the wrong relation, and WHO-WHERE-TAUGHT is a more suitable theme.

On the other hand, depending on user requirements, PREPARATION may be completely suitable as it is. If so, then if ClassroomNumber belongs in the database at all, it should be located in a different relation—perhaps SECTION-NUMBER, CLASS-SECTION, or some similar relation.

MULTIVALUED DEPENDENCIES, ITERATION 2

The discussion about many-to-many attribute value relationships may make the concept of multivalued dependencies easier to understand. The problem with the relation STUDENT (SID, Major, Activity) in Figure 5-9 is that it has *two* different many-to-many relationships, one between SID and Major and the other between SID and Activity. Clearly, a student's various majors have nothing to do with his or her various activities. Putting both of these many-to-many relationships in the same relation, however, makes it appear as if there is some association.

Major and Activity are independent, and there would be no problem if a student had only one of each. SID would functionally determine Major and Activity, and the relation would be in DK/NF. In this case, both the relationships between Major and SID and Activity and SID would be many to one.

Another way of perceiving the difficulty is to examine the key, (SID, Major, Activity). Since STUDENT has many-to-many relationships, all of the attributes have to be in the key. Now what theme does this key represent? We might say the combination of a student's studies and activities. But this is not one thing; it is plural. One row of this relation describes only part of the combination, and in order to get the whole picture, we need all of the rows about a particular student. In general, a row should have all of the data about one instance of the relation's theme. A row of Customer, for example, should have all the data we want about a particular customer.

Consider PREPARATION in Example 2 in the section on domain/key normal form. The key is (Fname, Class). The theme this represents is that a particular professor is prepared to teach a particular class. We need only one row of the relation to get all of the information (the relation might include NumberOfTimesTaught, AverageCourseEvaluationScore, and so on) we have about the combination of that professor and that class. Looking at more rows will not generate any more information about it.

As you know, the solution to the multivalued dependency constraint problem is to split the relation into two relations, each with a single theme. STU-MAJOR shows the combination of a student and a major. Everything we know about the combination is in a single row, and we will not gain more information about that combination by examining more rows.

DESIGN TRADE-OFFS

In this chapter we examined the concepts of normalization and demonstrated how to create tables that are in domain/key normal form. The process we used is usually suitable, but sometimes the result of normalization is not worth the cost. In this last section we look at two ways in which that can happen.

■ DE-NORMALIZATION

As you know, normalized relations avoid modification anomalies, and on that ground they are preferred to unnormalized relations. Judged on other grounds, however, normalization is sometimes not worth it.

Consider this relation:

CUSTOMER (CustNumber, CustName, City, State, Zip),
where CustNumber is the key.

This relation is not in DK/NF because it contains the functional dependency Zip → (City, State), which is not implied by the key, CustNumber. Hence, there is a constraint not implied by the definition of keys.

This relation can be transformed into the following two DK/NF relations:

CUSTOMER (CustNumber, CustName, Zip)
where the key is CustNumber
CODES (Zip, City, State)
where the key is Zip

These two tables are in domain/key normal form, but they most likely do not represent a better design. The unnormalized table is probably better because it will be easier to process and the disadvantages of duplicating the City and State data are not very important.

In summary, relations are sometimes purposely left unnormalized or are normalized and then de-normalized. Often this is done to improve performance. Whenever data must be combined from two separate tables, the DBMS must perform additional work. In most cases, at least two reads are required instead of one.

■ OPTIMIZATION

We typically create normalized tables by splitting unnormalized tables into two or more. In some cases, there is a better way of obtaining a normalized design. For example, consider the relation

COLLEGE (CollegeName, Dean, AssistantDean)

and suppose that a college has one dean and from one to three assistant deans. In this case, the key of the table is (CollegeName, AssistantDean). This table is not in domain/key normal form because the constraint, CollegeName → Dean, is not a logical consequence of the table's key.

COLLEGE can be normalized into the relations

DEAN (CollegeName, Dean)

and

ASSISTANT-DEAN(CollegeName, AssistantDean)

But now whenever a database application needs to obtain data about the college, it must read at least two rows and possibly as many as four rows of data. An alternative to this design is to place all three AssistantDeans into the COLLEGE table, each in a separate attribute. The table would then be

COLLEGE1 (CollegeName, Dean, AssistantDean1, AssistantDean2, AssistantDean3)

COLLEGE1 is in domain/key normal form because all of its attributes are functionally dependent on the key CollegeName. But something has been lost. To see what, suppose that you wanted to determine the names of the COLLEGEs that had an assistant dean named 'Mary Abernathy'. To do this, you would have to look for this value in each of the three AssistantDean columns. Your query would appear something like this:[6]

---

[6]These statements are examples of SQL, a relational language that we will discuss in detail in Chapter 10. For now, just think of them intuitively; you will learn the format of them in that chapter.

```
SELECT    CollegeName
FROM      COLLEGE1
WHERE     AssistantDean1 = 'Mary Abernathy' OR
          AssistantDean2 = 'Mary Abernathy' OR
          AssistantDean3 = 'Mary Abernathy'
```

Using the normalized design with ASSISTANT-DEAN, you would need only to state

```
SELECT    CollegeName
FROM      ASSISTANT-DEAN
WHERE     AssistantDean = 'Mary Abernathy'
```

In this example there are three possible solutions, each with advantages and disadvantages. The choice among them is an artistic one; there is no hard and fast rule stating how to select among them. The best choice depends on the processing characteristics of the applications that use this database.

◆ SUMMARY

The relational model is important for two reasons: It can be used to express DBMS-independent database designs, and it is the basis for an important category of DBMS-products. Normalization can be used as a guideline for checking the desirability and correctness of relations.

A relation is a two-dimensional table that has single-valued entries. All entries in a given column are of the same kind; columns have a unique name; and the order of the columns is not important. Columns are also called attributes. No two rows of a table are identical, and the order of the rows in the table is not important. Rows are also called tuples. The terms *table, file,* and *relation* are synonymous; the terms *column, field,* and *attribute* are synonymous; and the terms *row, record,* and *tuple* are synonymous.

A functional dependency is a relationship between attributes. Y is functionally dependent on X if the value of X determines the value of Y. A determinant is a group of one or more attributes on the left-hand side of a functional dependency. For example, if X determines Y, then X is the determinant. A key is a group of one or more attributes that uniquely identifies a tuple. Every relation has at least one key; because every row is unique, in the most extreme case, the key is the collection of all of the attributes in the relation. Although a key is always unique, the determinant in a functional dependency need not be. Whether or not attributes are keys and whether or not they are attributes are determined not by an abstract set of rules but by the users' semantics.

When updated, some relations suffer from undesirable consequences called modification anomalies. A deletion anomaly occurs when the deletion of a row loses information about two or more entities. An insertion anomaly occurs when the relational structure forces the addition of facts about two entities at the same time. Anomalies can be removed by splitting the relation into two or more relations.

There are many types of modification anomalies. Relations can be classified by the types of anomaly that they eliminate. Such classifications are called normal forms.

By definition, every relation is in first normal form. A relation is in second normal form if all nonkey attributes are dependent on all of the key. A relation is in third normal form if it is in second normal form and has no transitive dependencies. A relation is in Boyce–Codd normal form if every determinant is a candidate key. A relation is in fourth normal form if it is in Boyce–Codd normal form and has no multivalued dependencies. The definition of fifth normal form is intuitively obscure, and so we did not define it.

A relation is in domain/key normal form if every constraint on the relation is a logical consequence of the definition of domains and keys. A constraint is any constraint on the static values of attributes whose truth can be evaluated. As we defined them, domains have both a physical and a semantic part. In the context of domain/key normal form, however, domain refers only to the physical description.

An informal way of expressing domain/key normal form is to say that every relation must have only a single theme. For example, it might concern PROFESSORs or STUDENTs but not both PROFESSORs and STUDENTs at the same time.

Normalization is a process of analyzing relations. It is also possible to construct relations by a process of synthesis by considering the relationships among attributes. If two attributes functionally determine each other, they have a one-to-one relationship. If one attribute functionally determines the other, but not the reverse, the attributes have a one-to-many relationship. If neither attribute determines the other, they have a many-to-many relationship. These facts can be used when constructing relations as summarized in Figure 5-20.

In some cases, normalization is not desirable. Whenever a table is split into two or more tables, referential integrity constraints are created. If the cost of the extra processing of the two tables and their integrity constraint is greater than the benefit of avoiding modification anomalies, then normalization is not recommended. In addition, in some cases, creating repeating columns is preferred to the standard normalization techniques.

GROUP I QUESTIONS

5.1   What restrictions must be placed on a table for it to be considered a relation?

5.2   Define the following terms: relation, tuple, attribute, file, record, field, table, row, column.

5.3   Define *functional dependency*. Give an example of two attributes that have a functional dependency, and give an example of two attributes that do not have a functional dependency.

5.4   If SID functionally determines Activity, does this mean that only one value of SID can exist in the relation? Why or why not?

5.5   Define *determinant*.

5.6   Give an example of a relation having a functional dependency in which the determinant has two or more attributes.

5.7   Define *key*.

5.8   If SID is a key of a relation, is it a determinant? Can a given value of SID occur more than once in the relation?

5.9   What is a deletion anomaly? Give an example other than one in this text.

5.10   What is an insertion anomaly? Give an example other than one in this text.

5.11   Explain the relationship of 1, 2, 3, BC, 4, 5, and D/K normal forms.

5.12   Define *second normal form*. Give an example of a relation in 1NF but not in 2NF. Transform the relation into relations in 2NF.

5.13   Define *third normal form*. Give an example of a relation in 2NF but not in 3NF. Transform the relation into relations in 3NF.

5.14   Define *BCNF*. Give an example of a relation in 3NF but not in BCNF. Transform the relation into relations in BCNF.

5.15 Define *multivalued dependency*. Give an example.

5.16 Why must multivalued dependencies exist in pairs?

5.17 Define *fourth normal form*. Give an example of a relation in BCNF but not in 4NF. Transform the relation into relations in 4NF.

5.18 Define *domain/key normal form*. Why is it important?

5.19 Transform the following relation into DK/NF. Make and state the appropriate assumptions about functional dependencies and domains.

> EQUIPMENT (Manufacturer, Model, AcquisitionDate, BuyerName, BuyerPhone, PlantLocation, City, State, ZIP)

5.20 Transform the following relation into DK/NF. Make and state the appropriate assumptions about functional dependencies and domains.

> INVOICE (Number, CustomerName, CustomerNumber, CustomerAddress, ItemNumber, ItemPrice, ItemQuantity, SalespersonNumber, SalespersonName, Subtotal, Tax, TotalDue)

5.21 Answer Question 5.20 again, but this time add attribute CustomerTaxStatus (0 if nonexempt, 1 if exempt). Also add the constraint that there will be no tax if CustomerTaxStatus = 1.

GROUP II QUESTIONS

5.22 Consider the following relation definition and sample data:

PROJECT Relation

ProjectID	EmployeeName	EmployeeSalary
100A	Jones	64K
100A	Smith	51K
100B	Smith	51K
200A	Jones	64K
200B	Jones	64K
200C	Parks	28K
200C	Smith	51K
200D	Parks	28K

PROJECT (ProjectId, EmployeeName, EmployeeSalary)
Where ProjectId is the name of a work project
> EmployeeName is the name of an employee who works on that project
> EmployeeSalary is the salary of the employee whose name is EmployeeName

Assuming that all of the functional dependencies and constraints are apparent in this data, which of the following statements is true?

a. ProjectID → EmployeeName

b. ProjectID → EmployeeSalary

c. (ProjectID, EmployeeName) → EmployeeSalary

d. EmployeeName → EmployeeSalary

e. EmployeeSalary → ProjectID

f. EmployeeSalary → (ProjectID, EmployeeName)

Answer these questions:

g. What is the key of PROJECT?

h. Are all nonkey attributes (if any) dependent on all of the key?

i. In what normal form is PROJECT?

j. Describe two modification anomalies from which PROJECT suffers.

k. Is ProjectID a determinant?

l. Is EmployeeName a determinant?

m. Is (ProjectID, EmployeeName) a determinant?

n. Is EmployeeSalary a determinant?

o. Does this relation contain a transitive dependency? If so, what is it?

p. Redesign this relation to eliminate the modification anomalies.

5.23 Consider the following relation definition and sample data:

PROJECT-HOURS Relation

EmployeeName	ProjectID	TaskID	Phone	TotalHours
Don	100A	B-1	12345	12
Don	100A	P-1	12345	12
Don	200B	B-1	12345	12
Don	200B	P-1	12345	12
Pam	100A	C-1	67890	26
Pam	200A	C-1	67890	26
Pam	200D	C-1	67890	26

PROJECT-HOURS (EmployeeName, ProjectID, TaskID, Phone, TotalHours)

Where EmployeeName is the name of an employee

ProjectID is the name of a project

TaskID is the name standard work task

Phone is the employee's telephone number

TotalHours is the hours worked by the employee on this project

Assuming that all of the functional dependencies and constraints are apparent in this data, which of the following statements is true?

a. EmployeeName --→ ProjectID F

b. EmployeeName →→ ProjectID T

c. EmployeeName → TaskID F

d. EmployeeName →→ TaskID T

e. EmployeeName → Phone T

f. EmployeeName → TotalHours F

g. (EmployeeName, ProjectID) → TotalHours T

h. (EmployeeName, Phone) → TaskID F

i. ProjectID → TaskID F

j. TaskID → ProjectID F

Answer these questions:

k. List all of the determinants.

l. Does this relation contain a transitive dependency? If so, what is it?

m. Does this relation contain a multivalued dependency? If so, what are the unrelated attributes?

n. Describe the deletion anomaly that this relation contains.

o. How many themes does this relation have?

p. Redesign this relation to eliminate the modification anomalies. How many relations did you use? How many themes does each of your new relations contain?

5.24 Consider the following domain, relation, and key definitions:

Domain Definitions

EmployeeName	in	CHAR(20)
PhoneNumber	in	DEC(5)
EquipmentName	in	CHAR(10)
Location	in	CHAR(7)
Cost	in	CURRENCY
Date	in	YYMMDD
Time	in	HHMM where HH between 00 and 23 and MM between 00 and 59

Definitions of Relation, Key, and Constraint

EMPLOYEE (EmployeeName, PhoneNumber)

   Key: EmployeeName

   Constraints: EmployeeName → PhoneNumber

EQUIPMENT (EquipmentName, Location, Cost)

   Key: EquipmentName

   Constraints: EquipmentName → Location

                  EquipmentName → Cost

APPOINTMENT (Date, Time, EquipmentName, EmployeeName)

   Key: (Date, Time, EquipmentName)

   Constraints: (Date, Time, EquipmentName) → EmployeeName

Modify the definitions to add this constraint: An employee may not sign up for more than one equipment appointment.

DATABASE DESIGN USING ENTITY-RELATIONSHIP MODELS

• • • • • • • • • • • • • • •

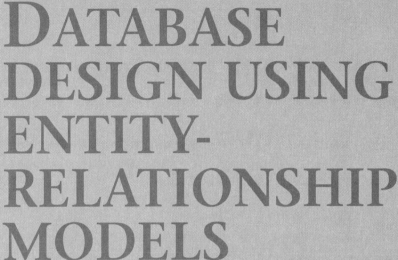

In Chapter 3 we discussed the specification of data models using the entity-relationship model, and in Chapter 5 we studied the relational model and normalization. In this chapter, we bring these subjects together to illustrate the transformation of users' requirements expressed in entity-relationship models into relational database designs. These designs are independent of any particular DBMS. In Chapter 7 we show how to transform semantic object data models into similar designs.

This chapter has two main sections. In the first, we show how to transform entity-relationship data models into relational designs. Normalization is important to this process because entities can contain more than one semantic theme. After demonstrating how to represent entities, we examine the representation of relationships using the relational model.

The second section applies the concepts described in the first section, illustrating the transformation of entity-relationship models into the representation of four common data structures. These structures are special cases of E-R constructs, and the techniques shown in the first section are applied to represent them with relations. We give these structures special attention because they occur so frequently as common patterns of entities and relationships.

TRANSFORMATION OF ENTITY-RELATIONSHIP MODELS INTO RELATIONAL DATABASE DESIGNS

Chapter 3 demonstrated how to express user data requirements in an entity-relationship model. With this model, those things that users want to track are represented by **entities,** and the relationships among those entities are represented by explicitly defined **relationships.** This section describes how to transform entities and relationships into the terms of the relational model.

■ REPRESENTING ENTITIES WITH THE RELATIONAL MODEL

In general, the representation of entities by means of a relational model is straightforward. We begin by defining a relation for each entity. The name of the relation is the name of the entity, and the attributes of the relation are the attributes of the

FIGURE 6-1   *Representation of an Entity with a Relation: (a) CUSTOMER Entity and (b) Relation Representing CUSTOMER Entity*

CUSTOMER entity contains

CustNumber
CustName
Address
City
State
Zip
ContactName
PhoneNumber

(a)

CUSTOMER (<u>CustNumber</u>, CustName, Address, City,
State, Zip, ContactName, PhoneNumber)
(b)

entity. Then we examine each relation according to the normalization criteria discussed in Chapter 5. It may or may not be necessary to change this initial design.

The example in Figure 6-1(a) is the entity shown in Figure 3-1. The CUSTOMER entity contains the following attributes: CustNumber, CustName, Address, City, State, Zip, ContactName, and PhoneNumber. To represent this entity with a relation, we define a relation for the entity and place the attributes in it as columns in the relation. If we know from the data model which attribute identifies this entity, that attribute will become the key of the relation. Otherwise, we must ask the users or otherwise investigate the requirements to determine what attribute or attributes can identify an entity. In this case, we assume that CustNumber is the key. In this figure, as in others to follow, the keys of the relations are underlined.

THE ROLE OF NORMALIZATION   During the requirements phase, the only stipulation placed on an entity is that it be important to the user. No attempt is made to determine whether the entity fits any of the criteria for normalization discussed in Chapter 5. Therefore, once a relation has been defined for an entity, it should be examined according to the normalization criteria.

Consider, for example, the CUSTOMER relation in Figure 6-1(b). Is it in DK/NF? To find out, we need to know the constraints on this relation. Without a full description of the underlying requirements, we do not know all of the constraints, such as all of the domain constraints. But we can discover some of the requirements just from the names of the attributes and knowledge about the nature of the business.

First, CustNumber determines all of the other attributes, because the unique values of CustName, Address, City, State, Zip, ContactName, and PhoneNumber can be determined from a given value of CustNumber. There are other constraints, however, that arise from other functional dependencies. Zip determines City and State, and ContactName determines PhoneNumber. As we stated in Chapter 5, to create a set of relations in DK/NF, we need to make these additional functional dependencies a logical consequence of domains and keys, and we can do that by defining the three relations shown in Figure 6-2. Observe that the key of CUSTOMER is CustNumber, the key of ZIP-TABLE is Zip, and the key of CONTACT is ContactName.

The design in Figure 6-2 is in DK/NF, and there will be no modification anomalies. That is, we can add new zip codes and new contacts without having to add a customer with the new zip code or contact. Furthermore, when we delete the last

FIGURE 6-2   *Representing the Customer Entity with Relations in Domain/Key Normal Form*

CUSTOMER (<u>CustomerNumber</u>, Address, Zip, ContactName)

ZIP-TABLE (<u>Zip</u>, City, State)

CONTACT (<u>ContactName</u>, PhoneNumber)

Interrelation constraints:

    Zip in CUSTOMER must exist in Zip in ZIP-TABLE
    ContactName in CUSTOMER must = a ContactName in CONTACT

customer in a given zip code, we do not lose the city and state for that zip code. But as we pointed out at the end of Chapter 5, most practitioners would consider this design too pure; breaking out Zip, City, and State will make the design hard to use. Hence, a better design would probably result by leaving Zip, City, and State in the CUSTOMER relation.

In other examples it is clearer that a pure DK/NF design is preferable. Consider the SALES-COMMISSION entity in Figure 6-3(a). If we attempt to represent this entity with one relation, as shown in Figure 6-3(b), the result is a confused mess of attributes with many potential modification anomalies.

This relation obviously contains more than one theme. On examination, it contains a theme about salespeople, a theme about sales during some period, and a theme about sales commission checks. The relations in DK/NF that represent this entity are shown in Figure 6-3(c). Intuitively, this design seems superior to that in Figure 6-3(b); it is more straightforward and better fitting.

To summarize the discussion so far, when representing an entity with the relational model, the first step is to construct a relation that has all of the entity's attributes as columns. Then the relation is examined against the normalization criteria. In many cases the design can be improved by developing sets of relations in DK/NF.

DK/NF relations are not always preferred, however. If the relations are contrived and difficult to work with, a non-DK/NF design may be better. Performance can also be a factor. Having to access two or three relations to obtain the data needed about a customer may be prohibitively time-consuming.

Regardless of our decision about whether to normalize, we should examine every entity's relation(s) against the normalization criteria. That is, if we are going to sin, we should make an informed and conscious decision to do so. In the process, we also learn the types of modification anomalies to which the relations are vulnerable.

REPRESENTATION OF WEAK ENTITIES   Weak entities require special treatment when creating the relational design. Recall that a weak entity depends for its existence on another entity. If the weak entity is existence dependent but not ID dependent, it can be represented using the techniques described in the last section. The existence dependency needs to be recorded in the relational design so that no application will create a weak entity without its proper parent (the entity on which the weak entity depends). Moreover, a processing constraint needs to be implemented so that when the parent is deleted, the weak entity is also deleted. These rules should be described in the relational design.

This situation is slightly different if the weak entity also is ID dependent. In Figure 6-4(a), LINE-ITEM is an ID-dependent weak entity. It is weak because its

FIGURE 6-3   *Entity with Appropriate Normalization: (a) SALES-COMMISSION Entity, (b) Representing SALES-COMMISSION with a Single Relation, and (c) Representing SALES-COMMISSION with Domain/Key Normal Form Relations*

SALES-COMMISSION entity contains

SalespersonNumber
SalespersonName
Phone
CheckNumber
CheckDate
CommissionPeriod
TotalCommissionSales
CommissionAmount
BudgetCategory

(a)

SALES-COMMISSION (SalespersonNumber, SalespersonName, Phone, CheckNumber, CheckDate, CommissionPeriod, TotalCommissionSales, CommissionAmount, BudgetCategory)

Functional dependencies:
    CheckNumber is key
    SalespersonNumber determines SalespersonName, Phone,
        BudgetCategory
    (SalespersonNumber, CommissionPeriod) determines
        TotalCommissionSales, CommissionAmount

(b)

SALESPERSON(SalespersonNumber, SalespersonName, Phone,
    BudgetCategory)
SALES (SalespersonNumber, CommissionPeriod,
    TotalCommissionSales, CommissionAmount)
COMMISSION-CHECK (CheckNumber, CheckDate, SalespersonNumber,
    CommissionPeriod)

(c)

FIGURE 6-4   *Relational Representation of a Weak Entity: (a) Example Weak Entity, (b) Relation Representing LINE-ITEM with No Key, and (c) LINE-ITEM Relation with Proper Key (Partly from INVOICE)*

(a)

LINE-ITEM (LineNumber, Qty, ItemNumber, Description, Price, ExtPrice)
(b)

LINE-ITEM (InvoiceNumber, LineNumber, Qty, ItemNumber, Description, Price, ExtPrice)
(c)

logical existence depends on INVOICE, and it is ID dependent because its identifier contains the identifier of INVOICE.

When creating a relation for an ID-dependent entity, we must ensure that both the key of the parent and the key of the entity itself appear in the relation. For example, consider what would happen if we merely established a relation for LINE-ITEM and did not include the key of INVOICE. Such a relation is shown in

Figure 6-4(b). What is the key of this relation? Because LINE-ITEM is ID dependent, it does not have a complete key, and, in fact, this relation could very well have duplicate rows. (This would happen if two invoices had the same quantity of the same item on the same line.) The problem is that the relation in Figure 6-4(b) has no unique identifier.

Thus, for an ID-dependent weak entity, it is necessary to add the key of the parent entity to the weak entity's relation, and this added attribute becomes part of the weak entity's key. In Figure 6-4(c), we have added InvoiceNumber, the key of INVOICE, to the attributes in LINE-ITEM. The key of LINE-ITEM is the composite {InvoiceNumber, LineNumber}.

■ REPRESENTING HAS-A RELATIONSHIPS

There are two types of relationships in the E-R model: HAS-A relationships among entities of different logical types and IS-A relationships among entities that are subtypes of a common logical type. In this section we consider HAS-A relationships; later we discuss IS-A relationships.

REPRESENTING ONE-TO-ONE RELATIONSHIPS   The simplest form of binary relationship is a one-to-one (1:1) relationship, in which an entity of one type is related to no more than one entity of another type. In the example of EMPLOYEE and AUTO, suppose that an employee is assigned exactly one automobile and an auto is assigned to exactly one employee. An E-R diagram for this relationship is shown in Figure 6-5.

Representing a 1:1 relationship with the relational model is straightforward. First each entity is represented with a relation, and then the key of one of the relations is placed in the other. In Figure 6-6(a), the key of EMPLOYEE is stored in AUTO, and in Figure 6-6(b), the key of AUTO is stored in EMPLOYEE.

When the key of one relation is stored in a second relation, it is called a **foreign key.** In Figure 6-6(a), EmployeeNumber is a foreign key in AUTO, and in Figure 6-6(b), LicenseNumber is a foreign key in EMPLOYEE. In this figure, foreign keys are shown in italics, but sometimes you may see foreign keys depicted by a dashed underline. In still other cases, foreign keys are not denoted in any special way. In this text, when there is a danger of confusion, we show foreign keys in italics, but most of the time, they do not receive any special notation.

For a 1:1 relationship, the key of either table can be placed as a foreign key in the other table. In Figure 6-6(a) the foreign key EmployeeNumber is placed in AUTO. With this design, we can navigate from EMPLOYEE to AUTO or from AUTO

FIGURE 6-5

Example of a 1:1 Relationship

EMPLOYEE ——— <1:1> ——— AUTO

FIGURE 6-6

Alternatives for Representing 1:1 Relationships: (a) Placing the Key of EMPLOYEE in AUTO and (b) Placing the Key of AUTO in EMPLOYEE

EMPLOYEE (<u>EmployeeNumber</u>, EmployeeName, Phone, . . .)

AUTO (<u>LicenseNumber</u>, SerialNumber, Color, Make, Model, . . .*EmployeeNumber*)

(a)

EMPLOYEE (<u>EmployeeNumber</u>, EmployeeName, Phone, . . .*LicenseNumber*)

AUTO (<u>LicenseNumber</u>, SerialNumber, Color, Make, Model, . . .)

(b)

to EMPLOYEE. In the first case, we have an employee and want the auto assigned to that employee. To get the employee data, we use EmployeeNumber to obtain the employee's row in EMPLOYEE. From this row, we obtain the LicenseNumber of the auto assigned to that employee. We then use this number to look up the auto data in AUTO.

Now consider the other direction. Assume that we have an auto and want the employee assigned to that auto. Using the design in Figure 6-6(a), we access the EMPLOYEE table and look up the row that has the given license number. The data about the employee who has been assigned that auto appear in that row.

We take similar actions to travel in either direction for the alternative design, in which the foreign key of LicenseNumber is placed in EMPLOYEE. Using this design, to go from EMPLOYEE to AUTO, we go directly to the AUTO relation and look up the row in AUTO that has the given employee's number as its value of EmployeeNumber. To travel from AUTO to EMPLOYEE, we look up the row in AUTO having a given LicenseNumber. From this row, we extract the EmployeeNumber and use it to access the employee data in EMPLOYEE. Here we are using the term *look up* to mean "find a row given a value of one of its columns." Later, when we discuss particular DBMS models, we demonstrate how this is done.

Although the two designs in Figure 6-6 are equivalent in concept, they may be different in performance. For instance, if a query in one direction is more common than a query in the other, we may prefer one design to the other. Also, if the DBMS product is much faster in lookups on primary keys versus lookups on foreign keys, we might also prefer one design to another.

QUESTIONABLE 1:1 RELATIONSHIPS   Figure 6-7 shows another 1:1 relationship, in which each EMPLOYEE has a JOB-EVALUATION and each JOB-EVALUATION corresponds to a particular employee. Observe from the hash marks that the relationship is mandatory in both directions. When the relationship is 1:1 and is mandatory in both directions, it is likely that the records are describing different aspects of the same entity, especially if, as is the case in Figure 6-7, both entities have the same key. When this occurs, the records should generally be combined into one relation. Learn to regard such 1:1 mandatory relationships with suspicion.

The separation of an entity into two relations can, however, sometimes be justified. One justification concerns performance. For example, suppose that the JOB-EVALUATION data are lengthy and are used far less frequently than are the other employee data. In these circumstances it may be appropriate to store JOB-EVALUATIONs in a separate table so that the more common requests for nonevaluation employee data can be processed faster.

Better security is the second justification for separating a single logical entity into two. If the DBMS does not support security at the data item level, the JOB-EVALUATION data may need to be separated in order to prevent unauthorized users from accessing them. Or it may be desirable to place JOB-EVALUATION in a separate table so that the table can be placed on disk media that are kept in special locked facilities.

Do not conclude from this discussion that all 1:1 relationships are questionable; only those that appear to describe different aspects of the same entity are suspect. For example, the 1:1 mandatory relationship between EMPLOYEE and AUTO is quite suitable because each relation describes a logically different thing.

FIGURE 6-7   *Suspect 1:1 Relationship*

| EMPLOYEE |——⟨1:1⟩——| JOB-EVALUATION |

REPRESENTING ONE-TO-MANY RELATIONSHIPS   The second type of binary relationship is one to many (1:N), in which an entity of one type can be related to many entities of another type. Figure 6-8 is an E-R diagram of a one-to-many relationship between professors and students. In this relationship, PROFESSOR is related to the many STUDENTs that he or she advises. As stated in Chapter 3, the oval means that the relationship between PROFESSOR and STUDENT is optional; that is, a professor need not have any advisees. The bar across the line at the other end means that a STUDENT row must correspond to a PROFESSOR row.

The terms **parent** and **child** are sometimes applied to relations in 1:N relationships. The parent relation is on the *one* side of the relationship, and the child relation is on the *many* side. In Figure 6-8(a), PROFESSOR is the parent entity, and STUDENT is the child entity.

Figure 6-8 shows two other one-to-many relationships. In Figure 6-8(b), a DORMITORY entity corresponds to many STUDENT entities, but a STUDENT entity corresponds to one DORMITORY. Furthermore, a dormitory does not have to have any students assigned to it, nor is a student required to live in a dormitory.

In Figure 6-8(c), a CUSTOMER is related to many APPOINTMENT entities, and a particular APPOINTMENT corresponds to only one CUSTOMER. Moreover, a CUSTOMER may or may not have an APPOINTMENT, but every APPOINTMENT must correspond to a CUSTOMER.

Representing 1:N relationships is simple and straightforward. First each entity is represented by a relation, and then the key of the relation representing the parent entity is placed in the relation representing the child entity. Thus, to represent the ADVISES relationship of Figure 6-8(a), we place the key of PROFESSOR, ProfessorName, in the STUDENT relation, as shown in Figure 6-9.

Figure 6-9 is an example of what is sometimes called a **data structure diagram,** in which relations are shown in rectangles with lines representing relationships and the key attributes are underlined. A fork, or crow's foot, on a relationship line indicates a many relationship.

FIGURE 6-8   *Examples of One-to-Many Relationships: (a) Optional-to-Mandatory 1:N Relationship, (b) Optional-to-Optional 1:N Relationship, and (c) 1:N Relationship with Weak Entity*

FIGURE 6-9   *Relational Representation of PROFESSOR and STUDENT Entities in Figure 6-8(a)*

FIGURE 6-10   *Relational Representation of the Weak Entity in Figure 6-8(c)*

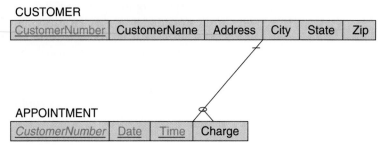

Referential integrity constraint:
CustomerName in APPOINTMENT must exist in CustomerNumber in CUSTOMER

In Figure 6-9, the fork at the STUDENT end of the relationship line means that there can be many STUDENT rows for each PROFESSOR. No fork at the other end means that each STUDENT can be advised by, at most, one PROFESSOR. As with E-R diagrams, hash lines are used to denote mandatory relationships, and ovals denote optional ones.

Notice that with ProfessorName stored as a foreign key in STUDENT, we can process the relationship in both directions. Given a StudentNumber, we can look up the appropriate row in STUDENT and get the name of his or her adviser from the row data. To obtain the rest of the PROFESSOR data, we use the professor name obtained from STUDENT to look up the appropriate row in PROFESSOR. To determine all of the students advised by a particular faculty member, we look up all rows in STUDENT having the professor's name as a value for ProfessorName. Student data is then taken from those rows.

Contrast this situation with one representing 1:1 relationships. In both cases, we store the key of one relation as a foreign key in the second relation. In a 1:1 relationship, however, it does not matter which key is moved to the second relation. But in a 1:N relationship, it does matter. *The key of the parent relation must be placed in the child relation.*

To understand this better, notice what would happen if we tried to put the key of the child into the parent relation (placing StudentNumber in PROFESSOR). Since attributes in a relation can have only a single value, there is room in any professor's record for only one student. Consequently, such a structure cannot be used to represent the "many" side of the 1:N relationship. Hence, to represent a 1:N relationship, we must place the key of the parent relation in the child relation.

Figure 6-10 shows the representation of the CUSTOMER and APPOINTMENT entities. Here we represent each entity with a relation. APPOINTMENT is an ID-dependent weak entity, so it has a composite key consisting of the key of the entity on which its key depends plus an attribute from itself. In this case, the key is (CustomerNumber, Date, Time). To represent the 1:N relationship, we would normally add the key of the parent to the child. In this case, however, the key of the parent (CustomerNumber) is already part of the child, so we do not need to add it.

REPRESENTING MANY-TO-MANY RELATIONSHIPS   The third and final type of binary relationship is many to many (M:N), in which an entity of one type corresponds to many entities of the second type, and an entity of the second type corresponds to many entities of the first type.

Figure 6-11(a) presents an E-R diagram of the many-to-many relationship between students and classes. A STUDENT entity can correspond to many CLASS entities, and a CLASS entity can correspond to many STUDENT entities. Notice that both participants in the relationship are optional: A student does not need to be

FIGURE 6-11   *Example of an M:N Relationship: (a) E-R Diagram of STUDENT to CLASS Relationship and (b) Sample Data for STUDENT to CLASS Relationship*

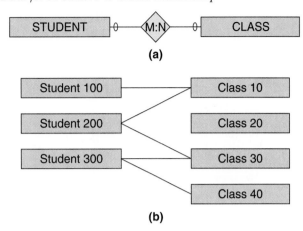

enrolled in a class, and a class does not need to have any students. Figure 6-11(b) gives sample data.

Many-to-many relationships cannot be directly represented by relations in the same way that one-to-one and one-to-many relationships are. To understand why this is so, try using the same strategy we did for 1:1 and 1:N relationships—placing the key of one relation as a foreign key in the other relation. First, define a relation for each of the entities; call them STUDENT and CLASS. Now try to put the key of STUDENT (say StudentNumber) in CLASS. Because multiple values are not allowed in the cells of a relation, we have room for only one StudentNumber, so we have no place to record the StudentNumber of the second and subsequent students.

The same problem will occur if we try to put the key of CLASS (say ClassNumber) in STUDENT. We can readily store the identifier of the first class in which a student is enrolled, but we have no place to store the identifier of additional classes.

Figure 6-12 shows another (*but incorrect*) strategy. In this case, we have stored a row in the CLASS relation for each STUDENT enrolled in one class, so there are two records for Class 10 and two for Class 30. The problem with this scheme is that we duplicate the class data and thus create modification anomalies. Many rows will need to be changed if, say, Class 10's schedule is modified. Also consider the

FIGURE 6-12   Incorrect *Representation of an M:N Relationship*

SID	Other STUDENT Data
100	. . .
200	. . .
300	. . .

STUDENT

ClassNumber	ClassTime	Other CLASS Data	SID
10	10:00 MWF	. . .	100
10	10:00 MWF	. . .	200
30	3:00 TH	. . .	200
30	3:00 TH	. . .	300
40	8:00 MWF	. . .	300

CLASS

FIGURE 6-13

Representing an M:N Relationship: (a) Relations Needed to Represent STUDENT to CLASS Relationship and (b) Example Data for STUDENT to CLASS Relationship

STUDENT (<u>StudentNumber</u>, StudentName)

CLASS (<u>ClassNumber</u>, ClassName)

STU-CLASS (<u>*ClassNumber*</u>, <u>*StudentNumber*</u>)

(a)

(b)

FIGURE 6-14

Data Structure Diagram for STUDENT to CLASS Relationship

insertion and deletion anomalies: How can we schedule a new class until a student has enrolled? And what will happen if Student 300 drops out of Class 40? Obviously, this strategy is unworkable.

The solution to this problem is to create a third relation that represents the relationship itself. Relation STU-CLASS has been defined in Figure 6-13(a). An instance of this relation is shown in Figure 6-13(b). Such relations are called **intersection relations** because each row documents the intersection of a particular student with a particular class. Notice in Figure 6-13(b) that there is one row in the intersection relation for each line between STUDENT and CLASS in Figure 6-11(b).

The data structure diagrams for the STUDENT-CLASS relationship appear in Figure 6-14. The relationship from CLASS to STU-CLASS is 1:N, and the relationship from STUDENT to STU-CLASS is also 1:N. In essence, we have decomposed the M:N relationship into two 1:N relationships. The key of STU-CLASS is the combination of the keys of both of its parents, (SID, ClassNumber). The key for an intersection relation is always the combination of parent keys.

■ REPRESENTING RECURSIVE RELATIONSHIPS

A recursive relationship is a relationship among entities of the same class. Recursive relationships are not fundamentally different from other HAS-A relationships and can be represented using the same techniques. As with nonrecursive HAS-A relationships, there are three types of recursive relationships: 1:1, 1:N, and N:M; Figure 6-15 shows an example of each.

Consider first the SPONSOR relationship in Figure 6-15(a). As with a 1:1 relationship, one person can sponsor another person, and each person is sponsored by no more than one person. Figure 6-16(a) shows sample data for this relationship.

FIGURE 6-15   *Examples of Recursive Relationships: (a) 1:1 Recursive Relationship, (b) 1:N Recursive Relationship, and (c) N:M Recursive Relationship*

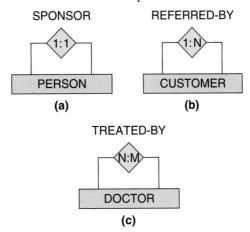

To represent 1:1 recursive relationships, we take an approach nearly identical to that for regular 1:1 relationships: We can place the key of the person being sponsored in the row of the sponsor, or we can place the key of the sponsor in the row of the person being sponsored. Figure 6-16(b) shows the first alternative, and Figure 6-16(c) shows the second. Both work, and so the choice depends on issues like performance.

FIGURE 6-16   *Example of a 1:1 Recursive Relationship: (a) Sample Data for 1:1 Recursive Relationship, (b) First Alternative for Representing a 1:1 Recursive Relationship, and (c) Second Alternative for Representing a 1:1 Recursive Relationship*

Person

Jones
Smith
Parks

Myrtle
Pines

(a)

Person   PersonSponsored

Person	PersonSponsored
Jones	Smith
Smith	Parks
Parks	null
Myrtle	Pines
Pines	null

(b)

Person   PersonSponsoredBy

Person	PersonSponsoredBy
Jones	null
Smith	Jones
Parks	Smith
Myrtle	null
Pines	Myrtle

(c)

FIGURE 6-17

Example of a 1:N Recursive Relationship: (a) Sample Data for the REFERRED-BY Relationship and (b) Representing a 1:N Recursive Relationship by Means of a Relation

Customer Number	Referred These Customers
100	200, 400
300	500
400	600, 700

(a)

CUSTOMER Relation

CustomerNumber	CustomerData	ReferredBy
100	. . .	null
200	. . .	100
300	. . .	null
400	. . .	100
500	. . .	300
600	. . .	400
700	. . .	400

(b)

This technique is identical to that for nonrecursive 1:1 relationships, except that both the child and parent rows reside in the same relation. You can think of the process as follows: Pretend that the relationship is between two different relations. Determine where the key goes, and then combine the two relations into a single one.

To illustrate, consider the REFERRED-BY relationship in Figure 6-15(b). This is a 1:N relationship, as shown in the sample data in Figure 6-17(a). When this data is placed in a relation, one row represents the referrer, and the other rows represent those who have been referred. The referrer row takes the role of the parent, and the referred rows take the role of the child. As with all 1:N relationships, we place the key of the parent in the child. In Figure 6-17(b), we place the number of the referrer in all the rows that have been referred.

Now consider M:N recursive relationships. Examine the TREATED-BY relationship in Figure 6-15(c) with the sample data shown in Figure 6-18(a). As with other M:N relationships, we must create an intersection table that shows all pairs of doctors. The name of the doctor in the first column is the one who provided the treatment, and the name of the doctor in the second column is the one who received the treatment. This structure is shown in Figure 6-18(b).

Recursive relationships are thus represented in the same way as are other relationships. The rows of the tables can take two different roles, however. Some are parent rows, and others are child rows. If a key is supposed to be a parent key and if the row has no parent, its value will be null. If a key is supposed to be a child key and the row has no child, its value will be null.

■ REPRESENTING TERNARY AND HIGHER-ORDER RELATIONSHIPS

Ternary relationships are represented using the techniques just described, but there is often a special consideration that needs to be documented as a business rule. Consider, for example, the entities ORDER, CUSTOMER, and SALESPERSON. In most cases, we can treat this ternary relationship as two separate binary relationships.

For example, assume an ORDER has a single CUSTOMER, but a CUSTOMER can have many ORDERs. Hence that relationship is binary N:1. Similarly, suppose

Example of an M:N Recursive Relationship: (a) Sample Data for the TREATED-BY Relationship and (b) Representing an M:N Recursive Relationship by Means of Relations

Provider   Receiver

Jones
Parks
Smith
Abernathy
Franklin

Smith
Abernathy
Jones
Franklin

(a)

DOCTOR relation

Name	Other Attributes
Jones	. . .
Parks	. . .
Smith	. . .
Abernathy	. . .
O'Leary	. . .
Franklin	. . .

TREATMENT-INTERSECTION relation

Physician	Patient
Jones	Smith
Parks	Smith
Smith	Abernathy
Abernathy	Jones
Parks	Franklin
Franklin	Abernathy
Jones	Abernathy

(b)

the ORDER has just one SALESPERSON, and a SALESPERSON has many ORDERs. That relationship is also binary N:1.

Both of these relationships can be represented using the techniques just described. We represent the first by placing the key of CUSTOMER in ORDER and the second by placing the key of SALESPERSON in ORDER. Thus, we have treated the ternary relationship among ORDER:CUSTOMER:SALESPERSON as two separate binary relationships.

Suppose, however, that the business has a rule that states that each CUSTOMER can place orders only with a particular SALESPERSON. In this case, the ternary relationship ORDER:CUSTOMER:SALESPERSON is constrained by an additional binary N:1 relationship between CUSTOMER and SALESPERSON. To represent the constraint, we need to add the key of SALESPERSON to CUSTOMER. The three relations will be as follows:

ORDER (OrderNumber, nonkey data attributes, *CustomerNumber, SalespersonNumber*)

CUSTOMER (<u>CustomerNumber</u>, nonkey data attributes, *SalespersonNumber*)

SALESPERSON (<u>SalespersonNumber</u>, nonkey data attributes)

The constraint that a particular CUSTOMER is called on by a particular SALESPERSON means that only certain values of CustomerNumber and SalespersonNumber can exist together in ORDER. Unfortunately, there is no way to express this constraint using the relational model. It must be documented in the design, however, and enforced either by the DBMS (if it has such capability) or by application programs.

Other types of such binary constraints are MUST NOT and MUST COVER constraints. In a MUST NOT constraint, the binary relationship indicates combinations that are not allowed to occur in the ternary relationship. For example, the ternary relationship PRESCRIPTION:DRUG:PERSON can be constrained by a binary relationship DRUG:PERSON that indicates drugs that a person is not allowed to take.

In a MUST COVER constraint, the binary relationship indicates all combinations that must appear in the ternary relationship. For example, consider the relationship AUTO:REPAIR:TASK. Suppose that a given repair consists of a number of TASKs, all of which must be performed for the REPAIR to be successful. In this case, in the relation AUTO:REPAIR:TASK, when a given AUTO has a given REPAIR, then all of the TASKs for that repair must appear somewhere in the relation.

None of the three types of binary constraints discussed here can be represented in the relational design. Instead, all of the relationships must be treated as a combination of binary relationships. The constraints, however, must be documented as part of the design.

■ REPRESENTING IS-A RELATIONSHIPS (SUBTYPES)

The strategy for representing subtypes, or IS-A relationships, is somewhat different from the strategy used for HAS-A relationships. Consider the example of CLIENT with attributes ClientNumber, ClientName, and AmountDue. Suppose that there are three subtypes of CLIENT, namely, INDIVIDUAL-CLIENT, PARTNERSHIP-CLIENT, and CORPORATE-CLIENT, with the following attributes:

INDIVIDUAL-CLIENT: Address, SocialSecurityNumber
PARTNERSHIP-CLIENT: ManagingPartnerName, Address, TaxIdentificationNumber
CORPORATE-CLIENT: ContactPerson, Phone, TaxIdentificationNumber

To represent this structure by means of relations, we define one relation for the supertype (CLIENT) and one relation for each subtype. Then we place each of the attributes of the supertype into the relation that represents it and each of the attributes of the subtypes into the relations that represent them. At this point, the subtype relations do not have a key. To create a key, we add the key of the supertype, or ClientNumber, to each of the subtypes. The final list of relations is

CLIENT (<u>ClientNumber,</u> ClientName, AmountDue)
INDIVIDUAL-CLIENT (<u>ClientNumber</u>, Address, SocialSecurityNumber)
PARTNERSHIP-CLIENT (<u>ClientNumber</u>, ManagingPartnerName, Address, TaxIdentificationNumber)
CORPORATE-CLIENT (<u>ClientNumber</u>, ContactPerson, Phone, TaxIdentificationNumber)

Note that with this structure, the relationship between a row in CLIENT and a row in one of the subtypes is 1:1. No client has more than one row in a subtype relation, and each subtype corresponds uniquely to one row of the supertype. Depending on the restrictions of the application, it might be possible for a row in CLIENT to correspond to multiple rows, each in a different subtype. But no row of CLIENT can correspond to more than one row in the *same* subtype relation.

It is possible for one or more of the subtypes to have a key of its own. For example, the application may call for a CorporateClientNumber that is distinct from ClientNumber. In that case, the key of CORPORATE-CLIENT is CorporateClientNumber. Since the relationship between CLIENT and CORPORATE-CLIENT is 1:1, it can be established by placing the key of one in the other. Most often, it is considered better design to place the key of the supertype relation in the key of the subtype relation. For this case, the structure of CORPORATE-CLIENT is

CORPORATE-CLIENT (<u>CorporateClientNumber,</u> ClientNumber, ContactPerson, Phone, TaxIdentificationNumber)

EXAMPLE DESIGN

Figure 6-19(a) is a copy of the E-R diagram introduced in Chapter 3 as Figure 3-9. It contains all of the basic elements used in E-R diagrams. To represent this diagram by means of relations, we begin by establishing one relation for each entity. We assume the keys as follows:

RELATION	KEY
EMPLOYEE	EmployeeNumber
ENGINEER	EmployeeNumber
TRUCK	LicenseNumber
SERVICE	InvoiceNumber
CLIENT	ClientNumber
ENGINEER-CERTIFICATION	(EmployeeNumber , CertificationName)
CERTIFICATION	CertificationName

FIGURE 6-19   *Relational Representation of an Example E-R Diagram: (a) E-R Diagram from Chapter 3 and (b) Relations Needed to Represent This E-R Diagram*

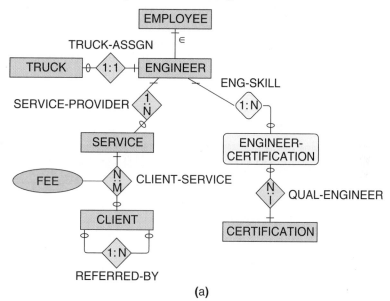

(a)

EMPLOYEE (<u>EmployeeNumber</u>, other nonkey EMPLOYEE attributes . . .)

ENGINEER (<u>EmployeeNumber</u>, other nonkey ENGINEER attributes . . .)

TRUCK (<u>LicenseNumber</u>, other nonkey TRUCK attributes, *EmployeeNumber*)

SERVICE (<u>InvoiceNumber</u>, other nonkey SERVICE attributes, *EmployeeNumber*)

CLIENT (<u>ClientNumber</u>, other nonkey CLIENT attributes, *ReferredBy*)

SERVICE-CLIENT (<u>InvoiceNumber</u>, <u>ClientNumber</u>, Fee)

ENGINEER-CERTIFICATION (<u>EmployeeNumber</u>, <u>CertificationName</u>, other nonkey ENGINEER-CERTIFICATION attributes)

CERTIFICATION (<u>CertificationName</u>, other nonkey CERTIFICATION attributes)

(b)

The next step is to examine each of these relations against the normalization criteria. The example does not tell us what attributes must be represented, so we cannot determine the constraints. We will assume that these relations are in DK/NF, although in practice we would need to check out that assumption against the attribute lists and constraints. For now, we will focus on the representation of relationships. The relations and their key attributes (including foreign keys) are listed in Figure 6-19(b).

The relationship between EMPLOYEE and ENGINEER is already represented, since the relations have the same key, EmployeeNumber. ENGINEER and TRUCK have a 1:1 relationship and so can be related by placing the key of one in the other. Since a truck must be assigned to an employee, there will be no null values if we place EmployeeNumber in TRUCK, and so we will do that.

For the 1:N relationship between ENGINEER and SERVICE, we place the key of ENGINEER (the parent) in SERVICE (the child). The relationship between SERVICE and CLIENT is M:N, so we must create an intersection relation. Since this relationship has an attribute, Fee, we add that attribute to the intersection relation. For the 1:N recursive relationship, REFERRED-BY, we add the attribute ReferredBy to CLIENT. The name *ReferredBy* implies, correctly, that the key of the parent—the one client doing the referring—is being placed in the relation.

Since ENGINEER-CERTIFICATION is ID-dependent on ENGINEER, we know that EmployeeNumber must be part of its key; thus the key is a composite (EmployeeNumber, CertificationName). The dependency relationship is 1:N and so will be carried by EmployeeNumber. Finally, the relationship between CERTIFICATION and ENGINEER-CERTIFICATION is 1:N, so we would normally add the key of CERTIFICATION (the parent) to ENGINEER-CERTIFICATION. But that key is already part of the relation, so we need not do this.

Study this example to make sure that you understand the various types of relationships and how they are expressed in terms of the relations. All of the elements of the E-R model are present in this diagram.

◆ TREES, NETWORKS, AND BILLS OF MATERIALS

Although neither the E-R model nor the semantic-object model makes any assumptions about patterns of relationships among entities, some patterns do occur often enough that they have been given special names. These patterns are trees, simple networks, complex networks, and bills of materials. We introduce the concept of these patterns here, in the context of the E-R model.

■ TREES

A **tree,** or **hierarchy,** as it is sometimes called, is a data structure in which the elements of the structure have only one-to-many relationships with one another. Each element has at most one parent. Figure 6-20 is an example of a tree. According to standard terminology, each element is called a **node,** and the relationships among the elements are called **branches.** The node at the top of the tree is called the **root** (what a metaphor—the roots of real trees are normally at the bottom!). In Figure 6-20, Node 1 is the root of the tree.

Every node of a tree, except the root, has a **parent,** which is the node immediately above it. Thus, Node 2 is the parent of Node 5; Node 4 is the parent of Node 8; and so on. As we stated earlier, trees are distinguished from other data structures in that every node has at most one parent. We say at most one parent because the root node has no parent.

The descendants of a node are called **children.** In general, there is no limitation on the number of children that a node may have. Node 2 has two children, Nodes 5 and 6; Node 3 has no children; and Node 4 has three children, Nodes 7,

FIGURE 6-20   *Example of a Tree*

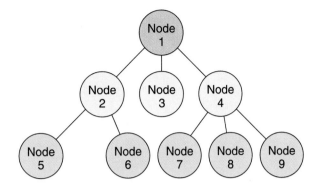

8, and 9. Nodes having the same parent are called **twins,** or **siblings.** For example, Nodes 5 and 6 are twins or siblings.

Figure 6-21(a) illustrates a tree of entities in which you can see several one-to-many relationships among entities in a university system. Colleges consist of many departments, which in turn have many professors and many administrative employees. Finally, professors advise many students who have received many grades. There are six different entity types in this structure, but all of the relationships are 1:N.

To represent a tree of entities using the relational model, we simply apply the concepts described in earlier sections of this chapter. First we transform each entity into a relation. Then we examine the relations generated against the normalization criteria and subdivide the relations if necessary. We represent the 1:N relationships by storing the key of the parent in the child. Figure 6-21(b) is a data structure diagram corresponding to the tree in Figure 6-21(a).

In summary, a hierarchy, or tree, is a collection of records organized in such a way that all relationships are 1:N. All records have exactly one parent, except the root, which has no parent. A hierarchy can be represented by a set of relations using the methods defined earlier. Hierarchies are common in businesses, especially in manufacturing applications.

■ SIMPLE NETWORKS

A **simple network** is also a data structure of elements having only one-to-many relationships. In a simple network, however, the elements may have more than one parent as long as the parents are of different types. For example, in the simple network shown in Figure 6-22, each STUDENT entity has two parents, an ADVISER entity and a MAJOR entity. The data structure in Figure 6-22 is not a tree because STUDENT entities have more than one parent.

Figure 6-23(a) shows the general structure of this simple network. Notice that all relationships are one to many but that STUDENT has two parents. In this figure, the parent records are on top, and the children records are beneath them. This arrangement is convenient but not essential. You may see simple networks depicted with parents beside or below the children. You can identify simple networks in such arrangements by the fact that a single record type participates as a child in two (or more) one-to-many relationships.

To represent a simple network of entities with the relational model, we follow the procedures described earlier. First we transform each entity into a relation and normalize the relations if necessary. Then we represent each 1:N relationship by storing the key of the parent relation in the child relation. The result of this process for the network in Figure 6-23(a) is shown in Figure 6-23(b).

FIGURE 6-21 *Representation of a Tree by Means of Relations: (a) Tree Composed of Entities and (b) Representation of This Tree by Means of Relations*

FIGURE 6-22 *Example of a Simple Network*

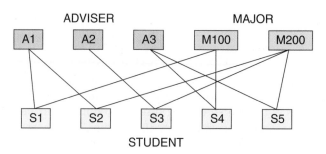

FIGURE 6-23 *Representation of a Simple Network by Means of Relations: (a) Simple Network Composed of Entities and (b) Its Representation by Means of Relations*

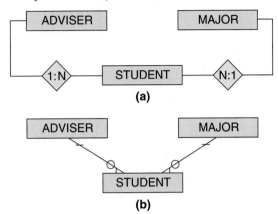

(a)

(b)

■ COMPLEX NETWORKS

A **complex network** is a data structure of elements in which at least one of the relationships is many-to-many. The complex network in Figure 6-24(a) illustrates the relationships among invoices, line items, parts, and suppliers. Two of the three relationships are 1:N, and the third is M:N. Since there is at least one many-to-many relationship, this structure is called a complex network.

As we just pointed out, M:N relationships have no direct representation in the relational model. Consequently, before this structure can be stored in relational form, we must define an intersection relation. In Figure 6-24(b), the intersection relation is part-supplier.

FIGURE 6-24 *Representation of a Complex Network by Means of Relations: (a) Complex Network Composed of Entities and (b) Its Representation by Means of Relations*

(a)

(b)

FIGURE 6-25 *Example of a Bill of Materials*

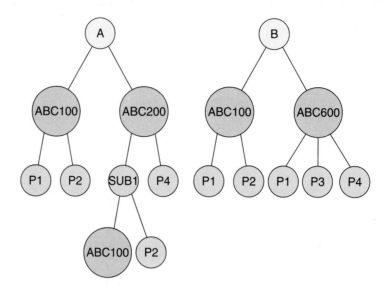

■ BILLS OF MATERIALS

A **bill of materials** is a special data structure that occurs frequently in manufacturing applications. In fact, such structures provided a major impetus for the development of database technology in the 1960s.

Figure 6-25 is an example of a bill of materials, which shows the parts that constitute products. When viewed from the standpoint of a given product, say Product A, this data structure is a hierarchy. But because a part can be used in more than one product, this structure is actually a network. For example, the part ABC100 has two parents, Product A and Product B.

A bill of materials can be represented by means of relations in several ways. The most common is to consider it as an M:N recursive relationship. A part (or product or assembly or subassembly or whatever) contains many elements. At the same time, there may be many elements that contain it. Figure 6-26(a) shows the

FIGURE 6-26 *Representation of a Bill of Materials with Relations: (a) Relations Representing a Bill of Materials and (b) Data for the ELEMENT RELATIONSHIP Intersection Relation*

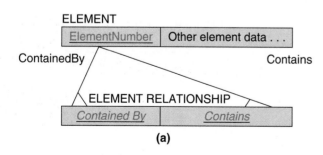

Contained By	Contains
A	ABC100
A	ABC200
B	ABC100
B	ABC600
ABC100	P1
ABC100	P2
ABC200	SUB1
ABC200	P4
ABC600	P1
ABC600	P3
ABC600	P4
SUB1	ABC100
SUB1	P2

Observe element A contains an ABC100 and element ABC100 is contained by an A

(b)

general data structure of the M:N recursive relationship, and Figure 6-26(b) shows an instance of the intersection relation created to represent this bill of materials.

SUMMARY

To transform entity-relationship data models, each entity is represented by a relation. The attributes of the entity become the attributes of the relation. Once the relation has been created, it must be examined against normalization criteria and divided into two or more relations if necessary.

There are three types of HAS-A relationships in the E-R model: 1:1, 1:N, and N:M. To represent a 1:1 relationship, we place the key of one relation into the other relation. One-to-one relationships sometimes indicate that two relations have been defined on the same entity and so should be combined into one relation.

To represent a 1:N relationship, we place the key of the parent in the child. Finally, to represent an M:N relationship, we create an intersection relation that contains the keys of the other two relations.

Recursive relationships are relationships in which the participants in the relationship arise from the same entity class. There are three types: 1:1, 1:N, and N:M. The types are represented in the same way as are nonrecursive relationships. For 1:1 and 1:N relationships, we add a foreign key to the relation that represents the entity. For an N:M recursion, we create an intersection table that represents the M:N relationship.

Ternary and higher-order relationships can be treated as combinations of binary relationships. If this is done, however, any binary constraints on the ternary relationship must also be represented in the design. Since it is not possible to enforce the constraint by the relational design, it must be documented as a business rule. Three types of such constraints occur: MUST, MUST NOT, and MUST COVER.

Supertype and subtype entities (IS-A relationships) are also represented by relations. One relation is defined for the supertype entity, and other relations are defined for each subtype. Usually the keys of the relations are the same, and the relationship among the rows is defined through those keys. If they are not the same, the key of the subtype relation can be placed in the supertype relation or the key of the supertype relation can be placed in the subtype. Most often, the key of the supertype relation is placed in the subtype relation.

Binary relationships can be combined to form three types of more complicated structures. A tree is a collection of record types in which each record has exactly one parent, except the root, which has no parent. In a simple network, records may have multiple parents, but the parents must be of different types. In a complex network, records have multiple parents of the same type. Another way of saying this is that in a complex network, at least one of the binary relationships is M:N.

A bill of materials is a data structure frequently seen in manufacturing applications. Such structures can be represented by M:N recursive relationships.

GROUP I QUESTIONS

6.1 Explain how E-R entities are transformed into relations.

6.2 Why is it necessary to examine relations transformed from entities against normalization criteria? Under what conditions should the relations be altered if they are not in DK/NF? Under what conditions should they not be altered?

6.3 Explain how the representation of weak entities differs from the representation of strong entities.

6.4   List the three types of binary relationships and give an example of each. Do not use the examples in this text.

6.5   Define *foreign key* and give an example.

6.6   Show two different ways to represent the 1:1 relationship in your answer to Question 6.4. Use data structure diagrams.

6.7   For your answers to Question 6.6, describe a method for obtaining data about one of the entities, given the key of the other. Describe a method for obtaining data about the second entity, given the key of the first. Describe answers for both of your alternatives in Question 6.6.

6.8   Why are some 1:1 relationships considered suspicious? Under what conditions should relations in a 1:1 relationship be combined into one relation?

6.9   Define the terms *parent* and *child* and give an example of each.

6.10 Show how to represent the 1:N relationship in your answer to Question 6.4. Use a data structure diagram.

6.11 For your answer to Question 6.10, describe a method for obtaining data for all of the children, given the key of the parent. Describe a method for obtaining data for the parent, given a key of the child.

6.12 For a 1:N relationship, explain why you must place the key of the parent in the child, rather than placing the key of the child in the parent.

6.13 Give examples of binary 1:N relationships, other than those in this text, for

a. An optional-to-optional relationship.

b. An optional-to-mandatory relationship.

c. A mandatory-to-optional relationship.

d. A mandatory-to-mandatory relationship.

Illustrate your answer using data structure diagrams.

6.14 Show how to represent the N:M relationship in your answer to Question 6.4. Use a data structure diagram.

6.15 For your answer to Question 6.14, describe a method for obtaining the children for one entity, given the key of the other. Also describe a method for obtaining the children for the second entity, given the key of the first.

6.16 Why is it not possible to represent N:M relationships with the same strategy used to represent 1:N relationships?

6.17 Explain the meaning of the term *intersection relation*.

6.18 Define three types of recursive binary relationships and give an example of each.

6.19 Show how to represent the 1:1 recursive relationship in your answer to Question 6.18. How does this differ from the representation of 1:1 nonrecursive relationships?

6.20 Show how to represent the 1:N recursive relationship in your answer to Question 6.18. How does this differ from the representation of 1:N nonrecursive relationships?

6.21 Show how to represent the M:N recursive relationship in your answer to Question 6.18. How does this differ from the representation of M:N nonrecursive relationships?

6.22 Explain how to use binary relationships to represent a ternary relationship. Give an example other than the ones in this text.

6.23 In your answer to question 6.22, define a binary constraint on the ternary relationship. Explain how to represent the constraint. Since the constraint cannot be enforced in the relational model, what should be done?

6.24   Give examples of MUST NOT and MUST COVER binary constraints other than the ones in this text.

6.25   Give an example of a supertype and subtypes, and show how to represent it using relations.

6.26   Define tree, simple network, and complex network.

6.27   Give an example of a tree structure other than one in this text, and show how to represent it by means of relations.

6.28   Give an example of a simple network other than one in this text, and show how to represent it by means of relations.

6.29   Give an example of a complex network other than one in this text, and show how to represent it by means of relations.

6.30   What is a bill of materials? Give an example other than the one in this text, and show how to represent your example by means of relations.

GROUP II QUESTIONS

6.31   Transform the entity-relationship diagram for the Jefferson Dance Club (Figure 3-12) into relations. Express your answer with a data structure diagram, and show the interrelation constraints.

6.32   Transform the entity-relationship diagram for San Juan Charters (Figure 3-14) into relations. Express your answer with a data structure diagram, and show the interrelation constraints.

P Key – f Key

DATABASE DESIGN WITH SEMANTIC OBJECT MODELS

This chapter discusses the transformation of semantic object models into relational database designs. First we describe the transformation of each of seven common types of semantic objects. Then we illustrate these concepts by showing the semantic object modeling and relational representation of several real-world objects. Since the best way to learn this subject is to work examples yourself, you are strongly encouraged to do the projects at the end of this chapter.

TRANSFORMATION OF SEMANTIC OBJECTS INTO RELATIONAL DATABASE DESIGNS

Chapter 4 introduced the semantic object data model and defined seven types of semantic objects. In this section, we present methods for transforming each of those seven types into relations. When working with semantic objects, normalization problems are less likely than they are when working with the entity-relationship models because the definition of semantic objects usually separates semantic themes into group attributes or objects. Thus, when transforming an object into relations, the relations are generally either already in domain/key normal form or are in very close to domain/key normal form.

■ SIMPLE OBJECTS

Figure 7-1 illustrates the transformation of a simple object into a relation. Recall that a simple object has no multivalued attributes and no object attributes. Consequently, simple objects can be represented by a single relation in the database.

Figure 7-1(a) is an example of a simple object, EQUIPMENT, which can be represented by a single relation, as shown in Figure 7-1(b). Each attribute of the object is defined as an attribute of the relation, and the identifying attribute, EquipmentNumber, becomes the key attribute of the relation, denoted by underlining EquipmentNumber in Figure 7-1(b).

The general transformation of simple objects is illustrated in Figure 7-2. Object OBJECT1 is transformed into relation R1. The attribute that identifies OBJECT1 instances is O1; it becomes the key of relation R1. Nonkey data is represented in this and subsequent figures with ellipses (. . .).

FIGURE 7-1   *Relational Representation of Example Simple Object: (a) EQUIPMENT Object Diagram and (b) Relation Representing EQUIPMENT*

```
EQUIPMENT
 ID EquipmentNumber
    Description
    AcquisitionDate
    PurchaseCost
```

(a)

EQUIPMENT (<u>EquipmentNumber</u>, Description, AcquisitionDate, PurchaseCost)

(b)

FIGURE 7-2   *General Transformation of Simple Object into a Relation*

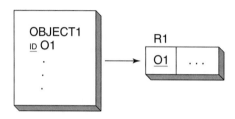

Since a key is an attribute that uniquely identifies a row of a table, only unique identifiers—those with the ID underlined—can be transformed into keys. If there is no unique identifier in the object, then one must be created, by either creating a new attribute that is a unique identifier or combining the existing attributes to form a unique identifier.[1]

■ COMPOSITE OBJECTS

A composite object is an object that has one or more multivalued simple or group attributes but no object attributes. Figure 7-3(a) shows an example composite object, HOTEL-BILL. To represent this object, one relation is created for the base object, HOTEL-BILL, and an additional relation is created for the repeating group attribute, DailyCharge. This relational design is shown in Figure 7-3(b).

In the key of DAILY-CHARGE, InvoiceNumber is underlined because it is part of the key of DAILY-CHARGE, and it is italicized because it is also a foreign key. (It is a key of HOTEL-BILL.) ChargeDate is underlined because it is part of the key of DAILY-CHARGE, but it is not italicized because it is not a foreign key.

---

[1]In some situations, database developers (or the DBMS) create a unique key, called a *surrogate key,* that identifies each row of a relation. Since it has no meaning, this key is hidden from the users by the application. When a user creates a new row in a form, the application creates, behind the scenes, a new value for the surrogate key, but the user never sees the key or is even aware of its existence. Such keys are used to give a unique identity to objects that do not have a unique identifier useful to the user. SALSA for the Desktop automatically creates surrogate keys and therefore does not require semantic objects to have a unique identifier. See also the discussion of SQL3 in Chapter 17.

FIGURE 7-3   *Relational Representation of Example Composite Object: (a) HOTEL-BILL Object Diagram and (b) Relations Representing HOTEL-BILL*

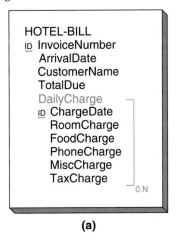

(a)

HOTEL-BILL (<u>InvoiceNumber</u>, ArrivalDate, CustomerName, TotalDue)

DAILY-CHARGE (*<u>InvoiceNumber</u>*, <u>ChargeDate</u>, RoomCharge, FoodCharge, PhoneCharge, MiscCharge, TaxCharge)

(b)

In general, composite objects are transformed by defining one relation for the object itself and another relation for each multivalued attribute. In Figure 7-4(a), object OBJECT1 contains two groups of multivalued attributes, each of which is represented by a relation in the database design. The key of each of these tables is the composite of the identifier of the object plus the identifier of the group. Thus, the representation of OBJECT1 is a relation R1 with key O1, a relation R2 with key (O1, G1), and a relation R3 with key (O1, G2).

The minimum cardinality from the object to the group is specified by the minimum cardinality of group attribute. In Figure 7-4(a), the minimum cardinality of Group1 is 1 and that of Group2 is 0. These cardinalities are shown as a hash mark (on R2) and an oval (on R3) in the data structure diagram. The minimum cardinality from the group to the object is, by default, always 1, because a group cannot exist if the object that contains that group does not exist. These minimum cardinalities are shown by hash marks on the relationship lines into R1.

As noted in Chapter 4, groups can be nested. Figure 7-4(b) shows an object in which Group2 is nested within Group1. When this occurs, the relation representing the nested group is made subordinate to the relation that represents its containing group. In Figure 7-4(b), relation R3 is subordinate to relation R2. The key of R3 is the key of R2, which is (O1, G1) plus the identifier of Group2, which is G2; thus the key of R3 is (O1, G1, G2).

Make sure that you understand why the keys in Figure 7-4(b) are constructed as they are. Also note that some attributes are underlined and italicized and some are simply underlined, because some attributes are both local and foreign keys and some are just local keys.

■ COMPOUND OBJECTS

The relational representation of compound objects is similar to the representation of entities. In fact, compound objects and entities are in many ways quite similar.

FIGURE 7-4

General Transformation of Composite Objects: (a) Composite Object with Separate Groups and (b) Composite Object with Nested Groups

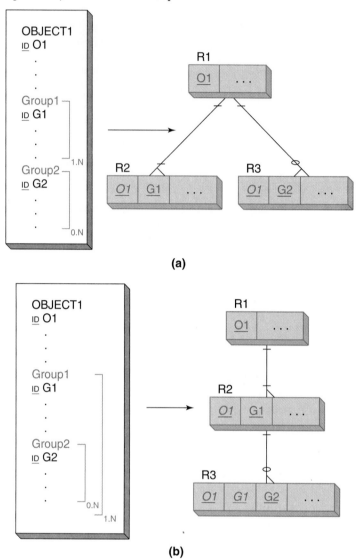

As we stated in Chapter 4, an object, OBJECT1, can contain one or many instances of a second object, OBJECT2, and OBJECT2 can contain one or many instances of the first object, OBJECT1. This leads to the object types shown in Figure 7-5.

All of these relationships involve some variation of one-to-one, one-to-many, or many-to-many relationships. Specifically, the relationship from OBJECT1 to OBJECT2 can be 1:1, 1:N, or N:M, whereas the relationship from OBJECT2 to OBJECT1 can be 1:1, 1:M, or M:N. To represent any of these, we need only address these three types of relationships.

■ REPRESENTING ONE-TO-ONE COMPOUND OBJECTS

Consider the assignment of a LOCKER to a health club MEMBER. A LOCKER is assigned to one MEMBER, and each MEMBER has one, and only one, LOCKER. Figure 7-6(a) shows the object diagrams. To represent these objects with relations,

FIGURE 7-5

Four Types of Compound Objects

		Object1 Can Contain	
		One	Many
Object2	One	**1:1**	**1:N**
Can	Many	**M:1**	**M:N**
Contain			

FIGURE 7-6

Example Relational Representation of 1:1 Compound Objects: (a) Example 1:1 Compound Objects and (b) Their Representation

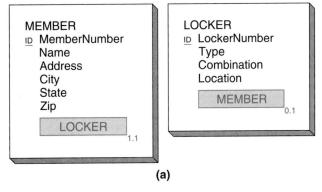

(a)

MEMBER (<u>MemberNumber</u>, Name, Address, City, State, Zip, *LockerNumber*)

LOCKER (<u>LockerNumber</u>, Type, Combination, Location)

(b)

we define a relation for each object, and, as with 1:1 entity relationships, we place the key of either relation in the other relation. That is, we can place the key of MEMBER in LOCKER or the key of LOCKER in MEMBER. Figure 7-6(b) shows the placement of the key of LOCKER in MEMBER. Note that LockerNumber is underlined in LOCKER because it is the key of LOCKER and is italicized in MEMBER because it is a foreign key in MEMBER.

In general, for a 1:1 relationship between OBJECT1 and OBJECT2, we define one relation for each object, R1 and R2. Then we place the key of either relation (O1 or O2) as a foreign key in the other relation, as in Figure 7-7.

■ REPRESENTING ONE-TO-MANY AND MANY-TO-ONE RELATIONSHIPS

Now consider 1:N relationships and N:1 relationships. Figure 7-8(a) shows an example of a 1:N object relationship between EQUIPMENT and REPAIR. An item of EQUIPMENT can have many REPAIRs, but a REPAIR can be related to only one item of EQUIPMENT.

The objects in Figure 7-8(a) are represented by the relations in Figure 7-8(b). Observe that the key of the parent (the object on the one side of the relationship) is placed in the child (the object on the many side of the relationship).

Figure 7-9 shows the general transformation of 1:N compound objects. Object OBJECT1 contains many objects OBJECT2, and object OBJECT2 contains just one

FIGURE 7-7

General Transformation of 1:1 Compound Objects

FIGURE 7-8

Example Relational Representation of 1:N Compound Objects: (a) Example 1:N Compound Objects and (b) Their Representation

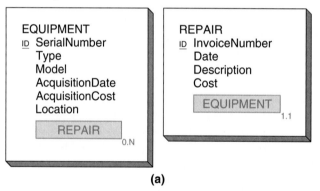

(a)

EQUIPMENT (<u>SerialNumber</u>, Type, Model, AcquisitionDate, AcquisitionCost, Location)

REPAIR (<u>InvoiceNumber</u>, Date, Description, Cost, *SerialNumber*)

(b)

OBJECT1. To represent this structure by means of relations, we represent each object with a relation and place the key of the parent in the child. Thus, in Figure 7-9 the attribute O1 is placed in R2.

If OBJECT2 were to contain many OBJECT1s and OBJECT1 were to contain just one OBJECT2, we would use the same strategy but reverse the role of R1 and R2. That is, we would place O2 in R1.

The minimum cardinalities in either case are determined by the minimum cardinalities of the object attributes. In Figure 7-9, OBJECT1 requires at least one OBJECT2, but OBJECT2 does not necessarily require an OBJECT1. These cardinalities are shown in the data structure diagram as an oval on the R1 side of the relation-

FIGURE 7-9   *General Transformation of 1:N Compound Objects*

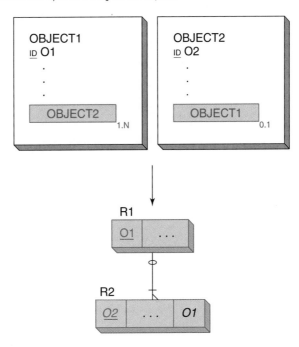

ship and as a hash mark on the R2 side of the relationship. These minimum cardinality values are simply examples; either or both objects could have a cardinality of 0, 1, or some other number.

■ REPRESENTING MANY-TO-MANY RELATIONSHIPS

Finally, consider M:N relationships. As with M:N entity relationships, we define three relations, one for each of the objects and a third intersection relation. The intersection relation represents the relationship of the two objects and consists of the keys of both of its parents. Figure 7-10(a) shows the M:N relationship between BOOK and AUTHOR. Figure 7-10(b) depicts the three relations that represent these objects: BOOK, AUTHOR, and BOOK-AUTHOR-INT, the intersection relation. Notice that BOOK-AUTHOR-INT has no nonkey data. Both the attributes ISBN and SocialSecurityNumber are underlined and in italics because they both are local and foreign keys.

In general, for two objects that have an M:N relationship, we define a relation R1 for object OBJECT1, a relation R2 for object OBJECT2, and a relation R3 for the intersection relation. The general scheme is shown in Figure 7-11. Note that the attributes of R3 are always O1 and O2. For M:N compound objects, R3 never contains nonkey data. The importance of this statement will become clear when we contrast M:N compound relationships with association relationships.

■ HYBRID OBJECTS

Hybrid objects can be transformed into relational designs using a combination of the techniques for composite and compound objects. Figure 7-12(a) shows SALES-ORDER, a hybrid object, and related objects. To represent this object by means of relations, we establish one relation for the object itself and another

FIGURE 7-10   *Relational Representation of Example N:M Compound Objects: (a) BOOK and AUTHOR Objects and (b) Their Relational Representation*

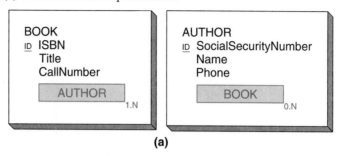

(a)

BOOK (<u>ISBN</u>, Title, CallNumber)

AUTHOR (<u>SocialSecurityNumber</u>, Name, Phone)

BOOK-AUTHOR-INT (*<u>ISBN</u>, <u>SocialSecurityNumber</u>*)
(b)

FIGURE 7-11   *General Transformation of M:N Compound Objects into Relations*

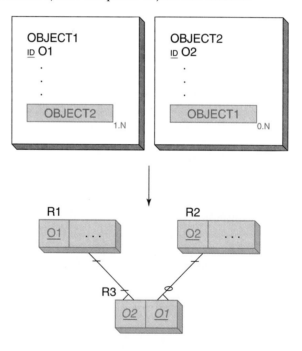

relation for each of the contained objects CUSTOMER and SALESPERSON. Then, as with a composite object, we establish a relation for the multivalued group, which is LineItem. Since this group contains another object, ITEM, we also establish a relation for ITEM. All of the one-to-many relationships are represented by placing the key of the parent relation in the child relation, as shown in Figure 7-12(b).

FIGURE 7-12   *Relational Representation of Example Hybrid Object: (a) Example Hybrid Object and (b) Relational Representation of SALES-ORDER and Related Objects*

(a)

SALES-ORDER (<u>SalesOrderNumber</u>, Date, Subtotal, Tax, Total, *Phone, SalespersonName*)

CUSTOMER (CustomerName, Address, City, State, Zip, <u>Phone</u>)

SALESPERSON (<u>SalesPersonName</u>, SalesPersonCode)

LINE-ITEM (*<u>SalesOrderNumber</u>, <u>ItemNumber</u>*, Quantity, ExtendedPrice)

ITEM (<u>ItemNumber</u>, ItemDescription, UnitPrice)

(b)

The example in Figure 7-12 is deceptively simple. As we mentioned in Chapter 4, there are actually four cases of hybrid objects, which are summarized in Figure 7-13.

Cases 3 and 4 are more common than Cases 1 and 2, so we consider them first. OBJECT1 in Figure 7-14 shows two groups; Group1 illustrates Case 3 and Group2 illustrates Case 4.

Group1 has a maximum cardinality of N, which means that there can be many instances of Group1 within an OBJECT1. Furthermore, since OBJECT2 is marked as ID unique, this means that a particular OBJECT2 can appear in only one of the Group1 instances within an OBJECT1. Thus OBJECT2 acts as an identifier for Group1 within OBJECT1.

(The SALES-ORDER in Figure 7-12 illustrates this case. ITEM is an identifier of LineItem, so a given ITEM can appear on only one LineItem in a particular ORDER. But an ITEM can appear on many ORDERs.)

FIGURE 7-13

Four Cases of Hybrid Object Cardinality

Case	Description	Example
1	OBJECT2 relates to one instance of OBJECT1 and appears in only one group instance within that object.	ITEM relates to one ORDER and can appear on only one LineItem of that ORDER.
2	OBJECT2 relates to one instance of OBJECT1 and appears in possibly many group instances within that object.	ITEM relates to one ORDER and can appear on many LineItems of that ORDER.
3	OBJECT2 relates to possibly many instances of OBJECT1 and appears in only one group instance within each object.	ITEM relates to many ORDERs and can appear on only one LineItem of that ORDER.
4	OBJECT2 relates to possibly many instances of OBJECT1 and appears in possibly many group instances within those objects.	ITEM relates to many ORDERs and can appear on many LineItems of that ORDER.

FIGURE 7-14

General Transformation of Hybrid Object into Relations

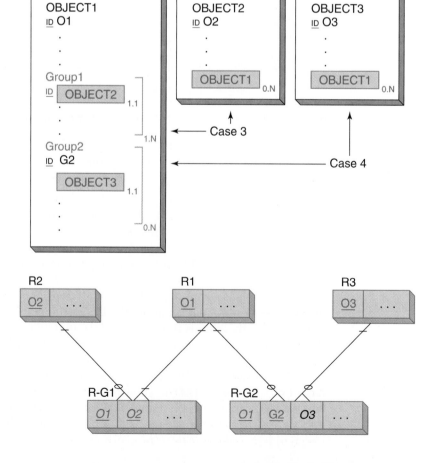

Consider the relational representation of Group1 in Figure 7-14. A relation, R1, is created for OBJECT1, and a relation, R2, is created for OBJECT2. In addition, a third relation, R-G1, is created for Group1. The relationship between R1 and R-G1 is 1:N, so we place the key of R1 (which is O1) into R-G1; the relationship between R2 and R-G1 is also 1:N, so we place the key of R2 (which is O2) in R-G1. Since an OBJECT2 can appear with a particular value of OBJECT1 only once, the composite (O1, O2) is unique to R-G1 and can be made the key of that relation.

Now consider Group2. OBJECT3 does not identify Group2, so OBJECT3 can appear in many Group2 instances in the same OBJECT1. (The SALES-ORDER in Figure 7-12 would be like this if ITEM were not ID unique in LineItem. This means that an ITEM could appear many times on the same ORDER.) Since OBJECT3 is not the identifier of Group2, we assume that some other attribute, G2, is the identifier.

In Figure 7-14, we create a relation R3 for OBJECT3 and another relation R-G2 for Group2. The relationship between R1 and R-G2 is 1:N, so place the key of R1 (which is O1) into R-G2. The relationship between R3 and R-G2 is also 1:N, so place the key of R3 (which is O3) into R-G2.

Now, however, unlike Group1, (O1, O3) cannot be the key of R-G2 because an O3 can be paired with a given O1 many times. That is, the composite (O1,O3) is not unique to R-G2, so the key of R-G2 must be (O1, G2).

Case 1 is similar to Case 3 except for the restriction that an OBJECT2 can be related to only one OBJECT1. The relations in Figure 7-14 will still work, but we must add the key of R1 (which is O1) to R2 and establish the restriction that (O1, O2) of R-G1 must equal (O1,O2) of R2.

Case 2 is similar to Case 4 except for the restriction that an OBJECT3 can be related to only one OBJECT1. Again, the relations in Figure 7-14 will work, but we must add the key of R1 (which is O1) to R3 and establish the restriction that (O1,O3) of R-G2 is a subset of (O1,O3) in R3 (see Questions 7.7 and 7.8).

■ ASSOCIATION OBJECTS

An association object is an object that associates two other objects. It is a special case of compound objects that most often occurs in assignment situations. Figure 7-15(a) shows a FLIGHT object that associates an AIRPLANE with a PILOT.

To represent association objects, we define a relationship for each of the three objects, and then we represent the relationships among the objects using one of the strategies used with compound objects. In Figure 7-15(b), for example, one relation is defined for AIRPLANE, one for PILOT, and one for FLIGHT. The relationships between FLIGHT and AIRPLANE and between FLIGHT and PILOT are 1:N, so we place the keys of the parent in the children. In this case, we place the key of AIRPLANE and the key of PILOT in FLIGHT.

FLIGHT contains a key of its own. Although it contains foreign keys, these keys are only attributes and are not part of FLIGHT's key. But this is not always the case. If FLIGHT had no key of its own, its key would be the combination of the foreign keys of the objects that it associates. Here that combination would be {AirplaneNumber, PilotNumber, Date}.

In general, when transforming association object structures into relations, we define one relation for each of the objects participating in the relationship. In Figure 7-16, OBJECT3 associates OBJECT1 and OBJECT2. In this case, we define R1, R2, and R3, as shown. The key of each of the parent relations, O1 and O2, appears as foreign key attributes in R3, the relation representing the association object. If the association object has no unique identifying attribute, the combination of the attributes of R1 and R2 will be used to create a unique identifier.

Note the difference between the association relation in Figure 7-16 and the intersection relation in Figure 7-11. The principal distinction is that the association table carries data that represent some aspect of the combination of the objects. The intersection relation carries no data; its only reason for existence is to specify which objects have a relationship with one another.

FIGURE 7-15 *Relational Representation of Example Association Object: (a) FLIGHT Association Object and Related Objects and (b) Relational Representation of AIRPLANE, PILOT, and FLIGHT Objects*

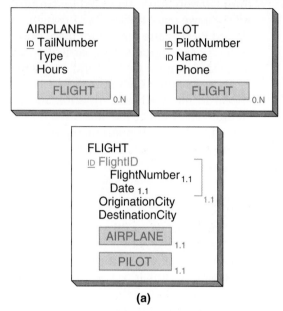

(a)

AIRPLANE (<u>TailNumber</u>, TypeHours)

PILOT (<u>PilotNumber</u>, Name, Phone)

FLIGHT (<u>FlightNumber</u>, <u>Date</u>, OriginationCity, DestinationCity,
      TailNumber, PilotNumber)

(b)

FIGURE 7-16 *General Transformation of Association Objects into Relations*

FIGURE 7-17   *Representation of Example Parent and Subtypes: (a) PERSON Parent and STUDENT and PROFESSOR Subtypes, (b) Relational Representation of Parent and Subtypes, and (c) Alternative Representations of the Parent Relation*

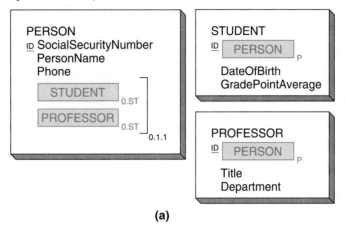

(a)

PERSON (<u>SocialSecurityNumber</u>, PersonName, Phone)

STUDENT (<u>SocialSecurityNumber</u>, DateOfBirth, GradePointAverage)

PROFESSOR (<u>SocialSecurityNumber</u>, Title, Department)

(b)

PERSON1 (<u>SocialSecurityNumber</u>, PersonName, Phone, PersonType)

PERSON2 (<u>SocialSecurityNumber</u>, PersonName, Phone, StudentType, ProfessorType)

(c)

■ PARENT/SUBTYPE OBJECTS

Parent (also called *supertype*) and subtype objects are represented in a way similar to that for parent and subtype entities. We define a relation for the parent object and one for each of the subtype objects. The key of each of these relations is the key of the parent.

Figure 7-17(a) shows a parent object, PERSON, that includes two mutually exclusive subtypes, STUDENT and PROFESSOR. Figure 7-17(b) shows a relational representation of these three objects. Each object is represented by a table, and the key of all of the tables is the same.

The relations in Figure 7-17(b) pose a problem, however. The application program still needs to look in both the STUDENT and PROFESSOR tables to determine the type of PERSON. If an entry is found in STUDENT, the person is a student; if an entry is found in PROFESSOR, the person is a professor. This is an indirect and possibly slow way to determine the type of a person, and if, as may happen, the PERSON is of neither type, both tables will have been searched for no reason. Because of this problem, a type indicator attribute is sometimes placed in the parent table.

Figure 7-17(c) shows two variations of a type indicator. In the first variation, relation PERSON1, the type of object is stored in the attribute PersonType. Possible values of this attribute are 'Neither', 'STUDENT', or 'PROFESSOR'. The application would obtain the value of this attribute and thereby determine whether a subtype exists and, if so, which type it is.

A second possibility is shown in the relation PERSON2, to which two attributes have been added, one for StudentType and another for ProfessorType. Each of the

FIGURE 7-18   *General Transformation of Parent/Subtype Objects into Relations*

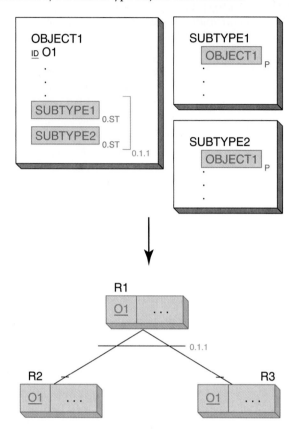

attributes is a Boolean variable; the allowed values are true or false. Note that if, as is the case here, a person can be of only one type, then if one of these values is true, the other one must be false.

In general, designs of type PERSON1 are better when the subtypes are mutually exclusive. Designs of type PERSON2 are better when the subtypes are not exclusive.

A general scheme for representing subtypes is shown in Figure 7-18. One relation is created for the parent and one each for the subtypes. The key of all of the relations is the identifier of the parent. All relationships between the parent and the subtype are 1:1. Note the bar across the relationship lines and the presence of the subtype group's cardinality. The value shown, 0.1.1, means that no subtype is required but, if present, at most one of the subtypes is allowed.

(Recall that in general, the format of group cardinality is **r.m.n.,** where *r* is a Boolean true or false depending on whether or not the subtype group is required, *m* is the minimum number of subtypes that must have a value within the group, and *n* is the maximum number of subtypes that may have a value within the group. In a group of five subtypes, therefore, the cardinality of 1.2.4 indicates that the subtype group is required, that at least two subtypes must have a value, and that a maximum of four subtypes may have a value.)

■ ARCHETYPE/VERSION OBJECTS

Archetype/version objects are compound objects that model various iterations, releases, or instances of a basic object. The objects in Figure 7-19(a) model software products for which there are various releases. Examples of such products are Excel, WordPerfect, and Paradox for Windows, and examples of releases are Release 2.0, Release 3.0, and Release 4.0 of Excel.

FIGURE 7-19   *Relational Representation of Example Archetype/Version Objects: (a) PRODUCT Archetype and RELEASE Version Objects and (b) Relational Representation of PRODUCT and RELEASE*

(a)

PRODUCT (<u>Name</u>, Description, TotalSales)

RELEASE (<u>*Name*</u>, <u>ReleaseNumber</u>, ReleaseDate, ReleaseSales)

(b)

FIGURE 7-20   *General Transformation of Archetype/Version Objectsand RELEASE Version Objects and (b)*

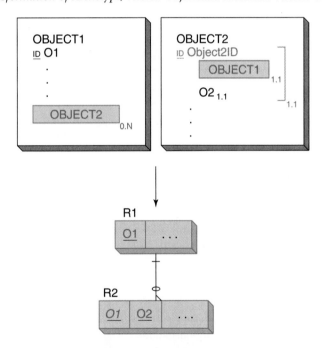

The relational representation of PRODUCT and RELEASE is shown in Figure 7-19(b). One relation is created for PRODUCT, and another is created for RELEASE. The key of RELEASE is the combination of the key of PRODUCT and the local key (ReleaseNumber) of RELEASE.

Figure 7-20 shows the general transformation of archetype/version objects. Attribute O1 of R2 is both a local and a foreign key, but O2 is only a local key.

SAMPLE OBJECTS

To reinforce the concepts presented so far, we now consider several example objects taken from actual businesses, presented in increasing order of complexity. We model the underlying object and represent it in relations using the methods described in this chapter.

■ SUBSCRIPTION FORM

Figure 7-21(a) shows a magazine subscription form. At least two object structures could represent this form. If the publishers of *Fine Woodworking* consider a subscriber to be an attribute of a subscription, a subscription could be a simple object represented as a single relation, as in Figure 7-21(b).

If this company has only a single publication and no plans to produce additional publications, the design in Figure 7-21(b) will work. If, however, this company has several publications and if a customer may subscribe to more than one of them, this design will duplicate the customer data for each publication. This will not only waste file space for the publisher but will also exasperate the customer because, for example, he or she will be required to submit address changes for each publication of the same publisher.

If the publisher has several publications or plans to have several publications, a better design would be to model subscriber as a separate object, as shown in

FIGURE 7-21 *Alternative Representations of Subscription: (a) Subscription Order Form, (b) Subscription Modeled as One Object, and (c) Subscription Modeled as Two Objects*

Fine Wood ▲▲▲▲Working   **To subscribe**

☐ 1 year (6 issues) for just $18 — 20% off the newsstand price.
  (Outside the U.S. $21/year.—U.S. funds, please)

☐ 2 years (12 issues) for just $34 — save 24%
  (Outside the U.S. $40/2 years—U.S. funds, please)

Name _____

Address _____

City _____ State _____ Zip _____
☐ My payment is enclosed. ☐ Please bill me.
Please start my subscription with ☐ *current issue* ☐ *next issue* .

(a)

SUBSCRIPTION
ID SubNumber
  StartDate
  EndDate
  AmtDue
  Name
  Address
  City
  State
  Zip
  PayCode

SUBSCRIPTION

SubNumber	StartDate	EndDate	AmtDue	Name	Address

City	State	Zip	PayCode

(b)

FIGURE 7-21   *(Continued)*

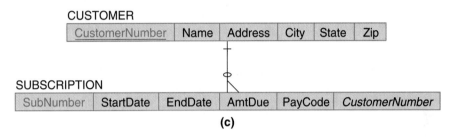

(c)

Figure 7-21(c). CUSTOMER is a 1:N compound object and is represented by the relations in this figure.

■ PRODUCT DESCRIPTION

Figure 7-22(a) shows the description of a popular packaged-goods product. Whereas Figure 7-21(a) shows a generic form with no data, Figure 7-22(a) shows an instance of a specific report with data about a cereal product. The reports for all of Kellogg's cereal products use this format.

Figure 7-22(b) shows a composite object that could underlie this report. We say *could* because there are many different ways that this object might be represented. Also, further investigation may reveal other objects that are not apparent in this one report. For example, USDA Recommendation may be a semantic object in its own right.

For illustration purposes, we make different assumptions about the Nutrient and USDARecDailyAllow groups. The CEREAL-PRODUCT object assumes that every element of the Nutrient group—namely, calories, protein, carbohydrate, fat, cholesterol, sodium, and potassium—is required in every instance of this object. We do not assume this for the USDARecDailyAllow group, because only one instance of this group must exist.

The report in Figure 7-22(a) has many interpretations and could be modeled in several different ways. In an actual development project, it would be important to obtain as many other reports about other cereal products and about the ingredients and nutritional information in this report. These other documents would most likely give additional structure to this semantic object.

Figure 7-22(c) shows the relational representation for the CEREAL-PRODUCT object. The minimum cardinality of 7 is shown by placing the numeral *7* next to the required hash mark on the relationship line. Foreign keys have been placed as described previously for composite objects.

■ TRAFFIC-WARNING CITATION

Figure 7-23(a) shows an instance of the traffic-warning citation form used in the state of Washington. The designer of this form has given us important clues to the underlying objects of this form. Notice that portions of the form are

FIGURE 7-22 *Cereal Product Representation: (a) Cereal Product Report, (b) CEREAL-PRODUCT Object Diagram, and (c) Relational Representation of CEREAL-PRODUCT*

(a)

(b)

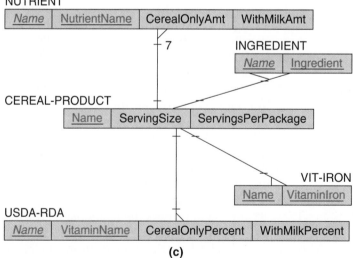

(c)

distinguished by rounded corners, indicating that different sections pertain to different objects. Also, some groups of attributes have names, indicating the need for group attributes.

Figure 7-23(b) is one way to illustrate the underlying objects of the traffic-warning citation. Although we cannot be certain from just this one form, there are

FIGURE 7-23   *Representation of a Correction Notice: (a) Example Form, (b) CORRECTION-NOTICE Object Diagram, and (c) Relational Representation of CORRECTION-NOTICE*

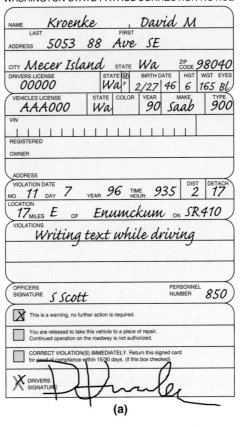

WASHINGTON STATE PATROL CORRECTION NOTICE

(a)

(b)

FIGURE 7-23 *(Continued)*

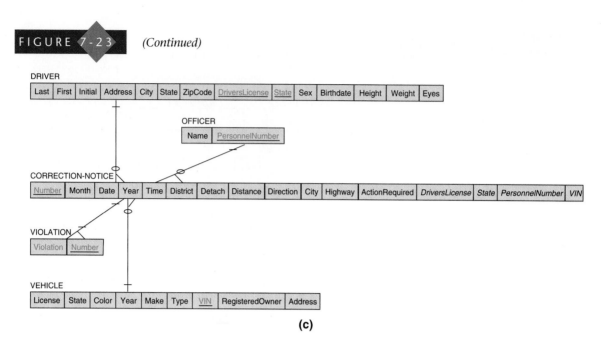

(c)

certain clues that lead us to believe that the driver, vehicle, and officer are independent objects. First, the data concerning each of these subjects are in a separate section on the form. But more important, each section has its fields that are undoubtedly identifying attributes of something apart from CORRECTION-NOTICE. For example, {DriversLicense, State} uniquely identifies a driver; VehicleLicense, State and VIN (Vehicle Identification Number) identify registered vehicles; and PersonnelNumber identifies an officer. These key fields obviously are determinants, so objects were defined for each. The relation representation of these diagrams appears in Figure 7-23(c).

SUMMARY

The transformation of semantic objects into relations depends on the type of object. Simple objects are represented by a single relation. The nonobject attributes are carried as attributes of the relation.

Composite objects require two or more relations for their representation. One relation contains the single-valued attributes of the object. Another relation is constructed for each multivalued simple or group attribute. The key of the relations representing the multivalued attributes is always a composite key that contains the key of the object plus an identifier of the composite group within that object.

At least two relations are required to represent a compound object. Each relation has its own distinct key. There are four different types of compound objects—one to one, one to many, many to one, and many to many—which are represented by inserting foreign keys. For one-to-one relationships, the key of either table is placed in the other table, and for one-to-many and many-to-one relationships, the key of the parent is placed in the child relation. Finally, for many-to-many relationships, an intersection table is created that carries the keys of both relations.

Hybrid objects are represented by creating a table for the multivalued group attribute of the composite object and placing the key of the relation representing the noncomposite object into that table. The four cases of hybrid are listed in Figure 7-14.

Association objects require at least three relations for their representation, one for each of the objects involved. Each relation has its own key, and the relation representing the association object contains, as foreign keys, the keys of the other two objects.

Parent and subtype objects are represented by creating a relation for the parent and one for each subtype. The key of all relations is normally the same. An identifier attribute is sometimes placed in the parent to indicate the object's type.

For archetype/version objects, one relation is created for the archetype object and a second is created for the version. The key of the version's relation always contains the key of the archetype.

◆ GROUP I QUESTIONS

7.1 Give an example of a simple object other than one in this text. Show how to represent this object by means of a relation.

7.2 Give an example of a composite object other than one in this text. Show how to represent this object by means of relations.

7.3 Give an example of a 1:1 compound object other than one in this text. Show two ways to represent it by means of relations.

7.4 Give an example of a 1:N compound object other than one in this text. Show how to represent it by means of relations.

7.5 Give an example of an M:1 compound object other than one in this text. Show how to represent it by means of relations.

7.6 Give an example of an M:N compound object other than one in this text. Show how to represent it by means of relations.

7.7 Give an example of a Case 1 (see Figure 7-13) hybrid object. Show how to represent it by means of relations.

7.8 Give an example of a Case 2 (see Figure 7-13) hybrid object. Show how to represent it by means of relations.

7.9 Give an example of an association and related objects other than one in this text. Show how to represent these objects by means of relations. Assume that the association object has an identifier of its own.

7.10 Do the same as for Question 9, but assume that the association object does not have an identifier of its own.

7.11 Give an example of a parent object with at least two exclusive subtypes. Show how to represent these objects by means of relations. Use a type indicator attribute.

7.12 Give an example of a parent object with at least two nonexclusive subtypes. Show how to represent these objects by means of relations. Use a type indicator attribute.

7.13 Find an example of a form on your campus that would be appropriately modeled with a simple object. Show how to represent this object by means of a relation.

7.14 Find an example of a form on your campus that would be appropriately modeled with a composite object. Show how to represent this object by means of relations.

7.15 Find an example of a form on your campus that would be appropriately modeled with one of the types of a compound object. Show how to represent these objects by means of relations.

7.16 Find an example of a form on your campus that would be appropriately modeled with a hybrid object. Classify the object according to Figure 7-14, and show how to represent these objects by means of relations.

7.17 Find an example of a form on your campus that would be appropriately modeled with an association and related objects. Show how to represent these objects by means of relations.

7.18 Find an example of a form on your campus that would be appropriately modeled with parent/subtypes objects. Show how to represent these objects by means of relations.

7.19 Find an example of a form on your campus that would be appropriately modeled with archetype/version objects. Show how to represent these objects by means of relations.

GROUP II QUESTIONS

7.20 In Figure 7-13, give a different example for each of the four cases in the right column. Show how each of your examples would be represented with relations.

7.21 Modify Figures 7-22(b) and (c) to add the reports shown in Figure 7-24.

7.22 Using the album cover shown in Figure 7-25 as a guide, perform the following tasks:

 a. Draw the object diagrams for the underlying objects ARTIST, ROLE, and SONG.

 b. Identify the relationships among those objects. What types of objects are they (simple, composite, and so on)?

 c. Indicate for each participant in a relationship whether it is optional or mandatory.

 d. Transform the object diagrams into relation diagrams.

 What is the key of each relation? What foreign keys appear in each relation?

FIGURE 7-24   *Reports for Question 7.21*

FDA REPORT #6272
Date: 06/30/93
Issuer: Kellogg's Corporation
Report Title: Product Summary by Ingredient

Corn	Corn Flakes
	Krispix
	Nutrigrain (Corn)
Corn syrup	Rice Krispies
	Frosted Flakes
	Sugar Pops
Malt	Rice Krispies
	Sugar Smacks
Wheat	Sugar Smacks
	Nutrigrain (Wheat)

(a)

SUPPLIERS LIST
Date: 06/30/93

Ingredient	Supplier	Price
Corn	Wilson	2.80
	J. Perkins	2.72
	Pollack	2.83
	McKay	2.80
Wheat	Adams	1.19
	Kroner	1.19
	Schmidt	1.22
Barley	Wilson	0.85
	Pollack	0.84

(b)

FIGURE 7-25   *Reports for Question 7.22*

West Side Story
Based on a conception of Jerome Robbins

Book by ARTHUR LAURENTS
Music by LEONARD BERNSTEIN
Lyrics by STEPHEN SONDHEIM

Entire Original Production Directed
and Choreographed by JEROME ROBBINS

Originally produced on Broadway by Robert E. Griffith and Harold S. Prince
by arrangement with Roger L. Stevens
Orchestration by Leonard Bernstein with Sid Ramin and Irwin Kostal

HIGHLIGHTS FROM THE COMPLETE RECORDING

Maria . . . . .KIRI TE KANAWA
Tony . . . . JOSE CARRERAS
Anita . . . . .TATIANA TROYANOS
Riff . . . . KURT OLLMAN
and MARILYN HORNE singing "Somewhere"

Rosalia . . . . Louise Edeiken	Diesel . . . . Marty Nelson
Consuela . . . . Stella Zambalis	Baby John . . . . . . Stephen Bogardus
Fancisca . . . . Angelina Reaux	A-rab . . . . Peter Thom
Action . . . . David Livingston	Snowboy . . . . .Todd Lester
Bernardo Richard Harrell	

1	**Jet Song** (Riff, Action, Baby John, A-rab, Chorus)	[3'13]
2	**Something's Coming** (Tony)	[2'33]
3	**Maria** (Tony)	[2'56]
4	**Tonight** (Maria, Tony)	[5'27]
5	**America** (Anita, Rosalia, Chorus)	[4'47]
6	**Cool** (Riff, Chorus)	[4'37]
7	**One Hand, One Heart** (Tony, Maria)	[5'38]
8	**Tonight** (Ensemble) (Entire Cast)	[3'40]
9	**I Feel Pretty** (Maria, Chorus)	[3'22]
10	**Somewhere** (A Girl)	[2'34]
11	**Gee OFicer Krupke** (Action, Snowboy, Diesel, A-rab, Baby John, Chorus)	[4'18]
12	**A Boy Like That** (Anita, Maria)	[2'05]
13	**I Have a Love** (Maria, Anita)	[3'30]
14	**Taunting Scene** (Orchestra)	[1'21]
15	**Finale** (Maria, Tony)	[2'40]

◆ PROJECTS USING SALSA FOR THE DESKTOP

You must install SALSA for the Desktop to do the following projects. See Chapter 4, Project 1, page 107 for information.

■ PROJECT 1

Use SALSA for the Desktop to create the model in Figure 7-10. To create the attributes, either drag and drop templates from the catalog that are close to those you need or create new templates. To change the properties of a template or attribute, click the right mouse button over the template or attribute you want to change. SALSA will display the property sheet. Here you can change whatever properties you want to change. Note that if you change the properties of a template, all of the attributes based on that template will inherit that change. If you change the properties of an attribute, only that attribute will change.

Generate the application by pressing the traffic light on the toolbar. Enter data for a few authors and data for a few books. Attempt to add a book without an author. If you have set the minimum cardinality of the AUTHOR attribute (in BOOK) to 1, SALSA will not let you add a book without an author.

Close your application and return to design mode. Click the Print Model Information choice under the File Menu. SALSA will display a list of reports about your model and generated application. (If you have not generated the application and entered some data, some of these choices will be disabled.) Print the following reports: Objects/Tables, Tables, Columns, Relationships.

Examine these reports and compare them to the relations in Figure 7-10(b). Annotate the reports to explain how each table and column correspond to your model. To do this, you need to know several facts about the databases that SALSA generates. First, SALSA creates a surrogate key called ID_ for each table. Thus, both BOOK and AUTHOR will have a key named ID_. Also, whenever SALSA generates a foreign key, it appends the characters _FK to the name of that attribute. Notice, too, that SALSA appends the characters _X to any table that serves as an intersection table. Finally, In these reports, you will notice a table called SALSASK_. This table is metadata; SALSA uses it to maintain surrogate keys values.

■ PROJECT 2

To do this project you will need to understand how to use and interpret the Print Model Information reports described in Project 1.

Use SALSA to create the CEREAL-PRODUCT object in Figure 7-22. Generate the application and add sample data. Print the Object, Object/Table, Table, and Relationship reports, and compare the results of SALSA to the design in Figure 7-22b. Explain differences between what SALSA generates and the tables in this figure.

Change CEREAL-PRODUCT by moving the NutrientName group inside the USDARecDailyAllow group (this is probably not a good model, but we are doing this as an exercise to understand semantic object design, so look past that issue for now). Generate the database and examine the data you added before. Observe how SALSA has changed your forms and reports. Return to design mode and print the Object, Object/Table, Table, and Relationship reports. Explain differences between the reports for the first version of CEREAL-PRODUCT and for this version of CEREAL-PRODUCT.

■ PROJECT 3

To do this project, you will need to understand how to use and interpret the Print Model Information reports described in Project 1.

Use SALSA to create the model in Figure 4-13. (You will have already done this if you worked the SALSA projects at the end of Chapter 4. If so, open the SALSA model you created for that project.) Generate the application, and add sample data to each object. Return to design mode, and print the Object, Object/Table, Table, and Relationship reports. Explain the reason for each table and relationship that SALSA has generated.

■ PROJECT 4

To do this project, you will need to understand how to use and interpret the Print Model Information reports described in Project 1.

Use SALSA to create a model for the data in Question 7.21 and Figure 7-22(b). Generate your application, and add sample data. Return to design mode and print the Object, Object/Table, Table, and Relationship reports. Explain the reason for each table and relationship that SALSA has generated.

■ PROJECT 5

To do this project, you will need to understand how to use and interpret the Print Model Information reports described in Project 1.

Use SALSA to create a model for an application to store data like that shown in Figure 7-25. To do this, you will need to make assumptions about the scope of the application. It is just for CDs? Is it for CDs and tapes? Is it for vinyl records? Is it only for albums of musicals based on plays? State the assumptions you make. Generate the application, and enter sample data. Return to design mode, and print the Object, Object/Table, Table, and Relationship reports. Explain the reason for each table and relationship that SALSA has generated.

8

DATABASE APPLICATION DESIGN

• • • • • • • • • • • • •

Chapter 8 discusses the design of database applications. Since this is not a text on systems development, we address only those aspects of application design that pertain directly to database processing.

This chapter assumes that the users' data model has been expressed in terms of semantic objects. Applications can be created from data models expressed in the entity-relationship constructs, but it will be easier to explain the concepts of this chapter if we use semantic-object data models.

We begin with a case that will be used to illustrate design concepts. This case will also be used in Chapter 11, where it is the basis for a discussion of database implementation. After the case description, we discuss the nature of database applications, object views, materializations, and the design of application forms and reports. Finally, the chapter concludes with a summary of application program design.

◆ CASE APPLICATION: VIEW RIDGE GALLERY

View Ridge Gallery is a small art gallery that sells contemporary fine art, including lithographs, original paintings, and photographs. All of the lithographs and photos are signed and numbered, and most of the art is priced between $1,000 and $25,000. View Ridge has been in business for twenty-seven years, has one full-time owner, three salespeople, and two workers who make frames, hang art in the gallery, and prepare art works for shipment.

View Ridge holds openings and other gallery events to attract customers to the gallery. Art is also placed on display in local companies and restaurants and in other public places. View Ridge owns all of the art that it sells; it holds no items on a consignment basis.

■ APPLICATION REQUIREMENTS

View Ridge wants to build database applications to satisfy the requirements shown in Figure 8-1. First, both the owner and the salespeople want to keep track of their customers and their art-purchasing interests. The salespeople need to know whom

FIGURE 8-1   *Summary of Requirements for the View Ridge Gallery Database Applications*

Track customers and their purchasing interests.

Record customers' art purchases.

Record gallery's purchases.

List the artists and works that have appeared in the gallery.

Report how fast an artist's works have sold and at what margin.

List current inventory.

List product reports to be used by the gallery's bookkeeper/accountant.

to contact when new art arrives, and they also need this information so that they can create personal written and verbal communications with their customers.

In addition, the database should record the customers' art purchases so that the salespeople can devote more time to the most active buyers. They also sometimes use the purchase records to identify the location of the art, because the gallery occasionally repurchases hard-to-find art for resale. The database application also should have a form for adding new works that the gallery purchases.

View Ridge wants its database application to provide a list of artists and works that have appeared in the gallery. The owner would also like to be able to determine how fast an artist's work sells and at what sales margins, and the database application should produce a list of current inventory for periodic physical inventory counts. Finally, View Ridge would like the database to produce reports that would reduce the work of the gallery's part-time bookkeeper/accountant.

■ DATABASE DESIGN

Figure 8-2(a) shows the structure of the objects required to support the gallery's database. CUSTOMER and ARTIST are compound objects, and WORK is a hybrid object whose unique identifier is the group {ARTIST, Title, and Copy}. The multivalued group Transaction represents the gallery's purchase and sale of the work. Since a given work can pass through the gallery several times (because of repurchases and trade-ins), Transaction is multivalued. WORK is a hybrid object because it contains the object attribute CUSTOMER in the multivalued Transaction group.

View Ridge wants to be able to track its customers' interests. In particular, it wants to know the artists in which a particular customer is interested and the customers who have an interest in a particular artist. These requirements are supported by placing the multivalued attribute ARTIST in CUSTOMER and the multivalued attribute CUSTOMER in ARTIST.

The relational representation of the View Ridge objects is shown in Figure 8-2(b). Since the CUSTOMER object does not have a unique identifier, one must be created to use as a key. Here we have added an identifying number, CustNumber. The maximum cardinality of the Phone and Address groups is 1, so the attributes in those groups can be placed in the CUSTOMER table. These groups, in fact, do not appear in the table as groups; instead, the group information is used later to construct forms.

The key of WORK consists of the key of ARTIST plus Title and Copy. The only nonkey attribute of WORK is Description. Since the Transaction attribute is multivalued, a table must be created for it. Its key is the key of the object in which it is contained plus the key of the group, which is DateAcquired. Note that CustNumber is carried as a foreign key in TRANSACTION.

FIGURE 8-2   *Database Design for View Ridge Gallery: (a) Objects Required for the View Ridge Gallery Database, (b) Relational Representation of View Ridge Gallery's Objects, and (c) Relational Representation Using Surrogate Keys*

(a)

CUSTOMER (<u>CustNumber</u>, Name, AreaCode, LocalNumber, Street, City, State, Zip)

WORK (<u>ArtistName</u>, <u>Title</u>, <u>Copy</u>, Description)

TRANSACTION (*<u>ArtistName</u>*, *<u>Title</u>*, *<u>Copy</u>*, <u>DateAcquired</u>, AcquisitionPrice, PurchaseDate, *CustNumber*, SalesPrice)

ARTIST (<u>ArtistName</u>, Nationality, Birthdate, DeceasedDate)

CUSTOMER-ARTIST-INT (<u>CustNumber</u>, <u>ArtistName</u>)

(b)

CUSTOMER (<u>CustomerID</u>, Name, AreaCode, LocalNumber, Street, City, State, Zip)

WORK (<u>WorkID</u>, ArtistName, Title, Copy, Description)

TRANSACTION (<u>TransactionID</u>, *WorkID*, DateAcquired, AcquisitionPrice, PurchaseDate, *CustomerID*, SalesPrice)

ARTIST (<u>ArtistID</u>, ArtistName, Nationality, Birthdate, DeceasedDate)

CUSTOMER-ARTIST-INT (*<u>CustomerID</u>*, *<u>ArtistID</u>*)

(c)

The ARTIST object is represented by a single table, and ArtistName can be used as the table key, since artists" names are modeled as being unique. The intersection table CUSTOMER-ARTIST-INT must be created to carry the M:N relationship between CUSTOMER and ARTIST.

The design in Figure 8-2(b) could be improved by replacing the data keys with surrogate keys. Recall that such keys are supplied by the DBMS or the application program as hidden identifiers that are maintained, behind the scenes, for the user. Such a design is shown in Figure 8-2(c), in which the names of the surrogate keys are constructed by appending the letters ID to the name of the table.

The design in Figure 8-2(c) is better because less data are duplicated. The columns (ArtistName, Title, Copy) need not be copied into the Transaction table. Since there may be many transactions for a given work, this savings may be appreciable. The cost is that if the DBMS does not support such keys, application programs must be developed to create and maintain the surrogate key values.

CHARACTERISTICS OF DATABASE APPLICATIONS

The purpose of a database application is to *create, update, delete, and display objects at the direction of the users while at all times protecting the security and integrity of the database.* Ideally, an application provides an easy-to-use interface for authorized users who are making authorized requests with valid and accurate data. Also ideally, it presents the equivalent of a closed door to unauthorized users, and it provides informative and helpful error messages to authorized users who are making unauthorized requests or mistakes or who are attempting to process invalid data. Often, however, these ideals cannot be fully achieved because of limitations in the DBMS products, development time and budget restrictions, limits in the developers' knowledge or abilities, and other constraints.

■ CREATE, UPDATE, DELETE, AND DISPLAY OBJECTS

The database application's first task is to *create, update, delete, and display objects.* As you know from earlier chapters, objects are not stored in the database. Rather, they are transformed and stored as sets of relations. Before objects can be processed, therefore, the application must construct them from the underlying relations or, as we sometimes say, the application must **materialize objects.**

Objects are created by obtaining data from users or other sources and storing them in the database. To update the data, the object data are read from the relations, and the appropriate changes are made. To delete the data, all object data are removed from the underlying relations. The data can be displayed by reporting them (on paper or other external media) or by showing object structures on display devices.

Creating, updating, and deleting objects are the bulk of the application's and the application developers' work. When objects are modified, the data must be correctly changed while the constraints are enforced. Although DBMS products should enforce many constraints automatically, in practice they enforce only a few. It thus falls on the application program to enforce domain, intrarelation, and interrelation constraints.

In addition, if the database is concurrently processed, updating must be controlled so that the actions of one user do not interfere with those of another. Finally, update processing must be structured so that in the event of a failure, the database can be recovered.

Few DBMS products support the querying of objects through an interface like QueryByForm. Instead, DBMS products provide features to query *relations.* Chapter 10 discusses SQL, the ANSI standard query language. This language is relation oriented, so the users themselves must construct objects from underlying relations. Since few users have the knowledge or patience to construct objects from relations, such languages are most often used only for querying simple objects. If the objects are more complex, users turn to an application program that constructs the object from the underlying relations.

■ PROVIDE FACILITIES FOR CONTROLLING PROCESSING

The next phrase in the purpose of a database application is *at the direction of the users.* That is, an application must provide a means for the user to direct and control activity. Three means are used. First, the user learns a set of **commands** to issue, like the following:

UPDATE CUSTOMER WHERE CustNum = 12345

SET CustBalance TO 1350

The advantage of command-driven applications is that they are direct and to the point; the user need not fuss with menus or other structures. The disadvantage

FIGURE 8-3   *Hierarchy of Menus for View Ridge Gallery—Not Using a Graphical User Interface*

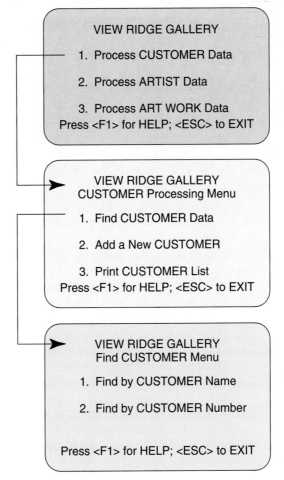

is that the end user must learn and remember the commands and their syntax. Teller processing at a bank or airline reservation processing are common command-driven applications.

The second means is application **menus.** Here the user is given one or more menus from which to make choices. Menus that the View Ridge Gallery could use are shown in Figure 8-3. Their advantage is that the end user need not remember command syntax or even which commands are suitable in a particular situation, because the system leads the user through the appropriate choices. The disadvantage of menu-driven applications is that they seem cumbersome to experienced users.

Today, most new applications provide a control via the features of a **graphical user interface** like that on the Apple Macintosh and that on computers using Microsoft's Windows. Such interfaces include pull-down menus, icons, dialogue boxes, mice support, and other facilities that greatly enhance the application's ease of use. Because of their intuitive nature and the standardized mode of processing, such interfaces have become common for new database applications. Figure 8-4 shows an example of GUI menus that View Ridge might use.

■ PROTECT SECURITY AND INTEGRITY

The phrase *while at all times protecting the security and integrity of the database* means that the application should be designed so that only authorized users can perform

FIGURE 8-4   *Graphical User Interface for Menus Shown in Figure 8-3*

authorized activities with valid data. Again, this is far easier to state as a goal than it is to accomplish in practice. Application designers, however, must keep this goal in mind.

There are many sources of errors and problems. Common sources are keystroke mistakes and erroneous input data (on source documents, for example). Also, end users sometimes perform operations out of sequence or perform invalid operations. Sometimes end users try to perform operations that they are not trained, qualified, or authorized to perform. Such problems are frequent and pervasive; therefore, applications must be designed either to prevent such problems or to mitigate the consequences of them when they do occur.

There are several ways in which the application developer can protect security and integrity. First, passwords and other controls can be established, as described in Chapter 12. Second, the developer can encode constraint enforcement into programs that update data. In addition, forms can be designed to eliminate errors. For example, a twenty-five-character text field can be displayed in a window of only twenty-five spaces. Menus can be designed so that only those commands suitable for a particular context can be executed from that context.

Security and integrity protection must be incorporated into the applications from the start. All too often, this is done only after problems have been detected, and at this point it is usually far more difficult to implement such protection.

■ A CONTINUUM OF APPLICATIONS

A database application is the interface between the user and the database. Although all applications have the functions described in the previous section, not all are equivalent. In fact, there is a continuum of applications. (See Figure 8-5.) On the high end, some provide extensive services on behalf of the user. They obtain data from several relations (or even several databases), combine them in accordance with an object structure, and display and manage updates of the data in a sophisticated GUI. While doing this, the application is constantly monitoring database integrity, ensuring that the user is not violating any constraints, and performing only authorized activities. All of these activities are organized and structured so as to maximize the application's performance.

At the other end of the spectrum are applications that do little more than list tables. In Chapter 10, in our discussion of SQL, we point out that the sophisticated end user could use this language as a bare-bones application. But such an application would only process data in tables; there would be little formatting, no object structuring, and little data integrity checking. Applications on the left-hand side of Figure 8-5 are relation oriented; they process just one table at a time. Those on the right-hand side of the continuum work with groups of relations—they **materialize objects and views.**

FIGURE 8-5   *An Application Continuum*

Unrestricted Use of Command Language on Relations (e.g. SQL)	Controlled Access to Relations	Uncontrolled Access to Objects	Secure and Controlled Access to Object Views

Low ◄——— Increasing Degree of Application Support ———► High

An Application Continuum

■ MATERIALIZING OBJECTS

One of the functions of a database application is to materialize objects. To understand this, consider the objects in Figure 8-2(a). Suppose that the gallery has just received a shipment of Mark Tobey lithographs and that the salespeople in the gallery want to know which customers have expressed an interest in Tobey's works. In this case, the salespeople do not want a list of all of the attributes in ARTIST; they just want the names and phone numbers of those customers who are interested in Mark Tobey. An example report is shown in Figure 8-6.

To produce the report in Figure 8-6, the database application must construct the object from the underlying relations. It must find the row in ARTIST for Mark Tobey, find all of the rows in the CUSTOMER-ARTIST-INT table that pertain to

FIGURE 8-6   *List of Customers Interested in a Given Artist*

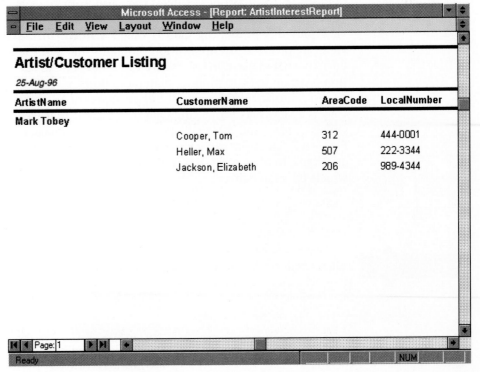

Microsoft Access - [Report: ArtistInterestReport]

File   Edit   View   Layout   Window   Help

Artist/Customer Listing

25-Aug-96

ArtistName	CustomerName	AreaCode	LocalNumber
Mark Tobey			
	Cooper, Tom	312	444-0001
	Heller, Max	507	222-3344
	Jackson, Elizabeth	206	989-4344

Page: 1

Ready   NUM

Mark Tobey, and, from each row, extract the value of CustNumber (according to the design in Figure 8-2[b]). This value of CustNumber is then used to look up the customers' names and phone numbers in the CUSTOMER table.

The process just described is what is meant by materializing an object. In general, such materialization is one of the most important functions of an application, as it saves the user from having to understand all of the tables and from having to learn how to bring the data in those tables together.

■ OBJECT VIEWS

In most applications, the users seldom want to see all of the data in an object at one time; they usually want to process a subset of the object's data. In Figure 8-6, for example, the salespeople did not want to see all of Mark Tobey's works, nor did they want to see all of the data about customers interested in Mark Tobey. They wanted only a subset of the ARTIST data.

The need to process subsets of objects occurs because although the users process the same object, they often do not see this object from the same perspective. For instance, the salespeople want to know who might buy a Tobey lithograph but the gallery owner wants to know how profitable Tobey's work has been for the gallery.

An **object view,** or **user view** or **view,** is a named subset of an object. A view is described by naming the object on which it is based and listing the attributes of the object that are visible from that view.

The creation of views is especially important to security and control. With views, sensitive data can be hidden from all but authorized users. For example, a personnel administration system contains an object called EMPLOYEE, which includes Salary. Because not all users may need to work with Salary data, one view can be defined for the EMPLOYEE object to enable those who need Salary to see it, and another view can be defined without Salary for those who do not need its data.

A view is a list of an object's visible attributes. In most cases, users want more than just a list of attribute values; they also want the view data to be formatted. That is, they want labels, lines, boxes, indentations, control breaks, and the like. A view plus this formatting data is called a **materialization.** Normally, object views are processed by application programs that add the formatting data to produce the materialization, and so we can restate one of the purposes of an application program to be to produce materializations of views of objects.

To summarize, a view is a list of attributes of an object. A materialization of a view is a view plus formatting data that exhibit that view in a particular format. Objects, views, and materializations have a hierarchical relationship, as shown in Figure 8-7. An object can have many views, and each view can have many materializations. In most cases, the application program receives the view data and constructs the materialization.

 Hierarchical Relationships of Object, View, and Materialization

FORM DESIGN

A **form** is a screen display used for data entry and edit. Read-only forms can also be used to report data, but in most cases, when developers speak of forms, they mean those used for data entry and edit.

Some forms are easy to use and result in few data entry errors. Others seem awkward and contrived and are difficult to use without creating errors. In this section, we discuss and illustrate several principles of good form design.

■ THE FORM STRUCTURE SHOULD REFLECT THE OBJECT STRUCTURE

First, to seem natural and be easy to use, *the structure of a form must reflect the structure of the object that it materializes.* Look at the form in Figure 8-8, which is a materialization of a view of the CUSTOMER object in the View Ridge database (Figure 8-2[a]).

The structure of this form reflects the structure of the CUSTOMER object. One section of the form has the basic customer data such as Name, Phone, and Address. The second section shows the customer's ARTIST interests. Finally, the third section lists the customer's purchases (of WORKs). Users find this form easy to use because the attributes are grouped in a way that reflects their understanding of the structure of the customer data.

In general, when designing a form, all of the data from a single relation should be placed in one contiguous section of the form. Assuming that the database is in domain/key normal form (which it should be), each relation should pertain to a specific theme, and the user should expect to have in one location all of the data for that theme. Thus CUSTOMER, ARTIST (labeled Interests) and WORK (labeled Purchases) are contiguous on the form in Figure 8-8.

FIGURE 8-8   *Materialization of View of CUSTOMER Object*

Microsoft Access - [CUSTOMER]

File   Edit   View   Records   Window   Help

CUSTOMER

CustomerName: Jackson, Elizabeth
AreaCode: 206
LocalNumber: 989-4344
Street: 123 - 44th Avenue
City: Seattle
State: WA
Zip: 98112

Interests

ArtistName
► Mark Tobey
Juan Miro
Dennis Frings
*

Assign ARTIST

[   ] [±] [Add]

Purchases

Title	Copy	ArtistName	
► South Toward Emerald Seas	106/195	Dennis Frings	
*			

Record: 1

Form View

There is one exception to this rule: Attributes in the base relation of the object (here, the relation CUSTOMER) are sometimes not placed contiguously. Suppose, for example, that CUSTOMER had a simple attribute named TotalPurchases. If we followed this rule, we would place TotalPurchases in the first section of the form. But it would be more sensible to the users to place that attribute at the end of the form, after all of the purchases have been listed.

The form in Figure 8-8 is not the only acceptable form of this view. Purchases could be placed before Interests, for example. The base CUSTOMER data could be rearranged to be more horizontal in appearance. CustomerName, AreaCode, and LocalNumber could be placed in one column, and Street, City, State, and Zip could be placed in another. All of these alternatives enable the structure of the form to reflect the structure of the underlying objects.

■ THE SEMANTICS OF THE DATA SHOULD BE GRAPHICALLY EVIDENT

Another characteristic of a well-designed form is that the semantics of the data are graphically evident. Consider the base customer data section of the CUSTOMER form in Figure 8-8. Observe that there is a small space between the data entry box for CustomerName and AreaCode but that there is no such space between AreaCode and LocalNumber. In fact, AreaCode and LocalNumber are placed adjacent to each other, and Street, City, State, and Zip are also placed adjacent to one another.

To understand why this is done, refer again to Figure 8-2(a). The CUSTOMER semantic object has a group attribute named Phone and another group attribute named Address. Since both of these attributes have a maximum cardinality of 1, they are—from the standpoint of the relational design—not really required. In fact, they do not appear in the relations in Figure 8-2(b) or (c). The only purpose of these group attributes is to semantically associate AreaCode with LocalNumber and Street and City, State, and Zip with one another.

The purpose of the vertical spacing in the CUSTOMER form is to make these associations graphically clear. Most users are comforted by the arrangement of the attributes in the CUSTOMER form. Knowing that phone number consists of AreaCode and LocalNumber, they find the graphically close association of those two to be very sensible.

■ THE FORM STRUCTURE SHOULD ENCOURAGE APPROPRIATE ACTION

The structure of forms should make it easy to perform appropriate actions and difficult to perform inappropriate or erroneous actions. For example, the field for entering State in the form in Figure 8-8 is small. Clearly, the user is supposed to enter only a two-digit state abbreviation. But a better design would allow only two digits to be entered, and the best design would present the states in a drop-down list and allow the user to choose from only that list.

In Figure 8-8, some fields in the form are white, and others are gray. The forms in this application have been designed so that the user can enter data only in the white spaces; the gray data items cannot be changed. Thus, the user cannot type into the Interests grid and instead must select from the combo box at the bottom of the grid. When the user clicks on the arrow, a drop-down list of available artists is displayed, as shown in Figure 8-9. If the user wants to add a new artist, he or she presses the button labeled Add, and the application brings the artist form to the screen.

Now suppose that the user wants to change some artist data—say, the spelling of Mark Tobey's name. The designer of the form in Figure 8-8 made it impossible to change that data in this form. Instead, the user places the mouse pointer on the name Mark Tobey and double-clicks the left button on the mouse. When this is

FIGURE 8-9

Form with Drop-down List Box

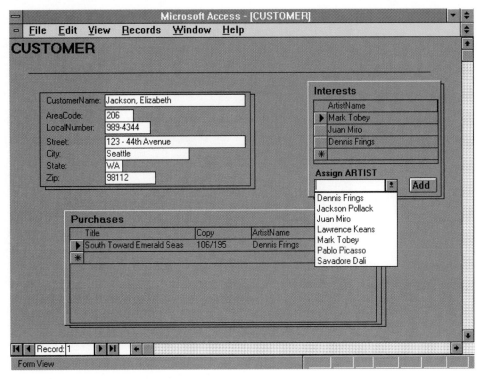

done, the application displays the ARTIST form shown in Figure 8-10. The user can then change the spelling of Mark Tobey in this form.

The form in Figure 8-8 cannot be used to change artist data, but the one in Figure 8-10 can. Why? The relationship between ARTIST and CUSTOMER is many to many. If the user could change artist data from the CUSTOMER form, the user would be changing data not only for this particular customer's linkage to that artist but also for all customers' linkages to that artist. This action, however, is not apparent in the form in Figure 8-8. According to that form, the user is aware only that Elizabeth Jackson is somehow connected to Mark Tobey.

When making changes in the artist data using the form in Figure 8-10, however, the user is aware that this change is affecting not only Elizabeth Jackson but also Tom Cooper and Max Heller. The structure of the forms thus makes it difficult for the user unknowingly to make mistakes.

■ FORMS IN A GUI ENVIRONMENT

A number of form features peculiar to GUI systems can dramatically facilitate the use of database applications.

DROP-DOWN LIST BOXES   A **drop-down list box** is a GUI control that presents a list of items from which the user can choose. There are two types of list boxes. With one type, the list is fixed; users cannot add to it. With the other, users can both add to and select from the list. The choice between the two types depends on the requirements of the application. The list box shown in Figure 8-9 has a fixed list; the users cannot add to the list.

List boxes have a number of advantages over data entry text boxes. First, human beings find it easier to *recognize* than to *recollect*. For example, in the form in Figure 8-9, it is easier to choose an artist's name from the list than it is to remember

FIGURE 8-10   *Materialization of View of ARTIST Object*

all of the artists' names. It is also easier to recognize a name than it is to spell it correctly. Finally, list boxes can be set up to display only those values present in the database, which means that the user cannot enter an invalid item.

OPTION BUTTONS AND GROUPS   An **option button,** or **radio button,** is a display device that enables users to select one alternative condition or state from a list of possibilities. For example, suppose the gallery decides that it needs to track the tax status of its customers. Assume that tax status has two possibilities, Taxable and Nontaxable, and that these possibilities are mutually exclusive. An option group like the one shown in Figure 8-11 could be used to gather this data. Because of the way that the option group works, if the user selects Taxable, then Nontaxable is automatically removed from the list. If the user selects Nontaxable, then Taxable is automatically removed.

Behind the form, the application program must store data in a table column that represents the radio button selected. For this example, the column is named TaxStatus. One of two possible ways for storing the option button data is used. One is to store an integer number from 1 to the number of buttons. In this example, one of the values 1 or 2 would be stored. The second option is to store a text value that describes the option chosen. The possibilities are Yes or No.

CHECK BOXES   **Check boxes** are similar to option buttons except that the alternatives in a group of check boxes are not mutually exclusive—more than one alternative may be chosen. Suppose, for example, that the gallery wants to record the type or types of art in which its customers are interested. The possible types are Lithographs, Oils, Pastels, and Photographs, shown in a series of check boxes in the version of the CUSTOMER form in Figure 8-12. The user selects or *checks* the appropriate boxes.

There are a number of ways of representing check boxes in relations. One common and simple way is to define a Boolean-valued column for each item in the

FIGURE 8-11   *CUSTOMER Form with Option Button Group*

FIGURE 8-12   *CUSTOMER Form with Check Boxes*

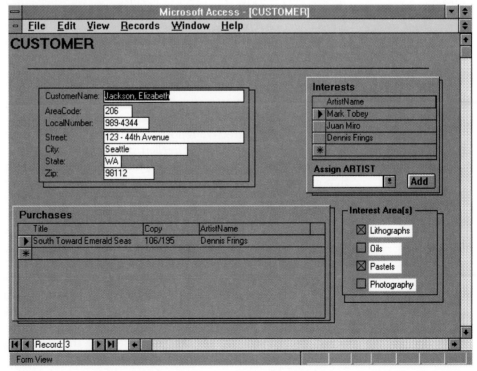

check box group. The value of each of such columns is binary; that is, it can be 1 or 0, representing yes or no. There are other possibilities, such as encoding bits in a byte, although they are not important to our discussion.

CURSOR MOVEMENT AND PERVASIVE KEYS

Another consideration in forms design is the action of the cursor. The cursor should move through the form easily and naturally. This usually means that the cursor follows the end user's processing pattern as he or she reads the source data entry documents. If forms are used to enter data over the telephone, the cursor should control the flow of the conversation. In this case, its movement should progress in a manner that the customer finds natural and appropriate.

Cursor movement is especially important during and after an exception condition. Suppose that in using the form in Figure 8-10, an error is made—perhaps an invalid state code is entered. The form should be processed so that the cursor moves to a logical location. For example, the application might display a list box of available state values and place the cursor on a logical position in the list—perhaps on the first state that starts with the first letter the user entered. When the state is selected, the cursor should move back to Zip, the next appropriate space on the form.

The actions of special-purpose keys such as ESC and function keys should be *consistent* and *pervasive*. If ESC is used to exit forms, use it consistently for this purpose and none other (except for actions that are logically equivalent to exiting from forms). The actions of the keys should be consistent throughout the application. That is, if ESC is used to exit from one form, it should be used to exit from all forms. If Cntrl-D is used to delete data in one form, it should be used to delete data in all forms. Otherwise, habits formed in one portion of the application must be disregarded or relearned in other portions of the application. This is wasteful, frustrating, and aggravating, and it causes errors. Although these comments may seem obvious, attention to such details is what makes a form easy and convenient to use.

REPORT DESIGN

The subject of report design, even more so than form design, has been discussed extensively in texts on application development. We will not duplicate or even attempt to summarize those discussions here but, rather, look at several concepts directly related to the notion of a report as a materialization of a semantic object.

REPORT STRUCTURE

The principles of effective report design are similar to those for form design. Just as with forms, *the structure of a report should reflect the structure of the underlying object.* This means that data from one table should generally be located in one contiguous group on the report. As with forms, one exception to this rule is that the base relation of the object (for example, the CUSTOMER relation for the CUSTOMER object) may be separated on the report. Attribute groups, like Phone, should also be located together and distinguished in some way.

Figure 8-13 shows a sample report for the View Ridge Gallery that lists the data for each work of art and the transactions for each work of art, computes the gross margin by work and artist, as well as a grand total.

The structure of the report in Figure 8-13 reflects the structure of the WORK object. The section for each work begins with the name of the work, which includes artist, title, and copy. Next is a section of repeating lines that shows the transactions for the work. Within each section, the name of the customer has been found from the CUSTOMER table.

FIGURE 8-13   *Sales Listing Report*

Sales Listing
15-Nov-96

ArtistName	Title		Copy		

Dennis Frings   South Toward Emerald Sea   106/195

DateAcquired	AcquisitionPrice	DateSold	Sold To	SalesPrice	GrossMargin
4/17/86	$750.00	5/3/86	Heller, Max	$1,000.00	$250.00
3/15/96	$1,200.00	5/11/96	Jackson, Elizabeth	$1,800.00	$600.00

Total margin for South Toward Emerald Seas, Copy 106/195   **$850.00**

Total margin for Dennis Frings   **$850.00**

Mark Tobey   Patterns III   27/95

DateAcquired	AcquisitionPrice	DateSold	Sold To	SalesPrice	GrossMargin
7/3/71	$7,500.00	9/11/71	Cooper, Tom	$10,000.00	$2,500.00
1/4/86	$11,500.00	3/18/86	Jackson, Elizabeth	$15,000.00	$3,500.00
9/11/95	$17,000.00	10/17/95	Cooper, Tom	$21,000.00	$4,000.00

Total margin for Patterns III, Copy 27/95   **$10,000.00**

Mark Tobey   Rhythm   2/75

DateAcquired	AcquisitionPrice	DateSold	Sold To	SalesPrice	GrossMargin
4/8/93	$17,000.00	7/14/93	Heller, Max	$27,000.00	$10,000.00

Total margin for Rhythm, Copy 2/75   **$10,000.00**

Total margin for Mark Tobey   **$20,000.00**
Grand Total: **$20,850.00**

We describe in Chapter 11 how this report is produced. For now, just note that its structure does, in fact, reflect the fundamental structure of the object. Because of this characteristic, the report seems useful and familiar to its users.

■ IMPLIED OBJECTS

Consider the request "Print all WORKs Sorted by Total Margin." At first glance, this appears to be a request to print a report about the object WORK. The words *sorted by,* however, indicate that more than one WORK is to be considered. In fact, this request is not based on the object WORK but, rather, is based on the object SET OF ALL WORKs. The report in Figure 8-13 shows data for multiple WORKs and is, in fact, based on the object SET OF ALL WORKs, not on the object WORK.

The human mind is so quick to shift from the object *OBJECT-A* to the object *SET OF ALL OBJECTS-A* that we normally do not even know there has been a change. When developing database applications, however, it is important to notice this shift because the application needs to behave differently when it occurs. Consider three ways in which sorting can change the nature of the base object: (1) sorting by object identifier; (2) sorting by nonidentifier, nonobject columns; and (3) sorting by attributes contained in object attributes.

FIGURE 8-14   *PHONE-REGION Object*

SORTED BY OBJECT IDENTIFIER   If the report is to be sorted by an attribute that is an identifier of object, the true object is the collection of those objects. Thus, an ARTIST report sorted by ArtistName is a report about the object SET OF ALL ARTISTS. For most DBMS report-writing products, a report about the object SET OF ALL X is no more difficult to produce than a report about object X. It is important to know, however, that there has been a shift in object type.

SORTED BY NONIDENTIFIER, NONOBJECT COLUMNS   When a user needs a report sorted by an attribute that is a nonidentifier of the object, the true object in the user's mind is most likely a totally different type of object. For example, the user wants to produce a report about ARTIST sorted by Nationality. Such a report is actually a materialization of a NATIONALITY object, not a materialization of the ARTIST object. Similarly, if the user asks for a report about CUSTOMER sorted by AreaCode, the report is actually based on an object called PHONE-REGION, or some similar object. Figure 8-14 shows an example PHONE-REGION object.

Some objects such as NATIONALITY or PHONE-REGION are **implied objects;** that is, their existence can be inferred by the fact that the user asked for such a report. If it makes sense to the user to ask for something as a sort value, then that something must be an object in the user's mind, regardless of whether it is modeled in the database or not.

SORTED BY ATTRIBUTES CONTAINED IN OBJECT ATTRIBUTES   The third way in which reports can be sorted is by attributes contained in object attributes. For example, the user might ask for a report about WORKs sorted by Birthdate of ARTIST. ARTIST is an object attribute of WORK, and Birthdate is an attribute contained in ARTIST. In this case, the user is actually asking for a report about an implied object (say, TIME or ARTISTIC PERIOD) that contains many ARTISTs, each of which includes many WORKs in the gallery.

Understanding this switch in objects may ease the task of developing the report. Proceeding as if WORK were the base object of the report will make the report logic contrived. If WORK is considered the base, the materializations of WORK objects that include ARTIST and Birthdate must be created for all WORK objects, stored on disk, and then sorted by Birthdate. On the other hand, if this report is about an implied object that contains ARTIST, which in turn contains WORK, then ARTIST objects can be created and sorted by Birthdate and WORK objects treated as multivalued rows in each ARTIST object.

APPLICATION PROGRAM DESIGN

Literally hundreds of books have been written about application program design, and it is not possible here to summarize even the basic schools of thought concerning this subject. Instead, we focus only on those aspects of program design that pertain directly to database processing.

■ THE STRUCTURE OF APPLICATION PROGRAM LOGIC

Some experts, notably Michael Jackson and those who follow his line of reasoning, state that the structure of a program should mirror the structure of the data that it processes.[1] If one adheres to that design philosophy, the data model and database design will offer rich and valuable guidelines for designing the structure of application logic.

Consider, for example, an application program that displays a CUSTOMER object. Pseudocode for the logic of such a program is shown in Figure 8-15. Observe the similarity in the structure of the object and that of the pseudocode. In the first

FIGURE 8-15   *Pseudocode for Program to Display CUSTOMER and Related WORK Objects*

Get CustNumber from User.

Display form headings for CUSTOMER.

Read CUSTOMER table using CustNumber as key.

Display Name, AreaCode, LocalNumber, Street, City State, Zip on form.

Read First WORK row using CustNumber as foreign key.

Display column headings for WORK display grid.

Do Until WORK.EndOfFile.

    Display ArtistName, Title, Copy, Description on form.

    Read ARTIST row using ArtistName as key.

    Display ArtistName, Nationality on form.

    Read First TRANSACTION row using (ArtistName, Title, Copy) as partial key.

    Display column headings for TRANSACTION display grid.

    Do Until TRANSACTION.EndOfFile.

        Display DateAcquired, AcquisitionPrice, PurchaseDate, SalesPrice on form.

        Read Next TRANSACTION row using (ArtistName, Title, Copy) as partial key.

    End Do.

    Display Column footings for TRANSACTION display grid.

    Read Next WORK row using CustNumber as foreign key.

End Do.

Display column footings for WORK display grid.

[Logic to process the ARTIST property of CUSTOMER could go here.}

Display column footings for CUSTOMER form.

[1]Michael Jackson, *Principles of Program Design* (New York: Academic Press, 1975).

FIGURE 8-16   *Example of a Mandatory-to-Mandatory Constraint: (a) Sample Mandatory-to-Mandatory Relationship and (b) Sample Data for It*

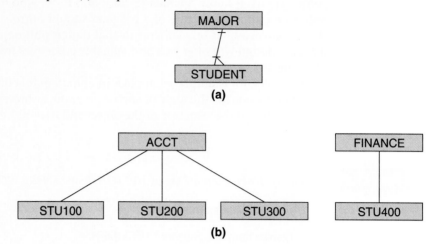

section, the program obtains a value for the key of CUSTOMER. Then the customer data are displayed, and a grid is set up to show the multivalued attribute WORK.

Next the program loops through all of the WORK rows that have CustNumber equal to the given number. For each such row, the identifying data are displayed, and ARTIST Nationality is obtained and displayed. Then another grid and loop are set up to process each of the TRANSACTION rows that pertains to this particular WORK.

In general, any program that processes a multivalued attribute must contain iteration logic structure for that attribute. If there are nested multivalued attributes, there will be nested iterations, and if there are serial multivalued attributes, there will be serial iterations in the program.

■ RELATIONSHIP CONSTRAINT CHECKING

The processing of updates for database applications differs in one important regard from the processing of updates in nondatabase applications: When processing updates, the application must be certain to preserve the constraints defined in the database data. In this section we consider constraints that arise from relationships, and in the next, we look at other types of constraints.

Figure 8-16 depicts the relationship between MAJOR and STUDENT relations. As shown in Figure 8-16(a), a MAJOR must have at least one STUDENT, and a STUDENT must have exactly one MAJOR. When users update either of these relations, the application program must make sure that these constraints are not violated (we assume in this section that such checking is not done by the DBMS). In Figure 8-16(b), for example, if a user attempted to delete the row for Student 400, the application program should deny this request. If the request were allowed, the row for FINANCE would not have a child row, and the mandatory constraint would be violated. Similarly, a new MAJOR, say BIOLOGY, cannot be added until there is a student who is majoring in that subject.

A row that exists inappropriately without a required parent or child is sometimes called a **fragment,** and child rows that exist without a mandatory parent are sometimes called **orphans.** One of the functions of an application program is to prevent the creation of fragments and orphans.

TYPES OF RELATIONSHIP CONSTRAINT   The means of preventing fragments depends on the type of constraint. Figure 8-17 shows examples of the four possible kinds of constraints: mandatory to mandatory (M–M), mandatory to optional (M–O), optional to mandatory (O–M), and optional to optional (O–O). These con-

FIGURE 8-17

Examples of the Four Types of Relationship Constraints: (a) Mandatory-to-Mandatory (M–M) Constraint, (b) Mandatory-to-Optional (M–O) Constraint, (c) Optional-to-Mandatory (O–M) Constraint, and (d) Optional-to-Optional (O–O) Constraint

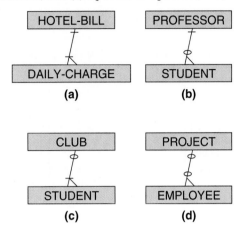

straints are shown on one-to-many relationships, but the same four types also apply to one-to-one relationships. We need not be concerned with many-to-many relationships constraints, as they will have been converted to one-to-many relationships by defining the intersection tables.

Constraints can be violated whenever there are changes in the key attributes (whether local or foreign), because changes in key values have the effect of changing the parent-child relationship. For example, in Figure 8-15(b), changing the major of Student 300 from ACCT to FINANCE reassigns that student to the finance department. Although this results in a change of parent, it does not cause a constraint violation.

Such a violation will be committed, however, if the major of Student 400 is changed to ACCT. When this is done, FINANCE no longer has any majors, and so the M–M constraint between MAJOR and STUDENT is violated. As another example, in Figure 8-17(a), a change in the HOTEL-BILL InvoiceNumber invalidates the relationship carried by the foreign key, InvoiceNumber, in DAILY-CHARGE. All of the DAILY-CHARGE rows for the changed invoice become orphans.

Figure 8-18 presents rules for preventing fragments for each of these types of constraints. Figure 8-18(a) concerns actions on the parent row, and Figure 8-18(b) concerns actions on the child rows. As these figures indicate, the possible actions are to insert new rows, modify key data, and delete rows. Figure 8-18 lists the rules for one-to-many relationships; the rules for one-to-one relationships are similar.

RESTRICTIONS ON UPDATES TO PARENT ROWS The first row of Figure 8-18(a) concerns M–M constraints. A new parent row can be inserted only if at least one child row is being created at the same time, which can be done by inserting a new child row or by reassigning a child from a different parent (however, this latter action may itself cause a constraint violation).

A change in the key of a parent is permitted in an M–M relationship only if the values in the corresponding foreign key in the child rows also are changed in the new value. (It is possible to reassign all of the children to another parent and then create at least one new child for the parent, but this seldom is done.) Thus, changing the Invoice in HOTEL-BILL is allowed as long as the Invoice is changed in all the appropriate DAY-CHARGE rows as well.

Finally, a parent of an M–M relationship can be deleted as long as all of the children also are deleted or are reassigned.

FIGURE 8-18   *Rules for Preventing Fragments: (a) Conditions for Allowing Changes in Parent Records and (b) Conditions for Allowing Changes in Child Records*

Proposed Action on Parent

Type of Relationship		Insert	Modify (key)	Delete
	M-M	Create at least one child	Change matching keys of all children	Delete all children OR Reassign all children
	M-O	OK	Change matching keys of all children	Delete all children OR Reassign all children
	O-M	Insert new child OR Appropriate child exists	Change key of at least one child OR Appropriate child exists	OK
	O-O	OK	OK	OK

(a)

Proposed Action on Child

Type of Relationship		Insert	Modify (key)	Delete
	M-M	Parent exists OR Create parent	Parent with new value exists (or create one) AND Sibling exists	Sibling exists
	M-O	Parent exists OR Create parent	Parent with new value exists OR Create parent	OK
	O-M	OK	Sibling exists	Sibling exists
	O-O	OK	OK	OK

(b)

In regard to M–O constraints, a new parent can be added without restriction, since parents need not have children. For the relationship in Figure 8-17(b), a new PROFESSOR row can be added without restriction. A change in the parent's key value, however, is permitted only if the corresponding values in the child rows are changed as well. If a PROFESSOR in the relationship in Figure 8-17(b) changes his or her key, the value of Adviser in all of that professor's advisees' rows also must be changed.

Finally, in a relationship with an M–O constraint, the parent row can be deleted only if all the children are deleted or reassigned. For the PROFESSOR-STUDENT relationship, all of the student rows would probably be reassigned.

For O–M constraints, a parent can be inserted only if at least one child is added at the same time or if an appropriate child already exists. For the O–M relationship between CLUB and STUDENT in Figure 8-17(c), for example, a new club can be added only if an appropriate STUDENT row can be created (by either adding a new student or changing the value of CLUB in an existing STUDENT). Alternatively, an appropriate student row may already exist.

Similarly, the key of the parent of an O–M relationship may be changed only if a child is created or if a suitable child row already exists. That is, the Ski Club can change its name to Scuba only if at least one skier is willing to join Scuba or if a student has already enrolled in Scuba. There are no restrictions on the deletion of a parent row in an O–M relationship.

The last type of relationship constraint, O–O, is shown in Figure 8-17(d). There are no restrictions on any type of update on rows in an O–O relationship. Both PROJECT and EMPLOYEE rows can be updated as necessary.

RESTRICTIONS ON UPDATING CHILD ROWS   The rules for preventing fragments when updating child rows are shown in Figure 8-18(b) and are similar to those in Figure 8-18(a). The one notable difference is that in several cases, child rows can be modified or deleted as long as sibling rows exist. For example, in an M–M constraint, a child row can be deleted as long as there are siblings in existence. (The last child never leaves home!) For the M–M constraint in Figure 8-17(a), a particular DAY-CHARGE row can be deleted as long as at least one remains.

With the exception of the considerations regarding siblings, the rules for avoiding fragments when processing child rows are similar to those for parents. Make certain you understand each statement in Figure 8-18(b).

Many of the rules in Figure 8-18 offer several alternatives, and the application program developer must select one of them. The choice depends on the requirements of the application. The point to remember is that you must consider such constraints when designing and developing application programs.

■ OTHER TYPES OF CONSTRAINT CHECKING

There are types of constraints besides those that arise from relationships. One common constraint is uniqueness. In some cases, the values of attributes or of composites of attributes must be unique. Many DBMS products are capable of enforcing this type of constraint, and if so, the application program is freed of the burden.

With regard to uniqueness, observe that requiring the composite (AreaCode, LocalNumber) to be unique is different from requiring the attributes (AreaCode) and (LocalNumber) to be independently unique. The second case is far more restrictive than the first. For example, in the first case, there can be only one (206, 325–1876). In the second case, there can be only one 206 and only one 325–1876. Some DBMS products do not support composite uniqueness, and, as you can see, this can be a problem.

Another common type of constraint is null, or unknown, values. For example, if the value of ShippingMode is null, this means that the shipping mode is either zero (for numeric attributes) or a blank (for text attributes). However, the meaning of the null value is ambiguous.

Nulls can arise in one of two ways. Either no value has ever been entered into the database, or no value is appropriate. These two are not logically the same. If ShippingMode has the value null, it might mean that the mode of shipment is unknown or that a value is inappropriate. A SALES-ORDER used for consulting services does not have a meaningful ShippingMode.

We discuss nulls further in later chapters. For now, it is enough to know that some DBMS products can enforce the constraint that *nulls are not allowed*. Others cannot, however, and in that case, the enforcement is up to the application program.

Finally, some constraints do not fall into any of these types. There might be the constraint that if the SALESPERSON resides in a region east of the Mississippi, the value of ShippingMode cannot equal 1-Day. Few DBMS products provide robust means of defining and enforcing such constraints. Today, almost all products require that such constraints be written into the application program.

■ THE USE OF APPLICATION PROGRAMS IN BACKUP AND RECOVERY

We address strategies for providing backup and recovery in Chapter 12. For now, however, you should know that the backup and recovery of concurrently processed databases require application programs to define transaction boundaries to the DBMS. These boundaries, called logical transactions or **logical units of work,** define a set of atomic actions. By atomic, we mean that either all of the actions are performed or none of them is.

To understand the need for atomicity, suppose that a user is entering data for a new WORK, and after several TRANSACTIONs have been created, the computer system fails. In this case, only a portion of the WORK data has been entered into the database. When the system recovers and the user reenters the WORK, it is possible that some TRANSACTIONs will be duplicated.

To prevent this from happening, the application program can define boundaries of atomicity for the DBMS. The means by which this is done varies from DBMS product to DBMS product, but in general, before processing any transactions, the application issues a command like START TRANSACTION (other terms are used synonymously). Then the application program processes the users' requests to a logically consistent end point (the end of a WORK object, for example).

If all processing has been done correctly, the application program will issue a command like END TRANSACTION, COMMIT, or some other equivalent command. At this point, the DBMS makes permanent all the changes in the database. If there has been a problem during processing, the application program will issue a command like ROLL BACK, thus telling the DBMS to remove all the changes made since the START TRANSACTION command. If the application program is abnormally terminated because of a system failure or an unexpected program termination, no END TRANSACTION command will be received, and the DBMS will remove the provisional changes.

The reason for introducing this topic here is that the definition of an object also defines the boundaries of the logical transaction. The start transaction is issued when the application program begins work on the object, and the end transaction is issued when all the object attributes have been processed.

◆ SUMMARY

The purpose of a database application is to create, update, delete, and display objects (or views of entities) at the users' direction while at all times protecting the security and integrity of the database. Before objects can be processed, they must be constructed, or materialized, from the underlying relations. When objects are updated, the data must be correctly modified while the constraints are enforced. Furthermore, if the database is concurrently processed, the updates must be controlled so that the actions of one user do not interfere with those of another.

The application must provide a means for the user to direct and control activities. Three strategies are used. With command-driven applications, the users are given a set of commands to do their work. The commands are direct and to the point, but users must memorize them and their syntax. Menu-driven applications provide a list of items from which users choose. Recently, a new style of control interface, the graphical user interface, has been devised and includes pull-down menus, icons, dialogue boxes, mice, and other facilities.

Database applications must protect the security and integrity of the database. They should be designed to enable authorized users to perform authorized activities, to provide accurate and helpful error messages when mistakes are made, and to prohibit unauthorized users and unauthorized activities.

Database applications differ in character along a continuum. At the high end, some applications offer extensive services on behalf of the user; they materialize complicated objects and present them in a sophisticated GUI. At the other end of the continuum, some applications do little more than list tables.

Applications materialize objects by combining data from one or more relations in accordance with the defined object structure. An object view is a subset of an object utilized by a particular user or group of users. Views can be described by naming the object on which they are based and listing the visible attributes. A materialization of a view is a view plus display data such as labels, lines, boxes, and other window dressing. An object can have many views, and a view of an object can have many materializations.

A form is a screen display that is most often used for data entry and edit, although forms are sometimes used for display. Not all forms are equal. For a form to be easy to use, its structure must reflect the structure of the object that it materializes. Forms should also make the semantics of the data graphically evident, and they should be structured so as to encourage the appropriate action.

Several form features are peculiar to GUI systems, including drop-down list boxes, option buttons, and check boxes. Such facilities are effective ways of materializing objects. Forms should be designed so that the movement of the cursor is natural to the user—for both normal use and exceptions. Moreover, the meaning and use of keys should be consistent throughout the application.

Reports also should be designed so that their structure reflects the structure of the object they materialize. Report sorting often implies the existence of other objects. If the sorting is done by the object identifier, the report concerns a collection of objects of this type. If the sorting is done by a nonidentifier attribute, the report concerns an object of a different type, called an implied object. If the sorting is done by an attribute contained in an object attribute, the report is about an implied object of that other object. The report will be easier to produce if the entry point of the object is considered to be the relation from which the sort field arises.

When designing application programs, the structure of the application program logic should also reflect the structure of the object that it processes. Multivalued attributes or groups require iteration structures.

Application programs have an important role in enforcing data constraints. There are four types of relationship constraints: M–M, M–O, O–M, and O–O. Changes in key values can alter relationships and possibly violate these constraints. Such changes should be disallowed when necessary.

Other types of constraints include attribute value uniqueness constraints and null values constraints. In some cases, composites of attributes are constrained to be unique. Null values indicate either that a value is unknown or that it is inappropriate. Sometimes the constraint is that null values are not allowed for attributes.

For backup and recovery in concurrent systems, application programs must define transaction boundaries with START TRANSACTION, END TRANSACTION, and ROLL BACK commands (or their equivalent). Object definitions can be used to establish these boundaries.

GROUP I QUESTIONS

8.1 State the purpose of a database application.

8.2 Explain the special tasks that the application must perform when adding, updating, or deleting objects.

8.3 Explain why relations are more frequently queried than objects.

8.4 What are the three principal means by which users control applications? Summarize the advantages and disadvantages of each.

8.5   What does GUI stand for, and how does it relate to database applications?

8.6   Summarize the role of database applications with regard to security and integrity.

8.7   Describe the continuum of applications discussed in this chapter.

8.8   Explain the difference between applications that are relation oriented and those that are semantic object oriented.

8.9   Explain the term *materialize objects*.

8.10 Define *view*. What constitutes a view?

8.11 Explain the difference between the terms *materialize an object* and *materialize a view of an object*.

8.12 Diagram the relationship of objects, views, and materializations.

8.13 Define *form*.

8.14 Explain the meaning of the phrase *a form should reflect object structure*. Why is a form with this characteristic easy to use?

8.15 Give a general rule for locating data on a form. What data should be physically contiguous?

8.16 Describe a circumstance in which it would make sense to place data from the base relation of an object at both the top and the bottom of a form that materializes a view of that object.

8.17 Explain the meaning of the phrase *data semantics should be graphically evident*. Why is this important?

8.18 Explain the meaning of the phrase *form structure should encourage appropriate action*.

8.19 What is a drop-down list box? Describe three advantages of such controls.

8.20 What is an option button? An option button group? Under what conditions would these controls be useful on a form? How would the underlying data be stored?

8.21 What are check boxes? Under what conditions would they be useful on a form? How would the underlying data be stored?

8.22 Describe the general design considerations regarding the cursor's movement on a form.

8.23 What is a pervasive key? Why are such keys desirable?

8.24 What should the relationship be between reports and object structures?

8.25 Explain why sorting implies a change in the object being processed.

8.26 Consider the object STUDENT with identifier StudentNumber and nonidentifier, nonobject attribute DateEnrolled. Suppose that STUDENT contains a single-valued object attribute DORMITORY, which contains an attribute DormName. Describe the object implied when producing reports about STUDENT that are sorted in the following way:

a. by Student

b. by DateEnrolled

c. by StudentLastName (a nonobject attribute of STUDENT)

d. by DormName

8.27 What general rule pertains to the relationship of the structure of a program and the structure of an object that it processes?

8.28 What is a fragment? An orphan?

8.29 Describe four types of relationship constraint. Give an example of each type, other than those in this book.

8.30 Explain the use of the rules in Figure 8-18 for each type of relationship constraint in your answer to Question 8.29.

8.31 What is a null value? What meaning does a null value have?

8.32 What role does an application have in enforcing rules concerning null values?

8.33 What role does an application have in enforcing rules concerning uniqueness constraints?

8.34 How does the statement that FirstName must be unique and LastName must be unique differ from the statement that (FirstName, LastName) must be unique? Which of these two statements is more restrictive?

8.35 What is a logical unit of work? What is a set of atomic actions? Why are these important?

8.36 What role does an application have in defining logical units of work?

GROUP II QUESTIONS

8.37 Consider a database application that is used to manage the access of students to a microcomputer lab at a university. Assume that the application is used to schedule student appointments for equipment at the lab and also to check out optional hardware or software. Assume, too, that only authorized students may use the lab and that therefore students must be preenrolled in the database before they can schedule an appointment. Finally, assume that when a student schedules an appointment, he or she must indicate the class for which the appointment is made. This means class data must also be stored. Finally, assume that the objects in Figure 8-19 are to be stored.

a. Transform the objects in Figure 8-19 into normalized relations, and indicate the key of each relation.

b. Design a data entry form for the STUDENT and the APPOINTMENT objects. Be certain your forms follow the design guidelines in this chapter.

FIGURE 8-19   *Objects for Question 8.37*

    c. Design a report to display the COMPUTER object. Be certain your report follows the design guidelines in this chapter. Explain how the underlying object changes when this report is sorted by ComputerNumber, by AcquisitionDate, and by StudentName.

    d. Show the basic logic of an application program that creates a new APPOINTMENT. Assume that all required CLASS, STUDENT, and COMPUTER objects already exist.

    e. Do you think there should be a separate object for SOFTWARE? Justify your answer. How would the application change if there were a separate SOFTWARE object?

8.38 Modify Figure 8-18 to describe the update rules for one-to-one relationships. Explain each entry.

PROJECT USING SALSA FOR THE DESKTOP

Use SALSA (for installation instructions, see the SALSA Projects at the end of Chapter 4, page 106) to create the semantic objects shown in Figure 8-2. Generate the application and open the WORK form. Evaluate this form on the basis of the form design principles in this chapter. In what ways does the form evidence or not evidence these principles? Comment on characteristics of the way that SALSA lets the user utilize the form. Would it be easy to use? Is the interface consistent? How could it be better? Print or preview the WORK report. Comment on the structure of this report in light of the principles discussed in this chapter. Add, modify, and delete data using all three forms. Does SALSA enforce the constraints listed in Figure 8-18? Explain why or why not.

Part IV considers database implementation using the relational model. It begins, in Chapter 9, with a discussion of relational data manipulation. First we look at the types of relational data manipulation languages, and then we explain the basic operators of relational algebra and illustrate their use.

Chapter 10 describes Structured Query Language, or SQL. This language has been endorsed by the American National Standards Institute as a standard for manipulating relational databases, and it also is the primary data manipulation language for commercial relational DBMS products. The concepts presented in these two chapters are illustrated in Chapter 11 where we describe the implementation of a database for the View Ridge Gallery case introduced in Chapter 8. The implementation uses Microsoft Access, a relational DBMS for personal computers.

DATABASE IMPLEMENTATION WITH THE RELATIONAL MODEL

CHAPTER

9

FOUNDATIONS OF RELATIONAL IMPLEMENTATION

• • • • • • • • • • • • •

This and the next two chapters discuss the implementation of relational databases. We begin in this chapter by describing relational data definition, reviewing relational terminology, and explaining how a design is defined to the DBMS. Next we turn to space allocation and database data creation. The remainder of the chapter addresses relational data manipulation: first, a survey of four types of relational data manipulation language (DML), then the three common modes of DML interfaces to the DBMS, and finally, the basic operators of relational algebra and example queries expressed in terms of relational algebra.

◆ DEFINING RELATIONAL DATA

Several tasks must be performed when implementing a relational database. First, the structure of the database must be defined to the DBMS. To do this, the developer uses a data definition language (DDL) or some equivalent means (such as a graphical display) to describe the structure. Then the database is allocated to physical storage media and filled with data. In this section we discuss each of these tasks, but first we review the relational terminology.

■ REVIEW OF TERMINOLOGY

As stated in Chapter 5, a **relation** is a table that has several properties:

1. The entries in the relation are single valued; multiple values are not allowed. Hence, the intersection of a row and a column contains only one value.

2. All the entries in any column are of the same kind. For example, one column may contain customer names and another, birthdates. Each column has a unique name, and the order of the columns is not important to the relation. The columns of a relation are called **attributes.** Each attribute has a **domain,** which is a physical and logical description of allowed values.

3. No two rows in the relation are identical, and the order of the rows is not important (see Figure 9-1). Each row of the relation is known as a tuple.

Figure 9-1 is an example, or occurrence. The generalized format, PATIENT (Name, Age, Gender, AccountNumber, Physician), is the relation structure and is

FIGURE 9-1   *Occurrence of PATIENT Relation Structure*

	Col 1 (or Attribute 1)	Col 2	Col 3	Col 4	Col 5
	Name	Age	Gender	Account Number	Physician
Row 1 (or Tuple 1)	Riley	56	F	147	Lee
Row 2	Murphy	17	M	289	Singh
Row 3	Krajewski	25	F	533	Levy
Row 4	Ting	67	F	681	Spock
Row 5	Dixon	17	M	704	Levy
Row 6	Abel	41	M	193	Singh

what most people mean when they use the term *relation.* (Recall from Chapter 5 that an underlined attribute is a key.) If we add constraints on allowable data values to the relation structure, we then have a **relational schema.**

Although relations are defined in the formal terms *relation, attribute,* and *tuple,* the informal terms *table, column,* and *row* are often used synonymously. Sometimes, too, the terms *file, field,* and *record* are used as synonyms. These terms are summarized in Figure 9-2.

CONFUSION REGARDING THE TERM *KEY*   The term **key** is a common source of confusion because it has different meanings in the design and the implementation stages. During the design, the term *key* refers to one or more columns that uniquely identify a row in a relation. As we explained in Chapter 5, we know every relation has a key because every row is unique; at the limit, the composite of every column in the relation is the key. Usually the key is composed of one or two columns, however.

During implementation, the term *key* is used differently. For most relational products, a key is a column on which the DBMS builds an index or other data structure. This is done to access rows quickly by means of that column's value. Such keys need not be unique, and often, in fact, they are not. They are constructed only to improve performance. (See the appendix for information about such data structures.)

For example, consider the relation ORDER (<u>OrderNumber</u>, OrderDate, CustNumber, Amount). From the standpoint of relational *design,* the key of this relation is OrderNumber, since the underline means OrderNumber uniquely identifies rows of the relation. From the standpoint of relational *implementation,* however, any of the four columns could be a key. OrderDate, for example, could be defined as a key. If it is, the DBMS will create a data structure so that ORDER rows can be quickly accessed by the value of OrderDate. Most likely, there will be many rows for a given value of OrderDate. Defining it as this type of key says nothing about its uniqueness.

Sometimes the terms **logical key** and **physical key** are used to distinguish between these two meanings of key. A logical key is a unique identifier, whereas a physical key is a column that has a special data structure defined for it in order to improve performance. A logical key need not be a physical key, and a physical key need not be a logical key.

INDEXES   Since a physical key is usually an index, some people reserve the term *key* for a logical key and use the term *index* for a physical key. In this text, we will do exactly that—use the term *key* to mean a logical key, and use the term *index* to mean a physical key.

FIGURE 9-2   *Summary of Relational Terminology*

Term	Meaning
Relation (or Table) (or File)	Two-dimensional table
Attribute (or Column) (or Field) (or Data Item)	Column of a relation
Tuple (or Row) (or Record)	Row in a relation
Domain	Physical and logical description of allowed values
Relation structure	Format of relation
Occurrence	Relation structure with data
Relational schema	Relation structure plus constraints
Key	Group of one or more attributes that uniquely identifies a tuple in a relation
Logical key	Same as key
Physical key (or Index)	A group of one or more attributes that is supported by a data structure that facilitates fast retrieval or rapid sequential access

There are three reasons for defining indexes. One is to allow rows to be quickly accessed by means of the indexed attribute's value. The second is to facilitate sorting rows by that attribute. For instance, in ORDER, OrderDate might be defined as a key so that a report showing orders by dates can be more quickly generated.

A third reason for building an index concerns uniqueness. Although indexes do not have to be unique, when the developer wants a column to be unique, an index is created by the DBMS. This index is used to ensure that no duplicated values are accepted by the DBMS. With most relational DBMS products, a column or group of columns can be forced to be unique by using the keyword UNIQUE when defining the appearance of a column in a table.

■ IMPLEMENTING A RELATIONAL DATABASE

In this text, we use the relational model to express database designs. Since we have done so, we can proceed directly from designing the database to implementing it. There is no need to transform the design during the implementation stage; we simply define the existing relational design to the DBMS.

The situation is different when we implement databases using DBMS products based on data models other than the relational model. For example, when imple-

FIGURE 9-3   *Example DDL Text File for Database Definition*

```
CREATE SCHEMA PHYSICIAN

CREATE TABLE PATIENT

    ( Name                CHARACTER VARYING (35) NOT NULL,
      Age                 SMALLINT,
      Gender              CHARACTER VARYING (10),
      AccountNumber       INTEGER NOT NULL,
      PhysicianName_FK1   CHARACTER VARYING (35) NOT NULL,

      PRIMARY KEY ( AccountNumber ),
      FOREIGN KEY ( PhysicianName_FK1 )
          REFERENCES PHYSICIAN
    )

CREATE TABLE PHYSICIAN

    ( PhysicianName       CHARACTER VARYING (35) NOT NULL,
      AreaCode            CHARACTER VARYING (3),
      LocalNumber         CHARACTER VARYING (8) NOT NULL,

      PRIMARY KEY (PhysicianName)
    )
```

menting a database for a CODASYL DBTG DBMS, we must convert the relational design to a CODASYL DBTG design and then define the converted design to the DBMS product. You will see examples of such design transformations in Chapter 18.

DEFINING THE DATABASE STRUCTURE TO THE DBMS   There are a number of different means by which the structure of the database is described to the DBMS, depending on the DBMS product being used. With some products, a text file is constructed that describes the database structure. The language used to describe such a structure is sometimes called the **data definition language,** or DDL. The DDL text file names the tables in the database, names and describes the columns of those tables, defines indexes, and describes other structures such as constraints and security restrictions. Figure 9-3 shows the typical data definition language used for defining a simple relational database for a hypothetical DBMS. A more realistic example of such a language for the DBMS product DB2 is shown in Chapter 13.

Some DBMS products do not require that the database be defined by DDL in text file format. One common alternative is to provide a graphical means for defining the structure of the database. With Access, for example, the developer is shown a graphical list structure and asked to fill in the table and column names in the appropriate places. We saw an example of this in Chapter 2 (Figure 2-4).

In general, graphical definition facilities are common for DBMS products on personal computers and textual DDL is common for DBMS products on servers and mainframes. ORACLE and DB2, for example, both employ text files for database structure definition. Figure 9-4 summarizes the database definition process.

Regardless of the means by which the database structure is defined, the developer must name each table, define the columns in that table, and describe the physical format (for example, TEXT 10) of each column. Also, depending on the facilities of the DBMS, the developer may specify constraints that the DBMS is to enforce. Column values can be defined to be NOT NULL or UNIQUE, for example. Some products also allow the definition of range and value constraints (Part less than 10000 or Color equal to one of ['Red', 'Green', 'Blue'], for example). Finally, interrelation constraints can be defined. An example is that DeptNumber in EMPLOYEE must match a value of DeptNumber in DEPARTMENT.

FIGURE 9-4   *Database Definition Process*

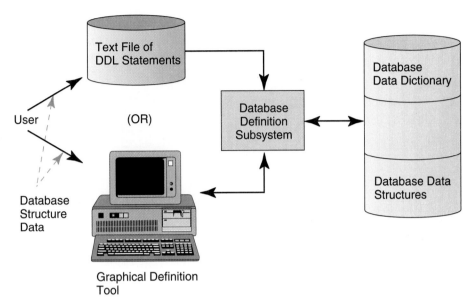

With many products, the developer can also define passwords and other control and security facilities. As shown in Chapter 12, a number of different strategies can be used. Some strategies place controls on data constructs (passwords on tables, for example), and others place controls on people (the user of password X can read and update tables T1 and T2).

ALLOCATING MEDIA SPACE   In addition to defining the structure of the database, the developer must allocate database structures to physical media. Again, the specific tasks depend on the particular DBMS product used. For a personal database, all that needs to be done is to assign the database to a directory and give the database a name. The DBMS then allocates storage space automatically.

Other DBMS products, especially those used for servers and mainframes, require more work. To improve performance and control, the distribution of the database data across disks and channels must be carefully planned. For example, depending on the nature of application processing, it may be advantageous to locate certain tables on the same disk, or it may be important to ensure that certain tables are not located on the same disk.

Consider, for example, an order object that is composed of data from ORDER, LINE-ITEM, and ITEM tables. Suppose that when processing an order, the application retrieves one row from ORDER, several rows from LINE-ITEM, and one row from ITEM for each LINE-ITEM row. Furthermore, the LINE-ITEM rows for a given order tend to be clustered together, but the ITEM rows are not at all clustered. Figure 9-5 illustrates this situation.

Now suppose that an organization concurrently processes many orders and has one large, fast disk and one smaller, slower disk. The developer must determine the best place to locate the data. One possibility is that the performance will be better if the ITEM table is stored on the larger, faster disk and the ORDER and LINE-ITEM data on the smaller, slower disk. Or perhaps the performance will be better if the ORDER and LINE-ITEM data for prior months' orders are placed on the slower disk and all the data for this month's orders are placed on the faster disk.

We cannot answer this question here, as the answer depends on the amount of data, the processing characteristics of the DBMS and the operating system, the size and speed of the disks and channels, and the application-processing requirements of all applications that use the database. The point is that factors such as these must be considered when allocating media space to the database.

FIGURE 9-5   *Example Data for Three Tables Representing an Order*

ORDER table	LINE-ITEM table			ITEM table	
Order Number	Order-Number	LINE-Number	ITEM-Number	ITEM-Number	ITEM-DESCRIPTION
100	100	1	10	10	A
200	100	2	70	20	B
300	100	3	50	30	C
	200	1	50	40	D
	200	2	10	50	E
	300	1	60	60	F
	300	2	10	70	G
	300	3	50		
	300	4	20		
	300	5	30		

Note: For a given order, LINE-ITEM rows are clustered, but ITEM rows are not.

CREATING THE DATABASE DATA   Once the database has been defined and allocated to physical storage, it can be filled with data. The means by which this is done depends on the application requirements and the features of the DBMS product. In the best case, all of the data are already in a computer-sensible format, and the DBMS has features and tools to facilitate importing the data from magnetic media. In the worst case, all of the data must be entered via manual key entry using application programs created from scratch by the developers. Most data conversions lie between these two extremes.

Once the data are input, they must be verified for accuracy. Verification is a labor-intensive and tedious but important task. Often, especially for large databases, it is well worth the time and expense for the development team to write verification programs. Such programs count the number of records of various categories, compute control totals, perform reasonableness checks on data item values, and provide other kinds of verification.

RELATIONAL DATA MANIPULATION

So far in this text, we have discussed the design of relational databases and the means by which such designs are defined to the DBMS. Whenever we have referred to processing relations, we have done so in a general and intuitive manner. Although this is fine for discussing designs, to implement applications we need clear, unambiguous languages for expressing processing logic.

■ CATEGORIES OF RELATIONAL DATA MANIPULATION LANGUAGE

To date, four different strategies for relational data manipulation have been proposed. **Relational algebra,** the first of the strategies, defines operators that work on relations (akin to the operators +, −, and so forth of high school algebra). Relations can be manipulated using these operators to achieve a desired result. But relational algebra is hard to use, partly because it is procedural. That is, when using relational algebra we must know not only *what* we want but also *how* to get it.

Relational algebra is infrequently used in commercial database processing. Although a few commercially successful DBMS products do provide relational algebra facilities, these facilities are seldom used because of their complexity. Even

FIGURE 9-6   *Four Categories of Relational DML*

- Relational algebra
- Relational calculus
- Transform-oriented languages (such as SQL)
- Query-by-example/Query-by-form

so, we will discuss relational algebra here, as it helps clarify relational manipulation and establishes a foundation on which to learn SQL.

Relational calculus is a second type of relational data manipulation. Relational calculus is nonprocedural; it is a language for expressing what we want without expressing how to get it. Recall the variable of integration in calculus, which ranges over an interval to be integrated. Relational calculus has a similar variable. For tuple relational calculus, the variable ranges over the tuples of a relation, and for domain relational calculus, the variable ranges over the values of a domain. Relational calculus is derived from a branch of mathematics called predicate calculus.

Unless you are going to become a theoretician of relational technology, you will probably not need to learn relational calculus. It is never used in commercial database processing, and the little use it once had is declining in importance. Therefore, we do not discuss relational calculus in this text.

Although relational calculus is hard to understand and use, its nonprocedural property is highly desirable. Therefore, DBMS designers looked for other nonprocedural techniques, which led to the third and fourth categories of relational DML.

Transform-oriented languages are a class of nonprocedural languages that transform input data expressed as relations into results expressed as a single relation. These languages provide easy-to-use structures for expressing what is desired regarding the data supplied. SQUARE, SEQUEL, and SEQUEL's offspring, SQL, all are transform-oriented languages. We study SQL in depth in the next chapter.

The fourth category of relational DML is graphical. **Query-by-Example** and **Query-by-Form** fall into this category. Products that support this category include Approach (from Lotus), Access, and SALSA for the Desktop. With a graphical interface, the user is presented a materialization of one or more relations. The materialization might be a data entry form, it might be a spreadsheet, or it might be some other structure. The DBMS maps the materialization to the underlying relation and constructs queries (most likely in SQL) on behalf of the user. The users are then causing the execution of DML statements, but they are unaware of that fact. The four categories of relational DML are listed in Figure 9-6.

■ DML INTERFACES TO THE DBMS

As we pointed out in Chapter 2, there are several different ways that users can interface to a database: They can use the form and report capabilities supplied by the DBMS; they can access the database via a query/update language; or they can process the database through application programs that access the database by means of DBMS commands.

DATA MANIPULATION BY MEANS OF FORMS Most relational DBMS products include tools for building forms. Some of these are created automatically when a table is defined, but others must be created by the developer, perhaps with intelligent assistance like that provided by Access's Wizards. A form may be tabular, like a spreadsheet, in which case it shows multiple rows at a time, or the form may show each row as an independent entity. Figures 9-7 and 9-8 show an example of

FIGURE 9-7   *Example of a Tabular Default Screen Form*

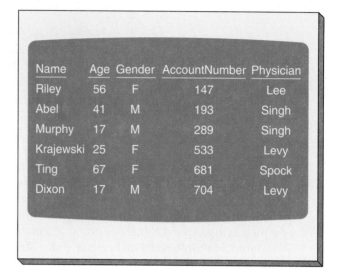

Name	Age	Gender	AccountNumber	Physician
Riley	56	F	147	Lee
Abel	41	M	193	Singh
Murphy	17	M	289	Singh
Krajewski	25	F	533	Levy
Ting	67	F	681	Spock
Dixon	17	M	704	Levy

FIGURE 9-8   *Example of a Single-Row Default Screen Form*

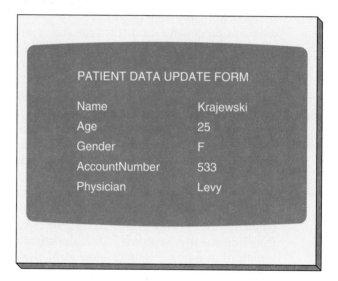

PATIENT DATA UPDATE FORM

Name	Krajewski
Age	25
Gender	F
AccountNumber	533
Physician	Levy

each for the PATIENT table in Figure 9-1. With most products, some flexibility is provided in the processing of the forms and reports. For example, rows can be selected for processing based on column values, and they can also be sorted. The table in Figure 9-7 is sorted by AccountNumber.

Many of the default forms present data from only a single relation at a time. If data are required from two or more relations, then customized forms must be created using DBMS tools. It is possible for both multitable and multirow forms to be created using such tools. The use of such tools is very specific to the product, however, and so we do not discuss them further here. Some of the tools for Microsoft Access are described in Chapter 11.

QUERY/UPDATE LANGUAGE INTERFACE   The second type of interface to a database is via a **query/update language,** or simply a **query language.** (Although most such languages perform both query and update, they are generally referred to as query languages.) With this type, the user enters query commands that specify actions on the database. The DBMS decodes the commands and carries out the appropriate actions. Figure 9-9 shows the programs involved in query processing.

FIGURE 9-9   *Programs Involved in Query Processing*

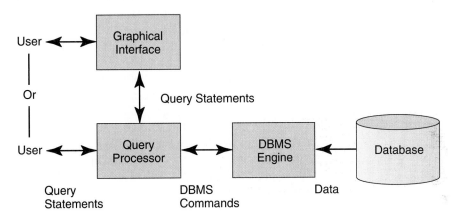

The single most important query language is SQL. To give you an idea of query languages, consider the following SQL statement that processes the relation PATIENT (Name, Age, Gender, AccountNumber, Physician) shown in Figure 9-1:

SELECT   Name, Age
FROM   PATIENT
WHERE   Age > 50

This SQL query statement extracts all the rows from the relation PATIENT in which the patient's age is greater than 50. It then displays the Name and Age for the qualifying rows in a second table.

Query languages were developed to provide a robust interface to the database that does not require writing traditional computer programs in a procedural language. This was especially important before the advent of the microcomputer. At that time, when most databases resided on mainframes, there was not enough processing power at the users' terminals to create and process the sophisticated forms and reports that are so common today. Query languages were thus a way of giving the nonprogramming user access to a database.

STORED PROCEDURE INTERFACE   Although query languages are simpler than computer-programming languages, they have generally proved to be too complicated for the average end user. Consequently, many end users have specialists write the query procedures, which are stored as files. Such procedures can be written to be parameter driven, thereby enabling the users to execute them when they change the data. As an example, the following command invokes a query procedure called BILLING and gives it a date value:

DO BILLING FOR BDATE = '9/15/1996'

Stored queries are similar in character to the BATCH files on DOS systems, although the commands are processed by the DBMS and not by the operating system (COMMAND.COM in DOS).

When query procedures are stored and processed in this way, there is, in fact, little difference in concept between them and the stored programs that are written in a traditional programming language. The primary justification for their use is productivity, as stored query procedures are often quicker for the specialist to write.

APPLICATION PROGRAM INTERFACE   The third type of data access interface is through application programs written in programming languages such as COBOL, BASIC, Perl, Pascal, and C++. In addition, some application programs are written in languages provided by the DBMS vendors, of which the dBASE programming language is the best known.

There are two styles of application program interface to the DBMS. In one, the application program makes subroutine calls to routines in a subroutine library provided with the DBMS. For example, to read a particular row of a table, the application program calls the DBMS read routine and passes parameters that indicate the table to be accessed, the data to be retrieved, the criteria for row selection, and the like.

Accessing the DBMS via a subroutine call can be complicated. The parameters to be passed may be complex, and often complicated shared data areas must be set up and maintained. Such programming is time-consuming and often error prone. To overcome these disadvantages, many DBMS products offer a second style of program interface in which they define a set of high-level data access commands. These commands—which are peculiar to database processing and not part of any standard language—are embedded in the application program code.

The application program, with embedded commands, is then submitted to a precompiler provided by the DBMS vendor. This precompiler translates the data access statements into valid subroutine calls and data structure definitions. In this process, the precompiler sets up parameter sequences for the calls and defines data areas that will be shared between the application program and the DBMS. The precompiler also inserts program logic to maintain the data areas. Then the precompiled routine is submitted to the language compiler. Figure 9-10 shows the relationships of the programs involved in this process.

In addition to its role in query processing, SQL is also used as a data access language in application programs. In this mode, SQL statements are embedded in the programs and translated into subroutine calls by a precompiler. Training costs and learning time are reduced, since the same language can be used for access to both query and application programs. There is one problem to be overcome, however. SQL is a transform-oriented language that accepts relations, manipulates them, and outputs a result relation. Thus, it deals with relations one at a time. Almost all application programs are row (record) oriented; that is, they read one row, process it, read the next row, and so forth. Such programs deal with a row at a time.

Thus, there is a mismatch in the basic orientation of SQL and application program languages. To correct for this mismatch, the results of SQL statements are assumed, in the application program, to be files. To illustrate, assume that the following SQL statement (the same as that earlier) is embedded in an application program:

FIGURE 9-10   *Processing Program with Embedded DML Statements*

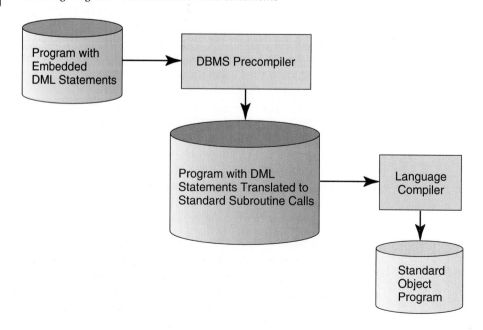

```
SELECT    Name, Age
FROM      PATIENT
WHERE     Age > 50
```

The result of these statements is a table with two columns and N rows. In order to accept the results of this query, the application program is written to assume that these statements have produced a file with N records. The application opens the query, processes the first row, processes the next row, and so forth, until the last row has been processed. This logic is the same as that for processing a sequential file. You will see examples of such application programs in Chapter 13. For now, just be aware that there is a mismatch in the basic orientation of SQL (relation oriented) and programming languages (row, or record, oriented) and that this mismatch must be corrected when programs access a relational database via SQL.

RELATIONAL ALGEBRA

Relational algebra is similar to the algebra you learned in high school, but with an important difference. In high school algebra, variables represented numbers, and operators like $+$, $-$, $\times$, and $/$ operated on numeric quantities. In relational algebra, however, the variables are relations, and the operators manipulate relations to form new relations. For example, the union operation combines the tuples of one relation with the tuples of another relation, thereby producing a third relation. In fact, relational algebra is *closed*, which means that the results of one or more relational operations are *always* a relation.

Relations are sets. The tuples of a relation can be considered elements of a set, and so operations that can be performed on sets can also be performed on relations. We first show four such set operators and then discuss other operators that are peculiar to relational algebra. Before proceeding, however, consider the following sample relations that we will use in this and the next chapter.

■ RELATIONAL OPERATORS

Figure 9-11 shows six relations and their attribute and domain definitions. Note that the attribute Name is used in several relations. When we refer to a specific attribute, we qualify it with its relation name. Accordingly, Name in CLASS is sometimes denoted as CLASS.Name.

Also, observe that the physical description of the Ages and the ClassSizes domains is the same, yet the domains are different. This is because their logical description is different; they are not the same semantically, since they do not represent the same attributes. The integer 21 in Ages represents 21 years, but the same integer 21 in ClassSizes refers to the number of people in a class. Thus the value 21 represents two entirely different characteristics.

In the following discussion, character values are shown in single quotes, and those characters not in quotes represent names. Thus 'ROOM' differs from Room because 'ROOM' is a value, whereas Room is, say, a domain name. In regard to numeric data, those numbers not in quotes refer to numeric quantities, and those numbers in quotes refer to character strings. Thus, 123 is a number, and '123' is a string of the characters '1', '2', and '3'.

UNION   The **union** of two relations is formed by adding the tuples from one relation to those of a second relation to produce a third relation. The order in which the tuples appear in the third relation is not important, but duplicate tuples must be eliminated. The union of relations A and B is denoted A + B.

For this operation to make sense, the relations must be **union compatible;** that is, each relation must have the same number of attributes, and the attributes in corresponding columns must come from the same domain. If, for example, the

FIGURE 9-11 *Examples of Relations and Domains: (a) Relation Definitions, (b) Attribute Domains, and (c) Domain Definitions*

1. JUNIOR (<u>Snum</u>, Name, Major)
2. HONOR-STUDENT (<u>Number</u>, Name, Interest)
3. STUDENT (<u>SID</u>, Name, Major, GradeLevel, Age)
4. CLASS (<u>Name</u>, Time, Room)
5. ENROLLMENT (<u>StudentNumber</u>, <u>ClassName</u>, PositionNumber)
6. FACULTY (<u>FID</u>, Name, Department)

(a)

	Attribute	Domain
1.	Snum	PeopleIdentifiers
	JUNIOR.Name	PeopleNames
	Major	SubjectNames
2.	Number	PeopleIdentifiers
	HONOR-STUDENT.Name	PeopleNames
	Interest	SubjectNames
3.	SID	PeopleIdentifiers
	STUDENT.Name	PeopleNames
	Major	SubjectNames
	GradeLevel	Classes
	Age	Ages
4.	CLASS.Name	ClassNames
	Time	ClassTimes
	Room	Rooms
5.	StudentNumber	PeopleIdentifiers
	ClassName	ClassNames
	PositionNumber	ClassSizes
6.	FID	PeopleIdentifiers
	FACULTY.Name	PeopleNames
	Department	SubjectNames

(b)

third attribute of one relation comes from the Ages domain, the third attribute of the second relation must also come from the Ages domain.

In Figure 9-11, the JUNIOR and the HONOR-STUDENT relations are union compatible because they both have three attributes, and the corresponding attributes come from the same domain. JUNIOR.Snum and HONOR-STUDENT.Number come from the domain PeopleIdentifiers; JUNIOR.Name and HONOR-STUDENT.Name have the domain PeopleNames; and JUNIOR.Major and HONOR-STUDENT.Interest have the domain SubjectNames. The relations JUNIOR and CLASS both have three attributes, but they are **union incompatible** because the three attributes do not have the same domain.

Figure 9-12 shows the union of the JUNIOR and HONOR-STUDENT relations. Note that the tuple [123, JONES, HISTORY], which occurs in both relations, is not duplicated in the union.

DIFFERENCE   The **difference** of two relations is a third relation containing tuples that occur in the first relation but not in the second. The relations must be union compatible. The difference of JUNIOR and HONOR-STUDENT is shown in Figure 9-13. As in arithmetic, the order of the subtraction matters, and so A − B is not the same as B − A.

FIGURE 9-11 *(Continued)*

Domain Name	Format
PeopleIdentifiers	Decimal (3)
PeopleNames	Char (8) (unrealistic, but handy for these examples)
SubjectNames	Char (10)
Classes	One of [FR, SO, JR, SN, GR]
Ages	Decimal from 0 to 100
ClassNames	Char (5)
ClassTimes	Char (5) format: DDDHH, where D is one of [M, T, W, R, F, or blank], and HH is decimal between 1 and 12
Rooms	Char (5) format: BBRRR, where BB is a building code, and RRR, is a room number
ClassSizes	Decimal from 0 to 100

(c)

FIGURE 9-12 *JUNIOR and HONOR-STUDENT Relations and Their Union: (a) Example JUNIOR Relation, (b) Example HONOR-STUDENT Relation, and (c) Union of JUNIOR and HONOR-STUDENT Relations*

Snum	Name	Major
123	JONES	HISTORY
158	PARKS	MATH
271	SMITH	HISTORY

(a)

Number	Name	Interest
105	ANDERSON	MANAGEMENT
123	JONES	HISTORY

(b)

Snum or Number	Name	Major or Interest
123	JONES	HISTORY
158	PARKS	MATH
271	SMITH	HISTORY
105	ANDERSON	MANAGEMENT

(c)

INTERSECTION The **intersection** of two relations is a third relation containing the tuples that appear in both the first and second relations. Again, the relations must be union compatible. In Figure 9-14 the intersection of JUNIOR and HONOR-STUDENT is the single tuple [123, JONES, HISTORY], which is the only tuple that occurs in both JUNIOR and HONOR-STUDENT.

FIGURE 9-13   *JUNIOR Minus HONOR-STUDENT Relation*

Snum	Name	Major
158	PARKS	MATH
271	SMITH	HISTORY

FIGURE 9-14   *Intersection of JUNIOR and HONOR-STUDENT Relations*

Snum or Number	Name	Major or Interest
123	JONES	HISTORY

FIGURE 9-15   *Examples of (a) STUDENT and (b) ENROLLMENT Relations*

SID	Name	Major	GradeLevel	Age
123	JONES	HISTORY	JR	21
158	PARKS	MATH	GR	26
105	ANDERSON	MANAGEMENT	SN	27
271	SMITH	HISTORY	JR	19

(a)

StudentNumber	ClassName	PositionNumber
123	H350	1
105	BA490	3
123	BA490	7

(b)

PRODUCT   The **product** of two relations (sometimes called the **Cartesian product**) is the concatenation of every tuple of one relation with every tuple of a second relation. The product of relation A (having *m* tuples) and relation B (having *n* tuples) has *m* times *n* tuples. The product is denoted A × B or A TIMES B. In Figure 9-15, the relation STUDENT has four tuples, and the relation ENROLLMENT has three. STUDENT TIMES ENROLLMENT therefore has twelve tuples, which are shown in Figure 9-16. (The resulting relation in Figure 9-16 contains some meaningless tuples. Other operations, shown later, would need to be performed in order to extract any meaningful information from this relation. This is simply an illustration of the product operator.)

PROJECTION   **Projection** is an operation that selects specified attributes from a relation. The result of the projection is a new relation with the selected attributes; in other words, a projection chooses columns from a relation. For example, consider the STUDENT relation data in Figure 9-15(a), from which the projection of STUDENT on Name and Major attributes, denoted with brackets as STUDENT [Name, Major], is shown in Figure 9-17(a). The projection of STUDENT on Major and GradeLevel, denoted as STUDENT [Major, GradeLevel], appears in Figure 9-17(b).

Note that although STUDENT has four tuples to begin with, the projection STUDENT [Major, GradeLevel] has only three. A tuple was eliminated because after the projection was completed, the tuple [HISTORY, JR] occurred twice. Because

FIGURE 9-16   *Product of the STUDENT and ENROLLMENT Relations in Figure 9-15*

SID	Name	Major	GradeLevel	Age	Student-Number	Class-Name	Position-Number
123	JONES	HISTORY	JR	21	123	H350	1
123	JONES	HISTORY	JR	21	105	BA490	3
123	JONES	HISTORY	JR	21	123	BA490	7
158	PARKS	MATH	GR	26	123	H350	1
158	PARKS	MATH	GR	26	105	BA490	3
158	PARKS	MATH	GR	26	123	BA490	7
105	ANDERSON	MANAGEMENT	SN	27	123	H350	1
105	ANDERSON	MANAGEMENT	SN	27	105	BA490	3
105	ANDERSON	MANAGEMENT	SN	27	123	BA490	7
271	SMITH	HISTORY	JR	19	123	H350	1
271	SMITH	HISTORY	JR	19	105	BA490	3
271	SMITH	HISTORY	JR	19	123	BA490	7

FIGURE 9-17   *Projections of STUDENT Relations: (a) STUDENT [Name, Major] and (b) STUDENT [Major, GradeLevel]*

Name	Major
JONES	HISTORY
PARKS	MATH
ANDERSON	MANAGEMENT
SMITH	HISTORY

(a)

Major	GradeLevel
HISTORY	JR
MATH	GR
MANAGEMENT	SN

(b)

the result of projection is a relation and because relations cannot contain duplicate tuples, the redundant tuple is eliminated.

Projection can also be used to change the order of attributes in a relation. For example, the projection STUDENT [Age, GradeLevel, Major, Name, SID] reverses the order of STUDENT attributes (see Figure 9-11 for the original order). This feature can sometimes be used to make two relations union compatible.

SELECTION   Whereas the projection operator takes a vertical subset (columns) of a relation, the **selection** operator takes a horizontal subset (rows). Projection identifies those *attributes* to be included in the new relation, and selection identifies those *tuples* to be included in the new relation. Selection is denoted by specifying the relation name, followed by the keyword WHERE, followed by a condition involving attributes. Figure 9-18(a) shows the selection of the relation STUDENT WHERE Major = 'MATH', and Figure 9-18(b) shows the selection of STUDENT WHERE Age < 25.

JOIN   The **join** operation is a combination of the product, selection, and (possibly) projection operations. The join of two relations, say A and B, operates as follows: First, form the product of A times B. Then do a selection to eliminate some tuples (the criteria for the selection are specified as part of the join). Then (optionally) remove some attributes by means of projection.

Consider the STUDENT and ENROLLMENT relations shown in Figure 9-15. Suppose we want to know the Name and Position Number of each student. To find this out, we need to join STUDENT tuples by matching ENROLLMENT tuples based on the SID. We denote such a join as STUDENT JOIN (SID = StudentNumber)

FIGURE 9-18 *Examples of Relational Selection: (a) STUDENT WHERE Major = 'Math' and (b) STUDENT WHERE Age < 25*

SID	Name	Major	GradeLevel	Age
158	PARKS	MATH	GR	26

(a)

SID	Name	Major	GradeLevel	Age
123	JONES	HISTORY	JR	21
271	SMITH	HISTORY	JR	19

(b)

FIGURE 9-19 *Examples of Joining STUDENT and ENROLLMENT Relations: (a) Equijoin and (b) Natural Join*

SID	Name	Major	Grade-Level	Age	Student-Number	Class-Name	Position-Number
123	JONES	HISTORY	JR	21	123	H350	1
123	JONES	HISTORY	JR	21	123	BA490	7
105	ANDERSON	MANAGEMENT	SN	27	105	BA490	3

(a)

SID	Name	Major	GradeLevel	Age	ClassName	PositionNumber
123	JONES	HISTORY	JR	21	H350	1
123	JONES	HISTORY	JR	21	BA490	7
105	ANDERSON	MANAGEMENT	SN	27	BA490	3

(b)

ENROLLMENT. The meaning of this expression is "Join a STUDENT tuple to an EN-ROLLMENT tuple if SID of STUDENT equals StudentNumber of ENROLLMENT."

To form this join, we first find the product of STUDENT and ENROLLMENT, an operation that was shown in Figure 9-16. Next we SELECT those tuples from the product where SID of STUDENT equals StudentNumber of ENROLLMENT (there are only three). This operation leads to the relation in Figure 9-19(a). Note that two attributes are identical: SID and StudentNumber (Snum). One of these is redundant, so we eliminate it (in this case, we choose StudentNumber) with projection. The result is the join in Figure 9-19(b). The join in Figure 9-19(a) is called the **equijoin,** and the one in Figure 9-19(b) is called the **natural join.** Unless otherwise specified, when people say join, they mean the natural join.

Because forming the product of two large relations is time-consuming, the algorithm used by a DBMS to join two relations will be different from that described here. The result will be identical, however.

Joining on conditions other than equality also is possible. For example, STUDENT JOIN (SID not = StudentNumber) ENROLLMENT, or STUDENT JOIN (SID < FID) FACULTY. The latter join would result in tuples in which the student numbers are lower than the faculty numbers. Such a join may have meaning if, say, PeopleIdentifiers were assigned in chronological order. Such a join would portray pairs of students and teachers in such a way that the student would appear to have been at the institution longer than the teacher had.

There is one important limit on the conditions of a join: The attributes in the condition must arise from a common domain, so STUDENT JOIN (Age = ClassSize)

FIGURE 9-20 *Summary of Relational Algebra Operations*

Type	Format	Example
Set operations	+, −, intersection, product	STUDENT [Name] − JUNIOR [Name]
Selection	Relation WHERE condition	CLASS WHERE Name = 'A'
Projection	relation [list of attributes]	STUDENT [Name, Major, Age]
Join	relation 1 JOIN (condition) relation 2	STUDENT JOIN (SID = StudentNumber) ENROLLMENT

ENROLLMENT is *illogical*. Even though the values of Age and ClassSize are compatible, they do not arise from the same domain. Semantically, this type of a join makes no sense. (Unfortunately, many relational DBMS products permit such a join.)

■ EXPRESSING QUERIES IN RELATIONAL ALGEBRA

Figure 9-20 summarizes the basic relational operations just discussed. Standard set operations include +, −, intersection, and product. Selection chooses specific tuples (rows) from a relation in accordance with the conditions for attribute values. Projection chooses specific attributes (columns) from a relation by means of the attribute name. Finally, join concatenates the tuples of two relations in accordance with a condition on the values of attributes.

We now turn to how relational operators can be used to express queries, using the relations STUDENT, CLASS, and ENROLLMENT from Figure 9-11; sample data are shown in Figure 9-21. Our purpose is to demonstrate the manipulation of relations. Although you will probably never use relational algebra in a commercial environment, these examples will help you understand how relations can be manipulated.

1. What are the names of all students?

STUDENT [Name]

This is simply the projection of the Name attribute of the STUDENT relation, and the result is

Duplicate names have been omitted. Although the names JONES and BAKER actually occur twice in the relation STUDENT, repetitions have been omitted because the result of a projection is a relation, and relations may not have duplicate tuples.

2. What are the student numbers of all students enrolled in a class?

ENROLLMENT [StudentNumber]

This is similar to the first query, but the projection occurs on the relation ENROLLMENT. The result is

100
150
200
300
400

Again, duplicate tuples have been omitted.

3. What are the student numbers of all students not enrolled in a class?

STUDENT [SID] − ENROLLMENT [StudentNumber]

This expression finds the difference of the projection of two relations: STUDENT [SID] has the student numbers of all students, and ENROLLMENT

FIGURE 9-21

Example Data for Relations Defined in Figure 9-11: (a) STUDENT Relation, (b) ENROLLMENT Relation, and (c) CLASS Relation

SID	Name	Major	GradeLevel	Age
100	JONES	HISTORY	GR	21
150	PARKS	ACCOUNTING	SO	19
200	BAKER	MATH	GR	50
250	GLASS	HISTORY	SN	50
300	BAKER	ACCOUNTING	SN	41
350	RUSSELL	MATH	JR	20
400	RYE	ACCOUNTING	FR	18
450	JONES	HISTORY	SN	24

(a)

StudentNumber	ClassName	PositionNumber
100	BD445	1
150	BA200	1
200	BD445	2
200	CS250	1
300	CS150	1
400	BA200	2
400	BF410	1
400	CS250	2
450	BA200	3

(b)

Name	Time	Room
BA200	M-F9	SC110
BD445	MWF3	SC213
BF410	MWF8	SC213
CS150	MWF3	EA304
CS250	MWF12	EB210

(c)

[StudentNumber] has the student numbers of all students enrolled in a class. The difference is the number of students not enrolled in a class. The result is

4. What are the numbers of students enrolled in the class 'BD445'?

ENROLLMENT WHERE ClassName = 'BD445' [StudentNumber]

This expression selects the appropriate tuples and then projects them onto the attribute StudentNumber. The result is

5. What are the names of the students enrolled in class 'BD445'?

STUDENT JOIN (SID = StudentNumber) ENROLLMENT WHERE ClassName = 'BD445' [STUDENT.Name]

To answer this query, data from both STUDENT and ENROLLMENT are needed. Specifically, student names must come from STUDENT, whereas the condition "enrolled in BD445" must be checked in ENROLLMENT. Since both relations are needed, they must be joined. After STUDENT and ENROLLMENT have been joined, the selection is applied, followed by a projection on student names. The result is

As we stated earlier, when two or more relations are considered, attribute names can be duplicated. Therefore, for clarity, the relation name may be prefixed to the attribute name. Thus, in our example, the projection is on [STUDENT.Name]. In this example, this prefix was added only for clarity, since the attribute names are different. But when attribute names are identical (a join involving STUDENT and CLASS yields two attributes, both called Name), the prefix is required. Consider the following query:

6. What are the names and meeting times of 'PARKS' classes?
To answer this, we must bring together data in all three relations. We need STUDENT data to find PARKS's student number; we need ENROLLMENT data to learn which classes PARKS is in; and we need CLASS data to determine the class meeting times.

STUDENT WHERE Name = 'PARKS' JOIN (SID = StudentNumber) ENROLLMENT JOIN (ClassName = Name) CLASS [CLASS.Name, Time]

This expression first selects PARKS's tuple and joins it to matching ENROLLMENT tuples. Then the result is joined to matching CLASS tuples. Finally, the projection is taken to print classes and times. The result is

We must specify CLASS.Name; simply specifying Name is ambiguous because both STUDENT and CLASS have an attribute called Name.

There are other, equivalent ways of responding to this query. One is

STUDENT JOIN (SID = StudentNumber) ENROLLMENT JOIN (ClassName
= Name) CLASS WHERE STUDENT.Name = 'PARKS' [CLASS.Name, Time]

This expression differs from the first one because the selection on PARKS is not done until after all of the joins have been performed. Assuming that the computer performs the operations as stated, this expression will be slower than the earlier one because many more tuples will be joined.

Such differences are a major disadvantage of relational algebra. To the user, two equivalent queries should take the same amount of time (and hence cost the same). Imagine the frustration if one form of a query costs $1.17 and another costs $4,356. To the unwary and unsophisticated user, the cost difference appears capricious. To eliminate this problem, the DBMS must optimize relational algebra expressions before processing them.

SUMMARY

Several tasks must be carried out when implementing a relational database. First, the structure of the database must be defined to the DBMS. Then file space needs to be allocated, and finally the database is filled with data.

The relational model represents and processes data in the form of tables called relations. The columns of the tables are called attributes, and the rows are called tuples. The values of the attributes arise from domains. The terms *table, column,* and *row* and *file, field,* and *record* are used synonymously with the terms *relation, attribute,* and *tuple,* respectively.

The use of the term *key* can be confusing because it is used differently in the design and implementation stages. During design, the term means a logical key, which is one or more attributes that uniquely define a row. During implementation, the term means a physical key, which is a data structure used to improve performance. A logical key may or may not be a physical key, and a physical key may or may not be a logical key. In this text we use key to mean logical key and index to mean physical key.

Since we are using the relational model to express database designs, there is no need to transform the design during the implementation stage. We simply define the relational design to the DBMS. Two ways of defining the design are to express it in a DDL text file and to use a graphical data definition tool. In either case, the tables, columns, indexes, constraints, passwords, and other controls are defined to the DBMS.

In addition to defining the database structure, the developers must allocate media space for the database. With multiuser systems, such allocation can be important to the DBMS's effective performance. Finally, the database is filled with data using tools provided by the DBMS vendor, programs developed by the vendor, or both.

The four categories of relational data manipulation language are relational algebra, relational calculus, transform-oriented languages, and query-by-example. Relational algebra consists of a group of relational operators that can be used to manipulate relations to obtain a desired result. Relational algebra is procedural. The transform-oriented languages offer a nonprocedural means to transform a set of relations into a desired result. SQL is the most common example.

There are three means of accessing a relational database. One is to use the form and report facilities provided by the DBMS. A second is to use a query/update language, of which SQL is the most common. A third is through application programs.

Application program interfaces can be either by subroutine call or special-purpose database commands that are translated by a precompiler. The processing orientation of the relational model is relation at a time, but the orientation of most programming languages is row at a time. Some means must be devised to correct for this mismatch.

Relational algebra is used to manipulate relations to obtain a desired result. The operators are union, difference, intersection, product, projection, selection, and join.

GROUP I QUESTIONS

9.1 Name and describe the three tasks necessary to implement a relational database.

9.2 Define *relation, attribute, tuple,* and *domain.*

9.3 Explain the use of the terms *table, column, row, file, field,* and *record.*

9.4 Explain the difference between a relational schema and a relation.

9.5 Define *key, index, logical key,* and *physical key.*

9.6 Describe three reasons for using indexes.

9.7 Under what conditions is it necessary to transform the database design during the implementation stage?

9.8 Explain the term *data definition language.* What purpose does it serve?

9.9 How can a database structure be defined other than through a text file?

9.10 What aspects of a database design need to be defined to the DBMS?

9.11 Give an example, other than the one in this text, in which the allocation of the database to physical media is important.

9.12 Describe the best and worst extremes for loading the database with data.

9.13 Name and briefly explain four categories of relational DML.

9.14 Describe how relational data can be manipulated by means of forms.

9.15 Explain the role of query languages in relational data manipulation. How do stored queries differ from application programs? Why are they used?

9.16 Describe the two styles of application program interface to the database. In your answer, explain the role of a precompiler.

9.17 Describe the mismatch between the orientation of the SQL and the orientation of most programming languages. How is this mismatch corrected?

9.18 How does relational algebra differ from high school algebra?

9.19 Why is relational algebra *closed?*

9.20 Define *union compatible.* Give an example of two relations that are union compatible and two that are union incompatible.

Questions 9.21 through 9.23 refer to the following two relations:

COMPANY (<u>Name</u>, NumberEmployees, Sales)

MANUFACTURERS (<u>Name</u>, PeopleCount, Revenue)

9.21 Give an example of a union of these two relations.

9.22 Give an example of a difference of these two relations.

9.23 Give an example of an intersection of these two relations.

Questions 9.24 through 9.28 refer to the following three relations:

SALESPERSON (<u>Name</u>, Age, Salary)

ORDER (<u>Number</u>, CustName, SalespersonName, Amount)

CUSTOMER (<u>Name</u>, City, IndustryType)

FIGURE 9-22   *Sample Data for Questions 9.24 Through 9.28*

Name	Age	Salary
Abel	63	120,000
Baker	38	42,000
Jones	26	36,000
Murphy	42	50,000
Zenith	59	118,000
Kobad	27	34,000

SALESPERSON

Number	CustName	SalespersonName	Amount
100	Abernathy Construction	Zenith	560
200	Abernathy Construction	Jones	1800
300	Manchester Lumber	Abel	480
400	Amalgamated Housing	Abel	2500
500	Abernathy Construction	Murphy	6000
600	Tri-City Builders	Abel	700
700	Manchester Lumber	Jones	150

ORDER

Name	City	IndustryType
Abernathy Construction	Willow	B
Manchester Lumber	Manchester	F
Tri-City Builders	Memphis	B
Amalgamated Housing	Memphis	B

CUSTOMER

An instance of these relations is shown in Figure 9-22. Use the data in those tables for the following problems:

9.24 Give an example of the product of SALESPERSON and ORDER.

9.25 Show an example of

SALESPERSON [Name, Salary]

SALESPERSON [Age, Salary]

Under what conditions will SALESPERSON [Age, Salary] have fewer rows than SALESPERSON does?

9.26 Show an example of a select on SALESPERSON Name, on SALESPERSON Age, and on both SALESPERSON Name and Age.

9.27 Show an example of an equijoin and a natural join of SALESPERSON and ORDER in which the Name of SALESPERSON equals the SalespersonName of ORDER.

9.28 Show relational algebra expressions for

a. The names of all salespeople

b. The names of all salespeople having an ORDER row

c. The names of salespeople not having an ORDER row

d. The names of salespeople having an order with Abernathy Construction

e. The ages of salespeople having an order with Abernathy Construction

f. The city of all CUSTOMERS having an order with salesperson Jones

STRUCTURED QUERY LANGUAGE

Structured Query Language, or SQL, is the most important relational data manipulation language in use today. It has been endorsed by the American National Standards Institute (ANSI) as the language of choice for manipulating relational databases, and it is the data access language used by many commercial DBMS products, including DB2, SQL/DS, ORACLE, INGRES, SYBASE, SQL Server, dBASE for Windows, Paradox, Microsoft Access, and many others. Because of its popularity, SQL has become the standard language for information interchange among computers. Since there is a version of SQL that can run on almost any computer and operating system, computer systems are able to exchange data by passing SQL requests and responses to one another.

The development of SQL began at IBM's San Jose research facilities in the mid-1970s under the name SEQUEL. Several versions of SEQUEL were released, and in 1980 the product was renamed SQL. Since then, IBM has been joined by many other vendors in developing products for SQL. The American National Standards Institute has taken over the role of maintaining SQL and periodically publishes updated versions of the SQL standard. This chapter discusses the core of SQL as described in the 1992 ANSI standard, which is often referred to as SQL92.[1] The most recent version, SQL3, concerns extensions to the language for object-oriented programming. That version is discussed in Chapter 17.

The constructs and expressions in a particular implementation of SQL (for example, in ORACLE or SQL Server) may differ in minor ways from the ANSI standard, in part because many of the DBMS products were developed before there was agreement on the standard and also because vendors added capabilities to their products to gain a competitive advantage. From a marketing perspective, simply supporting the ANSI standard was at times judged as not having enough sizzle.

SQL commands can be used interactively as a query language, or they can be embedded in application programs. In the latter case, they are processed by a pre-compiler, as described in Chapter 9. Thus SQL is not a programming language (like COBOL); rather, it is a *data sublanguage*, or *data access language*, that is embedded in other languages.

In this chapter, we present interactive SQL statements, which need to be adjusted and modified when they are embedded in programs, as illustrated in Chapter 13. This chapter is concerned only with data manipulation statements,

---

[1]International Standards Organization Publication ISO/IEC 9075: 1992, *Database Language SQL.*

although there also are SQL commands for data definition and control, examples of which are also given in Chapter 13.

SQL is a transform-oriented language that accepts one or more relations as input and produces a single relation as output. The result of every SQL query is a relation; even if the result is a single number, that number is considered to be a relation with a single row and a single column. Thus SQL, like relational algebra, is *closed*.

QUERYING A SINGLE TABLE

In this section, we consider SQL facilities for querying a single table. We will discuss multitable and update statements later in this chapter. By custom, SQL reserved words such as SELECT and FROM are written in capital letters. Also, SQL statements are normally written in multiple lines as illustrated in this chapter. SQL language compilers do not require either capitals or multiple lines, however. These conventions are used only to provide better clarity to humans who read the SQL statements.

We use the same set of six relations with which we illustrated relational algebra in Chapter 9. The structure of those relations is shown in Figure 10-1, and sample data for three of them appears in Figure 10-2.

FIGURE 10-1   *Relations Used for SQL Examples*

1. JUNIOR (Snum, Name, Major)
2. HONOR-STUDENT (Number, Name, Interest)
3. STUDENT (SID, Name, Major, GradeLevel, Age)
4. CLASS (Name, Time, Room)
5. ENROLLMENT (StudentNumber, ClassName, PositionNumber)
6. FACULTY (FID, Name, Department)

	Attribute	Domain
1.	Snum	PeopleIdentifiers
	JUNIOR.Name	PeopleNames
	Major	SubjectNames
2.	Number	PeopleIdentifiers
	HONOR-STUDENT.Name	PeopleNames
	Interest	SubjectNames
3.	SID	PeopleIdentifiers
	STUDENT.Name	PeopleNames
	Major	SubjectNames
	GradeLevel	Classes
	Age	Ages
4.	CLASS.Name	ClassNames
	Time	ClassTimes
	Room	Rooms
5.	StudentNumber	PeopleIdentifiers
	ClassName	ClassNames
	PositionNumber	ClassSizes
6.	FID	PeopleIdentifiers
	FACULTY.Name	PeopleNames
	Department	SubjectNames

FIGURE 10-2   *Sample Data Used for SQL Examples: (a) STUDENT Relation, (b) ENROLLMENT Relation, and (c) CLASS Relation*

SID	Name	Major	GradeLevel	Age
100	JONES	HISTORY	GR	21
150	PARKS	ACCOUNTING	SO	19
200	BAKER	MATH	GR	50
250	GLASS	HISTORY	SN	50
300	BAKER	ACCOUNTING	SN	41
350	RUSSELL	MATH	JR	20
400	RYE	ACCOUNTING	FR	18
450	JONES	HISTORY	SN	24

(a)

StudentNumber	ClassName	PositionNumber
100	BD445	1
150	BA200	1
200	BD445	2
200	CS250	1
300	CS150	1
400	BA200	2
400	BF410	1
400	CS250	2
450	BA200	3

(b)

Name	Time	Room
BA200	M-F9	SC110
BD445	MWF3	SC213
BF410	MWF8	SC213
CS150	MWF3	EA304
CS250	MWF12	EB210

(c)

■ PROJECTIONS USING SQL

To form a projection with SQL, we name the relation to be projected and list the columns to be shown. Using standard SQL syntax, the projection STUDENT [SID, Name, Major] is specified as:

SELECT   SID, Name, Major
FROM   STUDENT

The keywords SELECT and FROM are always required; the columns to be obtained are listed after the keyword SELECT; and the table to be used is listed after the keyword FROM. The result of this projection for the data in Figure 10-2 is

100	JONES	HISTORY
150	PARKS	ACCOUNTING
200	BAKER	MATH
250	GLASS	HISTORY
300	BAKER	ACCOUNTING
350	RUSSELL	MATH
400	RYE	ACCOUNTING
450	JONES	HISTORY

Do not confuse the keyword SELECT with the relational algebra operator selection. SELECT is an SQL verb that can be used to perform a relational algebra projection, selection, and to specify other actions. Selection, on the other hand, differs from SELECT because it is the relational algebra operation of obtaining a subset of rows from a table.

Consider another example:

SELECT   Major
FROM   STUDENT

The result of this operation is the following:

| HISTORY |
| ACCOUNTING |
| MATH |
| HISTORY |
| ACCOUNTING |
| MATH |
| ACCOUNTING |
| HISTORY |

As you can see, this table contains duplicate rows, and consequently, in a strict sense, this table is not a relation. In fact, SQL does not automatically eliminate duplicates because such removal can be very time-consuming and, in many cases, is not desirable or necessary.

If duplicate rows must be removed, the qualifier DISTINCT must be specified, as follows:

SELECT   DISTINCT Major
FROM   STUDENT

The result of this operation is the relation

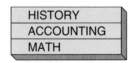

| HISTORY |
| ACCOUNTING |
| MATH |

■ SELECTIONS USING SQL

The relational algebra selection operator is also performed with the SQL SELECT command. An example is the following:

SELECT   SID, Name, Major, GradeLevel, Age
FROM   STUDENT
WHERE   Major = 'MATH'

This SELECT expression specifies the names of all the table's columns. FROM specifies the table to be used, and the new phrase, WHERE, provides the condition(s) for the selection. The format SELECT—FROM—WHERE is the fundamental structure of SQL statements. The following is an equivalent form of the preceding query:

```
SELECT    *
FROM      STUDENT
WHERE     Major = 'MATH'
```

The asterisk (*) means that all columns of the table are to be obtained. The result of both of these queries is

200	BAKER	MATH	GR	50
350	RUSSELL	MATH	JR	20

We can combine the selection and projection as follows:

```
SELECT    Name, Age
FROM      STUDENT
WHERE     Major = 'MATH'
```

The result is

BAKER	50
RUSSELL	20

Several conditions can be expressed in the WHERE clause. For example, the expression

```
SELECT    Name, Age
FROM      STUDENT
WHERE     Major = 'MATH' AND Age > 21
```

obtains the following:

BAKER	50

The conditions in WHERE clauses can refer to a set of values. To do this, the keywords IN or NOT IN may be used. Consider

```
SELECT    Name
FROM      STUDENT
WHERE     Major IN ['MATH', 'ACCOUNTING']
```

Notice that multiple values can be placed inside the brackets. This expression means "Display the names of students who have either a math or an accounting major." The result is

PARKS
BAKER
BAKER
RUSSELL
RYE

The expression

```
SELECT    Name
FROM      STUDENT
WHERE     Major NOT IN ['MATH', 'ACCOUNTING']
```

causes the names of students other than math or accounting majors to be presented. The result is

JONES
GLASS
JONES

The expression MAJOR IN means the value of the Major column can equal *any* of the listed majors. This is equivalent to the logical OR operator. The expression MAJOR NOT IN means the value must be different from *all* the listed majors.

■ SORTING

The rows of the result relation can be sorted by the values in one or more columns. Consider the following example:

SELECT   Name, Major, Age
FROM   STUDENT
WHERE   Major = 'ACCOUNTING'
ORDER BY Name

This query will list the accounting majors in ascending sequence by value of name. The result is

BAKER	ACCOUNTING	41
PARKS	ACCOUNTING	19
RYE	ACCOUNTING	18

More than one column can be chosen for sorting. If so, the first column listed will be the major sort field, the next column the next major sort field, and so on. Columns can also be declared to be ascending (ASC) or descending (DESC), as shown in the next statement:

SELECT   Name, Major, Age
FROM   STUDENT
WHERE   GradeLevel IN ['FR', 'SO', 'SN']
ORDER BY Major ASC, Age DESC

The result is

BAKER	ACCOUNTING	41
PARKS	ACCOUNTING	19
RYE	ACCOUNTING	18
GLASS	HISTORY	50
JONES	HISTORY	24

ORDER BY can be combined with any of the SELECT statements.

■ SQL BUILT-IN FUNCTIONS

SQL provides five built-in functions: COUNT, SUM, AVG, MAX, and MIN.[2] Although COUNT and SUM sound similar, they actually are different. COUNT computes the number of rows in a table, whereas SUM totals numeric columns. AVG, MAX, and MIN also operate on numeric columns: AVG computes the average value, and MAX and MIN obtain the maximum and minimum values of a column in a table.

---

[2]Sometimes built-in functions are referred to as *aggregate functions* to distinguish them from program languages' built-in functions such as SUBSTRING.

The query expression

```
SELECT    COUNT(*)
FROM      STUDENT
```

counts the number of STUDENT rows and displays this total in a table with a single row and single column:

With the exception of GROUP BY (considered below), built-in functions cannot be mixed with column names in the SELECT statement. Thus

```
SELECT    Name, COUNT (*)
```

is not allowed.

Consider the expressions

```
SELECT    COUNT (Major)
FROM      STUDENT
```

and

```
SELECT    COUNT (DISTINCT Major)
FROM      STUDENT
```

The first expression counts all majors, including duplicates, and the second counts only unique majors. The results are

```
8
```

and

```
3
```

respectively.

The built-in functions can be used to request a result, as in the preceding examples. In most implementations of SQL, and in the ANSI standard SQL, the built-in functions *cannot* be used as part of a WHERE clause.

■ BUILT-IN FUNCTIONS AND GROUPING

To increase their utility, built-in functions can be applied to groups of rows within a table. Such groups are formed by collecting those rows (logically, not physically) that have the same value of a specified column. For example, students can be grouped by major, which means that one group will be formed for each value of MAJOR. For the data in Figure 10-2, there is a group of HISTORY majors, a group of ACCOUNTING majors, and a group of MATH majors.

The SQL keyword GROUP BY instructs the DBMS to group together those rows that have the same value of a column. Consider

```
SELECT      Major, COUNT (*)
FROM        STUDENT
GROUP BY    Major
```

The result of this expression is

HISTORY	3
ACCOUNTING	3
MATH	2

The rows of the STUDENT table have been logically grouped by the value of MAJOR, and the COUNT function sums the number of rows in each group. The result is a table with two columns, the major name and the sum. For subgroups, both columns and built-in functions can be specified in the SELECT statement.

In some cases, we do not want to consider all of the groups. For example, we might form groups of students having the same major and then wish to consider only those groups that have more than two students. In this case, we use the SQL HAVING clause to identify the subset of groups we want to consider.

The following SQL statements can list the majors that have more than two students and also the count of students in each of those majors.

```
SELECT      Major, COUNT (*)
FROM        STUDENT
GROUP BY    Major
HAVING      COUNT (*) > 2
```

Here, groups of students having the same major are formed, and then groups having more than two students are selected. (Other groups are ignored.) The major and the count of students in these selected groups are produced. The result is

HISTORY	3
ACCOUNTING	3

For even greater generality, WHERE clauses can be added as well. Doing so, however, can create ambiguity. For example,

```
SELECT      Major, AVG (Age)
FROM        STUDENT
WHERE       GradeLevel = 'SN'
GROUP BY    Major
HAVING      COUNT (*) >1
```

The result of this expression will differ depending on whether the WHERE condition is applied before or after the HAVING condition. To eliminate this uncertainty, the SQL standard specifies that WHERE clauses are to be applied first. Accordingly, in the preceding statement, the operations are: select the senior students; form the groups; select the groups that meet the HAVING condition; display the results. In this case, the result is

HISTORY	37

(This query is not valid for all implementations of SQL. For some implementations, the only attributes that can appear in the SELECT phrase of a query with GROUP BY are attributes that appear in the GROUP BY phrase and built-in functions of those attributes. Thus in this query, only MAJOR and built-in functions of MAJOR would be allowed.)

QUERYING MULTIPLE TABLES

In this section we extend our discussion of SQL to include operations on two or more tables. The STUDENT, CLASS, and ENROLLMENT data in Figure 10-2 are used to illustrate these SQL commands.

■ RETRIEVAL USING SUBQUERY

Suppose we need to know the names of those students enrolled in the class BD445. If we know that students with SIDs of 100 and 200 are enrolled in this class, the following will produce the correct names:

SELECT   Name
FROM   STUDENT
WHERE   SID IN [100, 200]

Usually we do not know the SIDs of students in a class, but we do have a facility for finding those out. Examine the expression

SELECT   StudentNumber
FROM   ENROLLMENT
WHERE   ClassName = 'BD445'

The result of this operation is

These are the student numbers we need. Now when combining the last two queries, we obtain the following:

SELECT   Name
FROM   STUDENT
WHERE   SID IN
                (SELECT   StudentNumber
                 FROM   ENROLLMENT
                 WHERE   ClassName = 'BD445')

Observe that the second SELECT, called the subquery, is enclosed in parentheses.

It may be easier to understand these statements if you work from the bottom and read up. The last three statements obtain the student numbers for people enrolled in BD445, and the first three statements produce the names for the two students selected. The result of this query is

This strategy can be very useful, although for this operation to be semantically correct, SID and StudentNumber must come from the same domain.

Subqueries can consist of three or even more tables. For example, suppose we want to know the names of the students enrolled in classes on Monday, Wednesday, and Friday at 3 o'clock (denoted as MWF3 in our data). First, we need the names of those classes that meet at that time:

SELECT   CLASS.Name
FROM   CLASS
WHERE   Time = 'MWF3'

(Since we are dealing with three different tables, we qualify the column names with table names to avoid confusion and ambiguity. Thus, CLASS.Name refers to the column Name in the relation CLASS.)

Now we get the identifying numbers of students in these classes with the following expression:

```
SELECT      ENROLLMENT.StudentNumber
FROM        ENROLLMENT
WHERE       ENROLLMENT.ClassName IN
                (SELECT   CLASS.Name
                 FROM     CLASS
                 WHERE    Time = 'MWF3')
```

This yields

which are the numbers of the students in the class MWF3. To get the names of those students, we specify

```
SELECT      STUDENT.Name
FROM        STUDENT
WHERE       STUDENT.SID IN
                (SELECT ENROLLMENT.StudentNumber
                 FROM ENROLLMENT
                 WHERE ENROLLMENT.ClassName IN
                     (SELECT   CLASS.Name
                      FROM     CLASS
                      WHERE    CLASS.Time = 'MWF3'))
```

The result is

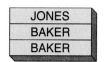

This strategy works well as long as the attributes in the answer come from a single table. If, however, the result comes from two or more tables, we have a problem. For example, suppose we want to know the names of students and the names of their classes. Say we need SID, StudentName, and ClassName. In this case, the results come from two different tables (STUDENT and ENROLLMENT), and so the subquery strategy will not work.

■ JOINING WITH SQL

To produce the SID, StudentName, and ClassName for every student, we must join the STUDENT table with the ENROLLMENT table. The following statements will do this:

```
SELECT      STUDENT.SID, STUDENT.Name, ENROLLMENT.ClassName
FROM        STUDENT, ENROLLMENT
WHERE       STUDENT.SID = ENROLLMENT.StudentNumber
```

Recall that a join is the combination of a product operation, followed by a selection, followed (usually) by a projection. In this expression, the FROM statement expresses the product of STUDENT and ENROLLMENT, and then the WHERE statement expresses the selection. The meaning is "Select from the product of STU-

DENT and ENROLLMENT those rows in which SID of STUDENT equals StudentNumber of ENROLLMENT." Finally, after the selection, the projection of the student number, name, and class name is taken. The result is

100	JONES	BD445
150	PARKS	BA200
200	BAKER	BD445
200	BAKER	CS250
300	BAKER	CS125
400	RYE	BA200
400	RYE	BF410
400	RYE	CS250
450	JONES	BA200

The WHERE clause can contain qualifiers in addition to those needed for the join. For example,

```
SELECT     STUDENT.SID, ENROLLMENT.ClassName
FROM       STUDENT, ENROLLMENT
WHERE      STUDENT.SID = ENROLLMENT.StudentNumber
AND        STUDENT.Name = 'RYE'
AND        ENROLLMENT.PositionNumber = 1
```

The additional qualifiers here are STUDENT.Name = 'RYE' and ENROLLMENT. PositionNumber = 1. This operation will list the student number and class name of all students named RYE who were first to enroll in a class. The result is

400	BF410

When data are needed from more than two tables, we can use a similar strategy. In the next example, three tables are joined:

```
SELECT     STUDENT.SID, CLASS.Name, CLASS.Time, ENROLLMENT.PositionNumber
FROM       STUDENT, ENROLLMENT, CLASS
WHERE      STUDENT.SID = ENROLLMENT.StudentNumber
AND        ENROLLMENT.ClassName = CLASS.Name
AND        STUDENT.Name = 'BAKER'
```

The result of this operation is

200	BD445	MWF3	2
200	CS250	MWF12	1
300	CS150	MWF3	1

■ COMPARISON OF SQL SUBQUERY AND JOIN

A join can be used as an alternative way of expressing many subqueries. For example, we used a subquery to find the students enrolled in the class BD445. We can also use a join to express this query:

```
SELECT     STUDENT.Name
FROM       STUDENT, ENROLLMENT
WHERE      STUDENT.SID = ENROLLMENT.StudentNumber
AND        ENROLLMENT.ClassName = 'BD445'
```

Similarly, the query "What are the names of the students in class MWF at 3?" can be expressed as

```
SELECT    STUDENT.NAME
FROM      STUDENT, ENROLLMENT, CLASS
WHERE     STUDENT.SID = ENROLLMENT.StudentNumber
AND       ENROLLMENT.ClassName = CLASS.Name
AND       CLASS.Time = 'MWF3'
```

Although join expressions can substitute for many subquery expressions, they cannot substitute for all of them. For instance, subqueries that involve EXISTS and NOT EXISTS (discussed in the next section) cannot be represented by joins.

Similarly, subqueries cannot be substituted for all joins. When using a join, the displayed columns may come from any of the joined tables, but when using a subquery, the displayed columns may come from only the table named in the FROM expression in the first SELECT. For example, suppose we want to know the names of classes taken by undergraduates. We can express this as a subquery:

```
SELECT    DISTINCT ClassName
FROM      ENROLLMENT
WHERE     StudentNumber IN
               (SELECT SID
               FROM STUDENT
               WHERE GradeLevel NOT = 'GR')
```

or as a join:

```
SELECT    DISTINCT ENROLLMENT.ClassName
FROM      ENROLLMENT, STUDENT
WHERE     ENROLLMENT.StudentNumber = STUDENT.SID
AND       STUDENT.GradeLevel NOT = 'GR'
```

But if we want to know both the names of the classes and the grade levels of the undergraduate students, we must use a join. A subquery will not suffice because the desired results come from two different tables. That is, the names of the classes are stored in ENROLLMENT, and the names of the students are stored in STUDENT. The following obtains the correct answer:

```
SELECT    DISTINCT ENROLLMENT.ClassName, STUDENT.GradeLevel
FROM      ENROLLMENT, STUDENT
WHERE     ENROLLMENT.StudentNumber = STUDENT.SID
AND       STUDENT.GradeLevel NOT = 'GR'
```

The result is

BA200	SO
CS150	SN
BA200	FR
BF410	FR
CS250	FR
BA200	SN

EXISTS AND NOT EXISTS

EXISTS and NOT EXISTS are logical operators whose value is either true or false depending on the presence or absence of rows that fit the qualifying conditions. For example, suppose we want to know the student numbers of students enrolled in more than one class.

```
SELECT    DISTINCT StudentNumber
FROM      ENROLLMENT A
WHERE     EXISTS
              (SELECT    *
               FROM      ENROLLMENT B
               WHERE     A.StudentNumber = B.StudentNumber
                 AND     A.ClassName NOT = B.ClassName)
```

In this example, both the query and the subquery refer to the ENROLLMENT table. To prevent ambiguity, these two uses of ENROLLMENT have been assigned a different name. In the first FROM statement, ENROLLMENT is assigned the temporary and arbitrary name A, and in the second FROM statement, it is assigned another temporary and arbitrary name, B.

The meaning of the subquery expression is this: Find two rows in ENROLLMENT having the same student number but different class names. (This means that the student is taking more than one class.) If two such rows exist, then the logical value of EXISTS is true. In this case, we present the student number in the answer. Otherwise, the logical value of the EXISTS is false, so we do not present that SID in the answer.

Another way of viewing this query is to imagine two separate and identical copies of the ENROLLMENT table. Call one copy Table A and the other copy Table B. We compare each row in A with each row in B. First we look at the first row in A and the first row in B. In this case, since the two rows are identical, both the StudentNumbers and the ClassNames are the same, so we do not display the SID.

Now look at the first row in A and the second row in B. If the StudentNumbers are the same and the ClassNames are different, we display the StudentNumber. Essentially, we are comparing the first row of ENROLLMENT with the second row of ENROLLMENT. For the data in Figure 10-2, neither the StudentNumbers nor the ClassNames are the same.

We continue comparing the first row of A with each row of B. If the conditions are ever met, we print the StudentNumber. When all of the rows in B have been examined, we move to the second row of A and compare it with all the rows in B (actually, if we are considering the *n*th rows in A, only those rows greater than *n* need to be considered in B).

The result of this query is

To illustrate the application of NOT EXISTS, suppose we want to know the names of students taking all classes. Another way of stating this is that we want the names of students such that there are no classes that the student did not take. The following expresses this:

```
SELECT    STUDENT.Name
FROM      STUDENT
WHERE     NOT EXISTS
              (SELECT  *
               FROM    ENROLLMENT
               WHERE   NOT EXISTS
                   (SELECT  *
                    FROM    CLASS
                    WHERE   CLASS.Name = ENROLLMENT.ClassName
                      AND   ENROLLMENT.StudentNumber= STUDENT.SID))
```

This query has three parts. In the bottom part, it finds classes the student did take. The middle part determines whether any classes were found that the student did not take. If not, then the student is taking all classes, and his or her name is displayed.

This query may be difficult to understand. If you have trouble with it, use the data in Figure 10-2 and follow the instructions. For that data, the answer is that no student is taking all classes. You might try to change the data so that a student does take all classes. Another way to look at this query is to try to solve it in a way other than with NOT EXISTS. The problems you encounter will help you understand why NOT EXISTS is necessary.

A final example combines many SQL concepts and illustrates the power of this data sublanguage. Suppose we want to know the names of graduate students taking classes only with other graduate students.

```
SELECT    A.Name
FROM      STUDENT A
WHERE     STUDENT.GradeLevel = 'GR'
          AND    NOT EXISTS
          (SELECT   *
          FROM      ENROLLMENT B
          WHERE     STUDENT.SID = B.StudentNumber
              AND       B.ClassName IN
              (SELECT   C.ClassName
              FROM      ENROLLMENT C
              WHERE     B.ClassName = C.ClassName
                  AND       C.StudentNumber IN
                  (SELECT   D.SID
                  FROM      STUDENT D
                  WHERE     C.StudentNumber =D.SID
                  AND       D.GradeLevel NOT = 'GR')))
```

The meaning of this query is "Present the names of students where there is no row in ENROLLMENT that matches the student with a class that is one of the classes that are matched with students who have a grade level other than graduate." The result of this query is

JONES

The last three queries are complicated, but you should not presume from this that SQL need always be this way. Actually, compared with the alternatives, SQL is simple. These last three queries are difficult only because we are solving queries that are logically quite complex. For most day-to-day problems, however, SQL queries are far simpler and more straightforward.

CHANGING DATA

SQL has provisions for changing data in tables by inserting new rows, deleting rows, and modifying values in existing rows. SQL also can change the data structure, although we will not explore this until we study DB2 in Chapter 13.

■ INSERTING DATA

Rows can be inserted into a table one at a time or in groups. To insert a single row, we state

```
INSERT    INTO ENROLLMENT
          VALUES (400, 'BD445', 44)
```

If we do not know all of this data—for instance, if we do not know PositionNumber—we could say

```
INSERT    INTO ENROLLMENT
          (StudentNumber, ClassName)
          VALUES (400, 'BD445')
```

PositionNumber could then be added later. Note that this causes the value of PositionNumber to have a null value in the new row.

We can also copy rows in mass from one table to another. For example, suppose we want to fill the JUNIOR table defined in Figure 10.1.

```
INSERT    INTO JUNIOR
              VALUES
              (SELECT SID, Name, Major
              FROM   STUDENT
              WHERE  GradeLevel = 'JR')
```

The contained SELECT, and all of the SQL SELECT expressions developed in the previous two sections, can be used to identify the rows to be copied. This feature offers quite powerful capabilities.

■ DELETING DATA

As with insertion, rows can be deleted one at a time or in groups. The following example deletes the row for Student 100:

```
DELETE    STUDENT
WHERE     STUDENT.SID = 100
```

Note that if Student 100 is enrolled in classes, this delete will cause an integrity problem, as the ENROLLMENT rows having StudentNumber = 100 will have no corresponding STUDENT row.

Groups of rows can be deleted as shown in the next two examples, which delete all enrollments for accounting majors as well as all accounting majors.

```
DELETE    ENROLLMENT
WHERE     ENROLLMENT.StudentNumber IN
              (SELECT  STUDENT.SID
              FROM     STUDENT
              WHERE    STUDENT.Major = 'Accounting')


DELETE    STUDENT
WHERE     STUDENT.Major = 'Accounting'
```

The order of these two operations is important, for if it were reversed, none of the ENROLLMENT rows would be deleted because the matching STUDENT rows would already have been deleted.

■ MODIFYING DATA

Rows can also be modified one at a time or in groups. The keyword SET is used to change a column value. After SET, the name of the column to be changed and then the new value or way of computing the new value is specified. Consider two examples:

```
UPDATE     ENROLLMENT
SET        PositionNumber = 44
WHERE      SID = 400
```

and

```
UPDATE     ENROLLMENT
SET        PositionNumber = MAX(PositionNumber) + 1
WHERE      SID = 400
```

In the second UPDATE statement, the value of the column is calculated using the MAX built-in function. Some implementations of SQL, however, may not allow the built-in function to be used as an argument in the SET command.

To illustrate mass updates, suppose the name of a course has been changed from BD445 to BD564. In this case, to prevent integrity problems, both the ENROLLMENT and the CLASS tables must be changed.

```
UPDATE     ENROLLMENT
SET        ClassName = 'BD564'
WHERE      ClassName = 'BD445'
UPDATE     CLASS
SET        ClassName = 'BD564'
WHERE      ClassName = 'BD445'
```

Remember that mass updates can be quite dangerous. The user is given great power—power that when used correctly can rapidly perform the task at hand but when used incorrectly can cause serious problems.

SUMMARY

SQL is today's most important relational data manipulation language. It has become the standard for information exchange among computers, and its popularity continues to grow. SQL statements that operate on a single table include SELECT, SELECT with WHERE, SELECT with GROUP BY, and SELECT with GROUP BY and HAVING. SQL also contains the built-in functions of COUNT, SUM, AVG, MAX, and MIN.

Operations on two or more tables can be done using subquery, joins, EXISTS, and NOT EXISTS. Subqueries and joins perform many of the same operations, but they do not completely substitute for each other. Subqueries require that the attributes retrieved arise from a single relation, but joins do not. On the other hand, some queries are possible with subqueries and EXISTS and NOT EXISTS that are impossible with joins.

The SQL statements for data modification include INSERT, DELETE, and UPDATE commands, which are used to add, remove, and change data values.

In this chapter we presented the basic SQL commands in generic form, and in Chapters 11 and 13 we use these commands to process a database using commercial DBMS products.

GROUP I QUESTIONS

The questions in this group refer to the following three relations:

SALESPERSON (Name, Age, Salary)

ORDER (Number, CustName, SalespersonName, Amount)

CUSTOMER (Name, City, IndustryType)

FIGURE 10-3   *Sample Data for Group I Questions*

Name	Age	Salary
Abel	63	120,000
Baker	38	42,000
Jones	26	36,000
Murphy	42	50,000
Zenith	59	118,000
Kobad	27	34,000

SALESPERSON

Number	CustName	SalespersonName	Amount
100	Abernathy Construction	Zenith	560
200	Abernathy Construction	Jones	1800
300	Manchester Lumber	Abel	480
400	Amalgamated Housing	Abel	2500
500	Abernathy Construction	Murphy	6000
600	Tri-City Builders	Abel	700
700	Manchester Lumber	Jones	150

ORDER

Name	City	IndustryType
Abernathy Construction	Willow	B
Manchester Lumber	Manchester	F
Tri-City Builders	Memphis	B
Amalgamated Housing	Memphis	B

CUSTOMER

An instance of these relations is shown in Figure 10-3. Use the data in those tables and show the SQL statements to display or modify data as indicated in the following questions:

10.1   Show the ages and salaries of all salespeople.

10.2   Show the ages and salaries of all salespeople but omit duplicates.

10.3   Show the names of all salespeople under thirty years old.

10.4   Show the names of all salespeople who have an order with Abernathy Construction.

10.5   Show the names and salary of all salespeople who do not have an order with Abernathy Construction, in ascending order of salary.

10.6   Compute the number of orders.

10.7   Compute the number of different customers who have an order.

10.8   Compute the average age of a salesperson.

10.9   Show the name of the oldest salesperson.

10.10 Compute the number of orders for each salesperson.

10.11 Compute the number of orders for each salesperson, considering only orders for an amount exceeding 500.

10.12 Show the names and ages of salespeople who have an order with ABERNATHY CONSTRUCTION, in descending order of age (use a subquery).

10.13 Show the names and ages of salespeople who have an order with ABER-NATHY CONSTRUCTION, in descending order of age (use a join).

10.14 Show the age of salespeople who have an order with a customer in MEM-PHIS (use a subquery).

10.15 Show the age of salespeople who have an order with a customer in MEM-PHIS (use a join).

10.16 Show the industry type and ages of the salespeople of all orders for companies in MEMPHIS.

10.17 Show the names of salespeople who have two or more orders.

10.18 Show the names and ages of salespeople who have two or more orders.

10.19 Show the names and ages of salespeople who have an order with all customers.

10.20 Show an SQL statement to insert a new row into CUSTOMER.

10.21 Show an SQL statement to insert a new name and age into SALESPERSON; assume that salary is not determined.

10.22 Show an SQL statement to insert rows into a new table, HIGH-ACHIEVER (Name, Age), in which, to be included, a salesperson must have a salary of at least 100,000.

10.23 Show an SQL statement to delete customer ABERNATHY CONSTRUCTION.

10.24 Show an SQL statement to delete all orders for ABERNATHY CONSTRUCTION.

10.25 Show an SQL statement to change the salary of salesperson JONES to 45,000.

10.26 Show an SQL statement to give all salespeople a 10 percent pay increase.

10.27 Assume that salesperson JONES changes his name to PARKS. Show the SQL statements that make the appropriate changes.

GROUP II QUESTIONS

10.28 Find out about a relational DBMS product such as Paradox for Windows, Microsoft Access, ORACLE, Informix, or other product. For the product you select, explain how its SQL syntax differs from that used in this chapter. Answer the following questions in your response:

a. How are single-table queries expressed?

b. What built-in functions does it have? What limits are set on their use?

c. How are subqueries expressed?

d. How are joins expressed?

e. Are EXISTS and NOT EXISTS supported? If so, how do they differ from the syntax shown in this chapter?

11

RELATIONAL IMPLEMENTATION FOR PERSONAL DATABASES

• • • • • • • • • • • • • • •

The goal of this chapter is to bring together the chapters on database and application design with the chapters on relational implementation and to show how all these topics are integrated in the development of a database application. To do this, we will build a database and application that meet several important application requirements for the View Ridge Gallery, a case introduced in Chapter 8.

The concepts of this chapter are illustrated using Microsoft Access, a Windows-based DBMS product. We use Access because it is modern and popular and has many features, and you are likely to encounter it sometime in your career. But this choice is not meant to be an endorsement of Access over other similar products such as Borland's Paradox for Windows and Lotus's Approach.

A database is a model of the users' model of their business activities; to implement a database, we must first have such a model. Here we assume that the model has already been developed and that it has been expressed in terms of semantic objects. We use the semantic objects shown in Figure 11-1 as the basis of our discussion. They are a subset of the objects described for the View Ridge Gallery in Chapter 8; that is, the model has been simplified by omitting the Transaction group property from the WORK semantic object. This has been done to avoid complexities that are not important to the purposes of this chapter.

CREATING THE DATABASE SCHEMA

Figure 11-2 shows the relations that represent the objects in Figure 11-1. These relations use data columns as keys; surrogate keys are not used. The N:M relationship between ARTIST and CUSTOMER is carried in the intersection relation ARTIST_CUSTOMER_INT. Note that the columns of this table are both local and foreign keys, so they are both underlined and italicized. The 1:N relationship from ARTIST to WORK is carried by the column ArtistName. Note that it, too, is both underlined and italicized in the WORK table.

To define these tables to Access, we must create a new database. This has been done in Figure 11-3. The dialog box is called the database container, and it has six tabs: Tables, Queries, Forms, Reports, Macros, and Modules. When the developer presses one of those tabs, a list of items of that category appears in the list box underneath the tabs. Hence, pressing the Tables button causes a list of tables to be displayed. But since this database is empty, nothing appears in this list in Figure 11-3.

FIGURE 11-1   *Modified View Ridge Gallery Objects*

FIGURE 11-2   *Relations Representing the Objects in Figure 11-1*

ARTIST (<u>ArtistName</u>, Nationality, Born, Died)

CUSTOMER (<u>CustomerNumber</u>, CustomerName, AreaCode, LocalNumber, Street, City, State, Zip)

ARTIST_CUSTOMER_INT (*<u>ArtistName</u>*, *<u>CustomerNumber</u>*)

WORK (*<u>ArtistName</u>*, <u>Title</u>, <u>Copy</u>, Description)

FIGURE 11-3   *An Empty Microsoft Access Toolbox*

In this text, we are concerned with only the first four tabs. The last two, Macros and Modules, pertain to the development of application program logic. Macros are groups of high-level actions, akin to what we earlier referred to as stored procedures. Modules are groups of Microsoft Visual Basic programs. Any further discussion of the functions of these buttons will take us too far afield from database processing, however, so consult the Access documentation or any of the many Access reference books for more information.

■ CREATING TABLES

To create a table in Access, the developer presses the Table tab and then the New button: This brings up a screen like that shown in Figure 11-4. To define the columns of the table (referred to as fields in Access), the developer types the names of the fields in the Field Name column of the form and enters the data type of each field in the second column. Only Number and Text fields are needed in this table. Other data types that are supported are Date/Time, Currency, Boolean, Counter (Access assigns a unique sequential number to each row of the table), and Memo (a large, variable-length text field). The third column of this form, labeled Description, can contain optional documentation about the column, but it is left blank in Figure 11-4. Notice the small key icon just to the left of the CustomerNumber Field Name. This means that CustomerNumber has been set to be the key of the table.

The bottom of the table definition form contains additional data about each property. In Figure 11-4, the focus is on the CustomerNumber field, so the additional properties of that field are shown in the bottom of this form. The Field Size is shown as Long Integer (this means a 32-bit integer); Decimal Places are set to automatic; values are required for the field; and the Indexed property has been set to Yes (No Duplicates). This means that Access is to create and maintain a unique index for the CustomerNumber property. The Indexed Property was automatically set by Access for this column when it was defined as a key column. If the developer knows that other columns are to be used to access directly a row or for sorting, those columns,

FIGURE 11-4   *Microsoft Access Table Definition Form*

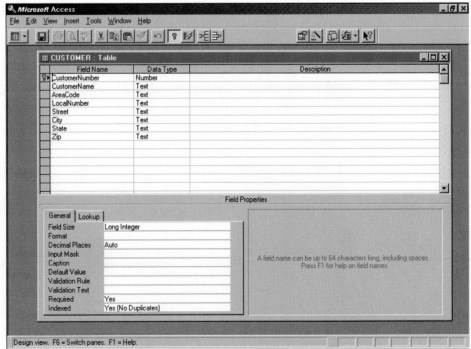

too, can be defined as Indexed. CustomerName is a likely candidate for a nonunique index because it has been marked as a nonunique identifier in Figure 11-1.

When the table definition has been completed, the developer closes the window, and Access prompts for a table name. The developer then enters the name CUSTOMER to save this table under that name.

The other tables in Figure 11-2 are defined in a similar manner. The column names are entered, the properties are set, keys are defined, and the table is saved under the appropriate name.

■ DEFINING RELATIONSHIPS

Once the tables have been created, the relationships among them can be defined. Access recognizes both one-to-one and one-to-many relationships. The advantage of defining relationships to Access is that when rows of two tables need to be connected (in a JOIN, a multitable form, or a report), Access uses the defined relationship as the default way of combining the two tables. This can spare the developer both time and confusion.

Figure 11-5 shows a form that is used to do this with Access. To open this form, the developer clicks Tools, Relationships. Relationships are created by dragging a column name from one table and dropping it on a column name in a second table. When this is done, Access displays the dialog box shown in Figure 11-5.

The table in this dialog box indicates that the ArtistName column of ARTIST is related to the ArtistName column in WORK. In this example, Enforce Referential Integrity has been checked, and, within that group box, both Cascade Update Related Fields and Cascade Delete Related Records have been checked. These have been checked because the key of WORK contains the key of ARTIST (an ID-dependency). Cascade Update means that if the user changes ArtistName in the ARTIST table, the change should be propagated to the WORK table. Similarly, Cascade Delete means that if an ARTIST row is deleted, then all of the WORK rows for that artist should be deleted as well.

FIGURE 11-5   *Defining a Relationship Between the ARTIST and WORK Tables*

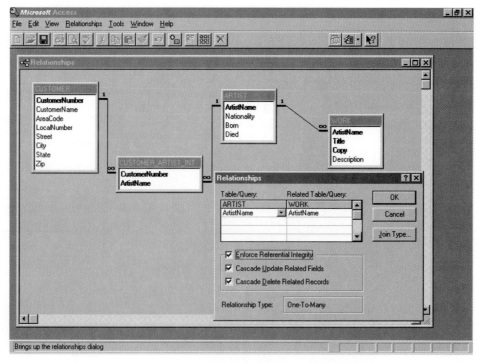

■ CREATING QUERIES

Queries are used for three purposes in Access: as a means for the user to pose ad hoc questions on the data, as the basis of forms and reports, and as the basis of multivalued controls such as combo boxes. In this section, we consider the development of queries that can be used for any or all of these purposes. Later we demonstrate how to bind a query to a form, report, or other control.

SINGLE-TABLE QUERIES   Queries can be defined either by using a variation of Query by Example, called graphical QBE, or by entering SQL statements directly. Figure 11-6 shows an example of defining a single-table query using QBE. The top part of this form is the table on which the query is based, with the key of the table in boldface type.

To include a field in the query, the field name is dragged from the table box and dropped on a column of the query grid in the bottom part of the form. If the column is to be used for sorting, the sort criteria are entered on the second row of the grid. If the box is checked, the column will appear in the result of the query. Search criteria can be added to the additional rows of the grid. For example, if the expression < 1950 were added to the Criteria row of the Born column in the grid in Figure 11-6, only those ARTISTs that were born before 1950 would be part of the query result.

Figure 11-7 shows an Access SQL expression equivalent to the query in Figure 11-6. Access SQL is quite similar to the standard SQL discussed in Chapter 10, except that the keyword *DISTINCT* has been changed to *DISTINCTROW*. Also, all Access SQL statements must be terminated with a semicolon.

MULTITABLE QUERIES   Figure 11-8 is a query of three tables. The developer has instructed Access to include these three tables in the query (by selecting the Show Table dialogue [not shown], which can be activated by the Query menu choice at the top of the form in Figure 11-8). The lines between the tables represent table relationships, which Access automatically draws. This first line shows that ARTIST is related to ARTIST_CUSTOMER_INT, by the field ArtistName in both tables.

FIGURE 11-6   *Access QBE for a Single Table Query*

FIGURE 11-7   *Access SQL for the Query in Figure 11-6*

FIGURE 11-8   *Access QBE for a Three-Table Query*

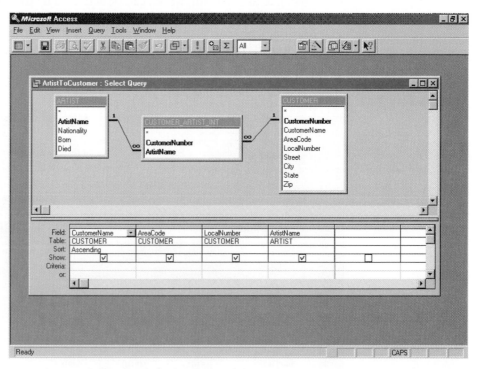

Those fields that are to appear in the query can also be dragged and dropped, as with a single-table query. For the query in Figure 11-8, CustomerName, AreaCode, LocalNumber, and ArtistName are to appear.

The SQL statement for the query in Figure 11-8 is shown in Figure 11-9. The join expression in this statement is similar to the syntax shown in Chapter 9 for

FIGURE 11-9   *Access SQL for the Query in Figure 11-8*

FIGURE 11-10   *Sample Results of Query in Figure 11-9*

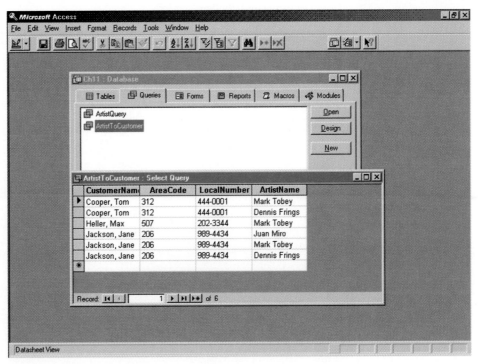

the relational algebra JOIN. The term INNER JOIN is used to indicate that rows having null values in join fields are to be dropped when forming the join.

The sample data for the query in Figure 11-9 are shown in Figure 11-10. Observe that the rows of this table are ordered by CustomerName, as indicated in the query definition.

CREATING FORMS

An Access form is used to display rows from a table or query. Since queries can combine several tables, an Access form may be based on data from several tables. When creating a form, the designer must first create the table or query and then bind that table or query to the form. The term *bind* means to logically associate the table or query with the form.[1]

Access forms consist of an arrangement of GUI controls. Examples of the types of controls available are labels, text boxes, combo boxes, and subform regions. Each control has a set of properties that can be changed. These properties govern characteristics such as caption, color, font type, font size, position on the form, width, and length. Some controls are bound to tables or columns of tables, and the particular entity to which a control is bound is a property that can be set or changed by the developer.

To create a new form, the developer presses the Form button in the database container and then presses the New button, thereby bringing up a blank form. He then places controls on the form. Figure 11-11 shows a form that is in the process of being created. The rectangle on the right is the Access Toolbox, which contains tools that can be used to create controls of various types. In Figure 11-11, the user has clicked the arrow tool, which is used to select controls on the form.

Figure 11-11 shows two controls. The first is the label "View Ridge Gallery," and the second is the label "Artist Dat." The second control is in the process of being created in Figure 11-11; that is, the user is typing the phrase "Artist Data" into the text label.

FIGURE 11-11   *Form Definition and Toolbox*

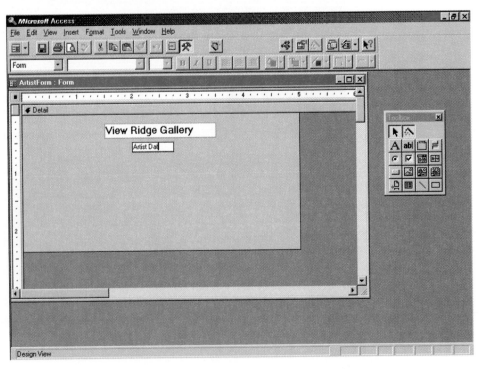

---

[1]Access provides many assistants or *wizards* to help ease the definition of forms and reports. We do not illustrate their use here because they hide many of the concepts that you need to learn. When developing an application with Access, however, most developers would make use of these wizards, at least as a starting point.

The properties of the form and the controls on the form can be viewed by opening a property window (a selection under the View menu choice). Figure 11-12 shows the property window with the properties of the text label being created. Note that the Caption property is set to Artist Data (the caption of the label). The other properties shown are not important to this discussion. Also, the property window has tabs as shown; these tabs are used to display properties of a given type. All of the properties can be viewed by clicking the All tab. The list is very long, however, and difficult to use, so normally one of the other tab groups is used.

■ BINDING A RELATION TO A FORM

As stated, forms can be used to show the data from the row of a table or query. To do this, the table or query must be bound to the form, and Figure 11-13 demonstrates how this is done. The properties of the form are made visible by clicking on a region of the form. Then the property Record Source is clicked. When this is done, a combo box containing the names of tables and queries is displayed, and the developer chooses a name from this list to bind that name to the current form. In Figure 11-13 the table ARTIST has been bound to the form, so at this point any of the columns of ARTIST are available to be bound to controls on the form.

■ BINDING A COLUMN TO A TEXT BOX CONTROL

Figure 11-14 shows the form after several text boxes have been created. Each text box has a label and a box that will contain column data. The first text box has the label "Artist Name" and has been bound to the column ArtistName. Nationality, Born, and Died have also been created.

In Figure 11-14, the developer is in the process of binding the Born column of the ARTIST table to a text box, by setting the Control Source property to Born. To make this association, the developer clicks on the Control Source entry field, and a list box appears with the names of all the columns in the table or query. Figure 11-14 shows the expanded list box.

 FIGURE 11-12   *Format Properties for a Text Label*

FIGURE 11-13   *Binding a Relation to a Form*

FIGURE 11-14   *Binding the Born Text Box to the Born Column*

■   SUBFORM CONTROL

The Artist Data form must contain a grid that has one row for each of the artist's works that the gallery has carried. (Look ahead to the finished form in Figure 11-19. The grid just referred to is labeled Works: and is at the bottom of the form.)

FIGURE 11-15   *Creating the Work Subform*

To create such a grid, the developer must first create a subform that has the required columns. Figure 11-15 shows the creation of such a form called WORK Subform. The Record Source of the form is the table WORK, and the subform contains three text boxes that have been bound to the Title, Copy, and Description columns of the WORK table, respectively.

Figure 11-16 shows how the subform is bound to the Artist Data form. A subform control has been drawn on the form and appears as a white rectangle in Figure 11-16, partially covered by the property list. The Source Object property of this subform control has been set to WORK Subform, the name of the subform created in Figure 11-15.

To match a row of ARTIST with the proper rows of WORK, the Link Child Fields and Link Master Fields properties must be set. Here they both are set to ArtistName, which means that the value of ArtistName in the master form (Artist Data) is to be matched with values of ArtistName in the subform. Since the subform is bound to the WORK table, all rows in WORK that have a value of ArtistName that matches the value of ArtistName in the Artist Data form are to be displayed.

■ BINDING A TABLE OR QUERY TO A COMBO BOX CONTROL

A combo box or a list box contains a list of values. Access allows combo or list boxes to contain multicolumn lists. Thus, several columns from a table or query can be bound to and appear in a combo or list box. In Figure 11-17, the CUSTOMER table is being bound to a combo box on the Artist Data form so that the user can click on the combo box to select a new customer that has an interest in the artist being displayed.

The combo box is bound to the table by entering CUSTOMER into the Row Source property (under the Data tab and not shown in Figure 11-17). The tab that

FIGURE 11-16   *Binding the Work Subform to the Artist Form*

FIGURE 11-17   *Binding a Procedure to a Combo Box Selection*

FIGURE 11-18   *Creating the Customer Subquery*

is showing in this figure is Event, which displays event properties. The developer can place the name of a Visual Basic procedure or Access macro in one of these properties, and the procedure or macro will be called when the event occurs. This process is called **trapping an event.** In Figure 11-17, the After Update property has been set to call a Visual BASIC function named AddIntersectionRow and is passing a parameter to that function, whose value is "ARTIST." This function, which was written by the developer, takes the values of ArtistName and CustomerNumber that have been bound to the form and adds a new row to the ARTIST_CUSTOMER_INT table, filling in those two values.

The subform region labeled Customer Subform in Figure 11-17 has been bound to a subform, as was done for the WORK subform. The Customer Subform, however, is bound not to a table but to a query named CUSTOMER Subquery, shown in Figure 11-18. This query contains ArtistName from the intersection table and CustomerNumber and CustomerName from the CUSTOMER table. The result of this query is to create a table with the artists' names bound to data concerning the customers interested in those artists.

The Link Child Fields and the Link Master Fields of the Customer Subform are set to ArtistName so that the master form (Artist Data) will be bound to the CUSTOMER Subform by Artist name. The result of all of these bindings is that when the user clicks on a customer name in the combo box, the function AddIntersectionRow is called. This function adds a row to the ARTIST_CUS-TOMER_INT table and causes the CUSTOMER Subquery to be requeried, which adds the new name to the query for the current ARTIST. The change in the subquery causes the Artist form to be repainted, and when it is, the new value of CUSTOMER is added to the CUSTOMER subform. The final form is shown in Figure 11-19, which is the way the form will appear when the user clicks the Customer List combo box.

FIGURE 11-19   *The Finished Artist Form*

CREATING REPORTS

The process of creating reports with Microsoft Access is similar to that for creating forms. In many ways, the creation of reports is easier, since reports are display-only documents.

Each report is based on a query. To create the query, the developer first must decide which columns of which tables will be required and then construct a query with those columns. For example, suppose that the salespeople at the View Ridge Gallery want a report, sorted by CustomerName, that includes the names of those artists in whom their customers have expressed an interest. Suppose, also, that the salespeople want a list of all the works by those artists that the gallery has ever carried.

Note the wording in the last paragraph. The works to be listed are not the works that the customers have purchased but all the works that the gallery has ever carried for the artists in whom the customers have expressed an interest.

Figure 11-20 shows the query that would be required for the report just described. It uses all four tables, although it does not show any columns from the ARTIST—CUSTOMER—INT table, which is used simply to link a CUSTOMER and an ARTIST. Sample results of this query are shown in Figure 11-21.

■ GROUPING

Report grouping offers a function similar to that of the SQL GROUP BY command. When a column is used for grouping, the underlying query or table is sorted by that column, and a group is defined for each set of rows with the same value of the column.

The report requirements indicate that the report data is to be grouped by customer and, within customer, grouped by artist. Then all of the works for a given

FIGURE 11-20   *Query to be Used for the Customer Interest Report*

FIGURE 11-21   *Sample Data for the Query in Figure 11-20*

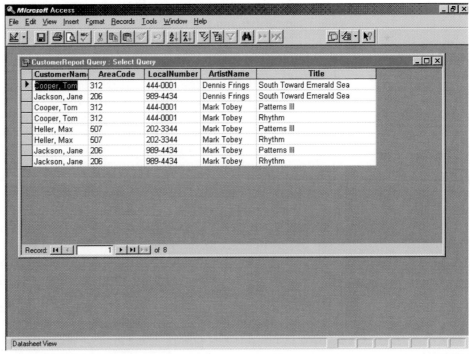

artist are to be listed. Figure 11-22 shows an example of the report for the sample data in Figure 11-21.

Examine the data for the first customer, Tom Cooper. Because he has expressed an interest in two artists, their works are listed after their names. The report is

FIGURE 11-22 *Example of the Customer Interests Report*

consistent, as the same works are listed for Mark Tobey under Tom Cooper as are listed for Mark Tobey under Max Heller. Again, the works shown are those that the gallery has carried, not the works purchased by a particular customer.

■ DEFINING THE REPORT

To create a report with Access, the developer presses the Report button in the database container window and then the New button. Next he enters the table or query on which the report is to be based. The result of these actions is the form in Figure 11-23. Notice that the Record Source property of the report will need to be set to CustomerReport Query, the name of the query in Figure 11-20.

To define the needed groups, the developer selects Sorting and Grouping from the View menu, and a subwindow like the one in Figure 11-24 appears. The names of columns to be used for the grouping are entered in the first column of this window. In Figure 11-24, the developer has typed CustomerName in the first row and ArtistName in the second. The Group Header and Group Footer properties of both these groups were set to yes, which causes Access to create a set of heading and footing areas for Customer and another set for ArtistName. Sometimes such headings and footings are called **report bands,** and a report writer that can support such bands is called a **banded report writer.**

Once this structure has been created, the labels and the text boxes are created and moved into the correct bands and positions within the bands. Additional formatting can be done by placing horizontal or vertical lines on the report. In this report a thick line has been drawn to be displayed before each new Customer group, as can be seen in Figure 11-24.

To improve the readability of this report, the developer has enlarged the font used to display the customer name and also has used boldface type for the customer and artist data and the headings of the work data.

FIGURE 11-23   *The Report Design Window*

FIGURE 11-24   *Defining Report Group Structures*

In addition to the bands shown here, it also is possible to create page headers and footers that are placed at the top and bottom of each page when the page is printed. The location of such headers and footers varies depending on the data and the characteristics of the printer used to print the report.

SUMMARY

A database is a model of the users' model, so a data model representation of the users' model must be created before implementation can start. The four main components of a database application are tables, queries, forms, and reports.

To create tables in Access, the developer initiates the table definition form and then enters the name and data type of each column (called *field* in Access) of that form. Other properties of the column are entered as well.

Relationships are defined in a separate form. Access recognizes both one-to-one and one-to-many relationships. Relationships are defined by identifying the column of the child table that matches the column on the parent table. Once the relationships have been defined, they are used as a default for joins and multitable forms and reports. A form of referential integrity can also be specified.

Queries are used for three purposes in Access: as a means of asking ad hoc questions about the data, as the basis of forms and reports, and as the basis of multivalued controls such as combo boxes. Queries can be defined using Access's version of QBE, or the SQL for the query can be entered directly.

Forms are created by binding various elements of the database to the form and its controls. A table or query is bound to the form itself; columns of the table are bound to text boxes; subforms are bound to subform controls; and tables or queries are bound to combo boxes. The form itself and every control on the form have properties including the binding of the control, its physical characteristics, and possibly the names of the macros of the Access Basic functions to be called when particular events take place.

Reports, like forms, are based on queries or tables. Grouping and sorting are supported. Headers and footers (also called **bands**) can be defined for each group that is defined. Once the structure of the report has been created, text labels, text boxes, and other graphical symbols are added to the appropriate positions of the form.

GROUP I QUESTIONS

11.1   What must exist before the database and database application can be implemented? Why?

11.2   Name two modern, GUI-based DBMS products other than Microsoft Access.

11.3   Redefine the relations in Figure 11-2 to use surrogate keys.

11.4   What is the Access database container? What does it contain?

11.5   What are the six components of an Access database?

11.6   What is an Access field? How does it differ from a table column?

11.7   List the field data types that are supported by Access.

11.8   What is a table key in Access? What is the difference between a key and an index in Access?

11.9   Briefly describe how relationships are defined in Access.

11.10 How is referential integrity supported by Access?

11.11 What are the three uses of queries in Access?

11.12 What are the two ways that queries can be created in Access? Which do you think is better? Why?

11.13 Explain the use of the term *bind* in regard to database application development in Access.

11.14 Explain how table or query data is made available to a form.

11.15 What is the purpose of a text box? What is bound to text boxes?

11.16 What is a subform control? What is it used for?

11.17 How are the rows of the main form connected to the rows of the subform?

11.18 What is the purpose of a combo box?

11.19 Describe the function of the combo box in the Artist Form in Figure 11-19.

11.20 Explain the meaning of the phrase *trapping an event.*

11.21 How is an Access macro or BASIC function bound to an event?

11.22 In the example in the text, the After Update property of the combo box was set to AddIntersectionRow. Describe the purpose of this function.

11.23 What is the essential difference between the functions of a form and those of a report?

11.24 What happens when a column is used for grouping?

11.25 What is a report band? What is its function?

GROUP II QUESTIONS

11.26 Obtain a copy of Microsoft Access. Implement the View Ridge Gallery example, but use the semantic objects shown in Figure 8-2(a). Use data keys rather than surrogate keys, and create a form for CUSTOMER that includes WORK data but not ARTIST data. (CUSTOMER relates directly to the Transaction group attribute, but that attribute is encapsulated in WORK and hence is hidden from CUSTOMER. Thus, the apparent relationship is between CUSTOMER and WORK.) Using these statements and the gallery's information needs, design the form for CUSTOMER and implement it using Access. Use the procedures outlined in this chapter to develop one of your forms. Use the Microsoft Access wizards to develop the others—at least as a starting point.

11.27 Obtain a copy of a GUI-based DBMS product other than Access, such as Paradox for Windows or Lotus Approach. Using that product, implement the database and application described in this chapter.

PROJECT USING SALSA FOR THE DESKTOP

Use SALSA for the Desktop to create the three objects in Figure 11-1. Generate a finished application. Compare the application that is generated with the one shown in this chapter. How are they similar? How are they different? SALSA generates SQL statements similar to those shown here, but they are done automatically and are not visible. Describe advantages and disadvantages of this approach. Under what circumstances would you use Access and under what circumstances would you use SALSA?

V

Part V presents technology and products for databases that are processed by more than one user. Chapter 12 surveys the basic multi-user systems architectures and discusses database reliability, security, and administration in the multi-user environment. Chapter 13 then describes the implementation of a relational database using DB2, IBM's primary database product for mainframes. Chapter 14 addresses client-server database systems and ODBC, a DBMS-independent standard for accessing server databases. Next, Chapter 15 discusses the sharing of enterprise data, including data administration and data warehouses. Finally, Chapter 16 presents database processing on intranets and on the Internet, and describes and illustrates multimedia database applications.

MULTI-USER DATABASE PROCESSING

INTRODUCTION TO MULTI-USER DATABASE PROCESSING

A **multi-user database** is a database in which more than one user processes the database at the same time. Examples of multi-user database applications are bank account processing, travel agency reservations processing, and distributor inventory processing. When more than one person processes a database, a number of important problems and issues arise. For one, it is possible for one user's work to interfere with another's (selling the same seat on the same airline flight, for example). Also, since not all users have the same skills, information requirements, and motivations, security and control become important. Further, when many users process the same database, administration of processing rights, responsibilities, and the control of change are necessary, and hence database administration becomes important.

This chapter discusses each of these dimensions of multi-user database processing. We begin with a survey of multi-user architectures and then discuss reliability, security, and administration, in turn.

MULTI-USER DATABASE PROCESSING ARCHITECTURES

A number of different system architectures are used for multi-user database processing. In the past, teleprocessing systems were the most common. But as microcomputers have become common on the desktop and more powerful as data servers, new multi-user database architectures have arisen. In this section, we introduce teleprocessing, client-server, file-sharing, distributed, and network database alternatives. After this introduction, teleprocessing systems are discussed. Client-server database systems are discussed in Chapter 14, enterprise database systems in Chapter 15, and network databases in Chapter 16.

TELEPROCESSING SYSTEMS

The classic method of supporting a multi-user database system is teleprocessing, which uses one computer and one CPU. All processing is done by this single computer.

Figure 12-1 shows a typical teleprocessing system. Users operate dumb terminals (or microcomputers that emulate dumb terminals) that transmit transaction

FIGURE 12-1   *Relationships of Programs in a Teleprocessing System*

messages and data to the centralized computer. The communications control portion of the operating system receives the messages and data and sends them to the appropriate application program. The program then calls on the DBMS for services, and the DBMS uses the data management portion of the operating system to process the database. When a transaction is completed, the results are returned to the users at the dumb terminals via the communications control portion of the operating system.

Figure 12-1 shows n users submitting transactions processed by three different application programs. Since there is little intelligence at the users' end (that is, the *terminals* are dumb), all commands for formatting the screen must be generated by the CPU and transmitted over the communication lines. This means that the users' interface is generally character oriented and primitive. Systems like this are called teleprocessing systems, since all inputs and outputs are communicated over a distance (*tele-* means "distance") to the centralized computer for processing.

Historically, teleprocessing systems have been the most common alternative for multi-user database systems. But as the price–performance ratio of computers has fallen and, in particular, with the advent of the microcomputer, other alternatives that require multiple computers have begun to be used.

■ CLIENT-SERVER SYSTEMS

Figure 12-2 is a schematic of one of these alternatives, called a **client-server system.** Unlike teleprocessing, which involves a single computer, client-server computing involves multiple computers connected in a network. Some of the computers process application programs and are designated as *clients*. Another computer processes the database and is designated as the *server*.

Figure 12-2 shows an example in which each of n users has his or her own client (application processing) computer: User$_1$ processes AP$_1$ and AP$_2$ on Computer 1. User$_2$ processes AP$_2$ on Computer 2, and User$_n$ processes AP$_2$ and AP$_3$ on Computer N. Another computer is the database server.

There are many options regarding computer type. Theoretically, the client computers can be mainframes or microcomputers. Because of cost, however, in almost all cases the client computers are microcomputers. Similarly, any type of computer can be the server, but again, because of cost, the server is most often a microcomputer. The clients and server are generally connected using a local area network (LAN).

FIGURE 12-2   *Client-Server Architecture*

Although it is rare for client computers to be anything other than micros, sometimes the server is a mainframe, especially when considerable power is required from the server or, for reasons of security and control, it is inappropriate to locate the database on a microcomputer.

The system in Figure 12-2 has a single server, although this need not always be the case. Multiple servers may process different databases or provide other services on behalf of the clients. For example, in an engineering consulting firm, one server might process the database while a second server supports computer-assisted design applications.

If there are multiple database processing servers, each one must process a different database in order for the system to be considered a client-server system. When two servers process the same database, the system is no longer called a client-server system; rather, it is termed a distributed database system.

■ FILE-SHARING SYSTEMS

A second multi-user architecture is shown in Figure 12-3. This architecture, called **file-sharing,** distributes to the users' computers not only the application programs but also the DBMS. In this case, the *server* is a file server and not a database server. Almost all file-sharing systems employ local-area networks of microcomputers.

The file-sharing architecture was developed before the client-server architecture, and in many ways it is more primitive. With file sharing, the DBMS on each user's computer sends requests to the data management portion of the operating system on the file server for file-level processing. This means that considerably more traffic crosses the LAN than with the client-server architecture.

For example, consider the processing of a query to obtain the Name and Address of all rows in the CUSTOMER table where Zip equals 98033. In a client-server system, the application program would send the following SQL command:

```
SELECT    NAME, ADDRESS
FROM      CUSTOMER
WHERE     ZIP = 98033
```

The server would respond with all qualifying Names and Addresses.

FIGURE 12-3   *File-Sharing Architecture*

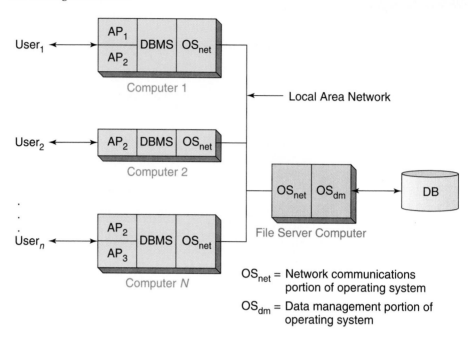

In a file-sharing system, the DBMS is on the local computer, and therefore no program on the file server is capable of processing the SQL statement. All such processing must be done on the user computer, so the DBMS must ask the file server to transmit the entire CUSTOMER table. If that table has indexes or other overhead associated with it, the overhead structures must be transmitted as well. Clearly, with file sharing, much more data need be transmitted across the LAN.

Because of these problems, file-sharing systems are seldom used for high-volume transaction-oriented processing. Too much data need be locked and transmitted for each transaction, and this architecture would result in very slow performance. There is, however, one database application for which this architecture makes sense: the query processing of downloaded, extracted data. If one or more users need access to large portions of the database in order to produce reports or answer queries, it can make sense to have a server that downloads large sections of data. In this case, the downloaded data are not updated and not returned to the database. We show examples of processing extracted data in Chapter 15.

File-sharing systems are also used for nondatabase applications, such as those that require large, fast disks to store large files such as large graphics, audio, and animations. They also are used to share expensive printers, plotters, and other peripheral equipment. Client-server and file-sharing systems are presented in more detail in Chapters 14, and 15.

■ DISTRIBUTED DATABASE SYSTEMS

A fourth alternative, shown in Figure 12-4, is a distributed database system, in which the database itself is distributed. In Figure 12-4, the database (or a portion of it) is stored on all N computers. As shown, Computers 1, 2, and N process both the applications and the database, and Computer 3 processes only the database.

In Figure 12-4, the dashed line around the files indicates that the database is composed of all the segments of the database on all N computers. These computers may be physically located in the same facility, on different sides of the world, or somewhere in between.

FIGURE 12-4   *Distributed Database Architecture*

OS_{net} =   Network communications portion of operating system

OS_{dm} =   Data management portion of operating system

DDBMS = Distributed DBMS

DISTRIBUTED PROCESSING VERSUS DISTRIBUTED DATABASE PROCESSING
Consider Figures 12-1, 12-2, 12-3, and 12-4 again. The file-sharing, client-server, and distributed database alternatives all differ from teleprocessing in an important way: They all use multiple computers for applications or DBMS processing. Accordingly, most people would say that all three of these architectures are examples of **distributed systems,** because applications processing has been distributed among several computers.

Observe, however, that the database itself is distributed only in the architecture shown in Figure 12-4. Neither the client-server nor the file-sharing architectures distribute the database to multiple computers. Consequently, most people would *not* refer to the file-sharing or client-server architectures as **distributed database systems.**

TYPES OF DISTRIBUTED DATABASES   There are a number of types of distributed database systems. First look at Figure 12-5(a), which shows a nondistributed database with four pieces, W, X, Y, and Z. All four pieces of these segments are located on a single database, and there is no data duplication.

Now consider the distributed alternatives in Figures 12-5(b) through (d). Figure 12-5(b) shows the first distributed alternative, in which the database has been distributed to two computers; pieces W and X are stored on Computer 1, and pieces

FIGURE 12-5

Types of Distributed Databases: (a) Nonpartitioned, Nonreplicated Alternative; (b) Partitioned, Nonreplicated Alternative; (c) Nonpartitioned, Replicated Alternative; (d) Partitioned, Replicated Alternative

Y and Z are stored on Computer 2. In Figure 12-5(c), the entire database has been replicated on two computers. Finally, in Figure 12-5(d), the database has been partitioned, and a portion (Y) has been replicated.

Two terms are sometimes used with regard to partitioning of databases. A vertical partition or **vertical fragment** refers to a table that is broken into two or more sets of columns. Thus, a table R(C1, C2, C3, C4) could be broken into two vertical partitions of P1(C1, C2) and P2(C3, C4). Depending on the application and the reason for creating the partitions, the key of R would most likely also be placed into P2 to form P2(C1, C3, C4). A horizontal partition or **horizontal fragment** refers to the rows of a table when they are divided into pieces. Thus, in the relation R, if the first 1000 rows are placed into R1(C1, C2, C3, C4) and the remaining rows are placed into R2(C1, C2, C3, C4), two horizontal partitions will result. Sometimes a database is broken into both horizontal and vertical partitions, and the result is sometimes called a mixed partition.

COMPARISON OF DISTRIBUTED DATABASE ALTERNATIVES   These alternatives are summarized on a continuum in Figure 12-6, arranged in increasing degree of distribution, from left to right. The nondistributed database is on the leftmost point of the continuum, and the partitioned, replicated database is on the rightmost point. In between these extremes is a partitioned database. The partitions are allocated to two or more computers and a database that is not partitioned, but each entire database is replicated on two or more computers.

The characteristics of the alternatives on this continuum are listed in Figure 12-6. The alternatives toward the right increase parallelism, independence, flexibility, and availability, but they also mean greater expense, complexity, difficulty of control, and risk to security.

One of these advantages is particularly significant to business organizations. The alternatives on the right of Figure 12-6 provide greater flexibility and hence can be better tailored to the organizational structure and the organizational process. A highly decentralized manufacturing company, for example, in which plant managers have wide latitude in their planning, will never be satisfied with an organizational information system with the structure of Figure 12-5(a) because the structure of the information system architecture and the structure of the company fight with each other. Thus, the alternatives on the right side provide a better and more appropriate fit to that organization than do those on the left.

 FIGURE 12-6   *Continuum of Database Distribution Alternatives*

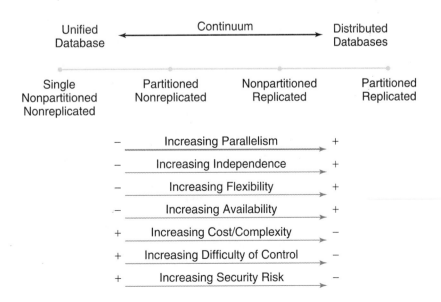

The greatest disadvantage is the difficulty of control and the resulting potential loss of data integrity. Consider the database architecture in Figure 12-5(d). A user connected to Computer 1 can read and update a data item in Partition Y on Computer 1 at the very same time that a different user connected to Computer 2 can read and update that data item in Partition Y on Computer 2.

Because of the difficulty of control and possible integrity problems, distributed databases are infrequently used for business information systems. Accordingly, we will not consider them further in this text.

■ INTRANET AND INTERNET DATABASE PROCESSING

With the advent of organizational intranets and with the rise in popularity of the Internet and the World Wide Web, it has recently become common to share databases over such networks. Most often, the client-server architecture is used in these environments. We discuss and illustrate such database applications in Chapter 16.

◆ DATABASE RELIABILITY

The term **database reliability** is used to refer to two distinct concepts: concurrency control and database recovery. **Concurrency control** consists of measures that are taken to prevent one user's work from interfering with another's. The goal of such measures is to ensure that the result of a user's work in a multi-user environment is the same as it would have been if the user had been working alone. **Database recovery** refers to the methods and techniques that are used to ensure that the database can be repaired or reconstructed after failure.

■ THE NEED FOR ATOMIC TRANSACTIONS

In most database applications, users submit work in the form of **transactions,** which are also known as **logical units of work** (LUWs). A transaction (or LUW) is a series of actions to be taken on the database such that either all of them are performed successfully or none of them is performed at all, in which case the database remains unchanged. Such a transaction is sometimes called **atomic,** since it is performed as a unit.

Consider the following sequence of database actions that could occur when recording a new order:

1. Change the customer record, increasing Amount Owed.
2. Change the salesperson record, increasing Commission Due.
3. Insert the new order record into the database.

Suppose the last step failed, perhaps because of insufficient file space. Imagine the confusion that would ensue if the first two changes were made but not the third one. The customer would be billed for an order never received, and a salesperson would receive a commission on an order that was never sent to the customer. Clearly, these three actions need to be taken as a unit—either all of them should be done or none of them should be done.

Figure 12-7 compares the results of performing these activities as a series of independent steps (Figure 12-7[a]) and as an atomic transaction (Figure 12-7[b]). Notice that when the steps are carried out atomically and one fails, no changes are made in the database. Also note that the commands Start Transaction, Commit Transaction, or Rollback Transaction must be issued by the application program to mark the boundaries of the transaction logic. The particular form of these commands varies from one DBMS product to another.

FIGURE 12-7

Comparison of the Results of Applying Serial Actions Versus a Multiple-Step Transaction: (a) Two out of Three Activities Successfully Completed, Resulting in Database Anomalies, and (b) No Change Made Because Entire Transaction Not Successful

<u>Before</u>

CUSTOMER

C-no	Order #	Description	Cost
123	1000	400 Baseballs	$2400

SALESPERSON

Name	Total-Sales
JONES	$3200

ORDERS

Order #
1000
2000
3000
4000
5000
6000
7000
FULL

<u>Action</u>

START

1. Add new-order data to CUSTOMER.

2. Add new-order data to SALESPERSON.

3. Insert new ORDER.

STOP

<u>After</u>

CUSTOMER

C-no	Order #	Description	Cost
123	1000	400 Baseballs	$2400
123	8000	250 Basketballs	$6500

SALESPERSON

Name	Total-Sales
JONES	$9700

ORDERS

Order #
1000
2000
3000
4000
5000
6000
7000
FULL

(a)

285

FIGURE 12-7 *(Continued)*

Before

CUSTOMER

C-no	Order #	Description	Cost
123	1000	400 Baseballs	$2400

SALESPERSON

Name	Total-Sales	
JONES	$3200	...

ORDERS

Order #	
1000	...
2000	...
3000	...
4000	...
5000	...
6000	...
7000	...

FULL

Transaction

```
Start Transaction
  Change CUSTOMER data
  Change SALESPERSON data
  Insert ORDER data
  If no errors then
    Commit Transactions
  Else
    Rollback Transaction
  End If
```

After

CUSTOMER

C-no	Order #	Description	Cost
123	1000	400 Baseballs	$2400

SALESPERSON

Name	Total-Sales	
JONES	$3200	...

ORDERS

Order #	
1000	...
2000	...
3000	...
4000	...
5000	...
6000	...
7000	...

FULL

(b)

CONCURRENT TRANSACTION PROCESSING   When two transactions are being processed against a database at the same time, they are termed *concurrent transactions*. While it may appear to the users that concurrent transactions are being processed simultaneously, this cannot be true, since the CPU of the machine processing the database can execute only one instruction at a time. Usually transactions are interleaved, which means that the operating system switches CPU services among tasks so that some portion of each of them is carried out in a given interval. This switching among tasks is done so quickly that two people seated at terminals side by side, processing the same database, may believe that their two transactions are completed simultaneously, but, in reality, the two transactions are interleaved.

Figure 12-8 shows two concurrent transactions. User A's transaction reads Item 100, changes it, and rewrites it in the database. User B's transaction takes the same actions, but on Item 200. The CPU processes User A until it encounters an I/O interrupt or some other delay for User A. The operating system shifts control to User B. The CPU now processes User B until an interrupt, at which point the operating system passes control back to User A. To the users, the processing appears to be simultaneous, but actually it is interleaved, or concurrent.

LOST UPDATE PROBLEM   The concurrent processing illustrated in Figure 12-8 poses no problems because the users are processing different data. But suppose that both users want to process Item 100. For example, User A wants to order 5 units of Item 100, and User B wants to order 3 units of the same item.

Figure 12-9 illustrates the problem. User A reads Item 100's record into a user work area. According to the record, there are ten items in inventory. Then User B reads Item 100's record into another user work area. Again, according to the record there are ten in inventory. Now User A takes 5, decrements the count of items in its user work area to five, and rewrites the record for Item 100. Then User B takes three, decrements the count in its user work area to seven, and rewrites the record for Item 100. The database now shows, incorrectly, that there are seven Item 100s in inventory. To review: We started with ten in inventory, User A took five, User B took three, and the database shows that seven are in inventory. Clearly, this is a problem.

   Example of Concurrent Processing of Two Users' Tasks

User A

1. Read item 100.
2. Change item 100.
3. Write item 100.

User B

1. Read item 200.
2. Change item 200.
3. Write item 200.

Order of processing at CPU

1. Read item 100 for A.
2. Read item 200 for B.
3. Change item 100 for A.
4. Write item 100 for A.
5. Change item 200 for B.
6. Write item 200 for B.

FIGURE 12-9   *Lost Update Problem*

User A

1. Read item 100
   (assume item count is 10).
2. Reduce count of items by 5.
3. Write item 100.

User B

1. Read item 100
   (assume item count is 10).
2. Reduce count of items by 3.
3. Write item 100.

Order of processing at CPU

1. Read item 100 (for A).
2. Read item 100 (for B).
3. Set item count to 5 (for A).
4. Write item 100 for A.
5. Set item count to 7 (for B).
6. Write item 100 for B.

Note: The change and write in Steps 3 and 4 are lost.

Both users obtained data that were correct at the time they obtained them. But when User B read the record, User A already had a copy that it was about to update. This situation is called the **lost update problem** or the **concurrent update problem.** There is another, similar problem, called the **inconsistent read problem.** With it, User A reads data that have been processed by a portion of a transaction from User B. As a result, User A reads incorrect data.

One remedy for the inconsistencies caused by concurrent processing is to prevent multiple applications from obtaining copies of the same record when the record is about to be changed. This remedy is called **resource locking.**

■ RESOURCE LOCKING

One way to prevent concurrent processing problems is to disallow sharing by locking data that are retrieved for update. Figure 12-10 shows the order of processing using a **lock** command. Because of the lock User B's transaction must wait until User A is finished with the Item 100 data. Using this strategy, User B can read Item 100's record only after User A has completed the modification. In this case, the final item count stored in the database is two, as it should be. (We started with ten, A took five, and B took three, leaving two.)

LOCK TERMINOLOGY   Locks can be placed either automatically by the DBMS or by a command issued to the DBMS from the application program or query user. Locks placed by the DBMS are called **implicit locks;** those placed by command are called **explicit locks.**

In the preceding example, the locks were applied to rows of data. Not all locks are applied at this level, however. Some DBMS products lock at the page level, some at the table level, and some at the database level. The size of a lock is referred to as the **lock granularity.** Locks with large granularity are easy for the DBMS to administer but frequently cause conflicts. Locks with small granularity are difficult to administer (there are many more details for the DBMS to keep track of and check), but conflicts are less common.

Locks also vary by type. An **exclusive lock** locks the item from access of any type. No other transaction can read or change the data. A **shared lock** locks the

FIGURE 12-10   *Concurrent Processing with Explicit Locks*

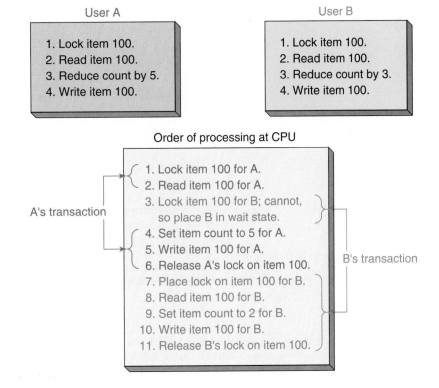

item from change but not from read. That is, other transactions can read the item as long as they do not attempt to alter it.

SERIALIZABLE TRANSACTIONS   When two or more transactions are processed concurrently, the results in the database should be logically consistent with the results that would have been achieved had the transactions been processed in an arbitrary serial fashion. A scheme for processing concurrent transactions in this way is said to be **serializable.**

Serializability can be achieved by a number of different means. One way is to process the transaction using **two-phased locking.** With this strategy, transactions are allowed to obtain locks as necessary, but once the first lock is released, no other lock can be obtained. Transactions thus have a **growing phase,** in which the locks are obtained, and a **shrinking phase,** in which the locks are released.

A special case of two-phased locking is used with a number of DBMS products, including DB2. With it, locks are obtained throughout the transaction, but no lock is released until the COMMIT or ROLLBACK command is issued. This strategy is more restrictive than two-phase locking requires, but it is easier to implement.

In general, the boundaries of a transaction should correspond to the definition of the semantic object it is processing. Following the two-phase strategy, the rows of each relation in the object are locked as needed. Changes are made, but the data are not committed to the database until all of the object has been processed. At this point, changes are made in the actual database, and all locks are released.

Consider an order entry transaction that involves an object CUSTOMER-ORDER that is constructed from data in the CUSTOMER table, the SALESPERSON table, and the ORDER table. To make sure that the database will suffer no anomalies due to concurrency, the order entry transaction begins by issuing all of its locks (on CUSTOMER, SALESPERSON, and ORDER) and concludes by making all the database changes and then releasing all its locks.

FIGURE 12-11   *Deadlock*

User A		**User B**	

User A
1. Lock paper.
2. Take paper.
3. Lock pencils.

User B
1. Lock pencils.
2. Take pencils.
3. Lock paper.

Order of processing at CPU

1. Lock paper for user A.
2. Lock pencils for user B.
3. Process A's requests; write paper record.
4. Process B's requests; write pencil record.
5. Put A in wait state for pencils.
6. Put B in wait state for paper.
** Locked **

DEADLOCK Although locking solves one problem, it introduces another. Consider what might happen when two users want to order two items from inventory. Suppose User A wants to order some paper, and if she can get the paper, she wants to order some pencils. Then suppose User B wants to order some pencils, and if he can get the pencils, he wants to order some paper. The order of processing could be that shown in Figure 12-11.

In this figure, users A and B are locked in a condition known as **deadlock,** or sometimes the **deadly embrace.** Each is waiting for a resource that the other person has locked. There are two common ways of solving this problem: preventing the deadlock from occurring or allowing the deadlock to occur and then breaking it.

Deadlock can be prevented in several ways. One way is to allow users to issue only one lock request at a time. In essence, users must lock all the resources they want at once. If User A in the illustration had locked both the paper and the pencil records at the beginning, the embrace would never have taken place.

The other strategy is to allow the deadlock to occur, detect it, and then break it. Unfortunately, there is only one way to break deadlock—kill one of the transactions. In the situation in Figure 12-11, one of the two transactions must be aborted. When that happens, the lock is released, and the other transaction can process the database unhindered. Obviously, any changes the killed transaction has made in the database must be undone; we discuss the techniques for this in the next section.

■ DATABASE RECOVERY

Computer systems can fail. Hardware breaks. Programs have bugs. Human procedures contain errors, and people make mistakes. All of these failures can and do occur in database applications. Since a database is shared by many people and since it often is a key element of an organization's operations, it is important to recover it as soon as possible.

Several problems must be addressed. First, from a business standpoint, business functions must continue. For example, customer orders, financial transactions, and packing lists must be completed manually. Later, when the database application is operational again, the new data can be entered. Second, computer operations personnel must restore the system to a usable state as quickly as possible and as close as possible to what it was when the system crashed. Third, users must know what to do when the system becomes available again. Some work may need to be reentered, and users must know how far back they need to go.

When failures occur, it is impossible simply to fix the problem and resume processing. Even if no data are lost during a failure (which assumes that all types of memory are nonvolatile—an unrealistic assumption), the timing and scheduling of computer processing are too complex to be accurately re-created. Enormous amounts of overhead data and processing would be required for the operating system to be able to restart processing precisely where it was interrupted. It is simply not possible to roll back the clock and put all the electrons in the same configuration they were in at the time of the failure. Two other approaches are possible: recovery via reprocessing, and recovery via rollback/rollforward.

RECOVERY VIA REPROCESSING   Since processing cannot be resumed at a precise point, the next best alternative is to go back to a known point and reprocess the workload from there. The simplest form of this type of recovery is to make a copy periodically of the database (called a **database save**) and to keep a record of all transactions that have been processed since the save. Then, when there is a failure, the operations staff can restore the database from the save and reprocess all the transactions.

Unfortunately, this simple strategy is normally unfeasible. First, reprocessing transactions takes the same amount of time as did processing them in the first place. If the computer is heavily scheduled, the system may never catch up.

Second, when transactions are processed concurrently, events are asynchronous. Slight variations in human activity, such as a user inserting a floppy disk more slowly or a user reading an electronic mail message before responding to an application prompt, may change the order of the execution of concurrent transactions. Therefore, whereas Customer A got the last seat on a flight during the original processing, Customer B may get the last seat during reprocessing. For these reasons, reprocessing is normally not a viable form of recovery from failure in concurrent processing systems.

RECOVERY VIA ROLLBACK/ROLLFORWARD   A second approach is periodically to make a copy of the database (the database save) and to keep a log of the changes made by transactions against the database since the save. Then, when there is a failure, one of two methods can be used. Using the first method, called **rollforward,** the database is restored using the saved data, and all valid transactions since the save are reapplied. (We are not reprocessing the transactions, as the application programs are not involved in the rollforward. Instead, the processed changes, as recorded in the log, are reapplied.)

The second method is **rollback,** in which we undo changes made by erroneous or partially processed transactions by undoing the changes they have made in the database. Then the valid transactions that were in process at the time of the failure are restarted.

Both of these methods require that a **log** of the transaction results be kept. This log contains records of the data changes in chronological order. Transactions must be written to the log before they are applied to the database. That way, if the system crashes between the time a transaction is logged and the time it is applied, then at worst there is a record of an unapplied transaction. If, on the other hand, the transactions were to be applied before they were logged, it would be possible (as well as undesirable) to change the database but have no record of the change. If this happened, an unwary user might reenter an already completed transaction.

In the event of a failure, the log is used both to undo and to redo transactions, as shown in Figure 12-12. To undo a transaction, the log must contain a copy of

FIGURE 12-12

Undo and Redo Transactions: (a) Removing Changes in the Database (Rollback) and (b) Reapplying Changes in the Database (Rollforward)

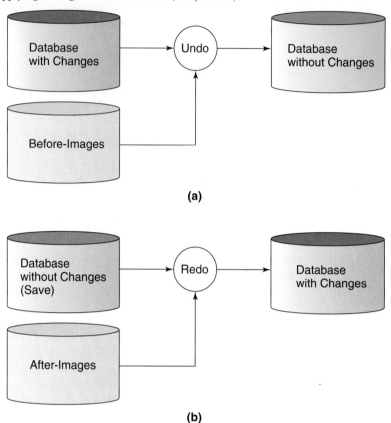

every database record (or page) before it was changed. Such records are called **before-images.** A transaction is undone by applying before-images of all its changes to the database.

To redo a transaction, the log must contain a copy of every database record (or page) after it was changed. These records are called **after-images.** A transaction is redone by applying after-images of all its changes to the database. Possible data items of a transaction log are shown in Figure 12-13(a).

For this example log, each transaction has a unique name for identification purposes. Furthermore, all images for a given transaction are linked together with pointers. One pointer points to the previous change made by this transaction (the reverse pointer), and the other points to the next change made by this transaction (the forward pointer). A zero in the pointer field means that this is the end of the list. The DBMS recovery subsystem uses these pointers to locate all records for a particular transaction. Figure 12-13(b) shows an example of the linking of log records.

Other data items in the log are the time of the action; the type of operation (START marks the beginning of a transaction, and COMMIT terminates a transaction, releasing all locks that were in place); the object acted on, such as record type and identifier; and finally, the before-images and after-images.

Given a log with both before-images and after-images, the undo and redo actions are straightforward (to describe, anyway). To undo the transaction in Figure 12-14, the recovery processor simply replaces each changed record with its before-image. When all before-images have been restored, the transaction is undone. To redo a transaction, the recovery processor starts with the version of the

FIGURE 12-13   *Transaction Log: (a) Data Items in a Log Record and (b) Log Instance for Three Transactions*

Transaction ID	Type of Operation
Reverse Pointer	Object
Forward Pointer	Before-Image
Time	After-Image

(a)

Relative
Record
Number

1	OT1	0	2	11:42	START			
2	OT1	1	4	11:43	MODIFY	CUST 100	(old value)	(new value)
3	OT2	0	8	11:46	START			
4	OT1	2	5	11:47	MODIFY	SP AA	(old value)	(new value)
5	OT1	4	7	11:47	INSERT	ORDER 11		(value)
6	CT1	0	9	11:48	START			
7	OT1	5	0	11:49	COMMIT			
8	OT2	3	0	11:50	COMMIT			
9	CT1	6	10	11:51	MODIFY	SP BB	(old value)	(new value)
10	CT1	9	0	11:51	COMMIT			

(b)

database at the time the transaction started and applies all after-images. As stated, this action assumes that an earlier version of the database is available from a database save.

Restoring a database to its most recent save and reapplying all transactions may require considerable processing. To reduce the delay, DBMS products sometimes use checkpoints. A **checkpoint** is a point of synchronization between the database and the transaction log. To perform a checkpoint, the DBMS refuses new requests, finishes processing outstanding requests, and writes its buffers to disk. The DBMS then waits until the operating system notifies it that all outstanding write requests to the database and to the log have been successfully completed. At this point, the log and the database are synchronized. A checkpoint record is then written to the log. Later, the database can be recovered from the checkpoint and only after-images for transactions that started after the checkpoint need to be applied.

Checkpoints are inexpensive operations, and it is feasible to take three or four (or more) per hour. In this way, no more than fifteen or twenty minutes of processing need to be recovered. Some DBMS products automatically checkpoint themselves, making human intervention unnecessary.

DATABASE SECURITY

Database processing can provide great value to organizations, but, unfortunately, such processing also increases organizational vulnerability. With a database, the company's data—a valuable resource—are centralized and made readily accessible. In fact, DBMS products are designed to maximize this accessibility.

FIGURE 12-14 *Example of a Recovery Strategy: (a) ORDER Transaction and (b) Recovery Processing to Undo an ORDER Record*

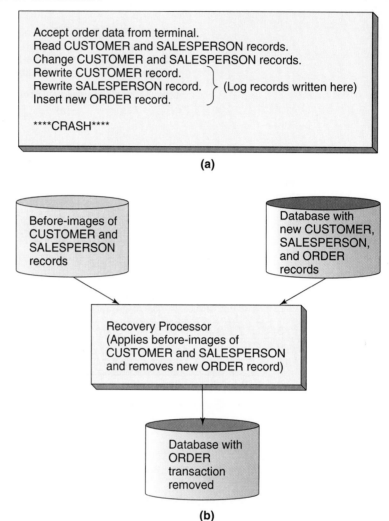

This situation is great for the authorized user. But, unfortunately, DBMS products are also easy for unauthorized users—and criminals—to use. Recognizing the problem of unauthorized use, most DBMS vendors have incorporated security features into their products. To the extent possible, these features allow only authorized users (people or programs) to access the data and restrict the types of processing on the data.

Not all users (and programs) are authorized to access all of the data. Further, some users need access to more data than other users, and some need more extensive processing rights as well. For example, some users need to modify or delete records, but other users need not.

In *Database Security and Integrity,* Fernandez, Summers, and Wood developed a model of database security.[1] Their model is essentially a table of processing permissions, or **authorization rules.** As shown in Figure 12-15, the table has four columns representing subjects, objects,[2] actions, and authorization constraints. A

[1]E. B. Fernandez, R. C. Summers, and C. Wood, *Database Security and Integrity* (Reading, MA: Addison-Wesley, 1981).
[2]This use of the term *object* is more general than *semantic object,* as it refers to some element or entity of the database or database application.

FIGURE 12-15   *Sample of Authorization Rules*

Subject	Object	Action	Authorization Constraint
PGM OE104J	ORDER Record	Insert	Amount less than $500,000
Sally Smith	ORDER Record	Read	None
Payroll Dept	EMPLOYEE Record	Read	Hourly workers
Payroll Dept	EMPLOYEE Record	Modify	Hourly workers
Payroll Dept	EMPLOYEE Record	Insert	Hourly workers
Payroll Supv	EMPLOYEE Record	Delete	Hourly workers
Payroll Supv	Read Permission of EMPLOYEE Records	Grant	To payroll personnel

row in this table indicates that the named subject has permission to take the indicated action on the listed object, subject to the stated authorization constraints. Thus, row 1 indicates that the program OE104J is authorized to insert ORDER records as long as the amount of the order is less than $500,000.

Although no DBMS product provides security in the form of this model, the model is an effective framework for understanding security capabilities and can help when determining and documenting users' processing rights and responsibilities. Consider the four columns in the model.

■ SUBJECTS

A subject is any identifiable user or user group that can process the database. Examples of subjects are particular people (Sally Smith), groups of people (everyone in the payroll department), people operating in particular roles (a teller making deposit transactions), application programs, and remote computers.

Determining whether someone who claims to be a subject really is that subject is difficult. People can be identified by fingerprints, voice prints, and passwords, to name a few techniques. Passwords are by far the most commonly used identifiers in a computer environment. Computer equipment is identified by hardware configuration (say, the line connected to port 4) and by the presence or absence of specialized signals. Programs are usually identified by name or specialized protocol.

In the database environment, the subject desiring access to an object provides his, her, or its identifier (name or password, for example). For verification, the DBMS looks up the name of the object and other data in a table and, if the identifier is found, determines what objects that user can access. If the object desired is on the authorized list for that user, then access is allowed.

■ OBJECTS

The second column of the security table in Figure 12-15 contains objects, the database units to be protected by security. Examples of objects (using relational terminology) are databases, relations, rows, columns, views, the DBMS, programs, transactions, and knowledge of status (for example, the existence or nonexistence of an attribute).

The term *granularity,* which was used earlier to refer to the size of locks, is also sometimes used to refer to the size of security objects. A security system that allows access to (or prevents access from) the entire database as a unit has large granularity. Conversely, a security system that allows access to or prevents access from a particular attribute has small granularity.

Small-granularity security systems allow close control over data. The users' access can be limited to the data needed to perform a function. On the other hand, security systems with small granularity require more overhead processing to administer. If a DBMS must check the authorization every time a user accesses any attribute of any row, processing will be slow and expensive.

Choosing the granularity of a security system involves a trade-off between closely tailored security and processing efficiency. As security increases, efficiency decreases since more processing is required. Deciding how much security is enough is an important part of system requirements.

■ ACTIONS

The action column in Figure 12-15 identifies what the subject can do to the object. Possibilities include reading, inserting, deleting, modifying, creating, destroying, and granting. Inserting and creating sound similar, but they differ as follows: Inserting means adding data to an existing structure, and creating means building the structure. Thus, a subject can insert a row (record) or create the structure of a table. Similarly, deleting means removing data, and destroying means eliminating data and structure.

The grant action refers to giving a permission (such as permission to modify data) to another subject. In Figure 12-15, the last row of the table specifies that the payroll supervisor has the authority to grant permission to payroll personnel to read employee records.

■ AUTHORIZATION CONSTRAINTS

Authorization constraints specify limitations on permissions concerning subject, object, and action. Several examples of authorization constraints are shown in Figure 12-15. For example, the payroll department can process EMPLOYEE records for hourly workers. If this table contains all the authorization constraints on the database, then the payroll department can process records *only* for hourly workers and not for supervisory or executive employees. Supervisory and executive payroll would be processed outside of the database system.

■ SECURITY IN DBMS PRODUCTS

No commercial DBMS provides as general a security capability as that shown in Figure 12-15. Rather, DBMS products usually offer a subset of these capabilities. The database developers, therefore, should determine security requirements and augment the capabilities of the DBMS product in areas where it is lacking.

SUBJECT-ORIENTED SECURITY   With subject-oriented security, the subject is defined to the DBMS, and each is allocated permissions. Before allowing the subject to perform a database action, the DBMS confirms that he or she or it has such authority. If the subject does not have permission, the DBMS will not permit the user's request. The table in Figure 12-16 illustrates permissions that have been as-

FIGURE 12-16   *Subject-oriented Security Example: Permissions Granted to the Program Processing ORDER Transactions*

| | | Objects | | |
		CUSTOMER Records	SALESPERSON Records	ORDER Records
Actions	Read	Y	Y	Y
	Insert	N	N	Y
	Modify	Y	Y	Y
	Delete	N	N	N
	Grant	N	N	N

signed to one subject. In this case, the subject is a program. The table tells us that all ORDER transactions are authorized to read CUSTOMER, SALESPERSON, and ORDER records. ORDER transactions may insert only ORDER records, but they may modify all three types of records. ORDER transactions are not authorized to delete any data, nor can they grant any rights to other subjects.

OBJECT-ORIENTED SECURITY   Another approach to security defines authorizations from the standpoint of objects. In this case, each object has an authorization matrix that shows what actions can be taken by various subjects on that object. Most often the subjects are defined by passwords. For example, in Figure 12-17 those subjects who can provide the password SESAME can read, insert, modify, and delete SALESPERSON records. People who supply the password ABALONE can read SALESPERSON records but take no other action.

CONSTRAINTS VIA PROGRAMMABLE EXITS   Constraints on authorization rules are not generally supported by DBMS products, although some DBMS products have an indirect way of enforcing authorization constraints. They exit to (call) user-written programs whenever a specified action is performed on a specified object. (The event properties described for Microsoft Access in Chapter 11 are examples of such exits.) The program can then provide the logic to enforce the constraint. Note that end users do not generally write such programs; rather, they are usually developed by professional programmers.

Consider an example. Suppose that no order in excess of $50,000 is to be accepted after 3:00 P.M. on a Friday or the day before a holiday. Instead, such orders are to be referred to a supervisor. In this case, the database designer specifies that whenever an ORDER record is created, a special program is to be called. This program will determine whether these conditions apply. If so, the program will not allow the insert and will instead send a message to a supervisor.

User exits provide a great deal of flexibility, as they can supplement the DBMS's capabilities or compensate for deficiencies in a particular DBMS product. Their advantages are their flexibility and greater control and security. But exits to user-written routines have disadvantages, as well. The user organization must develop and test these routines, and such routines add overhead to the system. They may need to be dynamically loaded (copied into computer memory from disk storage each time they are needed) and therefore degrade the system's performance.

In terms of security, then, a DBMS includes facilities for identifying subjects and allowing them to access the database, for restricting the actions that subjects can perform, for limiting objects that subjects can access, and for allowing user-developed routines to be incorporated into normal processing. Thus the *operation* of a security system is one function of the DBMS. Establishing the *policies and administration* of a security system is, however, a function of database administration.

FIGURE 12-17   *Object-oriented Security Example: Permissions Granted for SALESPERSON Records*

Object: SALESPERSON Record

		Subjects Who Know Password SESAME	Subjects Who Know Password ABALONE
Actions	Read	Y	Y
	Insert	Y	N
	Modify	Y	N
	Delete	Y	N
	Grant	N	N

DATABASE ADMINISTRATION

Both the terms **data administration** and **database administration** are used in industry. In some cases the terms are considered synonymous; in other cases, they have different meanings. In this text, we use the term *data administration* to refer to a function that applies to all of the organization. Sometimes the term *global database administration* is used instead of *data administration*. The term *database administration* refers to a function that is specific to a particular database, including the applications that process that database. This chapter addresses database administration. Data administration is discussed in Chapter 15.

Databases vary considerably in size and scope, from single-user personal database to large interorganizational databases like airline reservations systems. All of these databases have a need for database administration, although the tasks to be accomplished vary in complexity. For example, for a personal database individuals follow simple procedures for backing up their data, and they keep minimal records for documentation. In this case, the person who uses the database also performs the DBA functions, even though he or she is probably unaware of it.

For multi-user database applications, database administration becomes both more important and more difficult. Consequently, it generally has formal recognition. For workgroup applications, one or two people are given this function on a part-time basis. For organizationwide databases, database administration responsibilities are often too time-consuming and too varied to be handled even by a single full-time person. Supporting a database with dozens or hundreds of users requires considerable time as well as both technical knowledge and diplomatic skills and usually is handled by an office of database administration. The manager of the office is often known as the **database administrator;** in this case, the acronym **DBA** refers to either the office or the manager.

The overall responsibility of the DBA is to facilitate the development and use of the database. Usually, this means balancing the conflicting goals of protecting the database and maximizing its availability and benefit to users. The DBA is responsible for the development, operation, and maintenance of the database and its applications, specifically

• Managing the database structure

• Managing data activity

• Managing the DBMS

• Establishing the database data dictionary

■ MANAGING THE DATABASE STRUCTURE

Managing the database structure includes participating in the initial database design and implementation as well as controlling and managing changes to it. Ideally, the DBA is involved early in the development of the database and its applications, participates in the requirements study, helps evaluate alternatives, including the DBMS to be used, and helps design the database structure. For large, organizational applications, the DBA usually is a manager who supervises the work of technically oriented database design personnel.

Once the database has been designed, it is implemented using the DBMS product, and the database data are created. The DBA participates in the development of procedures and controls to ensure high integrity and quality of the database data.

CONFIGURATION CONTROL   After a database and its applications have been implemented, changes in requirements are inevitable. Such changes can arise from new needs, from changes in the business environment, from changes in policy, and so forth. When changes to requirements necessitate changes to the database structure, great care must be used because database structure changes seldom involve just one application.

Hence, effective database administration must include procedures and policies by which users can register their needs for changes, the entire database community can discuss the impacts of the changes, and a global decision can be made whether or not to implement proposed changes.

Because of the size and complexity of a database and its applications, changes sometimes have unexpected results. The DBA thus must be prepared to repair the database and to gather sufficient information to diagnose and correct the problem that caused the damage. The database is most vulnerable to failure after a change in its structure.

DOCUMENTATION   The DBA's final responsibility in managing the database structure is documentation. It is extremely important to know what changes have been made, how they were made, and when they were made. A change in the database structure may cause an error that is not revealed for six months; without proper documentation of the change, diagnosing the problem is next to impossible. Dozens of job reruns may be required to identify the point at which certain symptoms first appeared, and for this reason, it also is important to maintain a record of the test procedures and test runs made to verify a change. If standardized test procedures, test forms, and record-keeping methods are used, recording the test results does not have to be time-consuming.

Although maintaining documentation is tedious and unfulfilling, the effort pays off when disaster strikes and the documentation is the difference between solving and not solving a major (and costly) problem. Today, a number of products are emerging that ease the burden of documentation. Many CASE tools, for example, can be used to document logical database designs. Data dictionaries also provide documentation assistance, and other products that read and interpret the database data structures maintained by popular DBMS products are available.

Another reason for carefully documenting changes in the database structure is to use historical data properly. If, for example, marketing wants to analyze three-year-old sales data that have been in the archives for two years, it will be necessary to know what structure was current at the time the data were last active. Records that show the changes in the structure can be used to answer that question. A similar situation arises when a six-month-old backup copy of data must be used to repair a damaged database (although this should not happen, sometimes it does). The backup copy can be used to reconstruct the database to the state it was in at the time of the backup. Then transactions and structural changes can be made in chronological order to restore the database to its current state. Figure 12-18 summarizes the DBA's responsibilities for managing the database structure.

MANAGEMENT OF DATA ACTIVITY   Although the DBA protects the data, he or she does not process it. The DBA is not a user of the system, and, consequently, does not manage *data values*. Rather, the DBA manages *data activity*. The database is a shared resource, and the DBA provides standards, guidelines, control procedures, and documentation to ensure that the users work in a cooperative and complementary fashion when processing database data.

Because of the abundance of interrelated activity, database processing must be standardized. Providing database standards is one aspect of managing data activity: Every database field must have a standard name and format; every database record must have a standard name, format, and access strategies; and every database file must have a standard name and relationships with other files. The DBA establishes these standards in a manner that satisfies most of the needs of all the database users. Those organizations with an effective data administration will already have many of these standards, in which case the DBA may broaden them and ensure that they are enforced. Once established, the details of standardization are recorded in the DBMS **data dictionary,** which both the systems developers

FIGURE 12-18   *Summary of the DBA's Responsibilities for Managing the Database Structure*

> **Participate in Database
> and Application Development**
> • Assist in requirements stage and evaluation of
>   alternatives.
> • Play an active role in database design and
>   creation.
> • Develop procedures for integrity and quality of
>   database data.
> **Facilitate Changes to Database Structure**
> • Seek communitywide solutions.
> • Assess impact on all users.
> • Provide configuration control forum.
> • Be prepared for problems after changes are
>   made.
> • Maintain documentation.

and the users can query to determine exactly what data are being maintained, the names and formats of the data items, and their relationships.

Another aspect of managing data activity is establishing data proponents, access, and modification rights. Since the data are a shared resource, there may be problems regarding processing rights. The DBA and the relevant data proponents should consider each shared data item and determine the access and modification rights of particular applications and users. This should be done with regard for the greater community's benefit rather than that of one particular application, group, or user. Once processing rights have been determined, they can be implemented by the DBMS, by applications that process the database via the DBMS, or by both.

Another important function of database administration concerns database reliability. The DBA needs to ensure that proper programs and procedures have been established to control concurrent processing and to provide for database recovery. He or she must ensure that the techniques discussed earlier in this chapter are implemented and used.

Finally, the DBA is responsible for publishing and maintaining documentation regarding the data activity, including database standards, data retrieval and access rights, recovery procedures, and policy enforcement. Good documentation is especially important because it is needed by users throughout the organization. As with all documentation, keeping the documentation current is a major and unpopular task.

Many DBMS products provide utility services to assist in managing data activity. Some systems record the names of users and application programs that access (or are authorized to access) objects in the database. In this case, the DBMS data dictionary can be queried to determine which programs can access a particular record and what actions each can take. Figure 12-19 summarizes the DBA's responsibilities for managing data activity.

■ MANAGING THE DBMS

In addition to managing data activity and the database structure, the DBA must manage the DBMS itself. He or she should compile and analyze statistics concerning the system's performance and identify potential problem areas. Keep in mind that the database is serving many user groups. The DBA needs to investigate all

Summary of the DBA's Responsibilities for Managing Data Activity

- Establish database standards consistent with data administration standards.
- Establish and maintain data dictionary.
- Establish data proponencies.
- Work with data proponents to develop data access and modification rights.
- Develop, document, and train staff on backup and recovery procedures.
- Publish and maintain data activity standards documentation.

complaints about the system's response time, accuracy of data, ease of use, and so forth. If changes are needed, the DBA must plan and implement them.

The DBA must periodically monitor the users' activity on the database. DBMS products include features that collect and report statistics. Some of these reports may indicate, for example, which users have been active, which files and perhaps which data items have been used, and which access methods have been employed. Error rates and types can also be captured and reported. The DBA analyzes these data to determine whether a change to the database design is needed to improve performance or to ease the users' tasks. If change is necessary the DBA will make it.

The DBA should analyze run-time statistics on database activity and performance. When a performance problem is identified (by either a report or a user's complaint), the DBA must determine whether a modification of the database structure or system is appropriate. Examples of possible structure modifications are establishing new keys, purging data, deleting keys, and establishing new relationships among objects.

When the vendor of the DBMS being used announces new product features, the DBA must consider them in light of the overall needs of the user community. If she decides to incorporate the new DBMS features, the users must be notified and trained in their use. Accordingly, the DBA must manage and control changes in the DBMS, as well as in the database structure.

Other changes in the system for which the DBA is responsible vary widely, depending on the DBMS product as well as on other software and hardware in use. For example, changes in other software (such as the operating system or a communications control program) may mean that some DBMS parameters must be modified. The DBA must therefore also tune the DBMS product to other software in use.

The DBMS options are initially chosen when little is known about how the system will perform in the particular user environment. Consequently, operational experience and performance analysis over a period of time may reveal that a change is necessary. Even if the performance seems acceptable, the DBA may want to alter the options and observe the effect on performance. This process is referred to as *tuning*, or *optimizing*, the system. Figure 12-20 summarizes the DBA's responsibilities for managing the DBMS product.

■ ESTABLISHING THE DATABASE DATA DICTIONARY

A DBMS data dictionary is an important tool for the database administrator. It is actually a user-accessible catalog of data concerning the database, and its importance can be demonstrated by the following problem: A development team creates

FIGURE 12-20   *Summary of the DBA's Responsibilities for Managing the DBMS*

> • Generate database application performance reports.
> • Investigate user performance complaints.
> • Assess need for changes in database structure or application design.
> • Modify database structure.
> • Evaluate and implement new DBMS features.
> • Tune the DBMS.

a database consisting of twenty tables and 300 columns. Seventy-five application programs regularly process this database. Suppose that adhering to a new tax law requires changes in the way that employees' taxes are calculated and in the formats of the data fields that are used. Before modifying either the data or the programs, the manager of data processing should assess the impact of these changes (in order to allocate people and testing facilities, to develop user training, and so forth). He also needs to know which programs reference which data items.

If a data dictionary is in place, then a simple query (just like a query against data) can answer the manager's question. But if there is no cross-referencing mechanism in place, then each application program must be studied (usually by application programmers) to determine whether it references the data items in question. Obviously, the first approach is much faster and probably much more accurate.

Data dictionaries are not new. In fact, many data processing managers developed their own cross-referencing systems long before databases became popular. Now, however, many DBMS products include an integrated data dictionary option. IBM incorporates a user-accessible catalog in its DB2 relational database product. Other manufacturers offer similar options.

Some data dictionaries are active, and some are passive. An active data dictionary is one whose entries are automatically modified by the software whenever changes are made in the database structure. In contrast, passive data dictionaries need to be updated separately when changes are made in the database; otherwise, they will not accurately reflect the state of the database. Active data dictionaries usually cost more, but they ensure currency; however, they are not available with every DBMS product. Although passive data dictionaries are less expensive than active ones, more effort is required to keep them up-to-date. But either one greatly aids the DBA in recording and tracking data names, formats, relationships, and cross-references.

SUMMARY

Teleprocessing is the classic architecture for multi-user database processing. With it, users operate dumb terminals or micros that emulate dumb terminals. The communications control program, application programs, DBMS, and operating system all are processed by a single, centralized computer. Because all processing is done by a single computer, the user interface of a teleprocessing system is usually simple and primitive.

A client-server system consists of a network of computers, most often connected via a local area network. In nearly all cases, the user computers, called clients, are microcomputers, and in most cases, the server computer is also a micro, although mainframes can be used. Application programs are processed on the client computer; the DBMS and the data management portion of the operating system reside on a server.

File-sharing systems also involve networks of computers, and like client-server architectures, they usually consist of micros connected via local area networks. The chief difference between file-sharing systems and client-server systems is that the server computer provides fewer services for the user computers. The server, which is called a *file* server and not a *database* server, provides access to files and other resources. Consequently, both the DBMS and the application programs must be distributed to the users' computers.

With a distributed database system, multiple computers process the same database. There are several types of distributed databases: partitioned, nonreplicated; nonpartitioned, replicated; and partitioned, replicated. In general, the greater the degree of partitioning and replication, the greater the flexibility, independence, and reliability will be. At the same time, expense, control difficulty, and security problems increase. Because of these problems, distributed database processing is rarely used for business information systems.

Concurrent updates can be a problem if two users attempt to modify the same record at once. When this happens, anomalies can occur in the database. DBMS products solve this problem by locking the resources whenever the data might be changed. Locks prevent other users from accessing a record until the transaction is completed and the lock is released.

Concurrent processing can also be a problem if two users both lock resources that the other one needs. This situation, called deadlock, can be resolved by the DBMS by terminating one of the transactions and undoing any changes it made in the database.

In the event of a system failure, the database must be restored to a usable state as quickly as possible. Any transactions in progress at the time of the crash must be reapplied, and any processing that was done manually while the system was down must be entered. Recovery can be by means of straightforward reprocessing or rollback/rollforward. The latter strategy is almost always preferred.

Transaction logs must be maintained to ensure that all lost work is reapplied. Checkpoints can be taken more frequently than database saves. Although they require some overhead, checkpoints minimize the amount of reprocessing that needs to be done in the event of a failure.

Database security means allowing only authorized subjects to perform authorized actions on specified objects, subject to any managerial constraints. Once established by the DBA, many of these access and processing rights are enforced by the DBMS. Constraints that are not enforced by the DBMS can be enforced by user-written subroutines.

The scope of database administration is a particular database and the applications that process that database. Functions include managing the database structure, establishing frameworks to manage data activity, and managing the DBMS software. In addition, the database administration is responsible for establishing and managing the database data dictionary.

GROUP I QUESTIONS

12.1 Define multi-user database.

12.2 List the architectures that are used to support multi-user databases.

12.3 Sketch the architecture of a teleprocessing system. Name and identify the computer(s) and programs involved, and explain which computer processes which programs.

12.4   Why is the users' interface on teleprocessing applications generally character oriented and primitive?

12.5   Sketch the architecture of a client-server system. Name and identify the computer(s) and programs involved, and explain which computer processes which programs.

12.6   What types of processing hardware are used with client-server systems?

12.7   How many servers can a client-server system have? What restrictions apply to the servers?

12.8   Sketch the architecture of a file-sharing system. Name and identify the computer(s) and programs involved, and explain which computer processes which programs.

12.9   Explain how the processing of the following SQL query would differ in a client-server system and in a file-sharing system:

```
SELECT      StudentName, ClassName
FROM        STUDENT, GRADE
WHERE       STUDENT.StudentNumber = GRADE.StudentNumber
AND         GRADE.Grade = 'A'
```

Assume that the database contains two tables:

STUDENT (StudentNumber, StudentName, StudentPhone)

GRADE (ClassNumber, StudentNumber, Grade)

Also assume that the primary and foreign keys have indexes.

12.10 Explain why file-sharing systems are seldom used for high-volume transaction-processing applications.

12.11 Define the terms *partitioned* and *replicated* as they pertain to distributed database applications.

12.12 Define *transaction* and *logical unit of work*.

12.13 What is concurrent processing? Under what conditions is concurrent processing a problem?

12.14 Describe the lost update problem.

12.15 Explain the difference between explicit and implicit locks.

12.16 Define *lock granularity*. What are the general differences between large- and small-lock granularity?

12.17 Explain the difference between an exclusive and a shared lock.

12.18 Define *serializability*.

12.19 What is a two-phase locking, and how can it be used to prevent the lost update problem?

12.20 What is a deadly embrace?

12.21 Describe two ways in which a DBMS can handle a deadly embrace.

12.22 Explain how a database can be recovered by reprocessing. Why is database recovery by reprocessing usually not feasible?

12.23 Define *rollback* and *rollforward*.

12.24 Why is it important to write to the log before changing the database?

12.25 Describe the rollback process. Under what conditions is rollback more advantageous than rollforward?

12.26 Describe the rollforward process. Under what conditions is rollforward more advantageous than rollback?

12.27 Why is it usually advantageous to take frequent checkpoints of a database?

12.28 Define *subject, object, action,* and *authorization constraint* as they apply to database security.

12.29 How does a DBMS implement subject-oriented security?

12.30 How does a DBMS implement object-oriented security?

12.31 Explain the use of programmable exits for security.

12.32 Describe the need for database administration. What would be likely to happen if there were no database administration?

12.33 Explain how database administration is likely to vary among personal, workgroup, and organizational databases.

12.34 Summarize the DBA's responsibilities for managing the database structure.

12.35 What is configuration control? Why is it necessary for multi-user databases?

12.36 Describe two situations to which database system documentation is important.

12.37 Summarize the DBA's responsibilities for managing database activity. What are data access and modification rights? Why are they important?

12.38 Summarize the DBA's responsibilities for managing DBMS software.

12.39 What is the function of a data dictionary? Explain the difference between a passive and an active data dictionary.

GROUP II QUESTIONS

12.40 Interview the DBA of a local company, and determine whether it uses a data dictionary system. Is it integrated with the DBMS? If so, what are the advantages and disadvantages? If not, ask why the company chose that type of data dictionary. Find out whether the dictionary system is active or passive.

12.41 Interview the manager of a local small business that uses a microcomputer DBMS. Is there a DBA? If not, determine who in the company performs each of the DBA's functions. Also, find out whether any of the DBA's functions are not being performed. Why not? Find out what support the DBA (or people performing the DBA's functions) receives from the DBMS (for example, run-time statistics or a data dictionary).

RELATIONAL IMPLEMENTATION WITH DB2

• • • • • • • • • • • • • • •

The size and processing requirements for enterprise-wide databases greatly exceed the capacities of personal DBMS products. Accordingly, the DBMS products that are used for such databases are different in character from Access or other personal DBMS. To illustrate this difference, this chapter presents and discusses DB2, a DBMS product licensed by IBM. DB2 is intended primarily for large IBM mainframes, although versions of it are also used on the AS/400 family of smaller computers.

The chapter begins with a case that concerns information problems faced by the marketing department of a manufacturing company and then outlines the features and functions of an information system that can solve those problems. This information system has a relational database, and we define both the objects and the relations that should be stored in it. Next we turn to Database2 or, as it is more frequently called, DB2. We examine not only its data definition and data manipulation features but also those features that support concurrent processing, backup and recovery, and database security. Finally, we explore those portions of the relational application developed for the manufacturing company, including interactive DB2 queries and a COBOL program that contains embedded DB2 commands.

DB2 is typical of mainframe DBMS products designed to provide fast, highly reliable performance while processing hundreds of concurrent transactions per minute. Such products are complicated and thus require considerable expertise and knowledge on the part of systems and database administrators. Unlike microcomputer DBMS products, mainframe DBMS products are not designed to be easy to use and install but instead are intended to offer high performance and reliability. This chapter omits some important and useful features of DB2; see *DB2 System and Database Administration Guide* and *DB2 Application Programming Guide,* both published by IBM, for more information.

◆ CASE STUDY: KDK APPLIANCES

KDK Appliances manufactures major kitchen appliances, such as refrigerators, ranges, microwave ovens, and dishwashers. The company markets its products to independent dealers that then sell them to the public. Currently, its market is mainly the northeastern United States, but KDK plans to open soon new sales regions in the Midwest and in Canada. Each sales region is serviced by several salespeople

FIGURE 13-1   *Relationship Among KDK's Computers*

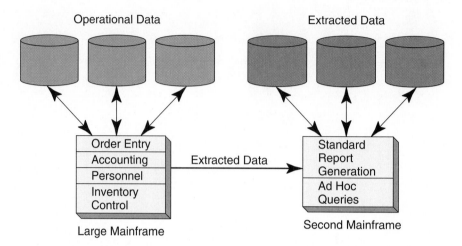

who call on dealers and explain KDK's product line, dealer-training program, incentives, and local advertising programs. It is possible for one dealer to work with more than one KDK salesperson.

KDK has a large mainframe computer that handles all order processing, inventory control, personnel, and accounting functions. Stored in this mainframe are files and databases that track sales and other data to meet various reporting requirements. The database structure and processing on this mainframe computer are far too complicated to present in a single chapter. Therefore, we will consider the work that would need to be done to create and process an extract of the operational database (see Figure 13-1). (See also Chapter 15 which discusses a related topic called *data warehousing*.)

■ PROBLEMS

The marketing department plays a key role in the success of the company's plans to expand. It now employs eight product managers (PMs), each responsible for a particular line of products (one for refrigerators, one for ranges, and so forth). As part of their duties, the PMs develop an annual product plan for each major product (for example, a major product is a particular refrigerator model or a specific type of microwave oven). The product plan establishes, among other things, the sales goals for the product and the budget for its marketing. These marketing expenses include advertising, dealer training, salesperson training, and dealer promotions.

In order to spend the marketing dollars wisely, the PMs want to access data stored in the computer. They need to know, for example, product sales by region and by salesperson and the effect of some aspect of marketing (say, advertising) on product sales.

Instant response time is not vital, because the PMs usually need quarterly, monthly, or weekly summaries of data. For example, immediate access to a particular order is not important. (In contrast, consider how important response time is when performing the order entry function on KDK's operational mainframe.)

KDK Appliances sponsors a co-op advertising program and employs several agencies to create advertising campaigns for various media, including newspapers (daily and weekly), periodicals (weekly and monthly), television, and radio. Much of KDK's advertising is shared with its dealers, which means that in addition to the advertising copy promoting a specific KDK product, a dealer's name, address, and logo appear in the ad (see Figure 13-2). Thus, although KDK products are the cen-

FIGURE 13-2 *Advertisement for a KDK Product*

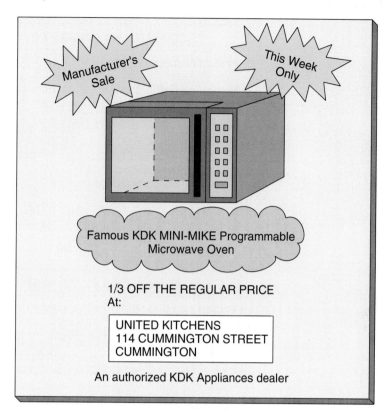

tral focus of the ad, a local dealer can share in the benefits by sharing the cost of the ad.

Some, though not all, dealers take advantage of this arrangement. The shared costs (percentages of the cost borne by KDK and by the dealer) vary from one ad to another and from one dealer to another, so the sales and marketing personnel must establish the shared costs of each ad.

None of the PMs is familiar with SQL or is willing to learn it, none is a programmer, and none has the time or interest to learn COBOL. Nonetheless, the PMs want the following questions answered: Which dealers participated in our shared advertising program this month? What was the total sales figure for product 45678 in March? How does that compare with its sales in April?

The goal of this chapter is to illustrate what would need to be done to create a database that would produce reports and answer queries that provide the information needed by PMs.

■ DEFINING OBJECTS

To develop the proposed system, the analyst first had to identify the semantic objects in which the PMs were interested. To start, the analyst and the PMs examined reports, transactions, and other entities. Let us first consider the reports and identify the underlying objects needed to construct them.

PRODUCT SALES SUMMARY REPORTS   Figure 13-3 shows three examples of the product sales summaries that the PMs need each month. Figure 13-3(a) is a sample PRODUCT SALES SUMMARY BY SALESPERSON report that contains data about products (product number, name, description, price), salespeople (name), and sales (total units sold by each salesperson). This suggests the existence of PRODUCT,

FIGURE 13-3   *PRODUCT SALES SUMMARY Reports: (a) SALES SUMMARY BY SALESPERSON Report,*
(b) SALES SUMMARY BY DEALER Report, and (c) SALES SUMMARY BY REGION Report

PRODUCT SALES SUMMARY BY SALESPERSON
- -

Product Number: 87224

Name/Description: Mini-Mike Programmable compact microwave
                  oven

Price: $194.99

SALESPERSON	UNITS SOLD
John Eberle	280
Margaret Gosselin	200
Hans Jensen	50
TOTAL	530

(a)

PRODUCT SALES SUMMARY BY DEALER
- -

Product Number: 87224

Name/Description: Mini-Mike Programmable compact microwave
                  oven

Price: $194.99

DEALER	UNITS SOLD
Lisbon Furniture and Appliances	30
Parks Department Store	200
United Kitchens	50
Gem Appliances	100
Rich Appliance Co.	100
Sounds Terrific	50
TOTAL	530

(b)

PRODUCT SALES SUMMARY BY REGION
- -

Product Number: 87224

Name/Description: Mini-Mike Programmable compact microwave
                  oven

Price: $194.99

REGION	UNITS SOLD
2	200
5	330
TOTAL	530

(c)

SALESPERSON, and SALE objects, but we will not be sure until all reports, transactions, and so forth have been examined.

The PRODUCT SALES SUMMARY BY DEALER report (Figure 13-3[b]) contains data about products (product number, name, description, price), dealers (name),

FIGURE 13-4   *DEALER ACTIVITY SUMMARY Report*

DEALER ACTIVITY SUMMARY

#6644   (617) 479-5555
J&S Department Store
75 Rock Road
Plymouth, MA 02787
- -
Purchases to Date

Invoice #	Date	Total
1013	01/02/92	15349.81
1071	02/01/92	22467.00
1296	03/02/92	18949.37
1380	04/01/92	36755.29
	TOTAL	93620.47

- -
Advertising to Date

Ad Name	Date	Ad Cost	Dealer's Share (%)
Ultra	02/10/97	250.00	67
Free Time	02/15/97	400.00	67
St. Paddy's Sale	03/14/97	600.00	67
Ultra	03/15/97	250.00	60

and sales (total units sold to each dealer). Thus, in addition to the objects mentioned, it is likely that a DEALER object will exist as well.

The third summary report, PRODUCT SALES SUMMARY BY REGION (Figure 13-3[c]), contains data about products (product number, name, description, price), regions (region number), and sales (total units sold in each region). In addition to the potential objects already identified—PRODUCT, SALESPERSON, SALE, and DEALER—another possible object is found: REGION.

DEALER ACTIVITY SUMMARY REPORT Figure 13-4 shows an example of the DEALER ACTIVITY SUMMARY report, which contains data about dealers (number, name, address, telephone number), sales (invoice number, data, invoice total), and advertisements (advertisement name, date, cost, and dealer's share). We have already identified DEALER and SALE (an invoice is the record of sale) as potential objects, and the DEALER ACTIVITY SUMMARY report suggests a few more attributes of these objects, such as the dealers' addresses, telephone numbers, and invoice numbers. This report also indicates that advertisements are possible objects.

Figure 13-5 illustrates our findings so far. The potential objects are PRODUCT, SALESPERSON, SALE (or INVOICE), REGION, DEALER, and ADVERTISEMENT. But this is by no means a complete and final list, as these objects show only the beginning of our investigation. Study the object diagrams in Figure 13-5, making sure you understand them before continuing.

SALES INVOICE DOCUMENT Product managers derive much information about product sales from one important document: the sales invoice. An invoice for each sale is completed by a salesperson. An *actual* invoice captures many details about the dealer; the product(s) sold; and the dollar amounts of the transaction, discounts, credits, balance due, and shipping charges. All invoice details are entered into KDK's large operational mainframe computer. Keep in mind that the PMs need only a subset of the data on an actual invoice. An invoice as viewed by a product manager is illustrated in Figure 13-6. It contains data about the invoice (number, sale date,

FIGURE 13-5   *Preliminary Objects for KDK Appliances*

FIGURE 13-6   *Product Manager's View of an Invoice*

```
INVOICE 1001                                          02/01/97
SOLD TO:                            SALES REP:  #5762
Lisbon Furniture and Appliances                Paula Jasinski
692 S. Ellington Rd.
South Windsor, CT   06114
```

	Number	Name	Price	Qty	Extended-price
1	80911	Kitchen Valet	$1,699.99	2	$ 3,399.98
2	87755	Mini-Mike	344.99	20	6,899.80
3	93861	E. Range-white	679.99	15	10,199.85
4					
5					
6					
				TOTAL	$20,499.63

total), salesperson (number, name), dealer (name, address), and items sold (line item number, product number, name, price, quantity sold, extended price).

It is easy to see that what we have just described as an *invoice* is really an embellishment of what we have been calling a *sale*. Because the PMs are more likely to use the term *invoice* than *sale* (this was discovered by talking to the PMs), we modify the object diagrams from Figure 13-5, replacing the SALE object with the updated INVOICE object. The results are shown in Figure 13-7.

ADVERTISING ACTIVITY   We noted earlier that KDK advertises its products to consumers in various media, such as print and television. An ad that can be run in,

Modified Objects for KDK Appliances

say, a newspaper is referred to as an *ad-copy*. Each ad-copy is given a title by the advertising agency that developed it. When a particular ad-copy is actually run in a newspaper on a certain date at a certain cost, it is referred to as an *advertisement*. Thus, an ad-copy called "Free Time" emphasizing the time-saving features of various KDK appliances might be run in several newspapers over a period of three or four months. Each time it is run, it is termed an advertisement.

As we already noted, each advertisement may be shared with a local appliance dealer, as long as the dealer agrees to share the cost of the ad. Because each ad-copy can target several products and because each advertisement can be shared with a dealer, the product managers need to track various aspects of advertising. After all, a large portion of each PM's budget is spent on advertising.

The underlying objects in the system's advertising are AD-COPY and AD-VERTISEMENT, and object diagrams for them are shown in Figure 13-8. This more complete definition of the ADVERTISEMENT object replaces the one in Figure 13-7.

FINAL VERSION Using object diagrams like the ones in Figures 13-7 and 13-8, the analyst reviewed with the PMs his understanding of the problems, thereby giving each of them an opportunity to correct or confirm what the analyst had done. One point that the analyst raised during this review concerned the REGION object. He wanted to be sure that the PMs did not need any data about a region. When the product managers agreed that they did not need any more data, the analyst decided to drop the REGION object. Thus modified, the object diagrams seemed acceptable, and the analyst went to the next step, translating the object definitions into relation definitions.

KDK Objects After Modification for AD-COPY Object

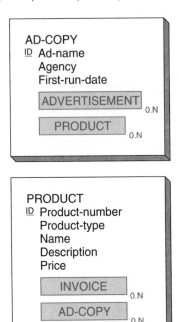

■ Defining Relations

To create a database to store this data, the object model needs to be transformed into a relational design. Consider the INVOICE object first.

INVOICE   INVOICE is a hybrid object because the line-item composite group contains an object attribute. Thus the INVOICE object is represented by several relations. One contains general information about an invoice, and another contains the line items associated with the invoice. The relations have a one-to-many relationship, and both relations are mandatory (see Figure 13-9). The formats of the two relations are

INVOICE (<u>Number</u>, Date, Total, *Salesperson.Number, Dealer.Number*)

LINE-ITEM (*<u>Invoice.Number</u>*, <u>Line-item-number</u>, *Product.Number*, Quantity, Extended-price)

Observe that the keys are underlined and the foreign keys are shown in italics. Those columns that are both local and foreign keys are shown in underlined italics. An example of the INVOICE and LINE-ITEM relations is given in Figure 13-10.

Relationship Between INVOICE and LINE-ITEM

FIGURE 13-10   *Sample Data in INVOICE and LINE-ITEM Relations*

Number	Date	Salesperson.Number	Dealer.Number	Total
10982	03/12/97	8555	2425	38549.05
75214	03/12/97	1755	4528	60472.95
63911	03/15/97	5762	6178	12249.92
41200	03/18/97	5762	6644	147997.70

INVOICE relation

Invoice.Number	Line-item-number	Product.Number	Quantity	Extended-price
10982	001	14365	50	14999.50
10982	002	74961	30	17999.70
10982	003	87033	15	5549.85
75214	001	87214	25	4874.75
75214	002	87224	100	25999.00
75214	003	87033	80	29599.20
63911	001	56271	3	3749.97
63911	002	80911	5	8499.95
41200	001	15965	200	129998.00
41200	002	74961	30	17999.70

LINE-ITEM relation

Notice that since several attributes are named *Number,* it is necessary to qualify the name of these attributes with their relation name. Hence, Invoice.Number is the Number attribute in Invoice. Product.Number is the Number attribute in Product. Also notice that the key for INVOICE (Invoice.Number) is part of the key for LINE-ITEM.

Three foreign keys appear in the INVOICE and LINE-ITEM relations, namely, Salesperson.Number, Dealer.Number, and Product.Number. These keys are needed to establish the one-to-many relationships between DEALER and INVOICE, between SALESPERSON and INVOICE, and between PRODUCT and INVOICE.

DEALER AND SALESPERSON   The DEALER object in Figure 13-7 is a compound object because it contains multivalued object attributes, INVOICE and ADVERTISEMENT. There is a 1:N relationship in both cases.

Similarly, the SALESPERSON object in Figure 13-7 is a compound object, and it has a 1:N relationship with INVOICE. In Figure 13-11 we have added the DEALER

FIGURE 13-11   *Result of Adding DEALER and SALESPERSON Relations to Figure 13-9*

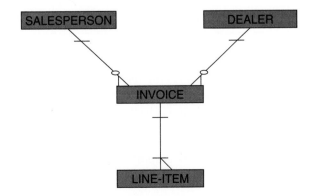

and SALESPERSON relations to the diagram from Figure 13-9. The relationships between SALESPERSON and INVOICE and between DEALER and INVOICE are mandatory to optional, which means that an invoice must be associated with a salesperson and a dealer but that a salesperson or a dealer does not have to have any invoices. The relation formats are

DEALER (<u>Number</u>, Name, Address-1, Address-2, City, State/Province, ZIP/Postal-code, Telephone)

SALESPERSON (<u>Number</u>, Name, Region)

Sample data for the SALESPERSON and DEALER relations are shown in Figure 13-12.

PRODUCT   Another object in Figure 13-7 is PRODUCT. According to the object diagram, there is an N:1 relationship between a product and an invoice. More specifically, there is an N:1 relationship between a line item and a product. A certain product—say, a dishwasher—can be found on line items from the various invoices issued to many different dealers, and this can be represented in relations as shown in Figure 13-13.

The relational format for the PRODUCT relation is

PRODUCT (<u>Number</u>, Name, Description, Price)

Sample data for the PRODUCT relation can be found in Figure 13-14.

ADVERTISEMENT AND AD-COPY   Two more objects, ADVERTISEMENT and AD-COPY (see Figure 13-8), need to be transformed into relations. A dealer can share the cost of several advertisements, but any advertisement features at most one dealer. Thus, there is a 1:N relationship between a dealer and an advertisement.

Similarly, one ad-copy can be run several times in many newspapers, so there is a 1:N relationship between an ad-copy and an advertisement. Adding these relations to the ones in Figure 13-13, we arrive at the result in Figure 13-15.

The next relationship to be incorporated is that between PRODUCT and AD-COPY. Each product can be featured in several ads, and each ad can specify several products. Thus, we have an N:M relationship between PRODUCT and AD-COPY.

Recall from Chapter 7 that many-to-many relationships are represented by creating an intersection relation containing only those keys from the two other relations. In this case, an intersection relation called PRODUCT-AD is defined, in which each row contains a product number and an ad-name. Here the PRODUCT-AD relation is added to the ones from Figure 13-15, and the result is Figure 13-16.

The formats for these three new relations are

AD-COPY (<u>Ad-name</u>, Agency, First-run-date)

ADVERTISEMENT (<u>Publication</u>, <u>Date</u>, <u>Ad-name</u>, Cost, Share-percent, *Dealer.Number*)

PRODUCT-AD (*<u>Ad-name</u>, <u>Product.Number</u>*)

Sample data for the AD-COPY and ADVERTISEMENT relations appear in Figure 13-17 and for PRODUCT-AD in Figure 13-18.

■ KDK Case Summary

All the objects identified earlier can be constructed from data stored in the relations we defined. Reports summarizing product sales based on various criteria (such as salesperson, region, and dealer), reports that analyze advertising, and much more can be readily extracted from the database.

The next step is to implement the database structure, that is, to define tables, fields, and constraints; to assign passwords; to establish security procedures; and to allocate file space. After doing that, application programs can be written to produce the required reports. Before turning to those tasks, consider the features and functions of DB2.

FIGURE 13-12 *Sample Data for SALESPERSON and DEALER Relations*

Number	Name	Region
1043	Ronald Hunt	1
2711	John Eberle	5
8555	Margaret Gosselin	2
5762	Paula Jasinski	4
1755	Hans Jensen	5
6042	Lawrence Smithers	1
2814	Maxine Whittier	3

SALESPERSON relation

Number	Name	Address-1	Address-2	City	State/ Province	ZIP/ Postal-code	Telephone
6178	Gem Appliances	1005 Farmington Ave.	-0-	W. Hartford	CT	06754	(203) 555-4312
2425	S. K. Lafferty	Prestige Park	Building 43	E. Hartford	CT	06832	(203) 555-6789
6624	Rich Appliance Co.	17 Whiting Street	Suite 4143	New Britain	CT	06588	(203) 555-6609
0212	Lisbon Furniture & Appliances	692 Ellington Road	-0-	South Windsor	CT	06551	(203) 677-4582
9356	Gallo's Appliance Outlet	P.O. Box 344	264 Park Road	W. Hartford	CT	06431	(203) 549-6772
4516	United Kitchens	114 Cummington Street	-0-	Cummington	MA	07231	(617) 438-0065
9101	Parks Department Store	21 Main Street	-0-	Worcester	MA	07488	(617) 756-2295
6644	J&S Department Store	75 Rock Road	-0-	Plymouth	MA	02787	(617) 479-5555
4528	Sounds Terrific	1433 W. Northeast Highway	Suite 5678	Boston	MA	07665	(617) 885-4000

DEALER relation

317

FIGURE 13-13   *PRODUCT Relation Added to Diagram in Figure 13-11*

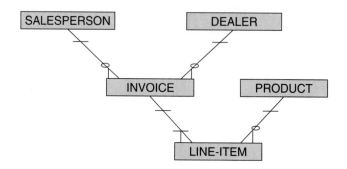

FIGURE 13-14   *Sample Data for PRODUCT Relation*

Number	Name	Description	Price
392761	Electric range–white	Electric range	$299.99
393861	Electric range–white	Electric range; self-clean; window	$679.99
393863	Electric range–toast	Electric range; self-clean; window	$689.99
393867	Electric range–avocado	Electric range; self-clean; window	$689.99
370351	Gas range–white	Gas range; 21-inch	$279.99
370353	Gas range–toast	Gas range; 21-inch	$289.99
374961	Gas range–white	Gas range; 36-inch; continuous clean	$599.99
374963	Gas range–toast	Gas range; 36-inch; continuous clean	$599.99
374976	Gas range–avocado	Gas range; 36-inch; continuous clean	$599.99
380551	Fifth-burner kit	Gas range 5th burner to replace griddle	$19.99
787214	Mini-mike	Compact microwave oven	$194.99
787224	Mini-mike	Programmable compact microwave oven	$259.99
787755	Mity-mike	Programmable solid-state full-size microwave oven	$344.99
787033	Mity-mike	#87755 with carousel	$369.99
415965	Ultra wash	Electronic dishwasher	$649.99
414365	Dishwasher	18-inch; 2-level dishwasher	$299.99
417375	Dishwasher–P	Dishwasher-portable	$409.99
416037	Dishwasher–sp	Space saver dishwasher	$249.99
556681	Porcelain-plus	Refrigerator; porcelain-on-steel; 25.8 cu ft	$1,599.99
556271	Quiet Cold	Frost-free refrigerator; ice maker	$1,249.99
580911	Kitchen Valet	Refrigerator; all-electronic; customized panels	$1,699.99
580922	KDK Limited Edition	Refrigerator; frost-free; special use compartments	$2,549.99
593252	Mini-fridge	Compact refrigerator	$99.00
593286	Mini-fridge	Compact refrigerator/freezer	$174.99
594605	Compact-fridge	3.6 cu ft compact refrigerator	$219.99
594911	Compact-fridge	#94605 with push-button defrost	$299.99

FIGURE 13-15   *Addition of AD-COPY and ADVERTISEMENT Relations to Those in Figure 13-13*

FIGURE 13-16   *Addition of PRODUCT-AD Relation to Those in Figure 13-15*

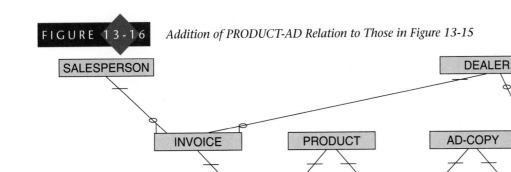

FIGURE 13-17   *Sample Data for AD-COPY and ADVERTISEMENT Relations*

Ad-name	Agency	First-run-date
Dishwashers	On-Target Ads	03/10/97
Free Time	Haskins	02/15/97
Microwaves	On-Target Ads	03/12/97
Presidents	Haskins	02/03/97
Ranges	On-Target Ads	02/01/97
St. Paddy's Sale	J&J Marketing	03/12/97
The Bachelor	J&J Marketing	01/04/97
The Fridge	Haskins	02/01/97
Ultra	J&J Marketing	03/10/97
Working Woman	Haskins	03/01/97

AD-COPY relation

Publication	Date	Ad-name	Cost	Share%	Dealer.Num
Herald	02/01/97	Ranges	300.00	25.	6644
Free Press	02/01/97	Ranges	320.00	33.	6178
Free Press	02/03/97	Presidents	450.00	50.	4528
Sentinel	02/15/97	Free Time	400.00	33.	6178
Herald	02/17/97	Free Time	350.00	50.	6178
Herald	02/19/97	Ranges	300.00	40.	4516
Sentinel	03/10/97	Dishwashers	400.00	50.	9101
Times	03/10/97	Ultra	250.00	33.	6644
Courier	03/11/97	Ultra	280.00	40.	0212
Sentinel	03/12/97	Working Woman	500.00	40.	9356
Times	03/14/97	St. Paddy's Sale	600.00	33.	6644
Times	03/14/97	The Bachelor	550.00	25.	4516
Herald	03/15/97	Ultra	250.00	40.	6644

ADVERTISEMENT relation

FIGURE 13-18   *Sample Data for PRODUCT-AD Relation*

Ad-name	Product.Number	Ad-name	Product.Number
Dishwashers	17375	Ranges	93861
Dishwashers	16037	Ranges	93863
Dishwashers	14365	Ranges	93867
Free Time	70351	Ranges	74967
Free Time	16037	Ranges	74963
Free Time	92761	Ranges	80551
Microwaves	87033	St. Paddy's Sale	15965
Microwaves	87224	St. Paddy's Sale	93867
Microwaves	87755	St. Paddy's Sale	94605
Microwaves	87214	St. Paddy's Sale	74967
Presidents	93286	The Bachelor	15965
Presidents	80551	The Bachelor	87755
Presidents	93861	The Bachelor	93867
Presidents	74961	The Fridge	56681
Presidents	80922	The Fridge	80922
Presidents	14365	Ultra	15965
Presidents	93252	Working Woman	93867
Ranges	92761	Working Woman	87033
Ranges	74961	Working Woman	87755

DB2: THE PRODUCT

Database2 (DB2) is IBM's relational database management system for large mainframe computers that run IBM's MVS operating system. Another earlier IBM DBMS is called IMS and is based on the hierarchical (DL/I), rather than the relational, model. DL/I is described in Chapter 18. You are far more likely to encounter databases using DB2 than those using IMS in your career, and we address it in some detail in the next sections.

■ KEY FEATURES

DB2 uses SQL to perform all database operations: data definition, data access, data manipulation, and authorization functions. The user enters the SQL statements at a computer terminal. This mode employs an interactive terminal interface program called DB2I, but SQL statements can also be embedded in application programs written in assembler language, COBOL, PL/I, FORTRAN, or C. Later in this chapter we present examples of both interactive commands and COBOL programs containing SQL instructions.

DB2 is well suited to a multi-user environment, as it allows users to create and modify tables, views, and other database structures; to define and modify database security parameters; and to execute various database utilities on-line. Most functions can be performed—within certain limits—even while others are using the database.

DB2's mechanisms for recovery in the event of a system failure are especially important in a multi-user environment. DB2 includes features for activity logging and transaction reprocessing, thus increasing system reliability. Because DB2 is just one of several subsystems that may be operating at the time of a system failure, its recovery processing is coordinated with that of other subsystems that may be present, such as CICS or other communications control programs.

DB2 enables a person—database designer, database administrator, or end user—to define and manipulate various constructs.[1] Constructs include databases, tables, views, and indexes, to name a few. In the next section, we examine DB2 constructs and some SQL data definition (DDL) statements.

■ DB2 DATA DEFINITION LANGUAGE

This section briefly describes each DB2 construct, including the resources that application programmers (and sometimes end users) need to understand, such as tables and views, as well as the resources that database designers and database administrators (DBAs)[2] need to understand, such as storage groups and table spaces. We also present SQL statements to define several objects for the KDK application. The DB2 constructs we study are tables, views, table spaces, indexes, index spaces, data bases, and storage groups. Although a few other DB2 constructs exist, they are not important to our discussion.

TABLES   Like all products based on the relational model, DB2 stores data as tables with rows and columns. DB2 can retrieve and change data in a table, insert and delete rows, and add new columns to an existing table.

VIEWS   A DB2 **view** is a virtual table derived from one or several base tables and not physically stored in the database (although the table data are). Views can be accessed and manipulated much as tables are, using many of the same SQL data manipulation statements used for tables. Indeed, a user often cannot tell whether he or she is processing a table or a view. Examples of a base table and a view of it are illustrated in Figure 13-19.

Database users, including application programmers and end users, need to know only about tables and views. But database designers and DBAs need to understand

FIGURE 13-19

Example of (a) EMPLOYEES (base table) and (b) EMPLOYEE-DIRECTORY (view of EMPLOYEES)

Name	Salary	Hire-date	Office	Extension
Walker	21800	12/88	321	246
Berg	36500	10/85	411	647
Dean	42900	02/91	308	795
Hsiu	36500	09/88	307	581
Cameratta	40000	03/83	419	669

(a)

Name	Office	Extension
Walker	321	246
Berg	411	647
Dean	308	795
Hsiu	307	581
Cameratta	419	669

(b)

[1] IBM uses the term *object* instead of construct, and we substitute this term here to avoid confusion between semantic objects and DB2 objects.
[2] DB2 allows separate passwords for *system administrators* and *database administrators*. A system administrator can access and change constructs for all databases on the DB2 system, whereas a database administrator is restricted to a particular database.

not only tables and views but also physical database storage, including table spaces, indexes, index spaces, data bases, and storage groups.

TABLE SPACES   A **table space** is a collection of one or more VSAM data sets (this is the name of standard nondatabase IBM mainframe files) used to store database data on magnetic disk. Both user and system tables are stored in table spaces (see Figure 13-20). A table space can hold approximately 64 billion bytes of data, although that size is not practical.

Table spaces are DB2's recoverable units. If the database system crashes, the table spaces will be recovered, not the databases or the individual tables. Perhaps you can see why huge table spaces (such as 64 billion bytes of data), though theoretically possible, are in reality seldom defined, as recovering a table space that large would be very difficult and time-consuming.

A table space can be either a **simple table space** or a **partitioned table space.** A simple table space can hold one or more tables, whereas a partitioned table space holds exactly one table. The DBA would probably define a partitioned table space for a very large table. Each partition would contain a part of the table based on the range of values in one or more columns. For example, each partition might contain taxpayer data based on Social Security Number. Partitions are independent of one another and can be reorganized and recovered individually.

Simple table spaces might contain several small, related tables. For example, the DBA might establish one table space for each user department and use each table space to store all the tables pertinent to a particular department. If an application requires exclusive use of a table, it issues a LOCK TABLE statement. This statement locks an entire table space and prevents other tables in it from being accessed. If separate table spaces "belong" to individual user departments, it is less likely that users from different departments will interfere with one another.

INDEXES   A DB2 **index** is an index as defined in earlier chapters. Indexes are used to reduce table access time and to place the table data in a logical sequence, regardless of its physical sequence. Multiple indexes can be defined for a single table. Consider the table in Figure 13-21(a). (In this example, the rows are numbered to

FIGURE 13-20   *Table Spaces and Tables*

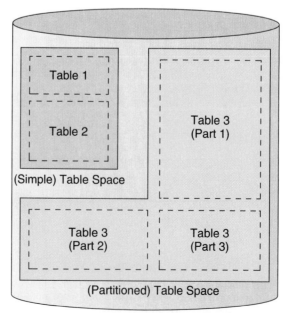

DASD (Disk) Volume

represent relative locations within the table, but in practice, record addressing is far more complex, as discussed in the appendix.) The rows might be stored in the sequence in which they appear in the figure. Now suppose that a user frequently needs to access the data by means of customer name. The index illustrated in Figure 13-21(b) can be used to find a specific name and the location of a row in the CUSTOMER table that has that name. Using the index will be much faster than sequentially searching the table.

Similarly, suppose another user often accesses the table by means of customer number. The index in Figure 13-21(c) would be useful in that case. Of course, the table in Figure 13-21 is very small, as it is only an example. KDK's real CUSTOMER table has thousands of rows. In fact, using indexes on such a small table would probably downgrade performance. Not only does index searching require time, but every addition or deletion to the CUSTOMER table also requires updating the indexes.

Subject to concurrent processing restrictions, indexes can be defined at any time. An index is a physical construct, completely separate from the table to which it is related. As we mentioned, DB2 automatically maintains an index once it is created. In fact, after an index is defined for a table, DB2 decides without any direction from a user or a programmer when, if ever, to use it. In other words, once an index has been defined, neither a user nor an application programmer actually references it.

INDEX SPACES   An **index space** is an area of disk storage in which DB2 stores an index (see Figure 13-22). When an index is created, DB2 automatically allocates an index space for it.

DATA BASES   IBM uses the term **data base** (two words) to define a collection of DB2 tables and indexes and the storage areas that hold them. Several DB2 data bases can exist on the same computer system. DB2 is designed to use a data base as an operational unit, meaning that it can *start* a data base (make it available), *stop* a data base (make it unavailable), and assign *authorization* to use a data base (allow users to access the data).

FIGURE 13-21   *Indexes on CUSTOMER Table: (a) CUSTOMER Table, (b) INDEX for Name, and (c) Index for CustomerNumber*

RowNumber	CustNumber	Name	CreditLimit	ZIPcode
1	10	Smith	3000	06413
2	20	Jones	3000	95060
3	30	Whittaker	2000	07814
4	40	Murphy	3000	62200
5	50	Wang	3000	08142
6	60	Youngblood	2000	62200
7	70	Jones	2000	95060

(a)

Name	RowNumber
Jones	2
Jones	7
Murphy	4
Smith	1
Wang	5
Whittaker	3
Youngblood	6

(b)

CustNumber	RowNumber
10	1
20	2
30	3
40	4
50	5
60	6
70	7

(c)

FIGURE 13-22   *DB2 Indexes Stored in Index Spaces*

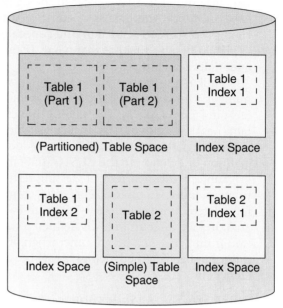

Users and application programmers do not deal directly with data bases any more than they deal with table spaces or indexes. Rather, they refer only to tables and views and are shielded from needing to know anything about the underlying database structures.

STORAGE GROUPS   A **storage group** is a group of disk volumes on which DB2 allocates space for user data bases (see Figure 13-23). DB2 manages its own data set[3] allocation unless the system administrator overrides this feature, thereby enabling DB2 to keep track of available disk space and locates tables, indexes, and other database constructs in that space. It also releases disk space for use when it becomes available, such as when an index or a table is dropped. The system administrator can also define, locate, and delete data sets. Sometimes this is done when tuning, or optimizing, data base performance.

FIGURE 13-23   *DB2 Storage Groups*

[3]Data set is an IBM term for a file. A data set is a named collection of data used to hold table and index data.

■ USING DB2 TO CREATE TABLES, VIEWS, AND INDEXES

DB2 uses its version of the SQL data definition language (DDL) to define the DB2 constructs. In this section and in the sections that follow, we will illustrate SQL DDL by defining several constructs—tables, views, and indexes—for the KDK application.

DEFINING A TABLE   DB2 uses the SQL CREATE statement to define its constructs. In Chapter 10 we examined only the data manipulation functions of SQL, and in this chapter we add data definition statements. Before defining a table, we must decide on the names of all the columns and their data types and lengths and whether we wish to allow null values.

The allowable DB2 data types for field values are summarized in Figure 13-24. As we stated earlier, a **null value** is a field value that is unknown or not applicable. A null value is different from a zero or a blank value. For example, a customer balance of zero is different from an unknown customer balance. You can prohibit null values from specific columns when you create a table by coding the phrase NOTNULL. If the column does not have this phrase, nulls will be allowed.

Consider the SALESPERSON relation for which sample data appear in Figure 13-12. The following CREATE statement defines it:

```
CREATE TABLE SALESPERSON
    (NUMBER          CHAR (4)         NOT NULL,
    NAME            CHAR (20)        NOT NULL,
    REGION          DECIMAL (1))
```

The next SQL statement creates the PRODUCT relation for the sample data shown in Figure 13-14:

```
CREATE TABLE PRODUCT
    (TYPE            CHAR (1)         NOT NULL,
    NUMBER          CHAR (5)         NOT NULL,
    NAME            CHAR (25)        NOT NULL,
    DESCRIPTION     CHAR (50),
    PRICE           DECIMAL (7,2)    NOT NULL)
```

DEFINING A VIEW   The CREATE statement can also be used to define a view. To do this, you include a SELECT statement that describes the view. The following CREATE statement defines a view of PRODUCT that includes only product numbers and prices:

```
CREATE VIEW PRICELIST
    AS    SELECT    NUMBER, PRICE
          FROM      PRODUCT
```

FIGURE 13-24   *Some Allowable DB2 Data Types*

INTEGER	31-bit signed binary values
SMALLINT	15-bit signed binary values
FLOAT	Floating-point values
DECIMAL(p,q)	Packed decimal values of p (1 to 15) digits; a number of decimal places (q) to the right of the decimal point may be specified
CHAR(n)	Fixed-length text data n (1 to 254) characters long
VARCHAR(n)	Variable-length text data up to n (1 to 32674) characters

The view PRICELIST can be manipulated in exactly the same way as a table is. Data is retrieved from a view using the same SQL statements used for a table. If the view is a subset of rows or columns of a single table, it can be used to update base table data. But views that are the result of a join operation cannot be used to update table data.

The next statement creates a view that contains only those rows in the PRODUCT relation for refrigerators (the Type field contains a 5):

```
CREATE VIEW REFRIGERATORS
    AS    SELECT    *
          FROM      PRODUCT
          WHERE     TYPE = '5'
```

By specifying SELECT * we include all of the columns, and by specifying WHERE TYPE = '5' we include only those rows for refrigerators. This view can be used to update base table data.

Consider a third view. Assume that KDK wants a particular user to have only restricted access to the DEALER and ADVERTISEMENT relations, that is, only those dealers who have participated in the advertising (see Figures 13-12 and 13-17). We might define an appropriate joined view in this way:

```
CREATE VIEW ACTIVEDEALER
    AS    SELECT    DEALER.NUMBER, DEALER.NAME, TELEPHONE,
                    ADVERTISEMENT.DATE, COST, SHARE-PERCENT
          FROM      DEALER, ADVERTISEMENT
          WHERE     DEALER.NUMBER = ADVERTISEMENT.DEALER-NUMBER
```

Since this view is based on a join, it cannot be used to update base table data.

DEFINING AN INDEX   Indexes are usually defined and dropped by the DBA or system administrator. As we mentioned earlier, neither users nor application programmers ever reference an index; rather, DB2 decides when to use it and which one to use.

One reason to use an index, as described in the previous section, is to increase processing performance. Several indexes can be defined for one table, thereby allowing rapid access on many different fields. Another reason for defining an index on a table is that an index can force the uniqueness of the values of a column (or multiple columns). For example, the dealer number in KDK's DEALER relation must be unique (although the dealer's name, address, ZIP, and so forth do not need to be unique). The way to establish the uniqueness of the dealer number field is to issue this CREATE statement:

```
CREATE    UNIQUE INDEX XDEALER
          ON DEALER (NUMBER)
```

In the next example, since UNIQUE is not specified, the resulting index might include duplicate telephone numbers. Incidentally, the index value is assumed to be ascending (ASC) unless otherwise specified (DESC):

```
CREATE    INDEX XDLRPHONE
          ON DEALER (PHONE DESC)
```

USING DB2 TO CHANGE A TABLE   Often when we design a database, we are unable to anticipate all of the user's needs. Even if we could, the needs change over time, and consequently we sometimes need to modify our database design. Notice that we are not talking about changing the data stored in the tables (that happens all the time, of course) but, rather, the structure of tables themselves.

DB2 offers two ways to modify table specifications: by dropping and then recreating the table and by using the ALTER statement. The ALTER statement can be used only for adding a column to an existing table.

To remove a column or to change a column's data type or length or to change whether null values are allowed, we must drop the table and re-create it. We illustrate how to drop a table in the next section. For now, just be aware that when you drop a table, you lose the table data as well as all the views and indexes based on that table.

To make structure changes other than adding a new column, follow these steps:

1. Define a new table with all the changes and a different name.
2. Copy the table data from the old table to the new one.
3. Define all indexes on the new table.
4. Drop the old table (this loses all the views of it, too).
5. Restore the original table name as a view of the new table. This allows applications that once referenced the old table to remain unchanged, because the new view is processed in exactly the same way as the old table.
6. Define views like the ones defined for the old table. These can be exact duplicates of the old views because you can base a view on another view, just as you can base a view on a table. (Of course, if a view contains a column that has just been dropped, that view is no longer valid.)
7. Authorize users to use the new table and views.

Clearly, this type of database modification is done only by a DBA or someone who is authorized by the DBA.

The second option for changing a table design uses the ALTER statement, with which we can add a column to an existing table. For instance, to add a salary column to the SALESPERSON relation, we would use the following statement:

```
ALTER     TABLE SALESPERSON
          (ADD SALARY DECIMAL (7,2))
```

■ USING DB2 TO DELETE TABLES AND VIEWS

The DBA periodically needs to eliminate tables from the data base. Users are rarely authorized to do this, because they could inadvertently delete data they do not realize that another user needs. In the previous section, we saw how the DBA might need to delete a table in order to change its structure.

Deleting a table erases not only the table but also all its dependent views and indexes. Thus, a table should not be dropped without careful thought. To delete the ADVERTISEMENT table from its database, KDK's DBA would issue the following DROP statement:

```
DROP     TABLE ADVERTISEMENT
```

The table and all its data would be deleted from the table space, as well as all the indexes and views associated with it.

The DROP statement can also be used to delete views. For instance, the DBA might authorize a user to create views and then to delete them when they are no longer useful. It is unlikely, however, that a user would be authorized to drop views that might be used by anyone else. That responsibility (and control) should remain with the DBA. This notwithstanding, however, we could delete the ACTIVE-DEALER view by issuing the following statement:

```
DROP     VIEW ACTIVEDEALER
```

Any applications that used that view (or views based on that view) would no longer work.

SUMMARY OF DB2 CREATION FACILITIES   DB2 allows the DBA or user to define, modify, and delete various database constructs—tables, views, table spaces, indexes, index spaces, data bases, and storage groups. Users and application programmers are concerned only with tables and views. In addition to tables and views, the DBA and database designers need to understand the underlying physical structures and database storage.

■ USING DB2 SQL TO MANIPULATE DATA

There are some differences between the DB2 statements used by interactive users and those used by application programmers that occur because of differences in the users' and the programmers' environments. Interactive users want results to be displayed immediately on a screen, whereas application programmers want the DBMS to place the values of columns and rows into program variables.

INTERACTIVE DATA MANIPULATION Interactive DB2, or DB2I, supports all of the SQL statements described in Chapter 10. Because the format is the same as shown in that chapter, we will not go over it again. The user simply types the commands, as shown in Chapter 10, at the DB2I prompt.

ACCESSING DB2 FROM COBOL DB2 application programs can be written in COBOL, PL/I, FORTRAN, C, and assembler language, and SQL statements can be embedded in programs written in any of these languages. The examples used in this text are embedded in COBOL programs.

As shown in Figure 13-25, all application programs that access DB2 must first be processed by the DB2 **precompiler.** The precompiler analyzes program source statements and processes those that are flagged as SQL statements (you will see how later). The precompiler inserts into the program the required table formats, which are already written in the host language and stored on disk. It also builds for each SQL statement a **data base request module,** or DBRM, which it stores for later use. Finally, the precompiler replaces the SQL statements with host-language call statements to access the DBRMs. As illustrated in Figure 13-25, the modified source code is then input to a standard language compiler for normal compilation.

The Bind process uses the DBRMs, database table definitions, available indexes, and other database data to determine the access paths for each SQL request. It stores these in the database data as an **application plan,** which is loaded when the first SQL call is executed.

To enable the DB2 precompiler to recognize the statements intended for it, all SQL statements are embedded in keywords. Specifically, every SQL statement is preceded by the keyword EXEC SQL and followed by the keyword END-EXEC. In COBOL, the keyword END-EXEC is followed by a period unless the SQL statement is located in an IF statement. The general format of a DB2 SQL statement in a COBOL program is

EXEC SQL statement END-EXEC.

Only one statement can be included between the keywords. Multiple SQL statements require multiple EXEC SQL . . . END-EXEC statements. DB2 SQL statements are embedded in the DATA DIVISION and the PROCEDURE DIVISION.

SQL STATEMENTS IN THE DATA DIVISION Two types of statements are embedded in the DATA DIVISION. The first describes data items that are used to pass database data between the application program and DB2. The second type describes the system data shared by the application program and DB2.

Figure 13-26 shows part of a COBOL program that processes the SALESPERSON table defined earlier. The DATA DIVISION includes data item definitions for all three columns of SALESPERSON. These columns have been renamed: NUMBER is SALESPERSON-NUM, NAME is SALESPERSON-NAME, and REGION is SALES-REGION. The correct correspondence of names is established in the PROCEDURE DIVISION.

FIGURE 13-25   *Steps in Developing an Application Program with DB2*

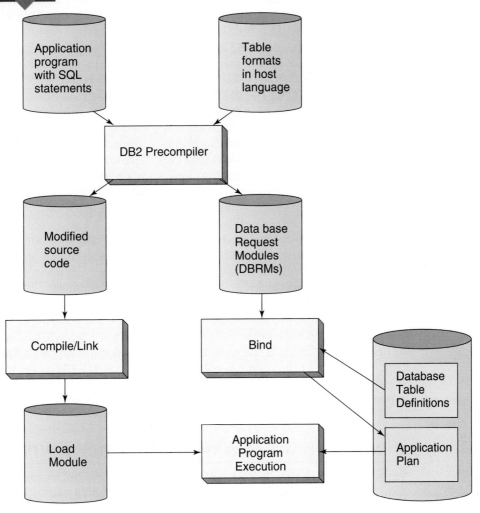

FIGURE 13-26   *SQL Statements Embedded in COBOL Program*

```
DATA DIVISION.
WORKING-STORAGE SECTION.
EXEC  SQL   BEGIN DECLARE SECTION          END-EXEC.
01       SALESPERSON.
         05       SALESPERSON-NUM           PICTURE X(4).
         05       SALESPERSON-NAME          PICTURE X(20).
         05       SALES-REGION              PICTURE 9  COMP-3.
EXEC  SQL   END DECLARE SECTION            END-EXEC.
EXEC  SQL   INCLUDE SQLCA   END-EXEC.
PROCEDURE DIVISION.
         MOVE '5762' TO SALESPERSON-NUM.
         EXEC SQL
              SELECT NAME, REGION
              INTO :SALESPERSON-NAME, :SALES-REGION
              FROM SALESPERSON
              WHERE NUMBER = :SALESPERSON-NUM
         END-EXEC.
```

The data types and lengths of data items do match, although COBOL uses a different vocabulary than SQL does. For example, when we created the table using SQL, we defined SPNUM as CHAR(4), whereas the equivalent COBOL definition for SALESPERSON-NUM is PICTURE X(4).

All the data items that DB2 and the application program share are grouped together, thereby enabling the precompiler to identify them. (We show these statements in the WORKING-STORAGE SECTION, but they could be located elsewhere in the DATA DIVISION.) The DECLARE SECTION is used to define those data items that will be used to transfer database data between the application program and DB2. That group of data item definitions is preceded by the DB2 keywords BEGIN DECLARE SECTION and is terminated with the message END DECLARE SECTION. In Figure 13-26, the definition of SALESPERSON is found in the DECLARE SECTION.

In addition to database data, the application program and the DBMS also need to share system data. For example, after each SQL statement is executed, DB2 sets a return code that indicates whether an error occurred. Both DB2 and the application program need access to this return code.

System data are defined in the program with the DB2 SQL message INCLUDE SQLCA (which stands for SQL Communications Area). When the precompiler processes this INCLUDE message, it inserts the data definitions in Figure 13-27(a) into the application program.

For brevity, Figure 13-27(b) describes only a few of the data items in SQLCA. Knowing all of them would contribute little to your understanding of DB2, but the one data item you must know is SQLCODE. SQLCODE is set by DB2 after each SQL command is executed. If the command is executed normally, SQLCODE is set to zero. If an unusual but normal condition occurs, SQLCODE is set to a positive value. For example, end-of-data is indicated by the value 100. If an abnormal, unexpected condition occurs, SQLCODE is set to a negative value. Insufficient VSAM file space is an example of an abnormal unexpected event.

■ SQL STATEMENTS IN THE PROCEDURE DIVISION

SQL statements in the PROCEDURE DIVISION instruct DB2 to perform some action. For example, the SELECT statement in Figure 13-26 causes DB2 to extract from the database the name and region of Salesperson 5762 and to place those values in the data items called SALESPERSON-NAME and SALES-REGION. This SQL statement is almost identical to the format followed when writing interactive SQL commands. The exception is the INTO clause that tells DB2 the name of the **host variable** (or variables) into which DB2 will place the value(s) it obtains from the database.

One problem for the DB2 precompiler is distinguishing between the data names defined in the database and those defined locally within the application program. If all names are unique, it can process the statements correctly. But it is impossible to guarantee that the application programmer will always choose data names not already used in the database. Consequently, a colon (:) precedes the names of program variables used within any embedded SQL statement.

As we stated in Chapter 9, COBOL (as well as many other programming languages) is designed to process data one record at a time. That is, a typical COBOL program retrieves one record, processes it, retrieves the next one, processes it, and so forth, until all the records have been handled. DB2, however, processes tables. That is, a DB2 SELECT statement always returns a table of data. (The example in Figure 13-26 is unusual in that it only returns one row; most SELECT statements return many rows.) This distinction between COBOL file processing and DB2 relation processing is important to the application programmer who might be tempted to think that SQL statements correspond to simple READ and WRITE statements. They do not.

FIGURE 13-27   *DB2 Communications Area: (a) COBOL Description of SQLCA and (b) Content of Selected SQLCA Data Items*

```
01   SQLCA.
     05   SQLCAID        PICTURE X(8).
     05   SQLCABC        PICTURE S9(9)  COMPUTATIONAL.
     05   SQLCODE        PICTURE S9(9)  COMPUTATIONAL.
     05   SQLERRM
          49   SQLERRML  PICTURE S9(4)  COMPUTATIONAL.
          49   SQLERRMC  PICTURE X(70).
     05   SQLERRP        PICTURE X(8).
     05   SQLERRD        OCCURS 6 TIMES
                         PICTURE S9(9)  COMPUTATIONAL.

     05   SQLWARN.
          10   SQLWARN0  PICTURE X(1).
          10   SQLWARN1  PICTURE X(1).
          10   SQLWARN2  PICTURE X(1).
          10   SQLWARN3  PICTURE X(1).
          10   SQLWARN4  PICTURE X(1).
          10   SQLWARN5  PICTURE X(1).
          10   SQLWARN6  PICTURE X(1).
          10   SQLWARN7  PICTURE X(1).
     05   SQLEXT         PICTURE X(8).
```

(a)

Data-item	Content
SQLCODE	Return code. Set by DB2 after each command. Zero indicates successful operation. Positive value indicates normal condition (such as end-of-data). Negative value indicates abnormal error.
SQLERRM	Error message. Set when SQLCODE is less than 0.
SQLERRP	Name of DB2 routine detecting error. Set when SQLCODE is less than 0.
SQLERRD	DB2 system status.
SQLWARN	Warning flags. Set for conditions such as data-item truncation (receiving data-item too small); null values encountered when processing SUM, AVG, MIN, or MAX; recovery from deadlock; and so forth.

(b)

The application programmer would be better served by thinking of DB2 as a vehicle for retrieving an entire input data set, or pseudofile, from the database. Then the data is processed one row at a time. To do this, the programmer defines a cursor within the application program.

A **cursor** is a pointer that operates on a SELECT statement, indicating the row to be processed within the pseudo-file generated by the SELECT statement. In Figure 13-28, for example, the cursor CURRENT is defined to operate on the SELECT statement that will retrieve the names of all the salespeople in Region 5. In subsequent statements the program uses CURRENT to process sequentially the retrieved rows. As you can see in Figure 13-28, the logic is similar to that of sequential file processing. The cursor is opened (similar to opening a file); the first row is fetched (similar to a read); and a loop is executed to process the rest of the data (similar to processing an entire file). The processing stops when SQLCODE is returned with a value of 100, indicating the end-of-data. For now we will ignore other types of error processing.

FIGURE 13-28   *Using the Cursor to Process Sequentially a Set of Database Records*

```
PROCEDURE DIVISION.
      .
      .
      .
      MOVE 5 TO SALES-REGION.
      EXEC SQL DECLARE CURRENT CURSOR FOR
            SELECT NAME FROM SALESPERSON
             WHERE REGION = :SALES-REGION
      END EXEC.
      .
      .
      .
      EXEC SQL OPEN CURRENT END-EXEC.
      EXEC SQL FETCH CURRENT INTO :SALESPERSON-NAME END-EXEC.
      PERFORM PROCESS-FETCH UNTIL SQLCODE NOT = 0.
      EXEC SQL CLOSE CURRENT END-EXEC.
      .
      .
      .
PROCESS-FETCH.
      (Instructions to process SALESPERSON-NAME go here.)
      EXEC SQL FETCH CURRENT INTO :SALESPERSON-NAME END-EXEC.
```

The format of the FETCH statement is

FETCH cursor-name INTO dataname(s)

The dataname(s) in the FETCH statement must match the column names identified in the SELECT statement in which the cursor is defined. More details about the programming techniques used with DB2 appear in the example at the end of this chapter.

■ DB2 CONCURRENT PROCESSING

Because DB2 allows concurrent processing, it must provide facilities to control and limit users' interference. This is done by means of locks. Two types of locks employed by DB2 are shared locks and exclusive locks. When an application reads database data, DB2 acquires a **shared lock** on the data, which allows other applications to read the same data. Applications that wish to modify those data must wait, however, until the lock has been released, to ensure that everyone has access to the most current data.

When an application needs to modify data (DB2 knows this by analyzing the SQL statements in the application), DB2 acquires an **exclusive lock** on the data, which prevents all other applications from accessing the data. When the application is finished with the data, the lock is released, thereby giving other applications access to the updated data. If DB2 did not acquire exclusive locks, a second application could possibly use the old version of the data while they were being updated by the first application, and this would compromise the integrity of the stored data.

In addition to choices regarding the type of lock, DB2 offers options regarding the level, or locksize. The two locking units in DB2 are table spaces and pages. (Recall that a table space is an area of disk storage in which one or several base tables are stored. Table spaces are made up of **pages,** 4k-byte blocks of disk space. Pages generally contain parts of tables.) Although you might expect DB2 to apply locks to tables or even to rows within tables, this is not the case. When an exclusive lock is acquired for a table space, no application can access the data in *any* table stored in that table space.

When establishing a new database, the DBA can specify the lock level within a table space, through the LOCKSIZE option of the CREATE TABLESPACE command. The format is

LOCKSIZE = ANY | PAGE | TABLESPACE

If the DBA specifies TABLESPACE, then locks (either shared or exclusive) will be applied to the entire table space in which a referenced table resides. This option improves the performance of the application, but in doing so it can seriously delay other applications needing access to something in that table space.

If the DBA selects PAGE, the locks initially are applied at the page level (DB2 may escalate the lock to the table level if it detects poor performance). Although locking at the page level results in fewer conflicts than does locking at the table space level, more resources are required to administer it.

Finally, if the DBA specifies ANY, then DB2 selects the appropriate level, depending on the number of pages that may be required to fulfill an application's needs. If only a few pages are referenced, page-level locks will be applied. On the other hand, if many pages are required, table space–level locks will be applied. ANY is the default value for the LOCKSIZE option, and so the DBA does not need to specify the LOCKSIZE option when creating a table space. By default, DB2 can be allowed to select the proper level of locking based on the type of SQL request and the number of pages involved.

As we mentioned, locks are completely transparent to end users and application programmers. DB2 automatically does all the necessary locking and unlocking.

COMMIT AND ROLLBACK   All DB2 table data modifications must be either committed or discarded. When a change is committed, it is final and becomes part of the actual database data. When a commitment is made, all the page locks placed on that data are released, and the updated data are made available to other applications. A commitment is automatically executed when an application terminates normally, but it can also be explicitly invoked with the SQL COMMIT statement.

Sometimes DB2 table modifications need to be discarded, for example, when an end user wants to terminate a transaction while it is being carried out. To discard the changes, the application program issues an SQL ROLLBACK statement, which returns the tables to their original state (the state after the most recent COMMIT), thus eliminating any pending updates to the table. At that point, all page locks are released, and other applications have access to the unchanged data.

DB2 AND DEADLOCK   When two or more applications are deadlocked, DB2 resolves the problem by examining the number of records that each application has written and terminates the application(s) with the fewest changes since the last commitment. The more active application is selected to continue processing.

■ DB2 BACKUP AND RECOVERY

DB2 stores the before-images and after-images of all database changes on a transaction log. Changes are written to the log before they are written to the database, and DB2 periodically checks itself. At the checkpoints, all changes residing in system buffers are written to the database, and a checkpoint record is written to the log. At the time of a checkpoint, therefore, the log and DB2 databases are synchronized.

DB2 can recover from a system failure by first applying all the before-images created since the most recent checkpoint and then applying all the after-images of committed transactions. As a result, all committed changes can endure the crash, although those transactions in progress at the time of the crash must be restarted.

Databases are stored on disks and are therefore vulnerable to physical damage. Should the disk be damaged, the database must be re-created from backup copies, which means that the users' organization must periodically save the database. In DB2, this is done by means of utility programs that copy table spaces (that is, the physical storage areas that contain table data). DB2 includes an option that allows the users' organization to make backup copies of only those pages in a table space that have been modified since the latest backup. This option can save much time because unchanged pages are not copied unnecessarily.

■ DB2 SECURITY

DB2 provides two types of security mechanisms to protect the database: restricting access via views and limiting processing capabilities to particular users.

VIEWS   Views provide data security at the field level. Remember that a view is a subset of columns, rows, or both derived from one or more base tables. To prevent a user from accessing any data in a base table except the fields that he or she needs to access, the DBA simply defines a view of the table and authorizes the user to access it but not the base table. We explained how to use SQL to create a view earlier in this chapter, so the following two examples are presented without further explanation.

The following SQL creates a view of KDK's DEALER table that allows access only to the dealers' names and telephone numbers:

```
CREATE VIEW DLRPHONES
    AS SELECT NAME, TELEPHONE
    FROM DEALER
```

The user of the next view is given access to only those dealers' records in the state of Massachusetts:

```
CREATE VIEW MASSDLRS
    AS SELECT *
    FROM   DEALER
    WHERE STATE/PROVINCE = 'MA'
```

LIMITING ACCESS TO DB2 RESOURCES   DB2 is able to control access to various database resources, including tables, views, databases, utility programs, the DB2 catalog, and table spaces. Because DB2 users (both end users and application programmers) access only tables and views, we will discuss only them. Though not shown here, system administrators and database administrators have access to all other database resources as well.

DB2 can control access to data in tables and views, so that users can be authorized to issue SELECT, INSERT, DELETE, and UPDATE statements against a table or view. The columns that may be updated can be specified, and the use of the ALTER command to change a table definition can be restricted.

IDENTIFYING USERS   Because DB2 is used in the MVS environment, many users can access it concurrently from a variety of other subsystems, such as IMS and CICS transaction managers, TSO, and batch jobs. Although you need not understand all these subsystems, it is important to know that each has a means of identifying authorized users. For instance, TSO terminal users have a log-on ID that identifies them; a batch job has a special parameter on the job card; and IMS users have a sign-on ID or a logical terminal name (thus, the equipment, not the person, is authorized to access the system). Other systems have similar authorization IDs.

DB2 uses the connecting subsystem's ID to identify the DB2 user and assigns capabilities to access resources according to permissions granted to those IDs. Permissions are given via the SQL GRANT statement:

GRANT capability resource-list
   TO authorization-ID-list
   (WITH GRANT OPTION)

The capabilities that can be granted to users are the following:

- ALTER   The definition of the specified tables may be altered.
- DELETE   Rows may be deleted from the specified tables or views.
- INSERT   Rows may be inserted into the specified tables or views.
- SELECT   Rows may be selected from the specified tables or views.
- UPDATE   The values for the specified list of columns in the specified tables may be updated.

The resource list for most users is simply the names of tables or views for which they will have the specified capabilities. The authorization-ID list is the list of user IDs to whom the specified authorization is being granted. The authorization-ID list can also be the keyword PUBLIC, which grants authority to all users. Here are some examples that illustrate the GRANT command:

- All users are allowed to look at the DEALER table:

  GRANT SELECT ON TABLE DEALER TO PUBLIC

- An application program can insert new records into the ADVERTISEMENT table:

  GRANT INSERT ON TABLE ADVERTISEMENT TO PROG87

- A user known by the ID TERM 14 is allowed to access the view DLRPHONES:

  GRANT SELECT ON VIEW DLRPHONES TO TERM 14

- Two users are allowed to change table definitions for the DEALER and SALES-PERSON tables:

  GRANT ALTER ON TABLE DEALER, SALESPERSON TO USER5, USER7

- An application program is allowed to delete SALESPERSON records:

  GRANT DELETE ON TABLE SALESPERSON TO PERS000

When the DB2 database is installed, the system administrator is given total control over all resources. He or she may grant authority to or revoke authority from any other individual, including DBAs, by means of the GRANT statement. Of course, the resources and capabilities available to the system administrator include many options besides those just described.

The GRANT statement contains an optional clause: WITH GRANT OPTION. When used, this clause enables the grantee to give others the same capabilities over the same resources. Thus one can pass along authorization to others. Consider this example:

GRANT SELECT ON AD-COPY TO MURPHY WITH GRANT OPTION

This gives Murphy permission to read the AD-COPY table and allows her to authorize other users to do the same.

In addition to the explicit authorization conveyed by the GRANT command, the creator of a construct is automatically given full authority WITH GRANT OPTION over that construct, and this cannot be revoked unless the construct itself is deleted from the database.

If authority is revoked (by means of the REVOKE command), it has a cascading effect; that is, the specified privilege is revoked not only from the named authorized ID but also from anyone else to whom that authorized ID granted this privilege. Suppose that User A were granted the authority to read a table with the GRANT option and subsequently granted that privilege to User B. When User A is transferred to another department and his authority to read the table is revoked, User B's authority stemming from the GRANT is also automatically revoked. The following illustrates this sequence of events:

1. DBA:

   GRANT SELECT ON TABLE PRODUCT TO USERA WITH GRANT OPTION
   (User A can now read the PRODUCT table.)

2. User A:

   GRANT SELECT ON TABLE PRODUCT TO USERB
   (Users A and B can now read the PRODUCT table.)

3. DBA:

   REVOKE SELECT ON TABLE PRODUCT FROM USERA
   (Neither User A nor User B can read the PRODUCT table.)

RELATIONAL IMPLEMENTATION USING DB2

This section discusses the implementation of KDK's application using DB2. A summary of KDK's database design appears in Figures 13-29 and 13-30.

First we create the database using interactive DB2 commands, and then we illustrate several on-line queries that product managers might execute. Finally, we present an application program that produces one of the standard reports that the PMs need.

■ CREATING THE DATABASE STRUCTURE

The interactive DB2 statements to create the database structure (KDKICB) presented in Figures 13-29 and 13-30 are shown in Figure 13-31 on page 338. As you can see, the statements are straightforward. Having completed the design earlier, we need only specify the format of each table and column using DB2.

FIGURE 13-29   *Summary of Relations for KDK Appliances*

INVOICE	(<u>Number</u>, Date, Total, Salesperson.Number, Dealer.Number)
LINE-ITEM	(<u>Invoice.Number</u>, <u>Line-item-number</u>, Product.Number, Quantity, Extended-price)
DEALER	(<u>Number</u>, Name, Address-1, Address-2, City, State/Province, ZIP/Postal-code, Telephone)
SALESPERSON	(<u>Number</u>, Name, Region)
PRODUCT	(<u>Number</u>, Name, Description, Price)
AD-COPY	(<u>Ad-name</u>, Agency, First-run-date)
ADVERTISEMENT	(<u>Publication</u>, <u>Date</u>, <u>Ad-name</u>, Cost, Share-percent, Dealer.Number)
PRODUCT-AD	(<u>Ad-name</u>, <u>Product.Number</u>)

FIGURE 13-30   *Table Descriptions for KDK's Database*

```
INVOICE
    Number                  Char (4)
    Date                    Numeric YYMMDD
    Total                   Numeric 9999.99
    Salesperson.Number      *
    Dealer.Number           *
LINE-ITEM
    Invoice.Number          *
    Line-item-number        Numeric 999 positive integer
    Product.Number          *
    Quantity                Numeric 999 positive integer
    Extended-price          Computed numeric 9(6).99
DEALER
    Number                  Char(4)
    Name                    Char(45)
    Address-1               Char(25)
    Address-2               Char(25)
    City                    Char(15)
    State/Province          Char(2)
    ZIP/Postal-code         Char(10)
    Telephone               Char(10)
SALESPERSON
    Number                  Char(4)
    Name                    Char(20)
    Region                  Numeric 9
PRODUCT
    Type                    Numeric 9
    Number                  Char(5)
    Name                    Char(25)
    Description             Char(50)
    Price                   Numeric 99999.99
AD-COPY
    Ad-name                 Char(15)
    Agency                  Char(30)
    First-run-date          Numeric YYMMDD
ADVERTISEMENT
    Publication             Char(10)
    Date                    Numeric YYMMDD
    Ad-name                 *
    Cost                    Numeric 9999.99
    Share-percent           Numeric 999.99
                            E.g., 30% is 30.00
    Dealer.Number           *
PRODUCT-AD
    Ad-name                 *
    Product.Number          *
```

*Definitions for foreign keys are shown in the foreign relations.

Keep in mind that this database will be used for reporting only—it will be neither updated nor altered. It is a snapshot of corporate operational data downloaded from the mainframe database to be analyzed by the product managers. All updates are made to the operational data in a carefully controlled environment. Therefore, other than authorizing each PM to access (SELECT) the tables, no other authority is granted. No one needs to alter, delete, or update any of the data. And because all the PMs are given access to all the columns in all the tables, no views are necessary.

■ EXAMPLES OF INTERACTIVE QUERIES

Figure 13-32 on page 339 shows four sample queries that could be made against KDK's database. The first lists the names of dealers who shared advertising with KDK during the month of March. The DB2 word DISTINCT eliminates duplicate names from the list. Although the name of a dealer who shared more than one ad with KDK should appear several times in the list, we will print it only once.

FIGURE 13-31   *Interactive DB2 Statements to Create Tables for KDK's Database*

```
CREATE   TABLE         INVOICE
         (NUMBER                         CHAR(4)          NOT NULL,
         DATE                            DECIMAL(6)       NOT NULL,
         TOTAL                           DECIMAL(7,2)     NOT NULL,
         SALESPERSON-NUMBER              CHAR(4)          NOT NULL,
         DEALER-NUMBER                   CHAR(4)          NOT NULL)
CREATE   TABLE         LINE-ITEM
         (INVOICE-NUMBER                 CHAR(4)          NOT NULL,
         LINE-ITEM-NUMBER                DECIMAL(3)       NOT NULL,
         PRODUCT-NUMBER                  CHAR(5)          NOT NULL,
         QUANTITY                        DECIMAL(3)       NOT NULL,
         EXTENDED-PRICE                  DECIMAL(8,2)     NOT NULL)
CREATE   TABLE         DEALER
         (NUMBER                         CHAR(4)          NOT NULL,
         NAME                            CHAR(45)         NOT NULL,
         ADDRESS-1                       CHAR(25),
         ADDRESS-2                       CHAR(25),
         CITY                            CHAR(15)
         STATE/PROVINCE                  CHAR(10),
         ZIP/POSTAL-CODE                 CHAR(10),
         TELEPHONE                       CHAR(10))
CREATE   TABLE         SALESPERSON
         NUMBER                          CHAR(4)          NOT NULL,
         NAME                            CHAR(20)         NOT NULL,
         REGION                          DECIMAL(1)).
CREATE   TABLE         PRODUCT
         (TYPE                           CHAR(1)          NOT NULL,
         NUMBER                          CHAR(5)          NOT NULL,
         NAME                            CHAR(25)         NOT NULL,
         DESCRIPTION                     CHAR(50),
         PRICE                           DECIMAL(7,2)     NOT NULL)
CREATE   TABLE       AD-COPY
         (AD-NAME                        CHAR(15)         NOT NULL,
         AGENCY                          CHAR(30),
         FIRST-RUN-DATE                  DECIMAL(6))
CREATE   TABLE         ADVERTISEMENT
         (PUBLICATION                    CHAR(10)         NOT NULL,
         DATE                            DECIMAL(6)       NOT NULL,
         AD-NAME                         CHAR(15)         NOT NULL,
         COST                            DECIMAL(6,2)     NOT NULL,
         SHARE-PERCENT                   DECIMAL(5,2),
         DEALER-NUMBER                   CHAR(4))
CREATE   TABLE         PRODUCT-AD
         (AD-NAME                        CHAR(15)         NOT NULL,
         PRODUCT-NUMBER                  CHAR(5)          NOT NULL)
```

This example uses the subquery technique. Recall from Chapter 10 that subqueries allow us to narrow the scope of our search through the database by qualifying one level of query with another. Reading from the bottom up, the first example in Figure 13-32 begins by building a list of numbers for those dealers who shared with KDK the cost of advertising during March. Then, moving up to the next SELECT statement, it extracts the dealers' names from the DEALER table for all whose numbers appeared in the first list. Finally, the DISTINCT option causes the DBMS to eliminate duplicate names.

The second example in Figure 13-32 also uses the subquery technique, only this time it is more complex. Once again we interpret the statement by reading it from the bottom up. We begin by building a list of product numbers for refrigerators (Type = '5'). Then we build a list of invoice numbers that contain line items for any of those products. Next we extract the dealers' numbers for all of those

FIGURE 13-32   *Sample Interactive DB2 Queries Against KDK's Database*

```
1.    List the dealers who participated in shared advertising during the month of March:
      SELECT DISTINCT NAME FROM DEALER
      WHERE DEALER. NUMBER IN
      SELECT DEALER-NUMBER
            FROM ADVERTISEMENT
            WHERE ADVERTISEMENT. DATE BETWEEN 970301 AND 970331
2.    List the dealers who purchased refrigerators (product type = 5) in March:
      SELECT DISTINCT NAME FROM DEALER
      WHERE DEALER. NUMBER IN
            SELECT DEALER-NUMBER FROM INVOICE
            WHERE DATE BETWEEN 970301 AND 970331
            AND INVOICE. NUMBER IN
                  SELECT INVOICE-NUMBER FROM LINE-ITEM
                  WHERE LINE-ITEM. PRODUCT-NUMBER IN
                        SELECT NUMBER FROM PRODUCT
                        WHERE TYPE = '5'
3.    List the products that were advertised in March:
      SELECT NUMBER, NAME, DESCRIPTION FROM PRODUCT
      WHERE PRODUCT. NUMBER IN
            SELECT DISTINCT PRODUCT-NUMBER FROM PRODUCT-AD
            WHERE PRODUCT-AD. AD-NAME = ADVERTISEMENT. AD-NAME
            AND ADVERTISEMENT. DATE BETWEEN 970301 AND 970331
4.    Print the total sales for product #94605 for the month of March. Then print it for the
      month of April:
      CREATE VIEW PRODUCTSALES
            (DATE, PRODUCT, EXTENDED-PRICE)
            AS SELECT DATE, PRODUCT-NUMBER, EXTENDED-PRICE
                  FROM INVOICE, LINE-ITEM
                  WHERE LINE-ITEM. INVOICE-NUMBER = INVOICE. NUMBER
                  AND LINE-ITEM. PRODUCT-NUMBER = '94605'
      SELECT SUM (EXTENDED-PRICE)
      FROM PRODUCTSALES WHERE DATE BETWEEN 970301 AND 970331
      SELECT SUM (EXTENDED-PRICE)
      FROM PRODUCTSALES WHERE DATE BETWEEN 970401 AND 970430
```

invoices occurring in March, and finally we build a list of dealers' names, eliminating duplicates. This is the list of dealers who purchased refrigerators during March.

The third illustration in Figure 13-32 extracts data from several tables in order to give the user the desired results. Product names and descriptions come from the PRODUCT table. Advertisements, which are dated, are stored in the ADVERTISEMENT table. But advertisements are not directly associated with any product—they are associated with advertising copy by means of the Ad-name column. Similarly, products are associated directly not with an advertisement but with advertising copy by means of the Ad-name column in the PRODUCT-AD table.

We begin by joining the PRODUCT-AD table and the ADVERTISEMENT table, matching on Ad-name. Then we extract unique (distinct) product numbers, but only for advertisements that ran in March. Finally, we extract from the PRODUCT table the name and description for each product number we have identified.

The fourth example of a query in Figure 13-32 begins by building a view (the join of two tables) and then selecting total sales figures from the view. The view is made up of sales data for Product 94605, taken from the INVOICE table (date) and the LINE-ITEM table (product number, extended price). Having established this subset of the larger base tables, we can ask DB2 to calculate the two sales totals by invoking the SUM built-in function in the SELECT statement. Two SELECT statements are needed, of course, one for each month.

■ APPLICATION PROGRAM EXAMPLE

Figure 13-33 presents a COBOL program that prints the report shown in Figure 13-3(c), entitled PRODUCT SALES SUMMARY BY REGION. In this section we examine the COBOL program, noting the placement of DB2 commands. Although this example is written in COBOL, SQL can also be embedded in PL/I, FORTRAN, C, and assembler language programs.

Looking at the WORKING-STORAGE SECTION of the DATA DIVISION, we find the definition of those variables that will hold data values as they are retrieved by DB2 from the database. These variables are defined following the SQL message BEGIN DECLARE SECTION. Notice that each SQL statement is surrounded by the precompiler keywords EXEC SQL and END-EXEC.

Within the DECLARE SECTION we have defined a sale record, made up of six fields. Later, in the PROCEDURE DIVISION, the data for this sale record can be found in four different database tables. The words END DECLARE SECTION signal the end of the DECLARE SECTION.

FIGURE 13-33   *COBOL Program to Produce PRODUCT SALES SUMMARY BY REGION Report*

```
        IDENTIFICATION DIVISION.
        PROGRAM-ID.    DB2-EXAMPLE.
        ENVIRONMENT DIVISION.
        CONFIGURATION SECTION.
        SPECIAL-NAMES.
             (special names go here)
        INPUT-OUTPUT SECTION.
        FILE-CONTROL.
             SELECT     (SELECT statements for nondatabase files go here)
        DATA DIVISION.
        FILE SECTION.
             FD          (FDs for nondatabase files go here)
        WORKING-STORAGE SECTION.
    *
    *        DECLARE VARIABLES FOR USE WITH DB2
    *
             EXEC SQL   BEGIN DECLARE SECTION    END EXEC.
        01    SALE-RECORD.
             05   PRODUCT-NUMBER             PICTURE X(05).
             05   PRODUCT-NAME               PICTURE X(25).
             05   PRODUCT-DESC               PICTURE X(50).
             05   QUANTITY-SOLD              PICTURE S999           COMP-3.
             05   UNIT-PRICE                 PICTURE S9 (5) V99     COMP-3.
             05   SALE-REGION                PICTURE S9             COMP-3.
             EXEC SQL   END DECLARE SECTION       END EXEC.
    *        REQUEST DB2 TO COPY INTO COBOL PROGRAM
    *        DEFINITIONS FOR DB2 COMMUNICATIONS AREA.
    *
             EXEC SQL   INCLUDE SQLCA              END-EXEC.
    *
    *        DEFINE NON-DATABASE VARIABLES
    *
        77    PRODUCT-NUMBER HOLD         PICTURE X(5).
        77    REGION-HOLD                 PICTURE X.
        77    SUM-UNITS-THIS-REGION       PICTURE 999            COMP-3 VALUE 0.
        77    SUM-UNITS-THIS-PRODUCT      PICTURE 99999          COMP-3 VALUE 0.
        01    PAGE-HEADER-1.
             05   FILLER                    PICTURE X(24)    VALUE SPACES.
             05   FILLER                    PICTURE X(31)
                  VALUE 'PRODUCT SALES SUMMARY BY REGION'.
             05   FILLER                    PICTURE X(25)    VALUE SPACES.
        01    GROUP-1.
             05   FILLER                    PICTURE X(16)
                  VALUE 'PRODUCT NUMBER:'.
```

The next instruction in the WORKING-STORAGE SECTION directs the pre-compiler to copy SQLCA into the COBOL program. Again, this is a list of parameters shared by the DBMS and the application program. The most important field in SQLCA is SQLCODE, as described earlier.

The remainder of the WORKING-STORAGE SECTION defines the work areas and report formats to be used by the program. These are normal COBOL entries that are not affected by the need to use DB2.

In the PROCEDURE DIVISION we find a mixture of SQL statements and ordinary COBOL instructions. The first sequence of instructions in the PROCEDURE DIVISION defines a cursor (C-1) that will be used to retrieve data from the database. The SELECT statement on which the cursor operates is lengthy, but it is easily understood. To print the report seen in Figure 13-3, we need a set of sales records containing product numbers, names and descriptions, prices, quantities sold, and regions, which are found in several different database tables.

FIGURE 13-33   *Continued*

```
            05  PRODUCT-NUMBER-OUT        PICTURE X(05).
            05  FILLER                    PICTURE X(59)      VALUE SPACES.
        01  GROUP-2.
            05  FILLER                    PICTURE X(16)
                VALUE 'DESCRIPTION:'
            05  NAME-OUT                  PICTURE X(25).
            05  FILLER                    PICTURE X(39)      VALUE SPACES.
        01  GROUP-3.
            05  FILLER                    PICTURE X(16)      VALUE SPACES.
            05  DESCRIPTION-OUT           PICTURE X(50).
            05  FILLER                    PICTURE X(14)      VALUE SPACES.
        01  GROUP-4.
            05  FILLER                    PICTURE X(16)
                VALUE 'PRICE:'
            05  PRICE-OUT                 PICTURE $(6).99.
            05  FILLER                    PICTURE X(55)      VALUE SPACES.
        01  COLUMN-HEADERS.
            05  FILLER                    PICTURE X(30)      VALUE SPACES.
            05  FILLER                    PICTURE X(24)
                VALUE 'REGION               UNITS SOLD'.
            05  FILLER                    PICTURE X(26)      VALUE SPACES.
        01  REGION-TOTAL-LINE.
            05  FILLER                    PICTURE X(32)      VALUE SPACES.
            05  REGION-OUT                PICTURE X.
            05  FILLER                    PICTURE X(13)      VALUE SPACES.
            05  UNITS-SOLD-OUT            PICTURE ZZ9.
            05  FILLER                    PICTURE X(31)      VALUE SPACES.
        01  PRODUCT-TOTAL-LINE.
            05  FILLER                    PICTURE X(36)      VALUE SPACES.
            05  FILLER                    PICTURE X(08).
                VALUE 'TOTAL'
            05  TOTAL-OUT                 PICTURE ZZZZ9.
            05  FILLER                    PICTURE X(31)      VALUE SPACES.
    PROCEDURE DIVISION.
        EXEC SQL
            DECLARE C-1 CURSOR FOR
            SELECT PRODUCT. NUMBER, PRODUCT. NAME,
                    PRODUCT. DESCRIPTION, LINE-ITEM. QUANTITY,
                    PRODUCT. PRICE, SALESPERSON. REGION
            FROM PRODUCT, SALESPERSON, LINE-ITEM, INVOICE
            WHERE LINE-ITEM. INVOICE. NUMBER = INVOICE. NUMBER
                AND INVOICE. SALESPERSON. NUMBER = SALESPERSON. NUMBER
                AND LINE-ITEM. PRODUCT. NUMBER = PRODUCT. NUMBER
            ORDER BY PRODUCT. NUMBER, SALESPERSON. REGION
        END-EXEC.
        OPEN OUTPUT REPORT-FILE.
        EXEC SQL   OPEN C-1              END-EXEC.
```

FIGURE 13-33   *Continued*

```
        EXEC SQL   FETCH C-1 INTO :SALE-RECORD     END-EXEC.
        MOVE PRODUCT-NUMBER TO PRODUCT-NUMBER-HOLD.
        MOVE SALE-REGION TO REGION-HOLD.
        PERFORM ISSUE-HEADERS.
        PERFORM PROCESS-AND-FETCH UNTIL SQLCODE = 100.
        EXEC SQL   CLOSE C-1 END EXEC.
        PERFORM ISSUE-REGION-TOTAL.
        PERFORM ISSUE-PRODUCT-TOTAL.
        CLOSE REPORT-FILE.
        EXIT PROGRAM.
    *
    PROCESS-AND-FETCH.
        IF PRODUCT-NUMBER NOT EQUAL PRODUCT-NUMBER-HOLD
        THEN PERFORM ISSUE-REGION-TOTAL
            PERFORM ISSUE-PRODUCT-TOTAL
        ELSE
            IF REGION-NUMBER NOT EQUAL REGION-HOLD
            THEN PERFORM ISSUE-REGION-TOTAL
            ELSE NEXT SENTENCE.
        ADD QUANTITY-SOLD TO SUM-UNITS-THIS REGION.
        ADD QUANTITY-SOLD TO SUM-UNITS-THIS-PRODUCT.
        EXEC SQL   FETCH C-1 INTO :SALE-RECORD     END-EXEC.
    ISSUE-REGION-TOTAL.
        MOVE SUM-UNITS-THIS-REGION TO UNITS-SOLD-OUT.
        MOVE REGION-HOLD TO REGION-OUT.
        MOVE REGION-TOTAL-LINE TO (printer record goes here).
        PERFORM WRITE-LINE.
        MOVE 0 TO SUM-UNITS-THIS-REGION.
        MOVE SALE-REGION TO REGION-HOLD.
    ISSUE-PRODUCT-TOTAL.
        MOVE SUM-UNITS-THIS-PRODUCT TO TOTAL-OUT.
        MOVE PRODUCT-TOTAL-LINE TO (printer record goes here).
        PERFORM WRITE-LINE.
        MOVE 0 TO SUM-UNITS-THIS-PRODUCT.
        MOVE PRODUCT-NUMBER TO PRODUCT-NUMBER-HOLD.
        PERFORM ISSUE-HEADERS.
    ISSUE-HEADERS.
        MOVE PAGE-HEADER-1 TO (printer record goes here).
        PERFORM WRITE-NEW-PAGE.
        MOVE PRODUCT-NUMBER TO PRODUCT-NUMBER-OUT.
        MOVE GROUP-1 TO (printer record goes here).
        PERFORM WRITE-LINE.
        MOVE PRODUCT-NAME TO NAME-OUT.
        MOVE GROUP-2 TO (printer record goes here).
        PERFORM WRITE-LINE.
        MOVE PRODUCT-DESC TO DESCRIPTION-OUT.
```

The SELECT specifies a join of four tables. The join conditions are specified in the where clause that starts

WHERE LINE-ITEM.INVOICE.NUMBER = INVOICE.NUMBER, etc.

Finally, the ORDER BY clause specifies that the rows (records) should be made available to the program sorted by region number within product number.

Having established the cursor, we now have a conceptual pseudofile that contains all the newly constructed sales records in the desired sequence. The rest of the program follows ordinary sequential file-processing logic, testing for two control-level breaks (one on region number and the other on product number).

First we open the output report file, and then we issue SQL statements to prepare the database data to be processed:

OPEN C-1

FIGURE 13-33   *Continued*

```
        MOVE GROUP-3 TO (printer record goes here).
        PERFORM WRITE-LINE.
        MOVE UNIT-PRICE TO PRICE-OUT.
        MOVE GROUP-4 TO (printer record goes here).
        PERFORM WRITE-LINE.
        MOVE COLUMN-HEADERS TO (printer record goes here).
        PERFORM WRITE-LINE.
WRITE-NEW-PAGE.
        (instructions for printing line at top of page go here).
WRITE-LINE.
        (instructions for writing a line go here).
```

We use the cursor to retrieve the first database row in the sale pseudofile,

FETCH C-1 INTO :SALE-RECORD

placing the data values into the fields we defined in the DECLARE SECTION. The word SALE-RECORD is preceded by a colon (:) to help the precompiler determine that SALE-RECORD is a program variable and not a database term. This FETCH SQL statement effectively reads the first sale record from the pseudofile.

The next instruction sequence saves the product number and region values in work areas and writes the first set of report headers. Now the program is ready to process the first record. The program starts the loop called PROCESS–AND–FETCH and remains in this program loop until no more "sale records" are left in the database (UNTIL SQLCODE = 100). When that eventually happens, the program closes the cursor, releasing those resources to other users of this database, and terminates the program normally.

Within the main program loop, PROCESS–AND–FETCH, we find only one SQL statement. The last command in the loop is

FETCH C-1 INTO :SALE-RECORD

This instruction, like an ordinary COBOL READ, reads the next sequential row from the pseudofile, replacing the one just processed. As we mentioned, the loop is executed until all appropriate data has been retrieved from the database. The remaining COBOL paragraphs contain no SQL statements. They are used simply to format and produce the SALES SUMMARY report and would be no different if a sequential input file had been used.

Note that because KDK database is being used exclusively for analyzing data, no database changes are illustrated. If changes in the table data were made in an application program, either the COMMIT SQL statement would be invoked whenever a change were to be made permanent (perhaps after each valid record update) or the ROLLBACK SQL command would be invoked if the program discovered an error partway through an update. Also, a COMMIT would automatically be invoked when the program terminated. However, COMMITs are unnecessary in this sample program because it does not update the database.

SUMMARY

KDK Appliances, a manufacturing company, needed to analyze sales data from its operational database. The most effective and least disruptive way to do this was to download sales data from the operational database onto a smaller mainframe.

Then the snapshot of the operational data could be studied by product managers so that they would have the data they needed to make timely decisions and to plan marketing strategies. KDK Appliances chose Database2 (DB2) as its relational database management system.

After identifying the various objects that the product managers needed, we developed a relational database design. First we drew a set of object diagrams and then converted them to relation diagrams. With the design completed, we turned to the database management system DB2 for implementation.

DB2 is an IBM product used to process relational databases on large computers operating under MVS. DB2 uses the language SQL to define, access, and manipulate data and to grant authorizations. SQL statements can be issued interactively or be embedded into application programs written in COBOL, PL/I, FORTRAN, C, or assembler language.

DB2 allows users to define various database constructs such as tables, views, table spaces, indexes, index spaces, data bases, and storage groups. Users—both on-line end users and application programmers—refer only to tables and views. The database administrator, or someone performing other system functions, is concerned with physical database storage and organization and thus deals with other DB2 constructs as well.

Database constructs can be defined, modified, and deleted, and DB2 includes SQL statements to perform all those functions.

SQL data manipulation language as implemented in DB2 contains all the relational functions studied in Chapter 10. In addition to reading a database, we can insert records, update stored data, and delete rows from a table. The SQL statements for these four functions are SELECT, INSERT, UPDATE, and DELETE.

When SQL statements are embedded in an application program, the entire program must first be processed by the DB2 precompiler. The precompiler finds all SQL statements (indicated in COBOL by the keywords EXEC SQL . . . END-EXEC) and translates them into equivalent host-language instructions. It builds database request modules, stores them on disk, and inserts call statements into the program to access them. Thus the application programmer needs to know little about the inner workings of the database management system, as the precompiler effectively shields the programmer from it.

In order to process a multiple-row query, the application programmer needs to define a cursor, a pointer that acts on a SELECT statement. Although the SELECT statement does not actually generate a file, you can imagine that a cursor defines a pseudofile in which DB2 will store the rows it retrieves. Then the set of retrieved rows can be processed one at a time, as if in a sequential file.

DB2 handles any problems of concurrent processing by using locks on portions of a database. Shared locks allow multiple concurrent access to the same data. But if any application needs to modify data, DB2 acquires an exclusive lock. No other application can access data that has an exclusive lock on it. When the lock is released, all applications have access to the updated data. The exclusive lock ensures the integrity of the data.

DB2 can lock either table spaces (which might include several tables) or pages (which contain tables or parts of tables). Locking pages causes less interference with other concurrent users but costs more to administer. Trade-offs like these are common in information processing.

DB2 logs all database changes before they are committed, or written, to the database. Database modifications that are not yet committed can be eliminated by issuing the ROLLBACK command. This might be necessary if a processing error is detected or a system failure occurs. The system log enables DB2 to recover data in the event of a system crash, by applying all before-images of the database since the latest checkpoint and then all after-images of the committed transactions (that had been logged). Any transactions in progress at the time of the crash must be restarted.

GROUP I QUESTIONS

13.1. Why did KDK Appliances decide to download only its sales data from its operational mainframe computer?

13.2 Why does the INVOICE in the downloaded data contain fewer fields than does the actual invoice used for operational processing?

13.3 What is the purpose of the PRODUCT-AD relation?

13.4 Describe two modes of DB2 access.

13.5 Define *table, view,* and *base table,* and describe their relationships with one another.

13.6 How can a view be used to make the database more secure?

13.7 Which database constructs are referenced by users and application programmers?

13.8 Describe the relationship among data base, storage group, table space, page, index space, table, and index.

13.9 Write the DB2 SQL statement that creates a table, an index, and a view. Assume that the table contains CustomerName, Address, and AccountNumber. Build an index on AccountNumber, assuming that the view presents unique customer names.

13.10 Show the DB2 statement to add a CustomerAge column to your answer to Question 13.9.

13.11 Write the DB2 statement(s) that would add these records to the customer table in your answer to Question 13.10:

Mike Thompson, Madison, 456, 45

Paula Hand, New Haven, 722, 20

Karen Munroe, Gales Ferry, 076, 27

13.12 Show the DB2 statement that drops the table, index, and view defined in Question 13.9.

13.13 Explain the role of the DB2 precompiler.

13.14 How does the precompiler know which instructions are SQL instructions and which belong to the host language?

13.15 Explain the role of the cursor in DB2 processing.

13.16 Explain the difference between a shared lock and an exclusive lock.

13.17 Why is an exclusive lock required when the data is going to be modified?

13.18 What two lock sizes are supported by DB2? What is the advantage of each over the other?

13.19 What is the purpose of the COMMIT statement? Of the ROLLBACK statement?

13.20 How does DB2 handle deadlock?

13.21 Explain how DB2 can recover from a system crash and from damage to the database.

13.22 Explain the role of the GRANT statement. How can GRANT authority be given to another user?

13.23 Explain the role of the REVOKE statement. What is the cascade effect of REVOKE?

GROUP II QUESTIONS

13.24 Locate a company that is using DB2. Determine how long it has had the system, why it chose DB2, and how well DB2 has worked out. Does the company use DB2 interactively, is it used in application programs, or both? Do users develop any on-line inquiries using DB2? If possible, obtain a copy of an application program, and explain the meaning of each embedded SQL statement. How does DB2 identify the application program as an authorized user? How often does the company back up its database? Does it copy the entire database, or does it back up only those pages changed since the previous backup? Has this company ever had to recover the database? What problems, if any, did it experience? Has performance ever been a problem? If so, what did the company do to improve it? Explain whether you believe that DB2 has been an effective DBMS for that company.

13.25 Locate a company that uses a mainframe relational DBMS other than DB2, and answer Question 13.24 for this DBMS.

CLIENT-SERVER DATABASE SYSTEMS AND ODBC

• • • • • • • • • • • • • • •

This chapter addresses client-server database processing. We begin with a description of the client-server architecture and describe the components of a client-server system and the functions of each. Then, using an example, we discuss reliability and present two strategies for concurrency control that are commonly used in client-server applications. We also address client-server security. Next we introduce ODBC, or the open database connectivity standard, and discuss its role in client-server database applications. We also describe ODBC conformance levels and illustrate use of ODBC with an example.

CLIENT-SERVER ARCHITECTURE

A **client-server** system is a network of computers in which some of the computers (called **clients**) process applications while other computers (the **servers**) provide services to the clients. A **client-server database** system is a client-server system in which at least one server stores and processes a database. While client-server database systems may consist of more than one database server, in this text we assume that if there are multiple servers, they process independent databases. Thus, all of a particular database is contained on a single server. If a database were spread over two or more servers, the systems would be a distributed database system, and such systems are beyond the scope of this chapter.

To understand client-server processing in more depth, consider Figure 14-1, which summarizes the programs involved in database processing. Application programs process the user interface, invoke application logic, and enforce some business rules. Application programs call the DBMS for database services; for relational databases, such service requests are generally expressed in some form of SQL. The DBMS processes the SQL (or other) statements and may enforce business rules as it does so. It returns data and error messages to the application program. In addition, the DBMS provides reliability and security functions as described in Chapter 12. Finally, the DBMS issues file input/output requests to the operating system.

All of these functions are required in any database system, regardless of its type. In the case of a personal database, all of the functions are performed on a single personal computer. In the case of teleprocessing, all of the functions are performed on a single computer, which is usually a mainframe that is connected to

FIGURE 14-1 *Programs Involved in Database Processing*

dumb terminals. In the case of file sharing, the application program and DBMS reside on the users' computers, and file management is performed by the computer that stores the shared files.

■ FUNCTIONS OF THE CLIENT AND SERVER COMPUTERS

With client-server database systems, the application program is placed on the client computers and the DBMS and operating systems (OS) file management programs are placed on the server computer as shown in Figure 14-2. Observe that a piece of the DBMS, called the **DBMS driver,** is placed on the client. The function of the DBMS driver is to receive processing requests from the application and format them for delivery to the DBMS. It also receives responses from the DBMS and formats them for the application. A layer of communications software is placed on both the client and the server. The role of this software is to interact with the communications hardware to send and receive messages between the DBMS driver and the DBMS.

Figure 14-3 summarizes the roles of the client and the server. The client computer manages the user interface, accepting data from the user, processing application logic, enforcing business rules, and generating requests for database services. The clients then transmit those requests to the server and receive results, which are then formatted for the user.

FIGURE 14-2 *Programs for Client-Server Database Applications*

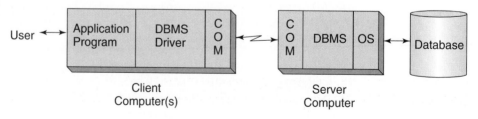

COM = Network Communications Software
OS = Operating System
Programs for Client-Server Database Applications

FIGURE 14-3   *Roles of the Client and Server Computers*

Client Roles	Server Roles
Manage the user interface.	Accept database request from clients.
	Process database requests.
Process application logic.	Format results and transmit to client.
Enforce business rules.	Enforce business rules.
Generate database requests. (SQL)	Perform integrity checking.
Transmit database requests to server.	Maintain database overhead data.
Receive results from server.	Provide concurrent access control.
Format results.	Provide recovery and security services.

The server accepts the clients' requests, processes them, and returns a response. While doing this, the server enforces business rules, performs database integrity checking, maintains the database overhead data, and provides concurrent access control. The server also performs recovery and security services.

■ ADVANTAGES AND DISADVANTAGES

A client-server system places the application processing closer to the user. This placement results in better performance, because several CPUs are processing applications in parallel. In addition, communications costs are reduced. Only the requests for DBMS processing and the responses to those requests need to be sent over the communications network, which means less communications traffic than in file-sharing systems.

Because multiple computers process applications and because those computers utilize the server for database processing, CPU power is available to make the users' interface much more elaborate. Sophisticated menus and forms are possible, with different colors, type fonts, and type sizes. Indeed, graphical user interfaces are becoming common for client-server applications.

One disadvantage of client-server systems concerns control. The client computers operate simultaneously and hence process applications in parallel. This introduces the possibility of the lost update and other multi-user control problems. Such problems are worse than in teleprocessing systems because the computers process in parallel. Multiple operating systems that direct multiple CPUs must coordinate their processing over communications media, and this differs from teleprocessing, in which all activity is governed by a single, local operating system.

CLIENT-SERVER DATABASE EXAMPLE

In order to understand client-server database processing, consider the example of the Customer Support Department at Legacy Systems, a microcomputer software publisher. Legacy has more than thirty products and an installed base of more than

100,000 customers. In addition to its software products, Legacy sells extended customer support. The customer support department uses a client-server system to keep track of customers and their queries.

The customer support department operates as follows: When customers call for service, the customer support personnel first ask for the customer's contract number, which consists of two parts, the customer number and the license number for a particular product. These numbers are then verified against Legacy's records before service is provided.

Customer support personnel create a record of each call so that when the customer calls again, the Legacy personnel have a record of what has transpired (the customer may be assigned a different support representative each time he or she calls). In addition, while assisting a customer, the support representatives often generate action items for departments within Legacy. For example, the representatives sometimes direct sales personnel to ship a replacement copy of a software product to a customer.

Legacy has installed a local area network of twenty-one microcomputers in the customer support department. One micro is the database server, and the other twenty process client application programs. The two types of application programs are the Customer Support application and the Customer Processing application. The Customer Support application is used by customer support representatives while they are serving customers, and the Customer Processing application is used to record new licenses, to produce mailing labels for newsletters and license renewal requests, and to update customer and other data. Each of the twenty application micros can process either application.

■ DATABASE CREATION

The creation of a client-server database follows the process you learned previously. The requirements are documented and a database design is developed using the entity-relationship or the semantic object model or some other modeling technique. The data model is then transformed into a database design. Almost all client-server DBMS products use the relational model, so the design is almost always a relational design.

LEGACY SYSTEMS DATABASE STRUCTURE   Figure 14-4(a) shows the five objects that need to be processed to support the Legacy Systems Customer Support Department applications. The CUSTOMER object contains multiple occurrences of the CALL and LICENSE objects; CALL contains CUSTOMER and multiple occurrences of the object ACTION-ITEM; ACTION-ITEM contains CALL and DEPARTMENT as well as data about the action to be taken; and DEPARTMENT contains data about Legacy's departments as well as multiple occurrences of ACTION-ITEM. ACTION-ITEM is an association object establishing the relationship between CALL and DEPARTMENT.

The structure of the database supporting these objects is shown in Figure 14-4(b). Legacy defines a customer as any entity having a license for one of its products, so a customer may be a person, a corporation, or some other organization. Hence, as shown in Figure 14-4(a), each CUSTOMER object may have many LICENSEs and many CALLs.

The creation of a client-server database is more like the creation of a mainframe database than that of a personal database. Because client-server databases are usually much larger than personal databases, the developer needs to pay more attention to factors that influence performance, such as the allocation of tables to physical devices and the structure and placement of indexes and related overhead. Also, since the server database will likely be a key component of the operation of one or more departments, the developers needs to pay more attention to the creation of concurrency control, backup and recovery, and security measures.

FIGURE 14-4   *Database Structure for Legacy Systems's Application: (a) Objects Processed by Legacy Systems's Customer Support and (b) Relational Structure Supporting These Objects*

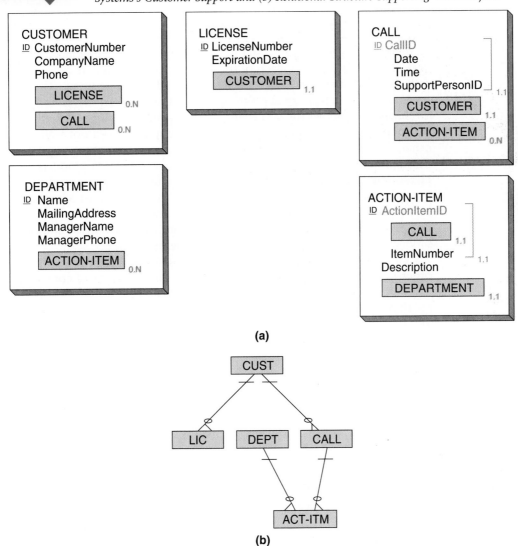

Server DBMS products give the developer much more control than personal DBMS products, but this control comes at the price of complexity and greater difficulty of use. For example, database structures are created using files of SQL data definition language instead of the graphical means used for personal DBMS products like Access. Also, the tools for managing the database structure tend to be more difficult to use than those for personal DBMS products. In most cases, a training period of weeks or months is required to learn to use a server DBMS product well.

Since a server database is used by many people, database administration is important. In particular, configuration control over the database structure is vital. Changes to the database need to be carefully planned and managed so that all of the applications can migrate to the changed structure without problem. In practice, accommodating change to the database has been much more difficult than most people expected. In truth, the problem is just as complicated as that of changing the structure of an enterprise database, but there is generally a smaller and less sophisticated staff available to make such change. Or there may be a competent and well-trained staff but one that is required to manage many server databases.

For these reasons, many companies have been frustrated at the difficulty and the slow pace of changing client-server database structures.

■ CLIENT DATABASE ACCESS

As stated, with client-server systems, the multiple client computers operate in parallel. For Legacy Systems, each of the twenty client computers can process applications in parallel while the server processes database requests. Thus, a client-server system can have greater throughput than can a teleprocessing system.

Figure 14-5 shows the processing of four transactions on two client computers and one server. Note that while the client computers need not wait for one another, they may need to wait for the server, since all database requests must go through it. To reduce the potential wait, most server DBMS products are **multi-threaded,** which means that they interleave database requests on the server computer. To do this, the DBMS processes a request to a point at which some delay occurs (to read data from the disk to memory, for example). During the delay, it can process a database request from a different client. This strategy is similar to that described for concurrency in teleprocessing systems.

Of course, if two requests involve the same data, then one must wait for the other to finish, and the system must provide for some type of concurrency control. At Legacy Systems, because a CUSTOMER can be an organization, it is possible that two customer support representatives may be dealing with the same CUSTOMER object at the same time. Two people who work for the same company, for example, may call about two different licenses on two different products. Two strategies for handling multi-user conflict are presented later in this chapter.

STATIC VS. DYNAMIC SQL   Applications on the client computer access the database using either static or dynamic SQL.[1] With **static SQL,** SQL requests are hard-coded into the application. Figure 14-6(a) shows an example of an SQL statement embedded in a portion of the Legacy Customer Support application. The structure of this statement is fixed; it always involves a SELECT of the CUSTOMER table. (The statement can be used to obtain data about different customers, so it can be used to select varying data, but the structure of the SQL statement is fixed.)

With **dynamic SQL,** the structure of the SQL statement is not determined until run time, when it is computed by the application program. Figure 14-6(b) shows

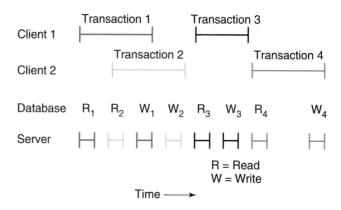

FIGURE 14-5   *Parallel Processing on Client-Server System*

---

[1]It is also possible to access a DBMS via what is termed a *native library.* Such a library is a collection of functions that provides services for defining and manipulating the database. The functions in the library serve the same role as SQL, but are unique to a particular DBMS, hence we do not consider them here.

a portion of a program that is used to process a query. The program examines which form fields have values and uses them to construct a WHERE clause, dynamically at run time. (Incidentally, this program is required because most server DBMS products do not provide QueryByForm, as personal DBMS products do.)

In general, the performance of static SQL statements is better than that for dynamic. Since static SQL statements are embedded in the application code, they can

FIGURE 14-6   *Static Versus Dynamic SQL*

Code in a declaration module:

```
EXECUTE SQL
      DEFINE CURSOR1 AS
      SELECT          CustomerNumber, Phone
      FROM            CUSTOMER
      WHERE           CustomerName = 0$      'set up where clause to receive a parameter
END EXECUTE
```

Code in processing module that uses the declaration:

```
Input Cname                              'get the value of Cname

Set CURSOR1.First USING Cname            'set the cursor to process the SQL statement

WHILE CURSOR1 < > 0                      'while there is a customer with this CName

      {do something with CustomerNumber, Phone}

      Set CURSOR1.Next USING Cname       'find next customer with this name

END WHILE
```

(a) Static SQL

```
Dim SQLString as string, AndWord as String
Dim Q as Query
'set initial values of string variables
AndWord = ""
SQLString = "SELECT CustomerNumber, CompanyName, Phone FROM CUSTOMER WHERE"

'if the CNumber textbox has a value, add it to the SQL string

If CNumber.Text < > "" then
      SQLString = SQLString + "CustomerNumber = " + CNumber.Text
      AndWord = " AND "
End If

'if the Cname textbox has a value, add it to the SQL String
If CName.Text <> "" then
      SQLString = SQLString + AndWord + "CompanyName = "+ CName.Text
      AndWord = " AND "
End If

'if the Phone textbox has a value
If Phone.Text < > "" then
      SQLString = SQLString + AndWord + "Phone = " + Phone. Text
End if

'open cursor on the computed SQL string

Set Q = QueryDef(SQLString)
```

(b) Dynamic SQL

be processed at compile time. The compiler can optimize the performance of the statement in light of indexes and database structure. In theory, such optimization could also be done for dynamic SQL at run time, but the time consumed in performing the optimization would likely more than offset the time saved by improving the performance of the statement.

■ ENFORCING BUSINESS RULES

Figure 14-3 indicates that business rules are processed both by the client and the server computers. While both are possible, in general it is better to process such rules on the server. To understand why, consider Figure 14-7. In Part (a), application programs on the client enforce business rules, and in (b) the DBMS on the server enforces rules.

If you compare these two figures, you will see why server rule processing is preferable. First, if the clients enforce rules, the checking logic must be included in

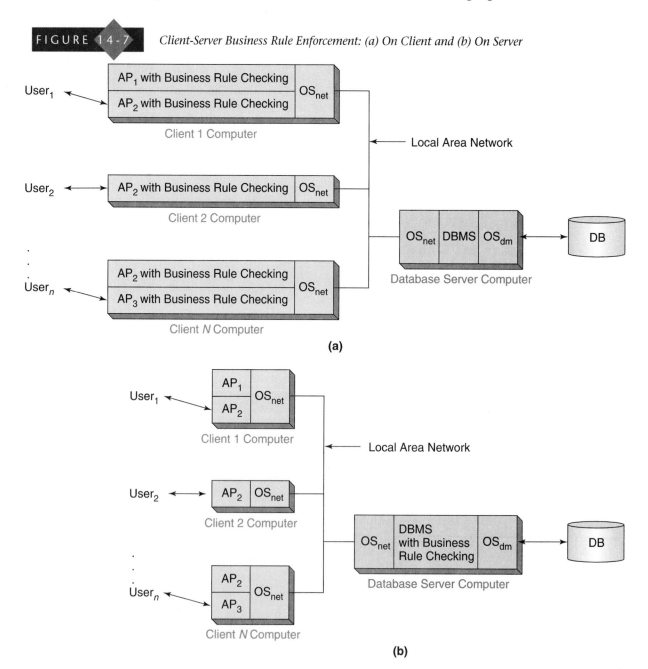

FIGURE 14-7 *Client-Server Business Rule Enforcement: (a) On Client and (b) On Server*

(a)

(b)

every application program. This means that code to enforce rules must be duplicated or copied from one application to another. If duplicated, the application programmers may understand the constraints differently and may make errors when programming them.

In addition, not all data changes are made via application programs. Users can make changes using a query/update language, and data can be imported en masse. When this is done, the program code that enforces rules will not be invoked, and, unless some special arrangement has been made, the business rules will not be enforced on data from these sources.

On the other hand, if the server enforces business rules, the rules need only be defined, coded, verified, and validated once. Furthermore, data changes from all sources will be checked for conformance. It will not matter whether a change is submitted by an application program or a query/update process or is imported. Regardless of the source, the DBMS will ensure that the business rules are enforced.

In some cases, however, server rule enforcement is not possible because the DBMS product does not provide sufficient capability. In that case, some rules may need to be enforced by the programs application program. Also, in some situations, business rules vary among applications, and, if so, it may be better to let each application enforce rules independently. Finally, when rules change, it may not be possible to rewrite every application to adapt to the new rules at once. It may be necessary to phase in the new rules across the applications; in this case, the rules may need to be enforced by the applications on the clients.

To summarize, when possible, it is better to enforce business rules on the server. If it is not possible, then they must be enforced by applications on the client.

■ TRIGGERS

A **trigger** is a database procedure that is automatically invoked by the DBMS when some event occurs. For example, in an inventory application, a trigger can be written to generate an order whenever the quantity of an item on hand falls below a certain threshold value.

Triggers are often used to enforce business rules. For example, at Legacy Systems, if a support representative is not allowed to provide support unless a valid LicenseNumber has been entered, then a trigger could be written on the event to create a new CALL row. When the support representative attempts to store a CALL record, the trigger would be invoked and would disallow it—and might even annotate the CUSTOMER record to indicate that an invalid service was performed.

To implement a trigger, the developer writes the trigger code and specifies the event under which the trigger is to be invoked. Later, when those conditions are realized, the DBMS calls the trigger. In a client-server system, the triggers reside on and are invoked by the server.

While they are very useful, triggers can also be a problem. In the presence of triggers, a user can cause activity on the database that he or she does not expect or even know about. A telemarketing person in order entry, for example, might want to reserve stock for a hot prospect. If he is not aware of the existence of the trigger, he may generate a dummy order to hold the stock. Later, if the prospect decides not to buy the stock, the user may return the stock to inventory. Meanwhile, unbeknownst to him, the trigger has generated orders for more of the product, orders that are unnecessary and that the user would not have generated had he been aware of them.

In a multi-user environment, trigger procedures sometimes need to invoke locks. The transaction that causes the event that invokes the trigger may have already obtained locks that conflict with the trigger. In this situation, a transaction can unknowingly come into deadlock with itself.

Finally, triggers can cascade and even form a closed loop. They cascade when one trigger creates a condition that causes another trigger to be invoked that creates a condition that causes a third trigger to be invoked, and so on. Triggers form loops when they cascade back to themselves. If this occurs, the DBMS must have some means of preventing an infinite loop.

As an aside, both DBMS-enforced constraint checking and triggers can be carried out by DBMS products in teleprocessing systems. There is no special characteristic of client-server systems that requires that only they have centralized constraint checking and triggers. In practice, however, these capabilities are more common on client-server DBMS products.

RELIABILITY AND SECURITY IN CLIENT-SERVER SYSTEMS

Client-server database systems are multi-user systems that are commonly used to support the operational activity of one or more departments. As such, reliability and security are important. We discussed these topics in Chapter 12; here we discuss how ideas in that chapter pertain particularly to client-server systems.

■ CONCURRENCY CONTROL

To illustrate concurrent processing control for client-server applications, consider the transaction logic shown in Figure 14-8, a transaction processed by customer support representatives at Legacy Systems. The support representative gets the customer and license data from the customer and uses them to read the appropriate row in CUST. Then the representative answers the customer's questions, updates the CUST data, and stores a new row in CALL. Finally, if the call results in an action item for one of Legacy's departments, a new row in ACT-ITM is stored.

Since several representatives could process the same customer data, it is necessary to protect against lost update and inconsistent read problems. There are two ways in which this can be done.

CONTROL BY MEANS OF PESSIMISTIC LOCKING   The first strategy, sometimes called *pessimistic locking* (because the locks are placed in anticipation of a conflict), is the same as that used in traditional teleprocessing systems such as DB2 (see Chapter 13). To implement this strategy, the DBMS places implicit locks on each DBMS command executed after the START TRANSACTION. These locks are then held until either a COMMIT or a ROLLBACK command is issued.

For the logic in Figure 14-8, an implicit lock is placed on CUST data when it is read at the start of the transaction. The lock is held until either a COMMIT or a ROLLBACK is issued. If the CUST data is valid, the customer's questions will be answered, and a new CALL record will be stored. The CUST data is also updated.

FIGURE 14-8   *Logic of the CALL Transaction*

```
START TRANSACTION
READ CUST DATA
IF VALID
      THEN ANSWER CUSTOMER'S QUESTIONS
              UPDATE CUST DATA
              STORE CALL DATA
              IF NEED LEGACY ACTION
                    THEN WRITE ACT-ITM DATA
              END-IF
              COMMIT TRANSACTION
      ELSE ROLLBACK TRANSACTION
END-IF
```

Finally, if necessary, a new ACT-ITM row is created, and both the new CALL and the new ACT-ITM records are locked until the COMMIT command is issued.

Figure 14-9 shows the time required for processing two CALL transactions. In Part (a), the transactions process different CUST data, so there is no data conflict. Client 2 waits while the server processes Client 1's CUST data request, but after that, both clients process in parallel to the end of the transactions.

Figure 14-9(b) shows two transactions trying to process the same row in CUST. In this case, Client 2 waits for data until Client 1 has finished processing its CALL transaction. Such waiting may be a problem. If the customer talking to the support representative on Client 1 has many questions, the CUST data will be locked for a long time—several minutes or more. Also, if the user has many data to enter regarding the call or an action item, this, too, will extend Client 2's wait. Perhaps the user at Client 2 can process his or her CALL transaction much faster than the user at Client 1 can. If so, the user on Client 2 may be able to read the data, change them, and replace them while the user on Client 1 is talking to the customer.

These problems will become even worse if the DBMS does not support row-level locking. Some DBMS products, for example, lock a page (a block of rows) rather than a row, and some even lock the entire table. If locking is performed at such large levels of granularity, pessimistic locks can result in appreciable and unnecessary delays. The situation depicted in Figure 14-10 assumes page-level locking. Two transactions are processing two different CUST rows that happen to be on the same page. In this case, Client 2 must wait for Client 1 to finish, even though the two transactions are processing different rows. Again, the delay may be substantial, and, in this case, it is also unnecessary.

FIGURE 14-9   *Locking on a Client-Server System*

FIGURE 14-10   *Page-Level Processing of Nonconflicting Data Requests on the Same Page*

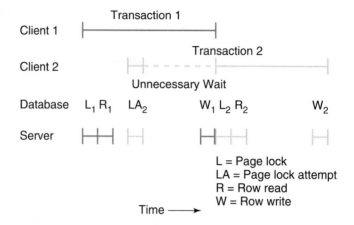

CONTROL BY MEANS OF OPTIMISTIC LOCKING   A second strategy, sometimes called *optimistic locking* (because no conflict is anticipated, but if there is one, one of the users must redo his or her work), is to defer the locking until the last possible moment and hope that there is no conflict. With this style, as much of the transaction is processed as possible before any locks are placed. Then the locks are obtained and held very briefly. To use this strategy, the DBMS must not apply any locks implicitly; instead, the application program must place the locks.

Figure 14-11 shows the CALL transaction logic using optimistic locking. The CUST data are read without any lock and without starting any transaction. A copy

FIGURE 14-11   *Logic of the CALL Transaction Using Delayed Locks*

```
READ CUST DATA
SAVE A COPY OF CUST DATA AS OLD-CUST
IF VALID
    THEN ANSWER CUSTOMER'S QUESTIONS
        CHANGE CUST DATA IN MEMORY
            -DO NOT WRITE TO DATABASE
        CREATE CALL DATA
            -DO NOT WRITE TO DATABASE
        IF NEED LEGACY ACTION
            THEN CREATE ACT-ITM DATA
                -DO NOT WRITE TO DATABASE
        END-IF
        START TRANSACTION
        LOCK CUST DATA
        READ CUST DATA
        IF CUST DATA = OLD-CUST
            THEN UPDATE CUST
                STORE CALL
                IF ACTION
                    THEN WRITE ACT-ITM
                END-IF
                COMMIT TRANSACTION
            ELSE ROLLBACK TRANSACTION
                INFORM USER DATA WAS CHANGED
                RESTART TRANSACTION
        END-IF
END-IF
```

FIGURE 14-12   *Delayed Lock Processing of Nonconflicting Data Requests on a Single Page*

of the data, as read, is stored as OLD-CUST. Then the customer is serviced and the CUST data are modified in memory. CALL data are created in memory, as are ACT-ITM data, if appropriate.

At this point all of the time-consuming aspects of the transaction have been completed, and the user has keyed in all of the data, so the transaction is started and a lock is obtained on the CUST data. The CUST data are reread. If the data just read are the same as OLD-CUST, then no other user has changed the data since the customer service call was started. In this case, the data are updated and stored; the locks are released; and the transaction is committed.

If CUST data do not equal OLD-CUST, then someone has changed CUST while the call was in process. In this case, the user is informed that the CUST data have been changed by another user, and the user again makes the changes in CUST. This latter action requires the user to repeat some work, but this should not be too much of a problem, since it should occur infrequently.

With delayed locks, the locks are held for very short periods of time, thus reducing the required waiting. Also, if two transactions are processing the same data in parallel, the one that finishes first will be the one whose changes are committed to the database. The faster transaction will not need to wait for the slower transaction to finish.

Finally, the delayed locking strategy is particularly useful if the DBMS locks at a level higher than the row. Two users processing different rows in the same page or table, for example, can process nearly in parallel. Since the locks are held for such a short period of time, the users minimize their interference. Figure 14-12 shows the two transactions in Figure 14-10. Unlike with implicit locking, there is almost no delay.

The problem with delayed locking is that transactions may need to be processed twice or even several times. Furthermore, the logic is more complicated, and so this scheme places a greater burden on the application programmer or client portion of the DBMS, or both.

■ RECOVERY

Recovery in client-server systems can be carried out in the same way that it is in teleprocessing. The server computer keeps a log of changes in the database, and the database is periodically backed up to tape or another medium. When failures occur, the server DBMS can perform both rollback and rollforward. These statements assume, however, a complete server DBMS. Unfortunately, not all products that are advertised as server DBMS products can support locking, constraint checking, backup, and recovery, as described here. As with any other product, the buyer should check for the features and functions he or she needs.

■ SECURITY

Features and functions for security in client-server systems vary according to the DBMS at the server and also according to the security system provided by the communications network that connects the clients to the server. In general, however, the security systems are some variant of subject oriented. The system administrator allocates names and passwords to users and assigns specific processing rights to tables and views for each name. When the users sign on to the system, they provide their name and password. Usually, users can change their password from the one assigned to them.

In some cases, several layers of security may be involved. The communications software might require a user name and password before granting access to the network, the operating system on the server might require another name and password before granting access to the database files, the DBMS might invoke a third name and password before granting access and permissions to tables and views, and the application might invoke yet a fourth name and password before granting access to specific records or fields.

As indicated in Chapter 12, security systems always involve a trade-off between ease of use and degree of protection. Such a four-level security system provides greater protection at the risk of frustrating the users who need to remember four names and passwords!

OPEN DATABASE CONNECTIVITY (ODBC) STANDARD

The **open database connectivity (ODBC)** standard is an interface by which application programs can access and process SQL databases in a DBMS-independent manner. This means, for example, that an application that uses the ODBC interface could process an ORACLE database, a SYBASE database, an INFORMIX database, and any other database that is ODBC compliant without any program coding changes. The goal is to allow a developer to create a single application that can access databases supported by different DBMS products without needing to be changed or even recompiled.

ODBC was developed by a committee of industry experts from the X/Open and SQL Access Group committees. A number of such standards were proposed, but ODBC emerged as the winner, primarily because it has been implemented by Microsoft and is an important part of Windows. Microsoft's initial interest in support of such a standard was to allow products like Microsoft Excel to access database data from a variety of DBMS products without having to be recompiled. Of course, Microsoft's interests have changed with the acquisition of FoxPro, the release of Access, and the continued success of SQL Server.

ODBC is important to client-server database systems because, in theory, it is possible to develop a client application that can process databases that are supported by different DBMS products. We say "in theory" because products vary in the way in which they comply with the standard. Fortunately, variance in conformance levels was anticipated by the ODBC committee, as you will learn.

■ ODBC ARCHITECTURE

Figure 14-13 shows the components of the ODBC standard. The application program, driver manager, and DBMS drivers all reside on the client computer. The drivers send requests to data sources, which reside on the server. According to the standard, a **data source** is the database, its associated DBMS, operating system,

FIGURE 14-13   *ODBC Architecture*

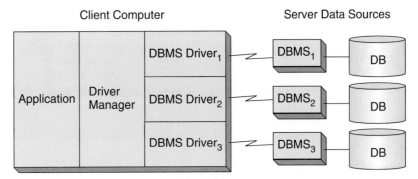

Application can process a database using any of the three DBMS products.

and network platform. An ODBC data source can be a relational database; it can also be a file server such as BTrieve, and it can even be a spreadsheet.

The application issues requests to create a connection with a data source, to issue SQL statements and receive results, to process errors, and to start, commit, and rollback transactions. ODBC provides a standard means for each of these requests, and it defines a standard set of error codes and messages.

The **driver manager** serves as an intermediary between the application and the DBMS drivers. When the application requests a connection, the driver determines the type of DBMS that processes a given ODBC data source and loads that driver in memory (if it is not already loaded). The driver manager also processes certain initialization requests and validates the format and order of ODBC requests that it receives from the application. The driver manager is provided by Microsoft and is included with Windows.

A **driver** processes ODBC requests and submits specific SQL statements to a given type of data source. There is a different driver for each data source type. For example, there are drivers for DB2, for ORACLE, for Access, and for all of the other products whose vendors have chosen to participate in the ODBC standard. Drivers are supplied by DBMS vendors and by independent software companies.

It is the responsibility of the driver to ensure that standard ODBC commands execute correctly. In some cases, if the data source is itself not SQL-compliant, the driver may need to perform considerable processing to fill in for a lack of capability at the data source. In other cases, where the data source supports full SQL, the driver need only pass the request through for processing by the data source. The driver also converts data source error codes and messages into the ODBC standard codes and messages.

ODBC identifies two types of drivers: single-tier and multiple-tier. A **single-tier** driver processes both ODBC calls and SQL statements. An example of a single-tier driver is shown in Figure 14-14. In this example, the data is stored in Xbase files (the format used by FoxPro, dBase, and others). Since Xbase file managers do not process SQL, it is the job of the driver to translate the SQL request into Xbase file manipulation commands and to transform the results back into SQL form. Single-tier drivers can be used to implement the file-sharing systems that were discussed in Chapter 12.

A **multiple-tier** driver processes ODBC calls but passes the SQL requests directly to the data source. While it may reformat an SQL request to conform to the dialect of a particular data source, it does not process the SQL. An example of the use of a multiple-tier driver is shown in Figure 14-15.

FIGURE 14-14   *ODBC Single-Tier Driver*

FIGURE 14-15   *ODBC Multiple-Tier Driver*

■ CONFORMANCE LEVELS

The creators of the ODBC standard faced a dilemma. If they chose to describe a standard for a minimal level of capability, many vendors would be able to comply. But if they did so, the standard would represent only a small portion of the complete power and expressiveness of ODBC and SQL. On the other hand, if the standard addressed a very high level of capability, then only a few vendors would be able to comply with the standard, and it would become unimportant. To deal with this dilemma, the committee wisely chose to define levels of conformance to the standard. There are two types: ODBC conformance and SQL conformance.

ODBC CONFORMANCE LEVEL   **ODBC conformance levels** concern the features and functions that are made available through the driver's application program interface (**API**). A driver API is a set of functions that the application can call to receive services. Figure 14-16 summarizes the three levels of ODBC conformance that are addressed in the standard. In practice, almost all drivers provide at least Level 1 API conformance, so the core API level is not too important.

An application can call a driver to determine which level of ODBC conformance it provides. If the application requires a level of conformance that is not present, it can terminate the session in an orderly fashion and generate appropriate messages to the user. Or the application can be written to use higher-level conformance features if they are available but to work around the missing functions if a higher level is not available.

For example, drivers at the Level 2 API must provide a scrollable cursor. Such a cursor is simply a marker of a position into a pseudofile that represents the results of a particular SQL SELECT statement. You saw examples of such cursors in the code that processed the DB2 database in Chapter 13. An application could be written to use cursors if they are available, but, if they are not, to work around the missing feature, selecting needed data using very restrictive WHERE clauses. Doing this would ensure that only a few rows were returned at a time to the application, and it would process those rows using a cursor that it maintained itself. Performance would likely be slower in the second case, but at least the application would be able to successfully execute.

FIGURE 14-16   *Summary of ODBC Conformance Levels*

Core API
- Connect to data sources
- Prepare and execute SQL statements
- Retrieve data from a result set
- Commit or rollback transactions
- Retrieve error information

Level 1 API
- Core API
- Connect to data sources with driver-specific information
- Send and receive partial results
- Retrieve catalog information
- Retrieve information about driver options, capabilities, and functions

Level 2 API
- Core and Level 1 API
- Browse possible connections and data sources
- Retrieve native form of SQL
- Retrieve catalog information
- Call a translation library
- Process a scrollable cursor

SQL CONFORMANCE LEVEL   SQL conformance levels specify which SQL statements, expressions, and data types a driver can process. Three levels are defined as summarized in Figure 14-17 on page 364. The capability of the minimum SQL grammar is very limited, and most drivers support at least the core SQL grammar.

As with ODBC conformance levels, an application can call the driver to determine what level of SQL conformance it supports. With that information, the application can then determine which SQL statements can be issued. If necessary, the application can then terminate the session or use alternative, less powerful means of obtaining the data.

EXAMPLE APPLICATION OF ODBC IN CLIENT-SERVER SYSTEMS

As stated, the goal of ODBC is to provide DBMS-independent access to data sources without requiring the application program to be changed or recompiled. To show how this goal can be realized in practice, consider Figure 14-18, which shows the important statements used in Microsoft Visual Basic to access an ODBC data source.[2]

---

[2]These statements show the syntax required for remote data objects in Visual Basic, Version 4.0, Enterprise Edition. The particular statements required and their syntax will likely change over time. Consider these statements only to be coding samples. If you want to write your own VB code to access an ODBC data source, see the Visual Basic product help documentation.

FIGURE 14-17   *Summary of SQL Conformance Levels*

Minimum SQL Grammar
- CREATE TABLE, DROP TABLE
- simple SELECT (does not include subqueries)
- INSERT, UPDATE, DELETE
- Simple expressions (A > B + C)
- CHAR, VARCHAR, LONGVARCHAR data types

Core SQL Grammar
- Minimum SQL Grammar
- ALTER TABLE, CREATE INDEX, DROP INDEX
- CREATE VIEW, DROP VIEW
- GRANT, REVOKE
- Full SELECT (includes subqueries)
- Aggregate functions such as SUM, COUNT, MAX, MIN, AVG
- DECIMAL, NUMERIC, SMALLINT, INTEGER, REAL, FLOAT, DOUBLE PRECISION data types

Extended SQL Grammar
- Core SQL Grammar
- Outer joins
- UPDATE and DELETE using cursor positions
- Scalar functions such as SUBSTRING, ABS
- Literals for date, time, and timestamp
- Batch SQL statements
- Procedure Calls

The purpose of the program segment is to read all of the customer data in the Legacy Systems CUST table (see Figure 14-4) and to replace the first three digits of any phone number beginning with "722" with the characters "360". This particular problem is arbitrary; we choose it only to illustrate ODBC application processing.

Visual Basic (VB) provides a set of object collections for processing ODBC databases. The collections are referred to as **remote data objects** or **rdo**. In Figure 14-18(a), three object variables are defined: CustEnv, CustConnection, and CustResultSet. The first is used to establish an ODBC environment (the communications connection), the second is used to establish a connection (the database connection), and the third is used to process a relation (which might be a table, a view, or the result of an SQL statement).

CustEnv is set using a call to the VB method rdoCreateEnvironment. The parameters that need to be passed to the method are summarized in Figure 14-18(b). Next, CustConnection is set using a call to the VB method OpenConnection. Observe that this method applied on the CustEnv object that was previously obtained. The third set statement causes a result set to be created under the object name CustResultSet. This object name is basically the name of a cursor over the result set. Note, too, in Figure 14-18(b) that the source parameter can name a table or view or can itself be an SQL statement that is to be executed dynamically.

Once the result set is established, the methods MoveFirst, MoveNext, and EOF can be invoked. This is done in the while loop in Figure 14-18(b). The logic here is

FIGURE 14-18 *Example of Visual BASIC Statements to Process an ODBC Database: (a) Code Example and (b) Parameters Used in Code Example*

```
Dim CustEnv as object, CustConnection as object, CustResultSet as object
Dim NewPhone as string

'First establish communications context
Set CustEnv = rdoCreateEnvironment (name, user, password)

'Now connect to database
Set CustConnection = CustEnv.OpenConnection(dsName, prompt, readonly, connect)

'Open table, view or SQL statement
'Example assumes source points to the Customer table or a view of it
Set CustResultSet = CustConnection.OpenResultset(source, type, locktype, options)

'Process rows of results
CustResultSet.MoveFirst

While CustResultSet.EOF = false

        If Left$(CustResultSet!Phone, 3) = "722" then
                CustResultSet.Edit
                NewPhone = Right$(CustResultsSet!Phone, 5)
                NewPhone = "360" + NewPhone
                CustResultsSet.Phone = NewPhone
                CustResultsSet.Update
        End If

        CustResultsSet.MoveNext
Wend

'Close objects
CustResultsSet.Close
CustConnection.Close
Cust.Env.Close
```

(a)

Statement	Parameter	Use
rdoCreateEnvironment	name	a name to be assigned to the environment
	user	a valid user name at the data source
	password	a valid password at the data source
OpenConnection	dsName	a registered ODBC data source name
	prompt	the style in which the user is to be prompted for connection information—this data may supplement or override the user and password provided in the rdoCreateEnvironment statement
	readonly	Boolean value indicating whether the data is to be readonly or updatable
	connect	optional, driver-dependent connection data
OpenResultset	source	the name of a table in the database or an SQL string that is valid for the database
	type	the type of cursor to create—forward only, dynamic, or other
	locktype	type of locking (pessimistic, optimistic, read-only)
	options	specify characteristics of rdoResultSet

(b)

typical sequential file processing; move to the first record, process it, read the next, and continue processing until the end of the file. At that point, the code closes the three object variables.

Do not be very concerned about the particular statements presented in Figure 14-18 or of their syntax. Your goal here should be to understand the nature of an application's interface to ODBC. Again, the benefit of this interface is that this application can be used to process any valid ODBC data source, regardless of the type of DBMS that is processing the database.

SUMMARY

A client-server system consists of a network of computers in which the client computers process applications while the server computers provide services to the clients. A client-server database systems is a client-server system in which at least one server stores and processes a database. A client-server system can have multiple servers. If it does, each server will process a different database. Those systems in which two or more servers process the same database are called distributed database systems.

Client computers run applications that manage the user interface, invoke application logic, enforce some business rules, and generate requests for database services, usually in the form of SQL. The DBMS on the server computer processes the SQL requests, enforces business rules, and generates error messages when required. The DBMS also provides reliability and security services.

Client-server systems place the application closer to the user, resulting in better performance and more sophisticated interfaces for the users. One disadvantage of client-server systems is control; because of parallel processing, conflicts caused by concurrency are more difficult to manage.

Server DBMS products are closer to mainframe DBMS products than they are to personal DBMS products. Server products allow the developer more control over file allocation and overhead data than do personal products, and they also provide more features for reliablity and security. The downside is that server DBMS products are more complicated and harder to use and require a longer training period. With client-server databases, database administration is important. Configuration control over the structure of the database is critical.

Client-server systems are often used for multi-user transaction-processing applications. Such systems can provide high performance because of the parallel processing among client and server computers. In addition, most server DBMS products are multithreaded, which means database requests are interleaved.

Applications can access a server DBMS using either static or dynamic SQL. The structure of static SQL is fixed at compile time, so such statements can be optimized for performance. Dynamic SQL structure is determined at run time; it is therefore more flexible, but it cannot be optimized.

Business rules can and usually are enforced at both the client and server computers. It is better to enforce business rules at the server because the code need not be duplicated and because the rules can be enforced against all data, regardless of their source. A trigger is a database procedure that is invoked when some event occurs; triggers are often used to enforce business rules.

Concurrency control is important in client-server systems; usually such control is provided using one of two styles of locking. Pessimistic locking requires implicit locks similar to the locks employed with traditional database applications. The data must be locked before they can be read for updating. With optimistic locking, the second style, as much of the transaction as possible is processed before obtaining a lock. Then the locks are obtained and the data are reread. If there has been no change, the transaction is committed to the database as processed. If there has been a change, the transaction is reprocessed as necessary. Optimistic locking is especially useful when locking is done at a level of granularity larger than a row at a time and when the transactions are likely to be lengthy because of slow human processing. Recovery in client-server systems is similar to recovery in teleprocessing database systems.

Recovery mechanisms for client-server systems are similar to those used for mainframe processing. Both rollback and rollforward strategies are used. Security in client-server systems is usually subject oriented; users have names and passwords. Several levels of security may be involved: network, server operating system, DBMS, and application.

ODBC, or the open database connectivity standard, provides an interface by which application programs can access and process SQK databases in a DBMS-independent manner. ODBC was developed by a group of industry experts and has been implemented by Microsoft. ODBC involves application program, driver manager, DBMS driver, and data source components. ODBC defines single-tier and multiple-tier drivers. Single-tier drivers process both ODBC and SQL statements. Multiple-tier drivers process only ODBC statements. SQL statements are passed through to the DBMS.

The creators of ODBC wisely allowed for various levels of conformance. In particular, there are three levels of API conformance and three levels of SQL grammar conformance. ODBC can be processed by many different application languages; a sketch of the commands and syntax for Visual Basic is shown in Figure 14-18.

GROUP I QUESTIONS

14.1   Define a client-server system and a client-server database system.

14.2   Is a system in which the database is partitioned on two different servers a client-server database system? Why or why not?

14.3   Sketch the architecture of a client-server system. Name and identify the computer(s) and programs involved, and explain which computer processes which programs.

14.4   List and describe the functions of an application in a client-server database system.

14.5   List and describe the functions of the DBMS in a client-server database system.

14.6   What is the function of the DBMS driver?

14.7   Summarize the advantages and disadvantages of a client-server database system.

14.8   How does a server DBMS differ from a personal computer DBMS?

14.9   Explain why configuration control is important for a client-server database system.

14.10 What does the term *multithreaded* mean? Why is it important?

14.11 Explain the difference between static and dynamic SQL. Which is better?

14.12 In general, where should business rules be enforced? Describe exceptions to your answer.

14.13 What is a trigger, and what is its purpose? What problems can occur when using triggers?

14.14 Describe how to control concurrency in a client-server system using pessimistic locking. First define the logic of a transaction, and then show how that logic would apply to a client-server system that has three clients and a single database server.

14.15 Describe how to control concurrency in a client-server system using optimistic locking. Use the same transaction logic and system as in your answer to Question 14.14.

14.16 How does recovery in a client-server system differ from that in a teleprocessing system?

14.17 Describe the general character of security in client-server database systems. Explain how there might be several levels of security.

14.18 What is ODBC?

14.19 Who developed ODBC, and who implemented it?

14.20 Why has ODBC been more successful than other, similar standards?

14.21 Name the components of the ODBC standard.

14.22 What role does the driver manager serve? Who supplies it?

14.23 What roles does the DBMS driver serve? Who supplies it?

14.24 What is a single-tier driver?

14.25 What is a multiple-tier driver?

14.26 Why are conformance levels important?

14.27 Summarize the three ODBC API conformance levels.

14.28 Summarize the three SQL grammar conformance levels.

GROUP II QUESTIONS

Questions 14.29 through 14.31 concern the following example: Consider a database having the following five tables:

SP (SPNumber, SPName, Region, TotalSalesMade)
CUST (CustNumber, CustName, CustPhone, Balance)
ORDER (OrderNumber, OrderDate, *SPNumber, CustNumber,* Amount)
LINE-ITEM (OrderNumber, LineItemNumber, *ItemNumber,* Qty, ExtendedPrice)
INVENTORY (ItemNumber, Description, UnitPrice, QuantityOnHand)

Assume that the following transactions exist:

T_1 Add/change/delete a row in CUST
T_2 Add/change/delete a row in INVENTORY
T_3 Add a new order by creating a new row in ORDER, new rows in LINE-ITEM, decrementing QuantityOnHand in INVENTORY, adding Amount of ORDER to Balance in CUST, and adding Amount of ORDER to TotalSalesMade in SP. Ensure that sufficient stock is in inventory for each item ordered. Do not allow any backorders.

Further assume that the organization has three users in the order-processing department. Each of these three users is authorized to process transactions of type T_1. Only one of them is authorized to process transactions of type T_2, and the other two users are authorized to process transactions of type T_3.

14.29 Sketch the architecture of a teleprocessing system to process these three transactions against this database. Describe the programs that would be required. Develop pseudocode or a flowchart of the logic to process transaction T_3. Also give an example of a concurrent-processing problem that could occur in this system, and explain how to prevent it.

14.30 Sketch the architecture of a client-server system to process these three transactions against this database. Explain the programs that would be required, and show where they would reside. Develop pseudocode or a flow-chart of the logic to process transaction T_3. Explain what data would need to be transmitted across the LAN to process this transaction. Also give an example of a concurrent-processing problem that could occur in this system, and explain how it could be prevented using the delayed-locking strategy. Discuss the advantages and disadvantages of this system compared with the teleprocessing system described in your answer to Question 14.29.

14.31 Sketch the architecture of a file-sharing system to process these three transactions against this database. Explain the programs that would be required, and show where they would reside. Develop pseudocode or a flow-chart of the logic to process transaction T_3. Explain what data would need to be transmitted across the LAN to process transactions of this type. Also give an example of a concurrent-processing problem that could occur in this system, and explain how that problem could be prevented using locks. What level of granularity of lock would be required? Discuss the advantages and disadvantages of this system compared with the client-server solution in Question 14.30.

15

SHARING
ENTERPRISE DATA

• • • • • • • • • • • • • • • • •

Data is an important organizational asset, an asset that can be used not only to facilitate the operations of a company but also for management, planning, forecasting, strategic analysis, and the like. Unfortunately, while many organizations have found that their databases effectively support organizational operations, they know that their databases are ineffectively used for analysis, planning, and other management purposes. In this chapter we address three topics that are important in increasing the return of the investment on enterprise data in databases: data administration, downloading of centralized data, and data warehousing.

DATA ADMINISTRATION

An organization's data are as much a resource as are its plant, equipment, and financial assets. Data are time-consuming and expensive to acquire, and they have utility beyond operations. Information derived from data can be used to assess the effectiveness of personnel, products, marketing programs and to determine trends in customers' preferences, buying behavior, and so forth. It can be used to simulate the effect of changes in products, sales strategies, and territories. The list of potential applications is so long that, in fact, data often serve to establish and maintain the organization's competitive advantage. Unfortunately, however, as long as the data are locked in operational databases, their utility is limited.

Because of the potential value of the organizational data resource, many organizations have established offices of data administration. The purpose of these offices is not just to guard and protect the data but also to ensure that they are used effectively.

In some ways, data administration is to data what the controller is to money. The responsibility of a controller is to ensure not only that financial assets are protected and accounted for but also that they are effectively used. Storing an organization's money in a vault can protect it, but it will not be effectively used. Instead, it must be invested in ways that advance the organization's goals and objectives. Similarly, with data administration, simply protecting the data is not enough. Data administration must also try to increase the utility of the organization's data.

■ NEED FOR DATA ADMINISTRATION

To understand the need for data administration, consider the analogy of a university library. The typical university library contains hundreds of thousands of books, journals, magazines, government reports, and so forth, but they offer no utility while they are on the bookshelves. To be useful, they must be made available to people who have an interest in and need for them.

Clearly, the library must have some means of describing its collection so that potential users can determine what is available. At first glance, this might seem like a trivial problem. You might say, "Well, build a card catalog." But much work must be done to be able to do that. How should the library's works be identified? How should they be described? Even more basic, what constitutes a work? How can we accommodate different ways of identifying works (ISBN, Dewey decimal system, government report number)? How do we help people find things that they may not know exist?

Other complications arise. Suppose the university is so large that it has several libraries. In this case, how are the collections to be managed as one resource? Furthermore, some departments may maintain their own libraries. Are these to be made part of the university system? Many professors have extensive personal libraries. Should these be part of the system?

■ CHALLENGES OF DATA ADMINISTRATION

The library analogy does not go far enough, however, as organizational data administration is considerably more difficult than library administration. First, it is not at all clear what constitutes a "work." Libraries contain books, periodicals, and so forth, but organizational data come in myriads of formats. Organizations have traditional data records, but they also have documents, spreadsheets, graphics and illustrations, technical drawings, and audio and video files. How should all of these be described? What are the basic categories of organizational data? These questions are important because their answers determine how the data will be organized, cataloged, managed, protected, and accessed.

Most organizations have many names for the same thing. For instance, a telephone number can be described as a PhoneNumber, Phone, TelephoneNumber, EmployeePhone, or DeptPhone. Which of these names is preferable? When a graphic designer places a telephone number on a new form, what label should he or she use? When a programmer writes a new program, what name should he or she use for the program variable that holds the telephone number? When a user wants to query for a customer area code while developing a buying trend analysis, which name should she use in her query?

There also are many ways of representing the data element. A phone number can be represented as a ten-digit integer, a ten-digit text field, a thirteen-digit text field in the form *(nnn)nnn-nnnn,* a twelve-digit text field in the form *nnn-nnn-nnnn,* or in still other formats. Which of these should be allowed? Which, if any, should be the standard?

Such differences between organizational data and library materials are minuscule, however, when compared with the next difference: People must be able to change organizational data.

Consider what would happen at the library if people checked out books, wrote in them, tore out pages, added pages, and then put the books back on the shelves. Or, even worse, suppose someone checked out three books, made changes in all three, checked them back in, and told the librarian: "Either change all of these or none of them."

Since data are a shared asset, limits must be placed on processing rights and responsibilities. For example, when an employee leaves the company, his or her records cannot be immediately deleted; they need to be maintained for several

FIGURE 15-1   *Challenges of Data Administration*

> • Many types of data exist.
> • Basic categories of data are not obvious.
> • The same data can have many names.
> • The same data can have many descriptions and formats.
> • Data are changed — often concurrently.
> • Political – organizational issues complicate operational issues.

years for management reporting and tax purposes. Hence, one department cannot delete data from the database just because that department is finished with them. The office of data administration needs to help define users' processing rights and responsibilities. This role is similar to that described for database administration in Chapter 12; there, however, the scope was a particular database. Here, the scope is the entire organization.

In addition to all of these operationally oriented challenges, there are organizational issues. For example, data and processing rights can mean organizational power; hence, changes in data control can mean changes in power. Thus, behind the tasks of data administration lie all sorts of political issues. A discussion of these is beyond the scope of this text, but they are important nonetheless. The challenges for data administration are summarized in Figure 15-1.

■ FUNCTIONS OF DATA ADMINISTRATION

Because of the challenges just described, data administration is complex. To protect the data asset while at the same time increasing its utility to the organization, a number of different functions or tasks must be performed. As shown in Figure 15-2, these activities can be grouped into several different categories.

MARKETING   First and foremost, data administration is responsible for declaring its existence and selling its services to the rest of the organization. Employees need to know that data administration exists and that there are policies, standards, and guidelines that pertain to organizational data and the reasons for them, and they need to be given reasons for respecting and following data administration rules, guidelines, and restrictions.

As Vinden points out, data administration must be, in the final analysis, a service function, and the users must perceive it in that way.[1] Thus, data administration activities must be communicated to the organization in a positive, service-providing light. Employees must believe that they have something to gain from data administration. Otherwise, the function becomes all cost and no benefit to the users, and it will be ignored.

DATA STANDARDS   For organizational data to be managed effectively, they must be organized coherently. If each department, function, or employee were to choose a different definition for a data item or for the means by which data items are to be named or described, the result would be chaos. It would be impossible even to compile an inventory of data, let alone manage it. Consequently, many organizations decide that important data items will be described in a standard way. For

---

[1] Robin J. Vinden, Data Dictionaries for Database Administration (Blue Ridge Summit, Pa.: TAB Books, 1990), p. 18.

FIGURE 15-2   *Functions of Data Administration*

> **Marketing**
> - Communicate existence of data administration to organization.
> - Explain reason for existence of standards, policies, and guidelines.
> - Describe in a positive light the services provided.
>
> **Data Standards**
> - Establish standard means for describing data items. Standards include name, definition, description, processing restrictions, and so forth.
> - Establish data proponents.
>
> **Data Policies**
> - Establish organizationwide data policy. Examples are security, data proponency, and distribution.
>
> **Forum for Data Conflict Resolution**
> - Establish procedures for reporting conflicts.
> - Provide means for hearing all perspectives and views.
> - Have authority to make decision to resolve conflict.
>
> **Return on Organization's Data Investment**
> - Focus attention on value of data investment.
> - Investigate new methodologies and technologies.
> - Take proactive attitude toward information management.

example, data administration may decide that every data item of importance to the organization will be described by a standard name, definition, description, set of processing restrictions, and the like. Once this structure is determined, the next question is, who will set the values of these standard descriptions? For example, who will decide the standard name or standard-processing restrictions?

In many organizations, the data administration group does not determine the standard descriptions. Instead, each item is assigned a **data proponent,** a department or other organizational unit in charge of managing that data item. The proponent is given the responsibility for establishing and maintaining the official organizational definitions for the data items assigned to it. Even though the data administration group may be the proponent of some data items, most proponents come from other departments.

You may encounter the term *data owner,* which is generally used in the same way that the term *data proponent* is used in this text. We avoid the term here because it implies a degree of propriety that does not exist. Both legally and practically, the organization is the one and only owner of the data. Although some group or groups have a legitimate claim to a greater degree of authority over particular data than others do, these groups do not own those data. Hence, we use the term *data proponent,* instead.

To summarize, the foundation of data administration is a system of data standards. The data administration group is responsible for working with users and management to develop a workable system of standards, which must be documented and communicated to the organization by some effective means. Procedures for assessing the employees' compliance with the standards also must be established.

DATA POLICIES   Another group of data administration functions concerns data policies. To illustrate the need for such policies, first consider data security. Every organization has data that are proprietary or sensitive, and data administration is responsible for developing a security system to protect them. Questions like the following need to be addressed: What security schemes should be put in place? Does the organization need a multilevel security system similar to that of the military? Or would a simpler system suffice? The security policy must also decide what is required for people to have access to sensitive data and what agreements they must sign to do so. What about employees of other organizations? Should sensitive data be copied? How should employees be trained with regard to security? What should be done when security procedures are violated?

A second type of data policy concerns data proponents and processing rights. What does being a data proponent mean? What rights does the proponent have that other groups do not? Who decides who will become a data proponent, and how can this be changed?

A third example of the need for data policy concerns the distribution of data, such as whether official data should be distributed on more than one computer and, if so, which, if any, should be the official copy. What processing should be allowed on distributed data? Should data that have been distributed be returned to the official data store? If so, what checks must there be to validate them before accepting them?

FORUM FOR DATA CONFLICT RESOLUTION   To be effective, organizational data must be shared, but humans have difficulty sharing. Consequently, the organization must be prepared to address disputes regarding data proponents, processing restrictions, and other matters.

The first responsibility of data administration in this regard is to establish procedures for reporting conflicts. When one user's or group's needs conflict with another's, the groups need a way to make their conflict known in an orderly manner. Once the conflict has been acknowledged, established procedures should allow all involved parties to present their case. Data administration staff, perhaps in conjunction with the data proponents involved, then must resolve the conflict. This scenario assumes that the organization has granted to data administration the authority to make and enforce the resulting decision.

Data administration provides a forum for resolving conflicts that apply to the entire organization. Database administration also provides a forum for resolving conflicts, but those that pertain to a particular database.

INCREASING THE RETURN ON THE ORGANIZATION'S DATA INVESTMENT   A final function for data administration is the need to increase the organization's return on its data investment. Data administration is the department that asks such questions as Are we getting what we should be getting from our data resource? If so, can we get more? If not, why not? Is it all worthwhile? This function involves all of the others: It includes marketing, the establishment of standards or policies, conflict resolution, and so forth. Sometimes this function also means investigating new techniques for storing, processing, or presenting data; new methodologies and technology; and the like.

The successful fulfillment of this role requires a *proactive* attitude toward information management. Relevant questions are whether we can use information to increase our market position, our economic competitiveness, and our overall net worth. Data administration must work closely with the organization's planning and development departments to anticipate rather than just react to the need for new information requirements.

Finally, data must be made available to their potential users. Availability means not only making it technically feasible for a highly motivated and skilled person to access data; it means that data must be provided to the users via means that are easy for them to use and in formats that are directly applicable to the work that must be done. We now turn to one way in which this is done, by downloading data from enterprise servers to users' departments and workstations.

DOWNLOADING DATA

With advent of powerful microcomputers, it has become feasible to download large quantities of enterprise data to departmental and user computers for local processing. Users can query these data using local DBMS products, and they can also import the data into spreadsheets, financial analysis programs, graphics programs, and other tools with which they are familiar.

In general, downloaded data can be used for query and reporting purposes only. They cannot be updated because once the data are removed from the operational database, they are no longer subject to concurrency control. Several users could update the same data and, if they were allowed to move them back, cause the lost update problem. In some applications, local data are merged with downloaded data. In these cases, users sometimes make unofficial changes to the data for the purposes of their analyses. Such changes, however, can cause consistency problems, as described later.

In some very rare situations, the applications processing the downloaded data are allowed to update and return the data to the source database. But, when this is done, elaborate manual procedures must be developed to ensure that data integrity problems do not occur when the data are returned. Since manual procedures are easily misunderstood, circumvented, or forgotten, they are not reliable. Hence, allowing users to update downloaded data is always risky and consequently is seldom done.

To understand more about the processing of downloaded data, consider a typical scenario.

■ UNIVERSAL EQUIPMENT

The Universal Equipment Company manufactures and sells heavy equipment for the construction industry. Its products include bulldozers, graders, loaders, and drilling rigs. Every product is assigned to a product manager in the marketing department who is responsible for product planning, advertising, marketing support, development of sales support material, and so forth. Each product manager is assigned a group of two or three related products.

Advertising is the product managers' largest budget item, so managers want to be able to measure the effectiveness of the ads they run. Universal's ads always contain a mail-in card to request information. The cards have a preprinted number unique to each ad appearance so that this number can be used to identify the ad that generated a particular lead. To facilitate lead tracking, the marketing department has developed a microcomputer database application that the product managers can use.

Figure 15-3(a) shows the semantic objects processed by this application. AD represents an advertisement; AD-APPEARANCE is the occurrence of a particular ad in a particular publication; PRODUCT represents a particular product such as a bulldozer; and PRODUCT contains two repeating groups, one on quotas and one on sales. The groups are multivalued because sales quotas are assigned for each quarter and product sales are recorded on a weekly basis.

The view of PRODUCT is quite simple. The complete PRODUCT object actually contains more attributes, such as AD. But because the other relationships are not needed for the product managers' application, we have omitted them. The database structure that supports these objects is shown in Figure 15-3(b).

FIGURE 15-3

Objects and Relations Supporting Universal's Product-Marketing Database: (a) Objects Processed by the Universal Product Managers and (b) Relational Structure Supporting These Objects

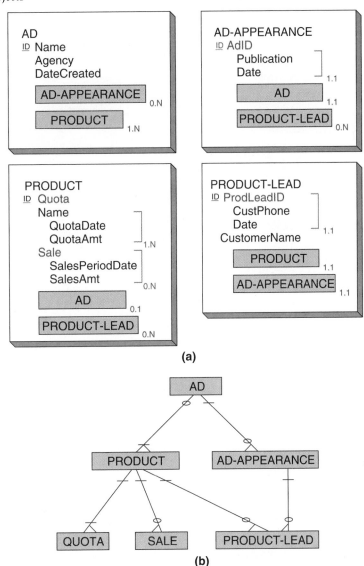

■ DOWNLOAD PROCESS

The product managers are assigned a microcomputer connected to other micros through a local area network in Universal's marketing department. To obtain sales and product-lead data, the micros call on a file server that serves as a gateway to Universal's mainframe (transaction-processing computer). The architecture is similar to that shown in Figure 15-4.

Every Monday, a key user in the marketing department runs a program developed by Universal's MIS department that updates the SALES, QUOTA, and PRODUCT-LEAD tables on the file server's database with data from the corporation's mainframe database. This program adds to the database the data from the previous week and also makes corrections. Product and sales data are imported for all related products to enable product managers to do comparative studies. Once the data have been downloaded to the file server, each product manager can

FIGURE 15-4 *Sharing of Downloaded Data with a Gateway Micro as the File Server*

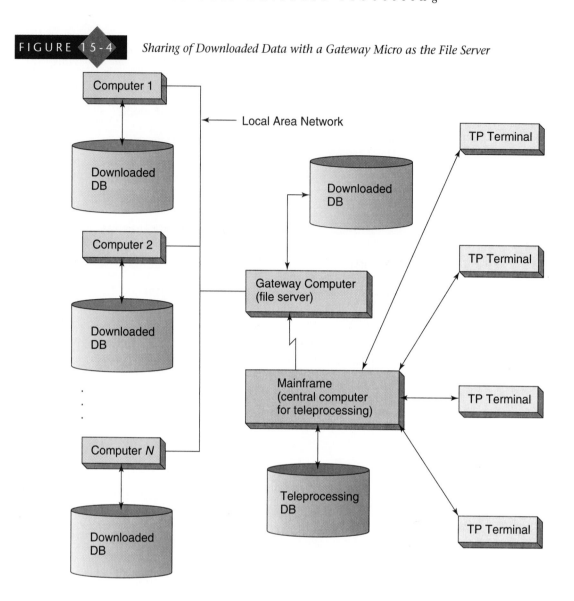

obtain the data of interest to him or her from that server. Controls ensure that the product managers do not obtain data for which access has not been authorized.

■ POTENTIAL PROBLEMS IN PROCESSING DOWNLOADED DATABASES

Downloading data moves the data closer to the user and increases the data's utility. Unfortunately, it may cause problems, including coordination, consistency, access control, and computer crime.

COORDINATION First consider coordination, using the PRODUCT-LEAD and AD-APPEARANCE tables for illustration. The PRODUCT-LEAD table is updated from data on the mainframe (leads are handled by sales personnel and are recorded on the mainframe). But the AD-APPEARANCE table is updated "locally" by the key user in the marketing department, who gets the data from reports prepared by the advertising manager and the advertising agency.

This situation could cause problems when an ad is run for the first time in a new issue or publication. For example, the ad could generate leads that are recorded on the mainframe database before the AD-APPEARANCE data is stored on the file server. Then, when those leads are downloaded, the program importing the data will have to reject the lead data, because such data violate the constraint that a PRODUCT-LEAD must have an AD-APPEARANCE parent. Thus, the activities of local updating and downloading must be carefully coordinated: The key user needs to insert AD-APPEARANCE data before importing data from the mainframe. Similar coordination problems can occur when updating SALES and QUOTA data.

CONSISTENCY   The second problem with downloaded data concerns **consistency.** Each of the product managers receives downloaded SALES and QUOTA data that they are not supposed to change. But what would happen if a product manager did change the data? In this case, the data in that product manager's database might not match the data in the corporate database, the data in the file server, and possibly the data in other product managers' databases. The reports produced by that product manager could therefore disagree with other reports. And if several product managers update data, many inconsistent data could be generated.

Clearly this situation calls for strict control by data administration. The database should be designed so that data cannot be updated. If this is not possible—say, the microcomputer database product will not enforce such a restriction, and the costs of writing programs to enforce it are prohibitively high—the solution to this problem is education. Product managers should be aware of the problems that will ensue if they change data, and they should be directed not to do so.

ACCESS CONTROL   A third problem is access control. When data are transferred to several computer systems, access control becomes more difficult. At Universal, for example, SALES and QUOTA data may be sensitive. For example, the vice president of sales may not want the sales personnel to learn about upcoming sales quotas until the annual sales meeting. But if fifteen product managers have copies of these data in their databases, it can be difficult to ensure that the data will be kept confidential until the appropriate time.

Furthermore, the file server receives all SALES and QUOTA data, which are supposed to be downloaded in such a way that a product manager receives only the SALES and QUOTA data for the products that he or she manages. Product managers can be quite competitive, however, and they may want to find the data for one another's products. Making this data accessible on the file server in the marketing department may thus create management problems.

COMPUTER CRIME   The fourth problem, a greater possibility of computer crime, is closely allied to access control. Whereas access control concerns inappropriate but legal activity, crime concerns illegal actions. Data on the corporate mainframe can be very valuable. Universal Equipment's sales and quota data, for example, are of great interest to its competitors.

When data are downloaded in bulk to the file server and then to one or many microcomputers, illegal copying becomes difficult to prevent. A diskette is easily concealed, and employees sometimes have modems with which they access work computers from off-site locations. In these situations, copying data over the telephone is nearly impossible to detect or prevent. The greater risk of computer crime is an important problem of downloaded databases. In fact, it alone might prohibit such a system from being developed, even though it would otherwise be an excellent solution. The potential problems of downloaded databases are summarized in Figure 15-5.

■ FILE-SHARING AND CLIENT-SERVER ALTERNATIVES

When processing downloaded data, either file-sharing or client-server architectures can be used. Consider Figure 15-6, which shows the file-server alternative. An extract of the operational database is made by the mainframe DBMS and delivered to a gateway computer, which saves that data on its own local files. The gateway does not have a DBMS, however, and its roles are only to coordinate

FIGURE 15-5   *Issues and Potential Problems Regarding Downloaded Data Applications*

Coordination
• Downloaded data must conform to database constraints.
• Local updates must be coordinated with downloads.
Consistency
• In general, downloaded data should not be updated.
• Applications need features to prevent updating.
• Users should be made aware of possible problems.
Access Control
• Data may be replicated on many computers.
• Procedures to control data access are more complicated.
Potential for Computer Crime
• Illegal copying is difficult to prevent.
• Diskettes and access via modem are easy to conceal.
• Risk may prevent the development of downloaded data applications.

FIGURE 15-6   *Processing Downloaded Data with File-Sharing System*

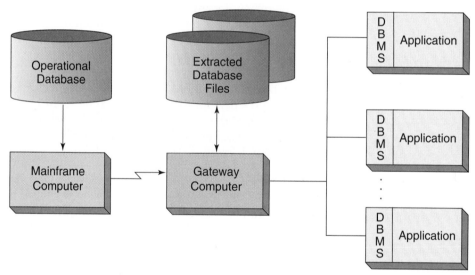

User Computers

communications processing and to provide file-processing services to the DBMS products that are located on the users' computers.

The user computer has a personal DBMS, which processes the data extract that resides on the gateway. This can be an advantage when processing downloaded data because each user can have his own private DBMS to query, sort, and report in whatever way he wants. Users need not contend with one another for DBMS services. Furthermore, since data are not normally updated, there is no need to provide centralized concurrency control.

In Figure 15-6 the gateway plays the role of the file server. Another file-sharing alternative was shown in Figure 15-4, in which the extracted data are passed through to the users' computers. In this variation, the gateway stores the extracted data and then sends some or all of them to the users' computers. This alternative

FIGURE 15-7   *Processing Downloaded Data with Client-Server System*

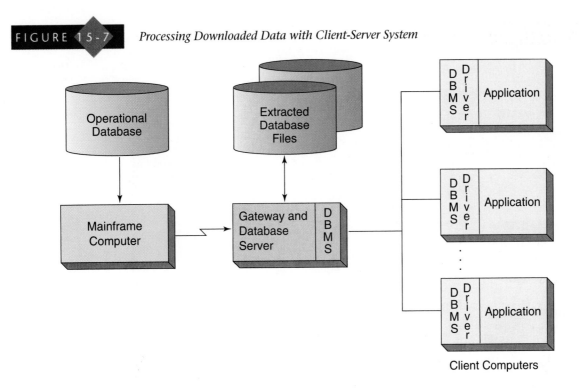

Client Computers

allows the gateway to further subset the extract (users get data about only the products they manage, for example), and it has better performance than the pure file-sharing systems shown in Figure 15-6 since the users' computers copy the data rather than repeatedly reading them. On the other hand, since the data are duplicated on each user computer, considerable file space may be required.

Figure 15-7 shows the processing of downloaded data with the client-server architecture. Here, the mainframe makes the extract and passes it to the gateway computer, which serves as both gateway and server DBMS. (Actually, the gateway computer and the server computer could be different. The important point is that in the department where the extracted data are used, there must be a local database server.) The users' computers have a DBMS driver but do not have a complete DBMS. The advantage of using the client-server model is that the entire extract need be stored only once on the server DBMS. The disadvantage is that the user computers must share the DBMS.

Any of these architectures can work, and one is not generally better than the other. Cost and performance vary among them, depending on the organization's license agreements with DBMS vendors, the size of the extracts, and the nature of the work performed on the users' computers.

To review, downloading data makes sense only if the users do not have to make official changes in the data and can live with data that are not up-to-date. They also make sense if the users' requirements necessitate repeated querying and reporting of the data in a way that would detrimentally impact performance on the operational database if the querying and reporting were to be done there.

DATA WAREHOUSES

Downloading does move the data closer to the user and thereby increase its potential utility. Unfortunately, while one or two download sites can be managed without problem, if every department wants to have its own source of downloaded data, the management problems become immense. Accordingly, organizations

FIGURE 15-8   *Data Warehouse*

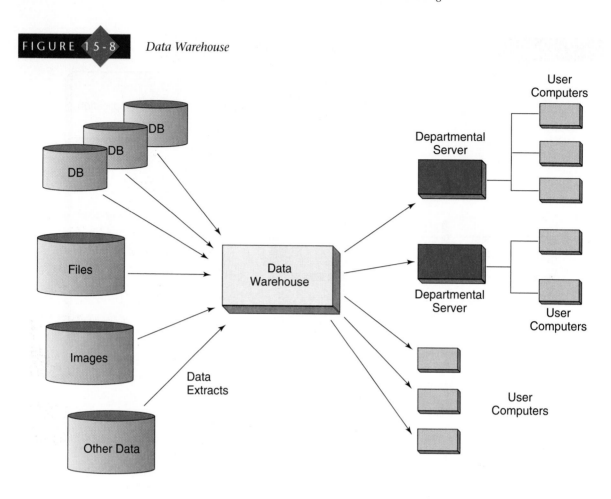

began to look for some means of providing a standardized service for moving data to the user and making them more useful. That service is called data warehousing.

A **data warehouse** is a store of enterprise data that is designed to facilitate management decision making. A data warehouse includes not only data but also tools, procedures, training, personnel, and other resources that make access to the data easier and more relevant to decision makers. The goal of the data warehouse is to increase the value of the organization's data asset.

As shown in Figure 15-8, the role of the data warehouse is to store extracts from operational data and make those extracts available to users in a useful format. The data can be extracts from databases and files, but it can also be document images, recordings, photos, and other nonscalar data. The source data could also be purchased from other organizations. The data warehouse stores the extracted data and also combines it, aggregates it, transforms it, and makes it available to users via tools that are designed for analysis and decision making.

■ COMPONENTS OF A DATA WAREHOUSE

The components of a data warehouse are listed in Figure 15-9. As stated, the source of the warehouse is operational data. Hence, the data warehouse needs tools for extracting the data and for storing them. These data, however, are not useful without metadata that describe the nature of the data, their origins, their format, limits on their use, and other characteristics of the data that influence the way they can and should be used.

Potentially, the data warehouse contains billions of bytes of data in many different formats. Accordingly, it needs a DBMS of its own to store and process the data. In fact, several DBMS products may be used, and the features and functions

FIGURE 15-9   *Components of a Data Warehouse*

- Data extraction tools
- Extracted data
- Metadata of warehouse contents
- Warehouse DBMS(s)
- Warehouse data management tools
- Data delivery programs
- End-user analysis tools
- User training courses and materials
- Warehouse consultants

of these may be augmented by additional in-house developed software that reformats, aggregates, integrates, and transfers data from one DBMS to another within the data warehouse. Programs may be needed to store and process nonscalar data like graphics and animations, also.

Since the purpose of the data warehouse is to make organizational data more available, the warehouse must include tools not only to deliver the data to the users but also to transform the data for analysis, query and reporting, and user-specified aggregation and disaggregation.

The data warehouse provides an important, but complicated set of resources and services. Hence, the warehouse needs to include training courses, training materials, on-line help utilities, and other similar training products to make it easy for users to take advantage of the warehouse resources. Finally, the data warehouse includes knowledgeable personnel who can serve as consultants.

■ REQUIREMENTS FOR A DATA WAREHOUSE

The requirements for a data warehouse are different from the requirements for a traditional database application. For one, in a typical database application, the structure of reports and queries is standardized. While the data in a report or query vary from, say, month to month, the structure of the report or query stays the same. Data warehouse users, on the other hand, often need to change the structure of queries and reports.

Consider an example. Suppose a company defines sales territories geographically—for simplicity, say one salesperson is assigned to each state or province in North America. Now, say a user of a data warehouse wants to investigate the impact on sales commissions if, instead of allocating salespeople geographically, staff are allocated to specific, named accounts. To compare these alternatives, sales must be grouped by company on the one hand and by state on another. Queries and reports with different structures will need to be created for this purpose.

Another difference is that users want to do their own data aggregation. For example, a user who wants to investigate the impact of different marketing campaigns may want to aggregate product sales according to package color at one time; according to marketing program at another; according to package color within marketing program at a third; and according to marketing program with package color on a fourth. The analyst wants the same data in each report; she simply wants to *slice and dice it differently.*

Not only do data warehouse users want to aggregate data in their own terms; they may also want to disaggregate them in their own terms, or, as it is commonly called, such users want to **drill down** their data. For example, a user may

FIGURE 15-10 *Categories of Requirements for a Data Warehouse*

- Queries and reports with variable structure
- User-specified data aggregation
- User-specified drill down
- Graphical outputs
- Integration with domain-specific programs

be presented a screen that shows total product sales for a given year. The user may then want to be able to click on the data and have them explode into sales by month; to click again and have the data explode into sales by product by month or sales by region by product by month. While database applications can be written to meet this need for a specific set of drill-down requirements, more often, the requirements vary by user and task. In fact, sometimes the users do not know how they want to drill down until they see the data and start drilling down; hence, drill-down tools need to be flexible.

Graphical output is another common requirement. Users want to see the results of geographic data in geographic form. Sales by state and province should be shown on a map of North America. A reshuffling of employees and offices should be shown on a diagram of office space. Again, these requirements are more difficult because they vary from user to user and from task to task.

Finally, many users of data warehouse facilities want to import warehouse data into domain-specific programs. For example, financial analysts want to import data into their spreadsheet models and into more sophisticated financial analysis programs. Portfolio managers want to import data into portfolio management programs, and oil drilling engineers want to import data into seismic analysis programs. All of this importing usually means that the warehouse data needs to be formatted in specific ways. These requirements are summarized in Figure 15-10.

■ CHALLENGES FOR DATA WAREHOUSES

So far, we've described data warehouses in an idealized way that makes them appear to be a panacea for management decision making. In point of fact, delivering the capabilities we have described is very difficult. There are a number of important challenges that must be met and problems that must be solved.

INCONSISTENT DATA Obviously, the data warehouse is useless, if not downright harmful, if the data that it provides are inaccurate. The issue goes beyond the quality of the data that the warehouse extracts from its sources. The source data can be accurate as extracted, but inaccuracies can be introduced by unwittingly integrating data that are inconsistent in timing or domain.

Consider the example of extracted data in Figure 15-11. One table is an extract of order data, and a second is an extract of checks that were written as bonuses to salespeople. Suppose that a data warehouse user wants to investigate the relationship of sales performance to sales bonuses. At first glance, it would seem that all that need be done is to sum the order amounts for each salesperson and compare the total to the bonus. The following SQL code will accomplish that task:

```
SELECT      SPName, Sum(OrderAmount), BonusAmount
FROM        ORDER, BONUS
WHERE       ORDER.SPNum = BONUS.SP#
GROUP BY    SpNum
```

FIGURE 15-11   *Example Extracts of Order and Bonus Data*

ORDER Table

SPNum	OrderNumber	OrderAmount
100	1000	$12,000
200	1200	$17,000
100	1400	$13,500
300	1600	$11,335

BONUS Table

SP#	SPName	BonusAmount
100	Mary Smith	$3,000
200	Fred Johnson	$2,500
300	Laura Jackson	$3,250

(As an aside, the typical data warehouse user probably does not know sufficient SQL to write this code, so it would need to be written for him or her or provided indirectly through some type of graphical query interface.)

Now suppose that these data were correct when extracted, and further suppose that they were obtained from two different information systems—order processing and accounts payable. Since they were obtained from two different systems, it is unknown whether the timing of the data is consistent. It might be that the order data were correct as of the last Friday of the month but that the bonus check data were correct as of the last day of the month. There is nothing in the data to indicate that difference, and, in fact, no one may note that such a difference exists. It may have a substantial impact on the results of the analysis, however.

In addition to timing differences, there can also be differences in the underlying domains. Consider the SALESPERSON and REGION tables in Figure 15-12, and suppose that someone wants to produce a report of total sales for each region. To do that, the following SQL needs to be executed:

FIGURE 15-12   *Salesperson and Region Data for Two Years*

SALESPERSON Table

SPName	Region	Year	TotalSales
Johnson	SO	1996	$175,998
Wu	NW	1996	$223,445
O'Connor	NE	1996	$337,665
Abernathy	SE	1996	$276,889
Lopez	SW	1996	$334,557
Johnson	SO	1997	$225,998
Wu	NW	1997	$276,445
O'Connor	NE	1997	$389,737
Abernathy	SO	1997	$362,768
Lopez	SO	1997	$419,334

REGION Table

SalesRegion	Manager
NW	Allen
NE	Brendlmann
SO	Currid

```
SELECT      SalesRegion, Sum(TotalSales)
FROM        REGION, SALESPERSON
WHERE       REGION.SalesRegion = SALESPERSON.Region
GROUP BY    Region
```

For the data shown, the result of this query will be a table having three rows, one each for the NW, NE, and SO sales regions. Because neither SE nor SW regions had a match in REGION, they were omitted from the join, and the sales from those regions will not appear in the result. This is most likely not what the user intended.

In actuality, between 1996 and 1997, this business changed its sales territories by merging the SE and SW sales regions into the SO region. Hence, all of the sales for salespeople in the SE and SW regions should have been added to the SO row in the query result. Put in database terms, the underlying domain of SalesRegion and Region are different. The domain of SalesRegion is the set of current regions; the domain of Region is the name of the region in which the sale occurred, at the time of the sale.

For the small amounts of data in Figures 15-11 and 15-12, these problems are obvious. If, however, there were thousands of rows of data, such problems could slip past the analyst, and incorrect information would be provided to the decision-making process.

To solve this problem, metadata must be created that describe both the timing and the domains of the source data. These metadata must be made easily accessible to the users of the data warehouse, and those users need to be trained on the importance of using such data.

TOOL INTEGRATION   Another serious problem for data warehouses concerns the integration of various tools that the users need. The paradigms of different products, in different product categories, are usually different. DBMS products are table oriented; spreadsheets are spreadsheet oriented; financial planning packages are plan oriented, and so on. As a result, the user interfaces in the products are dissimilar. Users may need substantial training to learn how to use several products from several categories, and they often have neither the time nor the inclination to learn them.

Even more serious, the process for exporting and importing data across products from different categories may be difficult. Consider the spreadsheet in Figure 15-13(a). This spreadsheet contains data about three themes: Departments, Managers, and Employees. To import this spreadsheet into a normalized database,

FIGURE 15-13   *Example of Conceptual Difference Between Spreadsheet and Database Products*

EmpNumber	EmpName	DeptNum	Manager	ManagerPhone	DeptCode
1000	Wu	10	Murphy	232-1000	A47
2000	O'Connor	20	Joplin	244-7788	D87
3000	Abernathy	10	Murphy	232-1000	A47
4000	Lopez	20	Joplin	244-7788	D87

(a)

EMPLOYEE(EmpNumber, EmpName, *DeptNum*)

DEPARTMENT(DeptNum, DeptCode, *Manager*)

MANAGER(Manager, ManagerPhone)

(b)

each of the themes will need to be allocated to separate tables like those in Figure 15-13(b). If the normalization is not done, considerable duplicated data will result as described in Chapter 5. The typical data warehouse user, however, will not understand the need for normalization nor have any idea about how to do it.

Finally, when products are acquired from different vendors, it is often difficult to get to the source of problems when they occur. For example, the vendor of the product that is exporting data may believe that a problem in the export/import process is due to the product that is importing the data, and the vendor of the product that is importing the data may claim the opposite. Since vendors are not experienced in using one another's products, nor are they motivated to encourage the use of other companies' offerings, technical support can be a nightmare.

MISSING WAREHOUSE DATA MANAGEMENT TOOLS   While there are many products and tools for extracting data from data sources and many tools for end-user query/reporting and data analysis, there is, at present, a lack of tools for managing the data warehouse itself. If the data warehouse consisted only of extracts from relational databases, and if the problems of timing and domain differences could be solved with training and procedures, then an off-the-shelf DBMS could be used to manage the data warehouse resources. In most cases, however, this is not the case.

Most data warehouses contain extracts from databases, files, spreadsheets, images, and external data sources. Since this is the case, these resources cannot be readily managed by a commercial DBMS, so the organization creating the data warehouse must write its own software. Usually this software has a commercial DBMS at its core, and the in-house data warehouse staff develops the additional features and functions necessary to manage the data warehouse resources.

The management of metadata presents another, similar problem. Few DBMS data dictionaries have sufficient capability to meet the metadata needs of the data warehouse. As stated, users need to know not only what's in the data warehouse but also where it came from, what its timing was, what the underlying domains of the data were, what assumptions were made when the data was extracted, and so forth. Data warehouse personnel will need to write their own metadata management software to augment the capabilities of the DBMS and other data dictionary products that they have.

Writing data management software is difficult and expensive. Once it is written, it must be supported. The vendors of the extraction programs and the data analysis programs will change their products, and any in-house developed software that uses them will need to be altered to conform to new interfaces. Further, the users' requirements will change, and this will necessitate adding new programs that will then need to be integrated with the data warehouse management software.

AD HOC NATURE OF REQUIREMENTS   Data warehouses exist to support management decision making. While a good portion of management decisions are regular and recurring, many other decisions are of an ad hoc nature. Questions like, Should we combine sales territories? Sell a product line? Consolidate warehouses? Adopt new Internet-based sales and marketing strategies? are not regular and recurring.

Computer systems, like bureaucracies, are slow and expensive to set up, are relatively inflexible, and work best with needs that follow a pattern. For that reason, such systems excel at tasks like order entry and reservations processing. It is most difficult, however, to design systems that readily respond to changing needs and requirements on an ad hoc basis. Thus, data warehouses have the most success in applications in which the variance in requirements follows a pattern. If a new requirement is similar in structure to an earlier one, that is, "consolidating the northern sales region will be like the process we followed when consolidating the southern region," then the data warehouse will likely be able to respond in a timely fashion. If not, then considerable time, expense, and anguish will probably need to be expended to meet the requirements.

FIGURE 15-14   *Continuum of Enterprise Data Sharing*

Data Downloading	Data Marts			Data Warehouse
	Particular Data Inputs	Particular Business Function	Particular Business Unit or Geographic Region	

Easier —————————————————————————— More Difficult

■ DATA MARTS

Because of the challenges just described, some organizations have decided to limit the scope of the warehouse to more manageable chunks. A **data mart** is a facility akin to a data warehouse but for a much smaller domain. Data marts can be restricted to a particular type of input data, to a particular business function, or to a particular business unit or geographic area.

Restricting a data mart to a particular type of data (e.g., database and spreadsheets) makes the management of the data warehouse simpler and probably means that an off-the-shelf DBMS product can be used to manage the data warehouse. Metadata are also simpler and easier to maintain.

A data mart that is restricted to a particular business function, such as marketing analysis, may have many types of data and metadata to maintain, but all of those data serve the same type of user. Tools for managing the data warehouse and for providing data to the users can be written with an eye toward the requirements that marketing analysts are likely to have.

Finally, a data mart that is restricted to a particular business unit or geographic area may have many types of input and many types of users, but the amount of data to be managed is less than for the entire company. There will be also be fewer requests for service, so the data warehouse resources can be allocated to fewer users.

Figure 15-14 summarizes the scope of the alternatives for sharing data that we have addressed in this chapter. Data downloading is the smallest and easiest alternative. Data are extracted from operational systems and delivered to particular users for specific purposes. The downloaded data are provided on a regular and recurring basis, so the structure of the application is fixed, the users are well trained, and problems such as timing and domain inconsistencies are unlikely to occur because users gain experience working with the same data. At the other extreme, a data warehouse provides extensive types of data and services for both recurring and ad hoc requests. Data marts fall in the middle. As we move from left to right in this figure, the alternatives become more powerful but also more expensive and difficult to create.

◆ SUMMARY

Data are an important organizational asset, one that can support both operations and management decision making. The purpose of the office data administration is not just to guard and protect the data asset but also to ensure that it is effectively used. One of the most important functions of data administration is to document the contents of the organization's data asset. This is a complicated task because data occur in many different formats in many different places in the organization. Data administration needs to help set organizational standards for names and formats of data items and also to define organizational processing rights and responsibilities. Finally, data are an asset, and their use can mean power; because of this, data administration must deal with organizational and political issues.

The specific functions of data administration include marketing its services, facilitating data standards and identifying data proponents, ensuring that appropriate data policies are established, and providing a forum for conflict resolution. All of these functions are aimed at the goal of increasing the return on the organization's data investment.

With the advent of powerful microcomputers, it became possible to download substantial amounts of enterprise data to users for local processing. Users can query and report on downloaded data using DBMS products on their own machines. In most cases, users are not allowed to update and return data because doing so could create data integrity problems. Even when downloaded data are not updated and returned, problems of coordination, consistency, access control, and possible computer crime can occur.

Either file-sharing or client-server architectures can be used when processing downloaded data. The advantage of file sharing is that each user has his or her own DBMS and need not contend with other users for DBMS services. Two variants of file sharing are possible, data can be stored on the file server or passed through to the local computers. If the latter, considerable file space may be required. With the client-server architecture, the extract is stored on a local server and each client user processes the database via the DBMS on the local server computer. The advantage of client server is that the extract need be stored only once. The disadvantage is that clients must share the DBMS services.

Downloading data can make sense for a few users or departments, but if many such systems need to be supported, the management problems for the MIS department become immense. Data warehouses have been developed as a way to give many users and departments better access to enterprise data.

A data warehouse is a store of enterprise data that is designed to facilitate management decision making. A data warehouse stores extracts of operational databases, files, images, recordings, photos, external data, and other data and makes these data available to users in a format that is useful to them.

The components of a data warehouse are data extraction tools, data extracts, metadata, one or more DBMS products, in-house developed warehouse data management tools, data delivery programs, user analysis tools, user training, and warehouse consultants. Typical requirements for a data warehouse include variable-structure queries and reports, user-specified data aggregation, drill-down, graphical outputs, and integration with domain-specific programs.

Data warehouses must overcome a number of important challenges. For one, when data are integrated, inconsistencies can develop due to timing and domain differences. Also, because of the many tools required in a data warehouse, tools will have different user interfaces and inconsistent means of importing and exporting data, and it may be difficult to obtain technical support.

Another challenge is that there is a lack of tools for managing the data warehouse itself. The organization may have to develop its own tools for managing nonrelational data and for maintaining appropriate metadata. Such development is difficult and expensive. Finally, the nature of many requests on the data warehouse is ad hoc; such requests are difficult to satisfy. As a result, some organizations have developed limited-scope warehouses called data marts.

GROUP I QUESTIONS

15.1 Explain why data are an important organizational asset.

15.2 Describe several example uses of data besides operational systems.

15.3 How is data administration similar to the job of a controller?

15.4 Briefly summarize the necessity for data administration.

15.5 List and briefly explain the challenges of data administration.

15.6 Describe data administration's marketing function.

15.7 What role does data administration take with regard to data standards?

15.8 Define data proponent.

15.9 What is the difference between data proponent and data owner?

15.10 Summarize data administration's role in regard to data policy.

15.11 Explain what is involved in establishing a forum for conflict resolution.

15.12 How can data administration help increase the return on an organization's data asset?

15.13 Explain the rationale for downloading data.

15.14 What limitations are normally placed on the processing of downloaded data?

15.15 At Universal Equipment, how do users obtain data extracts?

15.16 Summarize the coordination problem in processing downloaded databases.

15.17 Summarize the consistency problem in processing downloaded databases.

15.18 Summarize the access control problem in processing downloaded databases.

15.19 Why is computer crime a risk when processing downloaded databases?

15.20 Sketch and describe the use of file sharing for downloaded databases. What are the advantages and disadvantages?

15.21 Sketch and describe the use of client server for downloaded databases. What are the advantages and disadvantages?

15.22 Define data warehouse.

15.23 How does having a data warehouse compare to processing downloaded data?

15.24 List and describe the components of a data warehouse.

15.25 Explain what it means to change the structure of a query or report rather than change the data in a query or report.

15.26 Give an example, other than one in this book, of a user's need to aggregate data.

15.27 Give an example, other than one in this book, of a user's need to drill down data.

15.28 Explain two sources of data inconsistencies, and give an example, other than one in this book, of each.

15.29 Summarize the problems of having tools that use different paradigms and are licensed by different vendors.

15.30 Explain which data warehouse tools must be written in-house.

15.31 Why does the ad hoc nature of data warehouse requests pose a problem?

15.32 What is a data mart, and why would a company develop one?

15.33 List and briefly explain three types of data marts.

GROUP II QUESTIONS

15.34 Consider a company that has a national sales manager and fifteen regional salespeople. Each week, the salespeople download sales data from the mainframe and use it to update their sales projections for the next month. When they have done this, they connect via a modem to a server database and store their sales projections into that database. The manager then accumulates the sales data into a companywide forecast. What problems, issues, and difficulties might exist in this situation in terms of coordination, consistency, access control, and computer crime?

15.35 Consider the enterprise data that exists at your college or university. Does it seem to you that your institution makes good use of its data asset? What ways can you identify that the data asset is used for more than operational processing? In what ways do you think your college or university could take advantage of its data asset in the areas of:

- Student recruitment
- Fund-raising
- Program planning
- Student affairs
- Alumni affairs
- Other areas

15.36 Does your college or university have a data warehouse? If so, invite the manager of that facility to class and interview him or her. Compare your university's data warehouse to that described in this chapter.

INTERNET, INTRANET, AND MULTIMEDIA DATABASE PROCESSING

This chapter addresses the use of database technology in the context of public and private networks. We begin by briefly describing network environments of the Internet, the World Wide Web (WWW), and corporate intranets. Next, we summarize common database applications in those environments, and then we discuss alternative technologies for creating database applications. We conclude the chapter with a discussion of two multimedia database applications, including the semantic-object model and relational database designs for each.

Network database applications are important. Both public and private networks increase the demand for database applications because they provide a convenient way to deliver the application to the user. In fact, many believe that database applications are the next step in the commercialization of the Internet and that the number of Internet database applications will grow geometrically in the same way that other Internet applications have grown.

Both the technology and the products used for such applications are currently undergoing tremendous growth and change. After you have read this chapter to gain an understanding of the fundamental issues, get on the Internet to find out what products and technology are in use at the time you read this chapter.

NETWORK ENVIRONMENTS

A **network** is a collection of computers that communicate with one another using a standardized protocol. Some networks are **public;** anyone can utilize the network by paying a fee to a vendor who will provide access (or, like students, by joining an organization that has already paid to have access). Other networks are **private.** With these, only users who are preauthorized to connect to the network can gain access.

The most widely used public network is the Internet, and we begin with it.

■ THE INTERNET

The Internet is a public network of computers that communicate using a communications protocol called **Terminal Control Program/ Internet Protocol (TCP/IP).** This network was created by the Advanced Research Projects Agency

(ARPA) of the U.S. armed services in the 1960s. Initially, it was called ARPANET, and it connected major computing centers at military, university, and research institutions. Over time, more and more organizations joined the network, and it became desirable for nonresearch, commercially oriented organizations to join as well. In 1984, the military split its organizations off from ARPANET to form MIL-NET. ARPANET continued to grow in popularity with universities, research, and commercial organizations. Today it is referred to as the Internet. MILNET and the Internet are still connected, however.

A number of standard services are provided on the Internet. Any Internet user has access to **Internet mail services** for E-mail. Services for public **newsgroups** are provided by NetNews, an Internet facility that allows users with common interests to conduct public discussions with one another. Other services include **TelNet,** which allows an Internet user to sign on to a remote computer, and **FTP,** which allows users to send or retrieve files from remote computers.

In the beginning, almost all Internet servers ran some version of the UNIX operating system. Hence, the format and syntax of commands for accessing Internet services were UNIX-like. While this was acceptable, even an advantage, to technical users and computer programmers, it was off-putting to most people in business or at home. E-mail was popular because the complexity of UNIX was hidden by most mail applications, but TelNet, FTP, and other more sophisticated Internet services were not very popular among noncomputer experts. This situation changed with the advent of the World Wide Web.

THE WORLD WIDE WEB In 1989, Tim Berners-Lee of the European Particle Physics Laboratory (CERN) began work on a project that would enable researchers to share their work over the Internet. This project led to the development of the **hypertext transfer protocol (HTTP),** which is a TCP/IP-based protocol that enables the sharing of documents with embedded links to other documents over a TCP/IP network.

Berners-Lee and others proposed using a standard set of codes to mark text in documents both to indicate headings, emphasis, italics, and the like and also to indicate links to other documents. This language, called **hypertext markup language (HTML),** was a subset of an already accepted publishing industry markup language called the **standard generalized markup language (SGML).** Figure 16-1 shows an example of an HTML document, and Figure 16-2, on page 396 shows the way in which that document would appear to the client user.

In 1993, the National Center for Supercomputing Applications (NCSA) developed Mosaic, which was a client application for reading HTML (and other) documents. Later that year, Marc Andresen of NCSA proposed extending HTML to add the capability to add images and other types of media to HTML documents. Later Andresen and others left NCSA to form Netscape Communications, where they developed the Netscape Navigator. Today Mosaic, Netscape Navigator, and Microsoft's Internet Explorer are the most widely used Internet browsers.

Internet servers are programs that provide services in response to HTML commands. While many Internet server programs exist, the most popular are Unix servers developed by CERN and NCSA and a Windows NT Internet server from Microsoft.

The result of these products and technologies was the creation of a dynamic network of hypertext documents distributed across thousands of computers. This network of documents is called the **World Wide Web.**

INTERNET STANDARDS AND CHARACTERISTICS Three standards emerged from all of this activity that are important to network database applications. The first is HTML itself. Since, today, almost every computer has one or more browsers that can process HTML, it makes sense for Internet-oriented database applications to create forms and print reports in HTML format. We will say more about this later.

FIGURE 16-1   *Example of an HTML Document Source Code*

```
<HTML>
<HEAD>
<TITLE>Untitled</TITLE>
</HEAD>
<BODY>
<P>
<B><FONT SIZE=5 FACE="Arial">Internet Services Include<BR>
</FONT></B>
<UL>
<LI><FONT FACE="Arial">Mail</FONT>
</UL>
<P>
<FONT FACE="Arial"></FONT>
<UL>
<LI><FONT FACE="Arial">Newsgroups</FONT>
</UL>
<P>
<FONT FACE="Arial"></FONT>
<UL>
<LI><FONT FACE="Arial">TelNet</FONT>
</UL>
<P>
<FONT FACE="Arial"></FONT>
<UL>
<LI><FONT FACE="Arial">FTP</FONT>
</UL>
<P>
<FONT FACE="Arial"></FONT>
<UL>
<LI><FONT FACE="Arial">HTTP</FONT>
</UL>
</BODY>
</HTML>
```

Another important standard for database applications is the syntax by which documents are referenced on the Internet. The **universal resource locator (URL)** provides a standardized means to locate any document. A URL consists of three parts: a service name, a domain name, and a path name with (optionally) a file name. Thus, in the URL

http://www.companyx.com/dir1/myfile.abc

http:// is the name of the service (in this case hypertext transfer protocol), www.companyx.com is the name of a domain, and dir1/myfile.abc is the name of the path and file.

A third important standard that emerged from the Internet concerns the means by which URL files are to be processed. Not all files are HTML; some are graphics, or sound, or movie, or animation. When a server sends a file to a client, it also sends a code indicating the file's type. The client interprets the code to determine which program can process the file. The system of codes used is called **multipurpose Internet mail code (MIME).** The code was initially developed for mail, but today it is used more frequently in the processing of HTML documents. Figure 16-3 lists several types of files, their normal file extensions, and their

FIGURE 16-2   *HTML Source Code in Figure 16-1 as Shown in an HTML Browser*

FIGURE 16-3   *Sample MIME Types*

MIME Type	Name	File Extension
text/HTML	HyperText Markup	.htm, html
text/plain	Text	.txt
application/postscript	Postscript	.pdf, .ps, .ai
image/gif	Graphics Interchange Format	.gif
image/jpeg	Joint Photographic Experts Group	.jpg, .jpeg
audio/basic	mu-law	.au
audio/x-wav	Microsoft Wave File	.wav
audio/basic	Macintosh Sound File	.snd
video/quicktime	Macintosh Quick Time	.qt, .mov
video/x-msvideo	Microsoft Video	.avi

MIME types. Three-letter file extensions are used on Windows and Macintosh systems, and four-letter extensions are used on Unix.

MIME typing is important in database applications, not only for the obvious reason of generating standardized HTML, but also because MIME types can be extended. (In Figure 16-3, types preceded by x- are extended types.) Each server has a file that lists MIME types. An application-defined type can be added to this list, as well as to a similar list that is used by client browsers.

Thus, it is possible to create a database application that has a specific MIME type code. That code can be placed in the MIME lists on both the clients and the servers and associated with a given graphic image. When the user clicks on that image, the browser will check the MIME code and determine that it should invoke the database application. (It may need to call the server to download the application and then invoke it.) Thus, organizations can extend the MIME type system to include their own specific codes.

Two characteristics of WWW applications are especially noteworthy for database applications. First, WWW applications are request-oriented. WWW servers wait to be accessed and provide services when asked to do so. Unlike some traditional MIS applications, they do not poll or otherwise solicit application activity.

Second, WWW applications are stateless. The server receives a request, processes it, and then forgets about the client who made the request. No attempt is made to conduct a continuing session or conversation with a given client. This stateless characteristic poses no problems for web applications like those that display pages of promotional material. It is a problem for most database applications, however, because database applications usually involve the processing of a transaction, which may require several or many exchanges between the client and the server. We will return to this topic later in this chapter.

■ INTRANETS

The term *intranet* has several different interpretations. Most commonly, the term means a private, local or wide-area network (LAN or WAN) that uses TCP/IP, HTML, and related browser technology on client computers and web server technology on servers. Less commonly, the term is used to mean any private LAN or WAN that involves clients and servers.

Two characteristics of intranets differentiate them from the Internet. First, intranets are private. Either they are not connected to a public network at all, or they are connected to a public network via a **firewall,** which is a computer that serves as a security gateway. Firewall computers monitor the source and destination of traffic between the intranet and the Internet and filter it. Some firewalls operate so as to allow only certain traffic through; others operate so as to prohibit certain traffic; still others operate in both modes.

Because intranets are private, security is less of a concern. This does not mean that security is not a concern at all but rather that less elaborate security measures need to be taken. In most cases, computers on an intranet are known and supported by the organization that owns and maintains the intranet. Unauthorized activity and security problems are more easily identified and managed than on a public network.

The second major differentiating characteristic of an intranet is speed. Most users connect to the Internet via a modem. Since today's modems operate in the range of 28.8 kbs (thousands of bits per second), anyone planning an Internet application needs to size the application's transmission requirements accordingly. Large files cannot be transferred in a reasonable amount of time.

On the other hand, the transmission speed of a local area network can be in the range of 100,000 kbs. Hence, files downloaded on an intranet can be more than 1,000 to 10,000 times larger than those downloaded from the Internet.

Because of the speed difference, large bitmaps, sound files, and animations can be included in intranet applications. More important in the database world, large query responses can be transmitted to client computers. In addition, because of the increased speed, it is possible to download large program files to the client computer. This means, as you will see, that more of the application processing can be conducted on the client in an intranet than can be conducted on a client in the Internet.

◆ NETWORK DATABASE APPLICATIONS

In this chapter, we define a **network database application** as a database application in which the clients use an HTML-based browser like Netscape Navigator or Microsoft Internet Explorer and the server includes both an Internet server and database files. In all but file-processing systems, the server computer also includes a DBMS. (For file processing, as you will recall, the DBMS is located on the client computers.)

Several different types of network database applications are emerging. The term *publishing* is often used for these applications because of the request-oriented nature of Internet and intranet processing. That is, a server is available to be accessed by the client, when and if the client chooses to access it. The server does not solicit activity from the clients.

STATIC REPORT PUBLISHING   Some network database applications provide static report publishing. This means that the DBMS (or application program) generates a report, static form, or query response in HTML format and posts it to a web site. (A static form is a display-only data entry form. It is a picture of a data entry form that displays data but that cannot be used for data entry.)

Figure 16-4 shows an HTML report that was prepared from the database application in Chapter 11. Figure 16-5 shows the report in HTML format. This report was generated by Access using Microsoft's Internet Assistant for Access.

A report like the one in Figure 16-4 can be generated and a URL to that report file placed in an HTML web page. If the DBMS supports triggers or related functionality, the file containing the report can automatically be generated by the DBMS either after the passage of a certain amount of time or when a particular event occurs. For example, an application could post a daily sales summary report every hour onto a web page. Or the application could generate a new report every time daily sales increase by $100,000 or some similar figure.

Notice that the transmission traffic in static report publishing is one-way. The user provides no data; all of the data flow from the server to the user at the user's request. Because of this, no data about the state of the interaction between the client and the network server need be maintained by either.

DB QUERY PUBLISHING   A second type of network database application is query publishing. In this application, an HTML form is generated that has text boxes in

FIGURE 16-4

Example of Static Report Publishing

FIGURE 16-5   *HTML Code for the Report in Figure 16-5 Generated by Microsoft Access*

```
<HTML>

<TITLE>ARTIST</TITLE>

<BODY background = sky.jpg>

<TABLE BORDER=0 CELLSPACING=0 CELLPADDING=0 >
<TR HEIGHT=32 >
<TD WIDTH=4 ><BR></TD><TD WIDTH=860 ><B><I><FONT SIZE=5 FACE="Times New Roman"
COLOR=#000080>ARTIST</FONT></B></I></TD></TR>
</TABLE>
<TABLE BORDER=0 CELLSPACING=0 CELLPADDING=0 >
<TR HEIGHT=18 >
<TD WIDTH=4 ><BR></TD><TD WIDTH=188 ><B><I><FONT SIZE=2 FACE="Times New Roman"
COLOR=#000080>Nationality</FONT></B></I></TD><TD WIDTH=133 ><B><I><FONT SIZE=2
FACE="Times New Roman" COLOR=#000080>ArtistName</FONT></B></I></TD><TD WIDTH=41
ALIGN=RIGHT ><B><I><FONT SIZE=2 FACE="Times New Roman"
COLOR=#000080>Born</FONT></B></I></TD><TD WIDTH=44 ALIGN=RIGHT ><B><I><FONT SIZE=2
FACE="Times New Roman" COLOR=#000080>Died</FONT></B></I></TD></TR>
</TABLE>
<TABLE BORDER=0 CELLSPACING=0 CELLPADDING=0 >
<TR HEIGHT=18 >
<TD WIDTH=4 ><BR></TD><TD WIDTH=860 ><I><FONT SIZE=2 FACE="Times New Roman"
COLOR=#000080>Spanish</FONT></I></TD></TR>
</TABLE>
<TABLE BORDER=0 CELLSPACING=0 CELLPADDING=0 >
<TR HEIGHT=14 >
<TD WIDTH=192 ><BR></TD><TD WIDTH=133 ><FONT SIZE=1 FACE="Arial" COLOR=#000000>Juan
Miro</FONT></TD><TD WIDTH=41 ALIGN RIGHT ><FONT SIZE=1 FACE="Arial"
COLOR=#000000>1907</FONT></TD><TD WIDTH=45 ALIGN=RIGHT ><FONT SIZE=1 FACE="Arial"
COLOR=#000000>1994</FONT></TD></TR>
</TABLE>
<TABLE BORDER=0 CELLSPACING=0 CELLPADDING=0 >
<TR HEIGHT=18 >
<TD WIDTH=4 ><BR></TD><TD WIDTH=860 ><I><FONT SIZE=2 FACE="Times New Roman"
COLOR=#000080>U.S.</FONT></I></TD></TR>
</TABLE>
<TABLE BORDER=0 CELLSPACING=0 CELLPADDING=0 >
<TR HEIGHT=14 >
<TD WIDTH=192 ><BR></TD><TD WIDTH=133 ><FONT SIZE=1 FACE="Arial" COLOR=#000000>Dennis
Frings</FONT></TD><TD WIDTH=41 ALIGN=RIGHT ><FONT SIZE=1 FACE="Arial"
COLOR=#000000>1947</FONT></TD></TR>
</TABLE>
<TABLE BORDER=0 CELLSPACING=0 CELLPADDING=0 >
<TR HEIGHT=18 >
<TD WIDTH=4 ><BR></TD><TD WIDTH=860 ><I><FONT SIZE=2 FACE="Times New Roman"
COLOR=#000080>U.S./Swiss</FONT></I></TD></TR>
</TABLE>
<TABLE BORDER=0 CELLSPACING=0 CELLPADDING=0 >
<TR HEIGHT=14>
<TD WIDTH=192 ><BR></TD><TD WIDTH=133 ><FONT SIZE=1 FACE="Arial" COLOR=#000000>Mark
Tobey</FONT></TD><TD WIDTH=41 ALIGN=RIGHT ><FONT SIZE=1 FACE="Arial"
COLOR=#000000>1922</FONT></TD><TD WIDTH=45 ALIGN=RIGHT ><FONT SIZE=1 FACE="Arial"
COLOR=#000000>1987</FONT></TD></TR>
</TABLE>
<TABLE BORDER=0 CELLSPACING=0 CELLPADDING=0 >
<TR HEIGHT=15 >
<TD WIDTH=4 ><BR></TD><TD WIDTH=520 ><B><I><FONT SIZE=1 FACE="Times New Roman"
COLOR=#000080>Tuesday, December 17, 1996</FONT></B></I></TD><TD WIDTH=336 ALIGN=RIGHT
><B><I><FONT SIZE=1 FACE="Times New Roman" COLOR=#000080>Page 1 of
1</FONT></B></I></TD></TR>
</TABLE>


<A HREF="#">First</A>
<A HREF="#">Previous</A>
<A HREF="#">Next</A>
<A HREF="#">Last</A>

</BODY>

<BR><BR>

<IMG SRC = "msaccess.jpg">

</HTML>
```

which the user enters query criteria. For example, in the form in Figure 16-6, the user enters an order number and presses the submit query button. At that point the application sends a request to initiate a query for that order on the server. The server responds with order data or an error message.

From a database standpoint, there is nothing particularly unique about this query; such queries have been processed by DBMS products for many years. What is different about it, however, is that it is embedded in an HTML file that can be processed by any computer having a browser and access to the network. Hence, the query can be readily distributed. If a company wants its customers to be able to query orders, it need only distribute the URL of the web site having a link to this query page. In doing so, the company will most likely want to add a restriction to the query response so that it sends responses only to orders that originated at the client's company.

Unlike static report publishing, the data transmission for query publishing is two-way. In the example, the client provides an order number, and the server responds with query results. More realistically, the client would probably need to send identifying data as well.

If each query is considered to be an independent unit, then neither the client nor the server need maintain any data about the state of their interaction. It might be, however, that in order to reduce transmission traffic, queries should be remembered so that if the user enters the number of an order that has already been queried, the results can be obtained locally. In this case, the client computer would need to keep track of the queries that have been made and the responses to each.

APPLICATION PUBLISHING   Application publishing is a type of network database application that is closest to what we have called database applications in this book. Such applications have potentially many data entry forms and reports. They support transaction logic, provide concurrency control over database changes, and have all of the other database application characteristics.

Three factors limit application publishing on the Internet. First, because of slow transmission rates, only applications needing limited amounts of data can be

FIGURE 16-6   *Example of Query Publishing Form*

shared. Second, to date, Internet security lacks sufficient capability to be trusted for any but the least significant data. Until encryption is common, sharing account numbers, financial data, operational requests, and the like over the Internet is very risky. Most organizations are unwilling to accept the possibility that their transaction data might be read (or processed) by unauthorized users.

Third, the stateless nature of Internet transactions means that the client application needs to maintain session status. This means that the client application may need to be large and complex. This, in turn, means that a large client application will need to be downloaded over the network. But Internet transmission speeds are slow, and downloading a large application may be unacceptably slow.

These limitations do not necessarily apply to intranets, and it is likely that intranet application publishing will become common. In fact, the version of SALSA for the Desktop that is included with this text will generate an intranet application (see File, Share Application). This application requires that the client computer have either the SALSA Viewer or SALSA for the Desktop. This means that the client will be large, however.

NETWORK DATABASE ALTERNATIVES

Figure 16-7 summarizes the alternatives for network database application processing. In this figure, the vertical bar represents the split between client processing and server processing. For example, in the left bar, labeled "CGI with Perl," only the HTML browser and a small portion of the application are located on the client machine. All the rest of the application logic, the DBMS, and the database reside on the server. Since only a small amount of the application is located on the client, this is referred to as a **thin client** application.

The right vertical bar in Figure 16-7, labeled "File Processing," shows the alternative on the other end of the continuum. Here, the entire application and the DBMS reside on the client. The server only processes the database files. Since all of the application is located on the client, this is referred to as a **thick client** application.

We will consider each of these alternatives in turn from left to right. Notice that we are discussing *application design issues*; how the application is distributed over the network clients is more of a systems development topic than it is a database topic. Still, it is important for you to understand the role of these different alternatives.

■ CGI AND PERL

CGI stands for **common gateway interface,** and it refers to an HTML standard for defining forms and sending and receiving form data. **Perl (Practical**

FIGURE 16-7   *Continuum of Network Applications*

Extraction and Report Language)[1] is an interpreted programming language invented by Larry Wall; it is mentioned here because Perl is frequently used to create application programs that run on network servers. Perl is used not only because it is an effective programming language but also because it is free and portable. There are Perl interpreters for Unix, Windows NT, and Macintosh operating systems. Also, libraries are available for processing ODBC from Perl.

In actuality, any programming language can be used with CGI. If portability were not an issue, the server programs could be written in Visual Basic.[2] C++ and Java, which are portable, could be employed as well (see the discussion in the next section).

CGI emerged from the UNIX environment, and it has a definite UNIX flavor to it. According to this standard, input from the client form is transmitted either as parameters on the URL request that is sent to the server or in the standard UNIX input stream STDIN. Similarly, output from the server program is delivered back to the client on the standard UNIX output stream STOUT.

Figure 16-8 shows HTML for invoking the CGI interface. Figure 16-8(a) shows the HTML, and Figure 16-8(b) shows how this form would appear in a browser. CGI is invoked by the tag FORM; the keyword METHOD tells the browser to send the user's data (the order number) in the STDIN input stream. ACTION specifies the name of the program on the server that is to process the input stream, in this case CGI_EXAMPLE.

When the program receives this data, it processes it and replaces the HTML stream with its output. If the goal of the application is to create a form that looks like Figure 16-6, then the program CGI_Example would need to place HTML for that form on the STOUT stream.

The advantages of CGI are that it is standardized and simple to learn and use. As such, it is appropriate for simple query forms like that shown in Figure 16-8(b). Because of its simplicity, however, CGI is not appropriate for more sophisticated forms. Even requirements like masking of text boxes can be difficult to write and slow to execute. Also, since almost all of the application processing is done on the server, performance bottlenecks can occur at the server.

■ VBScript and Java Script

VBScript and Java Script are two "lightweight" programming languages that can be used to place programming logic into HTML pages. Both are interpreted, and both reside with the page. This means that when the page is downloaded from the web server, the script code is downloaded as well. Consequently, if there is a substantial amount of script code, the download process may be slow, especially on the Internet. On the other hand, once the page has been downloaded, all of the script is available and can be executed without further traffic over the network.

VBScript is a subset of Microsoft's Visual Basic. Figure 16-9 on page 404 shows an example of one way in which VBScript can be embedded into an HTML page.[3] The script for a button click event on a button named CalcButton has been placed in the HEAD section of the HTML form. The button is defined in the BODY section of the form. The form itself is shown in a browser in Figure 16-10 on page 405. When the user enters a number of hours and presses the Compute button, the code in the HEAD section of the form is executed. It will compute results and place them in the indicated text boxes.

---

[1] Also Pathologically Eclectic Rubbish Lister. That alias, together with Perl's copyleft notice may give you a sense of Perl.
[2] By the time you read this, there may be VB compilers and interpreters for environments other than Windows.
[3] There are a number of ways to embed VBScript into a form. They are similar in nature to the one shown here.

FIGURE 16-8   *HTML Using CGI Form*

```
<HTML>
<HEAD>
<TITLE>New Page</TITLE>
</HEAD>
<BODY>
<FORM METHOD="POST" ACTION="/CGI_EXAMPLE">
<EM>Please enter the Order Number:</EM>
<P>
Order Number:<INPUT TYPE=text NAME="OrdNum" SIZE=20><BR>
<P>
<INPUT TYPE=submit>
<INPUT TYPE=reset VALUE="Cancel">
<P>
</FORM>


</FORM>
</BODY>
</HTML>
```

(a)

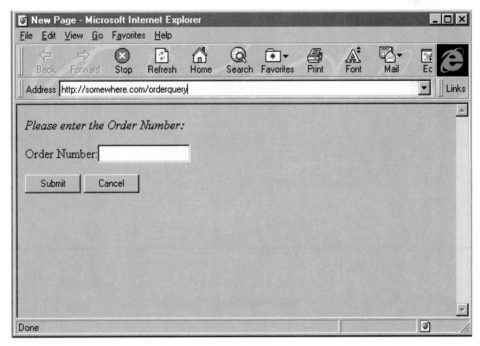

(b)

Java Script can be used in a similar way. In fact, script generation products are available that will generate script in either VBScript or Java Script languages. As an aside, Java Script is much closer in style and format to VBScript than it is to Java. Java, as you will learn, is an object programming language and is much closer to C++ than it is to Java Script.

As shown in Figure 16-7, VBScript and Java Script can be used to express more application logic than can be expressed in CGI. They are particularly useful for coding form processing tasks like masking edit controls, editing data values, filling

FIGURE 16-9   *HTML with VBScript Included*

```html
<HTML>
<HEAD>
<TITLE>Labor Estimation Sheet</TITLE>
<SCRIPT LANGUAGE="VBScript">
        <!--
        Sub CalcButton_OnClick()
        Dim LHours, LTotal, Tax, Total
        If LaborHours.Value = "" then
                MsgBox "Please enter a value for Labor Hours"
        End If
        LHours = LaborHours.Value
        LTotal = LHours * 65
        Tax = LTotal * .0891
        Total = LTotal + Tax
        LaborTotal.Value = LTotal
        TaxAmount.Value = Tax
        TotalBid.Value = Total
        End Sub
        -->
</SCRIPT>
</HEAD>
<BODY>
<HR>
<CENTER>
Enter the number of labor hours:
<BR>
(Standard labor rate is $65.00; tax is 8.91 percent)
<P>
<INPUT NAME="LaborHours">
<INPUT TYPE=BUTTON NAME="CalcButton" VALUE="Compute">
<BR>
Labor Total:
<INPUT NAME="LaborTotal">
<BR>
Tax Amount:
<INPUT NAME="TaxAmount">
<BR>
Total Bid:
<INPUT NAME="TotalBid">

</BODY>
</HTML>
```

combo boxes and list boxes, and responding to user activity. Once the form has been processed, however, the data must then be communicated back to the network server for processing. This can be done by using CGI, or by using Java and ActiveX.

◼ JAVA

Java is a programming language developed by Sun Microsystems, Inc. Some people believe that Java is the language that C++ should have been, while others refer to Java as a subset of C++. In any case, Java is an object programming language

FIGURE 16-10   *HTML from Figure 16-9 as Shown in a Browser*

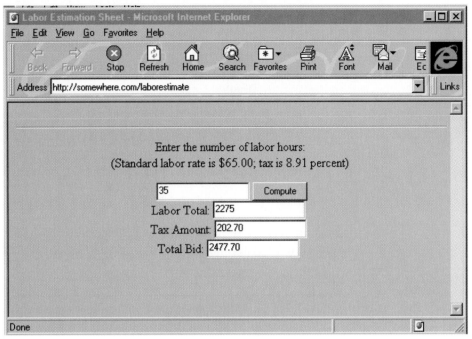

(see Chapter 17) that has better memory management and bounds-checking capabilities than C++.

When Java is compiled, the result of the compilation is a file of Java bytecode. This bytecode resides on the server, and when the user accesses an HTML page (or other resources) that has a Java program, the bytecode is transmitted to the client. This bytecode is then input to an interpreter that resides on the client.

Java was designed to be portable. Java bytecode is machine-independent; for it to run on a particular operating system, only the bytecode interpreter need be converted to the new operating system. There are Java bytecode interpreters for Unix, Windows, and Macintosh operating systems.

Unlike VBScript and Java Script, Java is a full and complete object-oriented programming language. This means that it can be used to write code for processing on the client side, code for processing on the server side, or both. Clearly, the more of the application that is written for processing on the client side, the larger the Java application will be, and the more bytecode will need to be downloaded. This means that startup times will be slower. On the other hand, once the code has been downloaded, the client computer will be able to process a larger share of the application, and the less likely it becomes that the network server will be a bottleneck.

There are libraries for binding Java to ODBC as well as for binding it directly to the native libraries of DBMS products. Figure 16-11 shows two ways that Java might be used. In Figure 16-11(a) some of the application tasks are handled by Java programs on the client, and some of them are handled by Java programs on the server. Java libraries are used to coordinate the transmission of data over the network.

Figure 16-11(b) shows a traditional client-server database application. Here, all of the application logic is processed on the client. The Java programs interface with the DBMS vendor's client software, which in turn transmits SQL requests and data to and from its counterpart on the server.

The major advantages of Java are machine portability and the fact that it is a modern, fully featured object-oriented programming language. The major disadvantage is that Java is less common than C++; hence, there are fewer Java

FIGURE 16-11   *Two Possible Network Database Applications: (a) Java Programs on Both Client and Server, and (b) Java Application Program on Client Only*

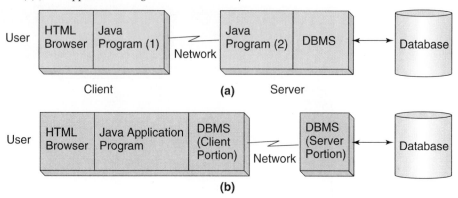

programmers and fewer prebuilt Java components. Also, as an object-oriented programming language, Java requires considerable skill and training.

◼ ACTIVEX

ActiveX is an architecture of program elements promulgated by Microsoft. It is a means by which independent programs can interface with one another in a generalized fashion. ActiveX is basically the same architecture that Microsoft had previously called COM (component object model) and prior to that had called OLE (object linking and embedding).

The goal of all of these technologies was to enable programs to interact with one another in a dynamic fashion. For example, users may want a Microsoft Word document to include a Visio drawing; without ActiveX (or some similar technology), Word and Visio would have to be written and compiled to work with one another. With ActiveX, programs can interface with one another dynamically; they need not be aware of one another at the time they are written.

To do this, an ActiveX program (say, Visio) accesses another ActiveX program (say, Microsoft Word) using an interface called **IUnknown.** If the program supports that interface (and we can bet that Microsoft Word does!), then the first program (Visio), using an interface called **Query Interface,** can determine what objects, methods, and properties the second program (Word) supports. Thus, ActiveX provides a standardized way of determining the appropriate interface to any unknown program.

ActiveX controls are programs that implement the COM (ActiveX) interface. As such, they can be called by other programs dynamically. ActiveX controls can be embedded on forms including HTML documents. Examples of ActiveX controls are a masked edit data entry box, a calendar, an Excel spreadsheet, a connection to a database table or query, and a connection to a live HTML report.

ActiveX documents are collections of ActiveX controls that can be displayed in a browser with no additional viewer required. A user, for example, could download a Powerpoint presentation in an ActiveX document, and the browser could display and edit the document without any additional program components. ActiveX documents are similar to HTML pages in that they serve as a browser-enabled container for graphics, text, input controls, and any other structure that is expressed as an ActiveX control. The Office Binder in Windows is an example of an ActiveX document.

ActiveX and Java have been inappropriately compared with each other in the popular press. Java is a programming language; ActiveX is an architecture that can be implemented with any number of different languages. One could write ActiveX controls in Java, or in C++, and, as of Version 5.0, in Visual Basic.

FIGURE 16-12   *Placing ActiveX Controls on an HTML Document with the ActiveX Control Pad*

Application developers can create their own ActiveX controls, or they can assemble existing ActiveX controls onto a HTML document or onto an ActiveX document. Since the controls support the COM interface, they can interact with one another by setting each other's properties, calling each other's methods, and so forth. (These terms are further explained in Chapter 17.)

Figure 16-12 shows the use of a Microsoft utility called the ActiveX Control Pad. This utility can be used to place ActiveX controls on an HTML page. In this figure, the user has already placed a label control on the HTML document and is in the process of adding a list box as well. In addition to adding controls to an HTML page, this utility can be used to write VBScript or Java Script that enables the controls to set one another's properties.

Considerable work is underway in ActiveX technology, and by the time you read this, there will undoubtedly be ActiveX controls for querying databases, for implementing ODBC commands, and for connecting to and processing any number of server databases.

ACCESS 97 SUPPORT FOR INTERNET APPLICATIONS

Access 97 includes features and functions for publishing database applications in both the Internet and intranet environments. It contains facilities to import, export, and link tables to HTML files, to process hyperlinks into or out of database applications, and to publish tables, forms, and reports in HTML format. Additionally, forms and datasheets (table data viewed in a spreadsheet-like format) can be saved as ActiveX Server pages. Import and export is straightforward and we need not address it here. Instead we will consider hyperlink processing and the publishing of data in HTML and as server pages.

■ HYPERLINK PROCESSING

To understand the processing of hyperlinks, first consider several terms. Microsoft defines **hyperlink address** to mean either a URL or UNC address. A URL is an Internet address like those previously discussed, for example, http:\\www.some-where.com.

UNC stands for **universal naming convention** and it refers to an address standard used on Windows 95 and NT. The general format of a UNC address is *servername* \ *sharename* \ *pathname* \ *filename*, where servername is the name of a network server, sharename is the name of a shared resource on that server, pathname is the name of a directory path within the sharename, and filename is the name of a file. UNC can be used in intranet environments to make device-independent file references so that network devices need not be associated with file names like d: or e:

Access 97 includes a new data type called **hyperlink.** Columns of tables can be defined to have this type; such columns are materialized in a particular way by Access as we will describe below. A hyperlink data item has the format *displaytext#address#subaddress*. Displaytext is a string of characters that is shown when the data item appears in tables or forms. Address is a hyperlink address, which can be either a URL or a UNC. Subaddress is a location within the source at the address. Only the address portion is required.

Valid example hyperlink values are "NOAA Site#http:\\www.noaa.gov", "PriceList#\\Deptserver\ShareOrder\PriceData\Orders.mdb#Form Price", and #http:\\www.somewhere.com#. In the first example, the string "NOAA Site" will be shown when the data value appears in a spreadsheet view of the table or in a form or report. The term will be associated with the URL http:\\www.noaa.gov. The second example uses a UNC to point to the form named Price on a database on a shared network device. The third example is the minimum possible hyperlink value; the full URL will appear in tables, forms, and reports since there no display text is provided.

To see how to use these concepts, suppose that you want to keep Internet addresses in a database application. The application could be as elaborate as you want. You could store keywords, locations, subjects, relationships to other objects, etc., for each hyperlink address. Or, you could place the hyperlink address for your customers on all of your customer forms and so forth.

For illustration, suppose we want to create a single table that has a surrogate key, a name, and a hyperlink. Figure 16-13 shows the Access table definition to do this. The attribute ID_ is the surrogate key, NameofWebSite is a text value, and WebID has been given the data type Hyperlink.

Figure 16-14 shows a form based on this table. The value of ID_ (the surrogate key) is automatically filled in by Access since ID_ has the data type AutoNumber. In a real application, this field would be hidden in the form. The user of this form has typed in the value "Site for Finding Weather Maps" in the NameofWebSite field and the string "NOAA Site#http:\\www.noaa.gov" in the WebID field. Since this field is of type hyperlink, only NOAA Site (the displaytext portion) appears.

When the user clicks on the WebID text box, Access 97 will automatically link to the related Internet site. Access causes Windows to start a web browser and send the URL value of http:\\www.noaa.gov to the browser. The user has thus linked from Access to a web site. Again, this simple application could be extended to provide quite an elaborate means of storing and querying URL or UNC addresses.

Another way to use hyperlink data is to bind it to controls such as labels, pictures, or command buttons. The form in Figure 16-14 has a button labeled Hyperlink. If the user clicks this button, the URL in the current value of WebID will be followed. To do this, however, a snippet of VB code must be written as shown in Figure 16-15 on page 410. This code traps the click event on the button (which is named HyperlinkButton) and sets the variable txt to point to the WebID text

FIGURE 16-13   *Defining a Hyperlink Data Type*

FIGURE 16-14   *Form Using a Hyperlink Data Type*

box. It then executes the Follow method on the Hyperlink property of WebID. The result is that Access links to the site as specified by the underlying URL. The same code could be placed on a label or a picture so that when the user clicks on either one, the application will link to the URL.

FIGURE 16-15 *Accessing a Hyperlink from a Button*

In addition to linking from a database application out to a URL or UNC site, the reverse is also possible. Other applications can link into an Access database table, form, or report. The details are similar to those shown here.

■ PUBLISHING TABLES, FORMS, AND REPORTS AS HTML DOCUMENTS

Tables (or queries on tables), forms, and reports can be published as HTML documents. Static HTML documents display data that was current at the time the HTML document was created. Tables, query results, forms, and reports can be published in static HTML format. Figure 16-4 is an example of a report that was published as static HTML.

Dynamic HTML documents display data that is current at the time the user accesses the HTML page. Tables, queries, and forms can be published as dynamic HTML, but reports may not. When a dynamic HTML document is accessed, the database is queried and results from the query are filled into the HTML document. To obtain this capability, the database must be located on a Windows NT server running Microsoft Internet Information Server or on a Windows 95 or NT workstation running the Personal Web Server. The database must also be accessible via ODBC.

When the developer saves a table, query, or form as a dynamic HTML document, Access creates two files and places them on the server. The first is called an Internet Database Connection file and has the file extension IDC. This file contains data necessary for the server to connect to the appropriate ODBC data source, run an SQL statement to obtain current values of required data, and provide ODBC-level security.

The IDC file has a pointer to a second file called an HTML Extension file; such files have the extension HTX. The HTX file contains a template of an HTML document; the server uses the results of the query from processing the IDC file to fill in data placeholders in the HTX file. The result of the merger of the query with the HTX file is a normal HTML page which is sent to the browser on the client. In this way, the client need only have a standard HTML browser to obtain dynamic HTML documents.

■ PUBLISHING FORMS AS ACTIVEX SERVER PAGES

Neither static nor dynamic HTML allows users to add, change, or delete database data. To do this over the web, the Access 97 developer must save an Access form as an ActiveX Server page. When this is done, Access creates an ActiveX Server Page file with the extension .ASP. This file is used by Microsoft's Internet Information Server, Version 3.0 or above, to process the form.

When the ASP file is created, the database form is converted to an ActiveX document and the form controls are converted to ActiveX controls. Also, Access creates server-side code to connect to the database. VBScript is also generated.

Using the ActiveX Server page, the user can add, change, and delete database data. However, there are important limitations. First, none of the VB code behind the form is saved as part of the ASP file, so application-specific logic will not be invoked. Also, no more than 64 users can be using the form at the same time, and there may be serious performance degradations with fewer users. If the workload is greater than this, Microsoft recommends converting the database to SQL Server.

Processing a database form with an ASP file is at present very much a work in progress. You can expect that significant changes will occur. Consult the Access developers web site for the latest information at http:\\www.microsoft.com.accessdev.

◆ MULTIMEDIA DATABASE APPLICATIONS

Earlier in this chapter we described static report publishing, query publishing, and application publishing network database applications. There is a fourth database application type that is also relevant for networks—multimedia. This section presents semantic-object models and relational database designs for two such applications. The first displays pictures and sounds in the form of a slide show, and the second extends the slide show application to include linked multimedia pages.

As of this writing, neither of these applications would be suitable for the Internet because they involve the transmission of many large binary files. They could be used on higher-speed intranets, however. They could also be used on personal computers if the images are stored locally.

■ A SLIDE SHOW MULTIMEDIA APPLICATION

Figure 16-16 shows a semantic object model for a database that tracks PICTURE, SOUND, and SLIDESHOW objects. As shown, the database stores a user-supplied name, a file name, and an optional description for each PICTURE or SOUND. Since

FIGURE 16-16 *Semantic Object Design for a Slide Show Multimedia Application*

a file name is stored, the database is linking to the image or sound. If the user changes the image or sound file, the next time the multimedia application is run, the changed file will be used.

An alternative design is possible if the underlying database supports binary large objects (BLOBs). With the alternative, an attribute to hold the binary data would replace the FileName attribute in PICTURE and SOUND. In this case, the picture or sound is embedded in the database. This means, however, that if the user changes the file externally, the changed file will need to be replaced into the database.

The SLIDESHOW object contains a multivalued group entitled Slide. This group contains an integer that represents the number of seconds the image is to remain on the screen and a link to the PICTURE to be shown. The minimum cardinality of Slide is zero, which is arguable. One could take the position that a slide shown cannot be a slide show without at least one slide. Within the group, both Seconds and the link to PICTURE are required. As shown, SLIDESHOW may or may not have a sound file.

A relational design for this database is shown in Figure 16-17. (As an aside, this document was created by generating the database in SALSA for the Desktop and printing the Model Information | Table report.) This database design is a straightforward application of the relational design techniques you learned in Chapter 7.

Figure 16-18 on page 414 shows pseudocode for an application to process this application. When the start button (or other control) is pressed, the code reads the sound filename and, if it is not null, starts it playing. Then, for each slide, it reads a slide file, displays it, and sets a timer. When the timer expires, the next slide is displayed.

To implement this code, the form needs a multimedia control for playing the sound file and a picture control for displaying the picture. Obviously, the controls need to be compatible with the type of files imported. Wave files need a control for playing .wav files, for example, and Gif images need a picture that displays .gif files.

■ A MULTIMEDIA APPLICATION WITH RECURSIVE PAGES

Figure 16-19 on page 414 shows a semantic object design for multimedia application that has recursive pages. The PICTURE, SOUND, and SLIDESHOW objects are similar to those shown in Figure 16-16. The only difference is that PICTUREs and SOUNDs can be used on PAGEs as well as on SLIDESHOW objects.

The PAGE object represents a screen display similar to an HTML page (and, in fact, these PAGEs could be materialized as HTML pages). A PAGE has an optional PICTURE, SOUND, SLIDESHOW, and text to be displayed. According to this design, each page has up to ten hot spots that link to other pages via the object HSLINK. The group Hotspot contains X and Y coordinates that store the location of the hot spots on the page. In addition, the CHILDLINK attribute links to an instance of HSLINK. The limit of ten is arbitrary; it could be twenty or fifty or five.

The HSLINK object contains label text plus two links back to page. The PARENTPAGE link is the paired link of CHILDLINK, and the CHILDPAGE link is the paired link of PARENTLINK. (This may seem backward at first reading. If so, make some example objects and trace the relationships through.)

The purpose of the SHOW object is to store the starting page of a particular multimedia program. To start a show, the user selects a particular instance of SHOW, and it loads the first PAGE of that show. From there, the user directs the processing by clicking on hot spots on the PAGE.

Figure 16-20 on page 415 shows the relational design for the model in Figure 16-16. As with Figure 16-17, this design was produced by SALSA for the Desktop and printed from it.

FIGURE 16-17   *Database Design for Model MM1.APM (Figure 16-16)*

PICTURE Table

Source Object or Item: PICTURE Object

Column Name	Data Type	Length	Null Allowed	Object Item Name	Index
Description	Memo		Yes	PICTURE.Description	
FileName	Text	50	No	PICTURE.FileName	Non-unique
ID_	Counter		No	SurrogateKey	PrimaryKey
PictureName	Text	25	No	PICTURE.PictureName	Unique

SOUND Table

Source Object or Item: SOUND Object

Column Name	Data Type	Length	Null Allowed	Object Item Name	Index
Description	Memo		Yes	SOUND.Description	
FileName	Text	50	No	SOUND.FileName	Non-unique
ID_	Counter		No	SurrogateKey	PrimaryKey
SoundName	Text	25	No	SOUND.SoundName	Unique

SLIDESHOW Table

Source Object or Item: SLIDESHOW Object

Column Name	Data Type	Length	Null Allowed	Object Item Name	Index
Description	Memo		Yes	SLIDESHOW.Description	
ID_	Counter		No	SurrogateKey	PrimaryKey
SlideShowName	Text	25	No	SLIDESHOW. SlideShowName	Unique
SOUND_ID_FK	Large Whole Number (± 2, 147,483,647)		Yes	ForeignKey	

SLIDESHOW_Slide Table

Source Object or Item: SLIDESHOW.Slide Item

Column Name	Data Type	Length	Null Allowed	Object Item Name	Index
ID_	Counter		No	SurrogateKey	PrimaryKey
PICTURE_ID_FK	Large Whole Number (± 2, 147,483,647)		No	ForeignKey	
Seconds	Whole Number (± 32,767)		No	SLIDESHOW.Slide.Seconds	
SLIDESHOW_ID_FK	Large Whole Number (± 2, 147,483,647)		No	ForeignKey	

FIGURE 16-18   *Pseudocode for Playing a SLIDESHOW*

```
On SLIDESHOW_CLICK(SLIDESHOW_PTR)
        Read SLIDESHOW_PTR.SOUND.FileName
        If SLIDESHOW_PTR.SOUND.FileName Not Null Then
                START_SOUND (SLIDESHOW_PTR.SOUND.FileName)
        End If
        Read First SLIDESHOW_PTR.Slide
        While SLIDESHOW_PTR.Slide Not Null
                Read SLIDESHOW_PTR.PICTURE.FileName
                Show SLIDESHOW_PTR.PICTURE.FileName
                Set Timer1 for Slide.Seconds Seconds
                Wait for Timer1
                Read Next SLIDESHOW_PTR.Slide
        Wend
End SLIDESHOW_CLICK
```

FIGURE 16-19   *Semantic Object Design for a Recursive Page Multimedia Application*

FIGURE 16-20   *Database Design for Model MM2.APM (Figure 16-16)*

PICTURE Table

Source Object or Item: PICTURE Object

Column Name	Data Type	Length	Null Allowed	Object Item Name	Index
Description	Memo		Yes	PICTURE.Description	
FileName	Text	50	No	PICTURE.FileName	Non-unique
ID_	Counter		No	SurrogateKey	PrimaryKey
PictureName	Text	25	No	PICTURE.PictureName	Unique

SOUND Table

Source Object or Item: SOUND Object

Column Name	Data Type	Length	Null Allowed	Object Item Name	Index
Description	Memo		Yes	SOUND.Description	
FileName	Text	50	No	SOUND.FileName	Non-unique
ID_	Counter		No	SurrogateKey	PrimaryKey
SoundName	Text	25	No	SOUND.SoundName	Unique

SLIDESHOW Table

Source Object or Item: SLIDESHOW Object

Column Name	Data Type	Length	Null Allowed	Object Item Name	Index
Description	Memo		Yes	SLIDESHOW.Description	
ID_	Counter		No	SurrogateKey	PrimaryKey
SlideShowName	Text	25	No	SLIDESHOW.SlideShowName	Unique
SOUND_ID_FK	Large Whole Number (± 2, 147,483,647)		Yes	ForeignKey	

SLIDESHOW_Slide Table

Source Object or Item: SLIDESHOW.Slide Item

Column Name	Data Type	Length	Null Allowed	Object Item Name	Index
ID_	Counter		No	SurrogateKey	PrimaryKey
PICTURE_ID_FK	Large Whole Number (± 2, 147,483,647)		No	ForeignKey	
Seconds	Whole Number (± 32,767)		No	SLIDESHOW.Slide.Seconds	
SLIDESHOW_ID_FK	Large Whole Number (± 2, 147,483,647)		No	ForeignKey	

(a)

FIGURE 16-20 *(Continued)*

PAGE Table

	Source Object or Item: PAGE Object					
Column Name	**Data Type**	**Length**	**Null Allowed**	**Object Item Name**	**Index**
ID_	Counter		No	SurrogateKey	PrimaryKey
PageName	Text	25	No	PAGE.PageName	Unique
PageText	Memo		Yes	PAGE.PageText	
PICTURE_ID_FK	Large Whole Number ($\pm$ 2, 147,483,647)		Yes	ForeignKey	
SLIDESHOW_ID_FK	Large Whole Number ($\pm$ 2, 147,483,647)		Yes	ForeignKey	
SOUND_ID_FK	Large Whole Number ($\pm$ 2, 147,483,647)		Yes	ForeignKey	

PAGE_HotSpot Table

	Source Object or Item: PAGE.HotSpot Item					
Column Name	**Data Type**	**Length**	**Null Allowed**	**Object Item Name**	**Index**
CHILDLINK_ID_FK	Large Whole Number ($\pm$ 2, 147,483,647)		No	ForeignKey	
ID_	Counter		No	SurrogateKey	PrimaryKey
PAGE_ID_FK	Large Whole Number ($\pm$ 2, 147,483,647)		No	ForeignKey	
X1	Whole Number ($\pm$ 32,767)		No	PAGE.HotSpot.X1	
Y1	Whole Number ($\pm$ 32,767)		No	PAGE.HotSpot.Y1	

HSLINK Table

	Source Object or Item: HSLINK Object					
Column Name	**Data Type**	**Length**	**Null Allowed**	**Object Item Name**	**Index**
CHILDPAGE_ID_FK	Large Whole Number ($\pm$ 2, 147,483,647)		No	ForeignKey	Unique
ID_	Counter		No	SurrogateKey	PrimaryKey
LabelCaption	Text	50	No	HSLINK.LabelCaption	Non-unique

SHOW Table

	Source Object or Item: SHOW Object					
Column Name	**Data Type**	**Length**	**Null Allowed**	**Object Item Name**	**Index**
Author	Text	25	Yes	SHOW.Author	Non-unique
Description	Memo		Yes	SHOW.Description	
FIRSTPAGE_ID_FK	Large Whole Number ($\pm$ 2, 147,483,647)		No	ForeignKey	
ID_	Counter		No	SurrogateKey	PrimaryKey
Title	Text	25	No	SHOW.Title	Unique

(b)

A portion of the logic of this application is shown in the pseudocode in Figure 16-21. The variables Level and HotSpot have a scope to all of the pseudocode. SHOW_CLICK converts the name of the first page of the given show to a pointer and then calls DISPLAY_PAGE to display the page. DISPLAY_PAGE stores the names of the pages of all hot spots on its page using the routine STORE_PAGE, and then it shows the PICTURE and starts the SOUND if appropriate. It also enables a button to play a SLIDESHOW if SLIDESHOW is not null. Finally, it displays the hot spots in the appropriate coordinates.

FIGURE 16-21   *Pseudocode for Displaying Recursive Pages*

```
Declare Level as Integer value = 0
Declare Hotspot(*,*) as string array

On SHOW_CLICK (SHOW_PTR)

        Declare PagePtr as pointer
        Set PagePtr = Pointer(SHOW_PTR.FIRSTPAGE.PageName)
        Call DISPLAY_PAGE(PagePtr)
End SHOW_CLICK

On HOTSPOT_CLICK (j)
        Declare PagePtr as pointer
        Set PagePtr = Pointer(HotSpot(Level, j))
        Call DISPLAY_PAGE (PagePtr)
End HOTSPOT_CLICK

Sub DISPLAY_PAGE (PagePtr)
        Call STORE_PAGE (PagePtr)
        If PagePtr.PICTURE.FileName Not Null Then
                Show PagePtr.PICTURE.FileName
        End If
        If PagePtr.SOUND.FileName Not Null Then
                START_SOUND (PagePtr.SOUND.FileName)
        End If
        If PagePtr.SLIDESHOW Not Null Then Enable SlideShow button
        Read First PagePtr.HotSpot
        While PagePtr.HotSpot Not Null
                Place PagePtr.HotSpot.HSLINK.LabelCaption
                        at {x-coord of PagePtr.HotSpot.HSLINK.X1 and
                        y-coord of PagePtr.HotSpot.HSLINK.Y1}
                Read Next PagePtr.HotSpot
        Wend
Sub STORE_PAGE (THISPAGE)
        Declare i as integer
        Level = Level + 1
        Read First THISPAGE.HotSpot
        i = 1
        While THISPAGE.HotSpot Not Null
                HotSpot(Level, i) =
                        THISPAGE.HotSpot.HSLINK.ChildMap.PageName
                Read Next THISPAGE.HotSpot
                i = i + 1
        Wend
End STORE_PAGE
```

When the user clicks on a hot spot, the event HOT_SPOT click is called with a parameter that indicates the index of the hot spot that has been clicked. This routine then calls DISPLAY_PAGE with a pointer to the correct page.

Figure 16-21 does not show the logic for ascending a level. This logic is left to the student as an exercise. Also, it would be possible to extend this design to allow for multiple pictures, sounds, or slide shows. It would also be possible to add another object type for movies or animations. All of these extensions are also left to you as exercises.

Either of these multimedia applications could be implemented as a personal database application, or they could be shared on an intranet. As mentioned previously, they probably are not feasible on the Internet due to the slow transmission speeds of most Internet client connections.

THE FUTURE FOR NETWORK DATABASE APPLICATIONS

By the time you read this chapter, much will have changed on the Internet and intranets. Most likely, there will be many more network databases and database applications than there are today. In the future, we can expect the number of such applications to increase geometrically. This will be especially true as new products and technologies are developed in several critical areas.

First, network security needs to be improved. While most intranets have adequate security using the security features of the server operating systems, there is still substantial risk because most intranet traffic is not encrypted. The security situation on the Internet is even worse. For databases to be as useful as they potentially can be, network security needs to be improved to the point that account numbers, transaction details, and even network cash can be transmitted at an acceptable level of risk.

Second, today's network database applications are too difficult to develop and maintain. New products and technologies need to be developed that will greatly increase the productivity of network database application developers. At present, many web sites have become stones around their developers' necks because of the difficulty and expense of maintaining the web sites.

Finally, new products and technologies need to be developed to increase the transmission speed on the Internet. Most multimedia applications are not yet feasible over the Net because of the limited speeds. As Internet transmission speed is increased, it is likely that the distinction between the Internet and intranets will disappear. Instead, each user will have access to a single network, one that can be local, departmental, enterprisewide, or even worldwide. Most experts believe that such networks should become like the telephone system. When I use the phone, I make no distinction among local, city, state, national, and international calls. So, too, will my computer network capability evolve.

Today and even more in the future, the skills required to develop database applications on the network will be in high demand. One can persuasively argue that, of all the applications of database technology, network database applications will be the most important in the next ten years. Follow this area closely.

SUMMARY

A network is a collection of computers that communicate using a standardized protocol. Public networks can be used by anyone who pays the required fee; users of private networks must be preauthorized to connect to the network. The Internet is a public computer network that uses the TCP/IP protocol. The Internet began as a military research project known as ARPANET. In 1984, MILNET split off from ARPANET, and over time ARPANET has come to be known as the Internet.

Services available on the Internet include mail, newsgroups, TelNet, FTP, and the World Wide Web. Initially, almost all Internet servers ran a version of UNIX, and Internet commands have a definite UNIX flavor to them. IN 1989, the hypertext transfer protocol or HTTP was proposed at CERN. The hypertext markup language (HTML), a subset of the standard generalized markup language (SGML), was proposed at the same time. In 1993, NCSA invented a graphical HTML display program known as Mosaic. Today Mosaic, Netscape Navigator, and Microsoft's Internet Explorer are the most popular web browsers. Internet servers include Unix servers from CERN and NCSA and a Windows NT server from Microsoft. HTML, URL, and MIME type codes are three standards that emerged from the web that are important to network database applications. Web applications are request-oriented and stateless.

The most common definition of an intranet is a private LAN or WAN that uses TCP/IP, HTML, and browsers. Intranets either are not connected to public networks or are connected via a firewall. Intranets have performance that is orders of magnitude faster than that of the Internet (28.8 kbs compared to 100,000 kbs).

A network database application is a database application in which the clients use an HTML browser and the server includes an Internet-style server. Three common types of network database applications are static report publishing, query publishing, and application publishing.

Network database alternatives are summarized in Figure 16-7. Alternatives that involve little client processing (thin clients) are CGI with Perl or a similar server language. Less thin clients involve some applications processing using VBScript or Java Script. Thicker client applications can be written in Java or may use one or more ActiveX controls. Traditional client-server database applications and file-processing applications involve the most processing on the client machines and require the thickest clients. ActiveX is an architecture that enables ActiveX components to work with one another via the IUnknown and Query Interfaces of Microsoft's COM. ActiveX documents are collections of ActiveX controls that can be displayed in a browser with no additional viewers required. They are analogous to HTML pages.

Access 97 includes features and functions for publishing database applications in both the Internet and intranet environments. Data can be imported, exported, and linked to HTML files; hyperlinks can be followed out of or into Access applications; and tables, forms, and reports can be generated in HTML format. Additionally, forms and datasheets (table data viewed in a spreadsheet-like format) can be saved as ActiveX Server pages.

Databases can be used to store the elements of multimedia applications. Linked media involve storing the name of the media (e.g., picture, sound) file. Embedded media involve storing the media bit streams in the database itself.

Network database applications are growing dramatically. In the future, they will grow even more as network security improves, as technologies and products are developed that increase the productivity of applications creators, and as the speed of the Internet increases.

GROUP I QUESTIONS

16.1   Explain the terms *network, public network,* and *private network* as they are used in this chapter.

16.2   Define *Internet.*

16.3   What is TCP/IP, and how it is used?

16.4   What is the difference between ARPANET and MILNET?

16.5   List and explain four Internet services besides the World Wide Web.

16.6   Why are many of the Internet service commands similar to UNIX?

16.7   What is HTTP, and how is it used?

16.8   What is HTML, and how is it used?

16.9   What is SGML, and how does it relate to HTML?

16.10 What is a browser? Name three popular browser products.

16.11 How is HTML important as a standard to network database applications?

16.12 What is a URL, and why is it important to network applications?

16.13 Give examples of three valid URLs.

16.14 What is MIME? Why is it important to network applications? To network database applications?

16.15 Explain why Internet applications are request-oriented. Why is this important to network database applications?

16.16 Explain why Internet applications are stateless. Why is this important to network database applications?

16.17 What is an intranet? How does it differ from the Internet?

16.18 What is a firewall, and what is its purpose?

16.19 Explain two characteristics of intranets that differentiate them from the Internet.

16.20 Define the term *network database application*.

16.21 Explain the purpose and nature of static report publishing.

16.22 Explain the purpose and nature of query publishing.

16.23 Explain the purpose and nature of application publishing.

16.24 Describe three factors that limit application publishing on the Internet.

16.25 Explain the meaning of each of the vertical bars in Figure 16-7.

16.26 Explain the difference between a thin client and a thick client.

16.27 What is CGI, and how is it used?

16.28 What is Perl? Can languages other than Perl be used with CGI?

16.29 Summarize the advantages and disadvantages of CGI.

16.30 What is VBScript, and how is it used?

16.31 What is Java Script, and how is it used?

16.32 How does VBScript relate to Visual Basic?

16.33 Explain one way that VBScript can be embedded in an HTML page.

16.34 What is Java, and why is it important?

16.35 What is Java bytecode, and how is it important to network database applications?

16.36 Illustrate two ways that Java could be used to implement a network database application.

16.37 What are the major advantages and disadvantages of Java?

16.38 What is ActiveX?

16.39 Why is it inappropriate to contrast ActiveX with Java?

16.40 What roles do the IUnkown Interface and Query Interface serve?

16.41 What is the difference between an ActiveX control and an ActiveX document?

16.42 What is a hyperlink?

16.43 Explain the format and use of a UNC.

16.44 Explain the format of a hyperlink data item. What portion does the user see?

16.45 What is the difference between static and dynamic HTML?

16.46 Explain the purpose of IDC and HTX files.

16.47 Explain the purpose of ASP files.

16.48 Explain the purpose of each of the attributes in the SLIDESHOW semantic object in Figure 16-16.

16.49 Explain the purpose of each of the columns in the SLIDESHOW_Slide table in Figure 16-17.

16.50 Explain the purpose of each of the attributes in the PAGE and HSLINK semantic objects in Figure 16-19.

16.51 Justify the statement that the CHILDLINK attribute in PAGE is paired with the PARENTPAGE attribute in HSLINK in Figure 16-19.

16.52 Explain the purpose of each of the columns in the PAGE_HotSpot and the HSLINK table in Figure 16-20.

16.53 What purpose does the Level variable serve in the logic in Figure 16-21? Write pseudocode to ascend a level and display the page one level up.

GROUP II QUESTIONS

16.54 Some industry analysts have said that the Internet offers the first real opportunity for companies to break the near monopoly that Microsoft has on the computer industry. First, do you agree or disagree that Microsoft has a near monopoly on the industry? If so, why? If not, what is the nature of the relationship between Microsoft and the computer industry? Second, how do you think the Internet offers an opportunity for other companies to better compete with Microsoft?

16.55 Both Java and Perl have the advantage of operating system portability. Since Microsoft Windows is installed on about 90 percent of the world's microcomputers, does portability matter? Is portability more important on the Internet than on an intranet? If you were a software vendor other than Microsoft, would you tout portability as an advantage? Or would you just develop your programs to run under Windows and not attempt to invest in other platforms?

16.56 Is a thin client better than a thick client? In formulating your answer, consider the type of application, whether the application is an Internet or an intranet application, the type of user, and the functions of the application. Can you develop general rules for deciding when to have a thin client and when to have a thick one?

PROJECTS USING SALSA FOR THE DESKTOP

A. Change the model in Figure 16-19 to include a MOVIE semantic object. Link the movie to the PAGE object. Explain how you might build the application to allow the user to invoke the MOVIE. Also create a PHOTOGRAPHER object and link it to PICTURE. Assume each PHOTOGRAPHER has a standard-use fee for including a PICTURE in a multimedia program. Add an attribute to SHOW that computes the use fee for all PICTUREs in a given SHOW.

B. Implement the model in Figure 16-16 and the code in Figure 16-17. You will need to display the picture using the Picture control, which you will need to place on the SLIDESHOW form. The logic in Figure 16-17 can be implemented using SALSA's script language and the timer event. To play sound, you will need to acquire a multimedia VBX control. When finished, your application should be able to accept the names of files having pictures and sounds and play them back.

VI

Part VI considers nonrelational database processing and presents what many would consider to be both the future and the past of this discipline. Chapter 17 addresses object-oriented database processing, a new style of database management that is not yet in widespread commercial use but that many believe will ultimately replace relational database processing. Others would disagree and claim that either relational database processing will coexist with object-oriented database processing or that the two will merge. In any case, object-oriented databases are beginning to appear, and they will likely play some important role in the future of database management.

Chapter 18 presents the hierarchical and network data models. The hierarchical model is discussed in terms of DL/I, a language developed by IBM and the basis of IMS and DL/I, which were at one time IBM's only database products. The network model is discussed in terms of the CODASYL DBTG model, a model that twenty years ago was proposed as a national standard but that today sees only very limited use. These models are an important part of the heritage of database processing, and you may encounter them. If you do work with them, it will likely be either in a maintenance mode or while converting them to another model and product.

NONRELATIONAL DATABASE PROCESSING

17

OBJECT-ORIENTED DATABASE PROCESSING

• • • • • • • • • • • • • • •

In the last ten years a new style of programming, called **object-oriented programming (OOP),** has emerged. This new style has demonstrated such significant advantages over traditional programming that almost all new development at software vendors is done in OOP. In addition, many corporations have decided to standardize on OOP for their new application development.

As you will learn in this chapter, OOP is a radical departure from traditional programming. Because of this difference, file processing and traditional, relational DBMS products are difficult to use for object storage. As a result, a new type of DBMS—the **object DBMS (ODBMS)**—has been developed. While ODBMS have significant advantages over traditional techniques for object storage, most data in commercial systems today are in relational format. Organizations are reluctant to spend the time and money necessary to convert all of their file and relational data into ODBMS format. Furthermore, current ODBMS lack some features that are essential in the commercial environment. Hence, at present, ODBMS are not seeing widespread use. This may change in the near future, however, and it is important for you to understand the characteristics of ODBMS, their advantages and disadvantages, and the differences between ODBMS and traditional DBMS. We begin with a brief introduction to OOP.

◆ A SKETCH OF OBJECT-ORIENTED PROGRAMMING

Object-oriented programming (OOP) is a way of designing and coding programs. OOP is substantially different from traditional programming, as it entails a new way of thinking about programming structures. Instead of viewing programs as sequences of instructions to be processed, OOP views programs as sets of data structures that have both data elements and program instructions.

Another way to understand the difference between traditional programming and OOP is that traditional programming is organized around logic first and data second, whereas OOP is organized around data first and logic second. To design a traditional program to create an order, for example, we would first develop a flowchart or pseudocode of the logic of the ordering process. The data to be processed would be documented as a part of the logic.

When developing an object-oriented program to create an order, we would first identify the objects involved, say, ORDER, SALESPERSON, ITEM, and CUSTOMER. We would then design those objects as data elements and programs that are shared or *exposed* to one another. Finally, we would create a flowchart or pseudocode of the behaviors of the objects.

■ OOP Terminology

An OOP object is an **encapsulated structure** having both **attributes** and **methods.** The term *encapsulated* means that it is complete in itself; programs external to an object know nothing of its structure and need to know nothing of its structure. The external appearance of an object is referred to as its **interface.** The interface consists of the attributes and methods that are visible to the outside world. The encapsulated internals of an object are referred to as its **implementation.**

The *attributes*[1] of OOP objects are arranged in a particular structure, and they are quite similar to the attributes of semantic objects. Finally, OOP objects contain *methods,* or sequences of instructions that the object executes.

For example, an OOP object may have a method (program) to display itself, one to create itself, and one to modify a portion of itself. Consider a method that modifies a CUSTOMER object. This method, which is part of the OOP object, is a program; to modify the OOP object, this program contains instructions to obtain data for the modification from the user or other source, and modify its data.

OOP objects interact by calling each other's methods. The CUSTOMER modify method, for example, invokes other objects' methods to obtain data, perform modifications on itself, and request services. These other objects' methods are called and may invoke yet other methods, and so forth. Since all the objects are encapsulated, none can or need to know the structure of any other object. This reduces complexity and promotes effective cohesion.

Many objects have methods in common. To reduce the duplication in programming, objects are subclassed from more general classes. An object, say O_1, that is a subclass of another object, say O_2, **inherits** all the attributes and methods of O_2. For example, an application may have a general class EMPLOYEE with two subtypes, SALESPERSON and ENGINEER. Methods that are common to all three object classes such as GetPhoneNumber are made a part of the EMPLOYEE class. The SALESPERSON and ENGINEER subclasses inherit those methods. Hence, when a program issues a call to GetPhoneNumber on either a SALESPERSON or an ENGINEER, the GetPhoneNumber method in EMPLOYEE is invoked. If the application requirements are such that ENGINEERs have a different way of providing phone numbers than other employees, then ENGINEER can have a special version of GetPhoneNumber as part of its class. That special version will be called when a program invokes GetPhoneNumber on ENGINEER. This characteristic is called **polymorphism.**

Several terms are commonly used in OOP discussions. The logical structure of an object—its name, attributes, and methods—is called an **object class.** A group of object classes is called an **object class library.** And instances of objects are called **object instances,** or simply **objects.**

Objects are created by calling object constructors, programs that obtain main memory and create the structures necessary to instantiate an object. Object destructors are programs that unbind objects and free memory. Objects can be **transient** or **persistent.** A transient object exists only in volatile memory during the

---

[1]The term *properties* is sometimes used instead of *attribute.* In the ODMG-93 standard, the term *property* is used instead of *attribute,* and *attribute* is used in a more restricted sense, as you will see. When reading the terms *class, type, property,* and *attribute,* pay attention to the context, as different authors use these terms slightly differently. Here we will use the terms in a way that is consistent with the source of the topic.

FIGURE 17-1   *Sample of CUSTOMER Object*

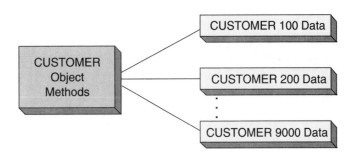

CUSTOMER Object Class

Object methods are stored once for each class
Object data is stored once for each object instance

execution of a program. When the program terminates, the object is lost. A persistent object is an object that has been saved to permanent storage, such as disk. A persistent object survives the execution of a program and can be read back into memory from storage.

The purpose of an ODBMS is to provide persistent object storage. An object is both data and methods; this means an ODBMS, unlike a traditional DBMS, should store object programs as well as data. Since each object of a given class has the same set of methods, the methods need be stored only once for the class; in contrast, data items must be stored once for each object instance. Figure 17-1 illustrates this point. In point of fact, few ODBMS today provide method persistence, but this is likely to change in the future.

OOP EXAMPLE

Figures 17-2 and 17-3 present a portion of an object-oriented interface and a sample method. To avoid details unimportant to this discussion, the code is written in a generic form that is consistent with object programming but is not in any particular object-oriented language. Consider this code to be something like pseudocode for an object program.

Figure 17-2 shows a portion of the interface of several objects used for order processing. Each object has a set of methods and attributes that it exposes. Every object has a constructor method (Create) and a destructor (Destroy). Some of the methods take parameters; the Assign method of SALESPERSON, for example, takes a pointer to the ORDER object and a value of ZipCode as its parameters. Attributes that are marked with (R) may only be read; attributes marked (RW) may be read or written (changed).

The notation in Figure 17-3 on page 429 needs explanation. First, the braces { } represent remarks—they are used here to describe the function of program code that needs to be written but has been left out of this example for brevity or because it is unimportant to this discussion. The Dim statement is used to declare variables and their types, as it does in Basic. LineItem is declared as a structure having the data elements listed in the brackets [ ]. The exclamation point (!) is used as a separator between an object and one of its methods. Thus, CUSTOMER!Find refers to the Find method of the CUSTOMER object. This character is pronounced "bang." A period is used as a separator between an object and one of its attributes. Thus, CustObj.ZipCode refers to the ZipCode attribute of the object pointed to by CustObj.

FIGURE 17-2   *Sample Objects, Methods, and Attributes*

Object	Methods	Attributes
EMPLOYEE	Create Save Destroy …	Number(R) Name(R) …
SALESPERSON (subclass of EMPLOYEE)	Create Save Destroy Assign(ORDER, ZipCode) …	TotalCommission(R) TotalOrders(RW) …
CUSTOMER	Create Save Destroy Assign(ORDER) Find …	Name(R) Phone(R) ZipCode(R) CurrentBalance(RW) …
ITEM	Create Save Destroy Find(Number) Take(ORDER, Quantity) Put(ORDER, Quantity) Find …	Number(R) Name(R) Description(R) Price …
ORDER	Create Save Destroy Print …	Number(R) Date(R) Total(R) CustomerName(R) SalespersonName(R) …

Two keywords are also used in Figure 17-3. **Nothing** is a special value of an object pointer that is used to represent a null value. In this figure, the expression

If CustObj = Nothing

means to compare the value of the object variable CustObj to the null object pointer. **Me** is an object pointer that references the object executing the code. When the code in Figure 17-3 is run, it will be run by an instance of the ORDER object, since it is an ORDER method. Me refers to the particular ORDER object that is executing the code.

The ORDER!Create method begins by obtaining data about the name of the customer placing the order; it is unimportant to our purposes how this value is obtained—it might be from a text box on a form. The Find method of CUSTOMER is then invoked to find a customer having the given name and to set a pointer to the object that has been found. The particulars of how an instance is found are encapsulated in CUSTOMER!Find, and we do not know how the selection is made, what happens if there is more than one customer that has that name, or other details.

The result of this operation is to set CustObj to either the value of a valid pointer to a CUSTOMER object or to the special value Nothing, which is the null pointer. If CustObj is null, then CustObj is set to a pointer to a new CUSTOMER object created by CUSTOMER!Create. As shown, the code assumes that a pointer to a valid customer object is returned at this point. In fact, CustObj should be

FIGURE 17-3   *Segment of an Object-Oriented Program*

```
ORDER!Create method
Dim CustObj as object, SPObj as object, ItemObj as object
Dim OrderTotal as Currency, OrderDate as Date, OrderNumber as Number
Dim LineItem as Structure
        [
        ItemNumber as Number,
        ItemName as Text(25),
        ItemQuantity as Count,
        QuantityBackOrdered as Count,
        ExtendedPrice as Currency
        ]

        {Get CustomerName from some source}
        Set CustObj = CUSTOMER!Find (CustomerName)
        If CustObj = Nothing then
                Set CustObj = CUSTOMER!Create(CustomerName)
        End If

        CustObj!Assign(Me)
        Set SPObj = SALESPERSON!Assign(Me, CustObj.ZipCode)

        {Get ItemNumber, Quantity of first ITEM from some source}
        Me.OrderTotal = 0
        While Not ItemNumber.EOF

                Me.LineItem!Create
                Me.LineItem.ItemNumber = ItemNumber

                Set ItemObj = ITEM!Find (ItemNumber)
                {process problem if ITEM not exist}

                Me.LineItem.ItemName = ItemObj.Name
                Me.LineItem.Quantity = ITEM!Take (Quantity)
                If Me.LineItem.Quantity <> Quantity Then
                        Me.LineItem.QuantityBackOrdered = Quantity - Me.LineItem.Quantity
                End If

                Me.LineItem.ExtendedPrice = Me.LineItem.Quantity* ITEM.Price
                Me.OrderTotal = Me.OrderTotal + Me.LineItem.ExtendedPrice

                ItemObj!Save
                Me.LineItem!Save
                {Get ItemNumber, Quantity of next ITEM from some source
                assume the source sets EOF to true when there are no more}
        While End

        SPObj.TotalOrders = SPObj.TotalOrders + Me.OrderTotal
        CustObj.CurrentBalance = CustObj.CurrentBalance + Me.OrderTotal

        SPObj!Save
        CustObj!Save
        ME!Save
End ORDER!Create
```

checked again to see if it is null, but, for brevity, we will omit all such checking in the rest of this program segment.

CUSTOMER exposes a method Assign that is to be called to assign a CUSTOMER to an ORDER. Because of encapsulation, we do not know what the Assign method does, but we do call it and pass Me, the pointer to the executing object. In fact, in this application, the Assign method is an example of what is called a **callback.** ORDER!Create is giving a pointer to itself to CUSTOMER so that CUSTOMER can keep track of which ORDERs it has. One reason for doing this is that when a CUSTOMER object is to be destroyed, it can call all ORDERs that are linked to it before it departs. In that way, ORDER can destroy its pointer to CUSTOMER when that pointer becomes invalid. There are many other uses for callbacks, as well.

Next, ORDER!Create sets SPObj to a salesperson object. We are passing the value of the customer's ZipCode, so it would seem that ZipCode has something to do with how a salesperson is assigned to us. Again, because of encapsulation, we do not know how this is done, however. By hiding the allocation methodology, the SALESPERSON object is free to change its allocation method without disturbing this or any other program's logic. In fact, no code in Figure 17-3 would need to be changed if SALESPERSON.Assign started using phases of the moon to allocate salespeople!

The next section of code fills in line item values. Observe that the keyword Me is used to refer to local data items. (In fact, in most OO languages, Me would be assumed and would not be necessary; we put it here for explicitness.) At the start of each repetition of the While loop, storage is allocated for another line item in the method LineItem!Create.

The method ITEM!Take is used to withdraw items from inventory. Notice that the logic assumes that if a number of items less than the quantity requested was allocated, then the balance of the items has been backordered. Also, observe that the changed ITEM is saved after each line item has been processed. Also, unlike with CUSTOMER or SALESPERSON, no callback is issued to ITEM. This means that the ITEM objects do not know which ORDERs are connected to them. Apparently, for this application, it is unimportant for the ITEM objects to know which ORDERs are using their data.

The loop continues until there are no more items to be placed on the order. At that point, totals are adjusted in the SALESPERSON and CUSTOMER objects, and both of those objects and Me are saved.

The segment of code in Figure 17-3 is typical of object-oriented code, and it brings to the surface a number of important issues for object-oriented database systems. In particular, How are the objects to be made persistent?

OBJECT PERSISTENCE

Figure 17-4 summarizes the data structures that exist after an ORDER has been created. In the order object, there are base order data, including ORDER.Number, ORDER.Date, ORDER.Total, as well as a repeating group for line items that have ItemNumber, ItemName, Quantity, a QuantityBackordered, and Extended Price. In addition, the base order data have a pointer to the CUSTOMER object assigned, a pointer to the SALESPERSON object assigned, and a pointer to each ITEM for each line item. These pointers are part of the ORDER object's data. To make this object persistent, all of this data must be stored. Further, although we do not know their structure, each CUSTOMER, SALESPERSON, and ITEM object must also be stored. The CUSTOMER and SALESPERSON objects are also storing a pointer back to ORDER as a result of the callbacks (!Assign methods) that were issued.

The pointers pose a particular problem. In most object-oriented languages, pointers are some form of in-memory address. Such addresses are valid only during the execution of the program; if the program terminates and is later restarted, the addresses of the objects will be different. Hence, when storing an object, the in-memory pointers need to be transformed into a permanent unique identifier that will be valid for the lifetime of the object, whether it is in memory or not. The process of transforming permanent identifiers into in-memory addresses is called **swizzling.**

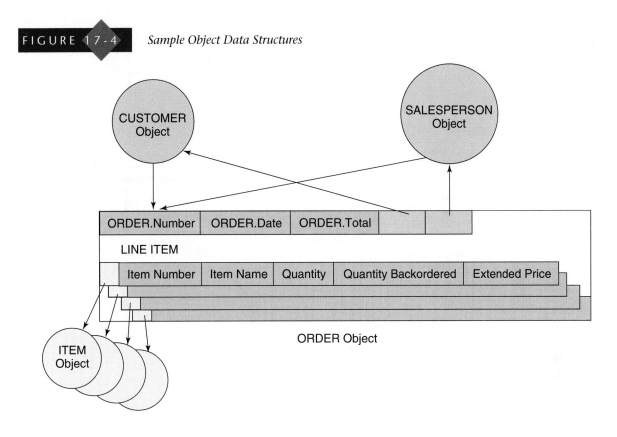

FIGURE 17-4   *Sample Object Data Structures*

FIGURE 17-5   *Tasks for Object Persistence*

- Save object instance data values
- Convert in-memory object pointers
  to permanent, unique IDs (swizzling)
- Save object class methods

Finally, recall that an object is defined as data values plus methods. Thus, to make an object persistent, we must save both the methods and the object values. Unlike data values, however, every object in a given class has the same methods, so we need store the methods only once for all object instances in the object class. The requirements for object persistence are listed in Figure 17-5.

Objects can be made persistent using traditional file storage, a relational DBMS, or an ODMBS. We now consider each of these.

■ OBJECT PERSISTENCE USING TRADITIONAL FILE STORAGE

Objects can be saved using traditional file storage, but doing so places a large burden on the programmer. Consider the data in Figure 17-4. The developer might decide to create one file to contain methods for all of the objects and a second file to contain the data for all of the objects. To do this, a generalized data structure will need to be developed to pack the methods and data into the files and to retrieve them when necessary. Figure 17-6 shows an example of such a file for storing just the data items. (Another will need to be developed to store the methods.)

FIGURE 17-6　*Using a Fixed-Length File to Hold Object Data*

RecordNumber	RecordCode	Contents	Link
1	ORDER	ORDER 100 data	4
2	SALESPERSON	SALESPERSON Jones data	null
3	CUSTOMER	CUSTOMER 10000 data	null
4	LINEITEM	LineItem of ORDER 100 data	5
5	LINEITEM	LineItem of ORDER 100 DATA	null
…	…	…	…

To use such a file, the programmer will write code in the Save methods to pack and unpack object data in these records, to find objects on demand, to manage unused file space, and so forth. Also, the developer will need to devise and implement swizzling and de-swizzling algorithms. Further, there is a bootstrap problem. All methods are stored in files, including the methods that store and read methods. How is the method that reads the first method to be obtained?

All of these problems are surmountable; they have been solved in operating system file-processing subsystems for many years. But, that is just the point. Such programming is slow, tedious, risky, and difficult, and it has already been done for traditional file processing. Why should such programming need to be done one more time?

Because of these problems, traditional file storage is viable for object persistence only when the application has a few simple objects whose structure does not change. Few business applications fall into this category.

■ OBJECT PERSISTENCE USING RELATIONAL DBMS

Another approach to object persistence is to use commercial relational DBMS products. This approach places a smaller burden on the developer than traditional file processing, because basic file management issues like record allocation, indexing, space management, and so forth are handled by the DBMS. The data management tasks left to the programmer are to define relational structures to represent the objects and to write the code to interface with the DBMS to get and put objects and to swizzle pointers.

Figure 17-7 shows the tables needed to store ORDER, LINEITEM, CUSTOMER, SALESPERSON, and ITEM objects. We've seen this design before. The only new element is a table to store object methods; this table contains a memo field that stores the method code.

To get or put an object, the programmer needs to write code to access the DBMS and cause it to process the object data. In most cases, SQL statements are embedded in the Save methods in a manner similar to that shown for DB2 in Chapter 13.

Relational databases represent relationships via foreign keys. This means that the application programmer must devise some means to use foreign keys to make relationships persistent. The most common way of doing this is to code the creation of a unique ID in the object's constructor method. This ID could be stored in the object's base table and exposed as a read-only property. Objects that need to link to the object can save the ID value. This strategy creates the problem that when an object is destroyed, it must notify all objects that are linked to it so that they can remove the pointer to the soon-to-be-destroyed object and take other action as appropriate. This is one reason for having callbacks like those shown in the Assign methods in Figure 17-3.

Object thinking and design bury relationships in context. Thus, when an ORDER object assigns itself to a SALESPERSON, it is concerned only with its side of

Relations Needed to Store EMPLOYEE, SALESPERSON, CUSTOMER, ITEM, and ORDER Objects

EMPLOYEE (<u>Number</u>, Name,...)

SALESPERSON (<u>*Number*</u>, TotalCommission, TotalOrders,...)

CUSTOMER (<u>Name</u>, Phone, ZipCode, CurrentBalance,...)

ITEM (<u>Number</u>, Name, Description, Price,...)

ORDER (<u>Number</u>, Date, Total, *SALESPERSON.Number*, *CUSTOMER.Name...*)

LINEITEM (<u>*ORDER.Number*</u>, <u>*ITEM.Number*</u>, ItemName, ItemQuantity,

           QuantityBackOrdered, ExtendedPrice,...)

METHODS (<u>ObjectName</u>, <u>MethodName</u>, MethodCode)

that relationship. If the ORDER wants to bind to many SALESPEOPLE, it does so. ORDER has no idea whether or not a SALESPERSON has a relationship to one or many ORDERs. Such knowledge is encapsulated in the SALESPERSON object and is no part of the ORDER logic.

This characteristic is either an advantage or a disadvantage, depending on how you think about it. Suppose that an ORDER can have several SALESPEOPLE and that a SALESPERSON can have many ORDERs. In database parlance, ORDER and SALESPERSON have an M:N relationship. Consequently, in the relational database world, an intersection table is defined to hold the identifiers of the ORDERs and SALESPEOPLE that are related to one another.

In the object world, SALESPERSON knows it has many ORDERs, and ORDER knows it has many SALESPEOPLE, but they do not know about each other. Hence, the data structures for carrying the relationship will be separated. ORDER will contain storage for many links to SALESPERSON, and SALESPERSON will contain storage for many links to ORDER. The sets of links will be isolated from each other.

Does this matter? No, not as long as there are no errors in the object processing. But there is risk because the object links are separate but not independent. If ORDER 1000 is linked to SALESPERSON A, then, by definition, SALESPERSON A is linked to ORDER 1000. In the relational DBMS world, since the relationship is carried in a row of an intersection table, deleting the row from one side deletes it from the other side automatically. But in the object world, the relationship could be deleted on one side but not on the other. Thus, ORDER 1000 might be linked to SALESPERSON A, but SALESPERSON A might not be linked to ORDER 1000. Clearly, this is an error and should not be allowed to occur, but it is possible if the relationships are defined from a purely object-oriented perspective.

Using a relational DBMS for object persistence is less work for the developer than using traditional file structures. There is still the need, however, for the developer to convert the objects into a relational design, to write SQL (or other code) to get and put the objects using the DBMS, and to swizzle. ODBMS are designed to accomplish these tasks.

■ OBJECT PERSISTENCE USING ODBMS

The third alternative for object persistence is to use an ODBMS. Such products are purpose-built for object persistence and hence save the most work for the application programmer.

An ODBMS is designed to be integrated with an object-oriented language. Thus, no special structures, such as SQL, need be embedded in the application code. For the example in Figure 17-4, it is possible that the Save methods are, in fact, methods provided by the ODBMS. Hence, by invoking the Save method, the programmer has invoked the ODBMS.

FIGURE 17-8   *Application Development Work for Object Persistence for Three Alternatives*

ODBMS	Relational DBMS	Traditional File Processing
• Invoke ODBMS Save methods	• Convert memory addresses to permanent ID and reverse (swizzling) • Define relational data structures • Create SQL (or other code) • Embed SQL in program	• Convert memory addresses to permanent ID and reverse (swizzling) • Define file data structures • Create object persistence code • Invoke object persistence code • Pack and unpack objects into file structures • Find objects on demand • Manage file space • Other file management tasks

Further, ODBMS products include a compiler (or are included with the compiler, depending on your point of view) that processes the source code and automatically creates data structures in the object database for storing objects. Hence, unlike with relational database or file processing, the object-oriented programmer need not transform objects into relation or file structures; the ODBMS does that automatically.

Finally, since ODBMS are designed for object persistence, some form of swizzling is built in. Thus, code like that in Figure 17-4 would be unaware of the problem. An object obtains a link to another object, and that link is a valid one, for all time. If the link takes different forms, the program is unaware of it.

This leads to a characteristic of ODBMS that is called single-level memory. With certain ODBMS, the program (hence, the programmer) need not know whether an object is in memory or not. If ORDER 1000 has a link to SALESPERSON A, then ORDER 1000 can use the exposed properties of SALESPERSON A without ever checking to see if those data are in memory or issuing a read or SQL statement. If SALESPERSON A is in memory, the ODBMS makes the link; if not, the ODBMS reads SALESPERSON A into memory and then makes the link.

Figure 17-8 compares the work required for each of the three alternatives for object persistence. Clearly, an ODBMS provides substantial benefit to the object-oriented programmer, so why are such products not in use everywhere? We consider that question in the next section.

COMPARING ODBMS AND TRADITIONAL DBMS

At this point you can probably understand why it is difficult to give a short and specific answer to the question, What is the difference between a relational DBMS and an ODBMS? They have completely different paradigms. It's not that comparing these two is like comparing apples and oranges; it's more like comparing them is like comparing a wrench to a gallon of gasoline. They both involve automobile transportation, but in very different ways.

To be able to answer the question, first consider the advantages and disadvantages of ODBMS, as listed in Figure 17-9.

■ ODBMS ADVANTAGES

The first advantage of ODBMS is that they are integrated with object-oriented programming languages. The programmer need not learn a programming language and then learn SQL. Using the language will automatically provide object persistence. Further, since ODBMS are designed for object-oriented programming,

FIGURE 17-9   *ODBMS Advantages and Disadvantages*

Advantages	Disadvantages
Integrated with programming language	Requires object-oriented programming
Automatic method storage (when available)	Little existing data in object form
User-defined types	Nonexistent (or poor) query and reporting tools
Complex data readily processed	
Automatic persistent object IDs	Limited concurrency control and transaction management
Single-level memory	Unproven performance
	Substantial change and learning required

method storage and management are automatic.[2] In theory, a programmer can code an instruction that causes object methods to be invoked and the ODBMS will find the appropriate methods, load them in memory, and cause them to be executed. The programmer need not be concerned with the storage and management of object code.

Second, ODBMS provide for the definition of user-defined types. Unlike traditional DBMS products where the basic data types are hard-coded in the DBMS and are unchangeable by the users, with an ODBMS the user can encode any type of structure that is necessary and the ODBMS will manage that type. (The object-oriented language compiler will perform type checking, as well.)

Because of user-defined types and because relationships are defined in context, it is easy to define complex data in an ODBMS. There is no need to define 1:1 or 1:N or N:M relationships and create the appropriate foreign key structures as with the relational DBMS. Instead, the programmer defines the relationship in context, and the ODBMS creates the necessary data structures in the database.

Finally, ODBMS automatically create persistent object IDs and provide swizzling. This not only saves programmers work, but it also enables the ODBMS to provide single-level memory so that the programmer need not be concerned with whether or not an object is located in memory.

■ ODBMS DISADVANTAGES

The disadvantages of ODBMS are listed in the second column of Figure 17-9. First, using an ODBMS requires object-oriented programming. While there are substantial advantages to such programming, not every company or department is willing to make the shift, at least not all at once. There are billions of lines of perfectly good program code already in existence. Such code is written in traditional style, and many companies believe that transforming it to object-oriented code would not be worth the enormous expense.

Moreover, most organizational data are in either file or traditional database format. Converting those data to an ODBMS is also very expensive. And, as with code, there is no compelling reason to make that switch.

---

[2]Again, ODBMS vary widely in their support for method management. Some provide very little support, others provide more.

A third disadvantage is that ODBMS do not, today, provide effective query and reporting tools. The application programmer must code query and reporting capabilities into his or her programs. This is laborious and expensive. In addition, query and reporting requirements often change, and users may want to change the structure of queries and reports themselves. This is not feasible when the relevant code is buried in object-oriented programs.

In addition, ODBMS are immature concerning concurrency control and transaction management capabilities. The features and functions for defining logical units of work, for committing and aborting transactions, and for rollback and rollforward are either nonexistent or are primitive as compared to traditional operational DBMS products. Also, the performance of ODBMS in high-volume, transaction-oriented environments is an unknown. Companies are reluctant to make the conversion investment and then find the new applications are unworkably slow.

Finally, as you have seen, ODBMS involves a new paradigm for both programming and database management. Programmers and database designers must invest considerable time and energy to learn this new paradigm and become proficient at it. Such change is always slow and is resisted by many people.

■ ARE ODBMS BETTER THAN TRADITIONAL DBMS?

There is no cut-and-dried answer to this question. It begs other questions like, Better for whom? For which application? In which settings? For applications in which the data are new (or readily converted), in which the programs are being written in an object-oriented language, in which there are complicated data types, and in which query and reporting requirements can be met by application programs, and setting aside performance issues, ODBMS appear to have significant advantages to the application programmer. Hence, ODBMS will likely be important in the future, at least for a large class of applications.

At the same time, ODBMS products are, at least today, only for the skilled object-oriented programmer. This leaves many out in the cold. Whereas one might justify the belief that all programmers should become object-oriented programmers anyway, there is a large class of nonprogramming creators of personal databases who are successful with relational products. These people would be overwhelmed with the knowledge requirements of object-oriented programming and ODBMS. For them, traditional database products are likely to continue to be a better choice for a long time.

In the next five years, the application of ODBMS will likely grow at a substantial rate, especially for applications that have complex data requirements and limited need for query and reporting such as engineering, graphics, and scientific applications. At the same time, the use of traditional DBMS products will also grow even more dramatically, especially in light of intranets and the Internet. So unless you are an object-oriented programmer or work in a specialized industry, continuing to develop your skills and knowledge in relational DBMS technology and products appears to be a better investment at the present time.

Most likely, these two technologies will merge in the future. If this happens, it will be possible for people and organizations to migrate to ODBMS features without having to convert programs and data to the new format. Evidence of this merger appears in the work of two different standards committees. We conclude this chapter with a brief survey of these two standards.

◆ ODBMS STANDARDS

A number of groups have been working toward the definition of an object database standard that could be used as a basis for the construction of ODBMS products. We survey the work of two of those groups here. The first group is a combination of ANSI and ISO (International Standards Organization) committees that has focused on extending the SQL92 standard for object processing. The second group is a consortium of object database vendors and other interested parties that builds on another important standard in the industry, the Object Management Group's Common Object Model and Interface Design Language. As you might expect, the first standard begins with a database perspective and moves toward object thinking. The second standard begins with an object perspective and moves toward data management thinking. Both standards are important, and both will likely serve as the basis for a number of important commercial ODBMS. It is too early to tell whether one standard will dominate the other. Consider the SQL standard first.

■ SQL3

SQL3 is an extension to the SQL92 database standard that includes support for object-oriented database management. Both the ANSI X3H2 and the ISO/IEC JTC1/SC21/WG3 standardization committees have worked to develop the draft of the SQL3 standard that we will discuss here. This standard is very much a work in progress, and changes from this draft are likely. Furthermore, SQL3 is a standard for products and not a product itself. There are, at present, no commercial DBMS products that implement this standard. You should view this section more as a description of the likely evolution of relational DBMS products than as a description of specific product features.

SQL3 arises out of the tradition of database management and not out of the tradition of object thinking. The goal of the committees working on SQL3 has been to describe a standard that is upward compatible with SQL92. This means that all of the features and functions of SQL92 would also work with SQL3. Consequently, SQL3 both looks like and is a relational database facility with object features added to it, as opposed to a new object-oriented database facility.

Three groups of new ideas are incorporated in SQL3: support for abstract data types, enhancements to the definitions of tables, and extensions to the language constructs to make SQL3 computationally complete.

ABSTRACT DATA TYPES   An **abstract data type (ADT)** is a user-defined structure that is equivalent to an OOP object. ADTs have methods, data items, and identifiers. ADTs can be subtypes of other ADTs; inheritance is supported. Either SQL (with the new language extensions) or an external language such as C11 can be used to express the logic of ADT methods.

An ADT can be used in an SQL expression, or it can be stored in a table, or both. If the ADT appears in one or more SQL expressions but is not stored in any table, then the ADT is transient; otherwise, it is made persistent by its storage in a table.

Figure 17-10 shows the definition of a sample ADT for an employee object type. The current syntax of SQL3 is shown in capital letters, and the developer-supplied code is shown in small letters. This specific syntax is unimportant, as it is likely to change. Instead, observe that this ADT, like an OOP object, has data items and functions (methods). The employee data items are: name, number, hiredate, currentsalary, and salary, a virtual data item (one that exists only as the result of a computation in a function). The functions are get_salary, change_salary, and remove_employee.

SQL defines two kinds of ADT: OBJECT ADTs and VALUE ADTs. An OBJECT ADT is an identifiable, independent data structure that is assigned an identifier called an **OID.** This identifier is a unique value that persists for the life of the object. If the programmer wants to be able to use the value of the OID to pass to other functions or to store in other tables, the expression WITH OID VISIBLE must be added to the first line of the object definition. This has been done in Figure 17-10.

OID values are pointers to objects; saving an OID value in a table saves a pointer to the object. This can be convenient, but it also creates a problem. When

FIGURE 17-10   *Sample ADT Definition in SQL3*

```
CREATE OBJECT TYPE employee WITH OID VISIBLE
        (name VARCHAR NOT NULL,
        number CHAR(7)
        salary UPDATABLE VIRTUAL GET with get_salary SET WITH change_salary,
        PRIVATE
        hiredate DATE
        currentsalary CURRENCY
        PUBLIC
        ACTOR FUNCTION get_salary (:E employee) RETURNS CURRENCY
        {code to perform security processing
         and return value of currentsalary if appropriate}
        RETURN salary
        END FUNCTION,

        ACTOR FUNCTION change_salary (:E employee) RETURNS employee
        {code to perform security processing
         and compute and set new currentsalary, if appropriate}
        RETURN :E
        END FUNCTION,

        DESTRUCTOR FUNCTION remove_employee (:E employee)
                                                RETURNS NULL
        {code to get ready to delete employee data}
        DESTROY :E
        RETURN :E
        END FUNCTION,
```

an ADT is destroyed, its OID is invalid, but that particular OID value may have been stored in rows of tables that are not even in memory when the ADT is destroyed. The SQL3 standard does not indicate what is to happen in this case. Apparently, programs are to be written to test whether an OID is valid before attempting to use it.

The second kind of ADT is a VALUE ADT. VALUE ADTs are not assigned OIDs and cannot exist except in the context in which they are created. If a VALUE ADT is created as a column in a table, it will be saved with that table. It will not be possible to refer to that ADT except through the name of the table. If a VALUE ADT is created in a function, then it will be transient and will be destroyed when memory for the function is released.

The code in Figure 17-10 defines the OBJECT ADT *employee* as a type. As such, the type name can be used in table definitions in the same way that SQL built-in data types can be used. In Figure 17-11, a table Dept is defined; it has a DeptName of type CHAR(10), a Manager of type employee, and an Admin, also of type employee. Thus, the ADT type is used as any other data type is used in a table definition.

 FIGURE 17-11   *Table Definition Using the Employee ADT*

```
CREATE TABLE Dept

            ( DeptName              char(10),
              Manager               employee,
              Admin                 employee INSTANCE
            )
```

When defining a column as having an ADT type, the keyword INSTANCE is used to indicate whether the object or a pointer to the object is to be stored. If INSTANCE is specified, then the object data is stored in the column. If INSTANCE is omitted, then a pointer to the object is stored in the column. If the ADT is a VALUE ADT, then INSTANCE is assumed.

In Figure 17-11, the manager column does not specify INSTANCE, but the admin column does. This means that each row of a dept table will contain a pointer to an employee in the Manager column and the actual data and methods for an employee in the Admin column.

The public data items of an object can be used in SQL statements just like regular table columns can be used. For example, consider the table in Figure 17-11 and the following SQL code:

```
SELECT     DeptName, Manager.OID, Manager.Name, Admin.OID, Admin.Name
FROM       Dept
```

When this code is executed, the DeptName, Manager.OID, Admin.OID, and Admin.Name would be extracted from the table. Behind the scenes, the DBMS would use the value of Manager.OID to find the instance of employee that it points to. The DBMS would then extract Manager.name from that object and return it as part of the response to this SQL statement. The result would be the same as if all of the Manager object were stored in the table. Clearly, if the OID that is stored in the table has become invalid because its object has been deleted, then the DBMS will need to process this error in some fashion.

Consider the SQL statement

```
SELECT     DeptName, Manager.Name, Manager.Salary
FROM       Dept
```

To process this statement, the DBMS will need to access the Dept table, obtain the OID of the manager, obtain the instance of employee that is that manager, and then invoke the get_salary function in employee that materializes the virtual column salary. The get_salary function may perform security checking when it is executed and so the user may be asked to provide a name or password or perform other tasks before the DBMS receives a response from get_salary. Once get_salary has returned a value or an error code indicating that no value will be forthcoming, the DBMS can format the data for that Dept. Similar processing will need to be done for each row of the Dept table.

Private data items are private to the functions in the object. Hence, the following SQL is invalid:

```
SELECT     DeptName, Manager.currentsalary
FROM       Dept
```

The only way currentsalary data can be extracted from an employee object is through the function get_salary.

Values can be assigned to columns just like other SQL statements. Thus, the SQL expression:

```
UPDATE     Dept
SET        Admin.Name = "Fred P. Johnson"
WHERE      DeptName = "Accounting"
```

will set the name of the admin object that is instantiated in the Accounting department.

Since some objects are represented by pointers and not by data values, some surprising results can occur. Consider the following SQL:

```
UPDATE    Dept
SET       Manager.Name = "Fred P. Johnson"
WHERE     DeptName = "Accounting"
```

This statement does not change the employee assignment so that a different employee whose name is "Fred P. Johnson" is assigned to Accounting. Instead, it changes the name of the employee who is currently the manager. The *employee* name is changed; this means that any other table that references this employee object will also have its name changed. If no employee has yet been assigned to Manager in the Accounting row, this statement will generate an error.

In order to replace the manager of the Accounting department with a different employee whose name is "Fred P. Johnson", the Manager object needs to be set to the correct object instance. The following SQL will do this:

```
UPDATE    Dept
SET       Manager =
          SELECT    employee.OID
          FROM      employee
          WHERE     name = "Fred P. Johnson"
WHERE     DeptName = "Accounting"
```

Conceptually, this statement is correct. Whether or not it would actually work with a DBMS that implemented SQL3 would, of course, be up to the designers of the DBMS. As stated, since SQL3 is a work in progress and since no product yet implements it, consider the discussion here to indicate the direction of the industry, rather than a fixed, industry-accepted syntax.

The definition of ADTs gives SQL3 the ability to define, store, and manipulate objects. Two other changes to SQL are also proposed in SQL3. We consider them next.

SQL3 TABLE EXTENSIONS SQL3 extends the definition of tables in several ways. First, SQL3 tables have a **row identifier,** which is a unique identifier for each row of a table. This identifier is the same as a *surrogate key,* the term we have used in prior discussions. Applications can use this identifier if it is made explicit by including the expression WITH IDENTITY in the table definition. Any table so defined is given an implicit column named IDENTITY. Values in the column can be used by the application, but it is not included in the results of a SELECT * expression.

Consider the table in Figure 17-12 and the next two SQL expressions:

```
SELECT    ProfessorName, Identity
FROM      PROFESSOR


SELECT    *
FROM      PROFESSOR
```

FIGURE 17-12   *Table Definition Using WITH IDENTITY*

```
CREATE TABLE PROFESSOR WITH IDENTITY
          (ProfessorName    char(10),
           Phone            char(7),
           Office           char(5)
          )
```

The result of the first SQL statement is a table with two columns; the first has the name of the professor, and the second has the value of the row identifier. The result of the second SQL expression is a table of three columns, which are ProfessorName, Phone, and Office.

The second extension to the table concept in SQL3 is the definition of three types of table: SET, MULTISET, and LIST. A SET table is a table with no duplicate rows; a MULTISET table may have duplicate rows and is equivalent to the table concept in SQL92. (This definition, of course, ignores the IDENTITY column, since with the IDENTITY column, no table has duplicate rows.) Finally, a LIST table is a table that has an order defined by one or more columns.

A third extension to the table concept in SQL3 is the **subtable.** A subtable is a subset of another table, called the **supertable.** A subtable inherits all of the columns of its supertable and may also have columns of its own. A table that has a subtable or a supertable has a row identifier defined implicitly. Figure 17-13 defines two types of professor: TENURED-PROFESSOR and NON-TENURED-PROFESSOR. The columns of TENURED-PROFESSOR are ProfessorName, Phone, Office, and DateTenureGranted. The columns of NON-TENURED-PROFESSOR are ProfessorName, Phone, Office, and NextReviewDate. Even though WITH IDENTITY is not specified for TENURED-PROFESSOR or NON-TENURED-PROFESSOR, both have an IDENTITY column because they are subtypes.

Reflect for a moment on the logical consequences of adding both ADTs and subtypes to the table construct. Both ADTs and tables can have subtypes, and the two are not the same. ADT subtypes define one generalization hierarchy, and table subtypes define another. One hierarchy may be nested in the other or the reverse, or they may be disjoint, or they may partially overlap. SQL3 is open to the criticism of excessive complexity here, and it will be interesting to see how much of this complexity is actually implemented in DBMS products.

SQL LANGUAGE EXTENSIONS   According to SQL3, ADT methods can be coded in the SQL language itself. To make this capability more robust, language elements are proposed that will make SQL computationally complete. The proposed additions are summarized in Figure 17-14.

To date, SQL has been a set-oriented language. SELECT statements identify a set of rows and operate upon them. The addition of the language statements in Figure 17-14 will change this characteristic. It will be possible to develop row-at-a-time logic within SQL itself. This change will make SQL more and more like a traditional programming language. This is necessary if SQL is to be used as the language for logic in ADT methods, but it also represents a change in the fundamental character of SQL.

FIGURE 17-13   *Subtable Definitions*

CREATE TABLE PROFESSOR WITH IDENTITY	
(ProfessorName	char(10),
Phone	char(7),
Office	char(5)
)	
CREATE TABLE TENURED-PROFESSOR UNDER PROFESSOR	
(DateTenureGranted	Date)
CREATE TABLE NON-TENURED-PROFESSOR UNDER PROFESSOR	
(NextReviewDate	Date)

FIGURE 17-14   *Proposed SQL3 Language Extensions*

Statement	Purpose
DESTROY	Destroy an object ADT; valid only in DESTRUCTOR functions
ASSIGNMENT	Allow the result of an SQL value expression to be assigned to a local variable, column, or ADT attribute
CALL	Invoke an SQL procedure
RETURN	Return a value from a value computation in a procedure or function
CASE	Select execution path on the basis of alternative values
IF THEN ELSE	Allow conditional logic
WHILE LOOP	Allow iterative logic

■ ODMG-93

The Object Data Management Group is a consortium of object database vendors and other interested industry experts that has applied the ideas of another group, the Object Management Group, to the problem of object databases. The first report on ODMG was produced in 1993 and is accordingly referred to as ODMG-93. This heritage of this standard is object programming and not traditional relational database management. Hence, it is based on the object as the fundamental construct, rather than on the table as the fundamental construct as we saw for SQL3.

ODMG-93 is a definition of interfaces for object data management products. The implementations of the ideas in ODMG-93 may be quite different. An ODMG-93 product that is designed for C++ object data storage and manipulation might have a completely different implementation from a product that is designed for Smalltalk object storage and manipulation. The two products could be very different and yet still both implement the ODMG-93 interfaces.

Since ODMG-93 arises out of the context of object programming, a detailed description of it requires substantial knowledge of OOP. Such a description is consequently beyond the scope of this text. Instead, we confine this discussion to fundamental ideas behind the ODMG-93 report. Figure 17-15 lists five core concepts as described by Loomis.[3]

OBJECTS ARE FUNDAMENTAL   According to the ODMG Object Model, the object is the fundamental entity to be stored and manipulated. Unlike SQL3, in which the fundamental entity is a table and objects are stored in columns of tables, in ODMG-93 the object is the basic entity. The ODMG concept is more like the one we described for the object program in Figure 17-3. That is, the application program defines objects in and of themselves, and it is up to the ODBMS to make those objects persistent. No other structure, such as a table, is required.

According to the ODMG model, objects can be **mutable** or **immutable.** Mutable objects can be changed; immutable objects are fixed, and no application is allowed to alter the state of any immutable object. The ODBMS is required to enforce immutability.

---

[3]Mary E. S. Loomis, *Object Databases, The Essentials.* Reading, MA: Addison-Wesley, 1995, pp. 88–110.

FIGURE 17-15 *Key Elements of the ODMG Object Model*

> • Objects are fundamental.
> • Every object has a lifelong persistent, unique identifier.
> • Objects can be arranged into types and subtypes.
> • State is defined by data values and relationships.
> • Behavior is defined by object operations.

EVERY OBJECT HAS A LIFELONG PERSISTENT IDENTIFIER The second fundamental concept in the ODMG object model is that each object is given a unique identifier that is valid for the lifetime of the object. Further, the identifier must be valid whether the object is stored externally or is in memory. The ODBMS is to perform swizzling transparently; the application program can use pointers to objects as if they are always valid.

The standard leaves the particular form of an object identifier open. Thus, different ODBMS vendors can use different means to specify object IDs. This means that object identifiers from different databases from different vendors are not necessarily compatible. For nondistributed databases, this is not likely to be a problem, since all of the objects in a given object database will have been created and stored by the same ODBMS.

In a distributed environment, the object identification problem is more difficult for two reasons: first, because object IDs in different ODBMS may have different formats, and, second, because object IDs are not necessarily unique across different databases. This issue is unaddressed by the ODMG-93 standard.

OBJECTS CAN BE ARRANGED INTO TYPES AND SUBTYPES The ODMG standard object model specifies that objects are arranged into groups by type. Objects are created to be of a given type. All objects of a particular type have the same data characteristics and behavior. Objects can be defined as subtypes of other objects. In this case, they inherit all of the data characteristics and behavior of their parent type. According to the standard, an object is created as an instance of a given type, and that instance cannot change its type.

The terms *type* and *class* are often used synonymously. According to Loomis, this is incorrect. An object class is a logical group of objects as defined in ODMG-93; such classes have subclasses that inherit from them. A type is the implementation of a class in a particular language. Thus, the class Employee is a logical definition of data and methods; it may have subclasses Salesperson and Accountant that inherit from Employee. An implementation of Employee in, say, C++, is called a type; implementations in C++ of Salesperson and Accountant are subtypes.[4] There may be another, different implementation of Employee in, say, Smalltalk. That implementation would be a different Employee type. Distinguishing between *class* and *type* helps to delineate logical definitions from particular implementations of those logical structures.

Object classes (and hence types) can have properties. The ODMG standard specifies that each class has a name and uniqueness constraints as its properties. All of the instances of an object class are called the object's **extent.** Any attribute or combination of attributes can be declared to be unique over the extent. Thus, in Employee, EmployeeNumber can be defined to be unique, as could {FirstName, LastName}, and so on. Since uniqueness requirements apply to the entire extent and not to any given object instance, such requirements are class properties and

---

[4]*Ibid.*, p. 96.

not class instance properties. Thus, the name Employee and the requirement that EmployeeNumber be unique are class properties. EmployeeNumber itself, however, is a property of an Employee instance.

Since ODMG is a standard for an interface and not for an implementation, no attempt is made to describe how types and subtypes should be stored or manipulated. Rather, the interface simply indicates that objects should be stored and retrieved by class and that inheritance should be provided.

STATE IS DEFINED BY DATA VALUES AND RELATIONSHIPS   According to the ODMG standard, the state of any object is represented by its properties. Such properties can be either attributes or relationships. An attribute is a literal value or a set of literal values. DateOfHire and CurrentSalary are literal values. PastSalary is a set of literal values. A relationship is a property that indicates a connection between one object instance and one or more other object instances. Department is an example of a relationship property.

The ODMG specifies a set of operations that can be performed on relationships, which are listed in Figure 17-16. Operations are distinguished by the maximum cardinality of the relationship. This is done because in the case of a 1:1 relationship, the properties are single-valued and no set of properties need be considered. In the case of a 1:N or N:M relationship, the number of elements in a property is plural; a set is created, and the program must be able to iterate over the elements of the set.

When objects have a relationship, the relationship must be made persistent when the object is made persistent. The standard does not specify how the relationship is to be represented and what means are to be used to swizzle the pointers among relationships. These issues must be solved when implementing an ODBMS, however.

BEHAVIOR IS DEFINED BY OBJECT OPERATIONS   The behavior of an object type is determined by its methods. All objects of a given type have the same methods, and objects of subtypes inherit those methods. If a subtype object redefines a method, then the redefinition will override the inherited method. If, for example, Employee has method Get_Salary, and if Salesperson, a subtype of Employee, also has a method called Get_Salary, the local method will be used for Salesperson!Get_Salary operations.

Objects interact by invoking one another's methods. Sometimes this is expressed by saying that objects pass messages to one another, where a message is a string like Salesperson!Get_Salary that includes the name of the object type and the name of the method of that type. Messages can, of course, include parameters.

FIGURE 17-16   *ODMG Relationship Operations*

Operation	Function
Set	Create a 1:1 relationship
Clear	Destroy a 1:1 relationship
Insert_element	Add an element to the many side of a 1:N or N:M relationship
Remove_element	Remove an element from the many side of a 1:N or N:M relationship
Get	Return a reference to an object in a 1:1 relationship
Traverse	Return a reference to a set of objects on the many side of a 1:N or N:M relationship
Create_iterator	Create a structure to process the elements of a set of objects obtained by a Traverse operation

The purpose of an ODBMS is to make objects persistent. The ODMG standard indicates that objects include methods, so method storage and management would seem to be included in the functions of an ODMG-compliant ODBMS. In truth, current ODBMS vary widely in their support for method storage. Some ODBMS, in fact, provide no support whatsoever for method persistence. Others provide some support, but not support for versioning of objects.

Method persistence is important, and likely the capabilities of ODBMS in this area will be improved in the future. No application is static; requirements change, and object behaviors must be adapted. Furthermore, methods can change without changing the underlying data properties of an object. Without method management, two instances of an object could be based on two different versions of methods.

Consider an example. Suppose that an instance of a Salesperson class, say Salesperson A, is created and stored using a version of the Set_Salary method. Now suppose that the means of computing salesperson salaries changes, and the Set_Salary method is altered accordingly. At this point, Salesperson B is created and stored. Now, Salesperson A and Salesperson B would appear, in their data properties, to be equivalent, but they are not. Without method management on the part of the ODBMS, there is no way to determine that Salespersons A and B represent different versions of the Salesperson object.

This situation is no different from what occurs today with application programs in non-ODBMS environments, so proponents of ODBMS would claim that ODBMS has not made the situation any worse. This, however, seems to be a cop-out. If objects are defined to include data properties and behavior properties, then object persistence cannot be claimed to pertain to one and not to the other. Too much of the promise of object thinking is left on the table if ODBMS do not support method management as well as data management.

SEMANTIC OBJECTS AND THE ODMG STANDARD   Semantic objects are very close to the ODMG standard in terms of data properties. A semantic object can have either data attributes or relationship attributes. If the maximum cardinality of a data attribute is greater than one, a set of data attributes is created. Similarly, groups of either data attributes or mixtures of data attributes and relationships (hybrid groups) can be defined. If the maximum cardinality of such a group is greater than one, then a set having such groups as its elements will be defined.

As we have discussed semantic objects in this text, they do not include behavior properties. If you install SALSA for the Desktop, the product included with this text, you will find that action items and action groups can be created and added to semantic objects. Action items are segments of code that are written in a Visual Basic-like language. Semantic objects that include action items do provide an implementation of the ideas of the ODMG standard, at least to the level described in this chapter. SALSA for the Desktop will store the action items with the database. Hence, method persistence is provided.

The major violation of the ODMG standard in SALSA for the Desktop is that it does not support subtype semantic objects. This restriction is due to this particular implementation of the semantic object model, and not to the model itself. Subtype objects are included in the model as discussed in Chapter 4.

SUMMARY

Object-oriented programming is a new style of programming that has emerged in the last ten years. It has substantial advantages over traditional programming, and many vendors and companies have standardized on it for their new applications. An object DBMS (ODBMS) provides for object storage. At present, ODBMS are not frequently used in commercial environments because most organizational data are in relational format. Also, ODBMS lack some essential features.

With object-oriented programming (OOP), programs are composed of objects that are encapsulated, logical structures that have data elements and behaviors. An interface is the external appearance of an object; an implementation is the encapsulated interior of an object. Objects can be subclassed; a subclass inherits the attributes and methods of its superclass. Polymorphism allows several versions of the same method to exist; the compiler invokes the proper version at execution time, depending on the class of the object.

An object class is the logical structure of an object; a group of object classes is called an object class library. Instances of an object class are called object instances or simply objects. Object constructors are methods that obtain memory and create object structures; object destructors unbind objects and free memory. Transient objects exist only during the execution of a program; persistent objects are saved to storage and survive the execution of a program.

Objects can be made persistent by using traditional file storage, using relational DBMS, or using ODBMS products. The use of traditional storage places considerable work on the application programmer and is feasible only for applications having a few simple objects whose structure does not frequently change. Relational DBMS can be used for object persistence, but the application developer must convert object structures to relations, write SQL, and develop swizzling algorithms. Using an ODBMS is the most direct and easiest means of object persistence.

The advantages and disadvantages of ODBMS are summarized in Figure 17-9. ODBMS appear to have significant advantages over relational DBMS for new applications written in OOP that have complicated data structures and limited query and reporting requirements. At present, relational DBMS appears to have advantages for other types of applications.

SQL3 is an extension to SQL-92 that provides for abstract data types (ADTs), enhancements to tables, and new features in the SQL language. ADTs, which are made persistent by embedding in tables, can be object or value; object ADTs have identifiers called OIDs. In SQL3, tables have a row identifier and can have subtypes. Three types of tables are defined: SET, MULTISET, and LIST. Figure 17-14 shows extensions to the SQL language proposed in SQL3.

The five basic elements of the ODMG-93 standard are that objects are the fundamental data structure, objects are given a lifelong persistent identifier, objects can be arranged in types and subtypes, object state is carried by data values and relationships, and object behavior is defined by object operations. Semantic objects as defined in Chapter 4 implement the ODMG standard for data attributes, but not for object behavior. Semantic objects as implemented in SALSA for the Desktop implement the ODMG standard for behavior and for data attributes, but not for types and subtypes.

◆ GROUP I QUESTIONS

17.1 Explain how object-oriented programming differs from traditional programming.

17.2 Why are relational databases more popular than object databases today?

17.3 Define an OOP object.

17.4 Define the terms *encapsulated, attribute,* and *method.*

17.5 Explain the difference between an interface and an implementation.

17.6 What is inheritance?

17.7 What is polymorphism?

17.8 Define the terms *object class, object class library,* and *object instance.*

17.9 Explain the function of object constructors and object destructors.

17.10 Explain the difference between a transient object and a persistent object.

17.11 Explain the difference in the notation CUSTOMER!Find and CUSTOMER.ZipCode.

17.12 What is the function of the keyword *NOTHING* in Figure 17-3?

17.13 What is the function of the keyword *ME* in Figure 17-3?

17.14 What is a callback, and why is one used?

17.15 What does the term *swizzling* refer to?

17.16 Briefly explain what tasks are required to use traditional file storage for object persistence.

17.17 Briefly explain what tasks are required to use a relational DBMS for object persistence.

17.18 Summarize the advantages and disadvantages of using an ODBMS for object persistence.

17.19 In what ways is an ODBMS better than a relational DBMS?

17.20 In what ways is a relational DBMS better than an ODBMS?

17.21 What is SQL3?

17.22 What is an abstract data type (ADT)?

17.23 Explain the difference between an object ADT and a value ADT.

17.24 What is an OID? How can one be used?

17.25 Explain what the DBMS must do when executing the following SQL on the ADT in Figure 17-10:

SELECT   DeptName, Manager.Phone, Admin.Phone
FROM   Dept

17.26 What happens when the following SQL is executed on the ADT in Figure 17-10:

UPDATE   Dept
SET   Manager.Name = "John Jacob Astor"

17.27 Code SQL that would need to be executed to change the instance of the manager of a department for the ADT in Figure 17-10.

17.28 What is a row identifier in SQL3?

17.29 Explain the differences among a SET, MULTISET, and LIST in SQL3.

17.30 Explain the differences among a subtable, a supertable, and a table.

17.31 What is ODMG-93?

17.32 List the five core concepts in ODMG-93.

17.33 What is the difference between a type and a class in ODMG-93?

17.34 What is the difference between a property and an attribute in ODMG-93?

17.35 What is an extent?

17.36 What are the properties of a class in ODMG-93?

17.37 In the ODMG standard, what values can properties have?

17.38 In the ODMG standard, what values can attributes have?

17.39 In the ODMG standard, what values can relationship properties have?

17.40 Why is method persistence important? Give an example of a problem that can occur when such persistence is not provided.

17.41 Explain how semantic objects conform to the ODMG standard and how they do not.

17.42 Explain how SALSA for the Desktop conforms to the ODMG standard and how it does not.

GROUP II QUESTIONS

17.43 Compare and contrast object-oriented programming with traditional programming. Evaluate the two on the following criteria:

   a. Ease of learning

   b. Ease of use

   c. Quality of code

   d. Changeability of code

   e. Data persistence

   f. Representation of object (entity) relationships

   For what types of applications do you think object-oriented programming should be used? For what types of applications do you think traditional programming should be used?

17.44 Contact a vendor of an ODBMS product, and evaluate that product's features and functions in terms of:

   a. Object definition

   b. Object storage facilities

   c. Swizzling

   d. Object relationships definition

   e. Object relationship processing

   f. Method storage and management

   g. Object query and reporting

   h. Concurrency control

   i. Transaction management

   j. Performance

PROJECT USING SALSA FOR THE DESKTOP

Install SALSA for the Desktop, and read its documentation regarding action items and action groups. Create an application with DEPARTMENT and PROFESSOR semantic objects. Create attributes for these two objects like those discussed in Chapter 4. Add an action item to the DEPARTMENT semantic object and an action group with two or more action items in it. Write code in an action item to determine if the department name includes the word *science* and, if so, to display a message box with the message "This is a science department." Drag and drop the action item in the DEPARTMENT object. Create the application, and observe how the action item is materialized in SALSA for the Desktop. Press the button to invoke your code.

   Consider SALSA for the Desktop as an implementation of the ODMG-93 interface standard. In what ways does it conform to the five major ideas of ODMG-93 as presented here? In what ways does it fail to conform? The ODMG standard is generally considered to be a standard for a programming language and development facility such as C++. SALSA for the Desktop, on the other hand, is an application generation product, intended for the nonprogrammer or the nonobject-oriented programmer. To what extent is it valid to consider SALSA for the Desktop to be an implementation of the ODMG-93 standard?

18

THE HIERARCHICAL AND NETWORK DATA MODELS

The hierarchical and network data models preceded the relational model, and they were at one time the workhorses of the database industry. Today, only remnants of both of these models survive, primarily in IMS, an IBM implementation of the hierarchical model DL/I, and in IDMS, an implementation of the network model known as the CODASYL DBTG model. Little new development is done in these products or models anymore; you are likely to encounter them only if you are employed to maintain existing code or to migrate an application in one of these systems to a relational DBMS. These models are an important part of the heritage of database processing, and understanding their basic concepts is worthwhile. Accordingly, this chapter surveys the major elements of these models.

LIBRARY EXAMPLE

We will use a case that involves the processing of library data to illustrate the nature and use of the hierarchical and network data models. The objects to be stored and processed are illustrated in Figure 18-1. This design contains composite objects 1:1, 1:N, and M:N compound objects and association objects. COPY is a composite object because it contains Due-date as a multivalued nonobject attribute. The 1:1 compound objects are STUDENT and VIDEO (students are allowed to check out only one videocassette at a time). The 1:N compound objects are PUBLISHER and TITLE. The M:N compound objects are AUTHOR and TITLE, because an author can write many books and a book can be written by many authors. The association object is COPY, which documents the relationship between a TITLE and the STUDENT who checks it out.

A relational design for these objects is shown in Figure 18-2. Note that there is one relation for each object and multivalued attribute. The names of the relations are slightly different from the object names in order to differentiate the two. In addition to these six relations, the relation DUE-DATE represents the repeating group in the COPY object, and the intersection relation TA-INT represents the M:N relationship between TITLE and AUTHOR.

FIGURE 18-1   *Six Objects Used by a University Library*

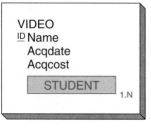

TITLE
Name
^{ID} Call#
PUBLISHER	1.1
COPY	0.N
AUTHOR	0.N

PUBLISHER
^{ID} Name
Address
Salesrep
Phone
| TITLE | 0.N |

AUTHOR
^{ID} Name
Affiliation
| TITLE | 1.N |

COPY
^{ID} Copy-ID
    Copy#
| TITLE | 1.1 | 1.1 |
Acqdate
| STUDENT | 0.1 |
Due-date 0.N

STUDENT
Name
^{ID} Student#
| COPY | 0.N |
| VIDEO | 0.1 |

VIDEO
^{ID} Name
Acqdate
Acqcost
| STUDENT | 1.N |

FIGURE 18-2

Relational Design for the University Database: (a) Relations for the University Library Database and (b) Relationship of University Database Relations

TTLE (Name, <u>Call#</u>, *PUB.Name*)

PUB (<u>Name</u>, Address, Salesrep, Phone)

AUTH (<u>Name</u>, Affiliation)

CPY (<u>Copy#</u>, *TTLE.Call#*, Acqdate, *STU.Student#*)

DUE-DATE (*Copy#*, *TTLE.Call#*, <u>DueDate</u>)

STU (Name, <u>Student#</u>)

VID (<u>Name</u>, Acqdate, Acqcost, *STU.Student#*)

TA-INT (*TTLE.Call#*, *AUTH.Name*)

(a)

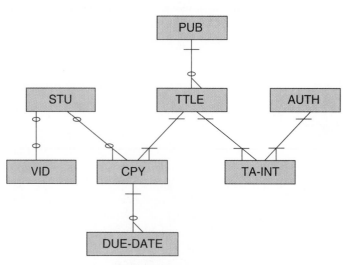

(b)

DATA LANGUAGE/I

IBM and North American Aviation jointly developed DL/I in the 1960s as an out-growth of data processing needs in the aerospace industry. DL/I is a language for processing a database, and its most popular implementation is IMS, or Information Management System, which for years was IBM's primary transaction process-ing–oriented DBMS (DB2 has now taken over this role). Actually, IMS is both a communications processor and a database management system, so it would be more correct to say that DL/I is implemented in IMS/DB, which is the database por-tion of IMS. DL/I uses hierarchies (trees) to represent relationships, which means that the users' objects must be transformed into tree representations before they can be processed using DL/I.

In DL/I terms, fields are grouped into **segments,** or the nodes of tree struc-tures. Remember from Chapter 6 that a **tree** is a collection of records and rela-tionships in which each record has at most one parent and all relationships are one to many between parent and child. (Throughout this discussion, we use the DL/I term *segment* rather than record or row.) DL/I refers to a particular tree structure (a collection of related segments) as a **data base record.** (*Data base* is two words in DL/I.) Since DL/I concerns only hierarchies, any network relationships must be transformed into hierarchies before they can be processed.

A sample STUDENT data base record is sketched in Figure 18-3. The forked line notation used throughout this text is not part of DL/I notation but is used here for consistency. Each STUDENT segment has Name, Number, and Address fields. Also, under each STUDENT segment are a variable number of JOB HISTORY and CLASS segments. An occurrence of the STUDENT data base record is shown in Figure 18-4.

In DL/I, a **data base** is composed of data base records, which can be occur-rences of the same record type or of several different record types. For example, a DL/I data base could consist of occurrences of the STUDENT data base record in Figure 18-3 and the FACULTY data base record in Figure 18-5. The data base would comprise all occurrences of each data base record type. Figure 18-6 summarizes the DL/I data structures.

Data base records are defined by means of a **data base description.** In the DBMS product IMS, a set of assembly-language macro instructions indicates the structure of each data base record. (Note that this is different from the relational language SQL we examined earlier. SQL includes both data definition and data ma-nipulation statements, whereas DL/I is for data manipulation only. This reflects DL/I's age, as it was developed before having a convenient means of defining data was judged important.) Figure 18-7 on page 453 depicts a portion of the data base description for the STUDENT data base record in Figure 18-3. The format of this description is unique to IMS.

Each segment description is headed by an SEGM macro that names the seg-ment, shows its total length, and gives the name of the parent if there is one. The

FIGURE 18-3   *STUDENT Data Base Record*

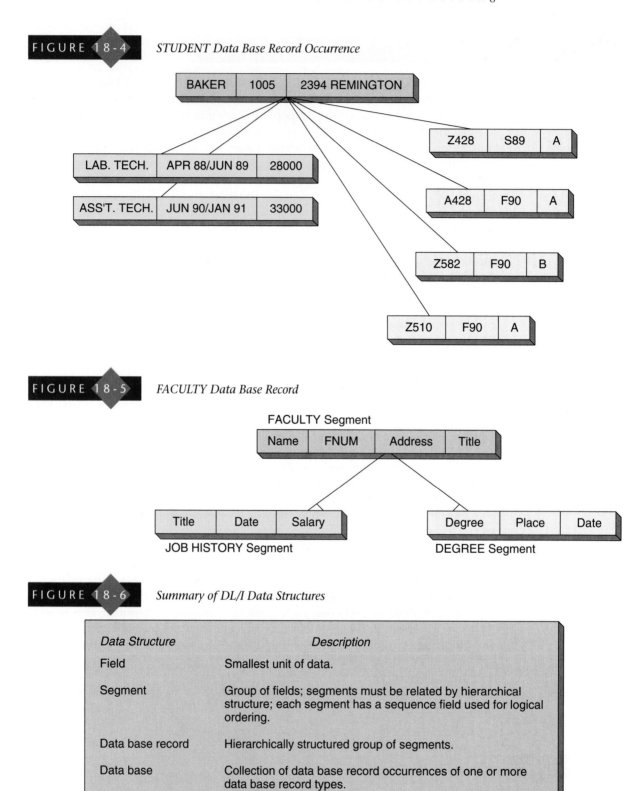

FIGURE 18-4   *STUDENT Data Base Record Occurrence*

FIGURE 18-5   *FACULTY Data Base Record*

FACULTY Segment

| Name | FNUM | Address | Title |

| Title | Date | Salary |
JOB HISTORY Segment

| Degree | Place | Date |
DEGREE Segment

FIGURE 18-6   *Summary of DL/I Data Structures*

Data Structure	Description
Field	Smallest unit of data.
Segment	Group of fields; segments must be related by hierarchical structure; each segment has a sequence field used for logical ordering.
Data base record	Hierarchically structured group of segments.
Data base	Collection of data base record occurrences of one or more data base record types.

first segment, or **root,** has no parent. Each field within a segment is represented by a FIELD macro that indicates the field's name, length, and starting position in the segment. One field in each segment is designated as the **sequence field** and is used to order the occurrences of a given segment type. The order is a logical one;

FIGURE 18-7 *Description of Data Base for STUDENT Data Base Record in Figure 18-3*

STUDENT segment description	DBD	NAME=STUDB
	SEGM	NAME=STU, BYTES=61
	FIELD	NAME=SNAME, BYTES=30, START=1
	FIELD	NAME=(NUM, SEQ), BYTES=11, START=31
	FIELD	NAME=ADDR, BYTES=20, START=42
JOB HISTORY segment description	SEGM	NAME=JOBHIST, PARENT=STU, BYTES=47
	FIELD	NAME=JOBTITLE, BYTES=30, START=1
	FIELD	NAME=(JDATE, SEQ), BYTES=11, START=31
	FIELD	NAME=SALARY, BYTES=6, START=42
CLASS segment description	SEGM	NAME=CLASS, PARENT=STU, BYTES=10
	FIELD	NAME=(CNAME, SEQ), BYTES=5, START=1
	FIELD	NAME=CDATE, BYTES=4, START=6
	FIELD	NAME=GRADE, BYTES=1, START=10

although it may appear to the application program that the segments are in order of sequence field, the physical ordering of the segments may be different.

In Figure 18-7, the STUDENT segment is named STU and is 61 bytes long. The STU record is composed of an SNAME field in bytes 1 through 30, a NUM field in bytes 31 through 41, and an ADDR field in bytes 42 through 61. (Because DL/I uses uppercase letters, all names are spelled in capitals.) The sequence field for STU segments is NUM.

JOB HISTORY segments are called JOBHIST and are composed of JOBTITLE, JDATE, and SALARY fields. CLASS segments are called CLASS and have CNAME, CDATE, and GRADE fields.

The data base description is assembled and can be stored in object form in a library to be called into main memory when needed. Consequently, each application programmer need only reference the data base description to have it copied into his or her program.

■ DL/I REPRESENTATION OF THE LIBRARY EXAMPLE

Since DL/I represents and processes only hierarchies, all database designs must be transformed into hierarchical designs. This is done by transforming any network relationships into multiple hierarchies with data duplication and then removing the data duplication by placing pointers to the source data in any duplicate segments. This process is illustrated in this section.

The relational design in Figure 18-2 is not a hierarchy because two relations, CPY and TA-INT, have more than one parent. We can transform this structure into hierarchical structures by creating two trees for each path from the parent to the child, for a total of four trees. This has been done in Figure 18-8(a) (only three trees appear because the middle tree in this figure holds two of them).

Consider this process for the CPY relation, first. Since both TTLE and STU are parents of CPY, we need to construct one tree for each of them. Thus you see in Figure 18-8(a) the STU/CPY/DUE-DATE tree (part of the left tree in that figure) and the PUB/TTLE/CPY/DUE-DATE tree (part of the middle tree). STU also has a child, VID, which we can add under STU without causing a problem, thereby completing that tree.

Now consider the TA-INT relation in Figure 18-2. The purpose of TA-INT is to represent many titles for a given author and many authors for a given title. Thus we want a tree with AUTH as parent and TTLE as child and a tree with TTLE as

FIGURE 18-8

Representing Hierarchies for DL/I Processing: (a) Logical Data Base Records for the Relations in Figure 18-2 and (b) Physical Data Base Records for the Relations in Figure 18-2

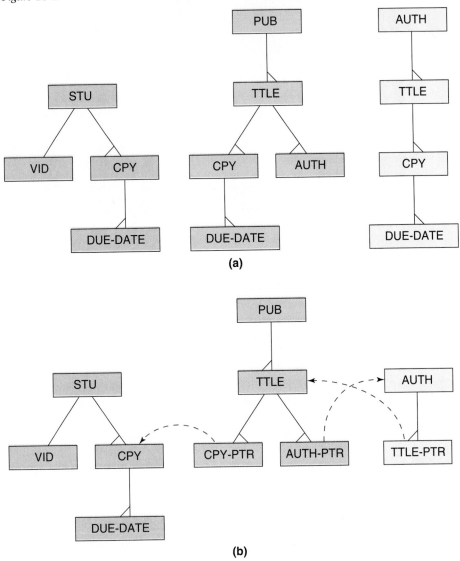

parent and AUTH as child. This representation is also shown in Figure 18-8(a). AUTH/TTLE/CPY/DUE-DATE is shown as a separate tree. The TTLE/AUTH relationship has been represented within the PUB/TTLE/CPY/DUE-DATE tree by adding the AUTH relation under TTLE. Figure 18-8(a) therefore shows four trees (two for each of the relations that have two parents), but two of them have been combined under the common parent TTLE.

The trees in Figure 18-8(a) have considerable data duplication. For example, the CPY segment appears in three different places. Since duplicated data not only waste file space but also can cause data integrity problems, we want to eliminate them. This can be done by storing the data in one place and storing pointers to the data in the other places. This is what is done with DL/I and what is illustrated in Figure 18-8(b).

DL/I divides a data base into physical and logical constructs. The terms physical data base (PDB) and **physical data base record** (PDBR) are used to describe the data as they exist in data storage. The terms **logical data base** (LDB) and

logical data base record (LDBR) are used to describe the data as they appear to the application programs that process them. LDBRs differ from PDBRs in either of two ways. An LDBR may be a subset of a PDBR, or an LDBR may contain portions of two or more PDBRs and represent tree structures that are not present in the PDBRs. The trees sketched in Figure 18-8(a) are LDBRs, as they represent data as they appear to an application program. Conversely, the trees sketched in Figure 18-8(b) are PDBRs; these are the physical data structures that are created on disk.

■ DL/I DATA MANIPULATION LANGUAGE

DL/I processes data in segments; DL/I statements can retrieve, update, insert, and delete segments. Unlike SQL, which can be used interactively or be embedded in application programs, DL/I statements must be embedded in application programs. DL/I has no interactive query language. (Keep in mind that DL/I was one of the earliest database languages, used exclusively for transaction processing by information systems professionals and not by end users.)

Using DL/I, the application programmer defines an input/output (I/O) work area that is shared by the application program and the DBMS product. To insert or update a segment, the application program places new data in the work area; the DBMS takes the data from there to modify the data base. When the DBMS retrieves data from the data base, it places it in the work area for the program to access. System status data, such as completion flags and error flags, are also placed in the work area by the DBMS so that the application program can examine them.

The DL/I syntax that is presented in this section represents functions that are embedded in application programs. The specific form of the functions depends on the language used and hence we present a generic form here. To understand these commands, consider the LDBR in Figure 18-9, which is based on the PUB/TTLE/AUTH-PTR/CPY-PTR PDBR in Figure 18-8(b).

GET UNIQUE (GU) GET UNIQUE (GU) is a command used to read a particular segment into the I/O work area. For example, the statement

GU   PUB(SALREP = 'JONES')

causes the first PUB segment with the SALREP value of JONES to be placed into the I/O work area. Thus, if the occurrences in Figure 18-10 are the first ones in the data base, the segment P2,NYC,JONES,(212)555–1776 will be placed in the work area. The following statements cause the first AUTH with name A3 of TTLE T2 to be placed in the work area:

FIGURE 18-9   *Sample LDBR for Data Base in Figure 18-8(b)*

FIGURE 18-10   *Two Occurrences of the LDBR in Figure 18-9*

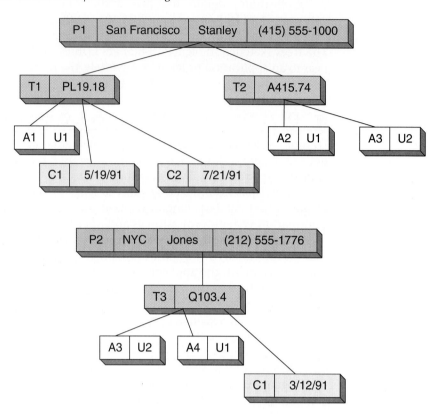

```
GU    PUB
      TTLE (TNAME = 'T2')
      AUTH (ANAME = 'A3')
```

If no such segment exists, the DBMS will set an appropriate return code in the work area.

The DBMS searches for the desired segment by starting at the first occurrence of the LDBR, at the first T2 occurrence of the TTLE segment (assuming that there could be more than one), and at the first A3 occurrence of the AUTH segment (again assuming that there could be more than one). The order of the segments is determined by the sequence fields in each segment (see Figure 18-7). For this LDBR, assume the following sequence fields:

SEGMENT	SEQUENCE FIELD
PUB	PNAME
TTLE	TNAME
AUTH	ANAME
CPY	COPY#

To find the first occurrence of AUTH A3 in TTLE T2, we examine the segments in the following order: P1 (PUB) segment, T1, T2 (TTLE segments), and, finally, A2, A3 (AUTH segments). The segment read into the work area is A3.

The qualifying data after the GU command are called a **segment search argument** (SSA). In general, an SSA is the name of a segment, which may be followed by a condition. As shown, there can be one SSA for each segment in the hierarchical path for the segment to be retrieved.

GET NEXT (GN)   GET NEXT (GN) is a command used to read the next segment. Next implies that there be a current segment to start from, so it is necessary to indicate a current segment before issuing a GN command. For example, the statements

```
GU    PUB
      TTLE (TNAME = 'T1')
GN    TTLE
```

cause the first TTLE segment in the data base with TNAME field equal to T1 to be placed in the I/O work area. This establishes a current position. (There most likely would be some program instructions to process that segment following the GU command, but we have omitted them.) The GN statement reads the next TTLE segment. For the occurrence in Figure 18-10, the T1 segment is read first, followed by the T2 segment. If a subsequent GN TTLE command is executed, the DBMS will attempt to find another TTLE segment under the current PUB segment. There is none for this occurrence, so it searches under the next PUB segment (P2) and reads the T3 occurrence of TTLE.

A third execution of GN TTLE causes the DBMS to look for the next TTLE segment. Since there are no more in the P2 occurrence of PUB, the DBMS searches the next LDBR occurrence for a TTLE segment and, if it finds one, places it in the work area. The search will continue to the end of the data base if necessary. If no TTLE segment remains in the data base, appropriate status data will be set.

When the GN statements are executed, the DBMS selects the next occurrence of the segment named. If there is no such occurrence under the current parent, the DBMS will switch to the next parent. The application program may need to know, however, when the DBMS selects a segment from a new parent. For example, if the second GN TTLE statement is executed as discussed in the preceding paragraph, the program may need to know that a new PUB segment has been retrieved.

To provide this information, when a segment is read, data regarding the path leading to the segment is placed in the work area. IMS places the *fully concatenated key* of the retrieved segment in the work area. This key is the concatenation of all sequence fields of segments leading to the segment, along with the sequence field of the segment. For example, the fully concatenated key for the A4 AUTH segment is P2 T3 A4. After the second GN TTLE command is executed as described, the DBMS returns the key P2 T3, and the application program can detect the new PUB segment by means of the change in PUB sequence field in the key. Now consider another example. The commands

```
GU    PUB
      TTLE(TNAME = 'T1')
GN    TTLE(CALL# > 'P')
```

cause the T1 TTLE segment to be read, followed by the next TTLE segment with a call number starting with a letter beyond P in the collating sequence. Consequently T3 is read next. The important point here is that sequential retrieval can be either *qualified* (with a condition after the segment name) or *unqualified* (with no condition).

Another type of sequential retrieval command requests the next segment regardless of its type. For example, the commands

```
GU    PUB
      TTLE(TNAME = 'T1')
GN
```

cause the T1 segment of TTLE to be read, followed by the A1 AUTH segment. A subsequent GN command reads the C1 CPY segment.

As an aside, this LDBR does not include DUE-DATE segments (or, as sometimes expressed in DL/I, this LDBR *is not sensitive to* DUE-DATE segments). When the GN commands are executed, no DUE-DATE data is presented to the application program; the DBMS automatically skips it. IMS never presents to an application any data to which the application is not sensitive.

GET NEXT WITHIN PARENT (GNP)   GET NEXT WITHIN PARENT (GNP) is a command that sequentially retrieves segments under one parent. When all segments under that parent have been read, end-of-data status is returned to the program. For example, when the commands

```
GU      PUB
        TTLE    (TNAME = 'T1')
GNP     TTLE
GNP     TTLE
```

are executed, the T1 and T2 segments of P1 are read. The second GNP command does not return data; rather, it causes the end-of-data status flag to be set. Contrast this with the statements

```
GU      PUB
        TTLE (TNAME = 'T1')
GN      TTLE
GN      TTLE
```

Here, the second GN command retrieves the T3 TTLE segment.

GET HOLD COMMANDS   GET HOLD UNIQUE (GHU), GET HOLD NEXT (GHN), and GET HOLD NEXT WITHIN PARENT (GHNP) operate like their Get counterparts except that they inform the DBMS to prepare for a change in or deletion of the retrieved segment. They are used with Replace and Delete commands. When the program replaces or deletes a segment, it first issues a Get Hold command for the segment. DBMS retrieves the segment and "holds" it; then Replace or Delete can be issued.

REPLACE (REPL)   Replace is used to modify data within a segment. For example, the commands

```
GHU     PUB
        TTLE (TNAME = 'T2')
```

(here the application program changes TTLE data)

```
REPL
```

cause the DBMS to retrieve the T2 TTLE segment and replace it with the changed data. (In this and several following examples, the program processing is in lower-case letters. Syntax is dependent on the language used and is omitted.)

The following instruction sequence sets the acquisition date of titles to 1/1/93.

```
GHU     PUB
        TTLE
        CPY
```

DOWHILE data remain

```
        Set ACQDATE = '1/1/93'
        REPL
        GHNCPY
        END-DO
```

The GHU command obtains the first CPY segment; GHN obtains subsequent ones.

DELETE (DLET)   Delete operates in conjunction with the Get Hold commands in a manner similar to Replace. The commands

```
GHU     PUB (PNAME = 'P1')
        TTLE (TNAME = 'T1')
        AUTH (ANAME = 'A1')
DLET
```

delete the A1 segment under T1 and P1 from the data base. When a segment is deleted, any subordinate segments are also deleted (including ones invisible to the application). Thus, the commands

```
GHU     PUB (PNAME = 'P1')
        TTLE (TNAME = 'T1')
        CPY (COPY# = 1)
DLET
```

delete not only the C1 copy segment under T1 and P1 but also all of the DUE-DATE segments under that copy. Therefore, any subordinate segments to which the application is not sensitive are deleted.

Deleting invisible data is dangerous and not recommended. In order to prevent it from happening, the database administrator, database designers, and application programmers must communicate clearly with one another and establish and enforce standards. They also should review the designs. Otherwise, application programmers may write application code that appears to them to be correct but that in fact is causing errors—errors that the programmers could not know might exist.

INSERT (INSRT)   Insert is used to create a new segment. For example, the statements (instructions to place new AUTH data in I/O work area)

```
INSERT  PUB (PNAME = 'P1')
        TTLE (TNAME = 'T2')
        AUTH
```

insert a new AUTH segment into the data base. Since the AUTH sequence field is ANAME, the new segment is logically inserted in order of that field. For example, if the new value of ANAME is A4, the new AUTH segment will be inserted logically as the last AUTH segment under the T2 parent.

FIGURE 18-11   *Summary of DL/I Data Manipulation Commands*

Name	Function
Get Unique (GU)	Retrieve a particular segment.
Get Next (GN)	Retrieve the next segment.
Get Next within Parent (GNP)	Retrieve the next segment under a particular parent.
Get Hold Unique (GHU) Get Hold Next (GHN) Get Hold Next within Parent (GHNP)	Similar to preceding commands but used to obtain a segment to be modified or deleted.
Replace (REPL) Delete (DLET)	Used in conjunction with Get Hold commands to modify or delete a segment.
Insert (INSRT)	Insert a new segment.

SUMMARY OF DL/I DATA MANIPULATION COMMANDS   Figure 18-11 summarizes the DL/I data manipulation commands, all of which operate on the logical structure of the data as seen by an application program. Since the physical structure of the data may be quite different from the logical structure, the DBMS must translate the logical activity into actions on the physical data structures. The application is independent of the physical structures and is freed from maintaining them.

THE CODASYL DBTG MODEL

The CODAYSL DBTG data model was developed by a group known as the CODASYL (Conference on Data Systems Languages) Data Base Task Group (hence CODASYL DBTG). The CODASYL committee is best known as the group that developed the standards for COBOL. The CODASYL data model evolved over several years, and several transaction-oriented DBMS products are based on it. Today, however, those DBMS products are nearly unknown.

Several reasons account for the decline of the DBTG model. First, it is complex and incohesive. For example, a statement in a schema definition can combine with a seemingly unrelated operation in an application program to produce strange and unexpected results. Consequently, designers and programmers must be very careful when building DBTG databases and applications. Second, the model has a decidedly COBOL flavor to it, and this similarity has been an issue in organizations in which COBOL is not the language of choice. Furthermore, the development of the CODASYL database model was heavily politicized, and so the committee had to contend with the tendency to include everyone's favorite idea. Finally, in fairness to this model, it originated very early in the history of database technology. Although it incorporated many important concepts, mistakes were also made. Indeed, some people believe that the model was developed too soon—before the essential concepts of database technology were known and had been explored.

■ CODASYL DBTG DATA DEFINITION LANGUAGE

The 1981 version of the CODASYL model provides three different types of database view. The **schema** is the complete logical view of the database, the entire database as viewed by the database administrator or other humans. A **subschema** is a view of the database as it appears to an application program. A subschema is a subset of the database and is also allowed to have records that are constructed by joining records in the schema. This is similar to a view composed of relation joins, as discussed in Chapter 13. The **data structure description** is the third type of view, and it maps schema records, fields, and relationships to physical storage. It is the view of the database as it appears in physical storage. Because data structure descriptions were introduced in a later version of the model, they were never used, and we omit them from the discussion here.

As shown in Figure 18-12, users interact with the database by means of an application program (no interactive query language exists). One or more users can execute a single program. Each user has a **user working area** (UWA) that contains database and control data for a particular user. The execution of a program by one of the users is called a **run-unit.** Figure 18-12 shows three run-units for Application Program A, and the application programs view the database through a subschema. The programs may share subschemas, or each may have its own.

FIGURE 18-12   *CODASYL DBTG Program/Data View Relationships*

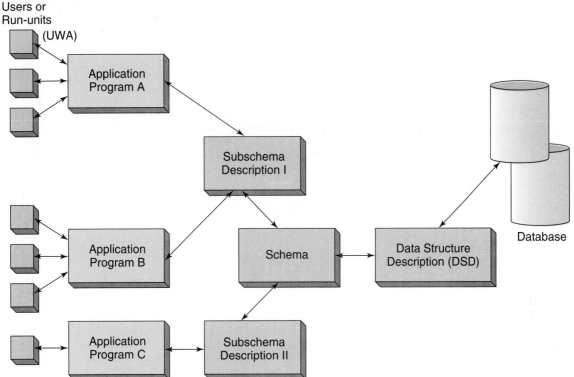

■ DATA DEFINITION CONSTRUCTS

Database designers use the basic data definition constructs in CODASYL DBTG to define schemas and subschemas. The three fundamental building blocks are data-items, records, and sets.

DATA-ITEMS   A **data-item** is a field that corresponds to an attribute or column in the relational model. Data-items have names and formats, and examples are Name, Character 25; Address, Character 40; Amount, Fixed 6.2. Although data-items come from domains, the domain concept is not recognized by the DBTG model.

RECORDS   A **record** is a collection of data-items, and Figure 18-13 shows several examples of DBTG records. Unlike the relational model, this model allows **vectors,** which are repetitions of a data-item (like GPA in Figure 18-13[b]), and it allows repeating groups, such as the data-items Course Name and Grade in Figure 18-13(c). Although such repeating groups are allowed, they are unnecessary and generally not recommended. Repeating groups were developed to represent composite objects, but a better way of representing them is with two record types and a set.

SETS   A **set** is a one-to-many relationship between records. Sets have *owners* and *members*. The owner of a set is the parent, and in Figure 18-14, ACCOUNTING is the owner of one set, and MARKETING is the owner of another set. Members of a set are the children in a one-to-many relationship. In Figure 18-14, Jones, Parks, and Williams are the members of the set owned by ACCOUNTING.

Figure 18-14 shows two occurrences of a general structure representing instances of a one-to-many relationship between the DEPARTMENT and FACULTY records.

FIGURE 18-13

CODASYL DBTG Record Types: (a) Record Composed of Data-Items, (b) Record Composed of Data-Items and a Vector Data-Aggregate, and (c) Record with Repeating Group

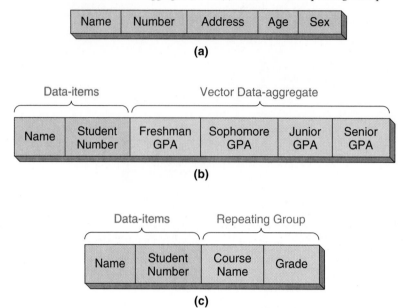

FIGURE 18-14   Two Occurrences of DEPT-FAC Set

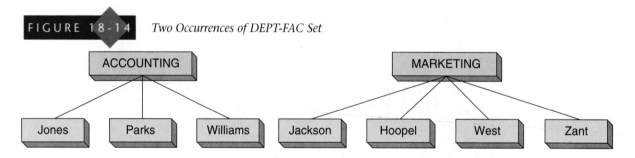

Figure 18-15 is a generalized representation of this relationship. The general structure, such as the one in Figure 18-15, is called the *set,* and examples of the structure, such as those in Figure 18-14, are called *instances,* or *occurrences,* of the set.

To define a set, we specify a set name and identify the type of record that will be the owner and the type (or types) of the records that will be the members. For example, in Figure 18-16, the set STU-MAJOR has MAJOR owner records and STUDENT member records; the set ORDER-ITEM has ORDER owner records and ITEM member records; and the set STU-HISTORY has STUDENT owner records and CLASS-GRADE member records.

The DBTG model has specific rules regarding set definition. First, a set can have only one type of record as owner, but one or more record types can be mem-

FIGURE 18-15   *General Form of CODASYL DBTG Set*

FIGURE 18-16   *Example of CODASYL DBTG Sets*

bers. Figure 18-17(a) shows the set ACTIVITY: The owner record is CLUB, and the member records are PROFESSOR and STUDENT. Figure 18-17(b) shows two instances of this set, in which both PROFESSOR and STUDENT records are members of the SKIING and BOWLING clubs.

According to the DBTG model, a member record can belong to only one instance of a particular set; that is, a record may not have two parents in the same set. This means, in Figure 18-17, that Professor Guynes can have only the SKIING parent record; he may not have BOWLING as well. Furthermore, Professor Pipkin can have only the BOWLING record as a parent and not SKIING as well. If faculty members are allowed to belong to more than one club, a DBTG set cannot be used to represent this relationship. In fact, if faculty members were allowed to belong to two clubs, this would be an instance of an M:N relationship.

Although a record cannot have two owners in the *same* set, a record may have two owners if they are in *different* sets. For example, a professor may have one

FIGURE 18-17   *Set with (a) Two-Member Record Types and (b) Example Occurrences of Them*

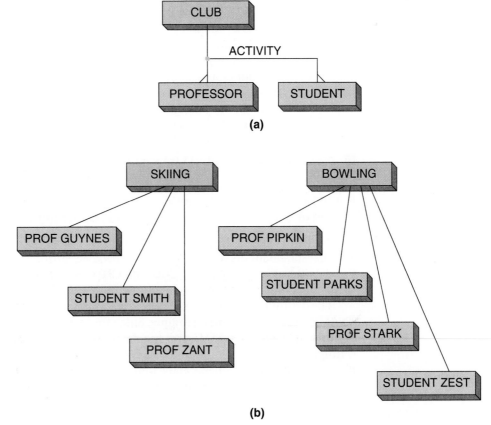

FIGURE 18-18 *Example of Two-Owner Record in Different Sets: (a) Record Belonging to Two Different Sets and (b) Instance of This Set Structure*

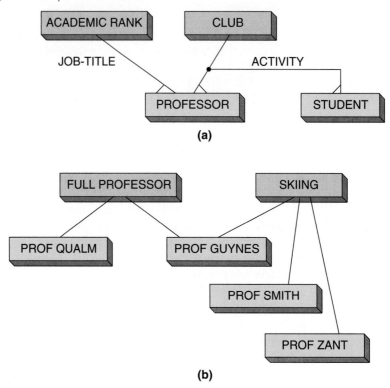

ACTIVITY owner and one JOB-TITLE owner. Figure 18-18 extends Figure 18-17 to allow this possibility. Professor Guynes, for example, has both SKIING and FULL PROFESSOR records as parents.

These restrictions on set membership mean that a set can readily be used to represent 1:1 and 1:N relationships and can directly represent composite objects, 1:1 and 1:N compound objects, association objects, and any hybrid objects that do not include an M:N compound object. M:N compound objects cannot be represented because M:N relationships cannot be represented directly with DBTG sets. The characteristics of sets are summarized in Figure 18-19.

■ A Schema Definition for the Library Database

Figure 18-20 presents a schema definition for the library database design shown in Figure 18-2. The schema definition has two main parts. The first concerns the definition of record structures, and the second, the definition of sets.

DEFINING RECORDS   Examine the definition of the PUB record in Figure 18-20. The first statement declares that values of PNAME must be unique. Following that, the data-items are described. Notice the CHECK statement that enforces the domain constraint that PNAME may not be null.

The definition of TTLE is next. Here, two different statements declare that both TNAME and CALL# are to be unique. Since these statements are separate, they imply that the value of TNAME and the values of CALL# each must be unique. This is different from declaring that a composite group is unique. An example of composite data-item uniqueness can be found in the definition of the next record, CPY, in which the DUPLICATES statement declares that the composite (CALL#, COPY#) must be unique.

FIGURE 18-19   *Summary of Set Characteristics*

- A set is a collection of records.
- There is an arbitrary number of sets in the database.
- Each set has one owner record type and one or more member record types.
- Each owner record occurrence defines a set occurrence.
- There is an arbitrary number of member record occurrences in one set occurrence.
- A record may be a member of more than one set.
- A record may not be a member of two occurrences of the same set.

FIGURE 18-20   *Definition of Library Schema*

```
SCHEMA NAME IS LIBRARY
      RECORD NAME IS PUB
            DUPLICATES ARE NOT ALLOWED FOR PNAME
            PNAME                   TYPE IS      CHARACTER    10
                                    CHECK IS     NOT NULL
            ADDRESS                 TYPE IS      CHARACTER    25
            SALPSN                  TYPE IS      CHARACTER    20
            PPHONE                  TYPE IS      FIXED        10

      RECORD NAME IS TTLE
            DUPLICATES ARE NOT ALLOWED FOR CALL#
            DUPLICATES ARE NOT ALLOWED FOR TNAME
            CALL#                   TYPE IS      CHARACTER    8
                                    CHECK IS     NOT NULL
            TNAME                   TYPE IS      CHARACTER    50
                                    CHECK IS     NOT NULL
            PNAME                   TYPE IS      CHARACTER    10
                                    CHECK IS     NOT NULL
      RECORD NAME IS CPY
            DUPLICATES ARE NOT ALLOWED FOR CALL#, COPY#
            CALL#                   TYPE IS      CHARACTER    8
                                    CHECK IS     NOT NULL
            COPY#                   TYPE IS      FIXED        2
                                    CHECK IS     NOT NULL
            ACQDATE                 TYPE IS      DATE

      RECORD NAME IS AUTH
            DUPLICATES ARE NOT ALLOWED FOR ANAME
            ANAME                   TYPE IS      CHARACTER    30
                                    CHECK IS     NOT NULL
            AFFILIATION             TYPE IS      CHARACTER    30

      RECORD NAME IS TA-INT
            DUPLICATES ARE NOT ALLOWED FOR CALL#, ANAME
            CALL#                   TYPE IS      CHARACTER    8
                                    CHECK IS     NOT NULL
            ANAME                   TYPE IS      CHARACTER    30
                                    CHECK IS     NOT NULL    7

      RECORD NAME IS STU
            DUPLICATES ARE NOT ALLOWED FOR STUDENT#
            STUDENT#                TYPE IS      FIXED        10
                                    CHECK IS     NOT NULL
            SNAME                   TYPE IS      CHARACTER    30
            SPHONE                  TYPE IS      FIXED
```

FIGURE 18-20   *(Continued)*

```
RECORD NAME IS VID
        DUPLICATES ARE NOT ALLOWED FOR VID#, VCOPY#
        DUPLICATES ARE NOT ALLOWED FOR STUDENT#
        VID#                        TYPE IS     FIXED           5
                                    CHECK IS    NOT NULL
        VCOPY#                      TYPE IS     FIXED           2
                                    CHECK IS    NOT NULL
        VNAME                       TYPE IS     CHARACTER      40
        STUDENT#                    TYPE IS     FIXED          10

RECORD NAME IS DUE-DATE
        DATE-DUE                    TYPE IS     DATE
                                    CHECK IS    NOT NULL

SET NAME IS PUBLISH
        OWNER IS PUB
        ORDER IS SORTED BY DEFINED KEYS
        MEMBER IS TTLE
        KEY IS ASCENDING TNAME

SET NAME IS T-A
        OWNER IS TTLE
        ORDER IS SYSTEM DEFAULT
        MEMBER IS TA-INT
        CHECK IS CALL# IN TTLE = CALL# IN TA-INT

SET NAME IS A-T
        OWNER IS AUTH
        ORDER IS SYSTEM DEFAULT
        MEMBER IS TA-INT
        CHECK IS ANAME IN AUTH = ANAME IN TA-INT

SET NAME IS COLLECTION
        OWNER IS TTLE
        ORDER IS BY DEFINED KEYS
        MEMBER IS CPY
        KEY IS ASCENDING COPY#

SET NAME IS CHECKOUT
        OWNER IS STU
        ORDER IS LAST
        MEMBER IS CPY

SET NAME IS VCHKOUT
        OWNER IS STU
        ORDER IS LAST
        MEMBER IS VID

SET NAME IS HISTORY
        OWNER IS CPY
        MEMBER IS DUE-DATE
        ORDER IS LAST

SET NAME IS TITLE-SEQ
        OWNER IS SYSTEM
        ORDER IS BY DEFINED KEYS
        MEMBER IS TTLE
        KEY IS ASCENDING TNAME
```

The remaining record definitions are similar, although one unusual statement appears in the definition of VID. In this record, STUDENT is required to be unique. Since a set is defined with STU as the parent and VID as the child, this relationship would normally be one to many, as the same value of STUDENT could appear in many different instances of VID. With the declaration that STUDENT must be unique, however, the same STUDENT can appear in only one VID record. This declaration therefore turns what would normally be a one-to-many relationship into the one-to-one relationship required in the design.

DEFINING SETS   In Figure 18-20, one set is defined for each one-to-many and one-to-one relationship shown in Figure 18-2. The first set, PUBLISH, represents the relationship between PUB and TTLE. The owner record of this set is PUBLISH, and the member record is TTLE. The records in the set are to be maintained in sorted order of TNAME, defined by two statements in the set definition. The first, ORDER IS SORTED BY DEFINED KEYS, indicates that the order is to be kept by a value of one or more data-items in the member record. The particular data-item is then identified by the statement KEY IS ASCENDING TNAME.

The remaining sets also are defined in Figure 18-20. The sets T-A and A-T represent the M:N relationship between titles and authors. The order is SYSTEM DEFAULT, which means that the application developers are not concerned about the order of the member records in the set. Other statements are similar to those for PUBLISH, except that these sets include a CHECK clause. Consider the set T-A. The CHECK clause in this set definition tells the DBMS to enforce the constraint that the values of CALL in TTLE and TA-INT must match.

■ SUBSCHEMAS FOR THE LIBRARY DATABASE

To illustrate the definition and use of CODASYL DBTG subschemas, we consider two subschemas for the library database. Figure 18-21(a) shows the structure of the PURCHASE subschema, used by application programs in the purchasing department. The second subschema, BORROW, is shown in Figure 18-21(b). BORROW is used by the checkout desk when books are lent.

PURCHASE SUBSCHEMA   The general format of a subschema description is shown in Figure 18-22. Each subschema description has three divisions. The TITLE DIVISION contains the name of the subschema; the MAPPING DIVISION contains alias descriptions; and the STRUCTURE DIVISION indicates the records, data-items, and sets in the schema that are present in the subschema.

Figure 18-23(a) on page 469 has a subschema description for PURCHASE. In the MAPPING DIVISION, the record TTLE is renamed BOOK, and the record DUE-DATE is renamed BORROWED. In addition, the set HISTORY is renamed USES, and the data-item DATE-DUE is named USE-DATE. The application program that accesses this subschema must use these aliases rather than the names in the schema description. AD is a keyword that stands for *alias definition*.

The RECORD SECTION of this subschema redefines the PUB record to omit the ADDRESS data-item. All the data-items in BOOK, CPY, and BORROWED should be part of the PURCHASE subschema. Finally, in the SET SECTION, the sets PUBLISH, COLLECTION, and USES are declared to be included in PURCHASE. SD is a keyword that stands for *set definition*.

BORROW SUBSCHEMA   The subschema BORROW is defined in Figure 18-23(b). The structure of the description is the same as that for PURCHASE. BORROW includes the BOOK (alias for TTLE), BORROWER (alias for STU), CPY, and DUE-DATE records. The sets included are COLLECTION, CHECKOUT, and RETURN (alias for HISTORY).

FIGURE 18-21   *Sample of Subschema Structures: (a) PURCHASE Subschema and (b) BORROW Subschema*

(a)

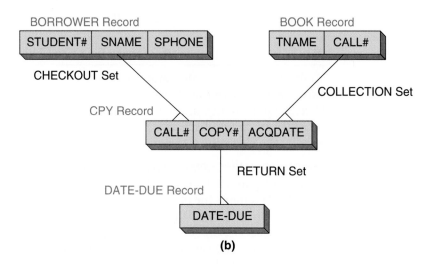

(b)

FIGURE 18-22   *Format of Subschema Description*

```
TITLE DIVISION.
 (subschema name)
MAPPING DIVISION.
ALIAS SECTION.
 (alternate names for records, sets, or data-items)
STRUCTURE DIVISION.
RECORD SECTION.
 (records and data-items that are to appear in the subschema)
SET SECTION.
 (sets to appear in the subschema)
```

FIGURE 18-23 *Example Subschema Definitions for Library Database: (a) PURCHASE Subschema Definition and (b) BORROW Subschema Description*

```
TITLE DIVISION.
SS PURCHASE WITHIN LIBRARY.
MAPPING DIVISION.
ALIAS SECTION.
AD      RECORD TTLE IS BOOK.
AD      RECORD DUE-DATE IS BORROWED.
AD      SET HISTORY IS USES.
AD      DATE-DUE IS USE-DATE.
STRUCTURE DIVISION.
RECORD SECTION.
01      PUB.
            05                          PNAME     PIC X(10).
            05                          SALPSN    PIC X(20).
            05                          PHONE     PIC 9(10).
01      BOOK ALL.
01      CPY ALL.
01      BORROWED ALL.
SET SECTION.
SD      PUBLISH.
SD      COLLECTION.
SD      USES.
```

(a)

```
TITLE DIVISION.
SS BORROW WITHIN LIBRARY.
MAPPING DIVISION.
ALIAS SECTION.
AD      RECORD TTLE IS BOOK.
AD      RECORD STU IS BORROWER.
AD      SET HISTORY IS RETURN.
STRUCTURE DIVISION.
RECORD SECTION.
01      BOOK.
            05                          TNAME     PIC X(50).
            05                          CALL#     PIC X(8).
01      BORROWER ALL.
01      CPY ALL.
01      DUE-DATE ALL.
SET SECTION.
SD      COLLECTION.
SD      CHECKOUT.
SD      RETURN.
```

(b)

■ CODASYL DBTG DATA MANIPULATION LANGUAGE

Most CODASYL DBTG data manipulation commands have two steps. First, a FIND command is issued to identify the record to be acted on. The FIND command does not read or otherwise process the indicated record; it simply identifies a record for the DBMS to locate. After a record has been identified, a second DML command can be issued to perform an operation on it. Typical patterns are FIND, GET; or FIND, MODIFY; or FIND, ERASE.

The only DML command that does not follow this pattern is STORE. Since this command inserts a new record into the database, there is nothing to be found before it is executed.

As we stated, every DBTG run-unit (a particular user connected to a particular program) has a user working area (UWA). The records in the subschema are stored in the UWA. For the PURCHASE subschema, there are four records in the UWA: PUB, BOOK, CPY, and BORROWED. For the BORROW subschema, they are BOOK, BORROWER, CPY, and DUE-DATE.

DBTG DML FOR SINGLE-RECORD PROCESSING   The following examples show how FIND is used in conjunction with other commands to process the database. The commands are shown in pseudocode form, and the particular syntax of each depends on the language in which they are embedded and on the particular implementation of the DBTG model.

Suppose we want to read the BORROWER record for STUDENT 150. The following commands will do this:

```
MOVE "150" TO STUDENT# IN BORROWER
FIND ANY BORROWER USING STUDENT#
GET BORROWER
```

The FIND command sets the current records of run-unit, BORROWER, and CHECKOUT to point to the record for Student 150. Then the GET command places the record into the BORROWER record area in the UWA. GET always operates on the current record.

Suppose we want to read all the CPY records for a book with the call number R726.8.L:

```
MOVE "R726.8.L" TO Call# IN CPY
FIND ANY CPY USING Call#
DOWHILE DB-STATUS = 0
    GET CPY
    (process CPY data)
    FIND DUPLICATE CPY USING Call#
END-DO
```

DB-STATUS, a DBNS-supplied return variable, is used here to control the loop processing. This code assumes that the DBMS will set DB-STATUS to a value other than zero at the end of data. A more sophisticated (and appropriate) algorithm would examine the value of DB-STATUS to ensure that no other condition or error had occurred. The first FIND specifies that ANY record can qualify, and the next FIND specifies DUPLICATE. This keyword means that the desired record must have the same value of CALL that the current record of CPY contains.

To illustrate the elimination of records, suppose we want to delete all CPY records for books having the call number R726.8.L:

```
MOVE "R726.8.L" TO Call# IN CPY
FIND FOR UPDATE ANY CPY USING Call#
DOWHILE DB-STATUS = 0
    ERASE CPY
    FIND FOR UPDATE DUPLICATE CPY USING Call#
END-DO
```

The logic is similar to that for the GET, except that the ERASE command is used in this example. Also, the words FOR UPDATE are added to the FIND command. These keywords inform the DBMS that an update is to occur, and, accordingly, the DBMS locks the record for the run-unit. This is similar to the DL/I GET HOLD commands described in the previous chapter.

To illustrate the modification of records, suppose that the BORROWER with STUDENT# of 150 changes her name to WILLIS:

```
MOVE "150" TO STUDENT# IN BORROWER
FIND FOR UPDATE ANY BORROWER USING STUDENT#
GET BORROWER
IF DB-STATUS = 0
    THEN MOVE "WILLIS" TO SNAME IN BORROWER
        MODIFY SNAME
    ELSE do error processing
END-IF
```

In this case, the MODIFY statement indicates that only the SNAME data-item has been changed. If no data-item is listed, the DBMS is to assume that the entire record (or this subschema's view of it) has been changed.

To create a new record, we first build it in the UWA and then issue a STORE command. The following statements insert a BORROWER record into the database:

```
MOVE "2000" TO STUDENT# IN BORROWER
MOVE "CALBOM" TO SNAME IN BORROWER
MOVE "5258869" TO PHONE IN BORROWER
STORE BORROWER
```

After the STORE command, the new record is the currents of run-unit, BORROWER, and CHECKOUT.

PROCESSING MULTIPLE RECORDS WITH SETS   Sets are used to process records by relationship. Three commands are used to insert and remove records from sets, and then several different formats of the FIND command are used to process the records in sets.

The DBTG model provides three commands for processing set members: CONNECT, DISCONNECT, and RECONNECT. The first command places a record into a set; the second removes a record from a set; and the third changes the set membership.

```
MOVE "R726.8.L" to Call#
MOVE "2" TO COPY#
FIND ANY CPY USING CALL#, COPY#
MOVE "150" TO STUDENT#
FIND ANY BORROWER USING STUDENT#
CONNECT CPY TO CHECKOUT
```

The first FIND command establishes copy 2 of R726.8.L as the current record of CPY. The second FIND then establishes Student 150 as the current record of the CHECKOUT set. The copy is then placed in the set with CONNECT.

DISCONNECT operates in a similar fashion. The current member record is removed from the current set. The following commands take copy 2 of R726.8.L from the set owned by Student 150:

```
MOVE "R726.8.L" to CALL#
MOVE "2" TO COPY#
FIND ANY CPY USING CALL#, COPY#
MOVE "150" TO STUDENT#
FIND ANY BORROWER USING STUDENT#
DISCONNECT CPY FROM CHECKOUT
```

SET MEMBERSHIP AND ERASE COMMANDS   If a record owns a set occurrence, special considerations will apply when the record is deleted. The application program can request that all children (and children of children, and so forth) be erased when the record is erased, or it can be more selective.

Suppose we want to delete a BOOK record and all of the CPY and DUE-DATE records that pertain to this book. The following statements can do this for the book whose call number is Q360.C33:

```
MOVE "Q360.C33" TO CALL#
FIND FOR UPDATE ANY BOOK USING CALL#
ERASE ALL BOOK
```

The keyword ALL in this ERASE command directs the DBMS to erase all CPY records (and all DUE-DATE records belonging to the set owned by CPY).

If ALL is not specified in the ERASE command, the result will depend on other considerations that are beyond the scope of this discussion.

USING SETS FOR RECORD RETRIEVAL   Once records have been placed in sets, set membership can be used to retrieve records by relationships. Suppose we want to process a view of the STUDENT object that contains both BORROWER and CPY records. Say we want to retrieve the call numbers of all the books on loan to Student 400. The following statements do this:

```
MOVE "400" TO STUDENT#
FIND ANY BORROWER USING STUDENT#
FIND FIRST CPY WITHIN CHECKOUT
DOWHILE DB-STATUS <> 0
    GET CPY
    (process CPY record to display CALL#)
    FIND NEXT CPY WITHIN CHECKOUT
END-DO
```

The first FIND command establishes the current records of both BORROWER and CHECKOUT. The next FIND command sets the current of CPY to the first record in the set owned by the BORROWER with STUDENT 400. The first record is then processed, and the next one is identified with the FIND NEXT command. In addition to FIND FIRST and FIND NEXT, this model also provides FIND LAST and FIND *n*th, where *n* is the ordinal position of the record in the set. This last option is useful only if the set members are ordered in some manner.

SUMMARY

DBMS products based on the hierarchical and network data models were created during the earliest years of database processing, and their importance lies in the existing databases whose structure is based on them. Almost no new databases use these models. Their chief importance to you is in maintaining existing applications or converting databases to the relational model.

The sole surviving hierarchical data model is the IBM language DL/I. The most important network model is the CODASYL DBTG data model, of which the DBMS product IDMS was the most important implementation.

DL/I uses terminology substantially different from that of the relational model. In DL/I, a row or record is called a segment. A segment is a group of fields. One field in the segment is designated as the sequence field; it is used to logically order the segments. A tree is made up of several related segments. An instance of a tree is a data base record (DL/I spells data base as two words). Data base records are defined by means of a data base description. A data base is composed of data base records of one or more types.

DL/I is hierarchical. Because the segments in a data base record can have at most one parent, in order to represent networks (relationships in which a child has more than one parent), the network must be decomposed into trees with data duplication. This duplication is then eliminated through the use of pointers or other data structures.

DL/I uses the term *physical data base record* (or PDBR) to refer to physically stored data and the term *logical data base record* (or LDBR) to refer to application views of data. An LDBR differs from a PDBR in one of two ways: It may be a subset of a PDBR, or it may contain portions of two or more PDBRs. An application view is a set of one or more LDBRs.

DL/I statements to retrieve, modify, insert, and delete segments must be embedded in application programs; thus, DL/I cannot be used interactively. DL/I data base requests are carried out by issuing subroutine calls from the application program.

Basic DL/I commands are GET UNIQUE, GET NEXT, GET NEXT within PARENT, GET HOLD UNIQUE, GET HOLD NEXT, GET HOLD NEXT within PARENT, REPLACE, DELETE, and INSERT. Each of these commands operates on an LDBR.

The most significant network data model is known as the CODASYL DBTG data model, named after the committee that developed it. The most significant difference between the network data model and the hierarchical data model is that simple networks can be represented directly in the network model. Thus, it was an improvement over the earlier hierarchical model.

The DBTG model introduced the concepts of both a data definition and a data manipulation language for DBMS products. Unlike DL/I, which has no database definition facilities, products based on the DBTG model provide both languages.

A schema is a logical view of the entire database as seen by the database administration. A subschema is a subset of the database, like a view in the relational model. A subschema is the application program's view of the database.

All user interactions with the database are carried out by means of application programs (there is no interactive query language in the model). An application program can be run by one or more users. Each user has his or her own user work area for passing data to and from the DBMS.

The building blocks used for DBTG data definition are data-items (or fields), records (collections of data-items), and sets (a set is a one-to-many relationship between records). These building blocks can be used to represent all the object types we have discussed in this text: composite, compound, and association. When defining the database, it is easy to transform the relational database definition into the DBTG database definition.

The DBTG model specifies a data manipulation language. Generally, the database is accessed in two steps: The first is used to identify the record to be acted on, and the second performs some operation. The DBTG FIND statement is used to identify a record. When executed, the FIND statement sets the value of one or more currency indicators.

DBTG commands are available to read, insert, modify, and delete database records. DBTG DML can be used to access and process individual database records and to process sets. The syntax shown in this chapter is generic; the exact syntax varies with the DBMS product.

GROUP I QUESTIONS

18.1 Explain the difference in the nature of DBMS products based on the hierarchical, network, and relational models.

18.2 Define the DL/I terms *field, segment, data base record,* and *data base.*

18.3 What DL/I structure corresponds to a node on a tree?

18.4 How are DL/I data base records defined? Does DL/I include data definition language as well as data manipulation language?

18.5 Why must simple networks be transformed into trees before they can be stored for processing by DL/I?

18.6 How does DL/I eliminate data duplication?

18.7 What is the difference between a physical data base record and a logical data base record? In what two ways does an LDBR differ from a PDBR?

18.8 Describe the function of each of the GET commands. Give an example of each.

18.9 Describe the function of each of the GET HOLD commands. Give an example of each.

18.10 Describe the function of each of the REPL, DLET, and INSRT commands. Give an example of each.

18.11 Explain the relationship among user, run-unit, application program, subschema, schema, database, and DBMS.

18.12 Define *data-item*. How are data-items related to domains? How are domains defined using the DBTG model?

18.13 Define *record* as used in the DBTG model.

18.14 Define the following terms and explain their purpose: set, owner, member, set occurrence.

18.15 Give an example of a set structure, and sketch two occurrences of this set.

18.16 Consider the following tree: School districts have schools, and schools have pupils (one record type) and teachers (another record type). Teachers have past assignments. Show a DBTG representation of this tree, and describe two occurrences.

18.17 Consider the following simple network: Fathers have children, and teachers teach children. Show a DBTG representation of this simple network, and describe two occurrences.

18.18 Consider the following complex network: Children have many hobbies, and a hobby is enjoyed by many children. Show a DBTG representation of this complex network, and describe two occurrences.

For Questions 18.19 through 18.22, provide pseudocode similar to that used in this chapter, based on the following model:

SALESPERSON with data-items NAME, AGE, SALARY

ORDER with data-items NUMBER, CUST-NAME, SALESPERSONNAME, AMOUNT

CUSTOMER with data-items NAME, CITY, INDUSTRY-TYPE

SET SALE with owner SALESPERSON and member ORDER

SET PURCHASE with owner CUSTOMER and member ORDER

18.19 Retrieve

   a. Customer with name ABC CONSTRUCTION.

   b. Order with number 12345.

   c. All orders for customer ABC CONSTRUCTION.

18.20 Delete all orders for salesperson PARKS.

18.21 Change the industry type of ABC Construction to type J (assume that INDUSTRY-TYPE is a character data-item).

18.22 Store a new SALESPERSON record: The name is CURTIS, the age is 39, and the salary is 65,000.

GROUP II QUESTIONS

18.23 Consider the following organizational chart:

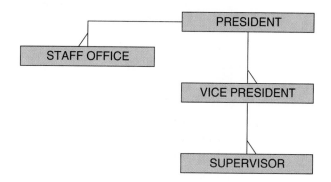

a. Sketch an occurrence of this structure.

b. What in this example constitutes a DL/I segment? A data base record? The total data base?

18.24 Sketch the hierarchical structure and logical pointers necessary to model the following data base records in DL/I:

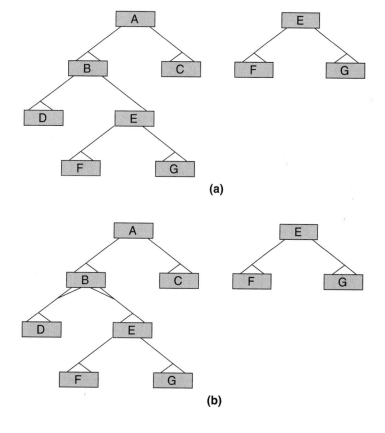

18.25 Assume that a data base consists of three separate PDBs, as follows:

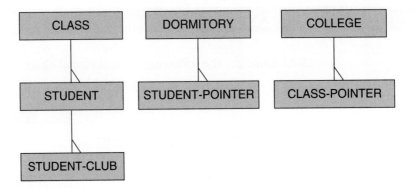

Describe the LDBR required to respond to the following requests:

a. Get the names of all students in a class taught by the College of Business.

b. Find the name of every student club that has at least one member living in Green Dormitory.

The data following Question 18.28 pertain to Questions 18.26 through 18.28. The sequence fields are underlined.

18.26 Describe the results of the following retrievals:

a. GU   FACTORY
          PRODUCT (COST = 40)
          PART

b. GU   FACTORY
          WREHOUSE (NAME = 'W2')
          DISTRBTR

c. GU   FACTORY
          PRODUCT (COST = 40)
          PART(NUM-REQ = 24)
   GN   PART
   GN   PART
   GN   PART
   GN   PART

d. GU   FACTORY
          PRODUCT (COST = 40)
   GNP   PART
   GNP   PART

18.27 What will happen when the last GN PART statement is executed in Question 18.26(c)? How will the user be able to detect this?

18.28 What will happen if another GNP PART statement is executed immediately after those in Question 18.26(d)?

18.29 Show the DL/I statements needed to specify the following actions:

a. Delete the PRT6 24 segment under PRD2.

b. Delete all data concerning warehouse W3.

c. Delete all data concerning factory F1.

d. Delete all products costing more than $45.

Segment	Fields
FACTORY	NAME, LOC
PRODUCT	NAME, COST
PART	NAME, NUM-REQ
WREHOUSE	NAME, LOCCODE
DISTRBTR	NAME

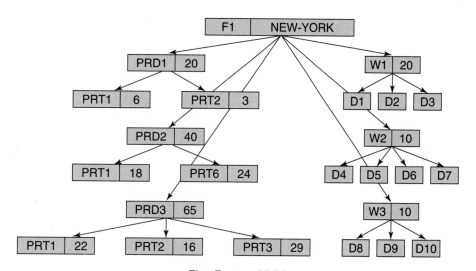

First Factory PDBR

18.30 Compare and contrast the DBTG model with the relational model. Which model is easier to understand? Which do you think would be easier to use? For what applications would the DBTG model be preferable to the relational model? For what applications would the relational model be preferable to the DBTG model?

18.31 Locate a company in your community that uses a CODASYL DBTG DBMS. Talk to some of the people who work there, and find out how the schemas and subschemas are designed. If possible, get a copy of a schema, subschema, and application program, and compare them with the concepts described in this chapter.

DATA STRUCTURES FOR DATABASE PROCESSING

• • • • • • • • • • • • • •

All operating systems provide data management services. These services, however, are generally not sufficient for the specialized needs of a DBMS. Therefore, to enhance performance, DBMS products build and maintain specialized data structures, which are the topic of this appendix.

We begin by discussing flat files and some of the problems that can occur when such files need to be processed in different orders. Then we turn to three specialized data structures: sequential lists, linked lists, and indexes (or inverted lists). Next we illustrate how each of three special structures discussed in Chapter 6—trees, simple networks, and complex networks—are represented using various data structures. Finally, we explore how to represent and process multiple keys.

Although a thorough knowledge of data structures is not required to use most DBMS products, this background is essential to database administrators and systems programmers working with a DBMS. Being familiar with the data structures also helps you evaluate and compare database products.

FLAT FILES

A *flat file* is a file that has no repeating groups. In Figure A-1, (a) shows a flat file, and (b) shows a file that is not flat because of the repeating field Item. A flat file can be stored in any common file organization such as sequential, indexed sequential, or direct. Flat files have been used for many years in commercial processing. They are usually processed in some predetermined order, say, in an ascending sequence on a key field.

PROCESSING FLAT FILES IN MULTIPLE ORDERS

Sometimes users want to process flat files in ways that are not readily supported by the file organization. Consider, for example, the ENROLLMENT records in Figure A-1(a). To produce student schedules, they must be processed in StudentNumber sequence. But to produce class rosters, the records need to be processed in ClassNumber sequence. The records, of course, can be stored in only one physical sequence. For example, they can be in order on StudentNumber or on ClassNumber, but not on both at the same time. The traditional solution to the

FIGURE A-1   *Examples of (a) a Flat and (b) a Nonflat File Enrollment Record*

Enrollment Record

StudentNumber	ClassNumber	Semester

Sample Data

200	70	88S
100	30	89F
300	20	89F
200	30	88S
300	70	88S
100	20	88S

(a)

Invoice Record

InvoiceNumber	Item(s)

Sample Data

1000	10	20	30	40
1010	50			
1020	10	20	30	
1030	50	90		

(b)

FIGURE A-2   *ENROLLMENT Data Stored as Sequential Lists: (a) Sorted by StudentNumber and (b) Sorted by ClassNumber*

Student-Number	Class-Number	Semester
100	30	89F
100	20	88S
200	70	88S
200	30	88S
300	20	89F
300	70	88S

(a)

Student-Number	Class-Number	Semester
300	20	89F
100	20	88S
100	30	89F
200	30	88S
200	70	88S
300	70	88S

(b)

problem of processing records in different orders is to sort them in student order, process the student schedules, then sort the records in class order, and produce class rosters.

For some applications, such as a batch-mode system, this solution, while cumbersome, is effective. But suppose that both orders need to exist simultaneously because two concurrent users have different views of the ENROLLMENT records. What do we do then?

One solution is to create two copies of the ENROLLMENT file and sort them as shown in Figure A-2. Since the data are listed in sequential order, this data structure is sometimes called a *sequential list*. Sequential lists can be readily stored as sequential files. This, however, is not generally done by DBMS products because sequentially reading a file is a slow process. Further, sequential files cannot be updated in the middle without rewriting the entire file. Also, maintaining several orders by keeping multiple copies of the same sequential list is usually not effective because the duplicated sequential list can create data integrity problems. Fortunately, other data structures allow us to process records in different orders and do not require the duplication of data. These include *linked lists* and *indexes*.

■ A NOTE ON RECORD ADDRESSING

Usually the DBMS creates large physical records, or blocks, on its direct access files. These are used as containers for logical records. Typically, there are many logical records per physical record. Here we assume that each physical record is addressed by its relative record number (RRN). Thus, a logical record might be assigned to physical record number 7 or 77 or 10,000. The relative record number is thus the logical record's physical address. If there is more than one logical record per physical record, the address must also specify where the logical record is within the physical record. Thus, the complete address for a logical record might be relative record number 77, byte location 100. This means the record begins in byte 100 of physical record 77.

To simplify the illustrations in this text, we assume that there is only one logical record per physical record, so we need not be concerned with byte offsets within physical records. Although this is unrealistic, it simplifies our discussion to the essential points.

■ MAINTAINING ORDER WITH LINKED LISTS

Linked lists can be used to keep records in logical order that are not necessarily in physical order. To create a linked list, we add a field to each data record. The *link* field holds the address (in our illustrations, the relative record number) of the *next* record in logical sequence. For example, Figure A-3 shows the ENROLLMENT records expanded to include a linked list; this list maintains the records in StudentNumber order. Notice that the link for the numerically last student in the list is zero.

Figure A-4 shows ENROLLMENT records with two linked lists: One list maintains the StudentNumber order, and the other list maintains the ClassNumber order. Two link fields have been added to the records, one for each list.

When insertions and deletions are made, linked lists have a great advantage over sequential lists. For example, to insert the ENROLLMENT record for Student 200 and Class 45, both of the lists in Figure A-2 would need to be rewritten. For the linked lists in Figure A-4, however, the new record could be added to the physical end of the list, and only the values of two link fields would need to be changed

ENROLLMENT Data in StudentNumber Order Using a Linked List

Relative Record Number	Student- Number	Class- Number	Semester	Link
1	200	70	88S	4
2	100	30	89F	6
3	300	20	89F	5
4	200	30	88S	3
5	300	70	88S	0
6	100	20	88S	1

Start of list = 2

ENROLLMENT Data in Two Orders Using Linked Lists

Relative Record Number	Student- Number	Class- Number	Semester	Student Link	Class Link
1	200	70	88S	4	5
2	100	30	89F	6	1
3	300	20	89F	5	4
4	200	30	88S	3	2
5	300	70	88S	0	0
6	100	20	88S	1	3

Start of student list = 2
Start of class list = 6

FIGURE A-5   ENROLLMENT Data After Inserting New Record (in Two Orders Using Linked Lists)

Relative Record Number	Student-Number	Class-Number	Semester	Student Link	Class Link
1	200	70	88S	4	5
2	100	30	89F	6	7
3	300	20	89F	5	4
4	200	30	88S	7	2
5	300	70	88S	0	0
6	100	20	88S	1	3
7	200	45	88S	3	1

Start of student list = 2
Start of class list = 6

FIGURE A-6   ENROLLMENT Data After Deleting Student 200, Class 30 (in Two Orders Using Linked Lists)

Relative Record Number	Student-Number	Class-Number	Semester	Student Link	Class Link
1	200	70	88S	7	5
2	100	30	89F	6	7
3	300	20	89F	5	2
4	200	30	88S	7	2
5	300	70	88S	0	0
6	100	20	88S	1	3
7	200	45	88S	3	1

Start of student list = 2
Start of class list = 6

to place the new record in the correct sequences. These changes are shown in Figure A-5.

When a record is deleted from a sequential list, a gap is created. But in a linked list, a record can be deleted simply by changing the values of the link, or the *pointer* fields. In Figure A-6, the ENROLLMENT record for Student 200, Class 30, has been logically deleted. No other record points to its address, so it has been effectively removed from the chain, even though it still exists physically.

There are many variations of linked lists. We can make the list into a *circular list,* or *ring,* by changing the link of the last record from zero to the address of the first record in the list. Now we can reach every item in the list starting at any item in the list. Figure A-7(a) shows a circular list for the StudentNumber order. A *two-way linked list* has links in both directions. In Figure A-7(b), a two-way linked list has been created for both ascending and descending student orders.

Records ordered using linked lists cannot be stored on a sequential file because some type of direct-access file organization is needed in order to use the link values. Thus, either indexed sequential or direct file organization is required for linked-list processing.

■ MAINTAINING ORDER WITH INDEXES

A logical record order can also be maintained using *indexes* or, as they are sometimes called, *inverted lists*. An index is simply a table that cross-references record addresses with some field value. For example, Figure A-8(a) shows the

FIGURE A-7   *ENROLLMENT Data Sorted by StudentNumber Using (a) a Circular and (b) a Two-Way Linked List*

Relative Record Number	Student-Number	Class-Number	Semester	Link
1	200	70	88S	4
2	100	30	89F	6
3	300	20	89F	5
4	200	30	88S	3
5	300	70	88S	2
6	100	20	88S	1

Start of list = 2

(a)

Relative Record Number	Student-Number	Class-Number	Semester	Ascending Link	Descending Link
1	200	70	88S	4	6
2	100	30	89F	6	0
3	300	20	89F	5	4
4	200	30	88S	3	1
5	300	70	88S	0	3
6	100	20	88S	1	2

Start of ascending list = 2
Start of descending list = 5

(b)

FIGURE A-8   *ENROLLMENT Data and Corresponding Indexes: (a) ENROLLMENT Data, (b) Index on StudentNumber, and (c) Index on ClassNumber*

Relative Record Number	Student-Number	Class-Number	Semester
1	200	70	88S
2	100	30	89F
3	300	20	89F
4	200	30	88S
5	300	70	88S
6	100	20	88S

(a)

Student-Number	Relative Record Number
100	2
100	6
200	1
200	4
300	3
300	5

(b)

Class-Number	Relative Record Number
20	3
20	6
30	2
30	4
70	1
70	5

(c)

ENROLLMENT records stored in no particular order, and (b) shows an index on StudentNumber. In this index the StudentNumbers are arranged in sequence, with each entry in the list pointing to a corresponding record in the original data.

As you can see, the index is simply a sorted list of StudentNumbers. To process ENROLLMENT sequentially on StudentNumber, we simply process the index sequentially, obtaining ENROLLMENT data by reading the records indicated by the pointers. Figure A-8(c) shows another index for ENROLLMENT, one that maintains ClassNumber order.

To use an index, the data to be ordered (here, ENROLLMENT) must reside on an indexed sequential or direct file, although the indexes can reside on any type of file. In practice, almost all DBMS products keep both the data and the indexes on direct files.

If you compare the linked list with the index, you will notice the essential difference between them. In a linked list, the pointers are stored along with the data. Each record contains a link field containing a pointer to the address of the next related record. But in an index, the pointers are stored in indexes, separate from the data. Thus, the data records themselves contain no pointers. Both techniques are used by commercial DBMS products.

■ B-TREES

A special application of the concept of indexes, or inverted lists, is a *B-tree,* a multilevel index that allows both sequential and direct processing of data records. It also ensures a certain level of efficiency in processing, because of the way that the indexes are structured.

A B-tree is an index that is made up of two parts, the sequence set and the index set (these terms are used by IBM's VSAM file organization documentation. You may encounter other, synonymous, terms). The *sequence set* is an index containing an entry for every record in the file. This index is in physical sequence, usually by primary key value. This arrangement allows sequential access to the data records as follows: process the sequence set in order, read the address of each record, and then read the record.

The *index set* is an index pointing to groups of entries in the sequence set index. This arrangement provides rapid direct access to records in the file, and it is the index set that makes B-trees unique.

An example of a B-tree appears in Figure A-9, and an occurrence of this structure can be seen in Figure A-10. Notice that the bottom row in Figure A-9, the sequence set, is simply an index. It contains an entry for every record in the file (although for brevity, both the data records and their addresses have been omitted). Also notice that the sequence set entries are in groups of three. The entries in each group are physically in sequence, and each group is chained to the next one by means of a linked list, as can be seen in Figure A-10.

Examine the index set in Figure A-9. The top entry contains two values, 45 and 77. By following the leftmost link (to RRN2), we can access all the records whose key field values are less than or equal to 45; by following the middle pointer (to RRN3), we can access all the records whose key field values are greater than 45 and less than or equal to 77; and by following the rightmost pointer (to RRN4), we can access all the records whose key field values are greater than 77.

Similarly, at the next level there are two values and three pointers in each index entry. Each time we drop to another level, we narrow our search for a particular record. For example, if we continue to follow the leftmost pointer from the top entry and then follow the rightmost pointer from there, we can access all the records whose key field value is greater than 27 and less than or equal to 45. We have eliminated all that were greater than 45 at the first level.

FIGURE A-9

General Structure of a Simple B-Tree

FIGURE A-10   *Occurrence of the B-Tree in Figure A-9*

RRN	Link1	Value1	Link2	Value2	Link3	
1	2	45	3	77	4	
2	101	7	102	27	103	Index Set
3	104	53	105	65	106	
4	107	84	108	89	109	

.
.
.

	R1	Addr1	R2	Addr2	R3	Addr3	Link	
101	1	Pointer to 6	3	Pointer to 8	7	Pointer to 12	102	
102	10	· · ·	13	· · ·	27	· · ·	103	
103	30	· · ·	35	· · ·	45	· · ·	104	Sequence Set
104	46	· · ·	47	· · ·	53	· · ·	105	(Addresses of
105	55	· · ·	57	· · ·	65	· · ·	106	data records
106	66	· · ·	73	· · ·	77	· · ·	107	are omitted)
107	78	· · ·	80	· · ·	84	· · ·	108	
108	86	· · ·	88	· · ·	89	· · ·	109	
109	91	· · ·	92	· · ·	94	· · ·	0	

B-trees are, by definition, balanced. That is, all the data records are exactly the same distance from the top entry in the index set. This aspect of B-trees ensures performance efficiency, although the algorithms for inserting and deleting records are more complex than those for ordinary trees (which can be unbalanced), because several index entries may need to be modified when records are added or deleted to keep all records the same distance from the top index entry.

FIGURE A-11   *Summary of Data Structures and Data Organizations Used for Ordered Flat Files*

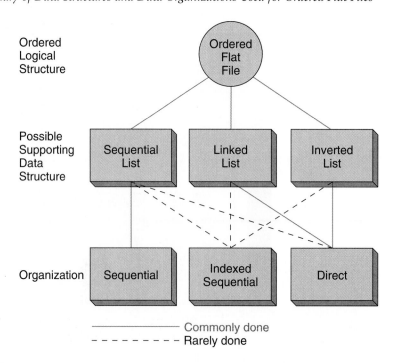

◼ SUMMARY OF DATA STRUCTURES

Figure A-11 summarizes the techniques for maintaining ordered flat files. Three supporting data structures are possible. Sequential lists can be used, but the data must be duplicated in order to maintain several orders. Because sequential lists are not used in database processing, we will not consider them further. Both linked lists and indexes can be used without data duplication. B-trees are special applications of indexes.

As shown in Figure A-11, sequential lists can be stored using any of three file organizations. In practice, however, they are usually kept on sequential files. In addition, although both linked lists and indexes can be stored using either indexed sequential or direct files, DBMS products almost always store them on direct files.

REPRESENTING BINARY RELATIONSHIPS

In this section we examine how each of the specialized record relationships discussed in Chapter 6—trees, simple networks, and complex networks—can be represented using linked lists and indexes.

◼ REVIEW OF RECORD RELATIONSHIPS

Records can be related in three ways. A *tree* relationship has one or more one-to-many relationships, but each child record has at most one parent. The occurrence of faculty data shown in Figure A-12 illustrates a tree. There are several 1:N relationships, but any child record has only one parent, as shown in Figure A-13.

FIGURE A-12 *Occurrence of a Faculty Member Record*

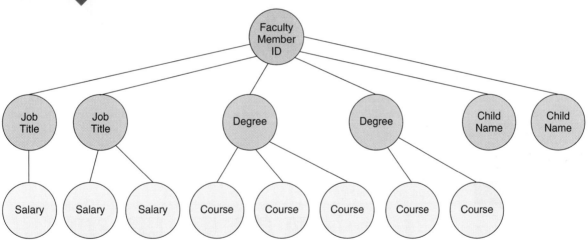

FIGURE A-13 *Schematic of a Faculty Member Tree Structure*

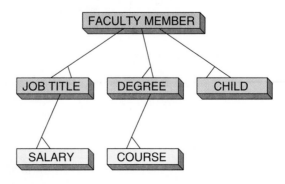

A *simple network* is a collection of records and the 1:N relationships among them. What distinguishes a simple network from a tree is the fact that in a simple network a child can have more than one parent as long as the parents are different record types. The occurrence of a simple network of students, advisers, and major fields of study in Figure A-14 is represented schematically in Figure A-15.

A *complex network* is also a collection of records and relationships, but the relationships are many to many instead of one to many. The relationship between students and classes is a complex network. An occurrence of this relationship can be seen in Figure A-16, and the general schematic is in Figure A-17.

FIGURE A-14   *Occurrence of a Simple Network*

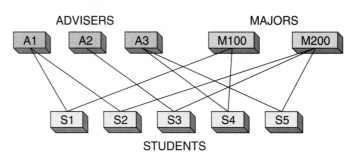

FIGURE A-15   *General Structure of a Simple Network*

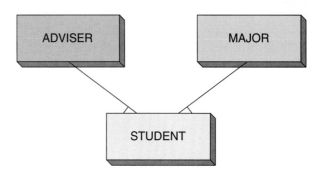

FIGURE A-16   *Occurrence of a Complex Network*

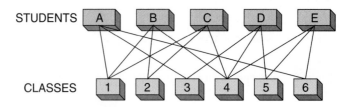

FIGURE A-17   *Schematic of a Complex Network*

We saw earlier that we can use linked lists and indexes to process records in orders different from the one in which they are physically stored. We can also use those same data structures to store and process the relationships among records.

■ REPRESENTING TREES

We can use sequential lists, linked lists, and indexes to represent trees. When using sequential lists, we duplicate many data, and furthermore, sequential lists are not used by DBMS products to represent trees. Therefore, we describe only linked lists and indexes.

LINKED-LIST REPRESENTATION OF TREES   Figure A-18 shows a tree structure in which the VENDOR records are parents and the INVOICE records are children. Figure A-19 shows two occurrences of this structure, and in Figure A-20, all of the VENDOR and INVOICE records have been written to a direct access file. VENDOR AA is in relative record number 1 (RRN1), and VENDOR BB is in relative record number 2. The INVOICE records have been stored in subsequent records, as illustrated. Note that these records are not stored in any particular order and that they do not need to be.

Our problem is that we cannot tell from this file which invoices belong to which vendors. To solve this problem with a linked list, we add a pointer field to every record. In this field we store the address of some other related record. For example, we place in VENDOR AA's link field the address of the first invoice

FIGURE A-18   *Sample Tree Relating VENDOR and INVOICE Records*

FIGURE A-19   *Two Occurrences of VENDOR-INVOICE Tree*

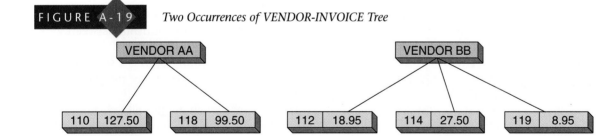

FIGURE A-20   *File Representation of the Trees in Figure A-19*

Record Number	Record Contents	
1	VENDOR AA	
2	VENDOR BB	
3	118	99.50
4	119	8.95
5	112	18.95
6	114	27.50
7	110	127.50

Tree Occurrences Represented by Linked Lists

Relative Record Number	Record Contents		Link Field
1	VENDOR AA		7
2	VENDOR BB		5
3	118	99.50	0
4	119	8.95	0
5	112	18.95	6
6	114	27.50	4
7	110	127.50	3

Inserting Invoice 111 into File in Figure A-21

Relative Record Number	Record Contents		Link Field
1	VENDOR AA		7
2	VENDOR BB		5
3	118	99.50	0
4	119	8.95	0
5	112	18.95	6
6	114	27.50	4
7	110	127.50	8
8	111	19.95	3	← Inserted Record

belonging to it. This is RRN7, which is Invoice 110. Then we make Invoice 110 point to the next invoice belonging to VENDOR AA, in this case RRN3. This slot holds Invoice 118. To indicate that there are no more children in the chain, we insert a 0 in the link field for RRN3.

This technique is shown in Figure A-21. If you examine the figure, you will see that a similar set of links has been used to represent the relationship between VENDOR BB and its invoices.

The structure in Figure A-21 is much easier to modify than is a sequential list of the records. For example, suppose we add a new invoice, say number 111, to VENDOR AA. To do this, we just add the record to the file and insert it into the linked list. Physically, the record can be placed anywhere. But where should it be placed logically? Usually the application will have a requirement like children are to be kept in ascending order on invoice number. If so, we need to make Invoice 110 point to Invoice 111 (at RRN8), and we need to make Invoice 111, the new invoice, point to Invoice 118 (at RRN3). This modification is shown in Figure A-22.

Similarly, deleting an invoice is easy. If Invoice 114 is deleted, we simply modify the pointer in the invoice that is now pointing to Invoice 114. In this case, it is Invoice 112 at RRN5. We give Invoice 112 the pointer that Invoice 114 had before deletion. In this way, Invoice 112 points to Invoice 119 (see Figure A-23). We have effectively cut one link out of the chain and welded together the ones it once connected.

INDEX REPRESENTATION OF TREES A tree structure can readily be represented using indexes. The technique is to store each one-to-many relationship as an index. These lists are then used to match parents and children.

Deleting Invoice 114 from File in Figure A-22

Relative Record Number	Record Contents		Link Field	
1	VENDOR AA		7	
2	VENDOR BB		5	
3	118	99.50	0	
4	119	8.95	0	
5	112	18.95	4	
6	114	27.50	4	← Deleted Record
7	110	127.50	8	
8	111	19.95	3	

Index Representation of VENDOR-INVOICE Relationship

Parent Record	Child Record
1	7
1	3
2	5
2	6
2	4

Simple Network Structure

Using the VENDOR and INVOICE records in Figure A-21, we see that VENDOR AA (in RRN1) owns INVOICEs 110 (RRN7) and 118 (RRN3). Thus, RRN1 is the parent of RRN7 and RRN3. We can represent this fact with the index in Figure A-24. The list simply associates a parent's address with the addresses of each of its children.

If the tree has several 1:N relationships, then several indexes will be required, one for each relationship. For the structure in Figure A-13, five indexes are needed.

■ REPRESENTING SIMPLE NETWORKS

As with trees, simple networks can also be represented using linked lists and indexes.

LINKED-LIST REPRESENTATION OF SIMPLE NETWORKS   Consider the simple network in Figure A-25. It is a simple network because all the relationships are 1:N, and the SHIPMENT records have two parents of different types. Each SHIPMENT has a CUSTOMER parent and a TRUCK parent. The relationship between CUSTOMER and SHIPMENT is 1:N because a customer can have several shipments, and the relationship from TRUCK to SHIPMENT is 1:N because one truck can hold many shipments (assuming that the shipments are small enough to fit in one truck or less). An occurrence of this network is shown in Figure A-26.

In order to represent this simple network with linked lists, we need to establish one set of pointers for each 1:N relationship. In this example, that means one set of pointers to connect CUSTOMERs with their SHIPMENTs and another set of pointers to connect TRUCKs with their SHIPMENTs. Thus, a CUSTOMER record will contain one pointer (to the first SHIPMENT it owns); a TRUCK record will contain one pointer (to the first SHIPMENT it owns); and a SHIPMENT record will have two pointers, one for the next SHIPMENT owned by the same CUSTOMER and one for the next SHIPMENT owned by the same TRUCK. This scheme is illustrated in Figure A-27.

A simple network has at least two 1:N relationships, each of which can be represented using an index, as we explained in our discussion of trees. For example, consider the simple network shown in Figure A-25. It has two 1:N relationships, one between TRUCK and SHIPMENT and one between CUSTOMER and SHIPMENT. We can store each of these relationships in an index. Figure A-28 shows the two indexes needed to represent the example in Figure A-26. Assume the records are located in the same positions as in Figure A-27.

FIGURE A-26 *Occurrence of the Simple Network in Figure A-25*

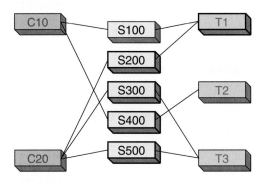

FIGURE A-27 *Representation of a Simple Network with Linked Lists*

Relative Record Number	Record Contents	Link Fields	
1	C10	6	
2	C20	7	
3	T1		6
4	T2		9
5	T3		8
6	S100	9	7
7	S200	8	0
8	S300	10	10
9	S400	0	0
10	S500	0	0

CUSTOMER Links   TRUCK Links

FIGURE A-28   *Representation of Simple Network with Index*

Customer Record	Shipment Record
1	6
1	9
2	7
2	8
2	10

Truck Record	Shipment Record
3	6
3	7
4	9
5	8
5	10

■ REPRESENTING COMPLEX NETWORKS

Complex networks can be physically represented in a variety of ways. They can be decomposed into trees or simple networks, and these simpler structures can then be represented using one of the techniques we just described. Alternatively, they can be represented directly using indexes. Linked lists are not used by any DBMS product to represent complex networks directly. In practice, complex networks are nearly always decomposed into simpler structures, so we consider only those representations using decomposition.

A common approach to representing complex networks is to reduce them to simple networks and then to represent the simple networks with linked lists or indexes. Note, however, that a complex network involves a relationship between two records, whereas a simple network involves relationships among three records. Thus, in order to decompose a complex network into a simple one, we need to create a third record type.

The record that is created when a complex network is decomposed into a simple one is called an *intersection record*. Consider the StudentClass complex network. An intersection record will contain a unique key from a STUDENT record and a unique key from a corresponding CLASS record. It will contain no other application data, although it might contain link fields. The general structure of this relationship is shown in Figure A-29. Assuming that the record names are unique (such as S1, S2, and C1), an instance of the STUDENT-CLASS relationship is illustrated in Figure A-30.

Notice that the relationship between STUDENT and the intersection record and that between CLASS and the intersection record both are 1:N. Thus, we have created a simple network that can now be represented with the linked-list or index techniques shown earlier. A file of this occurrence using the linked-list technique is shown in Figure A-31.

■ SUMMARY OF RELATIONSHIP REPRESENTATIONS

Figure A-32 on page 495 summarizes the representations of record relationships. Trees can be represented using sequential lists (although we did not discuss this

FIGURE A-29   *Decomposition of Complex Network into Simple Network*

FIGURE A-30   *Instance of STUDENT-CLASS Relationship Showing Intersection Records*

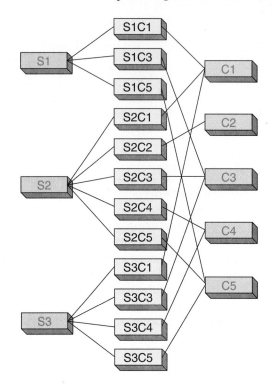

FIGURE A-31   *Occurrence of Network in Figure A-30*

Relative Record Number	Record Contents	Link Fields	
1	S1	9	
2	S2	12	
3	S3	17	
4	C1		9
5	C2		13
6	C3		10
7	C4		15
8	C5		11
9	S1C1	10	12
10	S1C3	11	14
11	S1C5	0	16
12	S2C1	13	17
13	S2C2	14	0
14	S2C3	15	18
15	S2C4	16	19
16	S2C5	0	20
17	S3C1	18	0
18	S3C3	19	0
19	S3C4	20	0
20	S3C5	0	0

STUDENT Links   CLASS Links

FIGURE A-32   *Record Relationships, Data Structures, and File Organizations*

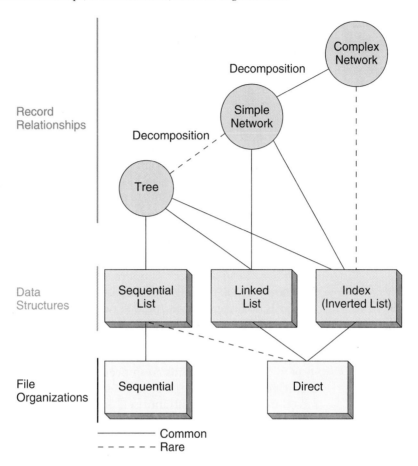

approach), linked lists, or indexes. Sequential lists are not used in DBMS products. A simple network can be decomposed into trees and then represented, or it can be represented directly using either linked lists or indexes. Finally, a complex network can be decomposed into a tree or a simple network (using intersection records), or it can be represented directly using indexes.

SECONDARY-KEY REPRESENTATIONS

In many cases the word *key* indicates a field (or fields) whose value uniquely identifies a record. This is usually called the *primary key.* Sometimes, however, applications need to access and process records by means of a *secondary key,* one that is different from the primary key. Secondary keys may be unique (such as a professor's name) or nonunique (such as a customer's zip code). In this section we use the term *set* to refer to all records having the same value of a nonunique secondary key, for example, a set of records having Zip Code 98040.

Both linked lists and indexes are used to represent secondary keys, but linked lists are practical only for nonunique keys. Indexes, however, can be used for both unique and nonunique key representations.

■ LINKED-LIST REPRESENTATION OF SECONDARY KEYS

Consider the example of CUSTOMER records shown in Figure A-33. The primary key is AccountNumber, and there is a secondary key on CreditLimit. Possible

CreditLimit values are 500, 700, and 1000. Thus there will be a set of records for the limit of 500, a set for 700, and a set for 1000.

To represent this key using linked lists, we add a link field to the CUSTOMER records. Inside this link field we create a linked list for each set of records. Figure A-34 shows a database of eleven customers, but, for brevity, only AccountNumber and CreditLimit are shown. A link field has been attached to the records. Assume that one database record occupies one physical record on a direct file using relative record addressing.

Three pointers need to be established so that we know where to begin each linked list. These are called *heads* and are stored separate from the data. The head of the $500 linked list is RRN1. Record 1 links to record 2, which in turn links to record 7. Record 7 has a zero in the link position, indicating that it is the end of the list. Consequently, the $500 credit limit set consists of records 1, 2, and 7. Similarly, the $700 set contains records 3, 5, and 10, and the $1000 set contains relative records 4, 6, 8, 9, and 11.

To answer a query like, How many accounts in the $1000 set have a balance in excess of $900?, the $1000 set linked list can be used. In this way, only those records in the $1000 set need to be read from the file and examined. Although the advantage of this approach is not readily apparent in this small example, suppose there are 100,000 CUSTOMER records, and only 100 of them are in the $1000 set. If there is no linked list, all 100,000 records must be examined, but with the linked list, only 100 records need to be examined, namely, the ones in the $1000 set. Using the linked list, therefore, saves 99,900 reads.

Linked lists are not an effective technique for every secondary-key application. In particular, if the records are processed nonsequentially in a set, linked lists are inefficient. For example, if it often is necessary to find the 10th or 120th or *n*th record in the $500 CreditLimit set, processing will be slow. Linked lists are inefficient for direct access.

FIGURE A-33   *CUSTOMER Record*

Account-Number	Name	Address	Credit-Limit	Account-Balance

Primary Key   Secondary Key

FIGURE A-34   *Representing CreditLimit Secondary Key Using Linked List*

Relative Record Number	Link	Account-Number	Credit-Limit	Other Data
1	2	101	500	
2	7	301	500	
3	5	203	700	
4	6	004	1000	
5	10	204	700	
6	8	905	1000	
7	0	705	500	
8	9	207	1000	
9	11	309	1000	
10	0	409	700	
11	0	210	1000	

HEAD-500 = 1
HEAD-700 = 3
HEAD-1000 = 4

In addition, if the application requires that secondary keys be created or destroyed dynamically, the linked-list approach is undesirable. Whenever a new key is created, a link field must be added to every record, which often requires reorganizing the database, a time-consuming and expensive process.

Finally, if the secondary keys are unique, each list will have a length of 1, and a separate linked list will exist for every record in the database. Since this situation is unworkable, linked lists cannot be used for unique keys. For example, suppose that the CUSTOMER records contain another unique field, say, Social Security Number. If we attempt to represent this unique secondary key using a linked list, every Social Security Number will be a separate linked list. Furthermore, each linked list will have just one item in it, the single record having the indicated Social Security Number.

■ INDEX REPRESENTATION OF SECONDARY KEYS

A second technique for representing secondary keys uses an index; one is established for each secondary key. The approach varies depending on whether the key values are unique or nonunique.

UNIQUE SECONDARY KEYS Suppose the CUSTOMER records in Figure A-33 contain Social Security Number (SSN) as well as the fields shown. To provide key access to the CUSTOMER records using SSN, we simply build an index on the SSN field. Sample CUSTOMER data are shown in Figure A-35(a), and a corresponding index is illustrated in Figure A-35(b). This index uses relative record numbers as addresses. It would be possible to use AccountNumbers instead, in which case the DBMS would locate the desired SSN in the index, obtain the matching AccountNumber, and then convert the AccountNumber to a relative record address.

NONUNIQUE SECONDARY KEYS Indexes can also be used to represent nonunique secondary keys, but because each set of related records can contain an unknown number of members, the entries in the index are of variable length. For example, Figure A-36 shows the index for the CreditLimit sets for the CUSTOMER data. The $500 set and the $700 set both have three members, so there are three account numbers in each entry. The $1000 set has five members, so there are five account numbers in that entry.

FIGURE A-35

Representing a Unique Secondary Key with Indexes: (a) Sample CUSTOMER Data (with SSN) and (b) Index for SSN Secondary Key

Relative Record Number	Account-Number	Credit-Limit	Social Security Number (SSN)
1	101	500	000-01-0001
2	301	500	000-01-0005
3	203	700	000-01-0009
4	004	1000	000-01-0003

(a)

SSN	Relative Record Number
000-01-0001	1
000-01-0003	4
000-01-0005	2
000-01-0009	3

(b)

Index for CreditNumber *Key in Figure A-33*

CreditLimit	AccountNumber				
500	101	301	705		
700	203	204	409		
1000	004	905	207	309	210

In reality, representing and processing nonunique secondary keys are complex tasks. Several different schemes are used by commercial DBMS products. One common method uses a values table and an occurrence table. Each values table entry consists of two fields, the first of which has a key value. For the CUSTOMER credit-limit key, the values are 500, 700, and 1000. The second field of the values table entry is a pointer into the occurrence table. The occurrence table contains record addresses, and those having a common value in the secondary-key field appear together in the table. Figure A-37 shows the values and occurrence tables for the Credit-limit key.

To locate records having a given value of the secondary key, the values table is searched for the desired value. Once the given key value is located in the values table, the pointer is followed to the occurrence table to obtain the addresses of those records having that key value. These addresses are then used to obtain the desired records.

When a new record is inserted into the file, the DBMS must modify the indexes for each secondary-key field. For nonunique keys, it must make sure that the new record key value is in the values table; if it is, it will add the new record address to the appropriate entry in the occurrence table. If it is not, it must insert new entries in the values and occurrence tables.

When a record is deleted, its address must be removed from the occurrence table. If no addresses remain in the occurrence table entry, the corresponding values table entry must also be deleted.

When the secondary-key field of a record is modified, the record address must be removed from one occurrence table entry and inserted into another. If the modification is a new value for the key, an entry must be added to the values table.

The index approach to representing secondary keys overcomes the objections to the linked-list approach. Direct processing of sets is possible. For example, the third record in a set can be retrieved without processing the first or second one. Also, it is possible to dynamically create and delete secondary keys. No changes are made in the records themselves; the DBMS merely creates additional values and occurrence tables. Finally, unique keys can be processed efficiently.

The disadvantages of the index approach are that it requires more file space (the tables use more overhead than the pointers do) and that the DBMS program-

Values and Occurrence Tables for CreditLimit Key in Figure A-33

Values Table   Occurrence Table

CreditLimit		AccountNumber				
500	— →	101	301	705		
700	— →	203	204	409		
1000	— →	004	905	207	309	210

ming task is more complex. Note that the *application programming* task is not necessarily any more or less difficult—but it is more complex to write DBMS software that processes indexes than it is to write software that processes linked lists. Finally, modifications are usually processed more slowly because of the reading and writing actions required to access and maintain the values in the occurrence tables.

SUMMARY

In this appendix we surveyed data structures used for database processing. A flat file is a file that contains no repeating groups. Flat files can be ordered using sequential lists (physically placing the records in the sequence in which they will be processed), linked lists (attaching to each data record a pointer to another logically related record), and indexes (building a table, separate from the data records, containing pointers to related records). B-trees are special applications of indexes.

Sequential lists, linked lists, and indexes (or inverted lists) are fundamental data structures. (Sequential lists, however, are seldom used in database processing.) These data structures can be used to represent record relationships as well as secondary keys.

The three basic record structures—trees, simple networks, and complex networks—can be represented using linked lists and indexes. Simple networks can be decomposed into trees and then represented; complex networks can be decomposed into simple networks containing an intersection record and then represented.

Secondary keys are used to access the data on some field besides the primary key. Secondary keys can be unique or nonunique. Nonunique secondary keys can be represented with both linked lists and indexes. Unique secondary keys can be represented only with indexes.

GROUP I QUESTIONS

A.1 Define a flat file. Give an example (other than one in this text) of a flat file and an example of a file that is not flat.

A.2 Show how sequential lists can be used to maintain the file in Question A.1 in two different orders simultaneously.

A.3 Show how linked lists can be used to maintain the file in Question A.1 in two different orders simultaneously.

A.4 Show how inverted lists can be used to maintain the file in Question A.1 in two different orders simultaneously.

A.5 Define a tree, and give an example structure.

A.6 Give an occurrence of the tree in Question A.5.

A.7 Represent the occurrence in Question A.6 using linked lists.

A.8 Represent the occurrence in Question A.6 using indexes.

A.9 Define a simple network and give an example structure.

A.10 Give an occurrence of the simple network in Question A.9.

A.11 Represent the occurrence in Question A.10 using linked lists.

A.12 Represent the occurrence in Question A.10 using indexes.

A.13 Define complex network, and give an example structure.

A.14 Give an occurrence of the complex network in Question A.13.

A.15 Decompose the complex network in Question A.14 into a simple network, and represent an occurrence of it using indexes.

A.16 Explain the difference between primary and secondary keys.

A.17 Explain the difference between unique and nonunique keys.

A.18 Define a file containing a unique secondary key. Represent an occurrence of that file using an index on the secondary key.

A.19 Define a nonunique secondary key for the file in Question A.18. Represent an occurrence of that file using a linked list on the secondary key.

A.20 Perform the same task as in Question A.19, but using an index to represent the secondary key.

GROUP II QUESTIONS

A.21 Develop an algorithm to produce a report listing the IDs of students enrolled in each class, using the linked-list structure in Figure A-4.

A.22 Develop an algorithm to insert records into the structure in Figure A-4. The resulting structure should resemble the one in Figure A-5.

A.23 Develop an algorithm to produce a report listing the IDs of students enrolled in each class, using the index structure shown in Figures A-8(a), (b), and (c).

A.24 Develop an algorithm to insert a record into the structure in Figure A-8(a), being sure to modify both of the associated indexes in Figures A-8(b) and (c).

A.25 Develop an algorithm to delete a record from the structure in Figure A-34, which shows a secondary key represented with a linked list. If all records for one of the credit-limit categories (say $1000) are deleted, should the associated head pointer also be deleted? Why or why not?

A.26 Develop an algorithm to insert a record into the structure shown in Figure A-34. Suppose the new record has a credit-limit value different from those already established. Should the record be inserted and a new linked list established? Or should the record be rejected? Who should make that decision?

GLOSSARY

Abstract data type: In SQL3, a user-defined structure having methods, data items, and identifiers. A version of an OOP object; persistence is provided by binding the ADT to a column of a relation.

Action/object menu: A system of menus in which the top menu refers to actions and the lowest menus refer to the objects on which those actions are taken.

ActiveX: An architecture of program elements developed and promulgated by Microsoft. ActiveX provides a means by which independent programs can interface with one another dynamically. ActiveX controls are program segments that conform to the ActiveX interface. See IUnknown and Query Interface.

ADT: See Abstract data type.

After-image: A record of a database entity (normally a row or a page) after a change. It is used in recovery to perform rollforward.

AI: Artificial intelligence. A group of related disciplines providing capabilities that in the past were attributed only to humans. Vision, robotics, and expert systems are branches of artificial intelligence. Sometimes a vague term, artificial intelligence is used in marketing literature to mean new and exciting.

Anomaly: An undesirable consequence of a data modification used primarily in discussions of normalization. With an insertion anomaly, facts about two or more different themes must be added to a single row of a relation. With a deletion anomaly, facts about two or more themes are lost when a single row is deleted.

API: See Application program interface.

Application: A business computer system that processes a portion of a database to meet a user's information needs. It consists of menus, forms, reports, queries, and application programs.

Application design: The process of creating the structure of programs and data to meet the application's requirements. Also the structure of the users' interface.

Application metadata: Data dictionary data concerning the structure and contents of application menus, forms, and reports.

Application plan: In DB2, a set of access paths for each SQL statement in an application program. It includes information about database tables' structures, available indexes, and data storage structures.

Application program: A custom-developed program for processing a database. It can be written in a standard procedural language such as COBOL, C, or BASIC or in a language unique to the DBMS.

Application program interface (API): A set of program procedures or functions that can be called to invoke a set of services. The API includes the names of the procedures and functions and a description of the name, purpose, and data type of parameters to be provided. For example, a DBMS product could provide a library of functions to call for database services. The names of procedures and their parameters constitute the API for that library.

Application view: That portion of a database processed by a particular application program.

Archetype/version object: A structure of two objects that represents multiple versions of a standardized item. For example, a SOFT-PRODUCT (the archetype) and PRODUCT-RELEASE (the version of the archetype). The identifier of the version always includes the archetype object.

Association object: An object that represents the combination of at least two other objects and that contains data about that combination. It is often used in contracting and assignment applications.

Atomic: A set of actions that is completed as a unit. Either all actions are completed or none is.

Atomic transaction: A group of logically related database operations that is performed as a unit. Either all of the operations are performed, or none of them is.

Attribute: (1) A column of a relation; also called a column, field, or data-item. (2) A property in an entity or semantic object. (3) A data or relationship property in an OOP object. (4) In the ODMG-93 model, an implementation of an object property in an OOP implementation such as C++ or Smalltalk.

Authorization rules: A set of processing permissions that describes which users or user groups can take particular actions against particular portions of the database.

Band: The section of a report definition that contains the format of a report section. There normally are bands for the report heading and footing, page heading and footing, and the detail line of the report. There are also bands for group or break points within the report.

Banded report writer: A report writer in which the sections of the reports are defined by bands. (See Band.)

Base table: In relational implementations, the table from which relational views are defined.

Before-image: A record of a database entity (normally a row or a page) before a change. It is used in recovery to perform rollback.

Bill of materials: A recursive data structure in which a part (or, in general, any element) can be both an assembly of other parts and a component of other assemblies.

Binary relationship: A relationship between exactly two entities or tables.

Bind: A verb meaning to connect a program variable or a GUI control to a column of a table or query.

Bottom-up database design: The design of a database that works from the detailed and specific to the general. Although this sort of design takes little time, it may result in a database that is too narrow in scope.

Boyce–Codd normal form: A relation in third normal form in which every determinant is a candidate key.

Branch: A subelement of a tree that may consist of one or many nodes.

Buffer: An area of memory used to hold data. For a read, data is read from a storage device into a buffer; for a write, data is written from the buffer to storage.

Built-in function: In SQL, any of the functions COUNT, SUM, AVG, MAX, or MIN.

Callback: An OOP design practice by which an object passes its identity to another object with the expectation that the called object will notify the calling object when some event occurs. Often the event is the destruction of the called object, but used for other purposes as well.

Candidate key: An attribute or group of attributes that identifies a unique row in a relation. One of the candidate keys is chosen to be the primary key.

Cardinality: In a binary relationship, the maximum or minimum number of elements allowed on each side of the relationship. The maximum cardinality can be 1:1, 1:N, N:1, or N:M. The minimum cardinality can be optional–optional, optional–mandatory, mandatory–optional, or mandatory–mandatory.

Cartesian product: A relational operation on two relations, A and B, producing a third relation, C, with C containing the concatenation of every row in A with every row in B.

CCP: Communications control program. A program that controls and administers transactions requests and responses in a teleprocessing system. The CCP routes transactions to the correct application programs and returns responses to the correct user terminal.

CGI: See Common gateway interface.

Check box: In a GUI environment, an element of the user interface in which a user can select one or more items from a list. Items are selected by clicking on them.

Checkpoint: The point of synchronization between a database and a transaction log. All buffers are force-written to external storage. This is the standard definition of checkpoint, but this term is sometimes used in other ways by DBMS vendors.

Child: A row, record, or node on the many side of a one-to-many relationship.

Child and twin pointer scheme: In DL/I, a technique used to represent segment relationships of a data base record in storage.

Child pointer: In the child and twin pointer scheme, the address of a child node.

Client computer: A microcomputer on a local area network with client–server architecture. In a database application, the client computer processes database application programs. Requests for actions on the database are sent to the database computer.

Client–server database architecture: The structure of a networked computing system in which one computer (usually a microcomputer) performs services on behalf of other computers (usually a microcomputer). For a database system, the server computer, which is called a database server, processes the DBMS, and client computers process the application programs. All database activities are carried out by the database server.

Client–server system: A system of two or more computers in which at least one computer provides services for one or more other computers. The services can be database services, communication services, printer services, or some other function.

COBOL: Common Business Oriented Language. The most widely used third-generation language for business applications.

CODASYL: Conference on Data Systems Languages. A nonprofit committee of vendor, user, and academic personnel who established and now maintain the conventions for COBOL. The DBTG, or DataBase task group, developed a network model that was popular in the 1970s and early 1980s but is now being phased out.

Column: A logical group of bytes in a row of a relation or a table. The meaning of a column is the same for every row of the relation.

Command: A statement input to a database application by which users specify the activity to be performed. Contrast this with Menu.

Commit: A command issued to the DBMS to make database modifications permanent. Once the command has been processed, the changes are written to the database and to a log in such a way that they will survive system crashes and other failures. A commit is usually used at the end of an atomic transaction. Contrast this with Rollback.

Common gateway interface: A standard for defining forms and sending and receiving form data in HTML documents.

Communications control program: See CCP.

Complex network: A collection of entities, objects, or relations and their relationships, of which at least one of the relationships is complex (many to many).

Composite group: A group of attributes in a semantic object that is multivalued and contains no other object attributes.

Composite key: A key with more than one attribute.

Composite object: An object with at least one multivalued attribute or attribute group. It is called a composite object because the key of the relation that represents the multivalued attribute or group is a composite key.

Compound object: An object that contains at least one other object.

Computed value: A column of a table that is computed from other column values. Values are not stored but are computed when they are to be displayed.

Concurrency: A condition in which two or more transactions are processed against the database at the same time. In a single CPU system, the changes are interleaved; in a multi-CPU system, the transactions may be processed simultaneously, and the changes on the database server are interleaved.

Concurrency transparency: In a distributed database system, the condition in which application programs do not know and do not need to know whether data is being concurrently processed. The DDBMS organizes update activities so that the results produced when concurrent processing is under way are consistent with the results that would occur if there were no concurrent processing.

Concurrent processing: In teleprocessing applications, the sharing of the CPU among several transactions. The CPU is allocated to each transaction in a round robin or in some other fashion for a certain period of time. Operations are performed so quickly that they appear to users to be simultaneous. In local area networks and other distributed applications, concurrent processing is used to refer to the (possibly simultaneous) processing of applications on multiple computers.

Concurrent update problem: An error condition in which one user's data changes are overwritten by another user's data changes. Same as Lost update problem.

Conflict: Two operations conflict if they operate on the same data item and at least one of the operations is a write.

Consistency: Two or more concurrent transactions are consistent if the result of their processing is the same as it would have been if they had been processed in some serial order.

Consistent schedule: An ordered list of transaction operations against a database in which the result of the processing is consistent.

Constraint: A rule concerning the allowed values of attributes whose truth can be evaluated. A constraint usually does not include dynamic rules such as "SalesPersonPay can never decrease" or "Salary now must be greater than Salary last quarter."

CPU: Central processing unit. The portion of the computer hardware that processes arithmetic and logic instructions. The term CPU usually includes main memory as well.

Currency indicator: In the CODASYL DBTG model, a variable that identifies the most recently accessed record or set. There are currency indicators for run-unit, record type, and set.

Cursor: An indicator of the current position or focus. (1) On a computer screen, a blinking box or underscore that indicates the position into which the next entry will be made. (2) In a file or embedded SQL SELECT, the identity of the next record or row to be processed.

Data access language: See Data sublanguage.

Data administration: The enterprisewide function that concerns the effective use and control of the organization's data assets. It can be a person but more often is a group. Specific functions include setting data standards and data policies and providing a forum for conflict resolution. Also see Database administrator.

Data base: In DL/I, a collection of data base records.

Database: A self-describing collection of integrated records.

Database administration: The function that concerns the effective use and control of a particular database and its related applications.

Database administrator: The person or group responsible for establishing policies and procedures to control and protect a database. He (she or it) works within guidelines set by data administration to control the database structure, manage data changes, and maintain DBMS programs.

Database data: The portion of a database that contains data of interest and use to the application end users.

Data base description: In DL/I, a data structure that describes the structure of a data base record.

Database machine: A special-purpose CPU designed specifically for processing a database. It is sometimes called a backend machine because it resides between the operating system and the data. The database machine has not been commercially successful, however, and is seldom used today.

Database manager (DBM): A program that processes some portion of a distributed database.

Database node: A computer that processes a database manager and its related database(s).

Data base record: In DL/I, a hierarchical arrangement of data segments. See Logical data base record and Physical data base record.

Data base request module: In DB2, a data structure that describes the SQL statements that need to be executed.

Database save: A copy of database files that can be used to restore the database to some previous, consistent state.

Database server: On a local area network with client–server database architecture, the microcomputer that runs the DBMS and processes actions against the database on behalf of its client computers.

Data definition language (DDL): A language used to describe the structure of a database.

Data dictionary: A user-accessible catalog of both database and application metadata. An active data dictionary is a dictionary whose contents are automatically updated by the DBMS whenever changes are made in the database or application structure. A passive data dictionary is one whose contents must be updated manually when changes are made.

Data dictionary and database administration subsystem: A collection of programs in the DBMS used to access the data dictionary and to perform database administration functions such as maintaining passwords and performing backup and recovery.

Dataflow diagram: A graphical display by system developers that illustrates business processes and the data interfaces. It also shows the flow of the system from the perspective of the data.

Data integrity: The state of a database in which all constraints are fulfilled. Usually refers to intertable constraints in which the value of a foreign key is required to be present in the table having that foreign key as its primary key.

Data-item: (1) A logical group of bytes in a record, usually used with file processing. (2) In the context of the relational model, a synonym for attribute.

Data Language I: See DL/I.

Data manipulation language (DML): A language used to describe the processing of a database.

Data mart: A facility similar to a data warehouse but for a restricted domain. Often the data are restricted to particular types, or to particular business functions, or to particular business units.

Data model: (1) A model of the users' data requirements expressed in terms of either the entity-relationship model or the semantic-object model. It is sometimes called a users' data model. (2) A language for describing the structure and processing of a database. See Hierarchical data model, Network data model, and Relational data model.

Data owner: Same as Data proponent.

Data proponent: In data administration, a department or other organizational unit in charge of managing a particular data item.

Data replication: A term that indicates whether any portion (or all) of a database resides on more than one computer. If so, the data are said to be replicated.

Data source: In the ODBC standard, a database together with its associated DBMS, operating system, and network platform.

Data structure diagram: A graphical display of tables (files) and their relationships. The tables are shown in rectangles, and the relationships are shown by lines. A many relationship is shown with a fork on the end of the line; an optional relationship is depicted by an oval; and a mandatory relationship is shown with hash marks.

Data sublanguage: A language for defining and processing a database intended to be embedded in programs written in another language—in most cases, a procedural language such as COBOL, C, or BASIC. A data sublanguage is an incomplete programming language, as it contains only constructs for data access.

Data warehouse: A store of enterprise data that is designed to facilitate management decision making. A data warehouse includes not only data, but also metadata, tools, procedures, training, personnel, and other resources that make access to the data easier and more relevant to decision makers.

DBA: See Database administrator.

DBM: Database manager. In a DDBMS, software that processes some portion of a distributed database in accordance with action requests received from distributed transactions managers (DTMs).

DBMS: Database management system. A set of programs used to define, administer, and process the database and its applications.

DBMS engine: A DBMS subsystem that processes logical I/O requests from other DBMS subsystems and submits physical I/O requests to the operating system.

DBTG: (1) A subcommittee of CODASYL that developed the DBTG network data model. (2) A network data model that models data as records and record relationships as sets. Only simple networks can be directly represented. Although the DBTG network data model is fading in popularity, it still is in use on mainframe computers.

DB2: Database 2. A relational DBMS developed and licensed by IBM for use on mainframe computers.

DDBMS: Distributed database management system. (1) The collection of DTMs and DBMs on all computers that processes a distributed database (see Chapter 16). (2) A commercial DBMS product that has been modified to allow processing a distributed database.

DDL: Data definition language. The portion of a data model used to define the structure of the database, views, and subschemas.

Deadlock: A condition that can occur during concurrent processing in which each of two (or more) transactions is waiting to access data that the other transaction has locked. It is also called a deadly embrace.

Deadlock detection: The process of determining whether two or more transactions are in a state of deadlock.

Deadlock prevention: A way of managing transactions so that a deadlock cannot occur.

Deadly embrace: See Deadlock.

Definition tools subsystem: The portion of the DBMS program used to define and change the database structure.

Degree: For relationships in the entity-relationship model, the number of entities participating in the relationship. In almost all cases, such relationships are of degree 2.

Deletion anomaly: In a relation, the situation in which the removal of one row of a table deletes facts about two or more themes.

Determinant: One or more attributes that functionally determine another attribute or attributes. In the functional dependency $(A, B) \rightarrow C$, the attributes (A, B) are the determinant.

Difference: A relational algebra operation performed on two union-compatible relations, A and B, that produces a third relation, C. Each row in C is present in A but not in B.

Distributed database: A database stored on two or more computers. Distributed data can be partitioned or not partitioned, replicated or not replicated.

Distributed database application: A business computer system in which the execution of transactions and the retrieval and updating of data occur across two or more independent and usually geographically distributed computers.

Distributed database management system (DDBMS): In a distributed database, the collection of distributed transaction and database managers on all computers.

Distributed database processing: Database processing in which transactions are executed and data is retrieved and updated across two or more independent and usually geographically separated computers.

Distributed database system: A distributed system in which a database or portions of a database are distributed across two or more computers.

Distributed system: A system in which the application programs of a database are processed on two or more computers.

Distributed two-phase locking: Two-phase locking in a distributed environment, in which locks are obtained and released across all nodes on the network. See Two-phase locking.

DL/I: Data Language I. A data model developed by IBM in the late 1960s to define and process hierarchical databases. The IBM DBMS product IMS is based on DL/I. Although IMS is still in widespread use on mainframes, such databases are being replaced by relational databases.

DML: Data manipulation language. The portion of a data model used to describe the processing of a database.

Domain: (1) The set of all possible values an attribute can have. (2) A description of the format (data type, length) and the semantics (meaning) of an attribute.

Domain/key normal form (DK/NF): A relation in which all constraints are logical consequences of domains and keys.

Download: Copying database data from one computer to another, usually from a mainframe or mini to a microcomputer or LAN.

Drill down: User-directed disaggregation of data; used to break higher-level totals into components.

Driver: In ODBC, a program that serves as an interface between the ODBC driver manager and a particular DBMS product. Runs on the client machines in a client-server architecture.

Driver manager: In ODBC, a program that serves as an interface between an application program and an ODBC driver. It determines the driver required, loads it into memory, and coordinates activity between the application and the driver. On Windows systems, it is provided by Microsoft.

DSD: See Data structure diagram.

DSS: Decision support system. An interactive, computer-based facility for assisting decision making, especially for semistructured and unstructured problems. Such a system often includes a database and a query/update facility for processing ad hoc requests.

DTM: Distributed transaction manager. In a DDBMS, software that receives processing requests from users or application programs and translates them into DBM requests for actions. A DTM can send requests to DBMs on nodes different from its own.

Encapsulated data: Properties or attributes contained in a program or object not visible or accessible to other programs or objects.

Encapsulated structure: A portion of an object that is not visible to other objects.

Entity: (1) Something of importance to a user that needs to be represented in a database. (2) In an entity-relationship model, entities are restricted to things that can be represented by a single table. Also see Existence-dependent entity, Strong entity, and Weak entity.

Entity class: A set of entities of the same type, for example, EMPLOYEE and DEPARTMENT.

Entity instance: A particular occurrence of an entity, for example, Employee 100 and the Accounting Department.

Entity-relationship diagram: A graphic used to represent entities and their relationships. Entities are normally shown in squares or rectangles, and relationships are shown in diamonds. The cardinality of the relationship is shown inside the diamond.

Entity-relationship model: The constructs and conventions used to create a model of the users' data (see Data model). The things in the users' world are represented by entities, and the associations among those things are represented by relationships. The results are usually documented in an entity-relationship diagram.

Entry-point relation: Used with regard to the relations representing an object. The entry-point relation is the relation whose key is the same as the key of the object it represents. The entry-point relation is normally the first relation processed. Also, the name of the entry-point relation is normally the same as the name of the object.

Enumerated list: A list of allowed values for a domain, attribute, or column.

Equijoin: The process of joining relation A containing attribute A1 with B containing attribute B1 to form relation C, so that for each row in C, A1 = B1. Both A1 and B1 are represented in C.

E-R diagram: See Entity-relationship diagram.

Exclusive lock: A lock on a data resource that no other transaction can either read or update.

Existence-dependent entity: Same as a weak entity. An entity that cannot appear in the database unless an instance of one or more other entities also appears in the database. A subclass of existence-dependent entities is ID-dependent entities.

Explicit lock: A lock requested by a command from an application program.

Export: A function of the DBMS, to write a file of data in bulk. The file is intended to be read by another DBMS or program.

Extent (of object): In the ODMG model, the union of all object instances. Attributes can be declared to be unique across an object's extent.

Extract: A portion of an operational database downloaded to a local area network or microcomputer for local processing. Extracts are created to reduce communications cost and time when querying and creating reports from data created by transaction processing.

Failure transparency: In a distributed database system, the condition in which application programs are isolated from failure.

Field: (1) A logical group of bytes in a record; used with file processing. (2) In the context of a relational model, a synonym for attribute.

File-processing system: An information system in which data is stored in separate files. There is no integrated data dictionary. The format of the files is usually stored in application programs.

File server: In a local area network, a microcomputer containing a file that it processes on behalf of other microcomputers on the network. The term file server is normally used for the resource-sharing architecture. See Client computer, Client–server database architecture, Database server, and Resource-sharing architecture.

Firewall: A computer that serves as a security gateway between an intranet and the Internet. Firewalls monitor the source and destination of network traffic and filter it.

First normal form: Any table that fits the definition of a relation.

Flat file: A file that has only a single value in each field. The meaning of the columns is the same in every row.

Force-write: A write of database data in which the DBMS waits for acknowledgment from the operating system that the after-image of the write has been successfully written to the log.

Foreign key: An attribute that is a key of one or more relations other than the one in which it appears.

Form: (1) A display on a computer screen used to present, enter, and modify data. A form is also called a data entry form or panel. (2) A paper document used in a business system to record data, usually concerning a transaction. Forms are analyzed in the process of building a data model.

Forms generator: A portion of the application development subsystem used to create a data entry form without having to write any application program code.

Formula domain: A domain whose values are computed by an expression containing arguments that are themselves domains.

Fourth normal form: A relation in third Boyce–Codd normal form in which every multivalued dependency is a functional dependency.

Fragment: A row in a table (or record in a file) in which a required parent or child is not present. For example, a row in a LINE-ITEM table for which no ORDER row exists.

FTP: File transfer protocol. A standard Internet service for copying files to or from a remote server.

Fully concatenated key: In DL/I, a composite of the sequence fields of a segment and the sequence fields of all its parents. The root occupies the leftmost position in the concatenated key, and the segment occupies the rightmost position.

Functional dependency: A relationship between attributes in which one attribute or group of attributes determines the value of another. The expressions $X \rightarrow Y$, "X determines Y," and "Y is functionally dependent on X" mean that given a value of X, we can determine the value of Y.

Generalization hierarchy: A set of objects or entities of the same logical type that are arranged in a hierarchy of logical subtypes. For example, EMPLOYEE has the subtypes ENGINEER and ACCOUNTANT, and ENGINEER has the subtypes ELECTRICAL ENGINEER and MECHANICAL ENGINEER. Subtypes inherit characteristics of their supertypes.

Generalization object: An object that contains subtype objects. The generalization object and its subtypes all have the same key. Subtype objects inherit attributes from the generalization object. A generalization object is also called a supertype object.

Granularity: The size of database resource that can be locked. Locking the entire database is large granularity; locking a column of a particular row is small granularity.

Graphical user interface: An interface having windows, graphical symbols, pop-down menus, and other structures that are often manipulated with a mouse pointer. Popular graphical user interface products are Windows from Microsoft and the Macintosh System Software from Apple.

Group identifier: An attribute that identifies a unique instance of a group within a semantic object or another group.

Growing phase: The first stage in two-phase locking in which locks are acquired but not released.

GUI: See Graphical user interface.

HAS-A relationship: A relationship between two entities or objects that are of different logical types, for example, EMPLOYEE HAS-A(n) AUTO. Contrast this with an IS-A relationship.

Hierarchical data model: A data model that represents all relationships using hierarchies or trees. Network structures must be decomposed into trees before they can be represented by a hierarchical data model. DL/I is the only surviving hierarchical data model.

Hierarchy: See Tree.

Horizontal partition: A subset of a table consisting of complete rows of the table. For example, in a table with ten rows, the first five rows.

Host variable: A variable in an application program into which a DBMS places a value from the database.

HTML: See Hypertext markup language.

HTTP: See Hypertext transfer protocol.

Hybrid object: An object containing a multivalued group that contains at least one object attribute.

Hypertext markup language: A standardized system of tagging text for formatting, locating images and other nontext files, and placing links or references to other documents.

Hypertext transfer protocol: A standardized means for using TCP/IP for communicating HTML documents over networks.

ID-dependent entity: An entity that cannot logically exist without the existence of another entity. An APPOINTMENT, for example, cannot exist without a CLIENT to make the appointment. The ID-dependent entity always contains the key of the entity on which it depends. Such entities are a subset of a weak entity. See also Strong entity and Weak entity.

Immutable object: In the ODMG standard, an object whose attributes cannot be changed.

Implementation: In OOP, a set of objects that instantiates a particular OOP interface.

Implicit lock: A lock that is automatically placed by the DBMS.

Implied object: An object that exists in the user's mind when he or she requests a report "sorted by x" or "grouped by x." For example, when the user requests all ORDERs sorted by OrderDate, the implied object is the set of all ORDER objects.

Import: A function of the DBMS, to read an entire file of data in bulk.

IMS: Information management system. A transaction-processing system developed and licensed by IBM. It includes IMS/DC, a communications control program, and IMS/DB, a DBMS that implements the DL/I data model.

Inconsistent read problem: An anomaly that occurs in concurrent processing, in which transactions execute a series of reads inconsistent with one another. It can be prevented by two-phase locking and other strategies.

Index: Overhead data used to improve access and sorting performance. Indexes can be constructed for a single column or for groups of columns. They are especially useful for columns used for control breaks in reports and for columns used to specify conditions in joins.

Index space: An area of disk storage in which DB2 stores an index.

Information-bearing set: In the CODASYL DBTG data model, a set in which the relationship between records is not represented in the data values. The relationship, though not visible in the data, is recorded in overhead data created and processed by the DBMS. Contrast this with Non-information-bearing set.

Inheritance: A characteristic of objected-oriented systems in which objects that are subtypes of other objects obtain attributes (data or methods) from their supertypes.

Insertion anomaly: In a relation, the condition that exists when, to add a complete row to a table, one must add facts about two or more logically different themes.

Insertion status: In the CODASYL DBTG model, a rule that determines how records are to be placed into sets. Records can be placed automatically by the DBMS or manually by the application program.

Interface: (1) The means by which two or more programs call each other; the definition of the procedural calls between two or more programs. (2) In OOP, the design of a set of objects that includes the objects' names, methods, and attributes.

Internet: A worldwide, public network of computers that communicate using TCP/IP.

Internet mail service: A standard service of the Internet that provides personal electronic mail.

Internet newsgroup: A standard service of the Internet that provides for public electronic mail.

Interrelation constraint: A restriction that requires the value of an attribute in a row of one relation to match the value of an attribute found in another relation. For example, CustNumber in ORDER must equal CustNumber in CUSTOMER.

Intersection: A relational algebra operation performed on two union-compatible relations, A and B, forming a third relation, C, so that C contains only rows that appear in both A and B.

Intersection relation: A relation used to represent a many-to-many relationship. It contains the keys of the relations in the relationship. When used to represent many-to-many compound objects, it has no nonkey data. When used to represent entities having a many-to-many relationship, it may have nonkey data if the relationship contains data.

Intranet: (1) A private local or wide area network that uses TCP/IP, HTML, and related browser technology on client computers and web server technology on serves. (2) Less commonly, any private LAN or WAN that involves clients and servers

Intrarelation constraint: A restriction on data values in a relation. For example, in PART (Part , Pname, Units), the rule is that if Part starts with a 1, then Units must equal Pounds.

I/O: Input/output. The process in the operating system that reads and writes data from and to peripheral storage devices.

IS-A relationship: A relationship between two entities or objects of the same logical type. In reference to ENGINEER IS-A(n) EMPLOYEE, both of these entities are employees and are of the same logical type. Contrast this with a HAS-A relationship.

IUnknown: An ActiveX interface in which one ActiveX program can call another, unknown ActiveX program. Once a connection has been established, the first program can use the Query Interface to determine what objects, methods, and properties the second program supports.

Java: An object programming language that has better memory management and bounds checking than C++. Used primarily for Internet applications, but also can be used as a general-purpose programming language. Java compliers generate Java byte code that is interpreted on client computers.

Join: A relational algebra operation on two relations, A and B, that produces a third relation, C. A row of A is concatenated with a row of B to form a new row in C if the rows in A and B meet restrictions concerning their values. For example, A1 is an attribute in A, and B1 is an attribute in B. The join of A with B in which A1 < B1 will result in a relation, C, having the concatenation of rows in A and B in which the value of A1 is less than the value of B1. See Equijoin and Natural join.

Key: (1) A group of one or more attributes identifying a unique row in a relation. Since relations may not have duplicate rows, every relation must have at least one key, which is the composite of all of the attributes in the relation. A key is sometimes called a logical key. (2) With some relational DBMS products, an index on a column used to improve access and sorting speed. It is sometimes called a physical key.

LAN: Local area network. A group of microcomputers connected to one another by means of communications lines in close proximity, usually less than a mile. See Client–server database architecture and Resource-sharing architecture.

LDBR: See Logical data base record.

List box: In a GUI environment, an element of the user interface in which a list of choices is presented in a rectangle. The user moves the cursor to shade the item to be selected from the list.

Location transparency: In a distributed database system, the condition in which application programs do not know and do not need to know where data are located. The DDBMS finds data, wherever they are located, without the involvement of the application program.

Lock: The process of allocating a database resource to a particular transaction in a concurrent-processing system. The size of the resource locked is known as the lock granularity. With an exclusive lock, no other transaction may read or write the resource. With a shared lock, other transactions may read the resource, but no other transaction may write it.

Lock granularity: The size of a locked data element. The lock of a column value of a particular row is a small granularity lock, and the lock of an entire table is a large granularity lock.

Log: A file containing a record of database changes. The log contains before-images and after-images.

Logical data base (LDB): In DL/I, the collection of all the logical data base records in the data base.

Logical data base record (LDBR): In DL/I, a hierarchy of segments as perceived by an application program. Such a structure may or may not exist physically; it may be taken from other structures using pointers and other overhead data.

Logical key: One or more columns that uniquely determine the row of a table or a record of a file. A synonym for a key. Contrast this with a physical key, which is a synonym for an index.

Logical unit of work: A group of logically related database operations that is performed as a unit. Either all of the operations are performed, or none of them is. A logical unit of work is the same as an atomic transaction. It is a term used with the DBMS DB2.

Look up: The process of obtaining related data by using the value of a foreign key, for example, when processing a row of ORDER (*OrderNumber*, Ord-Date, *CustNumber*, ...), using the value of CustNumber to obtain the related value of CustName from CUSTOMER (*CustNumber*, CustName, ...).

Lost update problem: Same as Concurrent update problem.

LUW: See Logical unit of work.

Mask: A format used when presenting data in a form or report.

Materialization: (1) The physical appearance of data in a form or report. (2) The appearance of a view of a semantic object in a form or report.

Maximum cardinality: (1) The maximum number of values that an attribute may have within a semantic object. (2) In a relationship between tables, the maximum number of rows to which a row of one table may relate in the other table.

Me: In OOP, a special pointer to the current object instance. For example, Me.Name refers to the Name attribute of the current object.

Member: In the CODASYL DBTG model, a record type that is on the many side of a one-to-many or set relationship.

Menu: A list of options presented to the user of a database (or other) application. The user selects the next action or activity from a list. Actions are restricted to those in the list. Contrast this with Command.

Metadata: Data concerning the structure of data in a database stored in the data dictionary. Metadata are used to describe tables, columns, constraints, indexes, and so forth. Compare this with Application metadata.

Method: A program attached to an object-oriented programming (OOP) object. A method can be inherited by lower-level OOP objects.

Method: In OOP, a program attribute of an object.

MIME: See Multipurpose Internet mail code.

Minimum cardinality: (1) The minimum number of values that an attribute may have within a semantic object. (2) In a relationship between tables, the number of rows to which a row of one table may relate in the other table.

Mixed partition: A combination of a horizontal and a vertical partition. For example, in a table with five columns and five rows, the first three columns of the first three rows.

Modeless processing: In a database application, the characteristic of inferring the mode of the user's processing from the user's actions, for example, on entering a key field, if the value exists in the database, inferring that an update is to occur; if the value does not exist in the database, inferring that an insert is to occur.

Modem: Modulator-demodulator. A device used to convert digital signals to analog signals and the reverse. It is most often used to communicate over telephone lines.

Modification anomaly: The situation existing when the storing of one row in a table records two separate facts or when the deletion of one row of a table eliminates two separate facts.

Multiple-tier driver: In ODBC, a two-part driver, usually for a client-server database system. One part of the driver resides on the client and interfaces with the application; the second part resides on the server and interfaces with the DBMS.

Multipurpose Internet Mail Code: A standardized list of symbols that indicate the type of a file embedded in an HTML document. Each MIME type code is associated with a program that processes files of that type. MIME types are defined for images, sounds, movies, etc. The code can be extended by adding new codes (and affiliated programs) to MIME code lists on clients and servers.

Multivalued attribute: The attribute of a semantic object that has a maximum cardinality greater than one.

Multivalued dependency: A condition in a relation with three or more attributes in which independent attributes appear to have relationships they do not have. Formally, in a relation R (A, B, C), having key (A, B, C) where A is matched with multiple values of B (or of C or both), B does not determine C, and C does not determine B. An example is the relation EMPLOYEE (EmpNumber, Emp-skill, Dependent-name), where an employee can have multiple values of Emp-skill and Dependent-name. Emp-skill and Dependent-name do not have any relationship, but they do appear to in the relation.

Mutable object: In the ODMG standard, an object whose attributes may be changed.

Natural join: A join of a relation A having attribute A1 with relation B having attribute B1 where A1 equals B1. The joined relation, C, contains either column A1 or B1 but not both. Contrast this with Equijoin.

Natural language interface: An interface to an application program or DBMS by which users can enter requests in the form of standard English or another human language.

Network: (1) A group of interconnected computers. (2) an intranet. (3) the Internet.

Network database application: A database application in which the clients use an HTML-based browser and the server includes both an Internet-style server and a database. The application could reside on either the Internet or an intranet.

Network data model: A data model supporting at least simple network relationships. The CODASYL DBTG, which supports simple network relationships but not complex relationships, is the most important network data model.

N.M.: An abbreviation for a many-to-many relationship between the rows of two tables.

Node: (1) An entity in a tree. (2) A computer in a distributed-processing system.

Non-information-bearing set: In the CODAYSL DBTG model, a set in which the child record type contains the key of the parent record type. The set ownership is implied by the value of the key in the child record instances.

Nonobject attribute: An attribute of a semantic object that is not an object.

Normal form: A rule or set of rules governing the allowed structure of relations. The rules apply to attributes, functional dependencies, multivalued dependencies, domains, and constraints. The most important normal forms are 1NF, 2NF, 3NF, Boyce-Codd NF, 4NF, 5NF, and domain/key normal form.

Normalization: The process of evaluating a relation to determine whether it is in a specified normal form and, if necessary, of converting it to relations in that specified normal form.

Nothing: In OOP, a null object reference. Used to set an object pointer to null, or to test an object pointer to determine if it is null.

Null value: A value that is either unknown or not applicable. A null value is not the same as a zero or blank, although in most commercial DBMS products, null values are represented by zeros or blanks.

Object: (1) A semantic object. (2) A structure in an object-oriented program that contains an encapsulated data structure and data methods. Such objects are arranged in a hierarchy so that objects can inherit methods from their parents. (3) In DB2, a term used to refer to data bases, tables, views, indexes, and other structures. (4) In security systems, a unit of data protected by a password or other means.

Object attribute: An attribute of a semantic object that represents a link to an object.

Object class: In object-oriented programming, a set of objects with a common structure.

Object class library: In object-oriented programming, a collection of object classes, usually a collection that serves a particular purpose.

Object constructor: In object-oriented programming, a function that creates an object.

Object destructor: In object-oriented programming, a function that destroys an object.

Object diagram: A portrait-oriented rectangle that represents the structure of a semantic object.

Object identifier: An attribute that is used to specify an object instance. Object identifiers can be unique, meaning that they identify one (and only one) instance, or nonunique, meaning that they identify exactly one object instance.

Object instance: The occurrence of a particular semantic object, for example, the SALESPERSON semantic object having LastName equal to Jones.

Object-Oriented Programming: A style of computer programming in which programs are developed as sets of objects that have data members and methods. Objects interface with one another by calling each other's methods.

Object persistence: In object-oriented programming, the characteristic that an object can be saved to nonvolatile memory, such as a disk. Persistent objects exist between executions of a program.

Object view: The portion of a semantic object that is visible to a particular application. A view consists of the name of the semantic object plus a list of the attributes visible in that view.

1:N: An abbreviation for a one-to-many relationship between the rows of two tables.

ODMG-93: A report issued by the Object Data Management Group, which is a consortium of object database vendors and other interested industry experts. The report applies the ideas of another group, the Object Management Group, to the problem of object databases. The first ODMG report was produced in 1993 and is accordingly referred to as ODMG-93.

OOP: See Object-oriented programming.

Open Database Connectivity Standard (ODBC): A standard interface by which application programs can access and process SQL databases in a DBMS-independent manner. ODBC was developed by a committee of industry experts from the X/Open and SQL Access Group committees and was incorporated as a part of Windows by Microsoft.

Option button: In a GUI environment, an element of the user interface in which the user can select an item from a list. Clicking on one button de-selects the button currently pressed (if any). It operates like the radio buttons on a car radio and in fact is the same as a radio button (see Radio button) but was introduced under a different name to avoid litigation among vendors.

Orphan: Any row (record) that is missing its parent in a mandatory one-to-many relationship.

Overhead data: Metadata created by the DBMS to improve performance, for example, indexes and linked lists.

Owner: (1) In the CODASYL DBTG model, a record type that is on the one side of a one-to-many or set relationship. (2) In data administration, the department or other organizational unit in charge of the management of a particular data item. An owner can also be called a data proponent.

Page: A unit of disk storage. In DB2, a 4K block of contiguous disk space used to hold the database, data dictionary, and overhead data.

Paired attribute: In a semantic object, object attributes are paired. If object A has an object attribute of object B, then object B will have an object attribute of object A; that is, the object attributes are paired with each other.

Parent: A row, record, or node on the one side of a one-to-many relationship.

Partition: (1) A portion of a distributed database. (2) The portion of a network that is separated from the rest of the network during a network failure.

Partitioned table space: In DB2, a table space that holds data for exactly one table.

Pathologically Eclectic Rubbish Lister: The programming language PERL, also known as Practical Extraction and Report Language.

PDBR: See Physical data base record.

PERL: The Practical Extraction and Report Language. An interpreted programming language developed by Larry Wall and originally for UNIX. PERL interpreters are now available for Windows and Macintosh. Often used for server programs on the Internet and on intranets.

Persistent object: An OOP object that has been written to persistent storage.

Pervasive key: In a database application, a key that performs the same function throughout the application. The meaning of the key always remains the same.

Physical data base record (PDBR): In DL/I, a hierarchy of segments stored in data base files.

Physical key: A column that has an index or other data structure created for it. A synonym for an index. Such structures are created to improve searching and sorting on the column values.

Pointer: An address to an instance of a data structure. The address of a record often is in a directly addressed file.

Polymorphism: In OOP, the situation in which one name can be used to invoke different functions. Polymorphism in which the functions are distinguished by having different parameter sequences is called parametric polymorphism. For it, names are resolved by the compiler at compile time. Polymorphism in which the functions are distinguished by object inheritance is called inheritance polymorphism. Such names are resolved at run time by determining the type of object being invoked.

Pop-down list box: In a GUI environment, the list box that appears when the user selects an icon that represents that box.

Precompiler: A program that translates the database access commands of a particular DBMS product. Such commands are embedded in an application program normally written in a third-generation language. The commands are translated into data structures and calls to DBMS-processing routines in the syntax of the third-generation language.

Primary key: A candidate key selected to be the key of a relation.

Processing-interface subsystem: The portion of the DBMS routines that executes commands for processing the database. It accepts input from interactive query programs and from application programs written in standard languages or in DBMS-specific languages.

Processing rights and responsibilities: Organizational policies regarding which groups can take which actions on specified data-items or other collections of data.

Product: A relational operation on two relations, A and B, producing a third relation, C, with C containing the concatenation of every row in A with every row in B. It is the same as a Cartesian product.

Program/data independence: The condition existing when the structure of the data is not defined in application programs. Rather, it is defined in the database, and then the application programs obtain it from the DBMS. In this way, changes can be made in the data structures that may not necessarily be made in the application programs.

Projection: A relational algebra operation performed on a relation, A, that results in a relation, B, where B has a (possibly improper) subset of the attributes of A. Projection is used to form a new relation that reorders the attributes in the original relation or to form a new relation that has only some of the attributes from the original relation.

Property: Same as an Attribute.

Proponent: See Data proponent.

Prototype: A quickly developed demonstration of an application or portion of an application.

QBE: Query by example. A style of query interface, first developed by IBM but now used by other vendors, that allows users to express queries by providing examples of the results they seek.

Query Interface: An interface in ActiveX (and Microsoft COM) that can be used to determine the objects, methods, and properties supported by an ActiveX program.

Query/update language: A language that can be employed by end users to query the database and to make changes in the database data.

Radio button: In a GUI environment, an element of the user interface in which the user can select one item from a list. Clicking on one button de-selects the button currently pressed (if any). It operates like the radio buttons on a car radio.

Read–write conflict: The situation in which two actions operate on the same data item. One of the actions is a read, and the other is a write.

Real output: Output transmitted to the client of an information system, such as an order confirmation. When produced in error, such outputs cannot be changed by recovering the database. Instead, compensating transactions must be executed.

Record: (1) A group of fields pertaining to the same entity; used in file-processing systems. (2) In a relational model, a synonym for Row and Tuple.

Recursive relationship: A relationship among entities, objects, or rows of the same type. For example, if CUSTOMERs refer other CUSTOMERs, the relationship *refers* is recursive.

Referential integrity constraint: The condition in a database in which all interrelation constraints are satisfied.

Relation: Same as a table. A two-dimensional array containing single-valued entries and no duplicate rows. The meaning of the columns is the same in every row. The order of the rows and columns is immaterial.

Relational database: A database consisting of relations. Usually such a database is structured according to the principles of normalization, although in practice, relational databases contain relations with duplicate rows. Most DBMS products include a feature that removes duplicate rows when necessary and appropriate. Such a removal is not done as a matter of course because it can be time-consuming and expensive.

Relational data model: A data model in which data is stored in relations and relationships between rows are represented by data values.

Relational schema: A set of relations with interrelation constraints.

Relationship: An association between two entities, objects, or rows of relations.

Replicated data: In a distributed database, data that is stored on two or more computers.

Replication transparency: In a distributed database system, the condition in which application programs do not know and do not need to know whether data is replicated. If it is replicated, the DDBMS will ensure that all copies are updated consistently, without the involvement of the application program.

Report: An extraction of data from a database. Reports can be printed, displayed on a computer screen, or stored as a file. A report is part of a database application. Compare this with a Form.

Report band: See Band.

Resource locking: See Lock.

Resource-sharing architecture: The structure of a local area network in which one microcomputer performs file-processing services for other microcomputers. In a database application, each user computer contains a copy of the DBMS that forwards input/output requests to the file server. Only file I/O is processed by the file server; all database activities are processed by the DBMS on the user's computer.

Retention status: In the CODASYL DBTG model, a rule that states whether or not a record must exist in a set. If FIXED, a record may never be removed from its original set. If MANDATORY, a record must be a member of a set once it is placed into a set. If OPTIONAL, a record may or may not reside in a set.

Rollback: The process of recovering a database in which before-images are applied to the database to return to an earlier checkpoint or other point at which the database is logically consistent.

Rollforward: The process of recovering a database by applying after-images to a saved copy of the database to bring it to a checkpoint or other point at which the database is logically consistent.

Root: The top record, row, or node in a tree. A root has no parent.

Row: A group of columns in a table. All the columns in a row pertain to the same entity. A row is the same as a Tuple and a Record.

Row identifier: In SQL3, a unique, system-supplied identifier, a surrogate key. The row identifier can be made visible by stating WITH IDENTITY in the table definition.

Run-unit: In the CODASYL DBTG model, the execution of an application program by a user. Several run-units may use the same application program concurrently.

Schedule: In a distributed database system, an ordered sequence of data requests.

Schema: A complete logical view of the database.

Screen: See Form.

Second normal form: A relation in first normal form in which all nonkey attributes are dependent on all of the key.

Segment: In DL /I, a collection of fields that is a node in a data base record.

Segment search argument: An expression in a DL /I that indicates the segment or segments to which the command is to be applied.

Selection: A relational algebra operation performed on a relation, A, producing a relation, B, with B containing only the rows in A that meet the restrictions specified in the selection.

Semantic object diagram: Same as Object diagram.

Semantic object model: The constructs and conventions used to create a model of the users' data. The things in the users' world are represented by semantic objects (sometimes called objects). Relationships are modeled in the objects, and the results are usually documented in object diagrams.

Semantic-object view: The portion of a semantic object that is visible in a form or report.

Sequence field: In DL/I, a field that is used to order logically the segments of a given type under a given parent. The order can be ascending or descending.

Serializable: A condition pertaining to two or more transactions in which the results of the processing are the same as they would have been if the transactions had been processed in some serial manner.

Set: In the CODASYL DBTG model, a structure that represents a one-to-many relationship among records. The parent record type is called the set owner, and the child record type(s) is (are) called the set member.

Set membership: In the CODASYL DBTG model, the records that belong to a particular set instance.

SGML: Standard generalized markup language.

Shared lock: A lock against a data resource in which only one transaction may update the data, but many transactions can concurrently read that data.

Shrinking phase: In two-phase locking, the stage at which locks are released but no lock is acquired.

Sibling: A record or node that has the same parent as does another record or node.

Simple network: (1) A set of three relations and two relationships in which one of the relations, R, has a many-to-one relationship with the other two relations. The rows in R have two parents, and the parents are of different types. (2) Any set of tables and relationships containing the structure defined in (1).

Simple object: An object that contains no repeating attributes and no object attributes.

Simple table space: In DB2, a table space that contains data from more than one table.

Single-tier driver: In ODBC, a database driver that accepts SQL statements from the driver manager and processes them without invoking another program or DBMS. A single-tier driver is both an ODBC driver and a DBMS; used for file-processing systems.

Single-valued attribute: In a semantic object, an attribute having a maximum cardinality of one.

SQL: Structured query language. A language for defining the structure and processing of a relational database. It is used as a stand-alone query language, or it may be embedded in application programs. SQL is accepted as a national standard by the American National Standards Institute. It was developed by IBM.

SQL3: SQL3 is an extension to the SQL92 database standard that includes support for object-oriented database management. Developed by both the ANSI X3H2 and the ISO/IEC JTC1/SC21/WG3 standardization committees.

Standard generalized markup language (SGML): A standard means for tagging and marking the format, structure, and content of documents. HTML is a subset of SGML.

Storage group: In DB2, a group of disk volumes on which database data is stored.

Strong entity: In an entity-relationship model, any entity whose existence in the database does not depend on the existence of any other entity. See also ID-dependent entity and Weak entity.

Subschema: A subset of a database that is processed by one or more applications. A subschema may also be called an application view; it is used primarily with the CODASYL DBTG model.

Subtable: In SQL3, a table that is a subtype of a second table, called a supertable.

Subtype: In generalization hierarchies, an entity or object that is a subspecies or subcategory of a higher-level type. For example, ENGINEER is a subtype of EMPLOYEE.

Supertable: In SQL3, a table that has one or more subtables defined on it.

Supertype: In generalization hierarchies, an entity or object that logically contains subtypes. For example, EMPLOYEE is a supertype of ENGINEER, ACCOUNTANT, and MANAGER.

Surrogate key: A column of unique values that is maintained by the application or the DBMS. This column is used as the primary key of the table.

Swizzling: In OOP, the process of converting a permanent object identifier into an in-memory address and the reverse.

Table space: In DB2, a collection of one or more VSAM data sets, or files, used to store database data on magnetic disk.

TCP/IP: Terminal Control Program/Internet Protocol.

TelNet: A standard service on the Internet that allows a user to log on to a server from a remote computer.

Third normal form: A relation in second normal form that has no transitive dependencies.

Top-down database design: The design of a database that works from the general to the specific. The resulting database can serve an organization's overall needs; the danger is that it may never be completed. See Bottom-up database design.

Transaction: (1) An atomic transaction. (2) The record of an event in the business world.

Transaction node: In a distributed database system, a computer that processes a distributed transaction manager.

Transform-oriented language: A data sublanguage such as SQL that provides commands and capabilities to transform a set of relations into a new relation.

Transient object: In OOP, an object that has not been written to permanent storage. The object will be lost when the program terminates.

Transitive dependency: In a relation having at least three attributes, R (A, B, C), the situation in which A determines B, B determines C, but B does not determine A.

Transparency: The hiding, from a system user, of the existence of some problem or characteristic.

Tree: A collection of records, entities, or other data structures in which each element has at most one parent, except for the top element, which has no parent.

Trigger: A procedure invoked when a specified condition exists in the data of a database. For example, when Quantity-on-Hand of an item reaches zero (or some specified amount), a procedure can be triggered to order more of the item.

Tuple: Same as Row.

Twin: A record or node that has the same parent as does another record or node.

Two-phase commitment: In a distributed database system, a process of commitment among nodes in which the nodes first vote on whether they can commit a transaction. If all the nodes vote yes, the transaction is committed. If any node votes no, the transaction is aborted. A two-phase commitment is required to prevent inconsistent processing in distributed databases.

Two-phase locking: The procedure by which locks are obtained and released in two phases. During the growing phase, the locks are obtained, and during the shrinking phase, the locks are released. Once a lock is released, no other lock will be granted that transaction. Such a procedure ensures consistency in database updates in a concurrent-processing environment.

Union: A relational algebra operation performed on two union-compatible relations, say A and B, forming a third relation, say C, with C containing every row in both A and B, minus any duplicate rows.

Union compatible: The condition in which two tables have the same number of attributes and the attributes in corresponding columns arise from the same domain.

Union incompatible: The condition in which either two tables have a different number of attributes or the attributes in corresponding columns arise from different domains.

Universal resource locator: The address of a file on the Internet.

URL: Universal resource locator. Sometimes uniform resource locator, but the meaning is the same.

User view: A particular user's view of a database.

User working area (UWA): In the CODASYL DBTG model, the area of main memory that contains data values pertaining to a particular run-unit.

UWA: See User working area.

VAR: Value-added reseller. A person, company, or group that develops database applications and sells them to other companies. The VAR adds value to the DBMS product by building the application.

Vertical partition: A subset of the columns of a table. For example, in a table with ten columns, the first five columns.

View: (1) The subset of a database that can be processed by an application. (2) An object view.

Weak entity: In an entity-relationship model, an entity whose logical existence in the database depends on the existence of another entity. See also ID-dependent entity and Strong entity.

Write–write conflict: The situation in which two write actions operate on the same data item.

WYSIWIG: What you see is what you get. A term used with form and report generators, in which the DBMS re-creates exactly what the developer types on the screen while developing forms and reports.

Bibliography

■ INTERNET RESOURCES

WEB SITES OF DATABASE PUBLICATIONS

Check these sites for recent articles on database topics:
Database Programming and Design – http://www.dbpd.com

Databased Advisor – http://www.advisor.com

DBMS Magazine – http://www.dbmsmag.com

PC Magazine – http://www.pcmag.com

WEB SITES FOR VENDORS OF DATABASE AND INTERNET PRODUCTS

Microsoft – http://www.microsoft.com (see the Internet Developers site for recent news about Internet and database applications products)

Oracle – http://www.oracle.com

Perl – http://www.perl.com

Sun – http://www.sun.com (check here for information about Java)

Wall Data, SALSA – http://www.salsa.walldata.com

WEB SITES FOR DATABASE STANDARDS

ODBC – http://www.liv.ac.uk/middleware/html/odbc.html

ODMG – http://www.odmg.org

SQL3 – http://info.gte.com/ftp/doc/activities/x3h7/by_model/SQL3.html

SQL92 – http://waltz.ncsl.nist.gov

■ BOOKS AND PUBLICATIONS

ANSI X3. *American National Standard for Information Systems—Database Language SQL*. ANSI, 1992.

Bruce, T. *Designing Quality Databases with IDEF1X Information Models*. New York: Dorset House, 1992.

Chamberlin, D. D., et al. "SEQUEL 2: A Unified Approach to Data Definition, Manipulation, and Control." *IBM Journal of Research and Development 20* (November 1976).

Chen, P. *Entity-Relationship Approach to Information Modeling*. E-R Institute, 1981.

Chen, P. "The Entity-Relationship Model: Toward a Unified Model of Data." *ACM Transactions on Database Systems 1* (March 1976).

Codd, E. F. "Extending the Relational Model to Capture More Meaning." *Transactions on Database Systems 4* (December 1979).

Codd, E. F. "A Relational Model of Data for Large Shared Data Banks." *Communications of the ACM 25* (February 1970).

Coffee, Peter. "No-sweat Database Design." *PC Week* (March 11, 1996).

Embley, D. W. "NFQL: The Natural Forms Query Language." *ACM Transactions on Database Systems 14* (June 1989).

Eswaran, K. P., J. N. Gray, R. A. Lorie, & I. L. Traiger. "The Notion of Consistency and Predicate Locks in a Database System." *Communications of the ACM 19* (November 1976).

Fagin, R. "Multivalued Dependencies and a New Normal Form for Relational Databases." *Transactions on Database Systems 2* (September 1977).

Fagin, R. "A Normal Form for Relational Databases That is Based on Domains and Keys." *Transactions on Database Systems 6* (September 1981).

Hammer, M., & D. McLeod. "Database Description with SDM: A Semantic Database Model." *Transactions on Database Systems 6* (September 1981).

IBM Corporation. *IBM Database 2 Concepts and Facilities Guide*. IBM Document GG24-1582.

Keuffel, Warren. "Battle of the Modeling Techniques." *DBMS Magazine* (August 1996).

Kroenke, David. "Waxing Semantic: An Interview." *DBMS Magazine* (September 1994).

Loomis, M.E.S. *Object Databases, The Essentials*. Reading, MA: Addison-Wesley, 1995.

Maier, D., J. Stein, A. Otis, & A. Purdy. "Development of an Object-oriented DBMS." *Conference Proceedings from the Object-oriented Programming Systems, Languages and Applications*. ACM SIGPLAN 21 (November 1986).

Moriarty, T. "Business Rule Analysis." *Database Programming and Design* (April 1993).

Nijssen, G., & T. Halpin. *Conceptual Schema and Relational Database Design: A Fact-Oriented Approach*. Englewood Cliffs, NJ: Prentice-Hall, 1989.

Nolan, R. *Managing the Data Resource Function*. St. Paul: West Publishing, 1974.

Rogers, Dan. "Manage Data with Modeling Tools." *VB Tech Journal* (December 1996).

Woelk, D., W. Kim, & W. Luther. "An Object-oriented Approach to Multimedia Databases." *ACM SIGMOD International Conference on Management of Data*, 1986.

Zloof, M. M. "Query by Example." *Proceedings of the National Computer Conference*, AFIPS 44 (May 1975).0

WALL DATA LICENSE AGREEMENT, SALSA® SOFTWARE

PLEASE READ THIS SOFTWARE LICENSE AND LIMITED WARRANTY STATEMENT CAREFULLY BEFORE USING OR REPRODUCING THE SOFTWARE. BY CLICKING ON THE ACCEPT BUTTON IN ORDER TO ACCESS THE SOFTWARE, YOU ARE AGREEING TO BE BOUND BY THE TERMS OF THIS LICENSE. IF YOU AGREE TO THE TERMS OF THIS LICENSE, DO NOT USE OR REPRODUCE THE SOFTWARE, PROMPTLY RETURN THE UNUSED SOFTWARE FOLLOWING THE RETURN INFORMATION IN SECTION 1, LIMITED WARRANTY, OUTLINED BELOW AND YOUR MONEY WILL BE REFUNDED.

1. **LICENSE.** Wall Data Incorporated ("Wall Data") grants you, the end user, the following rights to the Software enclosed in this package.

    For each license acquired, you may use one copy of the Software on a single computer. The primary user of a computer on which a copy of the Software is installed may make a second copy for his or her exclusive use on either a home or portable computer.

    You may also store or install a copy of the Software on a storage device, such as a network server, used only to install or run the Software on your computers over an internal network; however, you must acquire and dedicate a license for each separate computer on which the Software is installed or run from the storage device. A license for the Software may not be shared or used concurrently on different computers.

    You shall inform all users of the software of the terms and conditions of this Software License and Warranty Statement.

    Notwithstanding the above, you have the following license rights with respect to the SALSA model files (i.e. those files in the Software with an extension of ".APM") ("SALSA Models") and SALSA application files licensed directly from Wall Data (i.e. those files in the Software with an extension of ".SAR") ("SALSA Applications"). With respect to SALSA Models only, you are permitted unlimited use and distribution rights. With respect to SALSA Applications only, you may use only one copy of the SALSA Applications on a single computer; provided, however, you may make such one copy available for temporary use (i.e., in RAM) by others over the network, but such other users will have no right to download, make or install a copy of the SALSA Applications on a permanent memory device (i.e. hard disk, CD-ROM, or other storage device). You have no right or license to distribute, make copies of, or otherwise permit access by any other person of, the SALSA for the Desktop tools, if any, or the SALSA Viewer included with the Software.

    You have unlimited use and distribution rights concerning those applicants you create in connection with your authorized use of the Software (but not those applications included with the Software as licensed from Wall Data).

2. **PROOF OF LICENSE.** This software license is your proof of license to exercise the rights granted herein and must be retained by you.

3. **COPYRIGHT.** The Software is owned by Wall Data and is protected by United States copyright laws and international treaty provisions. There is no transfer to you of any title to or ownership of the Software. You must treat the Software like any other copyrighted materials (e.g., a book or musical recording) except that you make one copy of the Software solely for backup of archival purposes as long as you otherwise comply with the terms and conditions of this License Agreement. You may not copy the written materials accompanying the Software.

4. **OTHER RESTRICTIONS.** You may not rent or lease the software, but you may transfer your rights under this Wall Data Single User License Agreement on a permanent basis provided you transfer this software license, all copies of the Software, and all written materials and retain no copies, and the recipient agrees to the terms of this Agreement. Any transfer of the Software must include all prior and future versions of the Software. If the Software is an upgrade from another product, whether from Wall Data or another supplier, you may use or transfer the Software only in conjunction with that upgraded product (unless you destroy it) and in accordance with this License. You may not modify, adapt, translate, reverse-code, decompile, or disassemble the Software, or make any attempt to discover the source code to the Software.

5. **TERM.** This License is in effect until terminated. You may terminate it at any time by destroying the Software and all copies you have made. It will also terminate if you fail to comply with any term or condition of this Agreement. Upon such termination, you agree to destroy the Software and all copies you have made.

Limited Warranty

1. **LIMITED WARRANTY.** Wall Data warrants that, for ninety (90) days from the date of initial receipt of the enclosed software program, the Software will perform substantially according to the on-line documentation included with the Software. The duration of any implied warranties applicable to the Software is limited to the same ninety (90) day period. Some states/jurisdictions do not allow limitations on how long an implied warranty lasts, so the above limitation may not apply to you. Wall Data's and its suppliers' entire liability and your exclusive remedy for failure of the Software to comply with this Limited Warranty shall be, at Wall Data's option: (a) repair or replacement of the Software; or (b) return of the price you paid for the Software. To receive this remedy, you must return the Software to Wall Data with a copy of your receipt and a complete explanation of the problem within ninety (90) days of the date you initially received the enclosed software program. Any replacement Software will be warranted for the remainder of the original ninety (90) day warranty period or thirty (30) days from the date you receive the replacement, whichever is longer. This Limited Warranty applies only to the original recipient of the Software and is void if the failure of the Software has resulted from accident, abuse, or misuse.

2. **DISCLAIMER.** Wall Data does not warrant that the Software is free from all errors and omissions or is suitable for your intended use. TO THE MAXIMUM EXTENT PERMITTED BY APPLICABLE LAW, WALL DATA AND ITS SUPPLIERS DISCLAIM ALL OTHER WARRANTIES, EXPRESS OR IMPLIED, INCLUDING BUT NOT LIMITED TO, ANY IMPLIED WARRANTY OF MERCHANT ABILITY OR FITNESS FOR A PARTICULAR PURPOSE WITH REGARD TO THE SOFTWARE OF ANY RELATED SERVICES, THIS LIMITED WARRANTY GIVES YOU SPECIFIC LEGAL RIGHTS, AND YOU MAY ALSO HAVE OTHER RIGHTS WHICH VARY FROM STATE/JURISDICTION TO STATE/JURISDICTION.

3. **LIMITATION OF LIABILITY.** IN NO EVENT SHALL WALL DATA OR ITS SUPPLIERS HAVE ANY LIABILITY FOR COVER OR FOR ANY INDIRECT, INCIDENTAL, SPECIAL OR CONSEQUENTIAL DAMAGES (INCLUDING WITHOUT LIMITATION ANY LOSS OF PROFITS OR DATA, BUSINESS INTERRUPTION OR OTHER PECUNIARY LOSS) ARISING OUT OF THE USE OR INABILITY TO USE THE SOFTWARE OR PERFORMANCE OF OR FAILURE TO PERFORM ANY RELATED SERVICES, EVEN IF WALL DATA OR ITS SUPPLIERS HAVE BEEN ADVISED OF THE POSSIBILITY OF SUCH DAMAGES. SOME STATES DO NOT ALLOW THE EXCLUSION OR LIMITATION OF INCIDENTAL OR CONSEQUENTIAL DAMAGES, SO THE ABOVE LIMITATION OR EXCLUSION MAY NOT APPLY TO YOU. IN NO EVENT SHALL THE AGGREGATE LIABILITY OF WALL DATA AND ITS SUPPLIERS (WHETHER IN CONTRACT, WARRANTY, TORT (INCLUDING NEGLIGENCE), PRODUCT LIABILITY OR OTHER THEORY) (i)ARISING OUT OF THE USE OR INABILITY TO USE THE SOFTWARE EXCEED YOUR PURCHASE PRICE FOR THE SOFTWARE; OR (ii) ARISING OUT OF THE PERFORMANCE OF OR FAILURE TO PERFORM ANY RELATED SERVICES EXCEED THE PRICE YOU PAID FOR SUCH SERVICES DURING THE YEAR IN WHICH THE CLAIM AROSE. Further, Wall Data will not be liable for any delay or failure to perform any related services or any of its obligations under this Software License and Limited Warranty Statement as a result of any cause or conditions beyond Wall Data's reasonable control.